Jagdgeschwader 3 "Udet" in World War II

Also by Jochen Prien
JAGDGESCHWADER 53: Vol.1 March 1937 - May 1942
JAGDGESCHWADER 53: Vol.2 May 1942 - January 1944
JAGDGESCHWADER 53: Vol.3 January 1944 - May 1945
MESSERSCHMITT Bf 109 F/G/K SERIES (with Peter Rodeike)
(all available from Schiffer Publishing Ltd.)

Jagdgeschwader 3 "Udet" in World War II

Vol.II: II./JG 3 in Action with the Messerschmitt Bf 109

Jochen Prien & Gerhard Stemmer

Translated from the German by David Johnston

Schiffer Military History
Atglen, PA

Book Design by Robert Biondi.
Translated from the German by David Johnston.

Printed in China.
ISBN: 0-7643-1774-1

We are interested in hearing from authors with book ideas on military topics.

Published by Schiffer Publishing Ltd.
4880 Lower Valley Road
Atglen, PA 19310
Phone: (610) 593-1777
FAX: (610) 593-2002
E-mail: Info@schifferbooks.com.
Visit our web site at: www.schifferbooks.com
Please write for a free catalog.
This book may be purchased from the publisher.
Please include $3.95 postage.
Try your bookstore first.

In Europe, Schiffer books are distributed by:
Bushwood Books
6 Marksbury Avenue
Kew Gardens
Surrey TW9 4JF
England
Phone: 44 (0) 20 8392-8585
FAX: 44 (0) 20 8392-9876
E-mail: Bushwd@aol.com.
Free postage in the UK. Europe: air mail at cost.
Try your bookstore first.

Contents

Introduction

This book is the second of three volumes describing the operational career of the Messerschmitt Bf 109 with the *Gruppen* of Jagdgeschwader 3 "UDET"; a fourth volume describing the history of IV (Sturm.)/JG 3 will round out the series. This volume depicts the path of II/JG 3 from its formation in spring 1940 to its withdrawal from the *Geschwader* formation of JG 3 and incorporation into JG 7 in 1944. Also described is its successor *Gruppe*, which emerged from I/KG 1 by way of JG 7 and which served as II/JG 3 from November 1944 until the end of the war.

To date there has been no complete history of JG 3, which in itself comes as surprise, on the one hand because of the fame achieved by the "UDET" *Geschwader* and on the other because of the large number of publications available on the air war in the Second World War and the German fighter arm in particular. This work is not a *Geschwader* or *Gruppe* history in the sense of the author's previous works, instead it is intended as a photo album, albeit one with rather more text than usual on account of the absence of suitable publications which the reader might refer to. But in other respects this volume follows the pattern of the author's previous book on III and IV/JG 27 in that, true to its title, it essentially describes the development and use of the aircraft through a large number of photographs and line drawings with the operational history kept brief as a background to the photo section. The book is rounded off by detailed statistical appendices like those which appeared in my *Geschwader* histories.

Much has already been written about the Bf 109, and potential readers may wonder what would justify further examination of the operational career of the Bf 109 fifty years after the events. It is our opinion that there are two acceptable reasons for such a history: to serve as a memorial to the sacrifices directly or indirectly related to the aircraft's use, and to produce historical truth, exposing some of the many myths which have grown up around this aircraft. The response to our previous published works suggests that most readers accept this objective and the facts and commentaries which follow from it. Especially satisfying to the authors has been the approval of former pilots, technicians and ground personnel, who have been pleased to see an operational history of their unit and who also feel it appropriate and long overdue that the unit chronicle is presented within the framework of events instead of being dealt with in isolation.

The *Luftwaffe*'s fighter units were part of the *Wehrmacht*, which in turn was the instrument with which Adolf Hitler implemented his criminal plans against the states bordering the Reich. This is an indisputable historical fact. The *Wehrmacht* command accepted the tasks given to it by the leadership of the Reich and turned them into plans and actions. In doing so, they did not shy away from invading, occupying and exploiting neutral countries. In planning and executing an invasion of the Soviet Union, the *Wehrmacht* showed itself to be a willing tool of National-Socialism and its policy of conquest and enslavement. These are historical facts and a matter of record[1]. The question thus becomes unavoidable: what degree of guilt does the *Wehrmacht*, and its high command in particular, bear in the undisputed German war crimes, especially in the east, but also in the southeast and south? To examine this question in depth, however, would far surpass the self-imposed limits of this work and therefore this problem can only be alluded to.

This documentation is not intended as a reproach against any individual members of the *Wehrmacht* and consequently not against the fighter pilots and ground crews of the units being dealt with by the authors. On the contrary, the authors have made every effort to do justice to the operations and accomplishments of the *Luftwaffe*, to pay tribute to the fighter pilots where it is deserved and to provide understanding where their thoughts and actions are difficult to understand by present-day standards.

The air war was anything but an adventure, even though many publications still depict the war both as fate and as a test of manhood, whereas political and moral considerations and even reflections on the past are seen as negative thinking. It would be wrong and dangerous if, in viewing the following illustrations, one allowed the fascination which undoubtedly emanates from this technically and aesthetically impressive aircraft to force into the background the knowledge that it was not just an instrument of war, but a weapon which was designed for Adolf Hitler's criminal war of conquest and which played a significant role in it. In an era when flying was the greatest adventure and the dream of many a young man, service in the *Luftwaffe* offered the possibility of realizing this dream with the most modern and fastest aircraft extant. The thrill of flight was augmented by the picture of the fighter pilot which was painted by the schools, the party-run youth organizations and official propaganda. As well as adventure, they promised fame, recognition, honors and decorations. This struck a key with many ambitious young men and prompted them to volunteer for service in the *Luftwaffe*. For many, the awakening as to the true nature of the war, which was concealed behind the glitter and glory of the *Luftwaffe* and the adventure of flying, came too late.

The Messerschmitt Bf 109 may also be seen as a symbol in another respect, namely for the rise and fall of the *Luftwaffe*. When the war began the Messerschmitt fighter was superior to all enemy types; then, in 1940, it met an equal, the British Spitfire, for the first time. The type reached its peak of development in the F-series in 1941-42, and from 1943 on it fell farther and farther behind the Allied fighters. Instead of receiving a new aircraft able to meet the demands of the air war, the German fighter arm was forced to fight the great air battles over the Reich in 1944 with the now obsolescent "*Beule*". Only the most experienced pilots stood a chance of surviving against their technically and numerically far superior foe, while the young, inexperienced replacement pilots and their Messerschmitts were literally knocked out of the air in droves.

The Bf 109 can also serve as a symbol of another topic rarely mentioned in literature concerning the air war—the war profiteering of the German aviation industry during the years of the so-called "Third Reich". In the years from 1933 to 1945, the Messerschmitt AG experienced a dramatic rise in profits, from a meager 166,000 Reichsmark in 1933 to no less than 255,830,000 Reichsmark in 1943, an increase of 15,411%. This was in no small part due to the company's close contacts with leading officials of the Nazi Party. The Messerschmitt AG did not hesitate to use foreign workers and concentration camp inmates as labor to achieve this unbelievable rise and meet the production quotas worked out with the RLM.

The fighter pilots we see in this book cannot be blamed for all of this, for when Hitler assumed power on 30 January 1933 most were between eight and fifteen years old. Instead they were willing tools and consequently became the victims of an unholy alliance between meglomaniacal Philistines (the leaders of the National-Socialist movement), a power- and fame-hungry *Wehrmacht* command, and profit-seeking big business. For this reason, therefore, in spite of the briefness of the text the authors have allocated sufficient space to publish the names of all the pilots and ground crews

who lost their lives, were posted missing, were wounded or injured, or were taken prisoner while serving with *II Gruppe* of *Jagdgeschwader 3 "UDET"*. In the opinion of the authors, the overwhelming majority were victims of the criminal National-Socialist state, which lied to and deceived them about its true plans and intentions while demanding that they make the greatest sacrifices, and whose war crippled them and deprived them of the chance for a peaceful life. The viewer of these photographs must also keep in mind the countless other victims who came into contact with the Messerschmitt in one way or another, whether as forced laborers or concentration camp inmates forced to assist in producing the machine in the Messerschmitt factories, as members of the ground personnel who were lost far from home in Russia or Africa, or as pilots of enemy machines. Also victims were the relatives of fallen, missing and wounded pilots, families which lost a son or brother, women who lost a husband, children who lost their fathers. All of this and much more stands behind these photographs and gives cause to reflect on pictures from are own time which are depressingly similar. If this work succeeds in preserving this awareness or awakening it where it does not already exist, it will have achieved its underlying purpose.

This work is the result of research and the evaluation of sources by the authors, assisted by the following circle of people and former members of the *Gruppe* named in the acknowledgements. It is based on the published and unpublished sources cited in the bibliography and the many footnotes. The information derived from them and the conclusions and assessments expressed in this book reflect the authors' point of view exclusively. They were aware that a group of former members of the *Gruppe* had been working on a unit history for some time. Efforts to launch a cooperative effort involving the veterans group and a team of authors, including Jochen Prien, failed in 1986. Differing views on the form and content of the proposed history made cooperation impossible. Consequently, this work has not received the approval of the veterans group. Nevertheless, it is dedicated to all former members of II/JG 3, both to the fallen, whose memory it is intended to preserve, and to the survivors.

In closing, our thanks go to Hans Ring for his extensive and selfless assistance. Hans Lächler, Gunther Lauser, Walter Matthiesen and Peter Petrick provided photographs, while Winifried Bock worked tirelessly checking the appendices which accompany this book. A complete list of former members of II/JG 3 who contributed to the success of this project through their help and support and all contributing aviation historians is located at the end of the book.

Hamburg, September 1996
Jochen Prien and Gerhard Stemmer

Notes:

[1] In fact the formation of the *Gruppe* did not begin until later in the month as the soldiers transferred to the new unit arrived there. As an example, according to the "*Staffel* chronicler" Fw. Georg Alex (hereafter referred to as the "Writings of Georg Alex"), 4/JG 3 was not created at Zerbst until 13 February 1940. Also see the transfer dates of the pilots named below.

[2] See Ries/Dierich, p. 62 and the sketch map on p. 311.

Abbreviations

a.a.O.	am angegebenen Orte
Adju.	Adjutant
A.M.W.I.S.	Air Ministry Weekly Intelligence Summary
Ar	Arado
B.A.	Bundesarchiv
B.A./M.A.	Bumdesarchiv/Militärarchiv
Bf	Bayerische Flugzeugwerke
Bd.	Band
BMW	Bayerische Motorenwerke
Cat. E	Category E = *damaged beyond economical repair*
DB	Daimler Benz
Div.	Division
DK	Deutsches Kreuz in Gold
Do	Dornier
E.C.P.A.	Etablissement Cinematographique et Photographique des Armees
eins.	einsitzig
(Eins.)	Einsatz, als Zusatz zur Verbandsbezeichnung
EJG	Ergänzungsjagdgeschwader
EK I	Eisernes Kreuz I. Klasse
EK 11	Eisernes Kreuz II. Klasse
Erg.JGr.	Ergänzungsjagdgruppe
e. V.	endgültige Verniclitung
FBK	Flughafen-Betriebskompanie
FF	Flugzeugführer
FFS	Flugzeugführerschule
FhjFw.	Fahnenjunker-Feldwebel
FlijObfw.	Fahnenjunker-Oberfeldwebel
FhjUff:z.	Fahnenjunker-Unteroffizier
Fhr.	Fähnrich
Fl.E.A.	Flieger-Ersatzabteilung
Flg.	Flieger
Flgkpt.	Flugkapitän
Fl.-Kp.	Fliegerkorps
FlSt].	Fliegerstabsingenieur
Fn.	Fussnote
FSA	Fallschirmabsprung
FT	Funksprechgerät
FuG	Funkgerät
Fw.	Feldwebel
Fw	Focke Wulf
G.d.J.	General der Jagdflieger
Gefr.	Gefreiter
Gen.	General
GenLt.	Generalleutnant
GenMaj.	Generalmajor
GenO.	Generaloberst
Genst.	Generalstab
GFM	Generalfeldmarschall
GL	General-Luftzeugmeister
GQM	General-Quartiermeister
He	Heinkel
Hptm.	Hauptmann
HSS	Herausschuss
Jasta	Jagdstaffel
JFS	Jagdfliegerschule
JG	Jagdgeschwader
JGr.	Jagdgruppe
JK	Jagdkorps
Ju	Junkers
Jumo	Junkers Motor

Kdr.	Kommandeur
KG	Kampfgeschwader
KG	Kriegsgefangenschaft (nur in den Verlustmeldungen)
KGr.	Kampfgruppe
KTB	Kriegstagebuch
Lfl.	Luftflotte
Lfl.-Kdo.	Luftflottenkommando
LG	Lehrgeschwader
LKS	Luftkriegsschule
Lt.	Leutnant
Lw.	Luftwaffe
Maj.	Major
m.d.W.d.G.b.	mit der Wahrnehmung der Geschäfte beauftragt
MG	Maschinengewehr
MK	Maschinenkanone
rnw.N.	mit weiteren Nachweisen
NAG	Nahaufklärungsgruppe
n.b.	nicht bestatigt
N.N.	Name unbekamit (nomen nominandum bzw. nomen nescio)
NO	Nachrichtenoffizier
qbi	Schlechtwetter
OB	Oberbefehlshaber
Obfhr.	Oberfähnrich
Obfw.	Oberfeldwebel
Obgeft.	Obergefreiter
Oblt.	Oberleutnant
ObstIt.	Oberstleutnant
o.b.V.	ohne besondere Vorkommnisse
o.F.	ohne Feindberührung
OKH	Oberkommando des Heeres
OKW	Oberkommando der Wehrmacht
O.U.	Ortsunterkunft (gebräuchliche Absenderortsangabe)
Obw1n.	Oberwerkmeister
PK	Propagandakompanie
Pr.K.	Stiftung Preussischer Kulturbesitz
Pz.-Armee	Panzerarmee
Pz.-Div.	Panzerdivision
RAF	Royal Air Force
RLM	Reichsluftfahrtministerium
RM	Reichsmarschall
SG	Schlachtgeschwader
Sqn.	Squadron
StA.	Stabsarzt
Stfhr.	Staffelführer
StFw.	Stabsfeldwebel
StG	Sturzkampfgeschwader
StGefr.	Stabsgefreiter
Stkpt.	Staffelkapitän
Stuka	Sturzkampfbomber
TO	Technischer Offizier
uffz.	Unteroffizier
unverl.	unverletzt
USAAF	United States Army Air Force
USAF	United States Air Force
verl.	verletzt
verw.	verwundet
Viermot	viermotoriges Flugzeug, meist
w.b.	U.S.-Bomber B- 17 bzw. B-24 Airksam beschossen
WNr.	Werknummer
z.b. V.	zur besonderen Verwendung
ZG	Zerstörergeschwader

1

Formation of II/*Jagdgeschwader* 3

II/JG 3 was created at the beginning of 1940 as the second *Gruppe* of JG 3, which at that time consisted of just the *Geschwaderstab* and I *Gruppe*. Entered in the budget on 1 February 1940[1], the new *Gruppe* was established at Zerbst air base, a large, peacetime airfield approximately 35 kilometers southeast of Magdeburg[2]. Following the so-called "cell division"[3] method, in use since the start of the *Luftwaffe*'s expansion, it was created from personnel released by other *Jagdgruppen*, including I/JG 1, and elements of JG 2, II/JG 26 and I(J)/LG 2. The new *Gruppe*'s first *Kommandeur* was Hptm. Erich von Selle, who had formerly served as adjutant to the chief of the OKW[4]. The first *Staffelkapitän* of 4/JG 3 was Hptm. Alfred Müller, about whose earlier flying career nothing is known. 5 *Staffel* was formed under Oblt. Herbert Kijewski, who came from I(J)/LG 2, and finally 6/JG 3 was established by Oblt. Erich Woitke, who came from II/JG 26. Woitke had previously served in Spain, where he scored a total of four victories while flying with the *Jagdgruppe* J/88[5]. The following is a list of the new *Gruppe*'s command positions:

List of officers of II/JG 3 on 28 February 1940	
Gruppenkommandeur	Hptm. Erich von Selle
Gruppenadjutant	Lt. Franz von Werra
Hptm. beim Stabe	Maj. Julius-Georg von Plehn
Special Duties Officer	Hptm. Botho Teichmann[6]
Commander Headquarters Company	Oblt. Karl-Heinz Sandmann
Technical Officer	Oblt. Heinrich Sannemann[7]
Staffelkapitän 4/JG 3	Hptm. Alfred Müller
Staffelkapitän 5/JG 3	Oblt. Herbert Kijewski
Staffelkapitän 6/JG 3	Oblt. Herbert Woitke

At the end of March 1940 the *Gruppe* had a total of 27 pilots on strength[8]; further allocations in April 1940 brought II/JG 3 up to its authorized strength of forty pilots[9]. Little by little, personnel for the ground elements also arrived in Zerbst, where Hptm. Teichmann assigned them to the *Staffeln* and the individual platoons of the Headquarters Company[10] based on their area of expertise and training[11].

In the course of its formation, II/JG 3 was equipped with a mixed complement of Messerschmitt Bf 109 E-1, E-3 and E-4[12] fighters. The latter variant, which was introduced as a replacement for the Bf 109 E-3 in the spring of 1940, did not begin arriving until April[13]. The first of the *Gruppe*'s machines were picked up at Wiener Neustadt in February and ferried to Zerbst[14]. By the end of March[15] II/JG 3 was already reporting 34 Bf 109 Es on strength.

The weeks that followed were filled with numerous exercises for the air element and the ground personnel. While the former "flew themselves in" in numerous *Schwarm* and *Staffel* missions, the ground personnel were welded into a cohesive unit through various lectures as well as loading and transfer exercises which included practice setting up a front-line airfield[16]. It is noteworthy that the establishment of II/JG 3 took rather more time than that of III *Gruppe*, which was formed one month later. III/JG 3 was reported ready for operations on 28 March 1940, just four weeks after the start of its formation[17], whereas II *Gruppe* was allowed two-and-a-half months to complete this procedure. As a result, II/JG 3 was still at Zerbst when the French campaign began on 10 May 1940.

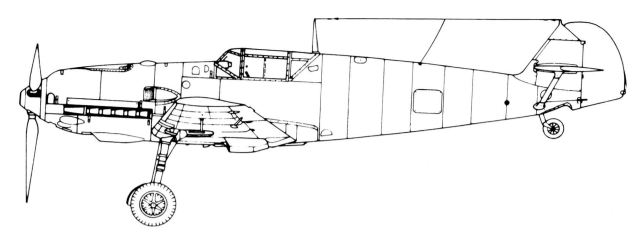

Line Drawing 1: Messerschmitt Bf 109 E-1

During the formation process, II/JG 3 received a full complement of Messerschmitt Bf 109 E-1 and E-3 fighters; in April 1940 the unit also received the first examples of the Bf 109 E. The latter were designated "cannon machines." All three variants were to form the equipment of II/JG 3 until autumn 1940, with the E-3s being increasingly replaced by E-4s, some new production aircraft, some converted machines. In contrast to the E-3 and E-4 with their two wing-mounted 20-mm MG FF and MG FF/M cannon respectively, the E-1's armament was limited to four 7.92-mm MG 17 machine-guns.

Length: 8.80 m   Engine: DB 601 A, 1,100 H.P.   Empty weight: 1 860 kg

Wingspan: 9.90 m   Takeoff weight: 2 573 kg

Height: 2.60 m   Armament: 4 MG 17

Notes:

[3] Also see Prien, JG 77 Part I, p. 14.

[4] After initial flight training at the Schleissheim Flying School and the Reichswehr's secret flying school at Lipetsk (there from 15/4 to 15/8/1930), by August 1935 Hptm. Erich von Selle had served in various reconnaissance units before being trained as a fighter pilot. He subsequently joined JG *"Richthofen"* from December 1935 until April 1937 and after an assignment to LKS Gatow as a tactics instructor served with *Stab*/JG 334 from 1/2/1938 to 28/2/1939 before becoming adjutant to the chief of the OKW. He was transferred to II/JG 3 effective 15 February 1940. Information provided by Erich von Selle, summary of his military career.

[5] Oblt. Erich Woitke was transferred to II/JG 3 effective 10/2/1940; he had served with 1(J)/88 in Spain from 26/5/1937 to 20/4/1938.

[6] Hptm. Botho Teichmann came from *Stab*/JG 3 and was transferred to II *Gruppe* effective 19/2/1940. Soon afterwards, on 6/6/1940, he assumed command of the Headquarters Company following the transfer of Oblt. Sandmann to III/JG 3.

[7] Oblt. Heinrich Sannemann came from I/JG 1 and was transferred to II/JG 3 effective 10/2/1940.

[8] Reporting date 30/3/1940, German Order of Battle, Statistics as of Quarter Years.

[9] 4/JG 3's initial complement of pilots was: Hptm. Alfred Müller, Lt. Heymann (special duties), Lt. Ewers (TO), Hptm. Dr. Ochs, Fw. Voget, Fw. Müller, Uffz. Gremm, Uffz. Kortlepel, Uffz. König, Uffz. Brüchert, Uffz. Dickow, Gefr. Müller—papers of Georg Alex.

[10] According to the so-called "Table of Organization" the Headquarters Company consisted of a finance platoon, workshop platoon, motor transport platoon, signals platoon and anti-aircraft platoon.

[11] Writings of Botho Teichmann dated 21/6/1953 – "On the History of Jagdgeschwader No. 3 (Udet)."

[12] In the beginning II/JG 3 also had on strength several He 51s and He 70 as well as several W 34s, Bf 108s and Go 145s used in the courier role.

[13] II/JG 3's strength and loss returns reveal that the *Gruppe* received very few Bf 109 E-3s.

[14] In addition to new-production Messerschmitt Bf 109 E-3s built by WNF (production batch with the Werknummer 5000) these obviously included a large number of repaired Bf 109 E-1s from the Amme Luther & Sack repair facility located on the Wiener Neustadt airfield.

[16] Account by Botho Teichmann, which speaks of a "*simulated*" front-line airfield; obviously, while this field was set up like a wartime airfield, it was not occupied by the air element.

[17] Compare Prien/Stemmer, III/JG 3, p. 1.

2

Operations in the French Campaign
19 May to 25 June 1940

On 10 May 1940 the units of the *Wehrmacht* launched an attack against France, Belgium, Luxembourg and the Netherlands. In keeping with the German plan of operations, the main weight of the offensive was initially in the northwest in the Netherlands and Belgium. Then, on 12 May 1940, German forces moved out of the hilly country of the Ardennes with the objective of crossing the Meuse at Sedan and Dinant. The river was crossed according to plan, and on 15 May 1940 the fast armored forces of Army Group A broke out of the Meuse bridgeheads and began driving north. Army Group A's objective was to advance in the direction of the Somme estuary, separate the fortified area of northern France from the rest of the country, and attack the strong Allied forces concentrated there from the rear. On 19 May 1940 the German forces reached the Canal du Nord, the area of the World War One battlefields on the Somme, and took Cambrai. By evening they were only 80 kilometers from the Atlantic[18].

It was on this day that II/JG 3 at Zerbst received orders to proceed immediately to France, where the *Gruppe* was to see its first action. For this purpose it was attached to *Stab*/JG 77, part of *I Fliegerkorps*, whose units were in turn part of *General* Hugo Sperrle's *Luftflotte 3*, which was committed over the focal point of the German advance in France[19]. The air element took off from Zerbst at about noon, however this initially consisted of just the *Gruppenstab* plus 4 and 6 *Staffel*. After an intermediate stop at Lippstadt, in the late afternoon the units arrived at the Philippeville forward airfield[20], where the *Geschwaderstab* of JG 77 was located. That evening Hptm. von Selle reported to the *Kommodore* of JG 77, *Oberst* Eitel Roediger von Manteuffel, and subordinated his *Gruppe* to him[21]. The air element was accompanied by a small detachment of technical personnel which had been flown to Philippeville by Ju 52. The main column of ground personnel followed by land transport. Until its arrival, the task of servicing II/JG 3's Messerschmitts was the responsibility of an airfield operating company of ZG 26[22]. 5 *Staffel*, on the other hand, was ordered to

Döberitz for the time being, with instructions to stand ready to follow the rest of the *Gruppe* to France.

On 20 May the spearheads of *General* von Kleist's armored group reached the Somme estuary; all British, French and Belgian forces still north and east of the "sickle cut" were now cut off from the French heartland. Meanwhile, this day saw II/JG 3 fly its first operational sorties—in the parlance of the day these were referred to as *Feindflüge* (combat flights)[23]. During one of these, at 4:25 in the afternoon, a mixed formation of seven Messerschmitts from the *Gruppenstab* and 4 *Staffel* encountered five Hurricanes east of Arras. The engagement, which was fought out at ground level, resulted in the *Gruppe*'s first four victories[24] but also its first fatal casualty. Lt. Peter Wisser of 5 *Staffel*[25] was killed when, in the heat of battle, he inadvertently flew into the ground. His Messerschmitt struck the ground, tumbled and burst into flames[26]. The remaining missions flown by the *Gruppe* on this day were uneventful, apart from an emergency landing at Aachen by a *Schwarm* which had lost its way; luckily none of the pilots was injured[27].

Because of the rapid advance by the German armored spearheads, the *Gruppen* under the command of *Stab*/JG 77 were barely able to cover the forward combat zone from their current bases on account of the Bf 109's limited range. For this reason, on 20 May and the morning of 21 May 1940 a large number of airfields were scouted in preparation for a move forward by the *Jagdgruppen*. One of these was the Nierguies forward airfield near Cambrai[28]. *Stab*/JG 77 plus I and II/JG 3 were ordered there, even though this airfield was already occupied by a *Jagdgruppe* and a *Stukagruppe* of *VIII Fliegerkorps*[29]. The air element of II/JG 3 took off from Philippeville for Cambrai at 1:35 PM, accompanied by five Ju 52s which had been assigned to the *Gruppe* to transport essential technical personnel. The *Gruppe* flew its first missions from its new base that afternoon, over the La Bassée—Lillers—St. Pol—Arras combat zone. 4 *Staffel* succeeded in shooting down two Moranes, however it suffered two losses in return: Lt. Ernst Ewers and Uffz.

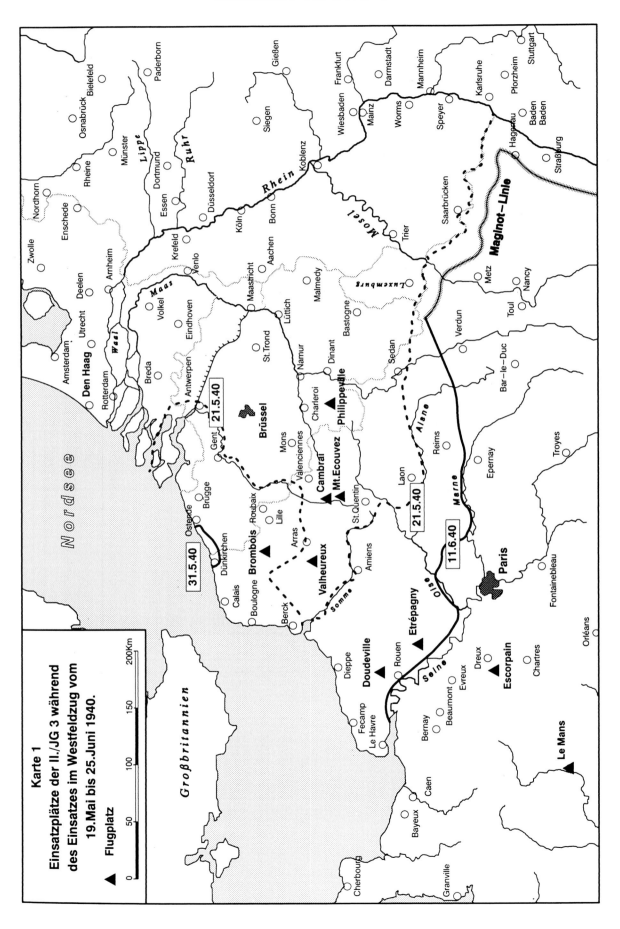

Karte 1
Einsatzplätze der II./JG 3 während
des Einsatzes im Westfeldzug vom
19.Mai bis 25.Juni 1940.

▲ Flugplatz

Rudolf Brüchert were both shot down over enemy territory near Arras and taken prisoner[30]. 6 *Staffel* also recorded a loss on this day: returning from a mission, Lt. Gottfried Pollach attempted an overshoot in his damaged machine; he crashed near Aachen airfield and was killed[31]. On account of the uncertain situation on the ground and fears that the airfield might be overrun by Allied forces during the night, at 8:30 PM the air elements of I and II/JG 3 received orders to return to Philippeville before nightfall.

22 May 1940: The French high command had meanwhile ordered a counterattack north across the Somme in order to restore ground contact with the forces cut off in Flanders, which would launch a simultaneous attack toward the south. But instead of a concentrated, coordinated offensive, the effort produced only several uncoordinated, ineffective attacks near Arras and Cambrai. After some initial success, the attacks were stopped and immediately thrown back by the German formations[32].

For the *Gruppen* under the command of *Stab*/JG 77, the day was marked by uncertainty over further developments in the Arras area. In the morning the air element of II/JG 3 moved up to Cambrai once again. From there it flew *Schwarm*- and *Staffel*-strength fighter cover missions over the battle zone around Arras all day, while cover was provided over the area around Douai and Cambrai only at the "main flying times"[33]. While II/JG 3's missions over the battle zone around Arras obviously failed to produce any tangible result[34], the *Gruppe* was nevertheless able to record two victories on this day. At 12:30 PM three Bréguet 690s appeared over the airfield; every Messerschmitt of I and II/JG 3 that was fueled and armed immediately scrambled after them. The fighters took off singly and rapidly overtook the French twin-engined machines, all three of which were shot down. Two victories went to Lt. Von Werra, *Gruppen-Adjutant* of II/JG 3; the second French machine was downed near Albert, approximately 50 kilometers southwest of Cambrai, after a determined, twenty-minute pursuit[35]. As on the previous day, the two *Gruppen* of JG 3 flew back to Philippeville before the onset of darkness. Meanwhile, the ground elements left behind at Cambrai spent a rather unsettled night. While it was becoming increasingly obvious to the command staffs that the French counterattack had collapsed and posed no threat, at about 10 PM approximately twenty-five rounds from heavy French guns fell around the airfield. The artillery fire inflicted no serious damage, however. Then, just thirty minutes later, French twin-engined aircraft appeared over the airfield; I/JG 3's anti-aircraft platoon and a nearby anti-aircraft gun belonging to the army succeeded in shooting down a Potez 63[36].

Early on the morning of 23 May the air element returned once again to Cambrai-Nierguies, but towards mid-morning it moved to Cambrai-South[37]. This day's missions, the majority of which were again over the Arras area and included low-level attacks against French troop concentrations as well as free chases and escort sorties for formations of bombers and Stukas, were uneventful. In any

event, the situation at the front had by now stabilized to the point where the *Gruppe* could remain in Cambrai when evening came. On the following day, 24 May 1940, the *Gruppe* was again tasked to fly missions over the Arras area. The *Gruppe* was also ordered to keep one *Schwarm* in the air over Cambrai airfield at all times throughout the day to provide air cover for the transport aircraft flying in supplies for the armored units of the 4th Army. During an afternoon mission[38] over the Arras area, a *Kette* from the *Gruppenstab* engaged ten Moranes north of Péronne. One of the French fighters was shot down by the *Gruppe*'s technical officer, Lt. Sannemann; the enemy pilot bailed out and was taken prisoner. That evening the *Gruppe* began yet another move; the air element flew from Cambrai-South to Mont St. Ecouvez-South[39], while the ground column followed from Philippeville. *I Fliegerkorps* had ordered *Stab*/JG 77 and the *Gruppen* under its command to occupy the group of airfields around Mont. St. Ecouvez, which included Ecouvez-North and Lesdain, during the next few days.

In the meantime, the armored units of Kleist's group had reached the line Lens—Béthune—Aire—St. Omer—Gravelines and were only about 18 kilometers from Dunkirk. Given the circumstances, the order for the panzers to halt came as a complete surprise: it was due in part to Hitler's desire to conserve his armored forces for the coming operations in the second part of the French campaign, but also to Göring's arrogant and unrealistic assurances that he could destroy the Allied forces surrounded in a tiny area around Dunkirk with "his" *Luftwaffe*[41].

Flying from Mont St. Ecouvez-South, on 25 May 1940 II/JG 3 saw most of its action over the area east of the line Lillers—Arras. There were no significant encounters with enemy aircraft. In the evening, the alert *Rotten* of II/JG 3 and I(J)/LG 2 were scrambled after heavy anti-aircraft fire near the airfield alerted those on the ground to a formation of French bombers flying by. During the pursuit of the escorted twin-engined machines, Uffz. Gremm of 4/JG 3 was able to shoot down a Potez-63, which came down in German-occupied territory near St. Quentin[42]. Meanwhile 5/JG 3 had arrived at Mont St. Ecouvez-South from Döberitz. The *Gruppe*'s landing was marred by a serious accident. Two Messerschmitts collided while on approach to the airfield, and Uffz. Max Bücher was killed in the crash of his machine. The other Messerschmitt was also destroyed, however its pilot escaped with a bad fright.

26 May 1940: After sitting immobile on the hills between Béthune and St. Omer for two days, the German armored units received orders to move east across the canal line and attack the surrounded Allied troops around Dunkirk. They were not to attack the city itself, however, as this was to be engaged by the *Luftwaffe* and the artillery alone. On the other side, the British issued orders to begin the evacuation of their own and allied troops from the mainland—"Operation Dynamo"; at this point approximately 350,000 British, French and Belgian soldiers were trapped at Dunkirk[43].

During the course of the day II/JG 3 flew several missions, mainly free chases but also some low-level attacks, over the Lille—Henin—Liétard area; none produced any tangible result. Early in the morning, however, during a free chase over the St. Omer—Dunkirk area, two *Schwärme* from 5 *Staffel* engaged two Hurricanes, one of which was shot down by Uffz. Heinzeller[44]. The British fighter crashed into the Channel[45]. The picture was much the same on the following day, 27 May. The *Gruppe* was again active mainly over and southeast of Lille, where, in addition to free chases, it was called upon to carry out strafing attacks on retreating Allied columns. In the afternoon the *Gruppe* was given an unusual task: responding to reports that a Henschel Hs 126 had been observed over the Valenciennes—Bouchain area apparently being flown by a French crew, a *Schwarm* from II/JG 3 was sent aloft to force the machine to land. The sortie proved uneventful, however, as the Hs 126 in question was not found[46].

While German army troops fought their way towards Dunkirk in the face of fierce resistance, on 28 May 1940 the *Luftwaffe*'s operations suffered when the weather deteriorated after midday. II/JG 3 flew several free chase and visual reconnaissance sorties over the Douai—Orchies area in the morning, all of which were uneventful. Then, in the afternoon, the *Gruppen* under *Stab*/JG 77 were ordered to stand down on account of the deteriorating weather[47]. The period of bad weather was of short duration, for by noon on the following day, 29 May 1940, mainly clear early summer weather had returned. Activity in the air was correspondingly intense, with the *Gruppen* of JG 77 alone logging a total of 158 sorties in 14 missions. The missions flown at noon concentrated on the area between Abbéville and Amiens, which corresponded to the 4th Army's western front, and all were uneventful. In the afternoon the *Gruppen* of JG 77, including II/JG 3, shifted their focus to the battle zone around Dunkirk[48]. *Staffel*-strength missions were flown there, with the fighters providing escort for bombers and Stukas and sweeping ahead of the bombers. During a late afternoon escort mission for I/KG 1, 4 *Staffel* and elements of I(J)/LG 2 fought a bitter air battle against a group of about 20 Hurricanes. A total of eleven victories was subsequently claimed, three of them by 4/JG 3[49], while the German *Jagdgruppen* returned without loss. In spite of this success, the German fighters had been unable to prevent several of the Hurricanes from getting through to the bombers and shooting down five Heinkels.

On 30 May 1940 bad weather kept II/JG 3 out of action. In the afternoon the *Gruppe*, together with I/JG 3 and I(J)/LG 2, was inspected at Mont St. Ecouvez by the commanding general of *I Fliegerkorps*, *General* Grauert, who expressed his appreciation for the units' operations during the fighting in the west to date, particularly over Dunkirk[50]. The bad weather over the northeast of France held on the morning of 31 May, but during the course of the mid-morning it cleared up sufficiently for the three *Gruppen* under *Stab*/

JG 77 to fly 107 sorties in the course of nine missions[51]. For II/JG 3 the day brought four escort missions in support of bomber and Stuka units[52]; however, none of these was over Dunkirk. II/JG 3 took off on its first mission at 1:55 PM together with elements of I(J)/LG 2. A total of 21 Messerschmitts escorted a Do 17 *Gruppe* of KG 76 into the Abbéville—Le Tréport area. There was no contact with enemy aircraft, however heavy, accurate anti-aircraft fire bracketed the formation[54]. Whereas II/JG 3 was escaped without loss, the Messerschmitt flown by Hptm. Trübenbach, the *Gruppenkommandeur* of I(J)/LG 2, was hit by flak and he was forced to put his machine down on its belly near Doullens[55]. At 4:02 PM twelve aircraft of 6 *Staffel* took off to provide escort for a *Staffel* of He 111s of KG 1 which had been tasked to fly armed reconnaissance over the Abbéville area. This mission also failed to result in contact with the enemy. A similar mission by nine Messerschmitts of 5 *Staffel* ninety minutes later proved more eventful: south of Abbéville the *Staffel* spotted a Breguet 690 which was shot down by Uffz. Heinzeller. The last mission of the day began at 8:05 PM, when a total of 31 Bf 109s of II/JG 3 and I (J)/LG 2 took off to escort Ju 87s of III/StG 51 attacking French troop concentrations near Huppy on the west bank of the Somme, southwest of Abbéville. Over the target area the formation encountered two British aircraft, a Wellington and a Blenheim, both of which were shot down in quick succession.

The first two days of June brought continued bright sunshine, enabling the *Gruppen* assembled at Mont. St. Ecouvez to fly missions over the battle zone on the western flank of the German breakthrough armies along the lower Somme between Abbéville and Amiens[56]. Allied aircraft were not in evidence and consequently there were neither victory claims nor losses. II/JG 3 flew its last mission over Dunkirk on the morning of 3 June 1940. Nine aircraft of 5 *Staffel* took off at 8:15 AM to provide fighter escort for a *Staffel* of II/StG 2, which was to attack field positions outside the city. There was an encounter with a number of Hurricanes east of Dunkirk and four were shot down; the Bf 109s and Ju 87s suffered no losses. That same afternoon witnessed the beginning of "Operation Paula", the *Luftwaffe*'s sole mass operation during the French campaign. A total of 1,200 machines from three air corps were committed to attacks on armaments industry targets in metropolitan Paris. These produced a number of confrontations with French fighters, some of which resulted in pitched battles. The *Gruppen* under the command of *Stab*/JG 77, which included I/JG 1 for this operation[57], put a total of 79 Messerschmitts into the air with takeoffs beginning at 1:45 PM. Their mission was to escort the Do 17s of KG 76 as they attacked airfields near Meaux in the southeast of Paris. The mission did not proceed as expected, however, for during the bombers' low-level approach two *Gruppenkommandeure* were wounded by ground fire. They were forced to turn back, and, as there was obviously a lack of radio communications, all the aircraft of their *Gruppen* followed them[59]. Meanwhile, over Compiègne and the area around Meaux, the escorting fighters became involved in air battles, some of them fierce, with French fighters, nine of which were shot down, including three Moranes which went to II/JG 3[60].

While the *Luftwaffe* was striking vigorously at the remnants of the French *Armée de l'Air*, on 3 June the British were able to evacuate another 26,746 from Dunkirk almost unhindered by German air attacks. II/JG 3 was not to take part in the final battles over Dunkirk, where by 4 June 1940 the British succeeded in evacuating 338,226 members of their expeditionary force to England, saving them from almost certain destruction[61]. While the fighting at Dunkirk was still going on, the *Luftwaffe* began its first regroupings in preparation for the second phase of the western campaign, the planned attack on the French heartland code-named "Case Red". These measures called for *Stab*/JG 77 to be withdrawn and replaced by *Stab*/JG 3[62]; while at the same time I(J)/LG 2 was to be replaced by III/JG 3, which had previously been subordinated to JG 26[63]. As well, the *Jagdgruppen* under the command of *Stab*/JG 77 were to transfer to the group of airfields around Valheureux, which had been scouted by the *Kommodore* of JG 77. This move was carried out on 4 June 1940. II/JG 3 went to Valheureux airfield, where *Stab*/JG 77 and, from the evening of 4 June, *Stab*/JG 3 were also stationed[64], while I/JG 3 transferred to Berneuil[65] and III/JG 3 to Valheureux-East. That evening the *Kommodore* of JG 3, Obstlt. Karl Vieck, took command of the three *Gruppen*, and for the first time all elements of the *Geschwader* were to go into action together. *Stab*/JG 77 subsequently remained at Valheureux until 9 June to brief the *Geschwaderstab* on operational procedures[66]. Twenty Messerschmitts flew an escort mission in support of a *Stukagruppe* on the early evening of 4 June. The mission, which was over the battle zone along the lower Somme, produced no tangible results for II/JG 3[67]. This mission was also a transfer flight for the participating aircraft, for they landed at Valheureux. Those elements of the *Gruppe* still at Mont St. Ecouvez set out for their new base as twilight was falling.

"Operation Red", the second phase of the French campaign and the actual battle for France, began on 5 June 1940. While the German ground attack made only very slow progress at first in the face of unexpectedly tough and determined resistance, the air forces of both sides were extremely active over the battle zone along the Somme and the Aisne-Oise Canal. During its missions over the battle zone west of Amiens on the first day of the German offensive, II/JG 3 recorded seven victories, including four by 4 *Staffel*, without loss to itself[68]. On the following day, 6 June, II/JG 3 scored a further five victories, including three more by 4/JG 3; this time, however, the *Gruppe* was itself forced to take three losses, all of which affected 4 *Staffel*. Lt. Rudolf Heymann was shot down in air combat near Cavillon, having previously shot down a P-36 for his third victory. Heymann bailed out, however his parachute failed to

open and he fell to his death. Fw. Erwin Dickow failed to return from a combat mission into the area south of Amiens; he was killed when his Messerschmitt went down vertically from great height and crashed[69]. Finally, Fw. August-Wilhelm Müller was shot down and wounded by the gunner of a Potez during air combat near St. Sauflieu southwest of Amiens. Müller succeeded in bringing down the French machine for his second victory before making a forced landing. He was taken to a field hospital where he ended up in the bed next to the pilot of the machine he had shot down[70].

The third day of the attack, 7 June 1940, saw II/JG 3 in action over the battle zone on the lower Somme as far as the area around Beauvais[71]. A total of five victories was claimed, all by 5 *Staffel*. Four of these came in an air battle with an escorted formation of Fairey Battles in the early evening. Oblt. Kijewski shot down a Spitfire for his second victory, while *Unteroffiziere* Heinzeller, Nelleskamp and Freitag each shot down a Battle. The *Gruppe* suffered no losses on this day. II/JG 3's missions during the next three days, escorting bombers and Stukas over the combat zone south of the lower Somme, were all uneventful, for neither successes nor losses were reported until 10 June.

Meanwhile the German ground offensive had gained further ground to the west against weakening French resistance. While Army Group B's advance resulted in the encirclement of strong British forces near Dieppe and St. Valéry on the Channel Coast, the units of Army Group A drove across the Aisne to begin the attack on Paris. The French abandoned the city on 13 June and that evening it was occupied by German soldiers without a struggle.

With Allied resistance weakening, after 10 June 1940 there was a clear drop in II/JG 3's level of activity[72], and the missions flown subsequent to that date produced just two victories—a Battle on 11 June and a Blenheim on 13 June. On 13 June 1940 the *Gruppe* was moved again, this time from Valheureux to Doudeville[73], a front-line airfield approximately 15 kilometers north of Rouen[74]. The next day several missions were flown from there, escort for bombers over the Paris area[75] and free chases over the coastal area on either side of Dieppe. Two more victories were recorded by 16 June. On 17 and 18 June II/JG 3's air element was moved forward to Escorpain, a front-line airfield near Dreux. In reality it was nothing more than a small, poorly-leveled wheat field, tightly enclosed by trees[76]. From there the *Gruppe* had to fly missions in pursuit of the French armies retreating towards the Loire. Uffz. Mias of 5/JG 3 scored one victory on 17 June. Then, on 18 June, when a free chase over the area around Orléans failed to produce contact with enemy aircraft, the fighters carried out strafing attacks on ground columns. It is not known if the *Gruppe* suffered any losses. On 18 June the *Gruppe* was again moved forward and flew from Escorpain to Le Mans, from where it flew several free chase missions as far as the lower Loire near Saumur and Nantes until 22 June. No further victories were recorded. During these days the *Gruppe*'s operational activities were restricted noticeably by a shortage of fuel, deliveries of supplies having become sporadic[77]. On the casualty list was Uffz. Fritz Mias of 5 *Staffel*, who on 19 June failed to return from a combat mission for reasons unknown. He was reported missing but soon afterwards arrived back at his unit unharmed.

On 23 June 1940 II/JG 3 made what was to be its last transfer for some time; the air element flew from Le Mans to Brombois, a front-line airfield five kilometers west southwest of Grandvilliers. II/JG 3 spent the last days of the French campaign there, apparently flying few missions during this time. The cease-fire took effect on 25 June 1940 and the guns fell silent in France, ending the first great chapter of World War Two.

The French campaign, which began barely three months after II/JG 3 was established, was the *Gruppe*'s first hard test in combat against the French and British air forces. During four weeks of operations it recorded 48 enemy aircraft shot down. Casualties during the same period totaled four pilots killed, two captured and one wounded. Material losses amounted to eleven Messerschmitts written off as total losses[78].

Notes:

[18] Compare Jacobsen/Rohwer, p. 22 and following pages.

[19] Compare Prien, JG 77 Part I, p. 269.

[20] According to the logbook of Heinrich Sannemann the transfer flight by the *Gruppenstab* took place from 12:32 to 1:15 PM from Zerbst to Lippstadt and from 4:00 to 5:32 PM from there to Philippeville.

[21] War diary of Stab/JG 77; it went on to say: *"According to a statement by the Kommandeur of II/JG 3, I/JG 77 is supposed to be exchanged for II/JG 3. There is no order concerning this."* In fact the exchange of the two *Gruppen* took place effective 22/5/1940. See Prien, JG 77 Part I, p. 295. On 20/5/1940 there were four *Gruppen* under the command of *Stab*/JG 77, namely I/JG 77, I(J)/LG 2 and I and II/JG 3.

[22] War diary of Stab/JG 77

[23] The term *"Feindflug"* or combat mission applied to a mission whose operational task required flight over enemy territory; consequently, according to the strict rules of the *Luftwaffe* bureaucrats scrambles to intercept enemy aircraft over friendly territory did not count as combat missions. This interpretation was subsequently broadened when events showed it to be unrealistic.

[24] According to *Stab*/JG 77's war diary the enemy aircraft were Spitfires, however they were in fact Hurricanes, as stated in the victory confirmations. As well, contrary to the *Stab*/JG 77 war diary four, not three, victories were claimed.

[25] According to the WASt. casualty report Lt. Wisser belonged to 5/JG 3; however, since 5 *Staffel* was still in Döberitz at this time and thus not in action over France, Lt. Wisser must have been attached to the *Gruppenstab* at this time.

[26] War diary of Stab/JG 77. Unless stated otherwise, subsequent information concerning the *Gruppe*'s losses is based mainly on two sources, namely the military casualty reports, which are currently held by the WASt. in Berlin, and the reports of the Quartermaster-General Dept. 6 concerning aircraft losses.

[27] Altogether the *Gruppen* under the command of *Stab*/JG 77 flew 18 missions on 20 May 1940 totaling 129 sorties. On this day successes were limited to three victories by II/JG 3.

[28] The airfield was usually recorded as Cambrai (as opposed to Cambrai-South).

[29] War diary of Stab/JG 77

[30] Curiously the *Stab*/JG 77 war diary contains no reference to this air battle; three engagements involving I/JG 3 are the only ones mentioned, and these resulted in six victories for no losses.

[31] No details of this engagement are known; this information is taken from the war diary of *Stab*/JG 77.

[32] Compare Jacobsen/Rohwer, p. 35; OKW War Diary 1940-41 Part II, p. 1164.

[33] According to the war diary of *Stab*/JG 77 the first missions to Arras began at 5:20 AM and went on until nightfall, while missions over the Douai—Cambrai area did not begin until 7:50 AM.

[34] Heinrich Sannemann's logbook records an engagement between 5 Messerschmitts and 5 Spitfires at noontime; their was no result apart from minor bullet damage.

[35] The third went to Lt. Fiel of I/JG 3—war diary of *Stab*/JG 77.

[36] War diary of Stab/JG 77

[37] Papers of Georg Alex, war diary of Stab/JG 77.

[38] According to Heinrich Sannemann's logbook the mission took place from 5:00 to 6:20 PM, while his victory report lists the time of the downing as 5:55 PM; according to *Stab*/JG 77's war diary, however, the engagement took place much earlier, at 3:35 PM.

[39] Also spelled Montécouvez.

[40] War diary of Stab/JG 77. Ecouvez-South was occupied by *Stab*/JG 77 and I and II/JG 3, while I(J)/LG 2 landed at Ecouvez-North.

[41] The most part this task was to fall to the units of *Luftflotte* 2; see Jacobsen/Rohwer, p. 40 and following pages; OKW War Diary 1940-41 Part II, p. 1064.

[42] One Ms 406 went to the Messerschmitts of I/JG 21, which happened to be in the same area and was able to intervene in the air battle.

[43] Compare Jacobsen/Rohwer, p. 46; OKW War Diary 1940-41 Part II, p. 1064.

[44] According to Josef Heinzeller it was a Dewoitine, contrary to the entry in the war diary of Stab/JG 77.

[45] The following observation in the war diary of *Stab*/JG 77 is noteworthy: *"From the direction in which the enemy flew away, it may be concluded that the enemy has withdrawn his air forces from the pocket in Flanders and the Artois and is flying his missions from England."*

[46] If this was in fact a Henschel; war diary of *Stab*/JG 77, which reveals that time of takeoff was 1:57 PM.

[47] The corresponding order was issued at 4:50 PM; by then the *Gruppen* under the command of *Stab*/JG 77 had been able to fly 11 missions totaling 64 Messerschmitt sorties.

[48] It was not until the afternoon of 29 May 1940 that the *Luftwaffe* was offered its second opportunity (in terms of weather) to launch concentrated attacks against the Allied forces surrounded at Dunkirk. The *Luftwaffe* achieved considerable success on this day, sinking five large ferries and three destroyers and damaging another seven destroyers. From the British standpoint these losses placed the continuation of "Operation Dynamo" in serious jeopardy, especially since this day's air attacks saw the port of Dunkirk blockaded and rendered unusable. Nevertheless, on this day the British succeeded in evacuating 47,310 men back to England. Compare in detail Jacobsen and Rohwer, p. 51; Bekker, p. 157, Prien, JG 77 Part 1, p. 302.

[49] Compare Prien, JG 77 Part 1, p. 51; Bekker, p. 157; Prien, JG 77 Part I, p. 302 and following pages. According to the war diary of *Stab*/JG 77 a total of 21 Messerschmitts from both *Gruppen* took part in this mission. I(J)/LG 2 subsequently claimed just six victories, however the instructional *Gruppe* in fact scored eight victories.

[50] War diary of *Stab*/JG 77.

[51] War diary *Stab*/JG 77.

[52] While the exact number of missions flown by II/JG 3 on this day is not known, entries in the war diary of *Stab*/JG 77 reveal that a total of about 35 to 40 sorties was flown in the four missions, an average of 1.5 missions per available aircraft. This does not seem like very many given the good weather that prevailed for most of the day and the fact that the fighting for the last positions held by Allied troops at Dunkirk was well within the *Gruppe*'s range. The reason for this comparatively modest effort is not known—as many as five or six missions per day would be flown during periods of heavy fighting in the east, and even during operations over England three *Gruppe* missions was often the rule. The war diary of *Stab*/JG 77 offers no clues in this regard.

[53] During the afternoon Dunkirk was struck by several air raids by units of *Luftflotte* 2; nevertheless, on 31 May 1940 a total of 68,014 men embarked for England.

[54] Logbook of Heinrich Sannemann; war diary of *Stab*/JG 77.

[55] Compare Prien, JG 77 Part I, P 306, 1817.

[56] On 1 June *Stab*/JG 77 reported that the *Gruppen* under its command flew 7 missions totaling 82 sorties, on 2 June it was 9 missions and a total of 88 sorties.

[57] See Prien/Rodeike/Stemmer, JG 27, P 57.

[58] Takeoff time from the war diary of *Stab*/JG 77; according to Heinrich Sannemann's logbook takeoff was at 2:00 PM.

[59] War diary *Stab*/JG 77.

[60] This operation was described as a great success for external consumption (see the OKW report of 4/6/1940, for example) however within the *Luftwaffe* command the value of "Operation Paula" was the subject of considerable dispute, especially since it had no obvious effects on the course of the battle in France.

[61] Compare Jacobsen/Rohwer, P 51 and following pages; Prien, JG 77 Part 1, P 306 and following pages; Jackson, P 21.

[62] Compare the extensive entries throughout the day in *Stab*/JG 77's war diary.

[63] Compare Prien/Stemmer, III/JG 3, P 24. I (J)/LG 2 left the command of *Stab/JG 77* effective the evening of 3 June and was subsequently placed under the command of the Jafü 2.

[64] *Stab*/JG 77 consisted of just an advance detachment; the headquarters was set up in Candas.

[65] Also one *Staffel* to Vignacourt.

[66] The main column, which had remained behind during the last move, stayed in Mont. St. Ecouvez.

[67] According to Heinrich Sannemann's logbook the mission times were 6:30 to 7:15 PM; on this day the *Gruppen* of JG flew three missions totaling 40 sorties. War diary *Stab*/JG 77.

[68] The *Kommodore* of JG 77 and JG 3 took part in several missions, with the former briefing Obstlt. Vieck on operational conditions; however, none of these missions resulted in enemy contact.

[69] According to the papers of Georg Alex this crash also occurred near Cavillon, where *"later a worthy cross made by the Staffel carpenter was erected in the chateau garden"*; the WASt. casualty report does not give a location of the loss.

[70] Papers of Georg Alex

[71] For example, between 9:15 and 10:20 in the morning the Messerschmitts of the *Gruppenstab* escorted several bombers engaged in armed reconnaissance; the mission was uneventful. Log book of Heinrich Sannemann.

[72] For example, three combat missions are recorded in Heinrich Sannemann's log book under 8 June, while a total of just four combat missions were flown in the period from 10 to 17 June.

[73] The spelling of this place name varies between the available references; in Heinrich Sannemann's log book it is spelled *Doudeauville*, while Botho Teichmann spelled it *Doudouville*.

[74] According to the papers of Georg Alex, on this day 4/JG 3 moved to Etrépagny, approximately 15 kilometers northwest of Gisors, and remained there until 16 June; the *Staffel* was obviously employed separated from the rest of the *Gruppe* during this time.

[75] The purpose of these missions is not clear, Paris having already been occupied on 13 June and the French forces having subsequently withdrawn to the west—however, the information here is based on entries in the logbook of Heinrich Sannemann under 13 and 14 June 1940.

[76] Georg Alex wrote: *"Several aircraft damaged as a result of striking treetops and grain heads lodged in the radiators."*

[77] Papers of Georg Alex

[78] Regrettably complete loss figures for the *Gruppe* are not available for this period.

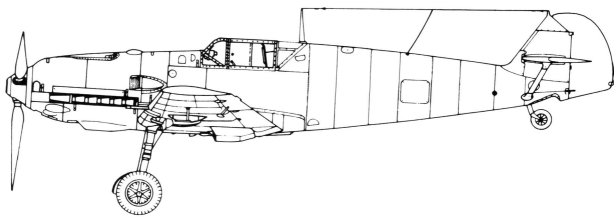

Line Drawing 2: Messerschmitt Bf 109 E-4

As well as the Bf 109 E-3, beginning in April 1940 II/JG 3 began receiving examples of the Bf 109 E-4, which was gradually to replace the E-3 as the unit's "cannon machine." The sole difference compared to the E-3 was the installation of the improved MG FF/M wing cannon.

Length: 8.80 m

Wingspan: 9.90 m

Height: 2.60 m

Engine: DB 601 A, 1,100 H.P.

Takeoff weight: 2 608 kg

Armament: 2 MG FF/M, 2 MG 17

Empty weight: 1 865 kg

A Bf 109 E-1 in an unmodified 1940 scheme after an engine-out belly landing, probably photographed during the French Campaign in May 1940. The relatively angular shape of the aircraft number suggests that this machine may have belonged to II/JG 3. Note the revised, angular shape of the cockpit canopy. (Berger)

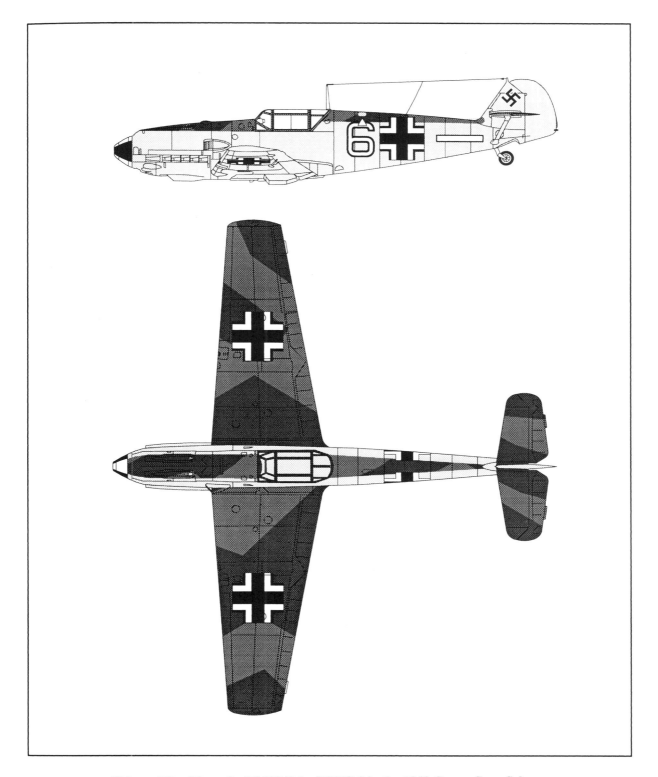

Side and Top View of a Bf 109 E-1 of II/JG 3 in the 1940 Camouflage Scheme

The machine depicted here is finished in the factory-applied scheme consisting of gray-green segments on the upper surfaces and pale blue fuselage sides and undersurfaces. Aft of the fuselage *Balkenkreuz* is the horizontal bar marking indicating the Second *Gruppe* as used by II/JG 3 from the beginning.

3

Operations over the Channel and Great Britain
July 1940 to February 1941

For II/JG 3, which had been in action only since 20 May 1940, the end of the fighting in France did not result in an opportunity to rest from operations and regain its strength after the hectic activity of the past weeks. Instead it went straight into operations against England. The *Gruppe* initially remained at Brombois, from where it was now called upon to defend the coast of France together with the other two *Gruppen* of the *Geschwader*, which had arrived at Grandvilliers (I/JG 3) and Dieppe (III/JG 3). On 29 June 1940 at Brombois II/JG 3 reported its strength as 34 pilots and 40 Bf 109 Es, of which 31 were serviceable[79]. New pilots were assigned to make good the losses suffered during operations in the French campaign and soon the *Gruppe* was back up to its authorized strength of forty pilots[80].

II/JG 3's operational activity was limited during all of July 1940, which was largely due to the onset of rainy weather at the beginning of the month which seriously restricted the activities of the *Luftwaffe* units on the Channel Coast. Sudden rainfalls often turned the flattened meadows used as airfields by the *Jagdgruppen* into bottomless morasses; taxiing the Messerschmitts under these conditions resulted in a large number of headstands and other usually harmless incidents[81]. Meanwhile a number of pilots were sent on flights to the home war zone on more or less official missions. For many this provided the welcome opportunity for a brief home leave[82]. Outings were also made to Antwerp and Brussels, where the pilots were able to enjoy some pleasant hours, each in his own way.

Since the British reckoned on a possible German invasion following the defeat of France and believed that the greatest danger would come (if at all) immediately after the end of the fighting in France[83], the fighter and bomber units of the RAF were sent into action over the English Channel almost daily to detect potential invasion preparations, strike at them, and tie up *Luftwaffe* forces. The result of this was that the German fighter units left along the Channel Coast after the cease-fire initially had to fly purely defensive missions before the scene of combat shifted to the waters be-

tween France and England in mid-July, when the *Luftwaffe* began attacking British coastal shipping in the Channel[84]. This resulted in some heavy fighting in the air, as on 30 June and 10 July 1940, however II/JG 3 does not appear to have been involved[85].

The period of relative quiet was short lived, for on 7 August 1940 II/JG 3 moved to Wierre-au-Bois, a forward airfield near Samer, about 12 kilometers southeast of Boulogne, which was to be the *Gruppe*'s new base of operations. The *Geschwaderstab* and the other two *Gruppen* also moved to the Channel Coast in these days—in some cases after a brief rest and refit—and occupied front-line airfields in the immediate vicinity of II/JG 3[86]. In the coming missions against Great Britain the *Geschwader* was to form part of *Luftflotte 2* and was thus under the command of the *Jafü 2*, *Oberst* Theo Osterkamp[87], who with five *Jagdgeschwader* under his command wielded the strongest concentration of fighters.

Meanwhile the *Luftwaffe*'s preparations for its planned air offensive against the British island kingdom were nearing their conclusion[89]; however, bad weather made it necessary to again postpone the start of the attack, which had originally been planned for 8 August 1940. II/JG 3 began operations from the Channel Coast on 11 August 1940, however the missions flown over the Channel and the south coast of England on that day were uneventful[90]. The result was the same on the following day, 12 August, when the *Gruppe* was sent to pick up a returning bomber formation in the evening[91]. In any case these missions gave the first direct impression of the operational conditions under which the *Gruppe* would be operating during its missions over England in the coming weeks. For the time being II/JG 3's area of operations was to be the waters off the Pas de Calais and off the southeast coast of England plus the county of Kent as far as London. The well-known limited range of the Bf 109 made deeper penetrations into the airspace over the British Isles impossible, while the return flight across the Channel (50 km at least) placed a considerable strain on the crews, as did any flights over water, especially if it was in an aircraft damaged in combat

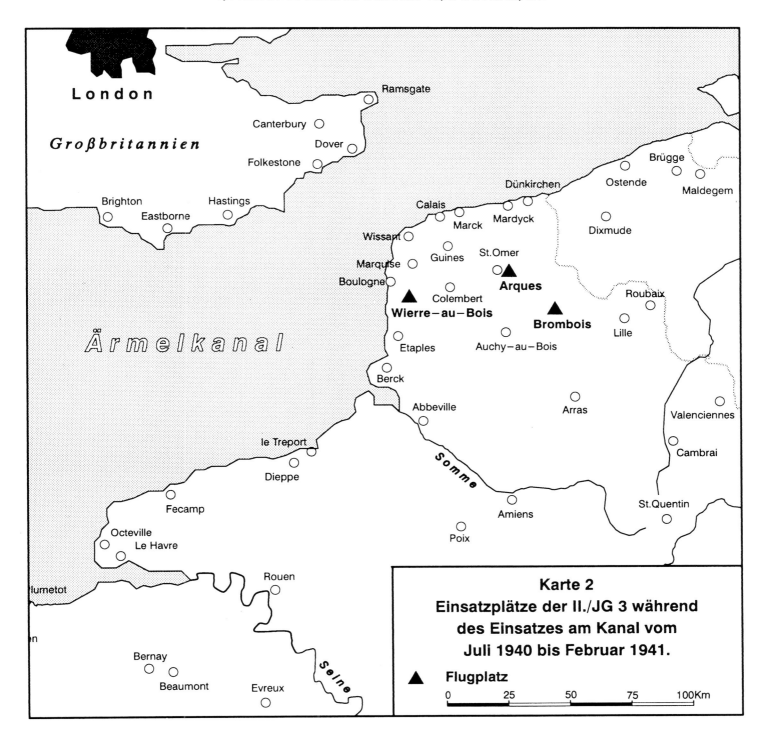

London

Großbritannien

Ramsgate

Canterbury

Dover

Folkestone

Brighton
Eastborne

Hastings

Ärmelkanal

Brügge

Ostende

Maldegem

Dünkirchen

Calais

Marck

Mardyck

Dixmude

Wissant

Guines

St.Omer

Marquise

Arques

Boulogne

Colembert

Wierre-au-Bois

Brombois

Roubaix

Lille

Etaples

Auchy-au-Bois

Berck

Abbeville

Arras

Valenciennes

le Treport

Somme

Cambrai

Dieppe

Fecamp

St.Quentin

Octeville
Le Havre

Amiens

Poix

lumetot

Rouen

Seine

Bernay

Beaumont

Evreux

Karte 2

Einsatzplätze der II./JG 3 während

des Einsatzes am Kanal vom

Juli 1940 bis Februar 1941.

▲ **Flugplatz**

0   25   50   75   100Km

with Hurricanes and Spitfires or one that was "thirsty"[92]. Operations over water also made it necessary for pilots to carry extensive emergency equipment to supplement their existing seat-type parachutes. This included a life vest, a one-man inflatable dinghy with a compressed air bottle for inflation, a bulky flare pistol with signal cartridges, a folding knife, emergency rations and a sea distress marker flag. All of these things had to be worn on the pilot's person, as a result of which the pilot's limited freedom of movement in the Messerschmitt's already cramped cockpit was restricted almost unbearably.

From this point on, the *Gruppen* of JG 3 flew mainly free chase and escort missions for bombers to England as well as defensive sorties over the Channel Coast[94]. As a rule these missions were flown in *Gruppe* strength, with II/JG 3 frequently providing escort for formations of bombers together with the other *Gruppen* of the *Geschwader*. Unlike the missions flown in the later stages of the French campaign, the missions to England were flown at ever higher altitudes in response to attacks from above by British fighters; it was not unusual for the Messerschmitts to operate at altitudes of 9 000 meters or higher.

13 August 1940 was to be the long awaited "*Adlertag*" (Eagle Day), even though it brought no significant improvement in the weather. But Hermann Göring, who had appeared in person at the Channel to "lead" the attack, ordered strikes against Fighter Command's ground organization to begin that afternoon[95]. A total of 485 bomber and approximately 1,000 fighter sorties were flown on this day[96], mainly against British airfields. The results were extremely poor, however. Hampered by bad weather and in some cases by defending British fighters, the attacks did not get through and so in the end only two airfields actually used by Fighter Command were hit and of the 47 aircraft destroyed on the ground on this day only one was a Spitfire[97]. The claims submitted by the German fighter pilots were also considerably exaggerated—the Royal Air Force's actual losses in air combat were 24 machines instead of the 74 claimed shot down by the *Luftwaffe*[98]. German losses amounted to 34 aircraft including nine Bf 109s[99]. II/JG 3 flew two missions on this day, and in each case the mission order was to "engage English fighter forces." Neither missions resulted in contact with the enemy and consequently both were unsuccessful[100].

The next day, 14 August 1940, brought heavy cloud which prevented the *Luftwaffe* from launching large-scale attacks against targets in the southeast of Great Britain. *Luftflotte* 2 carried out just one concentrated Stuka mission against targets in Kent and several free chases. At noon II/JG 3 escorted Stukas[101] over the Folkestone—Dover area. There was an engagement with British fighters and Obfw. Erich Labusga of 6 *Staffel* was shot down off Dover. He was posted missing in action. II/JG 3 recorded no successes on this day. Two days later, on 16 August, the *Gruppe* flew two missions, free chasing and escorting bombers over the Thames Estuary[102]. In the morning a free chase over the sea resulted in a fierce combat with a

number of Spitfires. Three of the British fighters were shot down for the loss of two Messerschmitts. The German fighters crashed into the sea, their pilots ending up "in the drink." Both men were fortunate, being picked up by the air-sea rescue service, however one of them, Hptm. Alfred Müller, *Staffelkapitän* of 4/JG 3, sustained such serious wounds that he was kept out of action for a long time. Oblt. Jost Kipper had to be placed in command of the *Staffel* in his place[103].

The 18th of August would be recorded as the "Hardest Day" in the fighting over Britain, resulting in the heaviest losses for both sides[104]. II/JG 3 was in action over Kent in the early afternoon[105], providing part of the forward escort for two bomber units whose targets were the British air bases at Kenley and Biggin Hill, however there was no contact with the enemy. A second mission flown in the early evening produced a much different result. This time the targets were the British fighter bases at Hornchurch and North Weald. Fierce fighting developed over Kent in which one victory was scored by Oblt. Westerhoff of 6 *Staffel* (4); on the other side of the coin three Messerschmitts sustained serious battle damage which forced them to head for home. Fw. August-Wilhelm Müller of 4/JG 3 crashed on landing at Wierre-au-Bois[106], but he was lucky and escaped injury. 6 *Staffel* suffered two casualties: seriously wounded in air combat, Uffz. Friedrich Becker crash-landed his battered Messerschmitt on Marquise airfield and succumbed to his wounds soon afterwards. Fw. Erich Dobrick, who was forced to belly-land his machine near Boulogne, was more fortunate; he escaped with relatively minor injuries.

In the following days up to 23 August, weather limited operations to attacks by small formations of bombers and free chase missions over southern England. II/JG 3 claimed one victory during this period (on 21 August), while no losses were suffered on operations. A slight improvement in the weather on 24 August 1940 resulted in an immediate upswing in operations by the *Luftwaffe* against the British Isles; this day also saw the start of a series of in some cases heavy air attacks on the Royal Air Force's ground organization in the southeast of Great Britain. On this day II/JG 3 was called upon to fly three *Gruppe*–strength missions[107], the first two to pick up returning bomber formations over the Channel and the third a free chase over Kent. No enemy aircraft were encountered. The *Gruppe* apparently saw no action on the following day, however it returned to action on 26 August 1940, providing escort for a Do 17 unit and picking up returning bomber formations over southeast England. II/JG 3 registered seven victories, and it is likely that all resulted from an air battle over the Canterbury area at about 1:30 PM during the first mission of the day[108]. These victories came at a high cost, however, for three pilots were killed or went missing. 4 *Staffel* was forced to place two pilots on the casualty list: Uffz. Willy Finke was shot down and killed in air combat near Reculver and Uffz. Emil Müller failed to return after last being seen in air combat in the Canterbury area. It must be assumed that he was killed when he crashed into the Channel while trying to nurse his damaged machine back to France. The third casualty was from 6/JG 3: Uffz. Fritz Buchner lost his life when he was shot down over the Thames Estuary and crashed into the sea.

On the following day steady rain and low cloud resulted in a break in operations. The weather was little better on 28 August, but nevertheless II/JG 3 flew three *Gruppe*-strength missions: the first saw it pick up a returning bomber unit over the Channel, the second was an escort mission for a Do 17 unit over southeast England (aborted after the bombers failed to arrive at the rendezvous point), and the third a free chase over the southeast of England. With a total of eleven victories, this was II/JG 3's most successful day during the fighting over England, while losses—one pilot slightly wounded (Obfw. Horst Götz of 5/JG 3) and three Messerschmitts shot down in air combat—were relatively light. The outstanding pilot of the day was unquestionably Oblt. Franz von Werra, who scored four victories to raise his total to eight, the best in the *Gruppe*[109].

The weather on 29 August 1940 was little better than on the previous days, consequently the *Luftwaffe*'s efforts over England were limited to numerous free chases—the task assigned the fighters was outlined in the following order:

Suppression of the enemy's fighter defense in the southeast of England through massed operations by the Jagdgeschwader.

In practice this meant that the German *Jagdgruppen* assembled on the Channel flew a total of 723 sorties[110] over the small area of southeast England which could be covered by the Messerschmitts with their limited range. II/JG 3's involvement was one *Gruppe*-strength mission: at 3:50 PM every serviceable Messerschmitt taxied out for takeoff at Wierre-au-Bois. Their mission order: free chase over the London—Hastings area[111]. Two victories were claimed by Oblt. Herbert Kijewski (3) and Oblt. Werner Voigt (2), both of 5/JG 3. On the debit side, 4 *Staffel* lost two pilots: *Staffelführer* Oblt. Jost Kipper was shot down near Hastings and crashed to his death with his Messerschmitt. The other pilot lost was Uffz. Walter Gericke, who was shot down in the same combat and crashed into the sea off Hastings. With the loss of Oblt. Kipper, Lt. Richard von Larisch assumed command of 4 *Staffel*.

The missions flown on the last two days of the month resulted in a number of clashes with British fighters. On 30 August II/JG 3 was able to report a victory by its *Kommandeur* Hptm. von Selle (5), who shot down a Hurricane in the Dungeness area during an early evening free chase mission[112]. The next day, however, the *Gruppe* was hit by two more total losses when Lt. Richard von Larisch, *Staffelführer* of 4/JG 3 for just two days, and Oblt. Karl Westerhoff of 6 *Staffel* were shot down during an evening bomber escort mission into the London area[113]. The former was shot down

and killed over London, while Karl Westerhoff came down in his blazing machine near Lydd. Seriously injured, he was taken prisoner. Lt. Von Larisch was succeeded by Oblt. Werner Voigt, who was transferred from 5 to 4/JG 3 to become the new *Kapitän* of 4 *Staffel*[114].

The first days of September saw the *Luftwaffe* continue its attacks against the forward British fighter bases in the southeast of England using small formations of bombers with a strong fighter escort. All of the German day fighter forces had meanwhile been concentrated in the area of the Pas de Calais in order to protect the bomber units of *Luftflotte 2* during their subsequent attacks on targets in the British Isles[115], while at the same time the bombers of *Luftflotte 3* had begun raiding targets by night.

While the first four days of the month were largely uneventful for II/JG 3 (apart from one Messerschmitt shot down and another damaged in air combat on the 2nd—neither pilot was injured), the missions of 5 September 1940 resulted in further encounters with British fighters. At 10:15 AM the *Gruppe* took off to escort bomber units attacking targets in the area south of London[116]. Over Kent it encountered a group of Spitfires, two of which were shot down by the *Staffelkapitän* of 6/JG 3, Oblt. Erich Woitke (4) for the loss of two Messerschmitts. One of these was flown by *Gruppen-Adjutant* Oblt. Franz von Werra; his machine damaged by friendly fire, he attempted to fly home alone, was pursued by a Spitfire and forced down near Marden. He was subsequently taken prisoner by the English unhurt[117]. The pilot of the other aircraft was more fortunate, for he managed to nurse his crippled machine out over the Channel, where he ditched and was later picked up by the air-sea rescue service, none the worse for his experience.

After almost four weeks of the so-called "intensified air war", disillusionment and helplessness were beginning to spread through the *Luftwaffe* command. Born of a total misreading of the facts and a dangerous overestimation the *Luftwaffe*'s capabilities, the boundless optimism that had culminated in the baseless expectation of softening up Great Britain with just eight days of bombing had disappeared. Moreover the objective of the German efforts continued to be anything but clear: talk was not of a landing in Great Britain, rather of an attempt to cut off Britain's supplies by destroying its ocean ports and production sites. In the prevailing confused atmosphere the *Luftwaffe*'s commanders obviously failed to appreciate that the recent days had brought it one step closer to achieving its objective of defeating the British fighter defense and that Fighter Command was in fact in bad shape. Instead of carrying on they now adopted a change of tactics: since the attacks against the RAF's ground organization had failed to achieve the desired results, beginning immediately terror attacks would be mounted against London as per Hitler's directive of 4 September. The decision was probably based on Adolf Hitler's belief (or more likely wishful thinking) that a series of concentrated day and night raids on the capital would make Great Britain ready to sue for peace[118,119].

"Operation *Loge*", the *Luftwaffe*'s assault against London, began on the late afternoon of 7 September 1940. 350 bombers in several waves, escorted by 648 fighters, were sent to attack docks, warehouses, oil tank farms and other targets in and around London. Beginning at 5:10 PM, II/JG 3 was in action escorting bombers to London[120], which was at the extreme range limit of the Bf 109 allowing the pilots only a brief period of air combat over the target area. It would not be long before the fighter pilots of the Royal Air Force adapted themselves to this weakness of their German opponent. They would climb to altitude west of London, safely beyond the range of the Messerschmitts, and wait for the moment when the German formations had to reverse course for the return flight. Among the German fighter pilots this maneuver was known as "the big panic turn over London". It was inevitably the signal for the Hurricanes and Spitfires to attack the German formations from above and behind. On this day, for the first time there was bitter fighting over the British capital against numerous Spitfires and Hurricanes which rose to defend it. II/JG 3 suffered no losses, while one victory was claimed by its *Kommandeur* Hptm. von Selle

On 8 September bad weather prevented a continuation of the daylight attacks on London[121], and it was not until the late afternoon of 9 September that further attacks were made on targets in the area of the British capital. Together with the other *Gruppen* of the *Geschwader* and III/ZG 76, II/JG 3 provided escort for the Heinkels of II/KG 1[122] as they attacked Farnborough airfield. The route to the target took the attackers into the area south of London and then west toward the target[123]. They ran into the concentration of defending British fighter squadrons there, resulting in fierce dogfights in which the Messerschmitts were hard-pressed to defend their charges against the attacking Hurricanes and Spitfires. For II/JG 3 the battle ended with two victories by 4 *Staffel*, these going to *Kapitän* Oblt. Voigt (3) and Obfw. Müller (3). The latter was himself shot down a short time later, and at about 6:55 PM he was forced to ditch in the Channel approximately 10 kilometers off Newhaven. Müller had the good fortune to be fished out of the water by the British rescue service and thus ended up a prisoner of war.

The weather remained changeable. No large attacks could be mounted on 10 September, while on the 11th 280 bombers and about 750 fighters were mustered for missions against targets in England. The following two days were again characterized by poor, mainly rainy weather, which restricted the *Luftwaffe* to weak fighter sweeps over the British coastal area. The only tangible result for II/JG 3 was one victory on 13 September by Uffz. Dilling (1) of 6/JG 3.

15 September 1940: In the morning there was a slight improvement in the weather which allowed the *Luftwaffe* to prepare for another major raid on London. Several waves of bombers totaling approximately 220 machines set out for the city with a powerful fighter escort. As a result there were relatively widespread air battles over the southeast of England in the early afternoon and evening

which were both fiercely fought and costly. II/JG 3 flew two *Gruppe*-strength bomber escort missions over England on this day[124] and was able to record two victories, one of them by technical officer Oblt. Sannemann (3)[125]. The fact that the *Gruppe* sustained no losses in men or machines in spite of the fierce dogfights with the British fighters, which for the first time appeared in large groups of up to 80 aircraft, must be considered a success. The *Luftwaffe* once again incurred painful losses, losing 63 aircraft[126]. Bomber losses were especially heavy[127].

The next two days brought more bad weather and operational activity was limited. On 18 September there was a brief resurgence in the *Luftwaffe*'s attacks, with a total of 359 bombers and 1,024 fighters being mustered for 33 missions by small formations of aircraft. Shortly before noon II/JG 3 flew a free chase mission over the London area[128], where it engaged British fighters, one of which was shot down by Oblt. Woitke (5). The *Gruppe* suffered no losses. Then rain set in, preventing further large-scale operations against England until 26 September 1940. During this period operations were limited to isolated fighter sweeps, as on 20 September, for example, when the *Gruppen* of the *JaFü 2* went free chasing over Kent in two large waves. II/JG 3 scored one victory, by Uffz. Heckmann of 5 *Staffel* (3), and suffered no losses. With Wierre-au-Bois airfield completely rain-soaked, making regular operations impossible for the foreseeable future, on 23 September 1940 II/JG 3 transferred to Arques, a front-line airfield southeast of St. Omer.

On 27 September there was a significant improvement in the weather, which made possible a resumption of air raids on London. Several attacks were flown against the British capital throughout the day, resulting in widespread fighting over the city and the southeast approaches, in which both sides suffered heavily. The *Luftwaffe*'s losses amounted to 19 Bf 109s, 19 Bf 110s and 17 Ju 88s, while the Royal Air Force lost 48 fighters[129]. II/JG 3 flew three missions on this day, the first a rendezvous with a returning formation of bombers and the other two escort for bombers to Canterbury[130]. Successes and losses balanced exactly—one victory against the loss of a Messerschmitt of 4/JG 3. The propeller pitch control mechanism of Gefr. Leo Suschko's machine was damaged in combat between London and Dover, causing the blades to immediately move to the feathered position; even though his engine was still producing power, there was no forward thrust. Leo Suschko was extremely fortunate to reach the middle of the Channel, where he was forced to ditch but was later picked up unhurt by the air-sea rescue service[131].

The last three days of September were much the same: weather permitting, free chase or bomber escort missions were flown over southeast England. These resulted in occasional encounters with British fighters, which usually avoided engaging in what they saw as useless and costly dogfights with the Messerschmitts, whose fighter sweeps posed no direct threat to the British position. During another bomber escort mission over London[132] on the afternoon of

29 September 1940, II/JG 3 fought a pitched battle with a unit of Hurricanes, six of which were shot down by the *Gruppe* without loss. II/JG 3 had not emerged from the battles of the past weeks unscathed, as the strength return at the end of September 1940 shows[133]: at this time II/JG 3 had 31 Messerschmitts on strength, however only twenty of these were serviceable. With so few available aircraft, each *Staffel* was only capable of putting five or six machines into the air. The pilot situation was not much better: the *Gruppe* had 24 pilots available against an authorized strength of 40. All were listed as fit for duty, however this was still just sixty percent of authorized strength.

On the last day of the month there was a change in the leadership of II/JG 3: Hptm. Erich von Selle left the *Gruppe* he had formed to become Ia (operations officer) on the staff of the *Nachtjagddivision* (Night Fighter Division). Hptm. Erich Woitke, the *Kapitän* of 6 *Staffel*, was temporarily placed in command of II/ JG 3.

The beginning of October 1940 brought another change in tactics by the *Luftwaffe*. In the following weeks the bomber units had to be almost completely withdrawn from daylight missions over England because of losses and lack of success. As a result, the fighters also had to assume the role of bomb carriers in subsequent attacks on England[134]. The aircraft of one *Staffel* from each of the *Jagdgruppen* stationed on the Channel Coast were equipped with bomb racks for the fighter-bomber (*Jabo*) role. The attacks by these *Jabos*, which could be described as pinpricks at best, were supposed to strike the decisive blow against the (as Göring imagined it) tottering island empire. This is a further example of the lack of realism and the unbroken overestimation of one's own capabilities which existed within the circle of the *Luftwaffe* command, for after the state of the fighting so far no one could realistically expect that the British position could really be shaken by a series of more or less random nuisance attacks. What the introduction of fighter-bomber *Staffeln* on the Channel did achieve was a serious weakening of the fighter force, for exactly one third of its aircraft were now converted into bomb carriers. Instead of being strengthened, the fighter arm, whose task it had once been to wear down the English fighter defense, was now so weakened that from this point on it was clearly at a numerical disadvantage[135].

As per orders, II/JG 3 now designated a *Jabostaffel*; the unit chosen was 5/JG 3 led by Oblt. Herbert Kijewski. In the days that followed, the unit's aircraft were fitted with bomb racks, the so-called ETCs[136], beneath the fuselage for carriage of a single 250-kg bomb. Even though there are no details available, it may be assumed that the pilots of 5/JG 3 had little, if any, opportunity to undertake practice bombing missions with their Messerschmitts; instead their first practice drops were also their first live drops in action over England[137].

After another largely uneventful *Gruppe*-strength bomber escort mission on 1 October[138], on 2 October 1940 the first escort

mission was flown in support of Bf 109 and Bf 110 *Jabos*, of which a total of 77 were committed on this day[139]. II/JG 3 flew three escort missions to London in support of the bomb-carrying Bf 109s of 5 *Staffel*, however none resulted in contact with the enemy[140]. After two more days of bad weather, with low cloud and frequent rain showers hindering further missions against England, on 5 October there was another clear upswing in operational activity. Although the weather had not improved significantly, throughout the entire day several waves of fighters and fighter-bombers attacked targets in the southeast of England and London[141]. II/JG 3 flew two escort missions over the coastal area around Folkestone and Dover, and once again there was no contact with the enemy[142]. The situation was similar in the days and weeks that followed: weather permitting, II/JG 3 flew missions in support of fighter-bomber attacks against targets in the southeast of England and in London[143]. Most of these missions were completed without contacting the enemy, especially if the attacks were aimed at targets in the coastal zone. If that was the case, the German fighters were usually back on "their own" side of the Channel before the British squadrons scrambled to intercept could reach the target area. Nevertheless, it was obvious to everyone that these attacks were not achieving any significant effect, and the *Jabos* were often forced to jettison their bombs over England. With the extra weight of the bombs the German fighters stood little chance against the Hurricanes and Spitfires. As a result of the constant fighter-bomber missions, the fighter pilots felt themselves being forced into the role of stopgap and scapegoat for other shortcomings of the *Luftwaffe* and its command, and there was a significant drop in morale as a result[144]. Furthermore, the continuous missions resulted in a noticeable drop in the *Gruppe*'s operational readiness, since not enough replacement machines were available[145]. The following account by Werner Voigt[146], then *Kapitän* of 4 *Staffel*, describes the events of 8 October 1940 and provides some insight into the operational conditions of these days:

> On 8 October 1940 my Staffel had three Me 109 E-4s on strength; these were flown by Obfw. Gremm, Obfw. Kortlepel[147] and myself. On this day we had already flown an escort mission to London for bomb-carrying Me 109s from 9:03 to 10:24 AM. After the machines had been refueled and rearmed, my Staffel provided the alert Rotte, which meant that Obfw. Gremm and Kortlepel taxied their machines to the takeoff point and waited there at cockpit readiness. Apart from my Staffel there was no one who could have done this, for 6 Staffel did not have a single serviceable machine. Orders were received for the Staffel's next mission, takeoff at 12:00 PM. Our II Gruppe's strength for this mission was as follows: from the Gruppenstab two Me 109 E-4s flown by the Kommandeur Hptm. Woitke[148] and the Technical Officer Oblt. Sannemann. 4 Staffel three Me 109 E-4s flown by Oblt. Voigt, Obfw. Gremm and

Obfw. Kortlepel. 5 Staffel six Me 109 Es with bombs under Oblt. Kijewski and 6 Staffel none. The mission order was the usual: protect 5 Staffel, which was to bomb London. Attack altitude: 4 000 m.

Shortly before our assigned takeoff time, Obfw. Gremm and Obfw. Kortlepel had to take off after an alert report was received. I could only hope that the two pilots would find an opportunity to rejoin the Gruppe after takeoff, as they knew the takeoff time, flight altitude and our flight path.

At 12:00 PM, 5 Staffel took off with six bomb-carrying machines, then the Kommandeur and his technical officer and I as the last machine. We overflew the English coast near Dover at a height of about 4 000 meters. I could hear over the radio that my two Oberfeldwebel were searching for us and just hoped that they would yet reach us in time. A devout wish that unfortunately was not satisfied. As usual in those days, the English fighters were waiting for us over London at a higher altitude. In the familiar state of desperation the bomber Staffel dropped its 'eggs' on London, the English attacked, I tried to count the English fighters, got to twenty and then stopped counting as time was becoming short. Then, on the Kommandeur's order, everyone dove into a layer of cloud over London at a height of 3 000 meters. I was the last to reach the layer and disappeared inside. After leveling out, however, I found myself in a hole in the layer and just as I disappeared into the next layer my machine was hit. Behind my head was a hole about three hands wide. After taking inventory, I flew out of the cloud at a height of 3 000 meters, saw no more enemy machines and took up a heading of 150° for Cap Gris Nez. I then discovered more hits in the first third of the right wing and thus, if I was unlucky, might also have been hit in the radiator.

I was unlucky. In spite of the open radiator flaps the temperature began to climb. I was now flying over a solid layer of cloud and when the temperature reached 120 degrees I switched off the engine and went into a glide until the temperature returned to 80 degrees. Then I started the engine again and carried on. In the process I noticed that the layer was slowly dropping towards the coast and in spite of the loss of height while gliding, I was able to stay above the cloud. I then transmitted to my formation several times what had happened to me and that I would probably have to make a forced landing, but would still try to reach the Channel. I received no acknowledgement, but several years later I learned that my formation had heard me and that the Kommodore, who was also in the air, had been able to follow the last part of my flight as I was trailing a long black-white banner of coolant.

Meanwhile the cloud layer and my machine and I had come down to about 800 meters, when the engine quit. I had to go into my last glide and hoped that I would find the French coast in front of me or at least the middle of the Channel. When I came out of the cloud layer at an altitude of about 600 meters I saw Folkestone below me; I recognized it immediately as it was on our familiar racetrack[149]. Cap Gris Nez, the object of my desires, beckoned in the distance! I was flying at about 220 kph, heading 150°. The flak began to fire and the sky in front of me became black with shell bursts. They must have considerably overestimated my speed, for the anti-aircraft shells all exploded in front of my machine and I did not receive a single flak hit. Since the end of the drama could no longer be avoided, I jettisoned my canopy and continued to head straight for the water. It was the only avenue still open to me. In a gentle left turn I overflew a sort of harbor and a tongue of land and then the water was beneath me. Cap Gris Nez disappeared on the horizon and I made my first and last water landing.

For Oblt. Werner Voigt this mission ended in captivity, after he was fished out of the water by the British rescue service. Four days later, Oblt. Gordon Gollob, who had been transferred to the Gruppenstab of II/JG 3 at the beginning of September, took command of 4 Staffel in his place. Oblt. Gollob originally came from the Zerstörer arm and had five victories to his credit; most recently he had held a position at the E-Stelle Rechlin[150].

On 15 October 1940 an improvement in the weather situation again allowed numerous fighters and fighter-bombers to see action over England[151]. II/JG 3 flew three Gruppe-strength missions in which its Jabos attacked targets in London[152]. The Gruppe sustained two losses: Gefr. Kurt Jahnke of 4/JG 3 was injured after he crashed near Le Portel from an altitude of 30 meters after suffering engine failure, while an aircraft of 5 Staffel was damaged in an emergency landing at Arques as a result of bullet damage sustained in combat. Two days later, on 17 October, another 4 Staffel machine was lost in air combat over the sea, however the aircraft's pilot escaped injury and was later picked up by the air-sea rescue service. Operations over England continued through the following weeks, and once again there was sustained, heavy air fighting over the southeast of Great Britain. Militarily, these battles had long since become pointless, yet they claimed further victims on both sides[153]. During this period II/JG 3 went on flying missions over England, even though little came of them, while men and machines began showing increased signs of wear and tear. Days deserving of mention in the second half of October are the 27th, when the Gruppe was again called upon to fly three fighter-bomber missions to London[154], all of which were completed without loss, the 29th, on which 5 Staffel lost one of its veteran pilots when Obfw. Horst Götz crashed near Arques airfield during a practice sortie, and the 30th, when the *Gruppe* lost two more pilots during another *Jabo* mission. Uffz. Alfred Fahrian and Gefr. Eugen Schuller were shot down by British fighters over Kent and both were taken prisoner with wounds. Gefr. Leo Suschko was extremely lucky once again: his Messerschmitt sustained radiator damage in a dogfight over Kent, however he managed to glide to the French coast, where he made a successful belly landing near Wissant[155]. II/JG 3 was stood down on the last day of the month. The extremely unsatisfactory balance from the *Gruppe*'s missions during October 1940 is reflected in losses of one pilot killed, three captured and one injured, plus six Messerschmitts written off as total losses, while it failed to record a single victory.

November 1940 began[156] as October had ended, with fighter-bomber raids[157] and once again several free chase missions were flown over southeast England. As in October, II/JG 3 was unable to score a single victory in November, however it was in turn spared any losses on operations. Operational activity dropped steadily in November on account of inclement autumn weather and the general exhaustion of the flying units, although heavy engagements were still to flare up now and then. Toward the end of the month there were several changes in the command structure of II/JG 3. On 24 November the new *Gruppenkommandeur* of II/JG 3 arrived at Arques; he was Hptm. Lothar Keller, who had most recently led 1/JG 3 and had 14 victories to his credit. He succeeded Hptm. von Selle, who had departed in September, and took over the duties of *Gruppenkommandeur* from Hptm. Erich Woitke, who had been acting *Gruppenkommandeur* since the departure of von Selle. The latter now left II/JG 3 to become *Gruppenkommandeur* of II/JG 52; his place as *Kapitän* of 6 *Staffel* was taken by Oblt. Heinrich Sannemann.

Since the beginning of the month the *Luftwaffe* had been withdrawing numerous units from operations and transferring them to Germany to rest and reequip. This affected the *Jagdgeschwader* in particular, whose *Gruppen* were worn out after months of operations on the Channel and in desperate need of overhaul. The *Gruppen* of JG 3 were not among the units pulled out of action in November, however. Instead, like JG 2 and JG 26, they had to remain in action for the time being and defend the French Channel Coast against air attack—they were back in the same place where it all had started five months earlier.

The last months of 1940 dragged on with the final skirmishes of the German air offensive that had begun in the summer. II/JG 3's operations during this period include little worthy of mention, apart from several *Jabo* missions against southeast England at the beginning of the month, all of which were completed without incident. On 5 December 1940, 4/JG 3 also began flying *Jabo* missions, its aircraft having been modified for the fighter-bomber role[159]. In December the *Gruppe* once again recorded neither victories nor operational losses, although conditions at Arques airfield, which had

been become soaked and muddy as a result of the autumn weather, resulted in a number of minor accidents. "Headstands" became frequent occurrences as the Messerschmitts taxied across the muddy airfield, resulting in bent propeller blades[160]. In spite of limited operational activity, there was little improvement in the number of aircraft available in these weeks, since deliveries of both new Messerschmitts and spare parts were lagging far behind requirements. This is reflected in the year-end strength return, when II/JG 3 reported a strength of 32 Bf 109 Es, of which 28 were serviceable. At the same time the *Gruppe* had available 28 pilots, however only 19 of these were listed as present and fit for duty[161].

A quick summary of II/JG 3's operations on the Channel reveals the following picture: the *Gruppe* had scored a total of 46 victories since arriving on the Channel at the end of June 1940. *Gruppenkommandeur* Hptm. von Selle and Oblt. Von Werra were the most successful pilots with four victories each, followed by Oblt. Voigt, Obfw. Kortlepel and Obfw. Götz with three. On the debit side the flying personnel had lost nine pilots killed or missing, six captured and four wounded. The *Gruppe*'s material losses in the same period amounted to 28 Messerschmitts written of as total losses, 24 of them as a result of enemy action.

At the beginning of 1941 II *Gruppe* was still at its base of operations at Arques; its mission remained unchanged: defend the Channel Coast against incursions by the Royal Air Force. In addition, whenever the winter weather permitted, constant patrols were flown off the French coast, usually in *Schwarm* or *Rotte* strength. There were also scrambles to intercept British fighters and bombers reported intruding into the *Gruppe*'s area of operations. January 1941 was largely uneventful, the high point being the downing of a Hurricane by Fw. Dilling (3) on the 10th. This was his first success with the *Gruppe*. Otherwise the *Gruppe* had neither victories nor losses in this month. On 4 February 1941 6 *Staffel* recorded the loss of a pilot: Uffz. Eduard Rybiak was killed while on a maintenance test flight when the Messerschmitt he was flying crashed near Vendeville for reasons unknown.

The level of operational activity increased noticeably as February 1941 wore on, after the Royal Air Force began a series of attacks against targets in occupied western Europe on 5 February. These so-called "Circus" missions, each of which involved formations of medium bombers escorted by several squadrons of fighters, were intended to draw the German air force into battle and (according to the long-range plans of the British commanders) destroy it[162]. The British raids carried out on 5 February were aimed at targets in the St. Omer—Etaples—Boulogne—Calais area and resulted in relatively widespread and heavy air battles with the defending German fighters. The outcome was a clear success for the latter, for they accounted for no less than 15 of the 17 enemy aircraft claimed shot down[163]. It is now known whether II/JG 3 took part in the air fighting on this day; the *Gruppe* reported neither victories nor losses.

Three days later, on 8 February 1941, II/JG 3 was obviously the victim of a British air raid on its base at Arques. One aircraft of the alert *Rotte* was damaged by gunfire, however its pilot was fortunate and got off with a fright. The RAF's next "Circus" operation took place two days later on 10 February 1941; two formations of Blenheims, each about ten strong, and about forty escort fighters flew into the Pas de Calais area. II/JG 3 engaged the second incursion, which occurred in the late afternoon, and scored one victory, which went to Hptm. Keller (16). The *Gruppe* sustained no losses.

The defensive mission on 10 February was the *Gruppe*'s last for some time, for on 15 February 1941 it received orders to return to the Reich, where II/JG 3 was to be rested and reequipped after its long tour of duty on the Channel. The next day the *Gruppe* handed its remaining Messerschmitts over to JG 51, and beginning on 16 February its various elements set out for home by road and rail[164]. In Germany the unit was to take up quarters in Darmstadt-Griesheim[165].

Notes:

[79] Reporting day 29 June 1940, German Order of Battle, Statistics as of Quarter Years

[80] For example, during the time at Brombois 4/JG 3 was assigned a total of five new pilots: Fw. Jansen, Uffz. Gericke and Gefreite Janke, Lucas and Suschko; on the other hand, Hptm. Dr. Ochs left the *Staffel* when he was transferred to III *Gruppe*, where he was to assume command of 9 *Staffel* on 1 July 1940. Writings of Georg Alex

[81] In most cases the damage was quite minor—a bent propeller blade for example—and the degree of damage was assessed at less than 5%. Consequently, these incidents were not reported. The only report of a taxiing accident was on 11 July and involved a Bf 109 E-3 which sustained 20% damage—see loss list in the appendices

[82] This also appears to have been the case in the two other *Gruppen*, as the logbook of Günther Lützow, at that time *Gruppenkommandeur* of I/JG 3, reveals. Heinrich Sannemann's logbook shows that he was Germany in his "Chevron Circle" from 3 to 5 July

[83] Bekker, p. 164. It seems more than doubtful, however, that Hitler ever in fact intended to attempt a landing in England. Also see the in-depth discussion of this question in Prien, JG 77 Part I, p. 325 and following pages and Prien and Stemmer, I/JG 3

[84] See Aders, JG 51, p. 55; Bekker, p. 163

[85] See Prien/Stemmer, III/JG 3, p. 36/

[86] *Stab*/JG 3 to Samer, I/JG 3 to Colembert and III/JG 3 to Desvres

[87] *Oberst* Theo Osterkamp had assumed this function on 21 July 1940 after handing JG 51 over to Maj. Werner Mölders

[88] Under the command of the *Jafü 2* (Commander of Fighters, *Luftflotte* 2) at the beginning of the fighting against England were JG 3, 26, 51, 52 and 54, while the *Jafü 3* based in the Cotentin Peninsula commanded three *Jagdgeschwader*, namely JG 2, 27 and 53. JG 27 was in turn directly subordinate to VIII *Fliegerkorps*

[89] For a detailed discussion of this topic see Ring, Bock and Weiss, p. 41 and following pages; Prien, JG 77 Part I, p. 337 and following pages. To sum up, however, it can be said that the *Luftwaffe* lacked both a proper concept for conducting the air war against Great Britain and the aircraft needed for a strategic air campaign. Furthermore the *Wehrmacht* was totally lacking in all the means necessary for a landing in Great Britain, so that a reasonable man could not seriously consider such an operation, to say nothing of making up his mind to carry it out. That a more or less random aerial campaign was nevertheless mounted over England in the months that followed, accompanied by loud beating of the propaganda drum and serious losses to irreplaceable personnel while achieving little, casts a revealing light on the state of mind of the then leading officers of the *Luftwaffe* as well as of the leadership of the Reich in general

[90] Two missions are recorded in the logbook of Heinrich Sannemann under this date: escort for a Bf 110 reconnaissance machine over the Channel and southern England from 10:20 to 11:43 AM and escort for Ju 87s attacking a British coastal convoy in the Channel from 2:20 to 3:40 PM. Both missions were recorded as uneventful

[91] Mission times 6:25 to 7:35 PM—logbook Heinrich Sannemann

[92] "Thirst" was fighter pilots' jargon for fuel shortage

[93] This seems as good a place as any to clear up one of the oldest and most inaccurate of the many legends that built up around the "Battle of Britain", namely that *countless* Messerschmitts crashed into the Channel or made crash landings on the French Channel Coast after running out of fuel. This claim cannot survive examination, neither in the case of I/JG 3 nor of the German fighter arm as a whole. I/JG 3 did not record a single Messerschmitt forced to ditch in the Channel after running out of fuel. The experiences of the other *Gruppen* based on the Channel were similar, as confirmed by the quartermaster reports: between 1 August and 30 November 1940 the day fighter units deployed on the Channel lost just two Bf 109 Es on account of fuel starvation while another eight were damaged in forced landings. One pilot was killed in these incidents and another was injured. It is possible that three other Bf 109 Es that went missing over the Channel under unknown circumstances during

the same period may also have been victims of fuel starvation, however this is far from certain. I/JG 54, which operated over Germany and Holland at the end of the period in question had three of its aircraft damaged slightly in belly landings resulting from fuel starvation. Thus the units involved in the so-called "Battle of Britain" did not suffer any worse in this regard than units deployed in other areas

[94] Writings of Karl-Heinz Langer

[95] German propaganda put it as follows: *"The German air force has opened the decisive battle against England!"* (original text from the Ufa newsreel of 19 August 1940). After only a few weeks it had become obvious to everyone that no decision had been achieved; in view of this, today it strikes one as odd that faith in the *Führer*'s "infallibility" and in the information released by the National-Socialist leadership remained intact among large segments of the population. The subsequent course of the battle was to provide many more examples of full-mouthed phrases and promises on the part of the leading figures of the Third Reich, especially Hitler and his mouthpiece Goebbels, which clearly did not lead to the promised success. The leadership's faith in the forgetfulness of the "folk comrades" was limitless

[96] Ring, *Luftschlacht*, p. 417

[97] Ring, *ibid.*; see also Mason, p. 240 and Ramsey, p. 354

[98] It should be noted, however, that many of the 74 victories claimed in the OKW communiqué of 14 August 1940 were not confirmed; once submitted, victory claims underwent protracted, careful examination before being confirmed. Regrettably, it is not known how many and which of the victory claims made on this day were in fact ultimately confirmed

[99] See also the overview in Ring, *Luftschlacht*, p. 424

[100] Logbook Heinrich Sannemann, takeoff times 6:28 AM and 4:20 PM

[101] Mission times from the logbook of Heinrich Sannemann 1:05 to 1:43 PM

[102] Mission times from the logbook of Heinrich Sannemann 12:32 to 1:45 PM and 5:15 to 6:40 PM

[103] Writings of Georg Alex; according to these Hptm. Müller had to be moved to an hospital in Germany and thus was no longer fit for front-line duty

[104] Alfred Price, *The Hardest Day*, p. 9, places the losses of the RAF on this day at 136 and the *Luftwaffe*'s at 100. This figure obviously includes machines which were damaged, for the *Luftwaffe* reported 70 aircraft as total write-offs. Also see the detailed account of this day's events in Price, where cited

[105] Mission times from the logbook of Heinrich Sannemann 1:17 to 2:35 PM

[106] According to the Quartermaster-General's report, this crash took place at Brombois; this may have been the result of a copying error, however, for there is no plausible reason why Fw. Müller should have flown all the way to Brombois when his home base at Wierre-au-Bois was clearly closer and there were no elements of II/JG 3 at Brombois. The same may apply to the loss report on 19 August—see loss lists in the appendices

[107] Mission times from the logbook of Heinrich Sannemann 11:23 AM to 12:33 PM, 2:10 to 2:42 PM, and 3:50 to 5:20 PM

[108] Mission times from the logbook of Heinrich Sannemann 12:25 to 1:50 PM and 3:40 to 4:55 PM

[109] According to the writings of Botho Teichmann, Franz von Werra allegedly employed a ruse to shoot down three Hurricanes. He attached himself to a flight of Hurricanes, followed them to their base, infiltrated himself into the landing sequence—even lowering his undercarriage—and then easily shot down his totally unsuspecting victims one after another before escaping at low level. As impressive as this account sounds, there is no reference to such a feat in any British records. One of the peculiarities of the so-called "Battle of Britain" is the degree of liberality for just this period in the normally very strict and orderly confirmation process employed by the *Luftwaffe*. Only by relaxing the rules in this way was it possible to confirm some victory claims which lacked air or ground witnesses, usually a precondition for confirmation. The reference to witnesses in the *Gruppe* war diary probably relates to this

In seeking an explanation for the allowances made in the evaluation of victory claims, one must take into consideration the nature of the air battles over England. Combats took place over British soil, which eliminated the possibility of ground witnesses. As well, since the majority of combats took place at high altitude, it was rarely possible for an eye witnesses to follow a Spitfire or Hurricane going down trailing smoke until it struck the ground, which was normally required according to the strict confirmation rules. A German pilot could not be expected to watch an enemy aircraft until it hit the ground just for the purpose of confirmation, since such a diversion would place him in great danger of being shot down by another British fighter. As understandable and proper as this loosening of the strict requirements in proving a victory claim was, it undoubtedly resulted in the confirmation of a number of questionable claims. Also noteworthy in this context is the obvious variations from *Geschwader* to *Geschwader* and in some cases even from *Gruppe* to *Gruppe* in the processing of victory claims that lacked the usual eye witnesses

[110] For the *Jagdgruppen* on the Channel, this equated to an average of just over *one* sortie per available and serviceable machine—a *mass* operation in the parlance of the leading *Luftwaffe* officers. The only question is, whom were they trying to deceive as to the actual conditions "on the Channel" with such trickery

[111] Mission times from the logbook of Heinrich Sannemann 3:50 to 5:25 PM

[112] Mission times from the logbook of Heinrich Sannemann 5:20 to 6:25 PM

[113] Mission times from the logbook of Heinrich Sannemann 6:25 to 7:50 PM. Another mission over the Thames Estuary from 11:25 to 11:50 AM was uneventful

[114] Writings of Georg Alex

[115] Stationed there at the end of August 1940 were JG 2, 3, 26, 27, 51, 52, 53 and 54 as well as I/JG 77 and I(J)/LG 2, while at the same time the remaining two *Gruppen* of JG 77 were based in Norway (II/JG 77) and Döberitz (III/JG 77), the latter to defend Berlin!

[116] Mission times from the logbook of Heinrich Sannemann 10:15 to 11:40 AM

[117] After two failed attempts to escape from England on 7 October and 20 December 1940, on 21 February 1941 von Werra succeeded in escaping from a prisoner of war camp in Canada. After an adventurous flight through the USA, Mexico and Spain, he returned to Germany on 18 April 1941. He was thus the only German soldier to succeed in escaping from captivity in Canada and returning home, a feat which ultimately contributed more to his fame than his success as a fighter pilot. The latter had already been acknowledged by the awarding of the Knight's Cross on 14 December 1940. This was obviously due to his lone actions, such as the one on 28 August 1940, for by the standards of the day his total of eight victories alone was insufficient to earn him the decoration. His subsequent path was a tragic one: after extensive debriefings in the RLM about his experiences in British captivity, in July 1941 he took over I/JG 53 in the east, where he recorded another 13 victories. His marriage is said to have resulted in a fundamental change in his personality, from daredevil to a sensible, mature man, as a result of which he adopted a more conservative attitude towards combat operations. On 25 October 1941 he suffered engine failure during a mission off the Dutch coast north of Vlissingen and died in the ensuing crash

[118] Also see Ring, *Luftschlacht*, p. 464; Prien, JG 77 Part I, p. 377 and following pages

[119] The change of objectives away from the destruction of the British fighters and their ground organization to attacks against purely industrial and economic targets was later often characterized as a decisive mistake on the part of the *Luftwaffe* command and the basis of the British victory. However, considerable doubts have been raised as to the validity of this claim, which in any case can only be understood against the background of the unproven, and in the opinion of the author for the reasons described previously inaccurate, assumption that the German efforts against England really were supposed to be a prelude to invasion. Quite apart from the moral reprehensibility of a bombing campaign against an opponent's civilian population, the decision to bomb London was certainly no clever tactical chess move, but this applied equally to the *Luftwaffe*'s entire effort against Great Britain in the late summer of 1940. Lacking a clear objective and with inadequate forces, what transpired there was a display of military ineptitude which ultimately cost the lives of about 2,000 German and 500 British airmen plus about 24,000 British civilians

[120] Logbook of Heinrich Sannemann

[121] At the same time, on this date II/JG 3 reported the shooting down of two Hurricanes, one of them by Fw. Kortlepel. No details of this victory are known

[122] Mission times from the logbook of Heinrich Sannemann 6:00 to 7:30 PM; according to him, however, the bombers being escorted were Ju 88s

[123] Mason, p. 373

[124] Mission times from the logbook of Heinrich Sannemann 12:00 to 1:25 PM and 2:45 to 4:02 PM

[125] This victory provides a graphic example of the extraordinary confirmation practice employed by the *Luftwaffe* during this time. Heinrich Sannemann's victory claim stated that there were no eyewitnesses because, having become separated from his unit, he had pursued a Spitfire alone and shot it down. In his report submitted several days later, Hptm. Woitke, by now acting *Gruppenkommandeur*, wrote: *"Given the nature of the air fighting over England, in most cases it is not possible to provide an eyewitness. This does not speak against the validity of the claim."* Hptm. Woitke was a capable reasonable leader who backed up the deserving and proven officers of his unit when he felt it was warranted, therefore his words require no commentary.

This did not apply to all units at this time, however, and certainly not for all the victory claims submitted without an eyewitness

[126] Compared to the 185 victories claimed by the British side on this day! This fantasy figure was the highest number of victories claimed by the British for any single day during the so-called "Battle of Britain," and it is the reason why 15 September is now celebrated as "Battle of Britain Day." The official German success reports also once again exceeded the enemy's actual losses—42 RAF fighters compared to 74 German victory claims.

[127] 57 of the German losses were due to enemy action, the rest were the result of accidents; 36 of the German aircraft lost were bombers. For a description of the events of this day and their (over-) evaluation, see Ring. *Luftschlacht*, p. 465

[128] Mission times from the logbook of Heinrich Sannemann 1:20 to 2:00 PM

[129] Ring. *Luftschlacht*, p. 467

[130] Mission times from the logbook of Heinrich Sannemann 9:30 to 10:50 AM, 12:55 to 2:20 PM and 3:56 to 4:28 PM

[131] Writings of Georg Alex

[132] Mission times from the logbook of Heinrich Sannemann 4:45 to 6:00 PM

[133] Reporting date 28 September 1940, German Order of Battle, Statistics as of Quarter Years

[134] Hermann Göring is said to have declared that the fighters were themselves responsible for now having to take over their (the bombers') role because they had failed in the role of bomber escort; for further information on the introduction of the *Jabos* see Ring, p. 500; Prien, JG 77 Part 1, p. 377 and following pages

[135] The British fighters had achieved a clear numerical superiority over their German counterparts by the end of September at the latest. At that time Fighter Command had approximately 1,050 Spitfires and Hurricanes, of which 730 were operational with front-line units. In addition the British had a reserve of 300-400 machines at the supply depots. The *Luftwaffe* likewise had approximately 730 aircraft, but almost no reserves. This situation was made even worse by the fact that in September deliveries of new and repaired aircraft lagged far behind actual losses—while 212 Messerschmitts were lost in action only about 190 new machines were delivered to the *Luftwaffe*

[136] *Einzelträger für C-Munition*; *C-Munition* was the *Luftwaffe* designation for air-dropped weapons, especially bombs

[137] Compare the introduction of fighter-bombers by JG 53, which was played out under similar portents; Prien, JG 53 Part 1, p. 224 and following pages

[138] Mission times from the logbook of Heinrich Sannemann 3:10 to 4:08 PM

[139] See detailed account in Prien, JG 77 Part I, p. 399 and following pages. The Jabo force consisted of 66 Bf 109s and 11 Bf 110s, including for the first time the Messerschmitts of 5/JG 3. As revealed by an official report submitted by II/JG 3 on 24 July 1941, these were already on their first bombing missions on this day

[140] Mission times from the logbook of Heinrich Sannemann 10:20 to 11:20 AM, 1:45 to 2:40 PM and 4:50 to 6:10 PM

[141] Mason, p. 432

[142] Mission times from the logbook of Heinrich Sannemann 12:00 to 1:00 PM and 4:12 to 4:50 PM

[143] II/JG 3's operational activities during the month of October 1940 are illustrated here using the logbook of Heinrich Sannemann: in that month he flew a total of 26 combat missions, all but one of them escort missions for Bf 109 fighter-bombers. Details of these missions are as follows: 1/10 – 1 escort mission for bombers; 2/10 – 3 escort missions for *Jabos*; 5/10 2 of the same; 7/10 – 2 of the same; 7/10 – 3 of the same; 8/10 – 2 of the same; 9/10 2 of the same; 10/10 – 2 of the same; 13/10 – 1 of the same; 15/10 – 3 of the same; 17/10 – 2 of the same; 27/10 – 3 of the same; 28/10 – 1 of the same; 30/10 – 1 of the same

[144] See Prien, JG 53 Part I, p. 247 and following pages, and Prien, JG 77 Part 1, p. 419 and following pages

[145] The German aircraft industry had yet to adapt itself to the requirements and conditions of a wartime economy, and as a result the production of new aircraft was not even sufficient to make good the ongoing losses at the front. For example, in August 1940 230 Bf 109s were written off, while all of 173 new machines were delivered by the industry. The corresponding figures for the Royal Air Force in the same period were 499 machines lost against the production of 476 aircraft; losses and production were therefore almost in balance; total production, however, was almost twice as high as in Germany (see Footnote 135)

[146] Letter written by Werner Voigt to the editors of KRISTALL dated 16 January 1964 to correct an article which it had published on the air war in 1940 (pre-publication of *ANGRIFFSHÖHE 4000*)

[147] In fact Anton Gremm and Erwin Kortlepel were not promoted to *Oberfeldwebel* until 1 November 1940—writings of Georg Alex

[148] In Werner Voigt's original report he still mistakenly refers to *Hptm. von Selle*

[149] "Racetrack" was the term used to describe the direct route always flown to London, which could not be changed to any significant degree on account of the limited range of the Bf 109.

[150] See Obermaier, p. 19; according to him, the transfer to *Stab*/JG 3 took place on 7 September 1940; writings of Georg Alex

[151] See Mason, p. 446 and following pages

[152] Mission times from the logbook of Heinrich Sannemann 9:30 to 10:45 AM, 1:05 to 1:45 PM and 4:20 to 5:30 PM

[153] Certainly one of the most disagreeable and cynical aspects of this final phase of the so-called "Battle of Britain" was that both Germany and Great Britain continued to beat the propaganda drum, though for very different reasons, even though the military and political leaders of both sides were well aware that the German strategic air offensive against England had failed and that an invasion of the island was completely impossible. Many people would lose their lives as a result. While the British still needed the specter of a German invasion as a means of pressuring the USA to enter the war at its side, the continuation of hostilities served the German command by allowing it to cover up its buildup, already under way, in preparation for the invasion of the Soviet Union. See Prien, JG 77 Part 1, p. 408 and following pages

[154] Mission times from the logbook of Heinrich Sannemann 8:15 to 9:30 AM, 12:00 to 12:45 PM and 5:15 to 6:05 PM

[155] Writings of Georg Alex

[156] The following comment in writings of Georg Alex is noteworthy: *"Batch of promotions: Gremm and Kortlepel Oberfeldwebel as well as the Iron Cross, First Class; Lucas and Suschko, the duty high cover Rotte, Unteroffizier and Iron Cross, Second Class."*

[157] According to an official assessment for the *Staffelkapitän* of 5/JG 3, Oblt. Herbert Kijewski, dated 24 July 1941, 5/JG 3 flew a total of 27 Jabo missions to England between 1 October and 31 December 1940. A total of 165 Bf 109 sorties were flown, on average slightly more than six aircraft per mission. A total of 41 250 kg of bombs was dropped. Oblt. Kijewski took part in all these missions and added

two more at the beginning of 1941; his personal *Jabo* balance was 29 missions over England with a total bomb load of 7 250 kg

[158] Data from the logbook of Heinrich Sannemann is once again used to illustrate. A total of nine combat missions are recorded there for November 1940, distributed as follows: 5/11 – 1 free chase and one *Jabo*; 11/11 – 2 *Jabo*; 15/11 – 1 *Jabo*; 17/11 – 1 *Jabo*, 1 free chase; 23/11 – 1 escort mission for returning bombers; 24/11 – 1 *Jabo*

[159] Writings of Georg Alex

[160] Because they involved damage of less than 5%, these incidents were not included in the Quartermaster-General's reports; however, several former technicians remember well that they occurred frequently in those weeks

[161] Reporting date 28/12/1940, German Order of Battle, Statistics as of Quarter Years. It is to be assumed that the nine pilots not with the *Gruppe* were at home on recovery leave, since the *Gruppe* had endeavored to grant its pilots a brief rest period in spite of the constant state of alert on the Channel

[162] One can see that the vast overestimation of one's own capabilities was certainly not the sole privilege of the German military

[163] The OKW communiqué of 6/2/1941 initially reported 14 fighters shot down, however the figure given here was obtained by adding all known German fighter victories on the Channel on 5/2/1941; the breakdown of claims was eight by III/JG 3, six by I/JG 3 and one by II/JG 26

[164] The last transport train, which departed on 19 December 1941, was involved in an accident near Metz at 9:25 in the evening, when the locomotive derailed, causing the cars at the front of the train to topple over. Two men were slightly injured in the accident—writings of Botho Teichmann

[165] Files of Heinrich Sannemann; these reveal that the stay in Darmstadt was officially from 20 February to 4 May 1941; however, see following chapter.

Above and below left: The "provisional command post" of II/JG 3 under the wing of a Bf 109 E-4 of the Gruppenstab, photographed at Wierre-au-Bois in August 1940. Seated at the table is the Gruppenkommandeur, Hptm. Erich von Selle, next to him in the brown flight suit is Lt. Heinrich Sannemann, the Gruppe Technical Officer. The aircraft wears an unmodified 1940 camouflage scheme and (barely visible) the Gruppe emblem of II/JG 3 in front of the cockpit. Lying on the wing is "Simba," a lion cub, which the Gruppe kept at that time as unit mascot. Below right: Lt. Heinrich Sannemann, Gruppe Technical Officer of II/JG 3, in the cockpit of his Messerschmitt, a Bf 109 E-4 coded "Chevron Circle," photographed at Wierre-au-Bois in August 1940. The machine, which Sannemann flew from June until the middle of November 1940, wears an unmodified 1940 camouflage scheme with the Gruppe emblem of II/JG in front of the cockpit. (Sannemann)

Above: Officers of the Gruppenstab *pass the time with Simba between missions. In the middle of the photo is the* Gruppen-Adjutant, *Oblt. Franz von Werra. Left: Oblt. von Werra and Sannemann study a map; while Franz von Werra is seen in the standard "attire" for the Channel at that time with a lifejacket over his tunic, Heinrich Sannemann wears the one-piece brown flight suit, which was rarely seen any more by this time. (Sannemann)*

The following photographs were taken at Wierre-au-Bois in August 1940 and depict the Gruppen-Adjutant *Lt. Franz von Werra with the* Gruppe *mascot Simba in the cockpit of his machine, a Bf 109 E-4 with the WerkNr. 1480 and the code "Black Chevron." This Messerschmitt wears an unmodified 1940 camouflage scheme; the* Gruppe *emblem is absent in the first photographs, but may be seen in the last pictures. Note the finish on the propeller spinner, black and white quarters, which was standard on aircraft of II/JG 3 at this time. (BA No. 384-407/408-1, 42, 43/Sannemann/Lützow)*

Inspection of II/JG 3 by General Grauert, the commanding general of I Fliegerkorps, photographed on the Wierre-au-Bois airfield in August 1940. Visible in the background are several of the unit's machines, which have been camouflaged with cut saplings. In these photographs, too, Simba is the center of interest. (BA No. 384-407/408-3, 12)

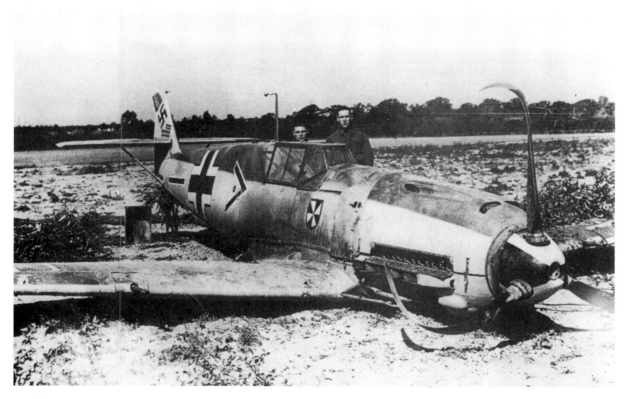

The following photographs depict the machine of Oblt. Franz von Werra, a Bf 109 E-4 with the WerkNr. 1480, after its belly landing near Marden in Kent on 5 September 1940. The machine still wears the unmodified 1940 camouflage scheme as well as the familiar black and white quartered finish on the propeller spinner. On the vertical fin are markings for eight victories and five aircraft destroyed on the ground; curiously, on the right side all of the bars were applied in front of the swastika, while on the left side one bar appears aft of the swastika. (Kent Messenger)

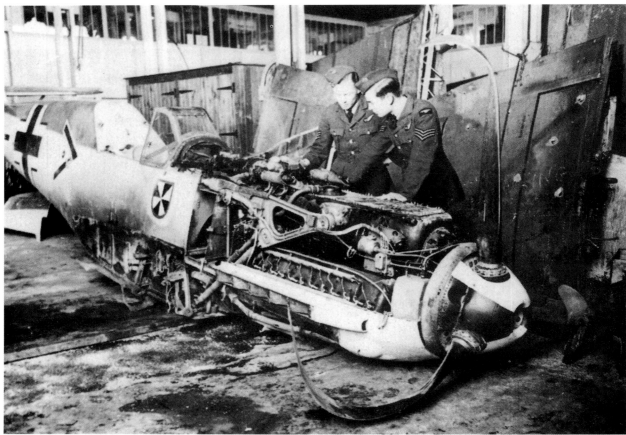

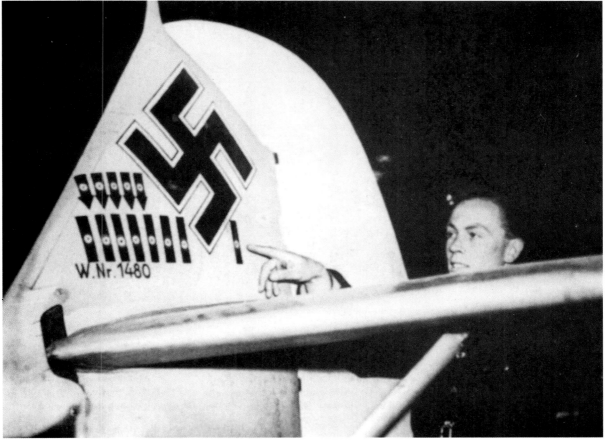

Two photographs of a Bf 109 E of 4 Staffel at Wierre-au-Bois in August 1940. The pilot may be Lt. Richard von Larisch. The aircraft wears a modified 1940 camouflage scheme with a soft overspray on the fuselage sides. On the other hand, the propeller spinner still wears the black and white quartered finish; the Gruppe emblem is visible in front of the cockpit. Note the octane triangle, which has been painted over the white aircraft number. (BA No. 385-585-16, 20)

Pilots of 5/JG 3 pass the time between missions with a game of skat. From the left are Uffz. Walter Ohlrogge, Obfw. Horst Götz, Uffz. Josef Heinzeller, Uffz. Fritz Mias and Lt. Horst Buddenhagen, photographed at Wierre-au-Bois in August 1940. Parked in the background are the Messerschmitts of 4 Staffel, including "White 1," possibly the aircraft of Hptm. Alfred Müller. Both machines visible here wear a modified 1940 camouflage scheme with a light overspray on the fuselage sides, standard on aircraft of II/JG 3 at this time. (Sannemann)

"Black 9" of 5/JG 3, a Bf 109 E-4, seen after a forced landing, photographed in late summer 1940 during II/JG 3's tour of duty on the Channel. Although the aircraft wears a camouflage finish with heavily-mottled fuselage sides, the overall effect is quite pale. The aircraft also obviously lacks any yellow identification markings. Note the emblem on the engine cowling, a white Scotch Terrier with the name "Schnauzl"; this was originally the personal emblem of Uffz. Josef Heinzeller, who came from 2(J)/LG 2 to 5/JG 3 when II/JG 3 was formed and there served as Schwarmführer. Uffz. Heinzeller obviously made the emblem into a marking for all the aircraft of his Schwarm. (Roletschek via Petrick)

The following illustrations are from a series of propaganda service photographs depicting several of 5/JG 3's Messerschmitts over the Channel; the photos were first published in the newspaper Völkischer Beobachter *on 9 September 1940. Above: Three Messerschmitts photographed from the fourth aircraft in the* Schwarm. *The "Schnauzl" emblem of Josef Heinzeller is plainly visible in this obviously slightly retouched photograph, while aircraft "Black 10" in the center wears an as yet unidentified emblem beneath the cockpit. (ADLER)*

Above: "Black 11," a Bf 109 E-4 with the WerkNr. 1155, probably the machine of Uffz. Fritz Mias, who flew in Uffz. Heinzeller's Schwarm *and thus wore the "Schnauzl" emblem on the engine cowling of his machine. Note the two victory bars in front of the swastika on the vertical fin. Below: "Black 14," another machine from Uffz. Heinzeller's* Schwarm. *In this photograph one can see both the* Gruppe *emblem in front of the cockpit and, just barely, the "Schnauzl" emblem on the engine cowling. (ADLER/ Petrick)*

Above: Another photo of "Black 14." In the background is "Black 10," which may also be seen in the photograph below. Note the as yet unidentified emblem on a circular white background beneath the cockpit. (Petrick.Matthiesen)

Above: An in-flight photo of "Black 8," a Bf 109 E-4 of 5/JG 3; though barely visible, this machine also wears the "Schnauzl" emblem on the engine cowling. Note the bright, probably yellow, rudder and the octane triangle, which once again covers part of the aircraft number. Below: "Made up to look like a pilot," a 5 Staffel technician on the wing of "Black 8," with mesh helmet and seat-type parachute. This is obviously a different machine than the one illustrated above. Note the obviously modified finish on the fuselage sides, which appears very dark in the area of the aircraft number. (ADLER/Lächler)

Above: "White 10" of 4 Staffel *in flight. Note the modified 1940 camouflage scheme with the lightly-mottled fuselage sides usually seen on aircraft of II/JG 3 and the angular shape of the aircraft number as used by the* Gruppen *of JG 3. The* Gruppe *emblem of II/JG 3 is visible in front of the cockpit. Also note the head armor in the folding hood, a feature introduced by the* Gruppen *based on the Channel in the late summer of 1940. Below: Two Messerschmitts of 4* Staffel, *photographed on Wierre-au-Bois airfield in September 1940; both aircraft wear the modified 1940 finish standard at that time. Also note the nagular shape of the aircraft numbers, a style used by all three* Gruppen *of JG 3 at that time. (Sannemann)*

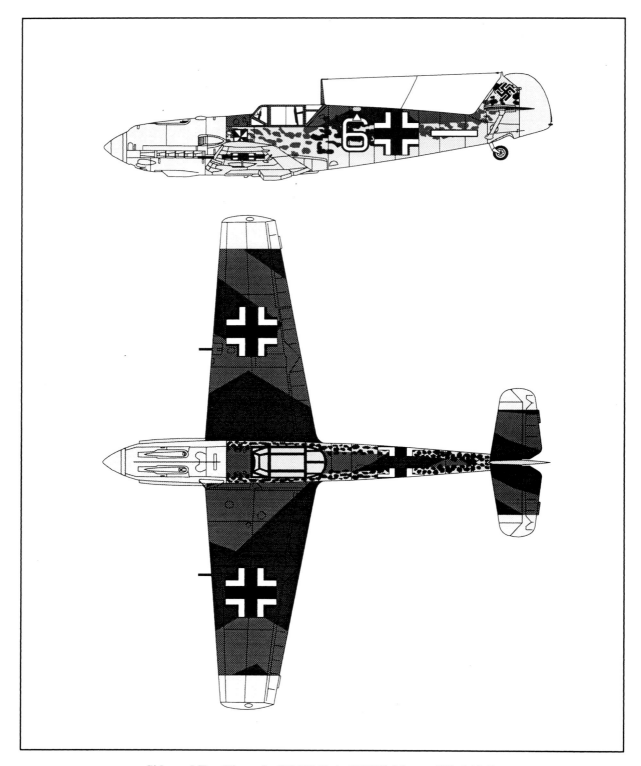

**Side and Top View of a Bf 109 E-4 of II/JG 3 in modified 1940
camouflage scheme with yellow identification markings.**

Beginning at the end of August 1940 II/JG 3 began applying yellow (and at first possibly also white) identification markings for better identification of friendly aircraft in the often confused combat situations over England. From that time on yellow became the basic identification color for German fighter aircraft, later supplemented by white markings in the Mediterranean Theater. In 1940 on the Channel, engine cowlings and rudders, and in some cases also wingtips and tips of the horizontal stabilizer, were sprayed yellow; on the other hand fuselage bands were not used at this time.

Photographs taken during a scramble by 4/JG 3 (probably posed for the propaganda service) at Wierre-au-Bois in September 1940. Both machines are finished in a 1940 camouflage scheme with lightly-mottled fuselage sides. Whereas the Gruppe emblem is barely visible on "White 4" in the foreground, it may clearly be seen on aircraft "White 1" in the background. (Sannemann)

Above left: Probably the same Messerschmitt as in the previous photo. Above right and below: Another 4 Staffel Bf 109 E-4 on the Wierre-au-Bois airfield. It appears that the sides of this aircraft's engine cowling received a bright identificationmarking, probably in yellow, while the green-gray splinter scheme on the fuselage spine was left intact. Note the rear-view mirror on the windscreen. (Sannemann/Petrick)

This aircraft may be Bf 109 E-1 Werknummer 6339, which was damaged in a crash-landing near Arques airfield on 28th September 1940. The aircraft wears the 1940 camouflage scheme with the familiar mottling on the fuselage sides. It quite obviously lacks any yellow identification markings. (Petrick)

The camouflage net over the revetment of "White 7," a Bf 109 E of 4 Staffel, is responsible for the numerous spots on the machine's finish; in fact, this Messerschmitt must have worn the usual lightly-mottled scheme used by II/JG 3. Below: On this Messerschmitt the sides of the engine cowling have obviously been sprayed yellow, while the original splinter scheme remains on the fuselage spine. Note the absence of any aing armament. (Petrick)

A Bf 109 E-1 of II/JG 3 taxiis out for takeoff. Clearly visible are the black and white quartered scheme on the propeller spinner and the lightly mottled finish on the fuselage sides. Below: A Bf 109 E-1, obviously newly delivered, on jacks in preparation for having its guns bore-sighted; the machine does not yet have an aircraft number and there are still traces of the factory code on the fuselage sides. Note that the aircraft wears a 1940 camouflage scheme which was obviously modified at the factory, with the mottling on the fuselage sides extendind down to the exhaust stacks. This Messerschmitt also lacks any yellow identification markings. (Petrick)

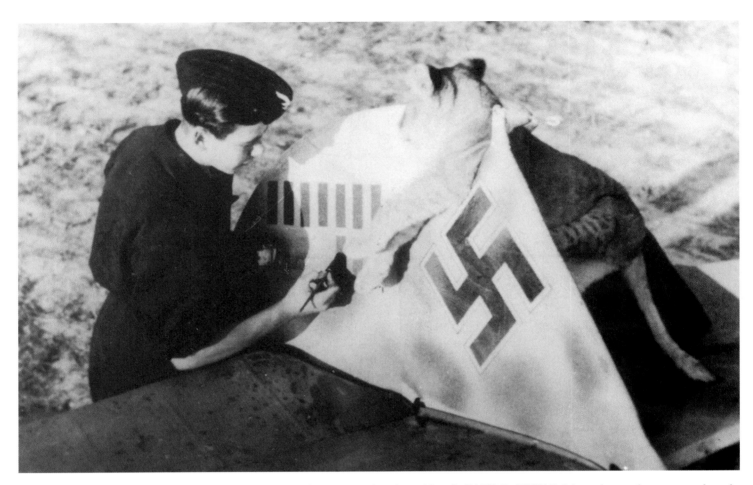

Gruppe *lion Simba watches with interest as the tenth victory bar is painted on the rudder of a Bf 109 E of II/JG 3. It is not known, however, to whom the aircraft belonged, for at this time none of the* Gruppe*'s pilots had claimed such a number of victories.*

After Oblt. von Werra failed to return, the lion remained for a while with II/JG 3, where he allegedly was allowed to roam freely. It is said that he was later poisoned with strychnine. (Sannemann)

Above: This photograph was probably taken on the same occasion; in contrast to the Messerschmitt illustrated previously, on this machine the victory bars have been placed around the swastika, as was the original practise. Once again, the name of the pilot responsible for the twelve victories is not known. Note the pale, probably yellow, ends of the horizontal stabilizer. Below: Three members of II/JG 3's ground crew with a tarpaulin-covered Messerschmitt, photographed on Wierre-au-Bois airfield in September 1940. (Sannemann/Petrick)

Above: Ground collision involving two Messerschmitts, probably of II/JG 3. Although the Gruppe *emblem is absent, the style of the modified 1940 camouflage scheme, the shape of the aircraft number and the superimposed octane triangle, and the finish on the propeller spinners of both machines suggest that they belonged to that* Gruppe. *Note that "Black 2" wears no yellow identification markings of any kind. Below: In the foreground an obviously newly-delivered machine, which has yet to receive any code markings but on which the remnants of the factory code may still be seen. Note the mottled fuselage sides and the clear color boundary in front of the cockpit. In the background are several Messerschmitts of 5 and 6* Staffeln, *including "Black 7" and "8". It is noteworthy that none of the machines illustrated here carry the* Gruppe *emblem of II/JG 3. (Payne/ Skibitzki)*

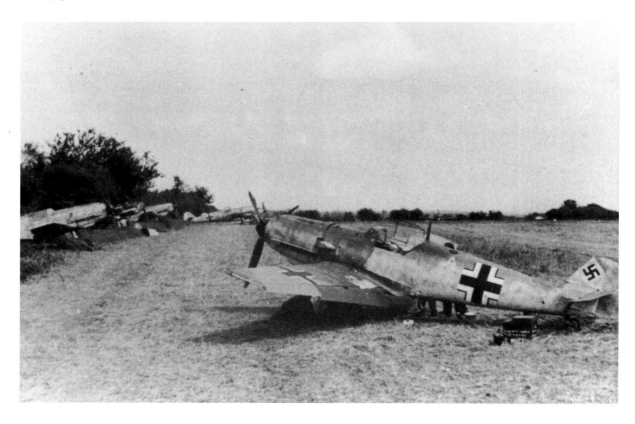

Above: Officers and pilots of II Gruppe *have assembled to witness the reception for Oblt. Herbert Kijewski,* Staffelkapitän *of 5/ JG 3; this photograph was probably taken on the occasion of the awarding of the Honor Goblet to Oblt. Kijewski, the main purpose of which was to acknowledge his success as leader of the* Jabostaffel. *Below: This photo, which shows a II/JG 3 band in front of three Messerschmitts, each accompanied by a number of soldiers from the ground personnel, was probably taken on the same occasion. (Sannemann)*

Pilots and technicians of 5/JG 3 with "Black 1," a rather darkly camouflaged Messerschmitt, probably a Bf 109 E-4/B. Note the head armor in the folding hood and the octane triangle partly superimposed on the aircraft number. Below: In-flight photo of "Black 4," another 5 Staffel aircraft, which clearly has a yellow engine cowling and rudder. Worthy of note is the swastika, which is still in the original position straddling the fin and rudder and which was largely overpainted when the rudder was sprayed yellow. (Lächler)

Technicians of 4 Staffel *servicing "White 3"; the men are wearing weatherproof clothing for protection against the rain. The aircraft wears the finish standard at that time, with lightly mottled fuselage sides and the familiar black and white propeller spinner. (ADLER)*

Above: Oblt. Georg Michalek, who occasionally flew with the Gruppenstab *of II/JG 3 and later assumed command of 4* Staffel, *in front of "White 8", a Bf 109 E of 4/JG 3. Below: Aircraft of 4* Staffel *taxi out for takeoff at Arques airfield. "White 1" in the foreground has the yellow wingtips and horizontal stabilizer tips introduced by II/JG 3 in September 1940. (Petrick/Sannemann)*

Above left: Oblt. Gordon Gollob, who assumed command of 4 Staffel after Oblt. Werner Voigt failed to return from a mission on 8 October 1940, prepares for a mission beside his Messerschmitt. It is noteworthy that Oblt. Gollob is wearing the old, one-piece, brown flight suit, which by this time was rarely worn by fighter pilots any more. His machine wears an obviously modified finish which appears quite dark on the upper surfaces, with the very dark color of the rudder being particularly noticeable. Part of the white aircraft number is just visible above the wingtip. Above right: A Messerschmitt from Fw. Josef Heinzeller's Schwarm, photographed on Arques airfield in autumn 1940, when 5/JG 3 had to assume the role of Jabostaffel within II/JG 3. A 250-kg bomb is visible under the fuselage. Also note the obviously yellow finish of the engine cowling, against which the "Schnauzl" emblem stands out clearly. Below: Uffz. Alfred Heckmann in front of his Bf 109 E following a mission over England in autumn 1940; the machine is coded "Black 6", his "personal" aircraft number. Heckmann was a member of 5/JG 3 since 5 February 1940, therefore from the time of its formation. The aircraft's finish obviously underwent much modification, in the process of which the octane triangle was oversprayed and totally obscured. (Petrick/Heinzeller/Schellhorn)

Above: Pilots of 4 Staffel on the engine cowling of a Messerschmitt, photographed at Arques in autumn 1940. This machine has an overall yellow engine cowling as introduced by II/JG 3 in autumn 1940. Note the capped propeller spinner, which still wears the familiar black and white quartered finish. Also note that all four of the pilots depicted here are still wearing the old, largely ineffective kapok life vests, which by this time had largely been replaced by the lighter, inflatable life vests in the Jagdgruppen. Below: Another group of pilots in front of an aircraft of 4/JG 3; the yellow finish on the engine cowling appears unusually dark here. Once again note the capped propeller spinner in the black and white quartered scheme. (Petrick)

Above: "White" of 4 Staffel *in a faded gray-green camouflage scheme, photographed in autumn 1940, probably at Arques. Several victory bars are just visible on the yellow rudder; this may be the aircraft of Obfw. Erwin Kortlepel, who had four victories at this time. Below: Uffz. Walter Ohlrogge, a pilot in 5/JG 3, in front of his machine; note the capped propeller spinner with a white tip. (Petrick/Struppek)*

Above: This photo may depict machines of 5/JG 3 at the beginning of 1941 at the end of the unit's deployment on the Channel. "Black 7" in the foreground wears a very faded gray-green camouflage finish with yellow engine cowling. The finish worn by "Black 3" in the background still resembles the 1940 camouflage scheme, but with a yellow engine cowling and rudder. Below: Parked Messerschmitts of 4/JG 3, possibly photographed at the beginning of 1941 prior to II Gruppe's withdrawal from operations. All of the machines depicted here wear the typical II/JG 3 finish derived from the 1940 camouflage scheme and overall yellow engine cowlings and rudders. (Held/Propaganda Aervice Photo)

An obviously considerably retouched photograph of "Black 14," a Bf 109 E of 5 Staffel, in France in autumn 1940. The Gruppe emblem of JG 3 in front of the cockpit, at least, has been heavily retouched. The engine cowling appears to be painted yellow as far as the cockpit and the rudder also appears to have a yellow finish. (unknown)

4

Rest and Refit and Return to Operations on the Channel February to June 1941

After returning to Germany at the end of February 1941, the entire *Gruppe* was first sent on a well-deserved rest leave. The "general leave period" for II/JG 3 obviously lasted well into March, with the pilots even enjoying a rollicking, carefree period during a ski vacation in Kitzbühel from 9 to 28 March 1941[166].

After the *Gruppe* had completely reassembled at Darmstadt-Griesheim, starting in mid-April 1941 it began receiving new machines[167]. In the course of its reequipment, II/JG 3 was issued a complete complement of Bf 109 F-2 fighters. This latest variant of the Messerschmitt fighter had begun reaching the front-line units in substantial numbers in February 1941, replacing the Bf 109 E[168]. In the three weeks that followed, the *Gruppe* had the opportunity to become familiar with its new machines, flying numerous practice missions. This period was largely uneventful, and there were no serious accidents. At the same time, the *Gruppe* was assigned new pilots to make good the losses it had suffered[169]. During those weeks at Darmstadt, the *Gruppe* was frequently inspected by the *Kommodore*, Maj. Günther Lützow, who took a keen interest in the state of the unit's regeneration, always with an open ear for the cares and concerns of all the men[170].

As April 1941 neared its end, there were increasing signs that the rest and refit period was about over, and soon orders were received to return to the Channel. On 25 April 1941 an advance party of ground personnel was dispatched to France, to the forward airfield at the Monchy-Breton, where II/JG 3 was to be based in the weeks to come. The air element subsequently flew there on 4 May[171].

The ratio of forces and operational conditions on the Channel front had not altered to the *Luftwaffe*'s advantage since the *Gruppe*'s withdrawal in February. On the contrary, as a result of the campaign in the Balkans and the sending of *Luftwaffe* units to North Africa and Sicily, a much weakened force was now left to carry on the air war against England. Moreover, attacks by the Royal Air Force against targets on the Dutch and German North Sea coasts meant that the *Jagdgeschwader* left in the west had to be spread out

even further. By the spring of 1941 only JG 2, 3, 26, 51 and 53 remained in northeastern France and western Belgium. Conversely the number of British fighters continued to grow steadily and there had also been a resurgence of the Royal Air Force's bomber force; as a result, in spring 1941 the RAF enjoyed a marked numerical superiority on the Channel[172]. In spite of this, there was a clear increase in the *Luftwaffe*'s offensive activities against England in that spring of 1941, but it was all for the purpose of deception and concealment—the *Wehrmacht*'s about face and the buildup in the east had to be concealed for as long as possible. The following is from an OKW directive issued at that time:

The widespread impression of an imminent invasion of England must be strengthened even further[173].

While the *Luftwaffe* bomber units carried out the heaviest raids of the entire war on targets in Great Britain during the spring nights of 1941[174], there was no resumption of the daylight raids of the previous autumn. Instead, the *Luftwaffe* limited its activities to fighter sweeps over the Channel and southeast England, and standing patrols and scrambles to intercept the frequent incursions by British bomber and fighter units[175]. Concerning German day fighter operations, there was a general order from the *Jafü 2* which stated that fighter sweeps were to be limited to the coastal areas of the British Isles in order to prevent the new Bf 109 F-2 from coming down on enemy territory and falling into the hands of the Royal Air Force[176].

The first days after the *Gruppe*'s arrival at Monchy-Breton were largely uneventful; the pilots took the opportunity conduct orientation flights to familiarize themselves with the new area of operations[177,178]. The first defensive missions took place on 7 May 1941, when RAF fighters carried out several fighter sweeps over the French coast. German fighters also engaged the fighter escort of a British convoy in the Channel, in order to clear the way for German bombers to attack. II/JG 3 claimed one Spitfire shot down. This was credited to the *Kapitän* of 4 *Staffel*, Oblt. Gollob (6). The only casualty suffered by the *Gruppe* was Uffz. Ernst Pöske, whose machine was damaged by enemy fire during an air battle over the Channel. Slightly wounded, Pöske was forced to belly-land his machine at Etaples. The German side claimed a total of nine victories on this day[179].

The next day, 8 May 1941, the *Gruppe* was again in action over the Channel, its orders to fly fighter sweeps over the south coast of England. Once again there were clashes with British fighters[180], in the course of which 4 *Staffel* suffered two losses. Lt. Karlheinz Ponec was forced to ditch his damaged machine in the sea off Gravelines, resulting in an immediate search effort by the air-sea rescue service. The *Gruppe* was in turn obliged to provide several *Schwärme* to provide fighter cover for the search aircraft. This had become standard practice since the previous summer and fall, when British fighters had frequently attacked and even shot down air-sea rescue machines. These escort missions resulted in another encounter with Spitfires, after which Lt. Joachim Pfeiffer was not seen again. He was reported missing. It is likely that he was shot down and went into the Channel with his machine. A pilot of 6/JG 3 was forced to belly-land his machine near Etaples, probably as a result of damage sustained in an air battle resulting from a late afternoon escort mission for the air-sea rescue service[181]. The pilot was not injured.

After this, combat activity diminished noticeably, with bad weather being at least partly responsible. Occasional fighter sweeps were flown over the English coast as well as a number of strafing attacks on British fighter bases near the coast. One such attack took place on the morning of 14 May, when 6 *Staffel* was ordered to strafe Hawkinge[182]. All in all, however, the rest of the month was uneventful for II/JG 3. Neither patrol flights nor occasional scrambles against reported incursions by British aircraft resulted in contact with the enemy. Consequently, in the period until the end of may 1941 the *Gruppe* reported neither successes[183] nor losses as a result of enemy action, although three machines were damaged in crash landings and in one case a failed takeoff. While the struggle against the Royal Air Force went on in this way from day to day, with neither side being able to gain any significant advantage over the other, in the east preparations for the planned invasion of the Soviet Union were proceeding apace. By 20 May 1940 the third echelon of the army's buildup had reached the eastern frontier, raising the total forces massed there to 120 divisions.

At the end of May there were growing rumors that II/JG 3's days in France were already numbered. In fact, before the end of the month the order arrived for the *Gruppe* to transfer to Hostynne in Poland, which at that time was called the *Generalgouvernement*. The loading of the ground elements aboard trains began immediately, and these subsequently began departing for the east on 1 June 1941[184]. After the departure of the ground elements it was obvious that the air element would soon follow. The *Gruppe* flew its last sorties in the west on 4 June 1941, several *Schwarm*-strength escort missions in support of a German coastal convoy. All were completed without incident.

Four days later, on 8 June 1941, the air element also received orders to transfer to the east; on that day the *Gruppe* flew to St. Dizier and then to Böblingen. On the following day it went to Breslau with an en route stop at Straubing[185].

Notes:

[166] The following appears in the writings of Georg Alex: *"Group ski vacation by the pilots; Stab, 5 and 6 Staffel in the Hotel Ehrenbachhöhle on the Hahnenkamm near Kitzbühel. Staffelkapitän Oblt. Gollob provided 4 Staffel with its own comfortable ski chalet: the Haus Sonnenbühel at the foot of the Ehrenbachhöhle."*

[167] According to the German Order of Battle, Statistics as of Quarter Years, Reporting Date 29/3/1941, at this time II/JG 3 still did not have a single machine; according to the logbook of Heinrich Sannemann, he took charge of his new Messerschmitt at Mannheim-Sandhofen on 16 April and ferried it to Darmstadt the same day.

[168] See technical data accompanying Line Drawing 4 on page 65.

[169] 4/JG 3's new arrivals in these days were Lt. Fuß, Lt. Pfeiffer, Uffz. Pöske, Fhr. Helm and Uffz. Bälz—writings of Georg Alex.

[170] On this topic, Georg Alex wrote: *"...visited the dispersals of the individual Staffeln, lengthy conversations with everyone."*

[171] Writings of Botho Teichmann; logbook of Heinrich Sannemann.

[172] Also see Prien, JG 53 part 1, p. 289 and following pages.

[173] OKW War Diary 1940/41 Part II.

[174] 4,354 sorties were flown against the island in March 1941 and 5,448 in April. The heaviest attacks on London took place during this time, such as on the night of 16-17 April when 681 bombers struck the British capital, and 19-20 April when 712 bombers took part. The series of attacks continued into May, when the principal targets were Liverpool, Glasgow and London.

[175] The "program" was rounded out by reconnaissance, weather reconnaissance and air-sea rescue missions over the sea as far as the Thames Estuary.

[176] The following telling entry appeared in the *Gruppe* war diary: *"It is extremely undesirable that machines end up over there."* From the writings of Karl-Heinz Langer.

[177] II/JG 3 had allegedly already reported the downing of a Lysander by the *Gruppenstabsschwarm* on 4 May 1941, however no details of the incident are known.

[178] According to the logbook of Heinrich Sannemann, for example, one such mission took place from 9:38 to 10:38 AM on 6 May.

[179] OKW communiqué of 8 May 1941.

[180] After which the German side claimed a total of seven victories—OKW communiqué of 9 May 1941.

[181] According to the logbook of Heinrich Sannemann, mission times 4:50 to 6:15 PM.

[182] Time of takeoff according to the logbook of Heinrich Sannemann was 5:30 AM; the mission was aborted.

[183] II/JG 3 did, however, report the downing of a Bristol Blenheim on 21 May 1941; no details of the claim are known.

[184] According to the writings of Botho Teichmann the first transport train left Arras at 11:46 AM on 1 June 1941.

[185] Logbook of Heinrich Sannemann; writings of Georg Alex.

Two Messerschmitts of II Gruppe, "Black 2" of 5 Staffel in the foreground and "White 4" of 4/JG 3 in the background, both Bf 109 F-2s. This photo was probably taken in spring 1941 when II/JG 3 converted to the F-model at Darmstadt. Note the Gruppe *emblem in front of the cockpit of "Black 2". (Skibitzki)*

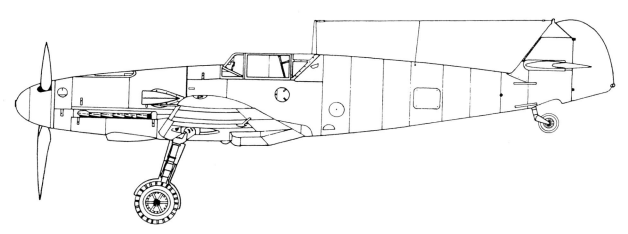

Line Drawing 3: Messerschmitt Bf 109 F-2

During the course of its rest and refit in the spring of 1941, as of mid-April II/JG 3 began receiving a complete complement of Bf 109 F-2 fighters. The F-series began replacing the Bf 109 E in service with front-line units in spring 1941. The "*Friedrich*" differed from the preceding Bf 109 E in a whole series of technical and aerodynamic refinements, making it clearly superior to the "*Emil*" in performance. However, the replacement of the wing-mounted guns with a single cannon mounted centrally between the cylinder banks and firing through the propeller spinner resulted in a clear reduction in firepower.

Length: 8.94 m	Engine: DB 601 N, 1,175 H.P.	Empty weight: 1 960 kg
Wingspan: 9.92 m	Takeoff weight: 2 750 kg	
Height: 2.60 m	Armament: 1 MG 151/20, 2 MG 17	

"Yellow 1", a Bf 109 F-2, was the aircraft of Staffelkapitän *Oblt. Heinrich Sannemann; the machine is seen here on the Monchy-Breton airfield in May 1941. It wears a gray-green camouflage scheme with heavily-mottled fuselage sides and an overall yellow engine cowling and rudder. Note the black protective finish aft of the exhaust stacks in the area of the wingroot, which was intended to conceal the exhaust stains on the fuselage sides. The* Gruppe *emblem of II/JG 3 is visible in front of the cockpit. (Sannemann)*

5

"Operation Barbarossa"
Operations in the East
22 June to 1 November 1941

By mid-June 1941 German preparations for the invasion of the Soviet Union were largely complete; the units of the *Wehrmacht* were arrayed along the German-Soviet demarcation line in position to launch "Operation Barbarossa", the attack on the Soviet Union, officially still Germany's ally[186]. The *Luftwaffe* had massed approximately two-thirds of its available forces for the operation, with three air fleets (1, 2 and 4) and part of a third (5) ready to strike.

The *Stab* and all three *Gruppen*[187] of JG 3 were to take part in the coming operation. At the beginning of its tour of duty in the east the *Geschwader* was under the command of *V Fliegerkorps* commanded by Gen. Ritter von Greim. The air corps was part of *Luftflotte 4* commanded by *Generaloberst* Löhr; it was assigned to operate over Army Group South commanded by *Generalfeldmarschall* von Rundstedt.[188]

The *Gruppe*'s ground elements arrived by train in Deblin on 4 June 1941. From there they traveled overland to Klemensow near Zamosc[189], approximately 70 kilometers southeast of Lublin. From there they were to prepare the forward airfield at Hostynne, 25 kilometers to the northeast and just inside the German-Soviet demarcation line, for the arrival of the air element and erect quarters[190]. The air element arrived at Breslau-Gandau on 9 June and initially remained there. Not until 18 June, after a brief interval at Cracow, did it fly to Hostynne, arriving there during the afternoon[191]. In the remaining days before the invasion activity was limited to technical work on the Messerschmitts[192], including the installation of bomb racks on all of 5 *Staffel*'s machines. Flying was restricted to maintenance test flights and the like.

At 5:00 in the afternoon on 21 June 1941, *V Fliegerkorps*, whose headquarters were in a forest camp near Lipsko[193], held a situation briefing for unit commanders and informed them of the coming attack[194]. That evening the *Gruppe* held a briefing for the *Staffelkapitäne*.

The German invasion of the Soviet Union began early on the morning of 22 June 1941. II/JG 3 flew its first missions shortly before 4:00 AM[195]. Its orders: *Staffel*-strength free chases and low-level attacks with guns and bombs against Soviet airfields in the Lvov area. At 4:30 AM, during one of these missions, Oblt. Walther Dahl, who was flying with the *Gruppenstab*, scored the *Gruppe*'s first victory in the east. The *Staffeln* of II/JG 3 flew numerous missions during the course of the day, the majority of them to the south, with emphasis on the area around Lvov. In addition to free chases and low-level attacks, in the afternoon bomber escort missions were also flown, with some pilots logging as many as five sorties[196]. The first missions in the early morning produced little contact with Russian aircraft, however the Russian air force recovered from the initial shock remarkably quickly, and the second group of missions, which began at about 6:30 AM, resulted in several fierce air battles[197], in which 4 *Staffel* claimed three victories and the *Gruppenstab* four. Four more victories were claimed in an early-evening engagement. With four claims, *Gruppenkommandeur* Hptm. Keller was the day's most successful pilot (17-20). II/JG 3 claimed a total of 16 enemy aircraft shot down on 22 June 1941[198]. The *Gruppe*'s losses were comparatively light, with just one Messerschmitt written off as a result of (probable) enemy action. Fw. Hermann Freitag of 5 *Staffel* failed to return from a mission into the Lvov—Brody area for reasons unknown and was at first reported missing. In fact Fw. Freitag was taken in by local farmers, who hid him until the arrival of German forces. As a result, he was able to rejoin the *Gruppe* unharmed on 2 July. For II/JG 3 this was the first example of the local population's willingness to assist. At that stage the local population still hoped that the German armies would liberate them from Soviet oppression, a hope that was to be cruelly disappointed[199]. One of 4 *Staffel*'s pilots was injured: the undercarriage hydraulics of Uffz. Leo Suschko's machine were damaged by enemy fire and he was obliged to attempt a forced landing in a field next to Hostynne

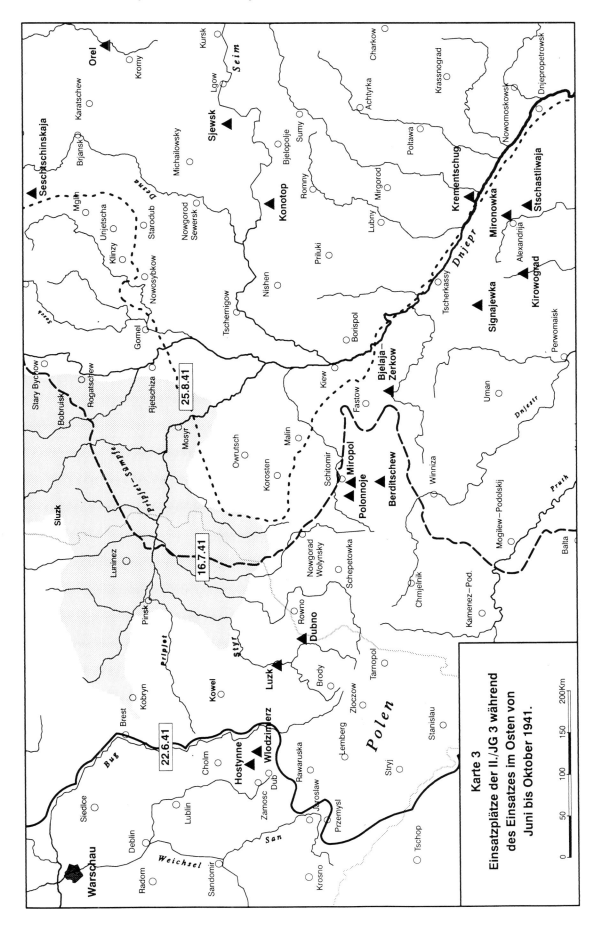

Karte 3

Einsatzplätze der II./JG 3 während des Einsatzes im Osten von Juni bis Oktober 1941.

airfield with one undercarriage leg retracted and the other extended. On landing he struck his head on the gunsight and sustained a minor concussion[200].

The second day of the war in the east, 23 June 1941, saw II/JG 3 in action mainly over the combat zone east of the former demarcation line, with emphasis on the area over Wlodzimierz. In addition to free chase missions and low-level attacks on Russian ground columns, in the afternoon the *Gruppe*'s fighters flew several *Schwarm*-strength missions to cover the erection of bridges over the River Bug. Once again there were frequent encounters with Russian aircraft, including for the first time large formations of twin-engined bombers. The SB-2, SB-3 and DB-3 bombers initially flew without fighter escort, and engaging them became one of II/JG 3's principal tasks. During its first, early-morning mission, 6/JG 3 alone shot down six SB-2s, a type which the Germans often referred to as the "Martin Bomber," without loss to itself. *Staffelkapitän* Oblt. Sannemann (4-5) and Fw. Dilling (5-6) each claimed two of the bombers[201]. Six more victories were recorded in an engagement at about 9:40 AM, in which 4 and 5 *Staffel* participated. The day's tally was sixteen victories with no pilot casualties, while four Messerschmitts were damaged in crash- or belly-landings.

In the two days that followed, the *Gruppe* continued to fly from the Hostynne airfield, operating over the battle zone on the east bank of the Bug. Providing fighter cover over the advance roads, especially the one from Hrubitschew through Wlodzimierz[202] to Lutsk, which had been designated "*Panzerstrasse Mitte*" (Tank Road Center) and which was a favorite target of the enemy bombers, assumed primary importance. Three victories were scored there on 24 June, however on this day II/JG 3 also lost two machines. During an early evening air battle southeast of Busk[203], Uffz. Eduard Kunz of 5 *Staffel* was shot down and wounded. He came down in Russian-held territory but was subsequently recovered by farmers, who took care of him and hid him from the Russian troops. His hiding place was soon betrayed, however, and the next day Uffz. Kunz was captured and taken to Zloczow hospital, where he succumbed to his serious injuries five days later. Obfw. Erwin Kortlepel of 4/JG 3 was more fortunate. His engine was hit in combat and he was forced to crash-land behind enemy lines. He, too, was taken in by local farmers and three days later he succeeded in returning to the *Gruppe* unharmed. 25 June 1941 was another lively day for the *Gruppe*, which in the end was able to claim 17 enemy aircraft shot down. In an early morning encounter with a formation of DB-3s, 6 *Staffel* scored another six victories without loss[204]. Oblt. Sannemann (6-7) and Fw. Dilling (7-8) once again accounted for two bombers each. A short time later, while on a free chase mission west of Lutsk, the *Stab* and elements of 4 *Staffel* shot down another seven DB-3s and a single I-16 *Rata*. Although there was an element of risk in engaging the slow Russian twin-engined bombers, shooting them down was comparatively easy and the offensive tactics employed

by the Russians contributed to this. The Russian bombers often flew without fighter escort, and when attacked by the Messerschmitts they took no evasive or defensive action, instead doggedly holding course for the target in an effort to accomplish their mission.[205] The result was tremendous losses among the SB-2s and DB-3s, while on the other side German fighter pilots were able to quickly rack up large scores[206]. Quite different from the operations of the *Stab* and the other two *Staffeln* were those of Oblt. Kijewski's 5 *Staffel*, II/JG 3's *Jabostaffel*. It was committed mainly to low-level attacks against Soviet airfields, vehicle columns and troop concentrations, as well as railway targets. Though its specialized ground attack role meant that it had fewer opportunities for air combat, it still managed a respectable number of enemy aircraft shot down. The Russian ground defenses made the *Staffel*'s low-level missions extremely uncomfortable affairs, the light flak and small arms fire proving especially lethal. Unlike the French and British in the west in 1940, Russian infantry were trained to fire on low-flying enemy aircraft with whatever weapons were available[207]. The cooling system of the Bf 109 was extremely vulnerable, and a single lucky hit by a rifle bullet could cause the coolant to escape and compel the pilot to make a forced landing. If he was unable to reach his own lines, this meant captivity or even worse for the unlucky pilot. On this day 5/JG 3 suffered its first total loss in its low-level attacks, when Horst Buddenhagen, one of the more promising new pilots with eight victories, flew into the ground south of Beresteczko. The Messerschmitt burst into flames on striking the ground and Buddenhagen was killed. As well, one of 4 *Staffel*'s pilots was wounded: Fhr. Albert Helm's aircraft was hit in the cockpit during combat and he was wounded in the face by splinters. In spite of his wounds he managed to reach his own lines, where he made a smooth belly landing.

The first days of the air war in the east were sufficient to show that the missions there were going to be fundamentally different from those in the west. Unlike on the Channel, in Russia missions were usually flown in *Schwarm* or even *Rotte* strength. This was due less to an intentional change in tactics than to the fact that the vastness of Russia[208] and the multitude of tasks assigned to the *Jagdgruppen* made it impossible for the available forces, which were completely inadequate, to employ entire *Staffeln* or *Gruppen*[209]. This situation was further aggravated by the rapidly diminishing number of serviceable machines[210]. As long as the *Luftwaffe* units maintained their initial technical and tactical superiority over the Russian air force this could go on, however any impartial observer would have to see that the *Luftwaffe*'s forces in the east fell far short of what was required to carry out the multitude of tasks assigned to them. Another difference from missions on the Channel was that the majority of air battles in the east were fought at altitudes of about 3 000 meters, but often less. This put them within range of the enemy's light and medium flak, for which the pilots soon developed a very healthy respect.

Meanwhile, the initially determined resistance by the Soviet armies on the left wing of Army Group South's front had lessened and the Russian troops had begun withdrawing to the east, allowing the German advance across the Bug to gain ground. On 26 June strong German armored forces crossed the line Dubno—Lutsk, took the latter town after fierce house-to-house fighting, and ended up north of the city advancing toward the Kovel line[211]. The units of *V Fliegerkorps* were ordered to support *Panzergruppe 1*'s advance to the east while simultaneously guarding the flanking areas against Soviet counterattacks[212]. As well, at this the *Gruppen* of JG 3 carried out their first transfers. In the morning the air element of II/JG 3 flew from Hostynne to Wlodzimierz, a forward airfield about 20 kilometers east of the unit's previous base. The ground elements followed over poor and often crowded advance roads, while during the course of the day Hostynne airfield was occupied by III/JG 3, which had been moved forward[213]. On its very first day of operations from Wlodzimierz, II/JG 3 flew a series of missions and scored a total of twelve victories in the process, including nine DB-3s shot down by 5 *Staffel* in a morning engagement in the Dubno area. On the other side of the coin, the *Gruppe* suffered an especially painful loss when it lost its *Kommandeur*; during a free chase mission west of Stoyanov[214], Hptm. Lothar Keller's machine was rammed by another Messerschmitt[215] and he crashed to his death. Hptm. Keller had scored six of his total of twenty victories during his short time with II/JG 3, and his accomplishments were honored with the posthumous awarding of the Knight's Cross on 9 July 1941. On the following day, the *Kapitän* of 4 *Staffel*, *Hauptmann* Gordon Gollob, was named to succeed Keller, and in turn Oblt. Karl Faust assumed command of 4/JG 3. 4 *Staffel* also mourned the loss of one of its pilots: Obfw. Anton Gremm, who had downed another DB-3 during an early afternoon mission, failed to return after an evening scramble to intercept a reported formation of eight SB-2s. He was listed as missing, until he was found dead by German troops several days later; he had probably fallen victim to return fire from the Russian twin-engined bombers[216]. A further casualty was reported by 6 *Staffel*: after returning from a defensive patrol over the advance roads, Lt. Ludwig Häfner made a forced landing at Hostynne, suffering minor injuries in the process[217].

27 June 1941: Under clear early summer skies the *Gruppe* flew missions over the battle zone north and northeast of Lvov. Once again its assigned task was to guard the German armored spearheads and provide fighter cover over the main roads designated *"Panzerstrasse Mitte"* and *"Nord"*[218]. The end result was two victories by the *Gruppe* against no losses. The picture was much the same on the following day, 28 June, with the Messerschmitts of II/JG 3 flying *Schwarm*-strength free chase and fighter cover missions over the battle zone east of the River Bug. A total of six victories was scored without loss. The final two days of the month also brought a series of encounters with Russian air units, in the course

of which the *Gruppe* scored several victories. Most of the missions flown during this time were free chases and fighter cover missions over the advance roads as well as occasional bomber escort sorties. Operational activity was, however, hindered by bad weather, for the unusually hot weather of the previous days led to a number of heavy thunderstorms. Sudden downpours flooded both roads and airfields, after which the storms dissipated as quickly as they had begun. On 29 June 1941 the *Gruppe* recorded four victories while suffering a single loss: during an evening *Schwarm*-strength free chase, there was an engagement with three SB-2s forty kilometers beyond the front. *Staffelkapitän* Oblt. Faust (4) and Uffz. Bälz (1) each accounted for one of the bombers, while Uffz. Leo Suschko was hit by return fire while attacking a third and was obliged to make a forced landing. Oblt. Faust observed Suschko's Messerschmitt going down trailing black smoke and believed that he saw it crash and explode; as a result, after returning to Wlodzimierz he reported that the pilot had been killed. In fact Uffz. Suschko managed a forced landing, after which the semi-conscious pilot was rescued by Ukrainian farmers. The latter cared for the injured pilot and hid him until the arrival of German troops two days later. As a result, Suschko was able to return to his *Staffel* two days later on 1 July[219]. II/JG 3 recorded four more victories on 30 June 1941, while losses were limited to a single machine which ran out of fuel and made a belly landing. Lt. Hans Fuß of 4 *Staffel* was extremely fortunate on this day. His machine was hit by shrapnel from an anti-aircraft shell, damaging the trim mechanism and making it almost impossible to control. Summoning all his strength and piloting skill, Fuß managed to nurse the machine back to Wlodzimierz, where he made a smooth landing.

Meanwhile, after only eight days of operations in the east, the first clear signs of a reduction in the *Gruppe*'s operational readiness were becoming apparent. Even though just seven Messerschmitts had been written off on operations to date, the number of serviceable machines had already sunk to no more than 20, or 50% of the *Gruppe*'s authorized strength on 22 June 1941[317]. The main reason for this was the almost complete absence of deliveries of new aircraft[221] or of engines and spare parts. As a result of this state of affairs an increasing number of machines with relatively minor defects could not be repaired and consequently had to sit idle. Another factor was overwork of the ground crews. Their strenuous labor began before sunrise and did not end even when the air element was stood down. The mechanics had to work through the short summer nights to repair defects that had appeared during the course of the day and have the "kites" ready to fly for the next day. It is not surprising, therefore, that the first signs of exhaustion were already becoming apparent[222].

At the beginning of July 1941 the front in the area of the northern wing of Army Group South came increasingly into movement. Faced with flagging resistance on the part of the Russian forces, the spearheads of the German 6th and 17th Armies advanced through

Dubno toward Berdichev and Zhitomir[223]. Consequently, in the first days of July the *Gruppe*'s zone of operations shifted to the area in front of Berdichev, where the fighting centered on towns such as Ostrog, Rovno and Novograd.

Operating from Wlodzimierz, II/JG 3 saw action over the battle zone west of Berdichev and Zhitomir in the first five days of the new month; in some cases the *Gruppe* was moved forward to Lutsk-South airfield during the day[224]. Once again the *Gruppe* flew free chase and fighter cover sorties over the advance roads, while 5 *Staffel* was mainly committed to low-level attacks with guns and bombs. The *Gruppe* scored four victories without loss[225] on 1 July, however this success was eclipsed on the following day, 2 July 1941, when II/JG 3 recorded no less than 23 victories in a series of air battles spread out through the entire day, with Obfw. Heinzeller (14-17) and Oblt. Franz Beyer (11-14) each accounting for four enemy machines. The *Gruppe* suffered one total loss on this day: Lt. Friedrich Kanzler of 5/JG 3 was killed when his machine crashed near Lutsk airfield shortly after taking off on a free chase sortie into the area around Ostrog. The missions of the next two days were largely uneventful, apart from one Messerschmitt damaged by anti-aircraft fire on 3 July 1941.

The rapid pace of the army's advance soon made it necessary for II/JG 3 to move again; during the afternoon of 4 July, therefore, the ground element's main transport column was ordered to set out for Dubno. Poor road conditions and heavy traffic slowed the column's progress, and when evening fell it was forced to halt 15 kilometers short of its destination and set up camp for the night in an open field. The next morning Ukrainian farmers reported that there were some straggling Russian soldiers hiding out in a nearby wood. Without any sort of reconnaissance, a squad of technicians and office workers armed with rifles, several machine-guns and hand grenades was sent to clear the wood. None of the men had any experience in infantry tactics. What began as a simple patrol operation ended in a bloody fiasco, for instead of the expected handful of demoralized Red Army soldiers, the wood was in fact held by a strong, well-equipped unit of cadets, who set an ambush for the approaching men of II/JG 3. The German patrol was badly mauled in the ensuing bitter, close-quarters fighting, before army troops came to the rescue the next day and cleared the wood. In the end the ground elements of II/JG 3 suffered casualties of six killed and two seriously wounded[226].

On 5 July 1941 the air element was again moved forward to Lutsk-South for the day's missions, the bulk of which were flown over the Polonnoye—Miropol area. II/JG 3 registered a total of eleven victories, including four by Fw. Ohlrogge of 5/JG 3 (7-10), while suffering no losses. In the evening the unit flew to Dubno-South, where those elements of the ground personnel which had already arrived had made the necessary preparations; the remaining elements of the main column, which had become involved in the forest battle near the airfield, did not arrive until the next day.

On 6 July the *Gruppe* was called upon to fly *Schwarm*-strength free chase missions over the battle zone around Berdichev and Zhitomir. Nine victories were scored, five of these by the *Kapitän* of 4 *Staffel*, Oblt. Faust (8-12). Once again the *Gruppe* suffered no total losses. Uffz. Bälz, who was flying in the *Stabsschwarm* on this day, enjoyed a singular piece of good luck. After his *Friedrich* was damaged in air combat, he managed to reach friendly territory, where he made a successful forced landing near Polonnoye airfield. The situation was much the same in the following days, with the air element being moved to forward airstrips for the day, in some cases to Polonnoye. On 7 July the Messerschmitts of II/JG 3 were again in action over the forward combat zone. Only two victories were claimed, both by Oblt. Beyer (14-15) in an evening engagement. II/JG 3 then scored four victories on 8 July and another ten on 9 July[227]; losses amounted to two Messerschmitts.

Berdichev fell into German hands on 7 July, followed two days later by Zhitomir. With the fortifications of the Stalin Line breached, the units of the 6th and 17th Armies now launched the next stage of the advance toward the Dniepr River. Operations were seriously hampered by periods of very bad weather, in which heavy rain transformed the mostly unpaved roads into bottomless morasses. Under these conditions progress was virtually impossible[228]. The flying units suffered accordingly under these conditions.

On 10 July II/JG 3 was ordered to move again; the air element flew from Dubno-South to Miropol[229], a forward airfield located approximately 10 kilometers east of Polonnoye where the main rail line from Rovno to Berdichev crossed the Sluch River. Since the serious road difficulties made it impossible for the ground elements to follow immediately, on the previous day a small advance detachment of technical personnel had been flown ahead by Ju 52. Meanwhile, in a laborious march, the main transport column carrying the ground elements crawled east over the softened and clogged roads[230]. The purpose of the *Gruppe*'s missions from Miropol: guard the advance roads being used by armored units in the Zhitomir—Kiev area[231].

The very first day of operations by II/JG 3 from its new airfield resulted in a series of missions over the area east of Zhitomir. After steady rain had ruled out flying in the morning, the first sorties were flown in the early afternoon. The result was a total of seventeen victories, including three each by Oblt. Kijewski (11-13), Obfw. Heinzeller (22-24) and Uffz. Lucas (2-4). One noteworthy sortie took place in the early evening, when a *Rotte* consisting of Oblt. Beyer and Uffz. Lucas of 4/JG 3 engaged five TB-3s. All of the enemy bombers were shot down in a running battle[232]. The following days' missions, which took the *Gruppe* into the area in front of Kiev, also resulted in numerous contacts with Russian formations. The *Gruppe* scored regularly—eight enemy machines destroyed on 11 July 1941, four on the 12th and another on the 13th—however, it also suffered a number of losses. On 11 July Oblt. Horst Beyer of 6/JG 3 failed to return from a cover mission over the ad-

II./Jagdgeschwader 3
Feldpostnr. L 30 633
Luftg.P.A. Breslau.
Az. 21 g Br.B.Nr. 579/41 geh.

Geheim!

Gefechtsstand, 24.7.1941.

Betr.: Neufestsetzung des Rangdienstalters
des Oberleutnant (Tr.O.) Kijewski, Herbert.

An
Jagdgeschwader 3.

Die Gruppe bittet, die Neufestsetzung des Rangdienstalters
des Oblt. Kijewski erwirken zu wollen.

Oblt. Kijewski ist am 1.7.1933 bei 12/I.R. 101 in
Arys (Fstpl.) eingetreten und am 1.4.1936 zum Leutnant be-
fördert worden. Er hat sich sowohl truppendienstlich als
auch als Jagdflieger vor dem Feind ausgezeichnet bewährt, be-
sonders als Führer seiner Staffel, die er zu hervorragenden
Erfolgen brachte.

Durch seine Umsicht, seine fliegerischen und taktischen
Kenntnisse blieben die Verluste innerhalb seiner Einheit die
denkbar geringsten. Er hat im Polenfeldzug, im Feldzug in
Westen, am Kanal im Kampf gegen England und nun im Rußland-
feldzug teilgenommen. Insgesamt flog er bis zum 18.7.1941
190 Feindeinsätze, davon 29 Jabo-Einsätze gegen England und
10 ebensolche gegen Rußland. 1/3 seiner Englandeinsätze sind
Jabo-Einsätze. Oberleutnant Kijewski hat seine Staffel immer
in diesen Einsätzen sicher zum Ziel und Erfolg geführt.
Unter den angegriffenen Jabo-Zielen befanden sich neben
London Flugplätze an der Südküste Englands, Fabrikanlagen,
Tankanlagen, Eisenbahnknotenpunkte, Truppenlager, Panzer, Ge-
schützstellungen u.ä. Oblt. Kijewski ist an diese schweren
Aufgaben mit ausgesprochenem Schneid und im Tiefangriff
herangegangen trotz sehr starker Bodenabwehr. Durch die Jabo-
Einsätze kam er naturgemäß zunächst zu wenigen Abschlüssen,
hat sich jedoch im Rußland-Feldzug rasch weitere Erfolge ge-
holt und bis zum 18.7.1941 15 Abschüsse erzielt. Die Gesamt-
abschüsse setzen sich zusammen:

Frankreich-Feldzug   2 Flugzeuge, Typ Spitfire
England-Einsatz   1   "   " Hurricane
Rußland-Feldzug   6 DB 3, 1 SB 2U, 1 TB 3,
                        2 einmot. Tiefangriffs-
                        flugzeuge neueren bisher
                        unbekannten Baumusters.

Major Herbert Kijewski (31.5.11-16.4.45)

Seine Staffel hat insgesamt 53.000 kg Bomben über Feind-
gebiet abgeworfen, davon Oblt. Kijewski persönlich 9 000 kg.
Die Gesamterfolge der Staffel sind folgende:
95 Abschüsse, 33 am Boden zerstörte und 31 beschädigte
Flugzeuge (nicht zur Anerkennung gemeldet), 11 Panzer
vernichtet, mehrere Lokomotiven zerstört, Geschütze,
Fahrzeuge, Kolonnen vernichtet.

Es ergeben sich aus seinen persönlichen Leistungen wie
aus den Erfolgen seiner Staffel die hohen soldatischen und
menschlichen Qualitäten, welche ihn unbedingt anerkannt
werden müssen. Oblt. Kijewski erhielt am 1.7.1940 das E.K.II,
am 7.7.1940 das E.K.I und am 24.12.1940 den Ehrenpokal für
besondere Leistungen im Luftkrieg.

Oblt. Kijewski ist 30 Jahre alt, an Lebensalter also
den meisten Offizieren seines Jahrgangs weit voraus. Die
Gruppe bittet, auch dies berücksichtigen zu wollen.

In erster Linie bittet die Gruppe, die Neufestsetzung
des Rangdienstalters auf Grund der hervorragenden Leistungen
des Oblt. Kijewski im Kriege vornehmen zu wollen.

sw. 24.7.41

m.d.W.d.G.b.

Hauptmann und Gruppenkommandeur.

vance roads in the area south of Kiev for reasons unknown. He was reported missing[233]. On the same day Obfhr. Albert Helm of 4 *Staffel* had a notable experience, which he was fortunate to survive. During an airfield scouting mission in the unit *Storch*, he strayed over Russian-held territory and came under heavy ground fire. Helm subsequently landed in a meadow behind the lines to inspect the damage. He just managed to get the battered machine back into the air before Red Army troops arrived on the scene. The *Storch* finally gave up the ghost soon after Helm regained friendly territory, and he was forced to set down again[234]. The next day, 12 July 1941, 4 *Staffel* was struck by an especially painful loss, when its *Kapitän*, Oblt. Karl Faust, failed to return from a mission into the area south of Kiev. A member of his *Schwarm* subsequently reported that Oblt. Faust had apparently been shot down by a Ju 88deep inside enemy territory, the bomber having apparently mistaken his Messerschmitt for an attacking Russian fighter. Oblt. Faust managed to nurse his crippled fighter to within about 15 kilometers of the front, where he carried out a smooth belly landing in a meadow. After ascertaining that the *Staffelkapitän* was apparently unhurt and that no Soviet soldiers were in the vicinity, the remaining aircraft flew to Miropol, from where a rescue attempt was launched at once. The Fieseler *Storch* took off and, following the directions provided by Oblt. Faust's "*Kaczmarek*" (wingman), found the landing site and the Bf 109. All efforts to locate the pilot proved fruitless, however. Then, several days later, the crew of a German armored scout car found Karl Faust's body near Chernyakhov. He had apparently been captured and shot by Soviet soldiers[235]. On 15 July, after the missing *Staffelkapitän*'s fate became known, Oblt. Georg Michalek was appointed the new leader of 4 *Staffel*.

The worrying drop in serviceability levels that had begun at the end of June had by now assumed disastrous proportions, for by the middle of the month II/JG 3 had available just a handful of serviceable machines. These were entrusted only to the *Gruppe*'s most successful pilots, who continued to add to their victory totals while the remaining pilots usually sat idle on the ground and only rarely flew combat missions[236]. In the days that followed, the *Gruppe*'s few remaining machines flew missions over Army Group South's northern area, with the focus of operations—if it could be called that in view of the drastic drop in the number of available aircraft—over the Zhitomir—Belaya Tserkov area after 16 July 1941. II/JG 3 was active over its new area of operations in the following days, in spite of variable weather conditions with frequent rain showers. These sorties produced seven victories on the 16th, two on the 17th and two more on 18 July, all without loss, after which bad weather largely brought operations by the *Gruppe* to a standstill[237, 238].

In these days there was a change in the command of 5 *Staffel*: Oblt. Herbert Kijewski was transferred to III *Gruppe*, where he initially assumed command of 8 *Staffel*[239]. Named as new *Kapitän* of 5/JG 3 was Oblt. Harald Moldenhauer, who had previously flown

with 2/JG 3 and who had a single victory to his credit[240].

The army's continued rapid advance made it necessary for II/JG 3 to move again on 20 July 1941. During the day the air element flew from Miropol to Berdichev; II *Gruppe* was soon to be the farther from the front than any of the other units of JG 3[241], for in the days that followed, *Stab*, I and III *Gruppe* were moved forward to Belaya-Tserkov, approximately 100 kilometers farther to the east. II/JG 3's mission continued to be fighter cover over the advance roads and free chases in the area southeast of Berdichev as far as Uman. For the first two days the weather was uncooperative and contacts with the enemy were few, consequently just two victories were recorded. On 23 July 1941, however, there was a return to fine weather; on this day the air element was also moved from Berdichev to Belaya-Tserkov, where the *Gruppe* was to support the three *Jagdgruppen* already stationed there (I and III/JG 3 and I/JG 53). The missions from Belaya-Tserkov were in three directions: north into the area around Kiev, east across the Dniepr between Kanev and Cherkassy, and south over the battle zone around Uman. 25 and 26 July were similar, with the air element once again being moved forward to Belaya-Tserkov[242]. While operating from there, the air element scored six victories on the 25th and ten more on the 26th. The only casualty was Lt. Gustav Frielinghaus of 6 *Staffel*: on 25 July[243] he was shot down north of Stawiszce after bringing down two DB-3 bombers. Frielinghaus attempted a forced landing, however his machine flipped over and he sustained minor injuries.

27 July 1941 brought more rain, which halted all operational flying. On this day II/JG 3 received orders to turn over its remaining machines to I/JG 53, as the *Gruppe* was to be reequipped with the Bf 109 F-4[244]. The pilots were flown by Ju 52 to Krosno to collect the new machines and on the morning of 28 July they hurriedly took charge of a full complement of Bf 109 F-4s. After a single "extended circuit" with which to familiarize themselves with the new type, at noon the pilots departed for Berdichev[245]. The *Gruppe*'s stay there would not be much longer, however, for on the following morning, 29 July 1941, the entire unit was transferred to Belaya-Tserkov[246]. While flying from there, by the end of the month the *Gruppe* scored two more victories without loss to itself[247].

The first days of August 1941 saw a return to mainly fine summer weather and during this time II/JG 3 was principally in action over the battle zone along the Dniepr. While the main thrust of the army's operations was aimed at encircling the Russian forces still holding out near Uman, approximately 200 kilometers south of Kiev, most of II/JG 3's missions led into the area of Kiev and to the north around Malin, where strong Soviet forces were still holding positions on the west bank of the Dniepr[248]. In the period until 6 August the *Gruppe* recorded five more victories, once again without loss to itself.

Meanwhile, the units of the German 17th Army, in cooperation with Panzer Group 1, had succeeded in encircling the bulk of three Soviet armies in the Uman area. By 8 August, after heavy fighting, the trapped enemy forces had been smashed. The strongest Soviet forces facing Army Group South had been decisively defeated and that the way into the Krivoy-Rog ore region and the Black Sea ports of Odessa and Nikolayev was open to German mobile units. Furthermore the way was cleared for an advance toward the lower Dniepr, where the area from Cherkassy to Zaporozhye lay open before the tank and motorized units of Army Group South—from there the German forces could launch an attack against Kiev and the entire southwestern front of the Soviets[249].

II/JG 3's next move came on 7 August 1941. From Belaya-Tserkov the *Gruppe* was moved forward to Signajewka, a front-line airfield near Shpola. The air element flew there during the late morning, for the most part in association with free chase sorties over the Smela—Alexandrija area[250]. In the days to come, the *Gruppe* was to be active mainly over the battle zone along the Dniepr between Kanev and Kremenchug as well as to the south, where strong Russian forces were still holding positions on the west bank of the Dniepr. Only a few missions led into the Kiev area. At first the *Gruppe*'s operational activities were considerably limited by frequent heavy downpours. Nevertheless, during its missions from Signajewka in the course of the next ten days, II/JG 3 recorded a total of 64 victories, including eleven on 8 August, seven on the 9th, eight on the 12th and 27 on 17 August 1941, the *Gruppe*'s most successful day of the entire summer campaign of 1941. The same names continued to feature prominently in the *Gruppe*'s victory list; *Gruppenkommandeur* Hptm. Gollob led all scorers, however Oblt. Michalek, Oblt. Sannemann, Obfw. Kortlepel and Fw. Ohlrogge were also very successful. The *Gruppe*'s losses for the same period were relatively minor, with one pilot killed, one captured and two Messerschmitts written off as a result of enemy action. Both losses came on 11 August, when the *Gruppe* flew several free chase sorties, escorted Ju 88 bombers and also carried out low-level attacks in the area south of Kiev. Oblt. Heinz Schoenefeldt of the *Gruppenstab*[251] and Lt. Herbert Glück of 5 *Staffel* were shot down during a strafing attack on a Soviet airfield south of Kiev. While Oblt. Schoenefeldt went down with his machine into a moor and was killed in the ensuing explosion, Lt. Glück was able to belly-land his Messerschmitt on another Soviet airfield southwest of Kiev and was subsequently taken prisoner[252].

Meanwhile, in the area of the left wing of Army Group South the German advance was making rapid progress toward the east and southeast; south of Kiev the units of the 17th Army and Panzer Group 1 had reached the Dniepr on a front of approximately 200 kilometers and in the south were advancing towards Dnepropetrovsk and Zaporozhye[253]. II/JG 3 had to be moved forward again in order to keep pace with the army; this began on the afternoon of 17 August 1941, when the first parts of the air element flew to Kirovograd-North airfield. A small advance detachment had already been transported there to prepare the field to accept the *Gruppe*. The aircraft

of 4 *Staffel* had just been refueled after arriving at Kirovograd, when Obfw. Kortlepel's *Schwarm* was scrambled to intercept a reported formation of Russian bombers. Immediately afterwards the four Messerschmitts came upon nine SB-3s, all of which were shot down. Obfw. Brenner (4-6) accounted for three of the enemy bombers, while Obfw. Kortlepel (15-16), Uffz. Suschko (6-7) and Uffz. Lucas (13-14) each accounted for two[254]. 5/JG 3, which arrived a short time later, encountered a formation of R-5s, small, single-engined biplanes used in the communications and night harassment roles, and shot down six. Fw. Ohlrogge accounted for three of the enemy (17-19). Losses amounted to one Bf 109 which made a forced landing at Kirovograd after being damaged in combat. The pilot of the aircraft escaped injury.

II/JG 3's primary mission during operations from Kirovograd was to protect the armored spearheads in the Dnepropetrovsk area, where the Russians still held a strong bridgehead on the west bank of the Dniepr[255]. Numerous free chase missions were flown there on 18 and 19 August; the *Gruppe* scored four victories without loss. On 20 August the *Gruppe* moved again, this time to Stschastliwaja, a front-line airfield about 25 kilometers southeast of Alexandrija[256]. Weather conditions were again hot and dry, and initially the *Gruppe* continued to fly free chase and area patrol missions from its new base over the Dnepropetrovsk combat zone and as far as Zaporozhye[257]. Russian air units were also extremely active over this area[258], resulting in regular contacts with the enemy and fierce air battles. By 25 August 1941 II/JG 3 was able to record a further 41 victories without loss, including 17 in one day on 21 August. On 25 August III Army Corps succeeded in taking Dnepropetrovsk and during the pursuit of the retreating Russian units it seized an undamaged floating bridge across the Dniepr. This was immediately used to cross the river and the first bridgehead was established on the east bank. Beginning on 26 August, II/JG 3's primary mission was to provide fighter cover for this bridge and the German bridgehead on the east bank. Russian close-support aircraft were in the air in large numbers, attempting to destroy the floating bridge, resulting in clashes with German fighters throughout the entire day. II/JG 3 claimed a total of seven victories, once again with no losses as a result of enemy action. One member of the *Stabsschwarm* was injured, however: the Messerschmitt flown by Uffz. Kuno Bälz crashed for unexplained reasons soon after taking off from Stschastliwaja on a free chase mission. The aircraft was wrecked and Bälz had to be taken to hospital in Alexandrija with serious injuries. The next five days again saw II/JG 3 in action, mainly over the area around Dnepropetrovsk; at times operations were again seriously hindered by heavy rainfalls. A further eleven victories were recorded by the end of the month, while the *Gruppe* suffered one fatal casualty when Gefr. Georg Reichhart of 5 *Staffel* was killed while taking off from Stschastliwaja on a combat mission.

By the end of the month the situation at Dnepropetrovsk and the bridgehead on the east bank of the Dniepr had firmed up considerably, and at the beginning of September II/JG 3's area of operations was to shift north towards the Kremenchug area, where units of the 17th Army were preparing to force a crossing of the Dniepr. As a result, on the afternoon of 1 September 1941 the *Gruppe* was moved once again, this time to Mironovka, not far from II/JG 3's former base at Alexandrija, where *Stab* and III/JG 3 were supposed to arrive the next day[259]. The primary mission for II/JG 3 and the elements of JG 3 assembled at Alexandrija was to defend the Dniepr crossings at Kremenchug and Derijewka and provide fighter cover over the area to the east, where units of the 17th Army had succeeded in quickly establishing a bridgehead on the left bank of the river. Powerful armored and infantry forces were to strike north from the bridgehead and drive into the rear of the strong Russian forces[260] still holding around Kiev and along the Dniepr. This operation formed the southern pincer of a planned battle of encirclement at Kiev, for at the same time north of Kiev the 2nd and 6th Armies had launched an attack towards the south[261].

The time at Mironovka was characterized by poor weather conditions with rain and fog[262], and as a result operations were kept to a low level[263]. In any event, on the first three days of the month the weather did permit a number of missions to be flown in defense of the bridge over the Dniepr at Kremenchug, which was the target of numerous attacks by Russian bombers and close-support aircraft[264]. During the course of these missions II/JG 3 scored a total of eight victories while suffering no personnel losses. Obfw. Heinrich Brenner of 4/JG 3 had a lucky escape on 1 September after his aircraft's cooling system was damaged in combat. After his engine seized, Brenner managed to glide to German-held territory, where he made a successful belly landing near Derijewka[265]. Bad weather prevented any missions from being flown for the next two days, however in spite of continued poor weather there was an upswing in operational activity on 5 September. On this day the Russian air force made no less than 19 attacks against the Dniepr crossings in the area of the 17th Army[266], however it achieved no significant success. The Messerschmitts of II/JG 3 flew several defensive missions over the bridges, however they failed to score. In the days that followed, II/JG 3's primary mission continued to be the defense of the bridges at Kremenchug. The *Gruppe* recorded four victories on 6 September, all by pilots of 4/JG 3[267,268]. It scored three more on the following day, 7 September, when the Russians committed a total of 83 machines to attacks against the crossing points[269]. Early on the morning of this day II/JG 3 was subjected to a fierce air attack against its airfield by a group of Soviet bombers with fighter escort. Fw. Lucas of 4 *Staffel*, who by chance was on a maintenance test flight in the vicinity of the airfield, spotted the enemy formation and radioed a warning back to base. The *Gruppe* immediately scrambled from Mironovka, however the bombs were already falling as the fighters took off. Miraculously, in spite of the hail of bombs and strafing Russian fighters, no serious damage was inflicted in II/JG 3's area[270]. A fierce low-level dogfight erupted over the airfield and one victory was scored by Fw. Lucas in return for the loss of a 4 *Staffel* pilot. The machine of Obfw. Heinrich Brenner blew up in midair after being hit by enemy fire, killing the pilot. 6 *Staffel* also recorded one loss on this day: while ferrying a new machine from Germany, Lt. Ludwig Häfner was obliged to make a forced landing near Przmysl. The machine overturned and the pilot received injuries serious enough for him to be taken to hospital in nearby Przmysl.

In the four days that followed, weather severely limited operations. In spite of the fact that Russian bombers and close-support aircraft were active over the combat zone in large numbers, during this period the *Gruppe* reported just three more victories. On 12 September a significant improvement in the weather allowed both sides to become more active in the air. As a result, during the course of the day no less than seventeen air attacks were recorded against targets inside the 17th Army's bridgehead on the east bank of the Dniepr[271]. On this day II/JG 3 was called upon to fly cover over the German armored spearheads and escort Stukas over the bridgehead east of Kremenchug, subsequently claiming a total of seven victories without loss. On the following day, 13 September, the *Gruppe* again flew missions over the bridgehead area around Kremenchug, where there were once again several clashes with groups of Soviet bombers and close-support aircraft[272]. The *Gruppe* emerged very successfully from these, scoring a total of 20 victories, 19 of which came in three large air battles in the early morning and evening. Losses were limited to one pilot wounded: Uffz. Edmund Mächler of 6/JG 3, who was shot down in air combat west of Derijewka. Early on the morning of 14 September 1941, II/JG 3's base at Mironovka was again the target of a Soviet air attack. Suddenly, a formation of Il-2s and escorting fighters appeared at low-level and sprayed the airfield with gunfire. There was no advance warning and therefore no time for defending fighters to get airborne. Georg Alex wrote: *"No one was in the slit trenches, we threw ourselves to the ground, where we lay and listened to the bullets whistle."* Luckily for II/JG 3, the Soviet attack again failed to inflict serious damage or casualties. When it was all over, several machines took off in pursuit of the attackers; after a lengthy chase, the *Stabsrotte* of *Gruppenkommandeur* Hptm. Gollob and adjutant Oblt. Dahl succeeded in bringing down two of the enemy. This was to be the only success of the day, for all of the missions flown over the bridgehead area east and north of Kremenchug were uneventful. This day marked the end of I/JG 3's deployment in the east, as it received orders to return to the Reich to rest and reequip. After handing its remaining aircraft, including all of three serviceable *Friedrichs*[273], and several pilots to II and III *Gruppe*[274], I/JG 3 departed for Germany on the same day[275].

Meanwhile, on the ground, movement had come to the front in the area of the Dniepr bridgehead. On 13 September German troops had begun an advance to the north and on the evening of the 14th near Lochwitza they established contact with the spearheads of the

2nd Army approaching from the north, completing the encirclement of five Russian armies[276]. Because of the army's rapid advance, on 15 September orders were issued for II/JG 3 to move again, this time to Kremenchug. While the air element completed the move on the same day[277], the move by the ground elements took all of three days, and the main column did not arrive at the new base of operations until the 17th[278]. In the days that followed, II/JG 3's mission while operating from Kremenchug was: defensive patrols and free chase sorties over the area around Poltava and Mirogorod, low-level attacks on Russian transport trains, and finally free chases in the Kharkov—Krasnograd area[279]. Even though the *Gruppe* was reinforced by III/JG 3, which was moved forward to Pirogi[280], on 17 September, given the small number of Messerschmitts[281] available, the completion of this myriad of tasks had to remain wishful thinking. This was yet another demonstration of how hopelessly inadequate the *Luftwaffe*'s forces in the east were[282]. At the same time, the transfer to Kremenchug meant that II/JG 3 would no longer be tied to the fighting in the Kiev area, where the Russian armies were desperately trying to break out of the encirclement, but instead would be responsible for defending the eastern flank of the German armies in the area southeast of Kiev.

The first missions from Kremenchug were flown on 15 September; these, and those of the following day, were uneventful. On 17 September the *Gruppe* was called upon to fly two missions, both low-level attacks on the Russian airfield of Kamyschna north of Mirogord[283]. Both resulted in engagements with Russian aircraft. Lt. Fuss of 4/JG 3 subsequently claimed one victory (15), while the *Gruppe* escaped without loss. Beginning on 18 September the focus of operations for both *Gruppen* of JG 3 moved into the Poltava area. On that day, during a fighter sweep and visual reconnaissance of the Russian-occupied airfields in the area[284], 6 *Staffel* recorded two victories. On the other side of the coin, the *Gruppe* was forced to place Gefr. Paul Brune of 5/JG 53 on the casualty list. At 7:55 AM he took off as part of a *Schwarm* assigned to free chase in the Poltava area. He was last heard from at about 9 AM when he called from the target area. Nothing more was heard of him after that, and the reason for his failure to return has not been determined. On the next day, 19 September, the mission was again strafing attacks against Soviet airfields which had been scouted during the previous day's sorties. A large number of enemy aircraft was destroyed on the ground; in addition, four victories were claimed, two by the *Stabsschwarm* and two by 4/JG 3. The cost to the *Gruppe* was four Messerschmitts damaged, however in only one case was this due to enemy action. Fhr. Eckart König, who had joined the *Gruppe* only the previous day, being assigned to 4 *Staffel*, ended his first combat mission, in which he had flown in the *Rotte* of Lt. Fuß, with a belly landing after running out of fuel. He was not injured[285].

In the days that followed, the *Gruppe* was employed mainly on free chase missions over the area of the front around Poltava and Kharkov, while continuing to escort bombers and provide fighter defense of the Dniepr crossings. The weather during this period was mainly clear and dry, although already rather cool[286], and this allowed both sides to maintain a high level of activity in the air. The result was frequent air battles, some of them quite large. The *Gruppe* scored a total of 26 victories by the end of the month; 28 September was the most successful day with eight enemy aircraft shot down, five of them by Hptm. Gollob. Casualties were limited to just two pilots reported missing temporarily: on 24 September Albert Helm of 4 *Staffel* was shot down by a Ju 88 in the Kharkov area and wounded in the forearm. He had just been promoted to *Leutnant* and this was his first combat mission as an officer[287]. In spite of his wound, Helm succeeded in reaching the German lines after an adventurous flight lasting four days, during which he disguised himself as a farmer for a time. He was immediately sent to Germany for medical treatment. Two days later, on 26 September, Uffz. Steinicke of 6/JG 3 failed to return from a mission in the Poltava area for reasons unknown. Several days later he, too, succeeded in regaining friendly territory unhurt.

On 30 September 1941 the *Gruppe*'s tour of duty in the south of the Eastern Front came to a temporary end when transfer orders arrived. These directed the unit to Sechtschinskaja, approximately 40 kilometers southeast of Roslavl. In contrast to the forward airfields the *Gruppe* had used recently, it was a very well-laid-out air base which before the commencement of hostilities in the east had housed a Soviet air force unit[288]. On its arrival there after a brief en route stop in Konotop[289], on 1 October 1941 the air element of II/JG 3 had just twelve serviceable Messerschmitts, while the number of pilots on strength with the *Gruppe* was 31[290]. For the ground elements the transfer meant the longest overland journey by truck to date, however in spite of rain-softened roads[291] the transfer was completed without serious incident[292] thanks to Hptm. Teichmann efficient command. The *Gruppe*'s transfer resulted in its removal from the command of *V Fliegerkorps* and assignment to *II Fliegerkorps*[293] and was part of the preparations far "Operation *Taifun*", the planned assault on Moscow. All available German forces were concentrated under the command of Army Group Center[294] in preparation for the attack, after the battle of Kiev had ended in a devastating defeat for the Russian armies[295].

The period until the start of the attack was largely uneventful, operational activity being limited by the low level of aircraft serviceability and the return of bad weather[296]. The men of II/JG 3 tried to make themselves as comfortable as possible at their new base of operations, with the worsening cold proving to be the greatest problem, especially since there was no heating fuel on the airfield. Georg Alex wrote: *"Everything that wasn't bolted or nailed down was burned."* The attack by the German armies along Army Group Center's front began on 2 October 1941. In the days that followed, II/JG 3's mission was to support the northeastwards advance towards Vyazma and Yukhnov by the units of Panzer Group 4 and the 4th Army. During the first three days of the attack the

Gruppe's fighters were engaged mainly in escorting Stukas and free chases over the battle zone east of the Desna[297]. The first two days produced no tangible results, however on 4 October II/JG 3 reported one enemy aircraft shot down by Hptm. Gollob (49). Gollob brought down two more on the following day, 5 October, including his fiftieth, while Obfw. Heckmann of 5 *Staffel* recorded his 25th victory on this day. For the next three days the focus of the *Gruppe*'s efforts lay in the Yukhnov area, where a further eight victories were scored. The *Gruppe*'s efforts were hindered quite considerably by bad weather. The first snow fell during the night of 7 October; while this quickly melted, afterwards the weather was mainly cloudy with frequent rain or snow showers.

Meanwhile, in spite of the catastrophic road conditions associated with the muddy period and the fierce resistance offered by Russian troops, by 9 October German army units again succeeded in encircling major Russian groupings in two separate pockets at Vyazma and Bryansk[298]. For II/JG 3 this meant that individual *Schwärme* had to be temporarily sent to Syevsk, a forward airfield approximately 100 kilometers south of Bryansk, on 7 and 8 October. III *Gruppe* was also based[299] there until the 8th. From Syevsk these units were supposed to intervene in the fighting over the fronts of Panzer Group 2 and the 2nd Army in the Bryansk area. From 9 to 11 October the air element operated from the Kirov and Orel airfields, which had fallen into German hands on 3 October, with the same mission. The *Gruppe* found both airfields to be completely rain-soaked and muddy. Bad weather so hindered operations from Orel that few missions could be flown; snow, rain and fog with ceilings as low as 50 meters at times made takeoffs impossible from the morass-like airfield. As a result, only four victories were recorded during this period, while two Messerschmitts were damaged in takeoff accidents resulting from the poor condition of the airfield. Luckily, neither pilot was injured. On 11 October Russian aircraft attacked Orel airfield. Obgefr. Martin Schemeit, an armorer in 6/JG 3 who was part of II/JG 3's small technical detachment, was seriously wounded by bomb splinters.

The missions on 11 October 1941 were to be II/JG 3's last over Army Group Center's combat zone. On the ground, the fighting around the pockets at Vyazma and Bryansk was to continue until 17 October, ending in another heavy defeat for the Soviet armies[300]. The units of Army Group Center then moved into their jump-off positions for the second phase of "Operation *Taifun*," the attack on Moscow itself. Prior to this, however, II/JG 3 received orders to transfer its air element and a small technical detachment, which was to be transported in several Ju 52s, to Chaplinka, a front-line airfield near Perekop, from where it was to take part in the campaign to conquer the Crimea. The transfer began on 13 October, but because of several en route stops necessitated by bad weather[301], it was not completed until 16 October. At Chaplinka the *Gruppe* was placed under the command of *Stab*/JG 77[302]. Also stationed at the field were III/JG 52 and III/JG 77. The new base was described as

extremely "*disconsolate*." Georg Alex wrote: "*Endless steppe, not a tree, not a bush. Quarters consist of an empty horse stall, half an hour's drive from the airfield by automobile over the worst roads.*"

II/JG 3's transfer to Chaplinka was part of preparations for the German attack on the Crimea, which was scheduled to begin on 18 October 1941[303]. Even though the *Luftwaffe* had massed several bomber, Stuka and fighter *Gruppen* for the attack, numerically it was still far inferior to the Russians in this area[304]. The first missions over the battle zone in front of Perekop and over the Crimea were flown on 17 October. The operational tasks for II/JG 3 and the other two *Jagdgruppen* consisted mainly of free chases and fighter escort for bomber and Stuka units. Russian air units were extremely active over the front, and there were several fierce air battles, especially in the late morning[305]. During the course of these, the *Gruppe* was able to claim eleven victories without loss to itself, including four by Lt. Fuß of 4 *Staffel* (19-22) and three by *Gruppenkommandeur* Hptm. Gordon Gollob, his 59th to 61st victories.

On 18 October 1941 the 11th Army began its attack on the Isthmus of Perekop and Ischum[306]. In spite of heavy casualties, German troops broke into the first line of the heavily-fortified and fiercely-defended positions everywhere and forced the Russian defenders to fall back to the south. The Soviet air force established a clear measure of numerical superiority in the area, and German troops were exposed to almost constant air attacks by enemy bombers and close-support aircraft[307]. The weather was warm and mainly sunny on this day, and II/JG 3 flew a series of free chase missions over the front-line area, most of which resulted in contact with large formations of enemy aircraft. The *Gruppe* subsequently reported a total of 16 victories, with the lion's share going to the *Gruppenstab*, which claimed twelve. The most successful pilot was Hptm. Gollob, who claimed nine enemy aircraft shot down (62-70). Losses totaled two Messerschmitts of 4 and 5 *Staffel*, which were damaged in combat and subsequently made forced landings. Neither pilot was injured. On the second day of the attack, 19 October 1941, the picture was much the same as the previous day—while German troops penetrated further into the Russian defense positions in heavy fighting, especially in the southern sector, taking the heavily-fortified strongpoint of Ischum, Russian air units continued to enjoy a clear numerical superiority in the air, taking advantage of this to launch waves of attacks against German army troops and their rear communications[308]. Early in the morning the *Jagdgruppen* assembled at Chaplinka were taken completely by surprise by a formation of Pe-2s, which appeared without warning and dropped their bombs across the airfield. *Waffenoberfeldwebel* Kühne was wounded by splinters and died in hospital several days later[309]. There is no information on aircraft losses[310]. The day's missions brought II/JG 3 ten more victories at the cost of just one casualty: Obfw. Keller of 6 *Staffel* was wounded in air combat but managed to bring his Messerschmitt back safely to Chaplinka. On 20 October the weather over the approach to the Crimea was again mainly warm and dry, allowing II/JG 3 to fly a whole series of missions over the front in the north of the peninsula. The Russians continued to enjoy clear aerial superiority[311], and on this day the *Gruppe* scored just one victory while sustaining no losses.

The weather over the Crimea now took a clear turn for the worse, which seriously limited activity in the air by both sides. Given the recent air superiority enjoyed by the Soviets, this came as a relief to the German ground forces, which continued to battle their way through the in-depth Russians positions in fierce, costly fighting. All of the missions flown in this inclement weather on 21 October failed to produce any tangible result. There was little improvement on 22 October, nevertheless there was an increase in activity in the air, resulting in a number of fierce battles with Russian fighters and close-support aircraft. From II/JG 3's standpoint the result was ten victories without loss, with Hptm. Gollob recording his 80th victory on this day. The next day, 23 October, was largely similar, with the *Gruppe* claiming another 15 victories, again without loss. On 24 October the mainly cloudy weather allowed only a few missions by II/JG 3, which subsequently reported two victories against one loss. While returning from a bomber escort and free chase mission, the aircraft of Fw. Hans-Georg Riedrich of 4 *Staffel* developed engine trouble. The engine caught fire and he was obliged to make a forced landing southeast of Ischum in Russian-held territory. The other members of his *Staffel* observed him being taken prisoner by Russian infantry[312].

The missions of the previous days had taken a toll on the *Gruppe*'s operational readiness; because of the continued completely inadequate deliveries of aircraft and spare parts, by the end of the month the *Staffeln* were each down to just two or three serviceable Messerschmitts, which were only flown by the most experienced pilots[313]. The missions of the following days all failed to produce any tangible result, while there was another casualty on 29 October. Fw. Fritz Mias of 5 *Staffel*, one of the "old hands" of the *Gruppe*, was seriously injured when his aircraft was written off in a failed takeoff at Chaplinka.

Meanwhile, on 27 October, German troops had forced the decisive breakthrough on the right wing of the front and were able to begin the drive into the interior of the Crimea[314]. The stubborn resistance previously offered by the Russian troops now quickly collapsed. German forces pursued the retreating enemy to the southwest and southeast, with German battle groups initially advancing toward the capital of Simferopol as a prelude to drives on Sevastopol and east toward Yalta and Feodosia and the Isthmus of Parpach[315]. Following the German breakthrough, it appeared that the ultimate decision had been reached in the Crimea, and the *Luftwaffe* began withdrawing the bulk of its forces, leaving the task of supporting the army to the remaining weak forces[316].

II/JG 3 flew its last combat missions over the northern Crimea on 31 October 1941, Two more victories were scored during free chase missions over the Alma-Tamak area on the west coast of the peninsula[317], these going to the *Kapitän* of 6 *Staffel*, Oblt. Sannemann (20), and Fw. Pöske of 5/JG 3 (14). While III/JG 77 was subsequently moved forward to Tokultschak for further operations over the Crimea, following the advancing army troops, II/JG 3 received orders withdrawing it from action and directing it to return to the Reich for rest and refit. The unit's few remaining machines were handed over to III/JG 77. Preparations were immediately begun for the transport of the *Gruppe* back to Germany, where it had been assigned to the Wiesbaden-Erbenheim airbase. Transport of the *Gruppe*'s ground elements, which had remained behind at Sechtschinskaja when the *Gruppe* was moved to Chaplinka, began at the same time. During this period the ground elements had more or less stood idle at Sechtschinskaja[318].

Four months of operations in Russian had come to an end and this is an appropriate place to drawn a brief interim balance. II/JG 3's operations in the preceding weeks may be seen as typical of the German effort in the east, which though seemingly a thorough success was in fact doomed from the start on account of insufficient forces. Blinded by the stunning initial combat successes, the *Luftwaffe* command had obviously failed to realize that it had not achieved a decisive defeat of the Soviet air force nor had it permanently weakened it. Instead the Soviets were regaining their strength and in many places, most recently in the Crimea, they had already achieved a clear numerical superiority. At the same time the German units were weakened by spreading themselves thin to cover the vast front, while combat and technical attrition, which could not be made good on account of the failure of supply, quickly eroded their operational strength and reduced them to weak remnants. When II/JG 3 returned to Germany at the beginning of November 1941, nineteen weeks had already passed instead of the eight called for in the plans for "Operation Barbarossa," which was supposed to "strike down" the Soviet Union in a blitz campaign. Soon afterwards, following the failure of the German attack on Moscow and the start of the Russian counteroffensive, an end to the war in Russia and with it the war as a whole had, as Hitler expressly informed his inner circle on 5 December 1941[319], moved into the unreachable distance.

In numerical terms the results of II/JG 3's operations in the summer campaign in the east in 1941 were impressive, for in a period equal to the time it had spent on the Channel, the *Gruppe* scored 504 victories, more than six times as many as in the previous campaign. On the other side of the ledger the *Gruppe* lost ten pilots killed or missing and nine more wounded or injured. Even though these figures seem rather trifling compared to the number of victories scored, they meant that the *Gruppe* had lost more than half of its authorized strength in pilots, at least temporarily, even though these losses were made good by the assignment of young, well-trained replacements, at least at the beginning. The loss of Hptm. Keller and Oblt. Faust, two important unit leaders, was unquestionably a heavy blow for II/JG 3, however the loss of experienced pilots like Lt. Buddenhagen, Obfw. Gremm, Obfw. Brenner and Fw. Mias[320] was equally serious. In purely material terms, during this period the *Gruppe* reported 27 aircraft written off with 60% or greater damage, while another 21 sustained 30-60% damage and 27 damage assessed at less than 30%.

In closing, a significant event for JG 3 which occurred during the time of II/JG 3's withdrawal from the front must be mentioned: on 17 November 1941, *Generaloberst* Ernst Udet, the Chief of Air Supply and Procurement and most successful surviving German fighter pilot of the First World War with 62 confirmed victories, had taken his own life. Udet, who achieved his high position in the *Luftwaffe* at Göring's urging, was anything but suited for this job in terms of personality and training; he was thus doomed from the beginning to fail in his official task of providing the *Luftwaffe* with the equipment it needed. Furthermore, he was incapable of coping

with the intrigues against him by leading members of the *Luftwaffe*, especially since there were few men in the *Luftwaffe* command who still backed him. Hermann Göring felt it necessary to conceal the true reasons for Ernst Udet's suicide, and he therefore invented the fiction that he had been killed while testing a new weapon. Udet was elevated to the status of hero and given a pompous state funeral, which precluded any uncomfortable questions about the circumstances of his death. Part of this repugnant propaganda campaign was the awarding of the title *"Jagdgeschwader Udet"* to JG 3 on 1 December 1941; this was done on Göring's order, even though Udet had had no close association with the unit and had played no significant part in its history while he was alive. It is, however, typical of this regime built on fraud and falsehood that its leadership did not have the courage to tell the believing people the truth about the suicide of this popular airman.

Notes:

[186] For information concerning the history leading up to "Operation Barbarossa" and the reasons behind it see Jacobsen and Dollinger, Vol. 3, p. 7; Jacobsen, Rohwer and Hofmann, p. 139 and following pages; introduction to the OKW War Diary 1940-41, p. 88 and following pages.

[187] Accordingly the *Stab* also moved to Hostynne, while I/JG 3 transferred to Zamocs-Dub and III/JG 3 to Moderovka.

[188] Also under the command of V *Fliegerkorps* were KG 51, KG 54, KG 55 and 4(F)/121.

[189] Also spelled Zamosch.

[190] Botho Teichmann wrote: *"I reported the Geschwader's arrival to corps (Oberst Plocher). Until 14 June everything was done to bring the unit to full operational readiness. The Kommodore Obstlt. Lützow took me with him on his flights to Luftgau-Kommando Breslau and RLM Berlin for various conferences, for it was very important to me to bring the entire Geschwader to the peak of performance where vehicles were concerned."*

[191] The logbook of Heinrich Sannemann states that the air element arrived at Hostynne at 5;16 PM. According to the war diary of I/JG 3, on this day its air element also transferred from Breslau to its designated base of operations at Zamosc-Dub, while III/JG 3 arrived at Moderovka at the same time. See Prien/Stemmer, III/JG 3, p. 105.

[192] This also included the application of yellow identification markings as per a general order dated 17/6/1941—OKW War Diary 1940-41 Part II, p. 416, which states: *"A special marking—bright yellow finish on the outer third of the wing undersides and a fuselage band level with the Balkenkreuz—has been ordered for all aircraft committed to the Barbarossa operation."*

[193] War diary I/JG 3.

[194] The German attack was in fact an invasion of a neighboring nation which was legally her ally based on existing and binding international treaties. There is uncertainty as to whether the Soviet command had similar plans for an assault against the German Reich at this time (there is evidence to support this theory), however the extensive surviving German records provide incontrovertible evidence that "Operation Barbarossa" was not a preemptive strike but instead was planned solely as a campaign of conquest and destruction. They also show that the German command was not aware of any invasion brewing in the east that would have required a counterstrike. Even the German propaganda did not expressly depict the invasion as a preemptive strike in the beginning; it was not until later, when the first great battles of encirclement revealed the almost limitless quantities of men and materiel available to the Soviets, that the theme of an invasion of the Reich successfully averted at the last minute was taken up. A detailed assessment of the German invasion would exceed the scope of this work, however, and therefore the reader is referred to the examination of this theme contained in Prien, JG 77 Vol. 2, p. 260 and following pages, as well as the general assessment by Wette and Überschar.

[195] For example, the logbook of Heinrich Sannemann shows that his first mission took place from 3:52 to 4:52 AM; the record book of Uffz. Werner Lucas of 4/JG 3 indicates that he took off at 3:55 AM for low-level attacks against airfields near Rawa Ruska.

[196] Like Heinrich Sannemann, for example, who flew a total of five missions, logging more than 5 1/2 hours in the air.

[197] It is worthy to note how different was the experience of the "neighboring" III/JG 3, which was based farther to the southwest at Moderovka; it had virtually no

contact with the enemy on this or the following day. See Prien/Stemmer, III/JG 3, p. 107.

[198] According to German accounts, a total of 322 Soviet machines were destroyed in aerial combat or shot down by flak on this day, while a further 1,489 were destroyed on the ground by bombing or strafing. On the other hand, German losses were 57 aircraft written off as a result of enemy action and another 54 damaged. See Prien, JG 77 Part 2, p. 639.

[199] In stark contrast to this was the behavior of many Soviet units, in which the surprise German assault produced powerless rage but also a boundless hatred for the German attacker, which in many cases resulted in atrocities against the first prisoners. Examples of this are provided by the fates suffered by the *Staffelkapitän* of 8/JG 3, Oblt. Willi Stange, who was killed by Russian soldiers after a successful forced landing on the first day of the war, and the *Kommodore* of JG 27, Maj. Schellmann, who was killed by Soviet militiamen at the outset of hostilities in the east. As repugnant and distasteful as such incidents were, there is no cause of justification for reproaches or even accusations on the part of the German side in view of the fate which the German leadership in cooperation with the *Wehrmacht* command had in mind for captured Russian soldiers and their political cadres in particular. In the end, approximately 3.3 million Russian prisoners of war died in German hands, while about 1 million German soldiers failed to return from Russian captivity (see Streit, p. 10 and following pages). The war was a catastrophe for both peoples, but this war was started by the German Reich alone, in whose name unspeakable atrocities were committed in those areas conquered by the *Wehrmacht*. These are easily forgotten or overlooked when the topic turns to the fury of the Red Army in the eastern provinces in 1944-45. The same applies to the subject of the treatment of prisoners: Russian captivity was unquestionably a hard, deprivation-filled and often cruel experience for most German soldiers, however it is often overlooked that the inhuman measures adopted by the German command at the start of the war resulted in the deaths by starvation and neglect of thousands of captured Red Army soldiers. Not until the beginning of 1942 was a slight change in the treatment of prisoners, however this was less due to humanitarian concerns than to the growing requirement for cheap labor for the German armaments industry (see Überschär/Wette, p. 159 and following pages).

[200] Writings of Georg Alex.

[201] Mission times according to the logbook of Heinrich Sannemann 5:40 to 6:25 AM.

[202] Also called Wladimir-Wolynsk.

[203] About 35 kilometers north-northeast of Lvov; the precise location of the crash was a swampy area approximately 2 kilometers east of the small town of Ostrowcz-Polny, 12 kilometers southeast of Lutsk. See appendix for the WASt. casualty report for Uffz. Kurz.

[204] Mission times according to the logbook of Heinrich Sannemann 6:30 to 7:30 AM; mission: protect *Panzerstrasse Mitte*.

[205] In many accounts the word *"stur"* (to persist obstinately) is used in this context, however it brings with it a subliminal derogation of or contempt for the Russian airmen which they surely do not deserve in view of their spirit of sacrifice; respect and bewilderment would be more appropriate, for in spite of the technical inferiority of their machines and the terrific losses they suffered at the hands of the German fighters, these men continued to carry out their orders in defense of their homeland even at the cost of their own lives. Less than three years later the same was to apply to the young, inexperienced German fighter pilots who fell in large numbers before

the guns of Allied fighters over the Reich and the invasion front on account of inadequate training as well as numerical and technical inferiority.

[206] More than once in these days there must have been cases in which not a single Russian machine returned from a mission. This had to have placed an unbelievable strain on the other crews who saw this and subsequently had to take off on missions themselves. Unfortunately very little is known about these days from the Russian viewpoint, apart from highly colored propaganda reports.

[207] Often, during low-level attacks, German aircrews saw Red Army soldiers throw themselves down on their backs, with no cover whatsoever, and open fire on the aircraft with their rifles.

[208] Indirectly this was the result of JG 3's combat orders for 26/6/1941, of which the III/JG 3 war diary states: *"Beginning at daybreak JG 3 will keep one Schwarm over Panzerstrasse Mitte at all times."* (author's emphasis)

[209] This shortcoming can not have seriously surprised anyone who kept the following simple fact in mind: in the late summer of 1940 the *Luftwaffe* had concentrated almost all of its fighter and bomber forces in a very small area on the Channel and was forced to realize that these were insufficient to achieve its objectives even over a limited area. Now, in the summer of 1941, approximately two-thirds of these same forces were supposed to suffice to achieve typically far-reaching objectives over a front approximately 1 600 kilometers long against an opponent who, though admittedly technically inferior, enjoyed a massive numerical advantage. This was a hopeless undertaking from the beginning, born of a fateful ignorance of and overbearing arrogance toward the enemy in the east, who had been branded "subhuman." In view of such crass military stupidity, the high opinion of German military commanders still expressed today by some quarters is quite amazing; even if they lacked the necessary ethical-moral fiber to categorically oppose or resist Hitler's declared "racial war of destruction" on grounds of decency or conscience, their expert military knowledge should at least have told them that they were helping bring ruin upon the Fatherland.

[210] See following text for explanation.

[211] Compare in detail the account in OKW War Diary 1940-41 Part II, p. 497 and following pages.

[212] Writings of Karl-Heinz Langer.

[213] See Prien/Stemmer, III/JG 3, p. 110; in most cases the transfer flight was obviously combined with a fighter cover mission over the *Panzerstrasse*—for example, see logbook of Heinrich Sannemann.

[214] From the WASt. casualty report, which states that the mission was *"Free chase over the area of Panzerstrasse Nord"*. The only reference to the aircraft type was a subsequent handwritten entry: *"Bf 109 F, 100%"*. Conversely, the writings of Botho Teichmann state that Hptm. Keller was flying a Fieseler *Storch* when he was rammed and subsequently crashed to his death; however, JG 3 did not file a loss report for a *Storch* under this date.

[215] It is impossible to determine from the surviving loss records whether this was a machine of JG 3 or another unit; obviously the other pilot involved in this incident was not hurt.

[216] According to the WASt. casualty report this loss took place on 27 June; the information presented here is taken from the writings of Georg Alex, which because of their concrete statements appear more believable than a loss summary compiled several days later.

[217] This loss may have taken place on 25 June, since the date in the WASt. casualty report cannot be confirmed.

[218] Logbook of Heinrich Sannemann.

[219] Writings of Georg Alex; these also state that Leo Suschko was bandaged *"with the silk from his parachute"* and fed.

[220] Reporting date 28 June 1941, German Order of Battle, Statistics as of Quarter Years, according to which II/JG 3 had 26 Bf 109 F-2s on strength on this day, of which 20 were serviceable, and 38 pilots, of which 30 were fit for duty.

[221] At this time German air armaments had yet to adapt to the requirements of a multi-front war; instead it continued to produce aircraft according to the procurement plans for the year 1940, which had long since been overtaken by events. These plans were slowly abandoned during the second half of 1941, as a result of which 2,764 Bf 109s were built instead of the 2,091 called for in the C-Amt plan of 1/10/1940; this increase in production of new aircraft was largely achieved at the expense of spare parts production.

[222] Concerning III/JG 3, see the writings of Karl-Heinz Langer, cited in Prien/Stemmer, III/JG 3, p. 111, Footnote 132.

[223] Also see OKW War Diary 1940/41 Part II, p. 503 and following pages.

[224] For example, the logbook of Heinrich Sannemann shows that he flew to Lutsk-South on the morning of 1, 3 and 5 July 1941.

[225] One of these victories was credited to the *Staffel*, because, as Georg Alex wrote, *"it proved impossible to reach agreement on who had fired last"*.

[226] Writings of Georg Alex; according to him, the army forces required almost a week, with tank and Stuka support, to completely wipe out the Russian troops hiding in the forest. This is backed up by the writings of Botho Teichmann.

[227] The following entries, which cover the period from 6 to 9 July 1941, are from the logbook of Heinrich Sannemann and illustrate the *Gruppe*'s activities at this time:

6/7/1941	Dubno-South	5:10 – 6:12 AM	free chase in Polonnoye area; combat with SB-2s, one victory
		10:55 AM – 12:10 PM	free chase in Polonnoye area, uneventful
		7:20 – 8:35 PM	free chase in Polonnoye area, uneventful
7/7/1941	Dubno-South	4:40 – 6:05 AM	fighter cover over Panzer-strasse Mitte, uneventful
		8:40 – 10:07 AM	fighter cover over Panzer-strasse Mitte, uneventful
8/7/1941	Dubno-South	12:20 – 1:05 PM	free chase over Miropol area, uneventful, landed Polonnoye
	Polonnoye	1:10 – 1:55 PM	free chase over Miropol area, uneventful, landed Dubno-South
	Dubno-South	5:20 – 5:55 PM	free chase and fighter cover over Panzerstrasse Mitte; combat with DB-3s, one victory
9/7/1941	Dubno-South	11:30 – 11:55 AM	transfer flight to Polonnoye
	Polonnoye	12:40 – 2:00 PM	escort for bombers to Zhitomir and Korosten

[228] See OKW War Diary 1940/41 Part II, p. 512 and following pages.

[229] The airfield was also known by the name Tyranovka, a small town near Miropol.

[230] It is likely that II/JG 3, like the other two *Gruppen* of the *Geschwader*, was for the time being forced to rely on Ju 52s for deliveries of fuel, since the normal surface supply system could not keep pace with the speed of the German advance—also see Prien/Stemmer, III/JG 2, p. 112.

[231] Writings of Georg Alex and Botho Teichmann; logbook of Heinrich Sannemann.

[232] Writings of Georg Alex.

[233] The missions recorded in the logbook of his *Staffelkapitän* Heinrich Sannemann over the area south of Kiev on this day are listed as "no enemy contact," but they also contain no reference to the loss of Beyer.

[234] Writings of Georg Alex; there is no reference to this loss in the WASt. casualty reports or the Quartermaster-General's reports.

[235] Writings of Georg Alex; WASt. casualty report.

[236] See the victory lists, but also the casualty lists, for this period, in which the names of the "*Experten*" appear almost exclusively. Conversely, the logbook of Heinrich Sannemann reveals that even though he was *Staffelkapitän* and one of the *Gruppe*'s most successful pilots with 11 victories, during the period from 12 to 18 July he flew just four combat missions; compare this to the two to five missions per day that had previously been the rule.

[237] The following is from the writings of Hptm. Hans von Hahn, the *Gruppenkommandeur* of I/JG 3 based at Polonnoye: *"We had many days off there because of bad weather; from time to time there were downpours which made flying activity impossible."*

[238] Worthy of note are the following data concerning the operations of 5/JG 3, the *Jabostaffel*, which are taken from an official assessment by Oblt. Kijewski dated 24 July 1941 and based on results achieved by 18 July: according to the report, by this date 5/JG 3 had achieved a total of 96 victories, 63 of them in the east. During its *Jabo* missions there it had destroyed 35 aircraft on the ground and damaged another 33, and destroyed 11 tanks and 3 locomotives plus an unspecified number of guns and vehicles. Also see the copy of the assessment.

[239] and who at the end of August, following the loss of Hptm. Andres, was to assume temporary command of the *Gruppe*; see Prien/Stemmer, III/JG 3, p. 118.

[240] Account by Harald Moldenhauer dated 11 August 1986.

[241] See Prien/Stemmer, III/JG 3, p. 119.

[242] Logbook of Heinrich Sannemann.

[243] Mission times according to the logbook of Heinrich Sannemann 4:20 to 4:55 PM, takeoff and landing at Belaya-Tserkov.

[244] Writings of Georg Alex.

[245] According to Heinrich Sannemann's logbook, on 28 July he carried out a "maintenance test flight" from 10 to 10:15 AM, and at 11:15 AM took off on the return flight to Berdichev.

[246] Concerning the Belaya-Tserkov airfield, the following comment in the writings of Georg Alex is noteworthy: *"Since this is a former Russian airfield, it is subject to repeated attacks, one air raid alarm follows the other."* The air attacks in question obviously had little effect, for there is no mention of personnel or material losses in the *Gruppe* reports.

[247] For the other two *Gruppen* of JG 3, operational conditions at Belaya-Tserkov in these days were anything but favorable. In addition to the steady rain, an outbreak of diarrhea, which affected more than half of the men and which was unaffected by available medicines, made it extremely difficult to maintain operations. It is not known if II/JG 3 was also affected by this wave of sickness, although it seems likely. Fortunately the problem subsided after a few days.

[248] Also see the OKW War Diary 1940/41 Part II, p. 447 and following pages.

[249] Also see the OKW War Diary 1940/41 Part II, p. 558 and following pages; Carell, p. 108.

[250] See logbook of Heinrich Sannemann, who took off on a free chase mission at 6:12 AM and landed at Signayevka at 7:35; there was no contact with enemy aircraft.

[251] A wartime source has stated that Schönefeldt scored 17 victories, however no reliable dates are available.

[252] WASt. casualty report; according to this Lt. Glück radioed that he was "under fire" before his belly landing.

[253] See the OKW War Diary 1940/41 Part II, p. 469 and following pages.

[254] Writings of Georg Alex.

[255] See the OKW War Diary 1940/41 Part II, p. 473 and following pages.

[256] As per standard practice, this transfer flight was also broadened to include a free chase; also see the logbook of Heinrich Sannemann, who flew free chase over the Dnepropetrovsk area from 5:30 to 6:50 AM, encountering no enemy aircraft. He subsequently landed at Stschastliwaja.

[257] Logbook of Heinrich Sannemann; writings of Georg Alex.

[258] See the repeated references to Soviet aerial activity in the Dnepropetrovsk area in the OKW War Diary 1940/41 Part II, p. 473 and following pages.

[259] Also see Prien/Stemmer, III/JG 3, p. 118.

[260] Altogether six armies with a total strength of over a million men.

[261] See the OKW War Diary 1940/41 Part II, p. 602 and following pages; Cartier, Vol. I, p. 334 and following pages.

[262] See the daily weather reports in the OKW War Diary 1940/41 Part II, p. 602 and following pages.

[263] See the logbook of Heinrich Sannemann, in which just three missions are recorded for the period from 2 to 10 September; the writings of Georg Alex also record missions on just four days during this period.

[264] Under the date 3 September, the following note appears under the heading "Air Situation," which was adopted by the *Wehrmacht* Command Staff for its situation reports on 2 September,: *"In the 17th Army's area, the enemy is concentrating his air activity against the LII Army Corps' crossing sites."*

[265] Writings of Georg Alex.

[266] OKW War Diary 1940/41 Part II, p. 613.

[267] Uffz. Lucas scored his victory during an early evening mission, in which he flew with 6 *Staffel*.

[268] The writings of Georg Alex reveal that on this day Leo Suschko of 4/JG 3 was sent on special leave to recover from the lingering effects of the concussions suffered in his two crash-landings. He did not return to the *Gruppe*, instead he was assigned to the reformed I/JG 3 in early 1942.

[269] OKW War Diary 1940/41 Part II, p. 617.

[270] *Gruppe* records contain no references to personnel or material losses associated with this attack.

[271] OKW War Diary 1940/41 Part II, p. 629.

[272] According to the OKW War Diary 1940/41 Part II, p. 632, nine Russian air attacks on the Derijewka bridgehead were reported on this day, while there is no report for the Kremenchug area.

[273] Writings of Hptm. Hans von Hahn.

[274] A total of twelve pilots of I/JG 3 remained in the east until the beginning of November 1941, being assigned to the *Stab*, II or III *Gruppe*; this group is known to have included *Oberfeldwebel* Lüth, Heesen and Ehlers, Fw. Hutter and *Unteroffiziere* Schiffer, Niedereicholz and Küpper. Lüth and Hutter are known to have gone to III/JG 3. During this period the pilots of I/JG 3 claimed a total of 20 victories, all of which were credited to I/JG 3.

[275] War diary I/JG 3.

[276] See the OKW War Diary 1940/41 Part II, p. 631 and following pages.

[277] Logbook of Heinrich Sannemann; writings of Georg Alex.

[278] Writings of Georg Alex: *"During the transfer to Kremenchug the main column got a foretaste of the Russian winter. After heavy downpours, the vehicles were left stuck in deep mud, no amount of pushing helped. Icy cold, spent the night in the vehicles in wet clothes. The next day, while avoiding an oncoming army unit, the vehicles slid into the ditch, up to the axles in mud. Tracked vehicles had to be summoned to extract them before we could continue."*

[279] See logbook of Heinrich Sannemann.

[280] See Prien/Stemmer, III/JG 3, p. 120.

[281] See the *Gruppe* strength report dated 27 September 1941, according to which 21 Bf 109s were available, of which just 12 were serviceable.

[282] The fact that such mission orders were nevertheless issued, which inevitably resulted in the already limited resources of the flying units being exhausted, casts a revealing light on the competence and mental state of the *Luftwaffe* command.

[283] Mission times according to the logbook of Heinrich Sannemann 11:30 AM to 12:40 PM and 3:05 to 4:10 PM.

[284] Logbook of Heinrich Sannemann.

[285] Writings of Georg Alex.

[286] See the repeated weather reports in the OKW War Diary 1940/41 Part II, for example under 24 September, where it says: *"Weather: cold, clear, roads good."* P. 657.

[287] Writings of Georg Alex.

[288] Georg Alex wrote: *"The new airfield is again a former Russian airfield, well known to the Russians. Consequently numerous night raids. 4 Staffel has been spared losses, other Staffeln have not."* Existing records do not list any losses for II/JG 3 as a result of Russian air attacks.

[289] In the writings of Botho Teichmann it says that the *Gruppe* arrived at Konotop on 22 September and remained there until 1 October. Regarding a victory by Obfw. Kortlepel on 22 September 1941, Georg Alex states that this was scored from Konotop. This seems rather unlikely, since Georg Alex himself states that II/JG 3 was at Kremenchug from 17 to 30 September 1941, which coincides with information in the victory and loss reports, and because entries in Heinrich Sannemann's logbook say that he was in action from Kremenchug until 30 September.

[290] Reporting Date 27 September 1941, German Order of Battle, Statistics as of Quarter Years. Actual aircraft strength was 21 Bf 109 F-4s, of which nine were unserviceable. Pilot strength was 43, of which 12 were away from the *Gruppe* because of wounds, secondment or other reasons.

[291] Unlike in the south, in Army Group Center's area at the end of September there had been, in some cases steady, rain. Under the date 1 October 1941 the OKW War Diary 1940/41 Part II says: *"Weather: cloudy. Roads…bottomless."* P. 671.

[292] Writings of Georg Alex. According to the writings of Botho Teichmann, the *Gruppe* had been at Konotop since 22 September and on 1 October moved on to Sechtschinskaja. See above.

[293] Writings of Karl-Heinz Langer.

[294] While the army units were still relatively well of in terms of personnel and material at this point in time, the *Luftwaffe*'s resources had been seriously weakened. Altogether, on 2 October 1941 II and VIII *Fliegerkorps*, which were responsible for air support for the coming offensive on a front of approximately 750 kilometers, had just 549 aircraft, of which 158 were bombers and 25 reconnaissance machines. The rest were fighters and transports.

[295] The number of prisoners taken in this one battle of encirclement was 665,000. In addition, vast quantities of war materiel and supplies were captured. See Cartier, p. 338 and following pages.

[296] See weather reports in the OKW War Diary 1940/41 Part II, p. 671 and following pages.

[297] See the writings of Georg Alex and the logbook of Heinrich Sannemann.

[298] See the OKW War Diary 1940/41 Part II, p. 681 and following pages.

[299] See Prien/Stemmer, III/JG 3, p. 121.

[300] Only three weeks after the Battle of Kiev, the Soviets lost the bulk of another nine armies. 663,000 Red Army soldiers were taken prisoner. See the OKW War Diary 1940/41 Part II, p. 736 and following pages.

[301] According to Heinrich Sannemann's logbook the transfer was carried out as follows: 13/10 Sechtschinskaja – Gomel; 14/10 Gomel – Belaya-Tserkov; 15/10 Belaya-Tserkov – Wosnessensk – Nikolayev; 16/10 Nikolayev – Mariupol – Chaplinka.

[302] For a detailed account of the fighting over the Crimea see Prien, JG 77 Part 2, p. 829 and following pages.

[303] Also see the OKW War Diary 1940/41 Part II, p. 700.

[304] See Prien, JG 77 Part 2, p. 829 and following pages.

[305] OKW War Diary 1940/41 Part II, p. 829 and following pages.

[306] Depending on how it was transcribed, the spelling of this town varies widely; for example, in the WASt. casualty report for Obfw. Riedrich of II/JG 3 it is spelled *"Juschim,"* while the OKW War Diary spells it *"Juschun".*

[307] OKW War Diary 1940/41 Part II, p. 708, which speaks of *"pronounced enemy air superiority"* and of *"waves of air attacks".*

[308] OKW War Diary 1940/41 Part II, p. 710.

[309] Because of the absence of the bulk of the ground elements, including the entire administrative apparatus of the *Gruppenstab*, the *Gruppe*'s reports during these days were very sketchy; most personnel loss reports are missing, including those for Obfw. Kühne and Obfw. Keller. Regarding this air attack, the following comment appears in the writings of Georg Alex: *"Wonderful escape by Obgefr. Oberröder during this attack. An aviation mechanic, he was running up the engine of his machine and could not hear the bombing attack above the noise of the motor. Suddenly the engine stopped. Bomb splinters had riddled the machine like a sieve. Oberröder climbed out safe and sound."*

[310] See above; III/JG 77 did not report any losses under this date, and there are also no loss reports for III/JG 52.

[311] Concerning this, the following extract from the OKW War Diary 1940/41 Part II, p. 712: *"Attack made difficult, especially by numerically superior enemy air force; our own fighter cover and the effect of our flak inadequate in the coverless narrows."*

[312] In the writings of Georg Alex, it states that Fw. Riedrich had only recently been transferred to 4 *Staffel* from *Stab*/JG 3, where he served as a courier pilot.

[313] On this topic, the following comment from the writings of Georg Alex: *"Only Hptm. Gollob and the Gruppenstab still have enough machines. The Stab, especially Gollob, is shooting down dozens of enemy aircraft here."*

[314] See the OKW War Diary 1940/41 Part II, p. 726 and following pages.

[315] See Prien, JG 77 Part 2, p. 840 and following pages.

[316] In fact, however, the German forces were unable to complete the conquest of the Crimea in the weeks that followed. Instead, strong Russian forces held on in the fortress of Sevastopol, and at the beginning of 1942 additional Russian forces landed at Feodosiya, temporarily threatening the German position in the east and southwest of the Crimea. See Prien, JG 77 Part 2, p. 844 and following pages.

[317] Mission times according to the logbook of Lt. Heinrich Sannemann 2:00 to 3:20 PM.

[318] Writings of Georg Alex and Botho Teichmann; according to these, the transfer (of the ground elements) took place from Sechtschinskaja to Wiesbaden via Smolensk, Minsk and Vilna.

[319] Feeling the effects of the setback before Moscow, the *Wehrmacht* Operations Staff diarist made the following entry in the war diary under 5/12/1941: *"When the catastrophe of the winter of 41/42 began, it was made clear to the Führer and to the Generaloberst* (Halder, the author)*, in particular, that from this culmination point of the new year of 1942 on, victory could no longer be achieved."*—OKW War Diary 1940-41 Part II, p. 1501 (emphasis by the author). For a further examination of this theme see Prien, JG 77 Part 2, p. 871 and following pages. Neither Adolf Hitler nor the military commanders of the armed forces drew the only possible conclusion from this accurate realization, namely to end the war as quickly as possible while trying to preserve the Reich. The senior *Wehrmacht* commanders had by this time sunk to the level of yes-men, as characterized by Cartier (Vol. I, p. 338).

[320] Even after recovering from the serious injury he suffered on 29 October 1941, Fw. Fritz Mias was no longer fit for front-line duty, and consequently he did not return to the *Gruppe*.

[321] See the reproduction of the order in the text.

1870. Tagesbefehl an die Luftwaffe

Kameraden der Luftwaffe!

Der Generalluftzeugmeister, Generaloberst Ernst Udet, ist am 17. November 1941 den Folgen einer bei der Erprobung einer neuen Waffe erlittenen schweren Verletzung erlegen. Ein kämpferisches Leben, das nur ein Ziel kannte — die fliegerische Erstarkung Deutschlands — ist damit beendet.

Mit Ernst Udet hat das Deutsche Volk den nächst Richthofen siegreichsten Jagdflieger des Weltkrieges, die fliegerische Jugend ein leuchtendes Vorbild, die deutsche Luftwaffe den kühnen und zielbewußten Wegbereiter verloren. In stolzer Trauer senken sich an der Bahre des Ritterkreuzträgers und Inhabers des Ordens »pour le mérite« die Fahnen seiner über alles geliebten Waffe. Ihr hat Generaloberst Udet in den dunklen Jahren nach Versailles, vor allem aber seit seinem Wiedereintritt in unsere Reihen den Weg zum Wiederaufbau und zum Sieg gebahnt. Als Generalluftzeugmeister sorgte er für die Rüstung, die die deutsche Luftwaffe der Heimat zum starken Schild, für den Feind zu einem furchtbaren Schwert werden ließ. In tapferstem persönlichem Einsatz hat Generaloberst Udet, beladen mit ungeheurer Verantwortung, oft selbst die letzte und entscheidendste Flugerprobung neuer Baumuster vorgenommen. Erst dann, wenn ein solches Flugzeug den höchsten Anforderungen des Kampfes entsprach, überließ er es den Kameraden an der Front. Sein Wort »Soldat sein, heißt an den Feind denken und an den Sieg und sich selbst darüber vergessen« ist uns das Vermächtnis eines Heldenlebens und bleibende Verpflichtung.

Sein Ruhm ist unsterblich. Darum erfülle ich heute den Willen des Führers und Obersten Befehlshabers der Wehrmacht und verleihe in seinem Auftrage dem Jagdgeschwader 3 den Namen:

Jagdgeschwader Udet.

So wird das Andenken an einen unserer Größten in der Luftwaffe für alle Zeiten verewigt sein.

Göring.

Reichsmarschall des Großdeutschen Reiches
und Oberbefehlshaber der Luftwaffe

Above: This "Yellow 1," a Bf 109 F-2, was the machine of Oblt. Heinrich Sannemann, the Kapitän *of 6 Staffel. Both photographs were probably taken shortly before the start of the war in the east—either at Breslau or Hostynne. The aircraft wears a gray-green finish with lightly mottled fuselage sides and a yellow fuselage band aft of the* Balkenkreuz, *as decreed by the order of 17 June 1941. Note the angular wheel wells and the absence of reinforcements for the tail section bearers in the photo on the right. Below: Servicing a Bf 109 F-2 of 6* Staffel, *photographed on a front-line airfield at the beginning of the war in the east. In these photographs a technician is seen cleaning the propeller pitch control mechanism. (Sannemann)*

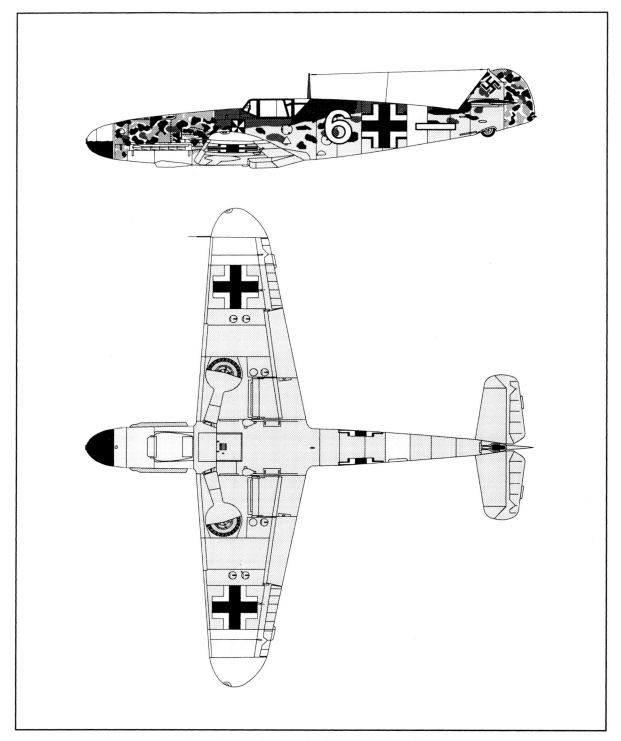

**Side and Top View of a Bf 109 F-2 of II/JG 3 with identification markings
for the RussianCampaign—June 1941**

A general order issued on 17 June 1941 decreed that, "*all aircraft engaged in the Barbarossa operation are to receive a special identification marking—a bright yellow finish on the outer third of the wing undersides and a fuselage band next to the Balkenkreuz.*" The Messerschmitts of II/JG 3 subsequently received a narrow yellow fuselage band, which was applied immediately behind the fuselage cross and which was the same width as a fuselage section—between Frames 6 and 7. Only rarely were machines seen whose fuselage band was displaced one fuselage section further aft. In the beginning the yellow finish on the wing undersurfaces extended past the wingtips almost to the *Balkenkreuz.*

Oblt. Heinrich Sannemann after returning from a mission on 12 July 1941, during the course of which his "Yellow 1" was hit on the armored windscreen by a bullet from a Soviet bomber he was attacking. Sannemann was extremely lucky to survive unhurt. The photographs clearly show the cockpit area and in particular details of the external armor-glass panel. The aircraft wears the emblem of II/JG 3 in front of the cockpit. (Sannemann)

Two photographs of "Black 4", a Bf 109 F-2 of 5/JG 3, following a belly landing; exactly when and where the photos were taken is not known. The aircraft wears the standard gray-green camouflage scheme together with a yellow engine cowling underside and yellow rudder. Note the yellow fuselage band, which here, contrary to standard practise, is one fuselage section aft of the Balkenkreuz. This machine obviously carries the Gruppe emblem of II/JG 3 on both sides of the fuselage. Note the retracted tailwheel. (Dr. Koos via Petrick)

Above: Pilots of 4 Staffel, *photographed on the Belaya-Tserkov airfield on 1 August 1941; the man in the middle is probably* Staffelkapitän *Oblt. Gerhard Michalek. In the background is "White 3", a Bf 109 F-4, being refueled from a tank truck. The dress worn by the pilot to the right of Michalek—short pants, fur-lined boots, a neckerchief and "nothing else"—is noteworthy. Below and following page: Under the guidance of a maintenance foreman, technicians of 4/JG 3 recover "White 7", a Bf 109 F-4 with the WerkNr. 8389, which on 1 August 1941 was obliged to make a forced landing on Belaya-Tserkov airfield after its*

horizontal tail surfaces were damaged by flak. In the last photo the men are setting up a tripod, which will be used to put the machine back on its feet again. Noteworthy details of this Bf 109 F-4 are the narrow yellow fuselage band in the style used by II/JG 3 as well as the external stiffeners over the tail section bearer, which appear quite massive in these views. (E.C.P.A. DAA 1132 L 13, 16-19)

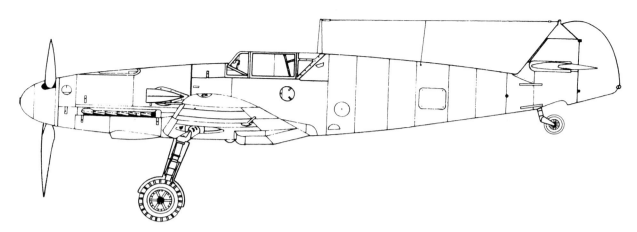

Line Drawing 4: Messerschmitt Bf 109 F-4

II/JG 3 converted from the Bf 109 F-2 to the Bf 109 F-4 at the end of July 1941. The F-4 differed from its predecessor mainly in the installation of the more powerful DB 601 E instead of the earlier N engine; the new power plant also used 87 octane B-4 fuel. Externally there was little difference between the early F-4 and the F-2; in particular these machines retained the narrow supercharger air intake and the external stiffeners on the aft fuselage.

Length: 8.94 m

Wingspan: 9.92 m

Height: 2.60 m

Engine: DB 601 N, 1,350 H.P.

Takeoff weight: 2 732 kg

Armament: 1 MG 151/20, 2 MG 17

Empty weight: 2 020 kg

Changing the engine of a Messerschmitt of II Gruppe *in the open air, photographed on a rain-soaked forward airfield in the east in late summer 1941. (Sannemann)*

Above: Several 6 Staffel *technicians at work on the recovery of "Yellow 2", a Bf 109 F-4 which made a belly landing, photographed in the east in late summer 1941. Note the spotted gray-green finish, the narrow fuselage band and the* Gruppe *emblem in front of the cockpit. The tailwheel was apparently torn off in the belly landing. Below: Lt. Max-Bruno Fischer's "Black 9" is towed back to its airfield after a landing away from base. Note Fischer's emblem beneath the cockpit and the narrow yellow fuselage band aft of the* Balkenkreuz; *Russia, summer 1941. (Punka via Petrick/Lächler)*

Two photographs of the tail section of Hptm. Gollob's Bf 109 F-4 after 33 victories, taken on Stschastliwaja airfield on 21 August 1941. Note the victory bars with pointed upper ends, a style rarely seen in the summer of 1941. Also noteworthy is the pale background of the swastika, which suggests that the machine's original finish had been retouched. (Lächler)

Above: A Bf 109 F-4 of 6/II/JG 3, photographed on a forward airfield in the east in the late summer of 1941. Note the narrow yellow fuselage band which partly covers the horizontal bar Gruppe *marking, the angular wheel wells, the old-style narrow air intake, and the external stiffeners on the rear fuselage; the latter suggest that this was an early production F-4. Five black victory bars are visible on the aircraft's rudder. Below: The already partly cannibalized wreck of a Messerschmitt of 4 Staffel, likewise photographed in the east in the late summer of 1941. Note the circular wheel well, the unusual broad, dark strip under the wing, the pilot seat lying next to the fuselage, and the propeller spinner in front of the aircraft. The* Gruppe *emblem of II/JG 3 is just visible between the legs of the technician standing on the wing. (Lächler)*

Above: Warming up the engines of the Messerschmitts of 6/JG 3, photographed in October 1941 after the first snowfall, probably on Sechtschinskaja airfield. Note the unusual finish on the engine cowlings of both machines depicted here, with very well defined blotches and a clear separation line between the pale sides and unusually dark upper surfaces. On both machines the cowling ring immediately aft of the spinner is very dark. The aircraft in the foreground apparently has a yellow spinner, while that of the machine in the background ("Yellow 2") appears to be black. Below: A Bf 109 F-4 of II Gruppe with a makeshift concealment of tarpaulins and saplings, photographed on a forward airfield in the east at the beginning of October 1941; this photo was obviously also taken after the first snow had fallen. (Sannemann)

Two photographs of aircraft of 5/JG 3, photographed in autumn 1941, probably during the period of operations over the approaches to the Crimea. Note the variety of finishes worn by the aircraft depicted here, which must be Bf 109 F-4s. All display the Gruppe emblem and narrow yellow fuselage band aft of the Balkenkreuz. *(Petrick)*

Four photographs of Oberst *Werner Mölders,* General der Jagdflieger *and in autumn 1941 local commander of fighter and close-support units operating over the Crimea, after returning from one of his "unofficial" missions. Because of the fact that Mölders was forbidden to fly, these missions were never recorded and any victories scored were not included in his victory list. In the first three photographs* Oberst *Mölders is seen in the cockpit of a Bf 109 F-4 of the* Gruppenstab *of II/JG 3 bearing the markings of the* Gruppenkommandeur, *while in the last photo he is seen standing in front of the aircraft. These photographs may have been taken after II/JG 3's withdrawal and the handover of its remaining aircraft to III/JG 77 at the beginning of November 1941. (Behling/Lächler)*

6

Operations in the Mediterranean Theater
January to April 1942

While a considerable part of the personnel of II/JG 3 was able to go on a well-earned leave immediately after returning from the east, those elements left behind at Wiesbaden-Erbenheim at once began working on the *Gruppe*'s reequipment. A complete complement of new machines, forty Bf 109 F-4 trop[322] fighters altogether, was received by the end of the year, replacing the F-4s previously flown. The reason for this was that II/JG 3 was to see action in the Mediterranean theater. As a first step, every member of the *Gruppe*, from the *Kommandeur* to the last enlisted man, was given a medical examination to determine whether or not he was suited for the tropics. Those who failed the examination subsequently left the unit and most were transferred to the new I/JG 3 then being formed[323]. In the weeks that followed, a number of young pilots arrived to fill the gaps created by operations in the east and the tropical selection process. The *Gruppe* soon reached its authorized strength of forty pilots, and by the end of the year even exceeded this by two[324]. The same process applied to the ground personnel, which was brought up to strength in a short time.

At the end of the year there were also a number of changes in the *Gruppe*'s command structure. *Gruppenkommandeur* Hptm. Gordon Gollob, who had been awarded the Oak Leaves on 26 October 1941 in recognition of his success in the east, left the *Gruppe* to take over the *Luftwaffe*'s test station (*E-Stelle*) at Rechlin. His place as *Kommandeur* of II/JG 3 was taken by Hptm. Karl-Heinz Krahl. Krahl had most recently commanded I/JG 2 based on the Channel, had 18 victories to his credit, all achieved in the west, and had worn the Knight's Cross since November 1940. The Headquarters Company also received a new commanding officer: on 20 December 1941 Oblt. Franke replaced Hptm. Botho Teichmann, who was transferred to the *Geschwaderstab*[325]. Oblt. Georg Michalek of 4 *Staffel* was promoted to *Hauptmann* and awarded the Knight's

Cross in recognition of his 38 victories. Coincident with this he was transferred to the new I/JG 3, where he became that *Gruppe*'s first *Kommandeur*. He was replaced as *Kapitän* of 4 *Staffel* by Oblt. Walther Dahl, who had previously flown in the *Gruppenstab*[326]. There were no changes in the leadership of 5 and 6 *Staffel* , with Oblt. Harald Moldenhauer and Oblt. Heinrich remaining as *Kapitäne*. After all these changes, the command list for II/JG 3 looked as follows:

List of Officers of II/JG 3 on 1 January 1942	
Gruppenkommandeur	Hptm. Karl-Heinz Krahl
Gruppenadjutant	Lt. Karlheinz Ponec
Gruppe Technical Officer	Lt. Gustav Frielinghaus
Commander Headquarters Company	Oblt. Franke
Staffelkapitän 4/JG 3	Oblt. Walther Dahl
Staffelkapitän 5/JG 3	Oblt. Harald Moldenhauer
Staffelkapitän 6/JG 3	Oblt. Heinrich Sannemann

After approximately two months of rest and refit and the receipt of a full complement of new aircraft[327], at the beginning of January 1942 the *Gruppe* received new orders: together with the *Stab* and III/JG 3, II/JG 3 was to transfer to Sicily for further operations. At that time strong forces of *II Fliegerkorps* were being concentrated on the island for the purpose of neutralizing the island fortress of Malta, from where British air and sea forces were raiding German-Italian supply traffic to North Africa. Recently almost half of all supply goods had been sunk while en route to North Africa[328]. Not surprisingly, news of the impending transfer to the sunny south was received with great relief by the *Gruppe*, for memories of its previous tour of duty in the east were still fresh and the prospect of a winter deployment there was an unhappy one.

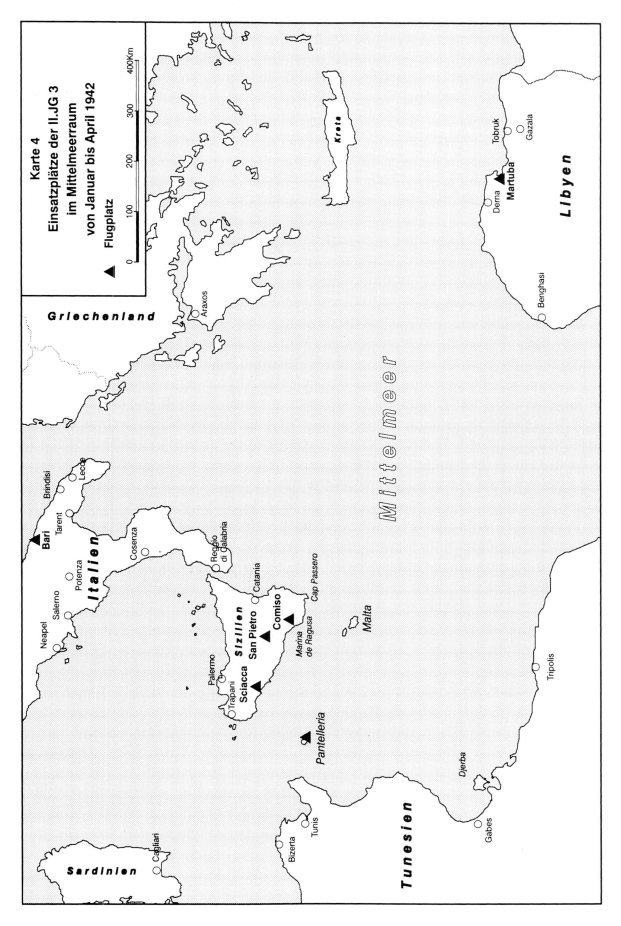

Karte 4
Einsatzplätze der II.JG 3
im Mittelmeerraum
von Januar bis April 1942

▲ Flugplatz

The first days of January were spent in preparations for the transfer, which was to be made by rail; this also applied to the air element, for orders were issued to disassemble the Messerschmitts and carefully load them aboard flatcars. The machines would then to be reassembled and test flown once the *Gruppe* reached its destination, Bari[329]. The first transport train carrying the disassembled Messerschmitts of 4/JG 3 and the technicians necessary to reassemble them departed Wiesbaden on 7 January 1942. Three days later it arrived in Bari, where the technicians immediately began reassembling the Messerschmitts so they could be test flown and ferried to Sicily. This work was completed by 17 January[330]. One after another, the transport trains carrying the other two *Staffeln* and the *Gruppenstab* arrived in Bari, where work immediately began to reassemble and test-fly their machines[331]. Meanwhile, the *Gruppe*'s remaining ground elements had already arrived in Sicily, where they were initially quartered at Comiso, a well-equipped Italian air base in the southeast of Sicily. Already stationed there were the *Geschwaderstab* and II *Gruppe* of JG 53, the *"Pik-As"* (Ace of Spades) *Geschwader*[332]. On 18 January 1942 the first serviceable machines of 4/JG 3 were ferried to Comiso[333], with the rest of the air element following by 24 January.

II/JG 3 began operations in the Mediterranean Theater on 19 January 1942, when a *Schwarm* from 4 *Staffel* escorted several Ju 88s to Malta[334]. At about the same time, however, the orders concerning the transfer of the *Geschwaderstab* and III/JG 3, elements of which had already arrived at Bari[335], were changed. As a result, neither unit would see action from Sicily; instead, after handing over those machines already at Bari to II/JG 3[336] and JG 53, they were to be transferred back to Germany. Since II/JG 3 was to be the only *Gruppe* of the *Geschwader* in Sicily, it was placed under the operational command of *Stab*/JG 53 under Maj. Günther von Maltzahn for subsequent operations. JG 53 *"Pik-As"* was in turn one of the units of II *Fliegerkorps*, which was in command of the planned offensive against Malta. On 19 January II/JG 3 moved from Comiso air base, which was already fully occupied by the units gathered there, to Sciacca, a forward airfield on the southwest coast of Sicily[337].

By mid-January 1942 the *Luftwaffe* had still not completed massing its forces for the planned air offensive on Malta. The "Directive for the Battle against Malta" had already been issued on 31 December 1941; it called for continuous air attacks on Malta by day and night, with the objective neutralizing the air and sea fortress[338]. In fact, however, because of cloudy, rainy weather, not much happened in Sicily for the first four weeks of the new year, apart from occasional attacks on Malta by small formations of bombers or fighter sweeps over the island by the German fighters already present in Sicily[339].

By the end of January II/JG 3 flew a number of missions, mainly free chases, over Malta from its base at Sciacca, however none produced any tangible result. The *Gruppe* did, however, experience a

number of accidents caused by airfield conditions or mechanical problems. On 27 January *Unteroffiziere* Edmund Mächler and Heinrich Rabe of 6/JG 3 were injured in crashes at Sciacca caused by undercarriage failure[341]. As well, four Messerschmitts were written off with damage in excess of 60%.

February 1942 also began quietly. *Generalfeldmarschall* Kesselring, the commander-in-chief of *Luftflotte* 2, had hoped to be able to step up the campaign against Malta, however these hopes were dashed. The unbearably low serviceable levels of the bomber and fighter units which had arrived in Sicily[342] and several fundamental shortcomings in the training and operational preparations of the bomber units made it necessary to postpone the start of the attack until the beginning of March[343]. Nevertheless, with a clear improvement in the weather at the beginning of the month, the *Luftwaffe* units gathered in Sicily experienced a noticeable increase in operational activity. For II/JG 3, this and the following three days brought several more free chase missions over Malta[344], however all were uneventful. Afterwards the weather became cloudy again, and the *Gruppe* apparently saw no action between the 8th and 11th of February[345].

After a moderate improvement in the weather on 12 February allowed a cautious resumption of the attacks, on the 13th the *Gruppe* flew several free chase missions over Malta. Most of these were uneventful, however in one instance a *Schwarm* from 4/JG 3 under Lt. Helm had an inconclusive skirmish with two Hurricanes in which the Messerschmitts did not open fire[346]. Nevertheless, on this day the *Gruppe* lost one pilot killed: while returning from a free chase mission over Malta, the Messerschmitt of the *Gruppe* adjutant, Lt. Karlheinz Ponec, developed engine trouble. Ponec radioed that his engine had stopped and that he was trying to reach the port of Agrigent, where he hoped to ditch[347]; however, the pilots of the remaining aircraft saw the machine crash into the sea about 5 kilometers south of Agrigent and its pilot was not seen again. A search was begun immediately, however this proved fruitless, and Lt. Ponec was reported missing two days later. That same day, 15 February 1942, II/JG 3 scored its first victory in the Mediterranean theater when, shortly after noon, Uffz. Vogel of 6 *Staffel* shot down a Beaufighter during a free chase over the sea (1)[348].

For the next few days the weather was mainly cloudy and rainy, and the few missions flown produced no tangible results. On 21 February 6 *Staffel* was transferred to Pantelleria, from where it was to fly escort for air and sea transports between Sicily and North Africa until the 27th. As far as can be determined, these missions were all uneventful, and the *Staffel* subsequently rejoined the rest of the *Gruppe*[349]. Meanwhile, on 22 February it was time for II/JG 3 to move again. Given the limited range of the Bf 109, Sciacca airfield was too far west for missions over Malta; consequently, the *Gruppe* was ordered to San Pietro, a forward airfield[350] 15 kilometers northwest of Comiso. The air element flew there the same day, while the ground elements traveled by road and arrived the following afternoon[351]. During the missions on the 22nd the *Gruppe* scored its second victory over Malta. While on a free chase mission, Fw. Münster of 4/JG 3 shot down one of a group of ten Hurricanes (13)[352]. In the days that followed, the skies clouded over again, and until the end of the month almost no more missions could be flown on account of inclement weather[353].

At the beginning of March 1942, too, attacks were limited to small and very small formations of aircraft. In spite of the limited forces committed, the attacks carried out to date had been sufficient to almost wipe out the British fighter defense on Malta, for in these days the German units rarely met British fighters during their missions over the island. Most of the free chase and bomber escort missions flown by the German fighters at this time were uneventful[354]. Nevertheless, in the first weeks of March II/JG 3 suffered three casualties, all the result of accidents. On 2 March, while ferrying a Kl 35 from Sciacca to San Pietro, Obgefr. Heinz Golke of 4 *Staffel* crashed from out of a steep turn and was seriously injured when the machine struck the ground. The cause of the accident is not known. Two days later, on 4 March, 5 *Staffel* was forced to place Uffz. Benedikt Wegmann on the missing list. On the way home after escorting Ju 88s to Malta, Wegmann's aircraft developed engine trouble and he radioed that he was bailing out. It was later learned that he had been captured by the British suffering from minor injuries[355]. Finally, on 7 March, Obfhr. Eckart König of 4/JG 3 struck an obstacle while taking off from Catania on a convoy escort mission. He was seriously injured in the ensuing crash.

Meanwhile, the British made efforts to bolster their badly battered fighter squadrons on Malta. On 7 March the first fifteen Spitfire Vs took from the deck of the aircraft carrier *Eagle*, which was at the limit of their range west of Malta, and flew to Ta Kali[356]. II/JG 3 first encountered one of these machines late on the afternoon of 10 March, when Hptm. Krahl shot down a Spitfire while escorting several Ju 88s (19)[357,358]. The very next day there was an encounter with a mixed force of about 25 Hurricanes and Spitfires, however the ensuing dogfight produced no tangible result[359]. All of the missions flown by II/JG 3 during the next nine days were uneventful, apart from one victory scored by Uffz. Beikiefer of 6 *Staffel* early on the evening of 18 March (2), when he shot down a Blenheim during a free chase mission southwest of Malta. Periods of bad weather during this period, especially on 16 and 17 March, saw to it that the *Gruppe*'s level of activity remained low, while its base of operations at San Pietro became completely rain-soaked. On 20 March 1942 a serious accident resulted in the death of a pilot. During a *Staffel* mission by 6/JG 3, in which it was supposed to drop cement practice bombs into the sea off Gela, the propeller of Uffz. Michael Beikiefer's "Yellow 3" struck the bomb of another machine, whereupon the Messerschmitt broke up and fell into the sea. A search was begun immediately, however no trace of the pilot could be found[361].

II Fliegerkorps's large-scale air assault on Malta began on 20 March with an attack by about 60 bombers on the British fighter base at Ta Kali. On the following day, a total of 210 bombers were sent against Ta Kali in several waves, while on 22 March the airfield at Hal Far was also attacked. The attacks met little opposition in the air, and the escorting *Jagdgruppen*, which included II/JG 3, had no contact with the enemy. Nevertheless, on 21 March 4 *Staffel* did lose one Messerschmitt: while over Malta at 6 000 meters, Uffz. Wolfgang Buttstädt's machine developed engine trouble. The DB 601 stopped almost immediately, but the pilot succeeded in gliding to a point just off the coast of Sicily[362] where he was forced to take to his parachute. He was picked up by the air-sea rescue service soon afterwards.

Whereas the first days' attacks were aimed at Malta's airfields, on 25 March the focus switched to the port installations of La Valetta. A short time earlier two freighters, the only ones from convoy MW 10 to reach Malta, had sailed into port and were now being unloaded. During the course of the afternoon thirteen machines of II/JG 3 were in the air over Malta, flying escort for a total of 25 Ju 87s of III/StG 3[363]. There was an engagement with a number of Spitfires and Hurricanes. A *Kette* of aircraft from 4 *Staffel* was attacked by eight Spitfires and the machine of Lt. Rudolf Wicklaus was badly damaged. Lt. Wicklaus subsequently bailed out approximately 30 kilometers north of Malta[364]. A Do 24 of 6 *Seenotstaffel* picked up the pilot some time later and flew him to Syracuse, where he was taken to hospital; Wicklaus was suffering from exposure but was otherwise unhurt. Another Messerschmitt of II/JG 3 was shot down during the course of this battle, however no details are known. II/JG 3 again escorted Stukas over Malta on 26 March 1942, and there was another engagement with defending British fighters[365]. Two victories were subsequently claimed by Lt. Fischer of the *Gruppenstab* (1) and Lt. Kirschner of 5/JG 53 (2), while the *Gruppe* lost one of its machines. After being hit by anti-aircraft fire, Uffz. Alfred Fischer of 6 *Staffel* was forced to abandon his aircraft north of Malta. Three hours later he was picked up uninjured by the air-sea rescue service[366]. II/JG 3's remaining missions prior to the end of the month were all uneventful.

While the Royal Air Force continued its efforts to deliver reinforcements to Malta for its battered fighter squadrons[367,368], the German side strove to increase the weight of its air attacks. The beginning of April saw further concentrated attacks by all available bomber units, with the four *Jagdgruppen* based on Sicily providing fighter escort. In practice this meant that the pilots of II/JG 3 had to fly two to three escort missions in support of Ju 87 and Ju 88 *Gruppen* each day; on the other hand, contact with or combat with defending fighters was comparatively rare[369]. Early on the evening of 1 April 1942, II/JG 3 once again escorted a large formation of Stukas to Malta. There was an engagement with a number of Spitfires, after which Uffz. Hans Pilz of 5 *Staffel* failed to return to San

Pietro. At 6:15 PM he had radioed that he was on the tail of an enemy machine over La Valetta at a height of 50 to 100 meters, then all trace of him disappeared. He was initially reported missing, but it was later learned that he had been captured injured by the British[370].

The missions on the following two days produced no result, and indeed until the end of the month the *Gruppe* reported no further losses or victories in air combat[371]. II/JG 3's operational activities were restricted considerably after it was forced to release a number of machines to JG 27 in Africa and replacements were not immediately forthcoming[372]. Single *Schwärme* continued to be deployed to Pantelleria for convoy escort duties and were thus lost for use over Malta[373]. Most significant, however, was the transfer of 6/JG 3 to North Africa to support JG 27; it remained there until 25 April, operating from Martuba[374]. On 10 April 1942 there was a change in the command of 4/JG 3: Oblt. Walther Dahl handed the *Staffel* over to Oblt. Albrecht Walz after being transferred to the *Geschwaderstab*.

The continuous fighting of the past weeks had inflicted such heavy losses on the British fighter defense, both in the air and on the ground, that it was scarcely able to offer serious resistance to the German attacks. As a result, from 11 April the German fighters were increasingly used in low-level attacks against British fighter bases on Malta. Given the strength of the British anti-aircraft defense, these attacks were understandably unpopular among the fighter pilots. Three days later, on 14 April 1942, II/JG 3 suffered a very painful loss during a low-level attack mission against Lucqa airfield. *Gruppenkommandeur* Hptm. Karl-Heinz Krahl was shot down by flak and crashed to his death not far from the airfield. Hptm. Krahl had commanded the *Gruppe* for just four months and had scored one victory over Malta. Soon afterwards Hptm. Kurt Brändle, who had formerly led 5/JG 53, was named to succeed. Pending his arrival at the end of April, the *Staffelkapitän* of 5/JG 3, Oblt. Harald Moldenhauer, was placed in temporary command of the *Gruppe*[375].

For the next three days strong winds and low cloud brought operations to a virtual standstill. Occasionally a *Rotte* was dispatched to conduct a visual reconnaissance of Malta, however all of these missions were uneventful. Not until 18 April 1942 did a significant improvement in the weather permit a resumption of the air attacks on the island, and once again the British fighter bases were the principal targets of the Ju 87 and Ju 88 units. No British fighters opposed the attacks on this and the following days, in which the elements of II/JG 3 left on Sicily took part. Not until 20 April were there contacts with enemy aircraft, however these produced no tangible results for II/JG 3. At this point it appeared that the air attacks of the past weeks had put Malta out of action as an air and sea base for some time, for in the last days of April there were few worthwhile targets left on the ground, while, in spite of repeated deliveries of new aircraft, the fighter defense was almost wiped out. Seri-

ous supply shortages, especially of fuel, ammunition and spares, contributed to this decline, as did losses in action[377].

The series of heavy air attacks against Malta was continued until 28 April 1942; the air offensive ended on this day, after the German command became convinced that the remaining British sea and air forces on the island could be held in check by continuous "harassment" and "destructive attacks"[378]. In spite of insistent pleas to seize the badly battered island fortress, which would have solved the problem of Malta for good, a considerable part of the forces assembled on Sicily under *II Fliegerkorps*[379] was withdrawn, as these were vital to the operations in the east which were then in preparation[380]. With the pressure relieved, in the following weeks the British air and sea forces on Malta recovered very quickly, and because of steady deliveries of fresh forces soon achieved numerical superiority over the German units left on Sicily and furthermore gained the initiative in the campaign against Axis supply traffic to Africa. Within just a few weeks the apparently decisive success of the German bombing offensive against Malta turned into a long-running and debilitating crisis spot, which was to be a contributing factor in the ultimate defeat of the Axis powers in North Africa and as a consequence in Sicily and Italy[381].

The end of II/JG 3's operations over Malta came on 25 April 1942, when elements of the *Gruppe* escorted bombers over the island for the last time. The withdrawal of the elements of the *Gruppe* stationed on Sicily began on the following day, 26 April. II/JG 3 was among the units earmarked for participation in the German summer offensive in the east, where operations were scheduled to begin at the end of May. On this day the *Stabsschwarm* plus 4 and 5 *Staffel* flew from San Pietro via Wiener Neustadt to Pilsen[382]. Several days later[383] 6 *Staffel* followed from North Africa; it, too, had flown its last mission on 25 April. On the same day, after turning its remaining Messerschmitts over to JG 27 at Martuba, the *Staffel* was transported in trucks to Derna and on the following day it was flown from there to Sicily[384]. Overall, 6/JG 3's deployment to the "Black Continent" had been extremely inauspicious, for since 7 April the *Staffel* had flown a total of just 20 missions, which involved just 64 Messerschmitt sorties[385]. While failing to score itself, the *Gruppe* had lost one pilot missing. On 13 April Uffz. Josef Fritz was shot down in air combat over the El-Adem area. It was later learned that he after a successful forced landing he had become a prisoner of the British. In addition, at least five machines sustained varying degrees of damage in crash-landings.

Thus ended II/JG 3's approximately three-month period of operations against Malta. Since it had been subordinated to the "Pik-As" *Geschwader* in those weeks, the *Gruppe*'s actions were somewhat overshadowed by the success of that unit[386]. The *Gruppe* was able to report six confirmed victories, while losses amounted to three pilots killed, six wounded or injured and three captured. In addition, 16 Messerschmitts were written off with damage in excess of 60 percent[387].

6/JG 3 Operations in North Africa
7 to 26 April 1942

07/04/42		8:20 – 9:45 AM	Transfer flight San Pietro to Tripoli
		11:10 AM – 1:05 PM	Tripoli to Arco Philaenorum
		2:30 – 4:55 PM	Arco Philaenorum to Martuba
09/04/42	3 Bf 109	4:28 – 5:28 PM	Familiarization flight, rendezvous with Stukas, n.c.*
10/04/42	3 Bf 109	11:06 AM – 12:02 PM	Familiarization flight, n.c.
	3 Bf 109	4:26 – 5:36 PM	Familiarization flight, n.c.
11/04/42	3 Bf 109	10:09 – 11:20 AM	High cover, n.c.; one Bf 109 aborted mission, landed 10:25 AM.
	3 Bf 109	4:10 – 5:04 PM	Escort for Stukas, n.c.
12/04/42	2 Bf 109	7:37 – 8:54 AM	Escort for Bf 110 reconnaissance machine to Gazala/Hacheim, n.c.
	1 Bf 109	10:43 – 11:36 AM	Fighter-bomber mission Mteifel area, together with a *Rotte* from III/JG 27
	2 Bf 109	2:06 – 2:52 PM	Fighter-bomber mission north of Hacheim, together with a *Rotte* from III/JG 27[376]
13/04/42	2 Bf 109	7:38 – 9:21 AM	Escort for Bf 110s, n.c.
	2 Bf 109	11:44 AM – 12:49 PM	Escort for a fighter-bomber *Schwarm* of III/JG 27 to El Adem, n.c.
	2 Bf 109	2:19 – 3:20 PM	Escort for fighter-bombers and free chase in El Adem area, combat with six P-40s and 1 Hurricane, Uffz. Fritz missing
	2 Bf 109	4:20 – 4:30 PM	Escort for Bf 110 reconnaissance machine, mission aborted because Bf 110 unserviceable
15/04/42	4 Bf 109	10:20 – 11:35 AM	Free chase El Adem area, n.c.
	4 Bf 109	2:05 – 3:05 PM	Free chase El Adem area, n.c.
20/04/42	6 Bf 109	11:06 AM – 12:15 PM	Free chase, n.c.
	4 Bf 109	2:39 – 3:35 PM	Defensive patrol over Derna, n.c.
23/04/42	6 Bf 109	11:03 AM – 12:15 PM	Free chase over Derna, n.c.
24/04/42	2 Bf 109	7:07 – 8:23 AM	Escort for Bf 110 reconnaissance machine, n.c
25/04/42	8 Bf 109	8:55 – 10:20 AM	Close escort for Stukas, combat with P-40s north of Gazala

(*no contact with enemy)

Notes:

[322] Reporting Date 27/12/1941, German Order of Battle, Statistics as of Quarter Years.

[323] Writings of Georg Alex. According to him, in these weeks the following personnel were among those that left the ground personnel of 4/JG 3: Fw. Glampke, Fw. Grünhagen (accountant and pay NCO), Uffz. Quandt, Uffz. Pavel (clothing stores) and Uffz. Preuss (weapons and equipment). They were replaced by Gefr. Engel (accountant and pay NCO), Uffz. Thürkow, Fw. Ortel (clothing stores) and Obgefr. Schudack (weapons and equipment).

[324] Reporting Date 27/12/1941, German Order of Battle, Statistics as of Quarter Years. According to this, on 27 December 1941 the *Gruppe* had on strength a total of 42 pilots, of which 25 were fit for duty with the *Gruppe* and another 17 who were convalescents or on detached duty.

[325] Writings of Botho Teichmann.

[326] The change of command took place on 13 December 1941. According to Georg Alex, after completing its rest and refit 4/JG 3 had the following pilots on strength: Oblt. Dahl, Oblt. Walz, Lt. Helm, Lt. Wicklaus, Lt. Fischer, Obfw. Kortlepel, Obfhr. König, Fw. Lucas, Fw. Hartenberger, Uffz. Schütte, Uffz. Münster, Uffz. Ebener, Uffz. Frese, Uffz. Buttstädt, Uffz. Huhndorf, Obgefr. Golke and Gefr. May.

[327] The following comments would seem to be appropriate here: the Quartermaster-General's loss reports record three losses by II/JG 3 in the second half of December during operations on the Dutch North Sea coast, however there are no other records which would suggest that elements or all of the *Gruppe* saw action in Holland. It may be assumed with certainty that this is a copying error and that the unit in question was I/JG 3, which in fact had been subordinated to the JaFü Holland/Ruhr Region by an order dated 9 December 1941. It subsequently moved to Katwijk and Vlissingen on 12-13 December in order to take over the role of defending coastal shipping and Holland. See I/JG 3 War Diary and Prien/Stemmer, I/JG 3.

[328] See the detailed account in Gundelach, Vol. I, p. 351 and following pages; Prien, JG 53 Part 1, p. 431 and following pages, especially 442 and following pages.

[329] The following information concerning 4/JG 3's operations in the Mediterranean Theater are taken from a condensed copy of the *Staffel* war diary, which will subsequently be cited as "War Diary 4/JG 3."

[330] War Diary 4/JG 3.

[331] For example, the logbook of Heinrich Sannemann records the first maintenance test flight in his "Yellow 1" at Bari on 20 January 1942.

[332] For a detailed account of operations on Sicily see Prien, JG 53 Part 1, p. 449 and following pages.

[333] War Diary 4/JG 3.

[334] War Diary 4/JG 3; involved were Lt. Helm, Obfhr. König, Obfw. Kortlepel, and Uffz. Schütte.

[335] See Prien/Stemmer, III/JG 3, p. 152.

[336] In addition to the Bf 109s that had already arrived at Bari, III/JG 3 also released several technicians to II/JG 3, including, for example, Fw. Helmut Hennig, who had previously served as a mechanic in the *Gruppenstab* of III/JG 3. Account dated 30/11/1985.

[337] War Diary 4/JG 3. The elements of II/JG 3 which arrived on Sicily later moved directly from Bari to Sciacca.

[338] See Gundelach, Part 1, p. 342 and following pages.

[339] See Prien, JG 53 Part 1, p. 449 and following pages.

[340] For example, the logbook of Heinrich Sannemann lists just four missions over Malta in January (on the 26th, 27th, 30th and 31st), all of which were uneventful.

[341] According to the WASt. casualty report. According to the logbook of Franz Schwaiger, then an *Unteroffizier* pilot in 6/JG 3, Uffz. Mächler went down with his machine and on impact sustained burns serious enough to require him to be taken immediately to hospital.

[342] At the beginning of February 1942 there were four *Jagdgruppen* assembled on Sicily with a total of 154 Messerschmitts, of which just 77 were serviceable. Of the 105 Ju 88s belonging to the four *Kampfgruppen* on Sicily, just 40 were reported serviceable. *Luftwaffe* strength reports, RL 2/v. 1747.

[343] See Gundelach, Part 1, p. 345 and following pages.

[344] 4/JG 3's war diary records missions by the *Staffel* on the 4th, 5th, 6th and 7th of February 1942. In each case these were apparently *Staffel*-strength missions, as for example on 4 February when Oblt. Dahl led a *Schwarm* with Lt. Helm, Uffz. Ebener and Uffz. Schütte.

[345] Diary of Franz Schwaiger: "Continued bad weather. Nothing special."

[346] War Diary 4/JG 3; the other pilots were Uffz. Münster, Uffz. Ebener and Gefr. May.

[347] WASt. casualty report.

[348] Mission times according to the logbook of Heinrich Sannemann 11:45 AM to 2:05 PM (!), time of victory 1:15 PM.

[349] According to his logbook, during these days Oblt. Heinrich Sannemann "shuttled" back and forth between Sciacca, Pantelleria and Tripoli. The *Staffel*'s planned return on 25 February was frustrated by bad weather. Franz Schwaiger wrote in his diary: *"We wanted to transfer again today, to San Pietro, but off the coast of Sicily we encountered such clag that we had to turn back. After an hour we all returned safely to Pantelleria."*

[350] Appeared as *"campo di fortuna"* (literally a lucky or chance field) on the Rome/Tripoli aviation map, special edition VI.1942; in fact, in the beginning it was no more than a simple landing field.

[351] War Diary 4/JG 3.

[352] According to 4/JG 3's war diary this victory was apparently submitted "without witnesses," however it appears to have been subsequently confirmed. Other participants in this mission were Lt. Helm and Lt. Wicklaus.

[353] The laconic entry in 4/JG 3's war diary: "25/2 – 1/3 bad weather", while Franz Schwaiger wrote in his diary: *"28/2 – 3/3/1942: At San Pietro. Poor airfield conditions as a result of rain. We are writing letters and resting."*

[354] See Prien, JG 53 Part 1, p. 475. Heinrich Sannemann's experiences may be seen as typical of II/JG 3's operations; according to his logbook, none of the Malta missions flown by him in March resulted in contact with enemy aircraft!

[355] WASt. casualty report, entry dated 18/4/1942.

[356] These 15 Spitfires were the first examples of this type to be used in the fighter role outside Great Britain; the aircraft were assigned to 249 Squadron.

[357] Time of the downing 5:10 PM, Hptm. Krahl's 24th victory. Franz Schwaiger wrote of this air battle: *"Today I flew my 130th mission, escort for a formation of bombers to Malta, encountered Spitfires for the first time. These attacked the Ju 88s very skillfully from in front and above, while a larger group of Hurricanes hung below. Unfortunately, I did not get a chance to fire, escorted the bombers home. One Ju 88 was heavily damaged by flak but nevertheless made it home safely. Hptm. Krahl shot down a Spitfire. The English fighters dove on us at an altitude of 5 000 meters."*

[358] According to Shores, *Spitfire Year*, p. 116, this was the very first Spitfire lost over Malta. The machine in question was one of four Spitfires of 249 Squadron and was flown by PO Murray. While he succeeded in bailing out, his parachute failed to deploy fully, he struck the ground hard and died in hospital later the same day. The information offered by Shores concerning the German units involved is inaccurate: Fw. Schade, who is credited with the victory, in fact claimed to have shot down a Spitfire at 11:10 AM on this day. This example serves to show that the efforts by various authors to prove who in fact shot down whom should be viewed with considerable skepticism, for in attempting to make the success and loss reports of both sides "fit" together, it is too easy to misinterpret the actual events and the associated claims and reports in order to "prove" the desired result. Where II/JG 3 is concerned, the same applies to the loss of Lt. Ponec and Uffz. Wegmann who, according to German sources, were lost for reasons other than enemy action, while Shores declares that they were lost as a result of air combat. If this were true, they should appear among the British claims. So as not to be misunderstood: it is not my intention to denounce a mistake in the work of another, deserving author—these are unavoidable, and there are undoubtedly some in this work—instead, it is my aim to point out what is, in my view, a misguided objective and, continuing with this theme, to encourage a style of work which promotes the *"corriger l'histoire"* in evaluating source material.

[359] War Diary 4/JG 3.

[360] Mission times according to the logbook of Heinrich Sannemann 2:00 to 2:45 PM.

[361] The day before, while returning from a bomber escort mission to Malta, Uffz. Beikiefer mistakenly attacked a *Kette* of Ju 88s, fatally wounded one of the gunners. Franz Schwaiger wrote in his diary: *"Beikiefer is completely shattered."*

[362] According to the WASt. casualty report and 4/JG 3's war diary, to within 30 kilometers south of San Pietro, or just a few kilometers off the coast.

[363] Mission times according to the logbook of Heinrich Sannemann 3:20 to 5:58 PM, however it is entered under *"o.F."* (no contact with the enemy).

[364] War Diary 4/JG 3; the pilots were Oblt. Dahl, Lt. Wicklaus and Obfw. Kortlepel.

[365] Mission times according to the logbook of Heinrich Sannemann 12:55 to 2:25 PM.

[366] Diary of Franz Schwaiger.

[367] According to RAF records, in March 1942 it lost 10 Hurricanes and 4 Spitfires in air combat over Malta and another 29 machines on the ground; during the same period the *Luftwaffe* flew 4,881 sorties to Malta, 2,903 of them by the fighters of JG 53 and II/JG 3.

[368] Eleven Hurricanes were flown into Malta on 27 March and seven Spitfires on 29 March.

[369] For example, the logbook of Heinrich Sannemann records just one air engagement (on 5 April) during the missions of 1-6 April 1942.

[370] WASt. casualty report; the capture report is dated 15 May 1942.

[371] Unlike JG 53, whose three *Gruppen* claimed 57 victories during their missions to Malta in the same period for the loss of four pilots in air combat. See Prien, JG 53 Part 1, p. 491 and following pages, 525 and 1670.

[372] For example, 4/JG 3 had already been required to release three Bf 109 F-4 trop to JG 27 on 31 March—War Diary 4/JG 3. Altogether, in March and April 1942 II/JG 3 had to release 10 Bf 109 F-4s to JG 27, six of them by the end of March and four in April. See aircraft complement lists in the appendices.

[373] Again using 4/JG 3 as an example, this meant that the *Schwarm* of Obfw. Freitag, Fw. Schütte, Uffz. Ebener and Gefr. May was deployed to Pantelleria on 7 April, leaving the *Staffel* with just three Bf 109 F-4 trop at San Pietro.

[374] See the table on Page 115, which is based on JG 27's takeoff log.

[375] Account by Harald Moldenhauer, 24/11/1986. He signed Hptm. Krahl's loss report as "*Oberleutnant and acting Gruppenkommandeur*" on 15 April. Hptm. Brändle, on the other hand, claimed a victory on 21 April 1942 while flying with 5/JG 53 See Prien, JG 53 Part 1, p. 504, and Part 3, p. 1670.

[376] Franz Schwaiger wrote in his diary: "*12/4/42. Today I flew my 160th mission, which was also my first fighter-bomber sortie. Oblt. Sannemann and I each carried four 50-kg fragmentation bombs; we found a worthwhile target in the desert near Mechili, a large number of parked vehicles. We approached these at low-level and dropped our bombs on the vehicles. While leaving the target area we came under heavy fire from an anti-aircraft gun, but, taking evasive action, we quickly got out of the gun's effective range. The effect of our bombs must have been very good.*"

[377] See Gundelach, *Mittelmeer*, p. 354 and following pages; Prien, JG 53 Part 1, p. 504 and following pages.

[378] See Gundelach, Mittelmeer, p. 362 and following pages.

[379] From the end of April two Ju 88 *Gruppen* of KG 77 and two *Jagdgruppen* (II/JG 3 and I/JG 53) left Sicily and were transferred to the east; during May 1942 other fighter and Stuka forces were sent to North Africa.

[380] One of the reasons why an attempt was not made to conquer Malta at this time was thus the shortage of air forces required for such an operation. By this time the *Luftwaffe* already had no reserves at all, making it impossible for it to complete the tasks assigned to it in the east and simultaneously support a landing on Malta and the continued offensive in North Africa. The latter operation was complicated by the almost total absence of the Italian air force, which could only be expected to offer very limited assistance for a brief period. In other words: even if the German command had seriously considered a landing on Malta, this could only have been possible at the price of at least temporarily weakening the *Luftwaffe* units available in the east, and there was no way that this could be reconciled with the priorities of Hitler's military objectives.

[381] See Gundelach, *Mittelmeer*, p. 399 and following pages; for an account of operations by JG 53 and JG 77 during this period see Prien, JG 53 Part 2 and JG 77 Part 3.

[382] War Diary 4/JG 3.

[383] According to the logbook of Heinrich Sannemann, 6/JG 3 transferred from San Pietro to Pilsen via Bari and Vienna during the period 4-6 May 1942.

[384] Diary of Franz Schwaiger.

[385] See the table above. In view of the duration of operations at Martuba, this meant that 6/JG 3 was only called upon to fly an average of slightly more than one mission per day with three aircraft, and that each of the twelve pilots flew only between five and six combat missions each. On the other hand, there were at least 13 days on which no missions were flown, and on these days the pilots took the opportunity to bask in the sun.

[386] 4/JG 3, for example, flew a total of 126 missions during this time, totaling 380 sorties. The result was two victories for the loss of four pilots wounded or injured and three machines written off—War Diary 4/JG 3.

[387] Of these, just four were the result of enemy action!

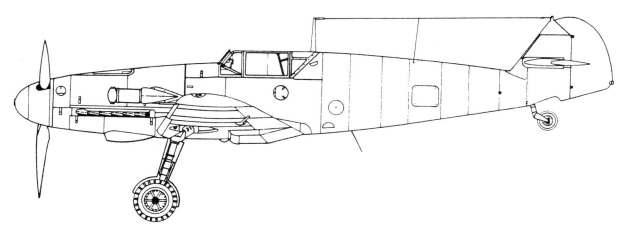

Line Drawing 5: Messerschmitt Bf 109 F-4/Z trop

Unlike the *Gruppen* of JG 53, for example, prior to commencing operations from Sicily II/JG 3 was issued the Bf 109 F-4 trop, a version designed for operational conditions in the North African desert; the most obvious identifying feature of the tropical version was the cylindrical sand filter in front of the supercharger air intake.

Length: 8.94 m
Wingspan: 9.92 m
Height: 2.60 m

Engine: Daimler Benz DB 601 E, 1,350 H.P. Empty weight: 2 083 kg
Takeoff weight: 2 895 kg
Armament: 1 MG 151/20, 2 MG 17

Many aircraft were also fitted with GM-1 nitrous-oxide injection, which provided a short-term increase in engine output. This installation was recognizable by a deeper oil cooler beneath the engine and often a propeller with broader blades. Installation of the GM-1 system resulted in the designation Bf 109 F-4/Z.

The following photographed depict the aircraft of Gruppenkommandeur *Hptm. Karl-Heinz Krahl, a Bf 109 F-4 trop with the WerkNr. 8665. This Messerschmitt originally belonged to the* Geschwaderstab *and was passed on to II Gruppe when it was recalled to Germany even before its arrival in Sicily. Mechanically, the machine was in rather poor condition when it was*

taken on strength by the Stabsschwarm *of II/JG 3 and consequently there were numerous "bugs" to be worked out before the* Gruppe *Technical Officer Lt. Frielinghaus was satisfied and it could be handed over to Hptm. Krahl. Subsequently the simple white chevron marking was turned into a double chevron and the emblem in front of the cockpit dating from its time with the* Geschwaderstab *(a combination of all three* Gruppe *emblems) was replaced by the* Gruppe *emblem of II/JG 3.*

The aircraft was flown regularly by Hptm. Krahl until he was issued a new Bf 109 F-4 shortly before his last mission; it was subsequently taken over by his successor, Hptm. Brändle, who was still flying it in the east in June 1942. On 9 July 1942 the machine was damaged during a maintenance test flight and was subsequently struck off strength. In these two photographs Hptm. Krahl is seen after returning from a sortie, awaited by the technicians who will immediately begin preparing it for the next mission.

Two more shots of the Kommandeur's aircraft. Above Helmut Henning, the first mechanic, is sitting in the cockpit; below several technicians of the maintenance section engaged in sporting activities during their free time, with "White Double Chevron" parked in the background. The change in the aircraft's finish is noteworthy. The machine originally wore the standard Africa scheme with a mid-fuselage separation line between the pale blue of the undersides and the sand-brown of the upper surfaces. Later the standard straight separation line between the two colors was "broken up," resulting in a wavy separation line. Note the external stiffeners for the tail section bearer on the rear fuselage. (all: Hennig)

Above: Gruppen-Adjutant *Lt. Max-Bruno Fischer seen climbing from the cockpit of his Bf 109 F-4 trop after returning from a mission over Malta in spring 1942. The machine wears the tactical marking "Chevron Bar" in black and Max-Bruno Fischer's personal emblem beneath the cockpit. Also note the irregular separation line between the sand brown upper surface color and the pale blue of the fuselage sides. Also note the armor-glass panel in front of the windscreen. Below: Technicians of the maintenance section with "White Chevron", another Bf 109 F-4 of the Gruppenstab of II/JG 3; once again the broken separation line between the colors on the upper and lower surfaces is clearly visible. (Fischer/Hennig via Lächler)*

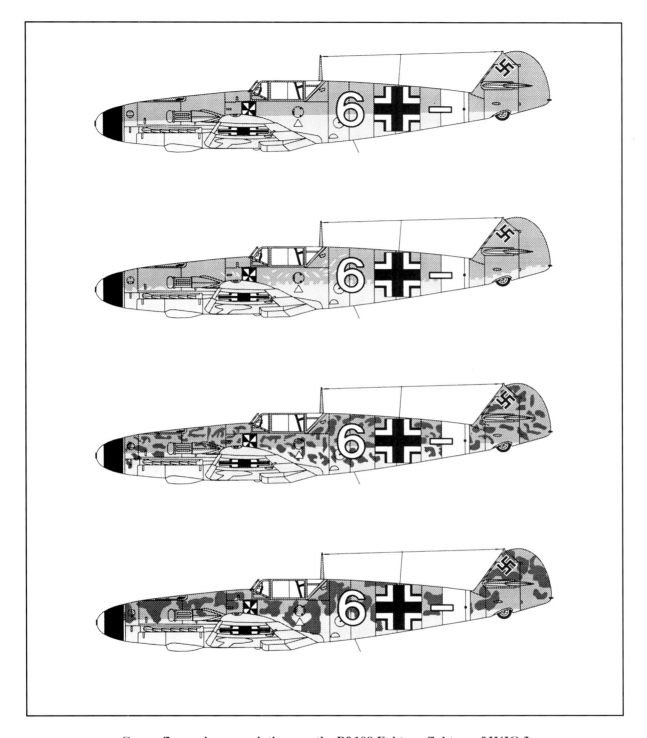

Camouflage scheme variations on the Bf 109 F-4 trop fighters of II/JG 3

The four Bf 109 F-4 trop shown here in side-view illustrate the variations of the Africa scheme worn by machines of II/JG 3 during its deployment in the Mediterranean Theater in spring 1942. At the top of the page is a Bf 109 F-4 trop in the standard, factory-applied Africa scheme of sand brown and pale blue with a high separation line. This was the scheme worn by most of the *Gruppe*'s aircraft after it reequipped. The second machine wears a variation of this scheme known only to have been used by II/JG 3, in which the separation line was more irregular and wavy. The third aircraft wears a finish consisting of the standard Africa scheme with a light application of dark green blotches, another variation which was occasionally seen. Finally, the last aircraft is finished in the Africa scheme with large, dark green blotches. The last three finishes must, however, have been the result of modifications at the unit level and were not applied at the factory.

The following photographs depict "Yellow 3", a Bf 109 F-4 of 6/JG 3 flown by Uffz. Franz Schwaiger. The aircraft is finished in the standard two-tone Africa scheme with the separation line halfway up the fuselage. In front of the cockpit is the Gruppe *emblem, while the name "Gisela" is visible on the engine cowling. Also note the finish on the propeller spinner with the yellow tip standard on 6* Staffel *aircraft. Also noteworthy is the external armor-glass panel in front of the windscreen. (Lorant)*

Above and below left: Two more photos of Uffz. Schwaiger's "Yellow 3". In the photograph below, which depicts Franz Schwaiger with four mechanics, the tip of the propeller spinner looks white rather than yellow. Also note the mount for the external fuel tank beneath the fuselage. All of these photos may have been taken at Sciacca in March 1942. Below right: The Gruppe *emblem of II/JG 3 beneath the cockpit of a Bf 109 F-4 trop; the spaces in the stencil used to spray the emblem are clearly visible. Above the emblem on the right, beneath the letters "WE" (horizontal position), may be seen the marking for lining up the machine during bore-sighting of the weapons. (Lorant/Sauer)*

Above: "White 10", a Bf 109 F-4 trop of 4 Staffel in an unmodified Africa scheme with low separation line, photographed on a forward airfield on Sicily in spring 1942; note the white fuselage band and the Gruppe emblem clearly visible in front of the cockpit. Below: "Black 3" of 5/JG 3, another Bf 109 F-4/Z trop in the two-tone Africa scheme, this time with a separation line about halfway down the fuselage. The engine cowling undersurface is obviously yellow, while the wing root area has retained a black protective finish. (Lächler)

Above: Lt. Josef Reisinger allegedly belly-landed his "Black 8", a Bf 109 F-4/Z trop of 5 Staffel, at San Pietro on 13 Mwrch 1942, however there is no reference to this incident in the Gruppe loss records. The aircraft wears the two-tone Africa scheme with a high separation line and its propeller spinner is apparently red, the Staffel color. Below: Pilots of 5/JG 3 with one of their Bf 109 F-4/Z trop fighters, which is parked in a blast pen; San Pietro, spring 1942. This aircraft carried an auxiliary fuel tank under the fuselage; note the overall black propeller spinner. (Lächler)

These two photographs of several Messerschmitts of 5 Staffel were taken on the same occasion. Above "Black 7" in front of a blast wall, below, in the foreground, "Black 8". Both are Bf 109 F-4/Z trop equipped with external fuel tanks, probably for escort missions over the sea. (Lächler)

Above: Pilots of 5 Staffel, *photographed at San Pietro in spring 1942; second from the left, standing, is Obfw. Walter Ohlrogge and on the far right Lt. Joachim Kirschner. Seated, on the right, is Obfw. Alfred Heckmann. Below: "Yellow 4", a Bf 109 F-4 of 6* Staffel, *photographed on a Sicilian airfield in spring 1942. This machine wears a "European" gray-green camouflage scheme with the white fuselage band used in the Mediterranean Theater. In front of the cockpit is the* Gruppe *emblem of II/JG 3, which was applied on both sides of the fuselage. (Ohlrogge via Struppek/Lächler)*

Pilots of 4/JG 3 with the Messerschmitt of their Staffelkapitän, *Oblt. Walther Dahl, a Bf 109 F-4 trop with the WerkNr. 8685, photographed at San Pietro in March 1942. The photos depict the* Staffelkapitän *after returning from a mission over Malta. Next to Oblt. Dahl is Obfw. Lortlepel, the oldest and most experienced* Oberfeldwebel *in the* Staffel. *Note the white fuselage band with the* Gruppe *bar superimposed. (E.C.P.A. DAA 1229 L 12-15)*

Aircraft of II Gruppe on San Pietro airfield in spring 1942; while "White 2" obviously wears a gray-green camouflage scheme, most of the other aircraft are finished in the two-tone Africa scheme. (Seiz)

These two photographs were allegedly taken on Pantelleria, to where II/JG 3 occasionally had to detach several Schwärme *to provide fighter cover for convoys sailing to North Africa. It appears that the machine in the foreground lacks the* Gruppe *bar aft of the fuselage* Balkenkreuz. *(Seiz)*

Obfw. Alfred Heckmann, one of 5 Staffel's most experienced pilots, in the cockpit of his "Black 10", a Bf 109 F-4 trop finished in the Africa scheme with prominent a prominent dark green dapple on the upper surfaces. Note the external armor-glass panel in front of the windscreen, the Gruppe *emblem of II/JG 3, and the white sidewalls on the mainwheel tires, a feature of tropical machines intended to protect the tires against the effects of the sun. Below: Obfw. Heckmann once again (right), seen here with Obfw. Ohlrogge in front of the nose of the Bf 109 F-4/Z trop. (Petrick/Ohlrogge via Struppek)*

Above: Pilots and members of the Gruppenstab *of II/JG 3 in front of their quarters on San Pietro airfield; standing, from the left: Fw. Fischer, Oblt. Waldhelm, Insp. Bauer, Oblt. Lang (HQ Comp.), HptFw. Schmidt and paymaster Engelke; seated: Obfw. Kortlepel, Lt. Wolf (HQ Comp.), Med. Officer Dr. Parday, Lt. Fuß (Gruppen-Adjutant of II/JG 3 after Lt. Ponec's failure to return), Hptm. Krahl and the* Gruppe *Technical Officer Lt. Frielinghaus. Below: Pilots of 4* Staffel *in front of one of their "Friedrichs," photographed at San Pietro in April 1942; in the center is Lt. Josef Reisinger. Note the aircraft's deep oil cooler, a clear indication that it is a Bf 109 F-4/Z trop, and the open sand filter. As usual, the tip of the propeller spinner is painted in the* Staffel *color white. (Hennig/BA No. 147-763)*

Above: New Bf 109 F-4 trop have arrived at a Sicilian airfield; both wear the standard Africa scheme with white spinners and fuselage bands as well as yellow engine cowling undersides. Both machines are obviously still wearing their factory codes. Below: A Bf 109 F-4 trop of II/JG 3, possibly of 5 Staffel, photographed on a Sicilian airfield in spring 1942. The machine is obviously wearing an unmodified Africa scheme with yellow engine cowling underside and a white fuselage band. Although difficult to see, the propeller spinner is two-tone, with the tip in the Staffel color red. Also note the auxiliary fuel tank under the fuselage, the external armor-glass panel, and the Gruppe emblem. (Seiz/Roletscheck/Petrick)

Above: Several pilots and mechanics of II/JG 3 have gathered in front of a machine of the Gruppenstab *and listen to a conversation between* Gruppenkommandeur *Hptm. Krahl (center, wearing forage cap) and a pilot. The machine in the background wears a black chevron staff marking, a style not introduced until toward the end of II Gruppe's tour of duty on Sicily. Below left:* Gruppenkommandeur *Hptm. Krahl seen leaving the cockpit of his Messerschmitt after a mission over Malta in April 1942. Worthy of note are the white staff marking, the aircraft of the* Gruppenstab *having worn only white chevron markings at first, and the irregular separation line between the sand brown of the upper surfaces and the pale blue of the fuselage sides. Below right: The fin and rudder of Obfw. Walter Ohlrogge's Messerschmitt, a Bf 109 F-4 trop with the WerkNr. 8654. Ohlrogge was 5* Staffel's *leading "Experte"; a total of 43 victories are recorded here, the first scored in the west and the remainder in the east. (BA/Fischer/ Sauer)*

Above: This photograph purportedly depicts Uffz. Karl-Heinz Steinicke of 6 Staffel with "White 7", a Bf 109 F-4 trop of 4/JG 3, prior to a mission. The machine obviously wears an unmodified Africa scheme with high separation line, a white fuselage band and probably a yellow engine cowling underside. In the original photo, the tip of the propeller spinner can be seen to be white. Below: A Bf 109 F-4 trop of 6/JG 3 on San Pietro airfield, photographed at the beginning of April 1942 just prior to the Staffel's transfer to North Africa. Note the sand filter in front of the supercharger air intake, the external fuel tank, and the propeller spinner with tip painted yellow, the Staffel color of 6/JG 3. (Steinicke/Sauer)

Effect: German plane that won't go back to base in Italy was brought down by Spitfire or anti-aircraft battery. Seven Stukas attacked one position in Malta recently. Seven were shot down.

Two photographs of the wreck of Hptm. Krahl's machine, which was shot down by anti-aircraft during a low-level attack on Ta Kali airfield on 14 April 1942. Krahl was killed when his Messerschmitt struck the ground. This aircraft, a Bf 109 F-4 with the WerkNr. 8784, was obviously finished in a gray-green scheme instead of the Africa scheme previously standard on the aircraft of II/JG 3.

The caption with the above photo is from a contemporary British press report on the downing of Hptm. Krahl's machine.

(unknown/Shores/NWMA)

Above: Aircraft of 6 Staffel on the Arco Philaenorum airfield, photographed on 7 April 1942 during the transfer to Martuba. Both Messerschmitts carry external fuel tanks under the fuselage. Note the finish on "Yellow 5" in the foreground with a noticeably wavy separation line between the sand brown of the upper surfaces and the pale blue of the fuselage sides. Also note the obviously yellow engine cowling undersides of both machines. Below: A special way of finding useful employment for damaged external fuel tanks… (Schwaiger/Sannemann)

One of the many aircraft graveyards that fell into Allied hands or were created by them at the end of 1942. A total of twelve Bf 109 fuselages may be seen here. The second aircraft from the front is the machine of Uffz. Josef Fritz of 6/JG 3, a Bf 109 F-4 trop with the WerkNr. 10 019, which was shot down in air combat over El Adem on 13 April 1942. This machine obviously wears a sand brown-pale blue Africa scheme with a light dapple in dark green on the upper surfaces. The Gruppe emblem of II/JG 3 is clearly visible in front of the cockpit. (I.W.M. CM 4038)

7

Return to Action in the East
From the Summer Offensive in the South of the Eastern Front 1942 to the Summer Battle at Kursk and Belgorod July-August 1943

Having withstood the winter crisis in the east, and with the army's strength restored to a reasonable level, in early 1942 Hitler's thoughts immediately turned to a resumption of the offensive. On 5 April 1942 Hitler issued Directive No. 41, which outlined the summer operations in the east. The plan called for the main German effort to be shifted to the southern wing of the Eastern Front, where a four-stage advance was to begin in June and end with the capture of Stalingrad and the conquest of the Caucasus[388]. In issuing his directive Hitler ignored the representations and concerns of the general staff, which rightly warned of an over-extension of their forces and recommended a consolidation of their own positions instead of Hitler's far-reaching plans for conquest[389]. Before the actual summer offensive could begin, it was necessary to conduct three preparatory offensive operations in Army Group South's area to address situations left over from the winter fighting: in the Crimea the Kerch Peninsula had to be retaken and the capture of the fortress of Sevastopol brought to a successful conclusion, while in the Ukraine the Russian salient before Izyum had to be eliminated and the Donets front restored[390]. The shortage of available air forces meant that it was impossible to carry out all three operations simultaneously, therefore the attack to retake the Kerch Peninsula—"Operation *Trappenjagd*" (Bustard Hunt)—was set to begin on 8 May 1942. As soon as it was completed the *Luftwaffe* units assembled in the Crimea were to be moved north to support the planned operation by Army Group von Kleist to pinch off the Russian salient in front of Izyum ("Operation *Fridericus I*"), which was set for 17 May. Once this was completed the air units would be able to return to the Crimea, where the attack on the fortress of Sevastopol ("Operation *Störfang*") was scheduled to begin on 7 June 1942[391].

Unnoticed by the Germans, the Russians had also prepared an offensive on the Donets front with the objective of recapturing Kharkov. The attack began on 12 May, taking the Germans completely by surprise and resulting in several days of fierce and at times confused fighting. In the end, however, German forces succeeded in heading off the Russian thrust and went ahead with their own preparations for "Operation *Fridericus I*," broadening the attack plan to include the encirclement and destruction of the Russian forces south of Kharkov[392]. As the German command had been five days earlier, the Soviet command was taken completely by surprise when the German attack began on 17 May 1942; but unlike the Russian attack, the German one was a success. German forces penetrated deep into the Russian positions in several places and were able to advance north toward Slavyansk and Barvenkovo[393].

*****

On 27 April 1942 II/JG 3 arrived at Pilsen from Sicily[394] with its own machines. For the next three weeks the *Gruppe* underwent a brief rest and refit in preparation for the coming operations associated with the summer offensive of 1942. By the end of the month the *Gruppe* was already able to report 40 Messerschmitts on strength, equal to its authorized strength. Another four Bf 109 F-4s were delivered at the end of the month[395]. In addition to thoroughly overhauling the machines and removing the sand filters and other tropical equipment, the tasks of the mechanics in those days included repainting the Messerschmitts, which were in tropical camouflage, in the familiar green-gray scheme with yellow fuselage band and wingtips for subsequent operations in the east[396].

At the end of April the new *Kommandeur*, Hptm. Kurt Brändle, assumed command of the *Gruppe* from Oblt. Harald Moldenhauer, who since the loss of Hptm. Krahl had commanded II/JG 3 in an acting capacity. As well, at the beginning of May there was a change in the command of 6 *Staffel*: in Pilsen Oblt. Heinrich Sannemann left the *Gruppe* after being transferred to LKS 3 Werder. His designated successor was Oblt. Hans-Jürgen Waldhelm, who had most recently seen action with JG 5 in Norway. At this time he had yet to score his first victory.

II/JG 3 Command List mid-May 1942

Gruppenkommandeur	Hptm. Kurt Brändle
Gruppenadjutant	Lt. Max-Bruno Fischer
Commander Headquarters Company	Oblt. Franke
Gruppe Technical Officer	Lt. Gustav Frielinghaus
Staffelkapitän 4/JG 3	Oblt. Albrecht Walz
Staffelkapitän 5/JG 3	Oblt. Harald Moldenhauer
Staffelkapitän 6/JG 3	Oblt. Hans-Jürgen Waldhelm

After barely three weeks of rest and refit, the transfer of II/JG 3 to the east, where it was to see action in the southern sector of the Eastern Front as part of VIII *Fliegerkorps*, began on 18 May 1942. According to the schedule of operations, the *Gruppe* was already too late to take part in the action to retake the Kerch Peninsula, and consequently it was immediately ordered into the area on the left wing of Army Group South, where it was assigned Chuguyev airfield as its base of operations. The air element began arriving at its new base on 19 May[397], joining the *Stab* and the other two *Gruppen* of the *Geschwader*[398].

From its new base of operations, II/JG 3 was initially called upon to fly free chase missions and patrols over the Kharkov area; as well, several times it escorted formations of bombers and Stukas into the combat zone on both sides of Kharkov[399]. The weather in those days was early-summer warm, and the Soviet air forces were also up in numbers, resulting in frequent encounters with Russian fighters and close-support aircraft. The first missions from Chuguyev were flown on 20 May. Hptm. Brändle scored the *Gruppe*'s first victory of its second tour of duty in the east, downing an R-5 at 3:49 AM. During the course of the day, the *Gruppe* claimed a total of six victories, including four Il-2s, without loss to itself.

In the meantime German troops had launched further attacks from the Donets line. The Russian attack on both sides of Kharkov broke down, whereupon German tank and infantry forces counter-attacked from the 6th Army's area in order to link up in the rear of the Russian 6th and 57th Armies positioned south of Kharkov and complete the encirclement of the Soviet forces[400]. For II/JG 3, on 21 May this meant flying missions over the combat zone in the area of the 6th Army northeast of Kharkov and over the southern wing near Izyum; mission assignments continued to be bomber escort and free chases, and the result at the end of the day was two victories. On the following day, 22 May 1942, the spearheads of the 6th Army and Army Group Kleist met near Bayrak on the Donets, clos-

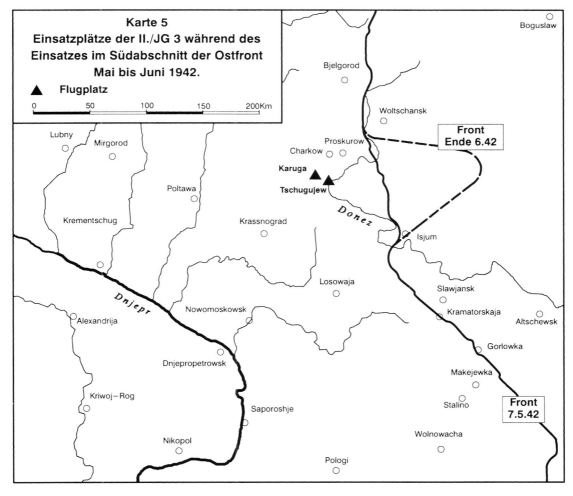

Karte 5
Einsatzplätze der II./JG 3 während des Einsatzes im Südabschnitt der Ostfront Mai bis Juni 1942.

▲ **Flugplatz**

0   50   100   150   200Km

ing the pocket around the Soviet forces south of Kharkov. II/JG 3 was again in action over the combat zone on both sides of the city on this day and it was able to score three victories for the loss of one pilot. 6 *Staffel* had to place Uffz. Robert Weinländer on the missing list after he was shot down by flak during a mission in the Volchansk area northeast of Kharkov. He was seen to parachute from his aircraft, however all trace of the pilot was then lost[401]. It was his third combat mission.

On the ground the focal point of the fighting in the days that followed was the area south of Kharkov, where the encircled Soviet forces launched furious counterattacks in an attempt to pierce the ring of German troops and break out to the east. On 23 May II/JG 3 scored eight more victories in the course of its missions, suffering no losses[402]. The *Gruppe* was largely inactive for the next two days, largely because of a period of rainy weather[403]. Few missions were flown, nevertheless one loss was recorded on 25 May, when Lt. Albert Helm of 4 *Staffel* was listed missing after being shot down by ground fire during low-level attacks in the Mikhailovskaya area southwest of Balakleya. Albert Helm had joined 4/JG 3 as a *Fähnrich* in March 1941 and had since scored five victories, all in the east. There was an improvement in the weather on 26 May and several missions were flown, free chases and Stuka escort over the Izyum-Balakleya area. The *Gruppe* subsequently claimed eight victories on this day and three more the day after, in each case without loss.

The battle of encirclement south of Kharkov ended on 28 May 1942 after the last resistance by the surrounded Russian armies was extinguished. 239,000 Red Army soldiers were taken prisoner and immense quantities of war materiel fell into German hands. Within a few days the Soviet command's attempt to encircle elements of Army Group South had been stood on its head and had ended with a devastating defeat for the Russian armies. This was to be the last significant German success in a major battle of encirclement, however, and it set the stage for the great summer offensive and ultimately set the German forces on the road that led to Stalingrad.

Even after the end of the battle of encirclement south of Kharkov, II/JG 3 remained at its recently-occupied base[404], while at the end of May the air element of III *Gruppe* was transferred to the Crimea to take part in "Operation *Störfang*", the attack on the fortress of Sevastopol[405]. While there was little activity on the ground in the area of front on both sides of Kharkov after 28 May, the Russian air force launched repeated attacks on the German positions in the Izyum area and east of Kharkov with strong formations of close-support aircraft, in some cases with fighter escort[406]. The weather was extremely variable during these days and at times quite cool, however it did not seriously restrict the operational activities of II/JG 3. By the end of the month the *Gruppe* scored an additional fifteen victories without loss, including twelve on 29 May. Lt. Fuß was the top scorer with four enemy aircraft shot down (31-34). On

31 May 1942 II/JG 3 reported a total of 34 machines on hand, which meant that it was already below authorized strength.

At the beginning of June 1942 the *Gruppe* continued operating over the area around Kharkov and south along the Donets. By then, I and II/JG 3 were the only *Jagdgruppen* left in action there, following the transfer of III/JG 77, which had most recently been based at Kharkov and Konstantinovka, to the Crimea[408]. During this period the *Gruppe*'s principal missions were fighter sweeps, defensive patrols over the German lines and rear areas, and escort for formations of bombers[409]. In the period that followed, roughly three weeks, II/JG 3 was able to score a total of 46 victories, including seven on the 11th, nine on the 13th and ten on the 24th of June, while losses totaled one pilot injured and three Messerschmitts damaged. On 13 June, while on a fighter cover mission over the advance roads, the machine of Uffz. Arthur Fischer of 4 *Staffel* developed radiator trouble, forcing him to make a belly landing near Pechenegi. Fischer sustained minor injuries in the landing. The next day an aircraft of 5/JG 3 sustained moderate damage when hit by flak near Anovka. During the same period two more of the *Gruppe*'s machines sustained considerable damage, the result of accidents or technical problems. As well, on 21 June a Kl 35 went missing while on a courier flight from Rogany to Shchigry. Nothing was ever heard of the crew of Obgefr. Emil Jazbec (pilot) and Uffz. Berthold Neumann of 5/JG 3 (passenger).

Meanwhile, by 22 June the units of the 11th Army that had launched the attack on Sevastopol on 7 June had achieved decisive breakthroughs into the fortress. It was therefore now possible for the units that had been withdrawn to support the assault to be returned to the front on the left wing of Army Group South, albeit somewhat later than originally planned, so that they might occupy their assigned airfields in preparation for the start of the main summer offensive planned for 28 June[410]. II/JG 3's period of operations from Kharkov also came to an end. On or about 24 June 1942[411], it moved to Shchigry, a spacious forward airfield approximately 50 kilometers east of Kursk; the *Stab* and the other two *Gruppen* of the *Geschwader* also assembled there[412]. During its first night on the new airfield II/JG 3 experienced a bombing raid by about 60 Russian bombers, however no serious damage was inflicted[413].

Shchigry airfield lay very close behind the front lines, a fact that was driven home to the assembled *Gruppen* of JG 3 on 25 June 1942 when, at about noon, the airfield came under artillery fire. While most of the men quickly took cover, a dozen Messerschmitts from all of the *Gruppen* assembled on the airfield scrambled from the field and headed for the front. There they discovered the Soviet battery responsible for the bombardment and silenced it with several strafing runs. A number of aircraft were supposedly destroyed by the artillery fire, however there is nothing in the surviving records to indicate that II/JG 3 suffered any such losses[414]. The Russian air force was also extremely active over this area, and during its mis-

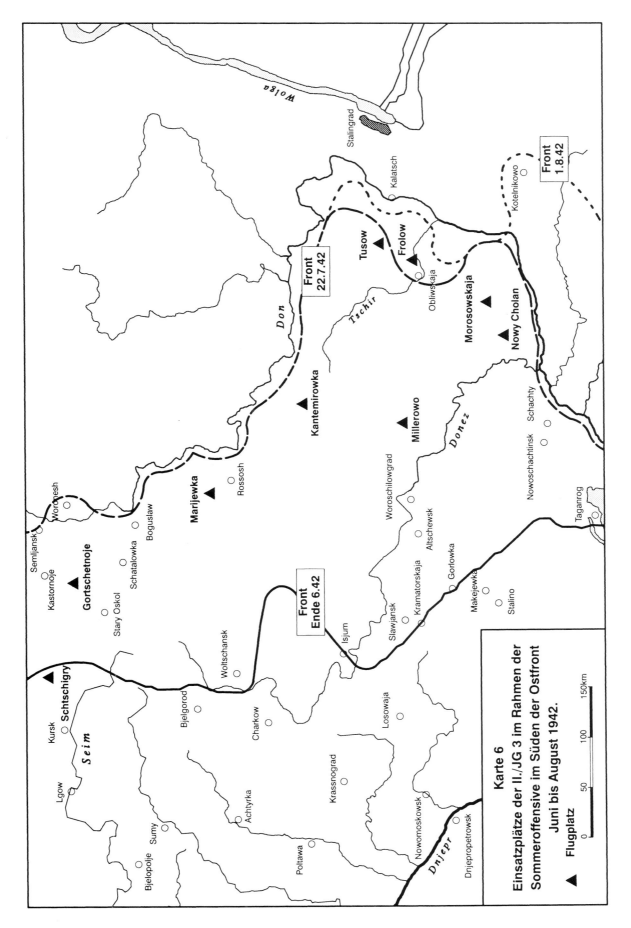

Wolga

Stalingrad

Kalatsch

Front 1.8.42

Kotelnikowo

Tusow

Frolow

Front 22.7.42

Don

Tschir

Obliwskaja

Morosowskaja

Nowy Cholan

Kantemirowka

Schachty

Millerowo

Donez

Woroschilowgrad

Nowoschachtinsk

Woronesh

Rossosh

Marijewka

Boguslaw

Taganrog

Semljansk

Schatalowka

Kastornoje

Stary Oskol

Gortschetnoje

Altschewsk

Kramatorskaja

Gorlowka

Makejewka

Stalino

Front Ende 6.42

Isjum

Slawjansk

Woltschansk

Schtschigry

Kursk

Lgow

Bjelgorod

Charkow

Losowaja

Seim

Krassnograd

Achtyrka

Nowomoskowsk

Bjelopolje

Sumy

Poltawa

Dnjepr

Dnjepropetrowsk

Karte 6

Einsatzplätze der II./JG 3 im Rahmen der Sommeroffensive im Süden der Ostfront Juni bis August 1942.

▲ **Flugplatz**

0 50 100 150km

sions on 26 and 27 June II/JG 3 had a series of encounters with formations of Russian fighters and close-support aircraft. Four enemy aircraft were shot down, including the first two P-40s, American types provided under Lend-Lease. This and other American types, especially the P-39 Airacobra and the twin-engined Douglas Boston, would appear in greater numbers in the weeks that followed[415].

The German summer offensive began on 28 June 1942 when Army Group von Weichs launched an attack from the area east of Kursk aimed at the upper Don and the capture of Voronezh. This advance by the left wing of Army Group South was supposed to screen the northern flank of the entire German summer offensive of 1942 while simultaneously creating the conditions necessary for the destruction of the Russian forces west of the Don. At first the pace of the German advance was surprisingly quick, for in contrast to their earlier method of fighting the Russian troops refused to stand and fight and instead conducted an orderly retreat everywhere. Only in the Voronezh battle zone was there a stiffening of resistance, and the German advance there did not proceed as quickly as planned.

To support the summer offensive, the *Luftwaffe* had concentrated powerful forces in the area of Army Group South in *Luftflotte 4*; at the start of the attack the two air corps under its command (*IV* and *VIII Fliegerkorps*) had available a total of 1,593 aircraft, including 325 fighters[416]. The primary mission of the air force units was once again to support the German ground forces.

The first day of the attack saw the three *Gruppen* of JG 3 in action from Shchigry over the battle zone east of Kursk, where they carried out fighter sweeps and strafing attacks against Russian troop columns in the rear area. One victory was recorded by II/JG 3 on this day, while the *Gruppe* lost one machine written off and another with considerable damage, although neither was due to enemy action. The picture was much the same in the days that followed: from Shchigry the Messerschmitts of II/JG 3 flew *Schwarm*- and *Rotte*-strength free chase and fighter cover missions over the spearheads of the armored units as well as several fighter-bomber missions against Russian vehicle and troop concentrations in the Kastornoye area. The 30th of June marked the beginning of a very successful period in which the *Gruppe* scored a large number of victories, and a number of pilots were able to increase their personal scores quite considerably. The balance at the beginning of this "hunting time" was nine victories scored on the 30th, eight on 1 July, ten on the 2nd, four on the 3rd and 15 on 4 July 1942. The only pilot casualty was Uffz. Karl Hamm of 6/JG 3, who was lost on 30 June during a free chase mission east of Kshen. He was last seen in pursuit of several Il-2s and was subsequently posted missing. On the other side of the coin, II/JG 3's aircraft complement had fallen to a barely tolerable level, for in those days the *Gruppe* had just 25 Messerschmitts, having received just two replacement machines in June[417].

In the first days of July, JG 3's area of operations shifted to the southeast as a result of the rapid advance by the German ground forces. The first transfer took place on 4 July, when the air element was moved forward to Gorshechnoye, a front-line airfield approximately 80 kilometers southwest of Voronezh, close behind the front lines[418]. On 5 July the skies were cloudy, and from Gorshechnoye II/JG 3 flew fighter cover missions over the area southwest of Voronezh, where German troops had forced a crossing of the Don and established three bridgeheads on the east bank. Throughout the day there were fierce air battles with large numbers of Russian close-support aircraft and bombers and their fighter escort. II/JG 3 registered four victories on this day, again without loss to itself[419], and six more followed the next day, 6 July 1942. On the same day the bulk of the ground personnel were moved from Shchigry to Gorshechnoye.

II/JG 3 continued to operate from Gorshechnoye in the days that followed; again the bulk of its missions were fighter sweeps, however it continued to fly fighter-bomber and strafing missions as well as escort missions in support of bombers and Stukas. The operational areas varied: on the one hand the *Gruppen* of JG 3 had to continue intervening in the bitter fighting in the Voronezh area, while on the other they also had to support the army's rapid advance southeast along the Don and to the west of it. The weather in those days was comfortably warm, with periods of cloud and occasional rain showers[420]. On 7 July 1942 the *Gruppe* claimed three victories during its missions over the battle zone around Voronezh. On the following day, 8 July, the focus of operations was once again the Voronezh area, where a total of ten victories was claimed. Losses amounted to one Messerschmitt damaged by flak near Perlovka, northwest of Voronezh.

The first phase of the summer offensive ended on 8 July 1942. The next step would begin on 9 July with an attack by the forces of the 1st Panzer Army from the area south of Kharkov. The objective of this move was to engage the bulk of the Soviet forces still west of the Don opposite Army Group South's front and encircle and destroy them together with the forces of Army Group von Weichs driving from the north[421].

Meanwhile, on 9 July II/JG 3 was again active over the combat zone around Voronezh, where in the course of several air battles the *Gruppe* was able to rack up another ten victories. The cost was one pilot missing: Uffz. Georg Schiller was not seen again after a combat with a formation of Russian bombers east of Voronezh. The *Gruppe* flew its last missions from Gorshechnoye early on the morning of the next day, 10 July 1942. At about 4:30 AM elements of all three *Staffeln* of II/JG 3 fought an engagement with a formation of Bostons and its fighter escort and seven victories were scored. Earlier, during a weather reconnaissance flight, Uffz. Vogel of 6 *Staffel* had reported two victories (14-15). On the loss side was a Messerschmitt of 4 *Staffel*: after shooting down a Boston for his seventh victory, Lt. Wolf Ettel was shot down by defensive fire from another bomber. He was forced to bail out 15 kilometers north of Voronezh, deep inside Russian territory. Reported missing by his unit, Ettel was able to complete the hazardous journey through enemy territory and four days later reached the German lines[423]. There were two more fierce air battles between 9 and 9:30 AM, after which II/JG 3 claimed another eight victories, three of them by its *Kommandeur* Hptm. Brändle (59-61). After returning from these early missions the pilots had to pack quickly, for that same morning the *Gruppe* was ordered to move south; its new base of operations was Maryevka, a forward airfield about 30 kilometers northwest of Rossosh, near Olkhovatka[424]. A small advance detachment of technical personnel flew to the new airfield in Ju 52 transports; these departed at about 10 AM with the air element providing the fighter escort. Meanwhile, at about noon the trucks of the main transport column departed for Maryevka, arriving three days later. The transfer was part of a shift in the *Luftwaffe*'s point of main effort. Beginning on this day, its units left their bases in the area east of Kursk and moved south, where they were to provide air support for the advancing 1st Panzer Army. In addition to II/JG 3, this transfer affected the *Stab* and the other two *Gruppen* of JG 3.

Meanwhile the German thrust from the area south of Kharkov had gained ground rapidly to the northeast; after crossing the Donets in the area of Lisichansk the army's fast units moved toward the Don, while elements of Army Group B simultaneously advanced southeast along the Don[425]. For II/JG 3 the following days until the 13th brought a series of missions over the Don region east of Rossosh, where a total of 13 victories were scored between the 11th and 13th of July. At this time operational activity was hampered by periods of very bad weather with sudden heavy rainfalls. As well, beginning on 13 July elements of II/JG 3 were moved forward to the Kantemirovka forward airfield, approximately 125 kilometers southeast of Maryevka, from where they flew missions in support of the army units advancing out of the Starobyelsk area[426]. While the *Gruppe* suffered no combat casualties during this time, it nevertheless took some painful losses. On 11 July Russian bombers attacked Maryevka airfield. Their bombs killed two—Uffz. Arthur Fischer, a pilot in 4/JG 3, and Fw. Günther Römmelt, *Schwarmmeister* in the headquarters company's repair platoon—and injured two more and damaged a machine of 6 *Staffel*. Two days later, on 13 July 1942, there was a serious accident at Kantemirovka: a Ju 87 of 2/StG 2 swung on takeoff and crashed into the parked machines of II/JG 3, destroying two Messerschmitts and seriously damaging two more. Fw. Werner Kloß of 5 *Staffel*, who was strapped into his machine in preparation for a mission, was seriously injured in the accident. As well, five technicians of 4 *Staffel* were killed and another injured[427].

On 14 July 1942 the spearheads of the German attack armies linked up near Millerovo, closing the pocket between the Donets and the Dniepr. The results were much less than the German command had expected, however, for the Russian units had succeeded in escaping encirclement through an orderly retreat. As a result of this, the German campaign plans were fundamentally altered and orders were now issued for the execution of simultaneous offensive operations against Stalingrad and the Caucasus region. Hitler's underlying basic misreading of the true conditions led to a total overtaxing of his forces and consequently to a situation which resulted in the dangerous over-extension of the German lines in the south of the Eastern Front[428].

On 15 July 1942 II/JG 3 received orders to move again, this time to Millerovo. Whereas the first elements of the air component arrived at the new base of operations in the afternoon, bad weather prevented the transfer of an advance detachment of technical personnel which was supposed to take place the same day. Early the next morning the elements of the *Gruppe* most recently deployed to Kantemirovka and the advance party of technical personnel also arrived at Millerovo. During its missions from Millerovo, II/JG 3's primary task was to provide air support for the army's motorized units; in addition to guarding the airspace over the armored spearheads it was to continue flying free chases. At Millerovo II/JG 3 received a large number of Bf 109 F-4s which had been released by other units after they had reequipped with the new Bf 109 G-2. While the addition of a total of 32 Bf 109 F-4s[429] significantly bolstered the unit's aircraft complement, which in recent weeks had fallen to a dangerously low level, it also meant that II/JG 3 could not expect to reequip with the new type for some time.

16 July 1942 was very humid with occasional thunderstorms[430]. An entire series of missions was flown on this day, resulting in a total of five victories. Losses were limited to one Messerschmitt which ran out of fuel and made a belly landing, and another machine which was slightly damaged following undercarriage failure at Millerovo. In neither case was the pilot injured. In the days that followed, the number of missions flown was limited by inclement, rainy weather. Whenever possible, the Messerschmitts of II/JG 3 were in the air over the battle zone along the Kalitva between Forschstadt and Morozovski. Two victories were scored on 17 July and one more on the 19th, while the missions of 20 July resulted in another five victories. That same day 5 *Staffel* mourned the death of one of its pilots: while taking off, Uffz. Horst Opalke crashed into a parked Ju 52. Both machines went up in flames and Uffz. Opalke, trapped in his cockpit, burned to death[431].

On 21 July 1942 it was time for the *Gruppen* of JG 3 to move again. Because of the army's continued rapid advance, II/JG 3 and the rest of the *Geschwader* were moved up to Novy-Cholan south of Tazinskaya[432]. The now familiar course of events was repeated, with a small detachment of key technical personnel being loaded aboard Ju 52s together with the most necessary equipment, ammunition and fuel and sent to the new base of operations, while the main transport column set out by road. Meanwhile, the air element had already flown ahead. The weather was again hot and dry as the air element flew top cover over the German armored spearheads and the Don bridges near Konstantinovskaya in the 4th Panzer Army's area of front. Four victories were claimed on this day without loss. During the missions from Novy-Cholan, individual *Schwärme* operated from the airfields of Morozovskaya[433] and Nikolayevska, which were nearer to the front. On 22 July II/JG 3 was again ordered to guard the Don crossings and conduct fighter sweeps. A total of seven victories was scored on this day, including four by Lt. Kirschner of 5 *Staffel* (15-18). The *Gruppe* recorded one loss: Fw. Ernst Pöske of 5/JG 3, one of the *Gruppe*'s most experienced pilots with 14 victories, was shot down in combat southeast of Melikhovskaya on the Don[434] and listed missing.

In the days that followed, II/JG 3's efforts were concentrated over the Don crossings. It also flew an increasing number of missions over the Kalach area[435], situated approximately 75 kilometers west of Stalingrad on the Don, where since 24 July German forces had been waging a battle of encirclement with the objective of breaching the first defense line in front of Stalingrad[436]. During the period from 23 to 27 July 1942, the *Gruppe* claimed a total of 56 victories during its missions over the area west of Kalach. The lion's share of these successes went to the "*Experten*," with Hptm. Brändle claiming ten, Fw. Münster nine, Lt. Ettel six and Lt. Kirschner, Fw. Lucas, Uffz. Ebener and Uffz. Schwaiger four each. The Il-2 close-support aircraft was appearing over the front in ever greater numbers, and the type figures prominently in II/JG 3's victory list at this time. These heavily-armored close-support aircraft, which usually came in small formations at very low altitude, were becoming a real problem, both for the ground troops who had to face their determined attacks, and for the fighter pilots, who were discovering that it was extremely difficult to shoot these machines down. The main reason for this was the inadequate armament of the Bf 109 F-4. The two rifle-caliber MG 17 machine-guns mounted above the engine were almost completely ineffective against the Il-2, and in many cases even strikes by shells from the engine-mounted 20-mm cannon had little effect. Only a few areas of the Il-2 were vulnerable to gunfire, in particular the oil cooler located beneath the fuselage[437]. Compared to its successes, the *Gruppe*'s losses in these days were extremely light, amounting to two machines damaged in air combat. There were no pilot casualties[438].

On the evening of 27 July 1942 the *Gruppen* of JG 3 received orders to move again; the *Geschwader* was to go to Frolov to continue supporting the units of the 6th Army advancing on Stalingrad. The new base of operations was located approximately 100 kilometers northwest of Stalingrad on the Archeda River[439]. On the evening of the same day the air elements landed at their new base after completing the last missions of the day[440]. The next day, 28 July 1942, they were to fly missions over the Kalach area from there. Frolov airfield had only recently been evacuated by the Russians and had been thoroughly mined and booby-trapped prior to their departure. Consequently, at first movement was limited to cleared and marked pathways[441].

Meanwhile the German advance toward Stalingrad had come to a halt. On 26 July strong forces of Army Group A had broken out of their bridgehead on the east bank of the Don and headed for the Caucasus, an advance that would require them to cover great distances, and consequently the fuel earmarked for the 6th Army was redirected to the Caucasus. As a result of this the bulk of the 6th Army's motorized units were stranded in the Don steppe for two weeks and the opportunity for a rapid advance on Stalingrad was squandered. The Russians took advantage of this unexpected breathing period and established a heavily-fortified bridgehead on the northwest bank of the Don near Kalach, blocking the most important Don crossings[442]. In the days that followed, there was heavy fighting in the area of the front before Kalach;, and both sides were very active in the air over this battle zone.

In the period from 28 to 31 July 1942, during its missions over the Kalach area II/JG 3 was able to score another 28 victories with no pilot losses and just one Messerschmitt damaged in air combat. On the last day of the month I/JG 53 arrived at Frolov, from where it was to support the *Gruppen* of JG 3 in their missions over the Stalingrad area. For this purpose it was placed under the *Geschwader*'s operational command[443]. On this day there were two changes in II/JG 3 at the command level: Oblt. Albrecht Walz handed command of 4 *Staffel* over to Hptm. Gerhard Wendt, who had been flying with the *Staffel* since the beginning of July 1942 for familiarization purposes. Wendt went to the *Gruppenstab*[444], where he took over the position of Lt. Hans Fuß, who in turn relieved Oblt. Waldhelm as *Staffelführer* of 6/JG 3[445]. Hans Fuß was one of the *Gruppe*'s most successful young pilots and already had 62 victories to his credit.

The picture was essentially the same in the early days of August 1942: from Frolov the *Gruppe* flew numerous *Schwarm*- and *Rotte*-strength missions over the Kalach area. The weather was fine, and there were frequent fierce air battles with Russian bombers and close-support aircraft, which appeared in ever greater numbers. II/JG 3 recorded a total of 27 victories between 1 and 6 August 1942, twelve of them on a single day, 6 August. These successes were offset by the loss of one pilot missing and one injured. On 1 August the aircraft of Uffz. Wolfgang Vogel of 6 *Staffel* developed a problem with its cooling system; he subsequently made a forced landing in enemy territory near Surovkino east of Oblivskaya and was posted missing. Obfw. Maximilian Seidler, also of 6/JG 3. Forced to come down behind the Russian lines after suffering engine failure during a free chase mission over armored spearheads in the Kalach area. Seidler sustained serious injuries in the forced landing. Before Soviet soldiers could reach the scene, however, a German armored patrol rescued him and took him to safety[446].

On 7 August 1942 the units of the German 6th Army attacked the Soviet blocking position in front of Kalach, in order to force a crossing of the river and open the road to Stalingrad. After fierce fighting, on the following day they succeeded in encircling elements of the Soviet 62nd Army still west of the Don. This was to be the last successful battle of encirclement carried out by German forces during the war in the east, however it would be several days before the last scattered remains of the shattered Russian army were wiped out and bridgeheads could be established on the far bank of the Don[447]. Meanwhile, farther west strong forces of the 4th Panzer Army had already crossed the Don and were advancing on Stalingrad from the south[478].

During this time II/JG 3 continued flying over the combat zone around Kalach; as well as free chases, these also included many low-level attacks in support of the advancing army troops. Missions were also flown in support of the spearheads of the 4th Panzer Army advancing toward Stalingrad from Aksai in the south[449]. By 10 August the *Gruppe* had scored an additional 37 victories, 23 of them on 7 August. Lt. Fuß claimed six victories on that day (63-68), while Hptm. Brändle recorded five (85-89). The *Gruppe* suffered no personnel losses in this period. Three Messerschmitts sustained varying degrees of damage, but only in case was this due to enemy action.

The *Gruppe*'s next move began on the afternoon of 10 August; its destination was Tuzov, a forward airfield in the large bend in the Don southwest of Kalach on the Liska[450]. This airfield was nothing more than a flat, treeless section of Don steppe surrounded by deep ravines produced by erosion, so-called "*balkas.*" There were no permanent structures or hangars and the pilots and ground personnel were forced to live in tents erected over slit trenches. In addition to all of JG 3, from 12 August Tuzov was also home to I/JG 53[451]. The blazing sun had completely dried out the airfield surface, and the Messerschmitts raised huge clouds of dust when they took off[452]. Supplies of fuel and ammunition were irregular and for the most part had to be flown in by Ju 52s[453]. In the early days at Tuzov, the missions assigned the *Gruppen* of JG 3 were unchanged: free chases over the battle zone around Kalach and south of Stalingrad[497] plus escort missions in support of Stukas and conventional bombers. Both sides would be very active in the air in the weeks that followed. The Russians sent unprecedented numbers of aircraft to the front, including growing numbers of modern machines such as the LaGG-3 and MiG-3, Boston and Pe-2 bombers and the ever-present Il-2. I-153s and I-16s also saw action there, but their numbers steadily dwindled.

The missions of 11 August 1942 brought II/JG 3 just two victories. The *Gruppe* once again escaped without loss, however one machine was damaged in a forced landing caused by engine failure. Early the next morning, on 12 August, a strong force of Il-2s with fighter escort attempted a low-level attack on Tuzov airfield in an effort to eliminate the German fighters known to be operating from there[455]. Before it could reach its target, however, the Russian formation was engaged by elements of I/JG 53, which were able to radio a warning back to base. As a result of this, at about 4:30 PM every serviceable Messerschmitt scrambled from Tuzov and en-

gaged the Il-2s in a long running fight. When the action was over, I/JG 53 claimed no less than 28 victories[456]. Four more were credited to I/JG 3[457], while the elements of III/JG 3 which took part in the engagement claimed two Il-2s. II/JG 3 came up empty-handed on this day.

II/JG 3 once again saw action over the area around Stalingrad on 13 August 1942, and beginning on this day the free chases were extended to east of the city, where the Russians were operating a series of airfields[458]. Once again, however, the *Gruppe*'s missions failed to produce any tangible result. In the evening another large formation of Il-2s, again with strong fighter escort, was detected heading for Tuzov airfield. The events of the previous day were repeated, for in spite of the impressive number of escorting fighters this formation, too, was badly mauled. The German fighters which took part in the interception claimed at least 33 victories, however II/JG 3 again played no part[459].

The following days were oppressively hot[460] and relatively quiet. There was a noticeable drop in the number of missions flown, and once again the *Gruppe* reported neither successes nor losses. On 15 August the units of the 6th Army launched an attack against the Russian forces still holding out on the west bank of the Don in the large northeast loop of the river north of Kalach. The purpose of the attack was to win bridgeheads on the east bank of the river from which to launch the assault on Stalingrad. The German attack gained ground in the face of fierce resistance. Bridging of the river began the next day, and the first bridgeheads were established on the east bank[461]. For II/JG 3 the result was a shift in emphasis: *Rotte-* or *Schwarm*-strength formations of Messerschmitts were kept in the air over the bridging sites all day to protect them against expected attacks by Russian bombers and close-support aircraft[462]. In the process, the pilots of II/JG 3 scored one victory on the 16th and four more on 17 August, in both cases without loss.

In spite of periods of poor weather with low cloud and frequent rain showers[463], in the days that followed, the Messerschmitts of II/JG 3 were again active over the Don crossings north of Kalach. A total of 25 victories were scored there by 22 August, eight on the 19th and seven more on the 20th. The top scorer during this period was Fw. Lucas of 4 *Staffel*, who scored seven victories to raise his total to 53. The *Gruppe* suffered just one casualty: on 18 August Uffz. Egon Spinner of 6/JG 3 was forced to abandon his aircraft near Ossino-Logovski after its engine caught fire. He struck the tailplane while bailing out and sustained minor injuries. One Messerschmitt was written off in a crash and three more sustained moderate damage. During the day orders arrived for the *Gruppe* to be withdrawn from action and sent back to Germany to reequip on the Bf 109 G[464].

On the morning of 23 August 1942 the 6th Army launched its attack from the Don bridgehead near Vertyachiy. Strong motorized forces set out for Rynok, the northern suburb of Stalingrad, and in the late afternoon reached the Volga there[465]. The attack was supported from the air by the Stuka and fighter *Gruppen* of VIII *Fliegerkorps*. For II/JG 3, the first day of the attack by the 6th Army was a day of hectic action, with pilots flying four or more sorties; it also brought a temporary end to missions over the combat zone in the approaches to Stalingrad. After several free chase missions over the breakthrough area east of the Don, in the evening all available aircraft were employed to escort large bomber formations attacking targets inside Stalingrad. This was the first mass attack on the city, however it was carried out with no interference from Russian fighters[466]. A total of nine victories was claimed at the end of the day, while losses were limited to one machine damaged in a takeoff

accident at Tuzov. During the day, news was received that Lt. Hans Fuß was to receive the Knight's Cross in recognition of his 70 victories; four days later, on 27 August 1942, it was announced that Hptm. Kurt Brändle had been awarded the Oak Leaves[467].

II/JG 3's part in the German summer offensive came to a temporary end. After handing its 22 remaining serviceable machines[468] to the other two *Gruppen* of the *Geschwader*, the *Gruppe* moved to Königsberg-Neuhausen, where, in the next three weeks, it was to rest and reequip on the new Bf 109 G-2. The first seven brand-new aircraft were received in August, and these were followed by 34 more in the first days of September. The pilots converted to their

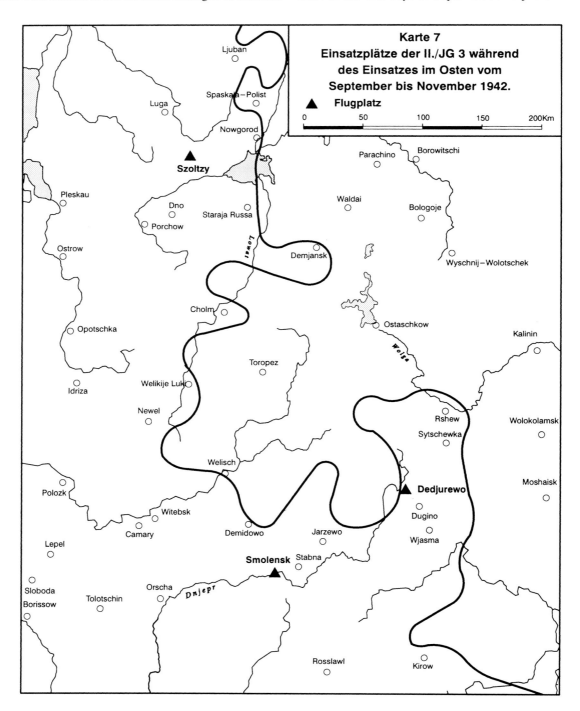

Karte 7
Einsatzplätze der II./JG 3 während des Einsatzes im Osten vom September bis November 1942.
▲ Flugplatz

new machines without problems, and the *Gruppe* was soon operational again. The break in operations also saw a change in the command of 5 *Staffel*: after two years of service at the front, Oblt. Moldenhauer was transferred to the headquarters of a *Jagddivision* (fighter division)[469]. His designated successor was Lt. Joachim Kirschner, who, with 34 victories, was one of the *Gruppe*'s most promising young officers[470].

The brief period of conversion training ended on 9 September 1942 with the receipt of an order for II/JG 3 to immediately transfer to Smolensk in the central sector of the Eastern Front, where the *Gruppe* was to be placed under the operational command of JG 51. An advance detachment of technical personnel left at once in three Ju 52s, which had been assigned specifically for that purpose. The air elements was to follow as soon as possible; the order read: *"All operational aircraft to Smolensk-North immediately, the rest as soon as ready. Next stage of flight 11/9"*[471]. However, the next day when the advance detachment arrived at Smolensk, waiting there was another order which cancelled the move to Smolensk and directed II/JG 3 to Dedyurevo, a front-line airfield approximately 25 kilometers southwest of Sychevka[472,473]. Consequently, the machines of the *Gruppenstab* and two *Staffeln* which arrived at Smolensk soon after the advance detachment were immediately sent on to Dedyurevo. By 12 September the entire *Gruppe* was assembled there[474]. II/JG 3 was then subordinated to *Lw.-Kdo. Ost*[475] for subsequent operations; initially, its area of operations was the area around Rzhev and Sychevka as far as Vyazma, which corresponded to the left wing of Army Group Center and the boundary with Army Group North's front[476].

In August 1942 the Russians had successfully relieved some of the pressure on their hard-pressed armies in the south by launching local assaults against various parts of Army Group North's front. Then, at the beginning of September, the fighting on the ground largely died down[477], however the Russians remained very active in the air over the front and the German rear. As a result, the German fighters based in that area (II/JG 3 plus the *Gruppen* of JG 51[478]) were instructed to fly free chases and fighter cover missions over the German main line of resistance plus occasional escort missions for bomber and Stuka units[479].

II/JG 3 resumed operations on 13 September 1942. On this day the *Gruppe* recorded six victories, all in an early morning engagement with a formation of bombers with fighter escort. The next day, 14 September, saw three more victories scored, however the *Gruppe* suffered a heavy loss: during a late afternoon fighter sweep Lt. Hans Fuß of 6/JG 3 shot down a Yak-1 for his 71st victory, after which his own machine was hit. The fuel tank was damaged, as a result of which the machine's engine stopped as Fuß was on approach to land at Dedyurevo. The aircraft immediately stalled, crashed and overturned several times, seriously injuring the pilot. Hans Fuß received medical treatment, however following an operation he developed gangrene and died eight weeks later in a hospital in Berlin[480].

II/JG 3 continued to score steadily during the second half of the month; it recorded a total of 39 victories between 15 and 30 September, including twelve on the 15th and nine more on the 23rd. Losses were held within strict limits, with one machine shot down and another damaged by ground fire. At the end of the month, Oblt. Paul Stolte took over the position of *Staffelkapitän* of 6/JG 3, left vacant after the crash in which Lt. Fuß was injured. Stolte had most recently commanded 3/JG 1 and had four victories to his credit, all scored in the west[481].

On 27 September II/JG 3 moved from Dedyurevo to Šolzy[482], an air base approximately 40 kilometers west of Lake Ilmen from which III/JG 3 had operated for several weeks at the beginning of the year[483]. Formerly a Soviet air force base, Šolzy was generously laid out, however the war had taken its toll and its permanent buildings and much of the nearby village had been destroyed and burnt out. From now on the *Gruppe*'s area of operations was to be the area around Lake Ilmen and surrounding Demyansk and Staraya Russa, where, since the second half of September, the German defense positions had been subjected to increasingly heavy Russian attacks, and where, since 27 September, a limited German counterattack had been under way with the objective of widening the land bridge south to Demyansk[484].

There is little to report about II/JG 3's missions in the weeks that followed[485]. The weather at the start of the month was mainly dry, although already very cool. The *Gruppe* scored a total of 16 victories without loss in its missions over the Demyansk battle zone and up to the Lovat between 4 and 7 October 1942. This was followed by a period of bad weather with steady rain, which more or less halted operations for several days. Things quieted down on the ground too, apart from isolated local clashes. Whenever the autumn weather permitted, II/JG 3 flew free chase missions over the area on both sides of Lake Ilmen, and by the end of the month it recorded 29 more victories. With just three Messerschmitts damaged, only one of them due to enemy action, losses remained extremely light. On the last day of the month the *Staffelkapitän* of 6/JG 3, Oblt. Paul Stolte, was injured slightly: after returning from a mission, while taxiing at Šolzy his machine rolled into a pothole and overturned. Fortunately, his injuries were such that they could be treated in the unit dispensary[486].

November 1942 saw II/JG 3 continue to operate over the battle zone on both sides of Lake Ilmen from Šolzy. By now winter had begun, the last rains having turned to snow. On most days the weather was poor with low cloud and restricted visibility, and consequently operational activity was very limited. On the ground, too, things remained quiet at first[487]. II/JG 3 recorded a total of ten victories during the month, three of them by Oblt. Werner Lucas, who had since been promoted to the officer ranks in recognition of his success in combat and become leader of 4 *Staffel* in place of Hptm. Gerhard Wendt, who was transferred to a staff position[488]. The

Gruppe's stay at _olzy ended on or about 25 November, when it was ordered to Smolensk[489]. On the ground, at the beginning of December the Russians began a series of attacks, some of them heavy, in the area south of Lake Ilmen. These were heavily supported by close-support units, and, while flying from Smolensk, on 3 December 1942 II/JG 3 shot down six enemy aircraft, including four Il-2s.

Meanwhile, the situation in the southern part of the Eastern Front had changed dramatically. By October at the latest, the German attack in the Stalingrad area had bogged down, and in the Caucasus the advance by Army Group A had ground to a halt. Against the bitter, at times self-sacrificial resistance of the Russian troops the Germans failed to achieve even one of the significant objectives of their summer offensive. In view of this state of affairs Stalingrad had lost all significance as a strategic position, for the last military-economic factor, namely halting shipping traffic on the Volga, lost its importance as ice in the river tied up traffic more effectively than the German armies ever could have[490]. But instead of pulling back the German forces deep in the Caucasus and on the Volga and drastically shortening his overextended lines in preparation for a second winter in Russia[491], Hitler ordered the battle for Stalingrad to go on until the entire city was in German hands. More and more, the struggle became a bloody slaughter with irrational motivations rather than a battle fought for conventional military reasons, in which whole battalions and regiments were recklessly and thoughtlessly sacrificed in order to take from the enemy the rubble of a single block of houses[492].

Meanwhile, on 18 November 1942, the forces of the 6th Army in Stalingrad had launched a final assault against the Russian forces holding on in the northern part of the city in hope of forcing a decision. The German assault troops succeeded in capturing more rubble in the area of the much fought over "*Barrikadi*" and "*Dzherzhinski*" factories, however this success was overshadowed by a Soviet offensive. On 19 November two Russian armies advanced out of the Don bridgeheads near Serafimovich and Kletskaya, achieving deep penetrations into the front held by the Romanian 3rd Army. On the following day the Red Army launched another attack south of Stalingrad and quickly achieved deep penetrations against the Romanian 4th Army. With the rapid collapse of the Romanian defense front, this Russian offensive posed a deadly threat to the German forces to the southeast, namely the elements of the 6th Army deployed in the area around Stalingrad[493].

In the face of the completely new situation created by the Russian attack north of Stalingrad, the German attack on the city was broken off. On 20 November 1942 the *Jagdgruppen* at Pitomnik, a front-line airfield 15 kilometers west of Stalingrad, received orders to put every available machine into the air to escort German bombers providing support to army troops withdrawing into the great bend of the Don. This order proved impossible to carry out, however, because bad weather halted all flying from Pitomnik. On the

following day, 21 November, orders were received from *VIII Fliegerkorps* for the *Stab* and I/JG 3 to remain inside the pocket then forming, while III/JG 3 was to proceed at once to Oblivskaya, a front-line airfield 150 kilometers west of Stalingrad, outside the pocket[494]. The next day, 22 November 1942, the Russian tank spearheads met near Kalach on the Don and completed the encirclement of the German and Romanian forces to the east. Twenty-two German and allied divisions with approximately 235,000 men, including the bulk of the 6th Army and elements of the 4th Panzer Army, had been cut off.

Following these dramatic developments at Stalingrad, on 7 December 1942 II/JG 3 received orders to immediately transfer to the Stalingrad area and rejoin the rest of the *Geschwader* there. The move, which was begun with a total of 35 machines, got under way on the following day. Because of bad weather, the transfer flight was not completed until 12 December. The *Gruppe* made a number of en route stops in which several Messerschmitts were damaged on account of poor weather and airfield conditions and had to be left behind. The rest of the air element arrived at Morozovskaya, a spacious airfield approximately 120 kilometers southeast of Millerovo[495]. From this airfield the *Gruppen* of JG 3 were to provide fighter escort for the air transports supplying "Fortress Stalingrad." For meanwhile, contrary to all military reason and ignoring all of the more or less clearly stated arguments by the leading officers on the scene, Hitler had ordered the 6th Army to adopt an all-round defensive posture on the Volga, hold the pocket and await further developments. One of the main reasons behind this order was Göring's promise that the *Luftwaffe* could supply the trapped 6th Army, with its approximately 235,000 German and allied troops, from the air. This promise was in reality impossible to keep and it contributed significantly to the ultimate demise of the 6th Army. Göring vastly overestimated his own possibilities[496], untroubled by any expert knowledge, and refused to listen to his commanders on the scene, *Generaloberst* von Richthofen, the commander in chief of *Luftflotte 4*[497], and *General* Fiebig, the commanding general of *VIII Fliegerkorps*, who advised him that supplying the 6th Army by air was totally impossible.

After this, the principle role of the *Gruppen* of JG 3 was fighter escort for the Ju 52 and He 111 units flying to Stalingrad; since the range of the Messerschmitts was insufficient to escort the slow transports there and back, in each case they had to land at Pitomnik and refuel[498]. The Messerschmitts then escorted the transports on the return flight, when they flew wounded out of the pocket. Rendezvous point, route of flight and altitude had to be changed daily, for the Russians soon stationed large numbers of anti-aircraft guns along the main approach corridor and also deployed numerous fighters in an attempt to seal off the air bridge. As well, an airfield defense *Staffel* was formed at Pitomnik, made up of volunteers from all three *Gruppen* of JG 3; its role was to clear the airspace over Pitomnik of enemy aircraft in order to protect the transport units

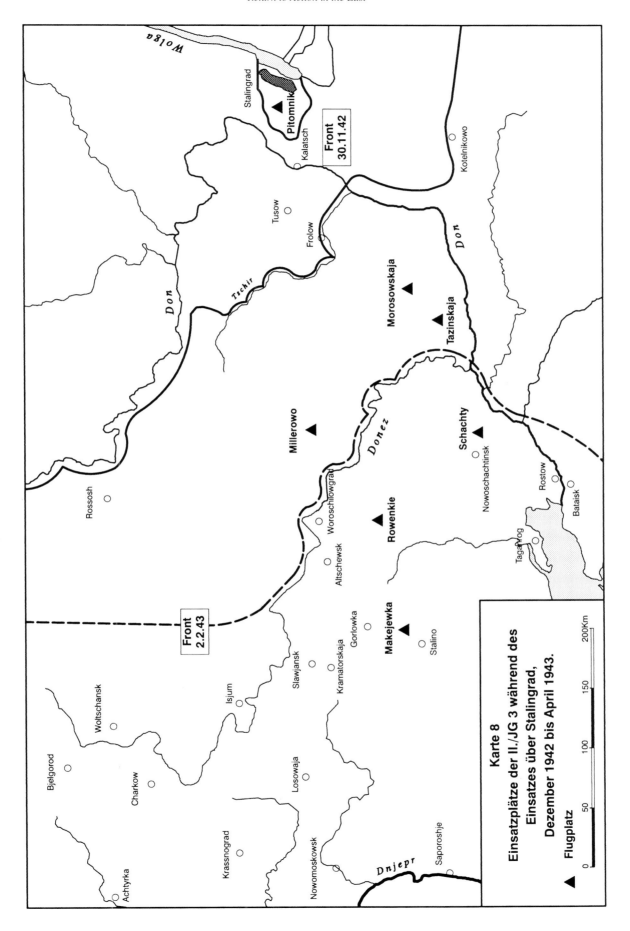

Karte 8
Einsatzplätze der II./JG 3 während des
Einsatzes über Stalingrad,
Dezember 1942 bis April 1943.

▲ Flugplatz

during takeoff and landing. Most of the *Staffel*'s pilots came from I and II/JG 3, and they were relieved after a few days and their places taken by other pilots who had flown into the pocket. In the following weeks, at least eleven pilots of II *Gruppe* served with the airfield defense *Staffel*, namely Oblt. Lucas, Lt. Frielinghaus, Obfw. Dilling, Fw. Ebener, Fw. Eyrich, Fw. Frese, Fw. Grünberg, Fw. Traphan, Uffz. Pissarski, Uffz. Bringmann and Uffz. May. Most of the *Staffel*'s ground personnel also came from I and II/JG 3. Working under the most primitive conditions, with totally inadequate equipment, no shelter from the icy cold and the most meager rations, this detachment saw to it that the few Messerschmitts at Pitomnik were kept airworthy[499].

On the same day that the air element of II/JG 3 arrived at Morozovskaya, armored forces of the LVII Panzer Corps under General Hoth launched an attack from the Kotelnikovo area aimed at relieving the 6th Army trapped at Stalingrad. Resistance was light at first and the attack quickly gained ground, taking the leading units to within 50 kilometers of the Russian ring around Stalingrad[500]. Beginning on this day the *Gruppen* of JG 3 were given another task, that of providing fighter cover over Army Group Hoth's attack area south of Stalingrad. On 13 December, in at best mediocre weather, II/JG 3 flew its first missions from Morozovskaya, all of which were uneventful. For the next two days bad weather put an end to all flying[501].

On 16 December 1942 three Russian armies launched another major attack, this time on the middle Don against the sector held by the Italian 8th Army; the poorly-equipped Italians offered little resistance and the Soviet troops quickly achieved a breakthrough. This posed another deadly threat to the south of the German eastern front, for the Russian drive was aimed at Rostov and threatened to cut off two entire army groups with approximately one and a half million men. Desperately, the German and Romanian troops of Army Group Hollidt, which was deployed to the east of the Russian attack area, tried to halt the advance of the Soviet armies. While this was going on, the leading elements of Army Group Hoth continued to fight their way toward Stalingrad against stiffening Soviet resistance, and on 22 December they got to within 48 kilometers of the pocket's southwest front. But then on the 23rd, the catastrophic developments in the area of front before Morozovskaya forced the abandonment of the relief attack and the redeployment of some of its forces to the battle zone at the Chir. After the commander in chief of the 6th Army, *Generaloberst* Paulus, was unable to bring himself to order his army to break out to the south, all hope of relieving the 6th Army in Stalingrad was gone. Instead, by this point at the latest, it had become an irreversible fact that the 6th Army had been written off. Nevertheless, it received orders to continue the hopeless battle to the end to occupy the Russian forces manning the encirclement front and prevent them from joining the Red Army's advance on Rostov aimed at trapping Army Groups A and Don[502].

During these crisis-filled and fateful days II/JG 3 continued to fly missions from Morozovskaya over the battle zone in the approaches to Stalingrad and at the Chir. Around the middle of the month there was a break in the weather which allowed a clear upswing in operational activity, and the *Gruppe* flew its first escort mission over the pocket on 16 December 1942. Several pilots, including Fw. Ebener of 4/JG 3, remained behind with the airfield defense *Staffel* at Pitomnik and in the days that followed flew missions from there[503]. II/JG 3 scored a total of 39 victories between 16 and 26 December; 13 of these were credited to Fw. Ebener in missions from Pitomnik over the Stalingrad pocket. In addition, many vehicles were destroyed in strafing attacks. Losses during the same period totaled two pilots wounded and one injured plus three Messerschmitts written off and three damaged. On 17 December Uffz. Wolfgang Buttstädt of 4/JG 3 was shot down by flak north of the Pitomnik airfield; slightly wounded, he was forced to bail out[504]. Four days later, on 21 December, the *Staffelkapitän* of 4/JG 3, Oblt. Lucas, was shot down while engaging a formation of Bostons north of Morozovskaya. Though slightly wounded, Lucas was able to parachute to safety[505]. The effort to supply Stalingrad from the air reached its apex at this time; 289 tons were delivered on 19 December and 291 tons the following day, the highest totals reached during the entire effort to supply the encircled city[506].

Meanwhile, on the ground the situation on the front along the Chir had deteriorated further. From the east, Russian troops had moved to within about 30 kilometers of Morozovskaya. On 27 December isolated groups of enemy soldiers were able to fight their way through the thin defense lines to a point near the airfield. There they were beaten back by an ad hoc force made up of men from the base flak and JG 3 ground personnel; two members of I/JG 3's ground personnel were wounded in this action. With II/JG 3's base of operations threatened, on 23 December an order was issued for the air element to temporarily move back to the Morozovskaya-South airfield[507]. At the same time, instructions were issued that, effective immediately, the pilots were to remain at the *Staffel* dispersals at all times so as to be able to get away from the airfield in the event of a sudden breakthrough by Russian tanks.

In the remaining days until year's end, II/JG 3 continued to fly missions over the battle zone south and west of Stalingrad and along the Chir; during the same period the handful of machines of the Pitomnik *Staffel* continued to operate over the pocket. A total of 19 victories were achieved between 27 and 31 December 1942, twelve of them over the pocket area, where Fw. Ebener accounted for four enemy aircraft in two missions on the 30th. Losses in this period amounted to one pilot missing: on 31 December Uffz. Fritz Köhler of 4 *Staffel* was shot down during low-level attacks in the Uryupin area and forced to bail out. A search for him was begun immediately, however he could not be found[508]. On the same day II/JG 3 reported a total of 17 Messerschmitts on strength, of which barely half were serviceable; the *Gruppe* had not received a single replacement aircraft during all of December.

The new year began with bad weather[509] which almost completely halted operations on 1 and 2 January 1943[510]. One day later, however, on 3 January, the continued advance of the Russian armored forces forced the *Gruppe* to immediately fall back. In spite of the continued bad weather, early in the morning every serviceable aircraft took off for Tazinskaya. The ground personnel followed soon afterwards after blowing up all of the bunkers on the airfield[511]. Only a few hours later, Russian tanks rolled past Morozovskaya airfield to Trofimenko, located approximately three kilometers west of Morozovskaya, and the next day occupied Morozovskaya. At Tazinskaya, the elements of JG 3 that had landed there were attached to *Fliegerdivision Donets*, an operational command consisting of the remnants of various bomber, Stuka, ground attack and fighter units, for further operations in support of the close-support units, while for subsequent escort missions in support of the Stalingrad airlift they remained under the command of *VIII Fliegerkorps*. The confusion in command relationships and operational conditions and the hopeless overtaxing of the badly battered units bore eloquent witness to the desperate state of the *Luftwaffe* in the south of the Eastern Front.

Little is known about II/JG 3's activities in the following days and weeks. After just two days at Tazinskaya, on 5 January 1943 what was left of the *Gruppe* moved again, to Shakhty, a forward airfield north of Rostov. Since this field was too far from Stalingrad for the limited range of the Messerschmitts, this move also brought an end to II *Gruppe*'s transport escort missions to Stalingrad. Meanwhile, the Airfield Defense *Staffel* remained at Pitomnik and continued flying missions over the pocket[512]. From Shakhty, the assembled remnants of II *Gruppe* and a detachment of III *Gruppe*, which was attached to II/JG 3 on 7 January, were required to fly defensive patrols, reconnaissance and free chase sorties over Army Group Hollidt's front, which had meanwhile fallen back to a line along the Donets north of Rostov. The narrow corridor north of Rostov was of decisive importance as an avenue of retreat for Army Group A, whose withdrawal had started at the beginning of the month. The army group's forces were now fighting their way west through ice and snow from the area of the Caucasus they had captured in summer. Against this relatively weakly defended sector, which was held by German and Romanian units, the Soviets now threw the bulk of two armies, whose tank spearheads reached a point about forty kilometers from Rostov on 7 January[513].

By 20 January 1943 II/JG 3 scored four victories without loss while flying from Shakhty. Meanwhile, at Pitomnik, the Airfield Defense Staffel shot down another 25 enemy aircraft before the airfield was overrun by Russian troops on 17 January. A total of six unserviceable Messerschmitts belonging to II *Gruppe* had to be left behind[514]. The pilots of the Pitomnik *Staffel* still inside the pocket made it to Gumrak under dramatic and chaotic conditions. They were flown out the next day and soon afterward rejoined their *Gruppe* in Shakhty. A *Schwarm* under Fw. Steinecke of 6 *Staffel*

was subsequently ordered to Svyerevo, where it was to provide fighter cover for the transport units still taking off for Stalingrad from there[515]. As well, several machines of II/JG 3 under the command of Oblt. Stolte and Fw. Förg plus several Bf 110 *Zerstörer* equipped with drop tanks were sent on long-range fighter missions to Stalingrad[516]. These efforts were nothing more than a desperate "showing of the flag" by the fighter arm, lacking any military purpose or effect.

At the end of January II/JG 3 was ordered to move again, from Shakhty to Rovenkie, a forward airfield about 50 kilometers south of Voroshilovgrad[517]. From there it was to intervene over the front of Army Group South, which was engaged in a fierce defensive struggle. The *Gruppe* was allocated a total of 46 Messerschmitts, allowing to reach its authorized strength, at least on paper[518]. The *Gruppe* remained at Rovenkie until 6 February 1943, when the continued Russian advance made it necessary to move the unit to Makeyevka, approximately 110 kilometers west of Rovenkie. During operations from Rovenkie II/JG 3 scored another 26 victories[519]. The *Gruppe* had no personnel casualties and equipment losses totaled one Messerschmitt shot down and two damaged. During the same period, however, a number of machines were damaged in accidents, some seriously, while one Messerschmitt was destroyed and two damaged in a Russian air raid on Rovenkie airfield on 5 February.

On 3 February 1943 the last fighting in the Stalingrad pocket came to an end; approximately 91,000 men, the remnants of the German 6th Army, were taken prisoner by the Russians[520,521]. This figure included those surviving members of the Pitomnik *Staffel*'s ground personnel who had not been flown out. Army Group A's retreat from the Caucasus was also almost over, the German divisions having succeeded in withdrawing west through the Rostov corridor and across the Strait of Kerch, avoiding total catastrophe for the German armies in the east. In mid-February 1943 the German armies were essentially back where they had been seven months earlier when they launched their great summer offensive. At this time, however, the German command was already planning a counter-offensive in the area of Army Group South; while its stated objective was to secure the industrial region around Stalino, its main purpose was to seize the initiative from the Red Army. The counteroffensive was to be carried out in three stages: first, the armored units of the 1st Guards Army, which had driven southwest in a narrow wedge, were to be cut off and the Soviet forces driven back toward the Donets. Afterwards, strong Soviet groupings in the Kharkov area were to be encircled and destroyed, and, finally, in conjunction with the 2nd Panzer Army, part of Army Group Center, the Russian salient west of Kursk was to be pinched off[522]. The first stage of the operation was scheduled to begin on 19 February 1943.

Periods of bad weather and very low cloud at first prevented II/JG 3 from flying more than a few missions from Makeyevka. During the period until 20 February the *Gruppe* claimed 20 enemy aircraft shot down, while suffering losses of one pilot killed and one slightly wounded plus three Messerschmitts written off and three more damaged as a result of enemy action. During a free chase mission in the Novocherkassk area on 10 February, Uffz. Willi Schick of 6/JG 3 was shot down in combat with La-5s and MiG-1s. He was subsequently reported missing. On the same day, Uffz. Günther Mohn of 5 *Staffel* was wounded in air combat over Slavyansk after shooting down a Boston, however he managed to return safely to Makeyevka[523].

At first II/JG 3 was not involved in the operations associated with the counter-offensive south and southwest of Kharkov, which began on 19 February 1943[524]. Instead, it was ordered to continue flying missions in support of the front along the Mius north of Taganrog. In the days after 20 February, that area was the scene of several fierce air battles against large numbers of Russian close-support aircraft and bombers and their fighter escort. II/JG 3 claimed a total of eleven victories on 22 February, including three each by Oblt. Kirschner, *Kapitän* of 5 *Staffel*, (54-56) and Fw. Steinecke of 6/JG 3 (10-12). One pilot was listed missing: Uffz. Heinrich May of 6 *Staffel*, an experienced and successful pilot with 18 victories to his credit, failed to return from a free chase mission following air combat over the area of Matveyev-Kurgan. In the days that followed, the *Gruppe* was involved in missions over the battle zone around Slavyansk, where units of the 1st and 4th Panzer Armies were advancing north to cut off and destroy the armored group of the Soviet 1st Guards Army, which had advanced far to the west. For II/JG 3, the following days brought a large number of free chase and bomber escort missions, but also low-level attack sorties against Russian march columns and troop concentrations in the area on either side of Slavyansk. The *Gruppe* scored a further eight victories by the end of the month without loss.

Meanwhile, the attack groups of the 4th Panzer Army had successfully concluded the first part of the counterattack and by the end of February had reached the line Barvenkovo—Lozovaya, averting the danger of a Soviet advance to the Dniepr. They were subsequently instructed to advance farther towards the upper Donets and then turn towards Kharkov. There was heavy fighting in the first days of March, especially in the Krasnograd area, in the course of which the Russian forces were driven back to the east and northeast in spite of stubborn resistance[525]. Despite periods of very bad weather, at this time II/JG 3 continued to operate over the front at the Donets and the Mius. As before, it was called upon to fly numerous low-level attack sorties in support of the army, plus free chase and reconnaissance missions. During the first four days of March 1943 the *Gruppe* was able to record just one victory, however in the same period it suffered no losses.

The second part of the German counter-offensive, whose objective was the recapture of Kharkov, began on 5 March 1943. On the ground, the focus of operations shifted farther north, however

II/JG 3 remained at Makeyevka to provide fighter cover over the Mius and Donets fronts[526]. As well, at various times parts of the air element were attached to III/JG 3. The latter unit was stationed at Pavlograd, from where it intervened in the fighting in the area around Kharkov and to the east[527]. In the following two weeks there was heavy fighting, which reached its climax on 16 March with the recapture of Kharkov by German forces. In the days that followed, the units of Army Group South were able to continue their advance to the north and east. On 18 March 1943 they took Belgorod, before the attack bogged down in the Oboyan area[528]. During its missions in support of army units along the Mius front and in the Kharkov area, by 20 March II/JG 3 scored a total of 65 victories without loss to itself. The most successful pilots in this period were Lt. Ettel with 15 victories, Fw. Dilling with 10, Oblt. Kirschner with six and Fw. Münster with five.

Beginning on 20 March 1943, the focus of II/JG 3's activities shifted to the southeast sector of the front in the area of the mouth of the Don. Together with the air element of III/JG 3, which flew from Pavlograd to Makeyevka each morning, flew its missions from there and then returned to its own airfield in the late afternoon[529], II/JG 3 flew escort missions in support of bomber and Stuka units attacking important Soviet rail junctions in the Rostov—Bataisk—Voroshilovgrad area. The *Gruppe* also flew free chase sorties over the same area. A total of 43 victories was scored between 21 and 27 March. Losses remained low, with one pilot slightly wounded and another injured in an accident. Both casualties occurred on 25 March. During a free chase mission over the Bataisk area, Oblt. Paul Stolte shot down an La-5. His own machine was hit immediately afterwards, however he was able to reach Makeyevka and land safely. After receiving treatment in the *Gruppe*'s medical dispensary, Paul Stolte was sent home for a complete recovery. Oblt. Gustav Frielinghaus assumed temporary command of 6/JG 3 in his place. Uffz. Günther Mohn of 5/JG 3 was injured while the alert *Rotte* was taxiing to position on Makeyevka airfield; his machine was rammed by a passing Bf 110 of 1/ZG 1 and heavily damaged.

On 28 March there was a brief interruption in the series of missions over the southern area, for on this day II/JG 3 was called upon to fly several free chase and bomber escort missions over the area east of Kharkov. Parts of the air element subsequently landed at Kharkov, but immediately afterwards flew back to Makeyevka. A total of three victories was scored, all by Lt. Wolf Ettel of 4/JG 3 (62-64). There were no losses. It appears that in the days that followed, II/JG 3 was again employed to escort bombers into the Bataisk area, and another 13 victories were recorded by 2 April 1943. At the end of April at Makeyevka, the *Gruppe* reported 40 Messerschmitts on strength, of which 25 were serviceable. Among these were six Bf 109 G-4s, the *Gruppe* having received the first seven of this type during the month[530]. Where flying personnel were concerned, the *Gruppe* was actually above its authorized strength,

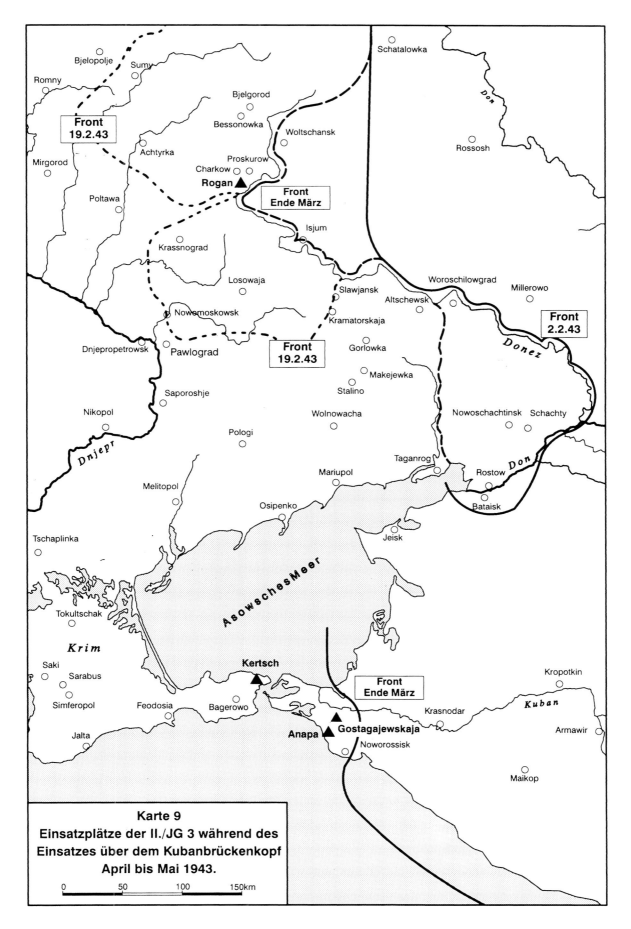

Front
19.2.43

Bjelopolje
Sumy
Romny
Bjelgorod
Bessonowka
Woltschansk
Schatalowka
Don
Rossosh
Achtyrka
Proskurow
Mirgorod
Charkow
Rogan ▲
Front
Ende März
Poltawa
Isjum
Krassnograd
Woroschilowgrad
Millerowo
Losowaja
Slawjansk
Altschewsk
Front
2.2.43
Nowomoskowsk
Kramatorskaja
Donez
Front
19.2.43
Gorlowka
Dnjepropetrowsk
Pawlograd
Makejewka
Stalino
Saporoshje
Nowoschachtinsk
Schachty
Nikopol
Wolnowacha
Dnjepr
Pologi
Taganrog
Mariupol
Rostow
Don
Melitopol
Bataisk
Osipenko
Jeisk
Tschaplinka
AsowschesMeer
Tokultschak
Krim
Saki
Kertsch ▲
Kropotkin
Sarabus
Front
Ende März
Kuban
Simferopol
Feodosia
Bagerowo
Krasnodar
Armawir
Jalta
Anapa ▲ **Gostagajewskaja** ▲
Noworossisk
Maikop

Karte 9
Einsatzplätze der II./JG 3 während des
Einsatzes über dem Kubanbrückenkopf
April bis Mai 1943.

0   50   100   150km

with 47 pilots; however, only 36 of these were with the *Gruppe* and fit for duty, while the rest were in Germany on rest leave or in hospital recovering from wounds[531].

On 5 April 1943 the *Gruppe* moved again: by order of *IV Fliegerkorps*, II/JG 3 transferred to Kerch in the eastern part of the Crimean Peninsula with all its aircraft and the most necessary personnel and equipment. There it was attached to *I Fliegerkorps*, while operationally it came under the command of JG 52. Several days later the *Gruppe* moved from Kerch to Anapa, a front-line airfield on the south coast of the peninsula[532]. II/JG 3's operational tasks there were Stuka escort and free chase missions over the Krymskaya area and the northern sector of the Kuban bridgehead, which was still held by the 17th Army and against which the Soviets were directing powerful attacks[533]. On 10 April at Anapa the *Gruppe* was subjected to a low-level attack by a group of Il-2s; two members of the technical personnel were slightly wounded by gunfire. On the same day a *Schwarm* from 6/JG 3 scored the first victories over the new area of operations. During the next two weeks the *Gruppe* saw action over the battle zone along the front of the Kuban bridgehead and the Soviet ports on the south coast. This proved to be an extraordinarily successful "hunting period" for the *Gruppe*; by the end of the month it scored no less than 204 victories while its own losses—two pilots killed and two wounded plus two Messerschmitts shot down and two damaged[534]—were comparatively light[535]. Oblt. Joachim Kirschner of 5/JG 3 and Lt. Wolf Ettel were the top scorers with 38 and 35 victories respectively, followed by Fw. Hans Grünberg with 15, Oblt. Gustav Frielinghaus with 13 and Uffz. Franz Cech with 10. On the casualty list was Uffz. Hans Pabst of 4/JG 3, who on 18 April was shot down into the sea of Novorossisk in combat with P-39s and LaGG-3s and listed missing. The next day flak claimed two victims in the Novorossisk area: Uffz. Oskar Fischer of 5 *Staffel* and Fw. Rasso Förg of 6 *Staffel* were both wounded by fragments but were able to reach friendly territory, the former belly-landing his machine near Krymskaya and the latter landing safely at Anapa. On 21 April 5 *Staffel* reported Lt. Lothar Myrrhe missing after he became separated from his unit during an engagement over the Novorossisk area and subsequently failed to return. By that time Lothar Myrrhe had scored 19 victories and was one of the *Gruppe*'s most promising replacement pilots.

Meanwhile, the spring thaw and the resulting muddy period had brought the fighting to a virtual standstill in the area of front held by Army Group South. Both sides were exhausted after months of uninterrupted fighting. After the frightful losses it had suffered during the past winter, the *Wehrmacht* desperately needed this forced pause in the fighting to at least partly rest and reequip its units. Meanwhile, Hitler was finalizing his plans for a renewed summer offensive in the east[536]. Contrary to all military reason, and ignoring the two-front war which the Reich was waging and the resulting need to husband his forces, Hitler decided to go on the offensive in the summer of 1943. Nevertheless, he could not ignore the fact that

the *Wehrmacht* no longer possessed sufficient forces to conduct an offensive with long-range objectives as in the two previous years. The *Führer* did, however, reckon that they were sufficient for a limited offensive, with the objective of destroying as many Soviet forces as possible and restoring something resembling a balance of forces on the Eastern Front[538]. The winter battles had left behind two distinct salients, the eastwards-facing Orel salient in the area of Army Group Center, and next to it the westwards-facing Kursk salient, which contained strong forces of the Central and Voronezh Fronts[539]. The latter was chosen as the target of the planned operation, code-named *"Zitadelle"*. Units of the 9th Army were to attack from the north and those of the 4th Panzer Army from the south, a total of 33 divisions, including 16 panzer and panzer-grenadier divisions which had only just been brought back up to strength after the losses of the winter. The objective was to pinch off the salient and destroy the Soviet forces trapped inside. Because of the uncertain situation in the Mediterranean, where the last German-Italian units in Tunisia were forced to surrender on 9 May 1943, after which the German command feared a landing on the European mainland which would require the dispatch there of all available reserves, the start date for *"Zitadelle"* was postponed a number of times. As a result, after the end of the muddy period, there was no large-scale fighting in the east in May and June 1943[540].

In the first days of May 1943, the air element of II/JG 3 was transferred from Anapa to Kharkov, from where missions were flown over the area east of Belgorod between 2 and 6 May 1943[541]. The initial missions were all uneventful, but early on the afternoon of 6 May there was a fierce air battle with a large group of Russian fighters over the Belgorod area, in the course of which II/JG 3 scored a total of twelve victories, including four by Lt. Ettel (101-104) and four by Oblt. Kirschner (110-113). The next day the *Gruppe* was transferred back to Anapa. II/JG 3 was back in action over the Kuban bridgehead on the afternoon of 7 May[543], scoring seven victories on that day and no less than thirty on the 8th. The *Gruppe* suffered no losses on either day. II/JG 3 remained at Anapa until 15 May, by which time it recorded another 50 victories. Casualties totaled one pilot missing: on 9 May Uffz. Vitmar von Langendorff of 4 *Staffel* was shot down in combat with a formation of Bostons and its fighter escort south of Krymskaya. He was not seen again[544]. More fortunate was Lt. Wolf Ettel of 4/JG 3, who on 11 May was hit by anti-aircraft fire after scoring his 120th victory and obliged to make a forced landing in no-man's-land. Ettel succeeded in reaching the German lines under heavy fire from Russian infantry. A few days later he left II/JG 3 after being transferred to III/JG 27 in Greece, where he was to form and lead 8/JG 27[545].

On the morning of 16 May 1943, II/JG 3's air element flew from Anapa to Varvarovka, a forward airfield about ninety kilometers southwest of Belgorod[546]. The ground personnel were also there, and for the first time in a long while the *Gruppe* was completely united. The next seven weeks were relatively quiet as far as combat

Karte 10
Einsatzplätze der II./JG 3
im Sommer 1943

▲ **Flugplatz**

| 0 | 50 | 100 | 150 | 200Km |

operations on the ground were concerned; both sides were busy concentrating their forces and both on the ground and in the air they displayed a reserve which was unusual for this time of year. II/ JG 3 continued to fly missions over the front on either side of Belgorod; most were free chases or bomber escort missions, and, less commonly, escort for reconnaissance aircraft[547]. A number of fighter-bomber missions were also flown, a number of the *Gruppe*'s missions having been fitted with bomb racks[548]. Unlike in other areas, in II/JG 3's area of operations Russian aircraft were active in large numbers and combats were frequent. As a result, by the end of the month the *Gruppe* was able to score a total of 24 victories. Nine of these were claimed early on 23 May, when elements of all three *Staffeln* escorted a formation of Stukas to Oboyan and became involved in an extended battle with Russian fighters[549]. One pilot was lost: on 29 May Lt. Reinhard Scholze of 4/JG 3 was hit by flak and crashed to his death east of Gresnoye. At the end of the month Oblt. Stolte rejoined the *Gruppe* after recovering from wounds and again assumed command of 6 *Staffel*. On the other

hand, at this time a number of pilots and ground personnel left the *Gruppe* to join IV/JG 3,which was in the formation stage. All in all, II/JG 3 released personnel equivalent to half a *Staffel*, and these were to form the core of the new 11/JG 3. Those who left included experienced pilots like Oblt. Gustav Frielinghaus of 6 *Staffel*, *Leutnant* Rachner of 4/JG 3, and Fw. Rasso Förg of 5 *Staffel*[550]. The resulting gaps were soon filled by the assignment of young replacement pilots and a corresponding number of men for the ground personnel.

June 1943 was much the same: operating from Varvarovka, the *Gruppe* saw action over the Belgorod battle zone and continued to have frequent clashes with Soviet aircraft. A total of 117 victories was claimed, and the early days of the month were especially hectic. Early on the morning of 3 June, for example, II/JG 3's air base was the target of a low-level attack by a group of Russian fighters. This was engaged, first by the alert *Rotte*, and then by aircraft of all three *Staffeln* which scrambled to intercept[551]. Fourteen enemy aircraft were claimed shot down in exchange for two

Messerschmitts shot down and two pilots injured. II/JG 3 continued to score steadily in the days that followed—five victories on 4 June, two on the 5th and 6th and eleven on the 8th. The *Gruppe's* success continued at a comparable rate until the end of the month. II/JG 3's losses for the month were one pilot killed, three missing and two injured; as well, a total of seven Messerschmitts were written off as total losses and five were damaged. On 2 June 6 *Staffel* reported Uffz. Werner Maisch missing after he became separated from his unit during a free chase mission and failed to return for reasons unknown. The next day two pilots were injured: an engine fire forced Uffz. Helmut Liebmann of 4/JG 3 to bail out northeast of Kharkov, while Lt. Karl-Ludwig Seewald of 6 *Staffel* was shot down in combat with Yak-1s southwest of Belgorod and was slightly injured while bailing out. Fw. Horst Lüdtke of 5/JG 3 became a casualty on 5 June. He was shot down near Oboyan during a bomber escort mission and was subsequently listed missing. Obgefr. Heinz Welsch, also of 5 *Staffel*, suffered the same fate three days later. During a bomber escort mission in support of Ju 87s west of Belgorod, he was shot down by La-5s and failed to return. On 16 June Lt. Herbert Fürst of 5/JG 3 crashed while attempting a forced landing following a maintenance test flight north of Kharkov-Rogany and was killed when his machine struck the ground.

After much hesitation, on 1 July 1943 Hitler ordered "Operation Zitadelle" to begin on 5 July. In the meantime, the Russians had used the unexpected respite to fortify their defensive positions against the coming German attack. The result was an in-depth defense position with countless bunkers and trenches supported by extremely strong artillery forces[552]. The German preparations included the massing of all available air forces. In the south of the Kursk salient around Belgorod were the units of *VIII Fliegerkorps* with approximately 1,000 bombers, Stukas, close-support aircraft and fighters[553], while in the northern attack sector the *1 Fliegerdivision* had massed approximately 700 more machines in the Orel area[554]. In spite of this concentration of forces, the *Luftwaffe* was clearly outnumbered, for the Soviets had assembled elements of three air armies—the 2nd, 16th and 17th—comprising a total of 2,650 aircraft. The Russian superiority was especially marked in the area of fighter aircraft, where somewhat more than 300 German machines from eight *Jagdgruppen* faced 1,062 on the Russian side[555].

II/JG 3 continued to operate from Varvarovka in the first days of July[556], scoring ten victories by 4 July 1943. The *Gruppe* recorded one total loss: on 4 July the aircraft of Fw. Alfred Fischer of 4/JG 3 was hit in the radiators southeast of Chuguyev. He was obliged to make a forced landing on the enemy side of the lines and was taken prisoner[557]. In these days II/JG 3 received the first examples of the Bf 109 G-6[558]; the new variant of the Messerschmitt which differed from the G-4 mainly in its heavier armament[559]. In the late afternoon of 4 July the *Gruppe* moved to its designated jump-off base of Rogany, a spacious forward airfield southeast of Kharkov. Operationally, the *Gruppe* was attached to JG 52[560], which in turn was under the command of *VIII Fliegerkorps* for the coming attack.

The German attack was supposed to begin early on the morning of 5 July 1943 with a concentrated air strike against Soviet airfields and bunkers, trenches and artillery positions of the Russian defense system. While the German units were still on the ground, large Russian formations—altogether 132 close-support aircraft and 285 fighters—were detected. Their targets were the principal German airfields in the area of *VIII Fliegerkorps*. Thanks to this early detection, II/JG 3 plus elements of JG 52 were able to get airborne[561], intercept the Russian formations and engage them in costly dogfights. These resulted in the destruction of about 120 enemy aircraft[562], including 29 by II/JG 3[563]. During the rest of the day the *Gruppe* flew numerous free chase missions over the 4th Panzer Army's attack front. In spite of their considerable losses in the morning battles, the Russian fighters continued to appear over the front in large numbers, and almost every mission resulted in contact with enemy aircraft. II/JG 3 scored another 48 victories, raising its total for this day to 77, making 5 July 1943 by far the most successful day in the *Gruppe's* history. Losses were relatively light, for at the end of the day four of the *Gruppe's* pilots were placed on the casualty list with injuries of varying severity, while just one machine was written off. The defensive mission in the morning resulted in two wounded: the aircraft of Uffz. Helmut Liebmann of 4/JG 3 was seriously wounded when his aircraft was hit in the cockpit during combat with Yak-1s. Liebmann was forced to crash-land his machine southeast of the airfield, however he was soon picked up and taken to a hospital. Obfw. Josef Schütte of 5 *Staffel*, an experienced and successful pilot with 40 victories, was also badly wounded in combat with Russian fighters. Fortunately, he was able to parachute to safety southwest of Volchansk. 6/JG 3 recorded two more pilot casualties during the day: Lt. Friedrich-Wilhelm Schmidt and Gefr. Hans Schilling were both slightly wounded in air combat near Belgorod, however both were able to reach the German lines and make forced landings there.

On the ground, the German attack gained ground slowly and at great cost in the face of stubborn Russian resistance. While the Germans lacked reserves with which to exploit potential breakthroughs, the Russians had ample reserves to throw into the battle and prevent the Germans from achieving a decisive breakthrough. The German air forces made every effort to support the army's advance, flying 15,057 sorties in the first five days[564]. The efforts of the two *Gruppen* of JG 3 reflect the intensity of the fighting; as long as technical availability permitted, in the following four days the pilots flew four or more sorties each day. Even though the Russians remained extremely active in the air, the *Gruppe* was unable to match its success of the first day of the offensive; nevertheless, it continued to score at an impressive rate. II/JG 3 reported 21 more victories on 6 July, 27 on 7 July, ten more on 8 July, and nine on 9 July. Losses remained relatively low, with just one pilot reported missing. On 7 July Lt. Wolfgang Cichorius of 4 *Staffel* failed to

Grünberg, Hans, Feldw.,
5./Jagdgeschwader Udet.

E.O., den 5.7.1943

Gefechtsbericht.

Am 5.7.1943 startete ich um o3.1o Uhr als Rottenflieger bei Oblt. Kirschner zur freien Jagd im Raum von Belgorod.

Als wir uns etwa 1o km nördl. des Platzes befanden, bekamen wir durch Funkspruch die Meldung, daß am Flugplatz Charkow-Nord von leichten Möbelwagen angegriffen wurde. Wir machten sofort kehrt und trafen den Verband IL-2 bei Jaruga. Nachdem ich sah wie Oblt. Kirschner bei Jaruga eine IL-2 abschoß, griff ich die letzte IL-2 an. Von hinten unten beschoß ich diese aus nächster Entfernung, worauf die IL-2 sofort aus dem Motor und Rumpf brannte. Die IL-2 flog brennend noch etw. 555 km und schlug dann brennend auf. Durch Aufschlagbrand wurde sie restlos vernichtet. Einen Fallschirmabsprung habe ich nicht beobachtet.

Der Aufschlag erfolgte um o3.3o Uhr im Planquadrat 6o237. Zeuge des Abschusses ist Feldw. Traphan.

[Unterschrift: Grünberg]

Traphan, Rudolf, F.laW.,
5. /Jagdgeschwader Udet.

E.O., den 5.7.1943

Luftkampfzeugenbericht.

Am 5.7.1943 startete ich um o3.25 Uhr auf Sicht von IL-2 mit Jagdschutz, die Charkow angriffen.

Wir flogen sofort auf einen Verband IL-2 zu, der Charkow-Nord angriff. Noch während des Anfluges sah ich, wie Feldw. Grünberg, der die schwarze 1 der Staffel flog, die letzte IL-2 von hinten unten angriff. Sofort nach dem Beschuß brannte die IL-2 und ging brennend nach unten weg. Durch Aufschlagbrand wurde diese restlos vernichtet. Einen Fallschirmabsprung habe ich nicht beobachtet.

Der Aufschlag erfolgte um o3.3o Uhr im Planquadrat 6o237.

[Unterschrift: Traphan]

---

37. Abschuß.

Anlage 1
zu Nr. 431

5./Jagdgeschwader Udet
(Truppenteil)

E.O., den 5.7.1943   o3.3o Uhr
(Ort, Datum)

Abschußmeldung, Zerstörungsmeldung.

1. Zeit (Tag, Stunde, Minute) und Gegend des Absturzes: 5. 7. 1943   o3.3o Uhr
   Planquadrat 6o237   Feldwebel Hans Grünberg
   (Insassen)

Höhe: 2oo m

2. Durch wen ist Abschuß / Zerstörung erfolgt?

3. Flugzeugtyp des abgeschossenen Flugzeuges: IL - 2

4. Staatsangehörigkeit des Gegners: UdSSR

   Werknummern bzw. Kennzeichen: Sowjetstern

5. Art der Vernichtung: Aufschlagbrand

6. a) Flammen mit dunkler Fahne, Flammen mit heller Fahne;
   b) Einzelteil weggeflogen, abmontiert (Art der Teile erläutern), auseinandergeplatzt;
   c) zur Landung gezwungen (diesseits oder jenseits der Front, glatt bzw. mit Bruch);
   d) jenseits der Front am Boden in Brand geschossen):

   Art des Aufschlages (nur wenn dieser beobachtet werden konnte):

   a) diesseits oder jenseits der Front:
   b) [senkrecht, flachem Winkel, Aufschlagbrand, Staubwolke:]
   c) nicht beobachtet, warum nicht?

7. Schicksal der Insassen (tot, mit Fallschirm abgesprungen, nicht beobachtet):

8. Gefechtsbericht des Schützen ist in der Anlage beigefügt.

9. Zeugen:
   a) Luft: Feldwebel Traphan
   b) Erde:

10. Anzahl der Angriffe, die auf das feindliche Flugzeug gemacht wurden: 1 Angriff

11. Richtung, aus der die einzelne Angriffe erfolgten: Von Hinten unten

12. Entfernung, aus der der Abschuß erfolgte: 3o m

13. Takt. Position, aus der der Abschuß angesetzt wurde: von hinten unten herangezogen

14. Ist einer der feindlichen Bordschützen kampfunfähig gemacht worden?   ./.

15. Verwandte Munitionsart: M.G., M.K.., 7.-Juni., 7.-Juni.

16. Munitionsverbrauch: kann nicht ausgegeben werden, da mehrere Maschinen beschossen

17. Art und Anzahl der Waffen, die bei dem Abschuß gebraucht wurden: 1 MG 151/2o und 2 MG 17
    Bf 1o9 G-4 2 Kanonen und 2 MG.)

18. Typ der eigenen Maschine (z. B. Me 1o9 F mit 2 Kanonen und 2 MG.):   Me 1 K. u. 2 M

19. Weiteres taktisch oder technisch Bemerkenswertes: keino

20. Treffer in der eigenen Maschine: nein

21. Beteiligung weiterer Einheiten (auch Flak):

[Unterschrift]
(Unterschrift)

Oberleutnant u. Staffelkapitän.

Zu Ziffer 5-7 ist Zutreffendes zu unterstreichen.

HB: Din A4 tatg. Heidelberger Gutenberg-Druckerei GmbH. 11. 43.

153

return from a free chase mission southwest of Prokhorovka for reasons unknown.

In the days that followed, the German attack became bogged down in the Russian defense system. Then, on 11 July, the Russians counterattacked with superior forces in the area of Army Group Center, first against the 2nd Panzer Army and then the 9th Army in the Orel salient, supported by five air armies with 5,000 aircraft. The Russian counterattack caused the offensive battle in the Kursk salient to become the defensive battle in the Orel salient. Furthermore, on 10 July Allied troops had landed in Sicily, beginning the attack from the south against what German propaganda had called "Fortress Europe," creating a dangerous situation there[565].

While the attack in the northern part of the Kursk salient had to be broken off, the German offensive effort in the southern sector at first continued. On 14 July, however, the order was given to cease the attack there, after it became obvious that no decisive success could be achieved. Furthermore, a strong buildup of Russian forces had been detected along the Donets and Mius front, obviously in preparation for an attack on the German defense positions. II/JG 3 continued flying missions over the battle zone around Belgorod and Oboyan. Its efforts focused on providing fighter cover for the German armored units against Russian close-support aircraft, which were appearing in ever greater numbers. A further 37 victories were claimed between 10 and 14 July 1943. On 12 July Uffz. Stienhans of 6 *Staffel* scored II/JG 3's 2,000th victory[566]. On the other side of the coin, the *Gruppe* reported two pilots missing: on 10 July, during an escort mission for He 111s, Lt. Hans Reiser of 4 *Staffel* was shot down southwest of Prokhorovka and was not seen again. The next day, while on a free chase mission over German armored spearheads in the Volchansk—Tomarovka area, Gefr. Hans Schilling of 6/JG 3 became separated from his unit and subsequently failed to return to Rogany for reasons unknown.

The breaking off of "Operation Zitadelle"[567] also marked the end of II/JG 3's attachment to *VIII Fliegerkorps*. The *Gruppe* was split up for subsequent operations. On 16 July part of the air element and some key technical personnel were transferred to Kutelnikovo, a forward airfield south of Ilovayskoye west of the upper Mius; the rest of the *Gruppe* and the bulk of the ground personnel remained at Rogany[568]. On this day the latter were subjected to a bombing raid on their airfield; one Messerschmitt was seriously damaged, but otherwise damage was negligible. Two aircraft were damaged in the final missions in the Belgorod area; in neither case was the pilot injured. On the other hand, in these days the *Gruppe* reported eleven victories, most of which were scored by the elements at Rogany. The elements of the *Gruppe* at Kutelnikovo were bolstered by 8/JG 3, which was temporarily subordinated to II/JG 3[569].

On 17 July 1943, following a heavy artillery bombardment, the Russian armies launched an attack against the German front on the Donets and Mius Rivers and achieved several deep penetra-

tions. They succeeded in crossing the Donets at Izyum and north of Slavyansk[570]. In spite of poor weather, both sides were very active in the air. In these days the elements of II/JG 3 at Kutelnikovo and the attached 8/JG 3 were used mainly in free chases and to provide fighter escort for close-support aircraft over the front on the upper Mius near Dmitriyevka, where there were frequent encounters with Russian units. Three victories were claimed on this day, while the *Gruppe* suffered no losses. In the days that followed, II/JG 3 continued to see action both over the battle zone around Belgorod and the area of front along the upper Mius[571], where heavy fighting continued on the ground. Periods of rainy weather at times considerably hindered operations and on some days there was apparently no flying at all[572]. In spite of this, by 27 July 1943 II/JG 3 scored another 48 victories, including Oblt. Lucas' 100th on the 21st and Oblt. Kirschner's 170th on the 27th. In the same period the *Gruppe* lost four pilots killed or missing and one injured plus five Messerschmitts written off through enemy action. On 18 July Uffz. Thomas Ametsbichler of 4/JG 3 was shot down and killed by flak southeast of Prokhorovka, in the Belgorod combat zone[573]. The next day, during a free chase from Kotelnikovo, Uffz. Helmuth Schirra, also of 4 *Staffel*, failed to return after an engagement with Il-2s near Dmitriyevka and was reported missing. The third casualty also affected 4 *Staffel*, for on 21 July Lt. Hermann Schuster failed to return after combat with Il-2s in the Permovaysk area and also had to be reported missing. With 35 victories to his credit, Schuster was one of the *Gruppe*'s most promising replacement officers. Three days later Uffz. Günther Mohn of 5 *Staffel* was forced to abandon his machine near the Kutelnikovo airfield, after flak had damaged his aircraft's undercarriage, making a belly landing impossible. Mohn struck the tail hard while bailing out and suffered further injuries on landing; however, his injuries could be treated in the *Gruppe* medical dispensary and he was able to return to action soon afterwards. Finally, on 27 July, Obfhr. Botho Katz of the *Gruppenstab* was shot down in air combat near Belgorod and was subsequently reported missing.

On 29 July 1943 the 6th Army launched a counterattack to restore the front at the Mius[574]. After two days of fighting against determined Russian resistance, the German attack gained ground to the east, and on 31 July the units of the 6th Army regained the former main line of resistance and drove the Russian troops back to their start positions. II/JG 3 supported the army's attack, and until 2 August 1943 flew a large number of missions from Kutelnikovo and Varvarovka airfields, escorting bombers and Stukas attacking targets in the front-line area, in addition to its familiar roles of free chase and fighter cover. When the German attack began, 8/JG 3's brief subordination to II *Gruppe* ended and it went to Makeyevka, where it was reunited with the rest of its *Gruppe*[575]. II/JG 3 recorded another 25 victories during this time, 17 of them on 31 July. Just one pilot became a casualty: Lt. Hartwig Dohse of 5 *Staffel*, a very promising young officer with 23 victories to his credit, failed to return from a free chase mission in the Marinovka area after combat with Russian fighters[576]. He remains missing.

The missions of 2 August 1943 were to be II/JG 3's last in the east. The next day the order arrived for it to move to the homeland, where the *Gruppe* was to operate as part of the Defense of the Reich. The transfer flight was made by the unit's aircraft, accompanied by several Ju 52s carrying key technical personnel. The bulk of the ground personnel followed by train[577]. After it was initially planned to assemble the *Gruppe* in Mönchen-Gladbach, several days later II/JG 3 was assigned Uetersen air base north of Hamburg for its planned refurbishment.

This brought to an end almost fifteen months of unbroken action in the east. During this time the men of II/JG 3 had experienced the heady advance of the German summer offensive of 1942, which had led directly to the catastrophe of Stalingrad, the tough, costly defensive fighting at the start of 1943, and finally the failed summer offensive of 1943, which marked the final turning point in the war in the east. The *Gruppe* had achieved considerable success during this time—a total of 1,538 victories since May 1942—and thus remained among the most successful *Jagdgruppen* in the east. This success had no decisive effect on the outcome of the fighting, however, indeed it was not enough to prevent the Russian air force from growing steadily in numbers. Unlike the *Luftwaffe*, the Russian air force received sufficient deliveries of aircraft from Soviet production and aid supplied by the western allies under Lend-Lease. In spite of their huge losses, the Russians always had sufficient numbers of replacement pilots. When the *Gruppe* left Russia at the beginning of August 1943, the days of *Luftwaffe* air superiority in the east were already gone for good.

Expressed in numerical terms, II/JG 3's balance at the end of its deployment in the east looks like this: against the already-mentioned 1,538 claimed victories, the *Gruppe*'s losses in flight personnel amounted to four killed and 22 missing, including two and one, respectively, as a result of non-combat-related accidents. In addition, two pilots are known to have been captured[578] and 18 were wounded or injured. Total losses thus almost equaled the *Gruppe*'s authorized strength; together with the wounded, some of whom were out of action for a long time, the loss rate was 130% of authorized strength and was even higher in relation to actual strength, which was usually lower than authorized. It is significant that II/JG 3 lost few unit leaders. The *Gruppe*'s personnel losses include just one *Staffelkapitän*, Lt. Hans Fuß, while Oblt. Lucas and Oblt. Stolte were both able to return to the *Gruppe* a short time after they were injured. As well, compared to other units[579] II/JG 3 lost relatively few "*Experten*". Those who were lost include Lt. Hermann Schuster of 4/JG 3, who went missing on 21 July 1943 after 35 victories, Lt. Hartwig Dohse of 5 *Staffel*, who also went missing after 23 victories, and Obfw. Josef Schütte of 5/JG 3, who was seriously wounded on 5 July 1943 after 40 victories[580].

Between 1 May 1942 and 2 August 1943 the *Gruppe* lost a total of 72 Messerschmitts written off or with damage in excess of 60%, 37 of which were due to enemy action. 54 machines sustained damage between 30% and 60%, and another 60 sustained damage of between 10% and 30%[581].

Notes:

[388] Compare in detail OKW War Diary 1940-41 Part I, p. 47 and following pages; Jacobsen and Dollinger, Vol. 4, p. 76 and following pages; Prien, JG 77 Part 2, p. 977 and following pages.

[389] See OKW War Diary 1940-41 Part I, p. 46 and following pages; Cartier, Vol. 1, p. 452. The fateful weakness of Hitler's campaign plan lay in the clear disproportion between intentions and means; for even after all available reserves had been moved in as well as a large number of divisions from the armies of Germany's allies, Army Group South had only 60 German divisions, nine of them armored, for the summer campaign along with 21 Italian, Romanian, Hungarian and Slovakian divisions. However, it would have required forces at least twice as strong to achieve the objectives of the summer campaign of 1942, code-named "Blue". Furthermore, the divisions of Army Group South had not received sufficient replacements to make good the losses they had suffered since the start of the war in the east and on average were at only 50% of their authorized strengths. The situation of the *Luftwaffe* was equally precarious as the number of serviceable aircraft available to its units had sunk on average to 50-60% of the level of 1 May 1941.

[390] Cartier Vol. I, p. 453 and following pages; OKW War Diary 1940-41 Part I, p. 49.

[391] OKW War Diary 1940-41 Part I, p. 49, 323; in view of this rapid series of operations requiring all available forces, it was foreseeable that the *Luftwaffe*'s resources would already be rather exhausted at the start of the actual summer offensive and that there would be a clear drop in operational readiness by this time.

[392] Compare in detail OKW War Diary 1940-41 Part I, p. 49, also 456 and following pages.

[393] OKW War Diary 1940-41 Part I, p. 366; Cartier Vol. I, p. 456-457.

[394] The transfer flight followed a route from San Pietro via Bari, Forli and Treviso to Munich-Riem and from there to Wiener-Neustadt. There a number of machines underwent engine changes, something that would not be possible in the east for some time. Letter from Wolf Ettel, 29/4/1942 (Busacker-Lührssen, p. 120).

[395] See aircraft complement lists in appendices.

[396] Consequently, the Messerschmitts of II/JG 3 were the only ones in the *Geschwader* at that time which were not finished in the splinter camouflage pattern derived from the factory-applied sand brown and pale blue Africa scheme (see Prien/Stemmer, III/JG 3, p. 215 and following pages).

[397] Log books of Gerd Schaedle, *Leutnant* and pilot in 6/JG 3, and Kurt Ebener. According to Franz Schwaiger's diary, the transfer led through Breslau, Krosno, Proskurov and Kirovograd to Chuguyev, where Franz Schwaiger arrived on 20/5.

[398] JG 3 landed at a group of airfields southeast of Kharkov, which included Rogany, Chuguyev and Yaruga. Contemporary records reveal a rather lax attitude toward the precise designations of these airfields—the names "*Kharkov*" and "*Kharkov-Rogany*" appear most frequently in the Quartermaster-General's reports for I/JG 3, but "*Rogany-East*" is also sometimes seen, which could easily refer to Chuguyev or Yaruga. Surviving records (confirmed by Walther Hagenah) indicate that "Rogany-East" and "Yaruga" were two designations for one and the same airfield. [399] Log book of Gerd Schaedle; diary of Franz Schwaiger.

[400] OKW War Diary 1942, Part I, p. 376; Bekker, p. 406; Cartier, Vol. I, p. 456-57.

[401] WASt. casualty report; diary of Franz Schwaiger.

[402] Three of the victories were scored during a mission by the *Stabsrotte* in the early morning; the following account was made by Helmut Hennig: "*The Kommandeur of II/JG 3, Hptm. Brändle, returned from the Rotte mission with his young adjutant Lt. Fuß. It had been a successful one, for both the Kommandeur and his wingman made victory passes over the airfield before landing. But while the Kommandeur then came in to land, Lt. Fuß approached the airfield again and flew over it, rocking his wings vigorously. I marshaled Hptm. Brändle to the dispersal and congratulated him on his victory, an I-61. To my surprise his only response was a mumbled, 'Thank you.' When I asked if his machine was otherwise alright, I received the characteristic answer: 'The whippersnapper has two.' By this he meant that Lt. Fuß had outdone his Kommandeur by one victory, which visibly annoyed him.*" Account dated 30/11/1985.

[403] OKW War Diary 1942, Part I, p. 379 and following pages; also the diary of Franz Schwaiger for 25/5.

[404] However, on 29 May elements, at least, of the *Gruppe* moved to Yaruga airfield, a few kilometers northwest of Chuguyev; see log book of Gerd Schaedle.

[405] Compare in detail Prien and Stemmer, III/JG 3, p. 174 and following pages; Prien, JG 77 Part 2, p. 1040 and following pages. The *Luftwaffe* planning for

operations leading up to the big summer offensive clearly shows once again just how inadequate the available air forces already were at this time. In order to be able to provide the necessary air support for the attack on Sevastopol, three bomber, three Stuka and three fighter *Gruppen* had to be moved to the Crimea by 6 June 1942, immediately following the battle near Kharkov. However, already by 10 June these same units plus another fighter *Gruppe* had to be moved back so as to be able to occupy their jump-off bases in time for the start of the summer offensive. The diarist of the OKW's military history department summed it up as follows: *"If Störfang begins as planned on 7 June, full air support by the Luftwaffe will only be possible on the first three days."* See OKW War Diary 1940-41 Part I, p. 380.

[406] See corresponding references in OKW War Diary 1942, Part I, p. 388 and following pages.

[407] According to aircraft movement reports, during the month of May the *Gruppe* had lost a total of nine machines on operations and transferred one to another unit; however, only four of these losses are confirmed by surviving WASt. and Quartermaster-General reports; see the loss lists in appendices.

[408] See Prien, JG 77 Part 2, p. 1037 and following pages.

[409] Log book of Gerd Schaedle; diary of Franz Schwaiger.

[410] Compare to original schedule in Footnote 391; instead the fighting at Sevastopol went on until the first days of July, when German troops finally succeeded in wiping out the last nests of Russian resistance.

[411] Log book of Gerd Schaedle. On the other hand, according to his log book, Kurt Ebener did not arrive there until 26/6. An advance detachment of technical personnel had already been moved up to Shchigry on or about 20 June 1942, to prepare the airfield to accept the air element.

[412] See Prien/Stemmer, III/JG 3, p. 176.

[413] Papers of Botho Teichmann.

[414] Papers of Botho Teichmann.

[415] In total, beginning in autumn 1941 the Soviet air force received approximately 20,000 aircraft from America and Great Britain; this figure included 4,958 P-39s, 2,400 P-63s, 2,097 P-40s, 2,908 Bostons, 862 Mitchells, 707 C-47s, 2,952 Hurricane IIs, 1,336 Spitfire Vs and IXs, and approximately 1,300 P-51s from British sources.

[416] According to the OKW War Diary 1940-41 Part I, p. 1311, reporting date 20 June 1942; of the named fighter aircraft only 236 were serviceable. The *Jagdgruppen* available at the start of the attack were JG 3 and JG 52 with all three *Gruppen*, I/JG 53 and II/JG 77.

[417] See aircraft complement list in the appendices; in addition, these were repaired machines and not new-production Bf 109 F-4s.

[418] Log book of Gerd Schaedle.

[419] Apart from two Messerschmitts of 4 *Staffel* damaged in a ground collision at Gorshechnoye.

[420] See *Luftwaffe* General Staff daily reports, OKW War Diary 1942, Part I, p. 483 and following pages.

[421] Also see OKW War Diary 1942, Part I, p. 486; Piekalkiewicz, *Stalingrad*, p. 26; Cartier, Vol. I, p. 476.

[422] The German armed forces continued to use German Summer Time, even in the east. Since the battle zone around Voronezh was much farther east than Germany, sunrise and sunset were considerably earlier than in the Reich. Consequently, in II/JG 3's area of operations it began to get light shortly after 2:00 AM.

[423] Ettel's victory took place at 4:31 AM; also see the letter from Ettel's father in *Jägerblatt*, No. 2-XI, February 1962, p. 8 and following pages.

[424] The airfield was located 5 km north of the town of Maryevka and 9 km northwest of Olkhovatka, Grid Square 35 East 91/3/8.

[425] Also see OKW War Diary 1942, Part I, p. 491 and following pages.

[426] According to the log book of Kurt Ebener, it remained at Kantemirovka until 16 July.

[427] See the ground personnel loss lost in the appendices.

[428] See OKW War Diary 1942, Part I, p. 57 and following pages; Cartier Vol. I, p. 477-78; Piekalkiewicz, *Stalingrad*, p. 27 and following pages.

[429] Altogether, in July 1942 II/JG 3 received 32 machines as replacements, 29 of which were handed down by other units. It is likely that the majority of the aircraft taken on strength by II/JG 3 came from III/JG 52 and I/JG 53, which reequipped with the Bf 109 G-2 at this time.

[430] OKW War Diary 1942, Part I, p. 502.

[431] WASt. casualty report.

[432] Novy-Kholan is better known by the name Tazinskaya; it may be assumed, however, that it was more than just an airfield with the name Tazinskaya. Novy-Kholan may therefore have been called Tazinskaya-South, in any case it was located in Grid Square 44 East 19/7/6. According to Kurt Ebener's log book, he arrived at the new field on 20 July 1942.

[433] According to Kurt Ebener's log book from 23 July 1942.

[434] Grid Square 44 East 08/5/2.

[435] The area *west of Kalach* was first mentioned in Franz Schwaiger's diary under 23 July.

[436] See OKW War Diary 1942, Part I, p. 525 and following pages.

[437] There was another method of attack, developed by pilots of II/JG 77, which involved concentrating fire on the horizontal stabilizer. Since the Il-2 was quite nose-heavy on account of its heavily-armored forward fuselage and motor, the loss of or heavy damage to the horizontal stabilizer resulted in a nose-down attitude which, at the low altitudes at which the Il-2s operated, usually resulted in the aircraft crashing into the ground. See Prien, JG 77 Part 2, p. 1127.

[438] As well, a Messerschmitt of 6 *Staffel* was destroyed when it struck an obstacle while taking off from Morozovskaya on 25 July.

[439] Grid Square 45 East 30/2/7; see Special Map Frolov.

[440] As usual, however, several machines which were unserviceable on this day did not follow until later; for example, on 28 July a Messerschmitt crashed while attempting a landing at Novy-Kholan in bad weather. See loss lists in the appendices.

[441] Papers of Alfred Gerdes, technician in III *Gruppe*. On 3 August a truck belonging to the Headquarters Company of III/JG 3 drove over a wooden box mine, killing both of those inside. See the loss list in Prien/Stemmer, III/JG 3, appendices.

[442] See Piekalkiewicz, *Stalingrad*, p. 38.

[443] It moved on to Bereska on 4 August 1942, however; see Prien, JG 53 Part 2, p. 538 and following pages.

[444] Hptm. Wendt's promotion to *Staffelkapitän* may have been due mainly to his rank and possibly his good connections to the staff of the *General der Jagdflieger*, for at this time he had neither long experience as a *Staffelführer* (he led 8/JG 26 from 16 March to 7 August 1940) nor the necessary success as a fighter pilot, having just one victory to his credit (acquired on 13 May 1940).

[445] Oblt. Waldhelm may have been relieved on account of his lack of success as a fighter pilot—after having failed to achieve a single victory with JG 5 in Norway and having scored just one with II/JG 3 in the east in the summer of 1942, a period of great success, he was transferred to the *Schlachtflieger* (close-support aviation). Waldhelm was killed in combat with P-40s on 3 February 1943, while serving with 1/SG 2 in Tunisia.

[446] WASt. casualty report.

[447] See OKW War Diary 1942, Part I, p. 558 and following pages.

[448] A total of 35,000 prisoners and extensive booty were brought in by 11 August, which meant however that this battle of encirclement could not be compared with the great battles of encirclement of summer 1941 or even with the success south of Kharkov in May 1942.

[449] For example, the first free chase mission southwest of Stalingrad is recorded in Franz Schwaiger's diary under 6 August 1942; meanwhile, on 2 August, Franz Schwaiger had been transferred to I *Gruppe*, where he was initially assigned to 2 *Staffel*.

[450] Grid Square East 39/3/4.

[451] In addition, during the course of the month elements of all three *Gruppen* of JG 52 used the airfield for a brief period as well as the two *Gruppen* of SchlG 1 and two transport *Gruppen*.

[452] Papers of Kurt Ebener.

[453] According to the papers of Karl-Heinz Langer, during the course of this several Ju 52s which approached the Tuzov airfield at low level landed next to the airfield and were wrecked in the balkas. The Quartermaster-General's loss reports contain no reference to such an incident, however, and the only loss involving a Ju 52 during I/JG 3's stay at Tuzov was an aircraft of KGr.z.b.V. 50 which sustained 10% damage in a landing accident (10/8/1942).

[454] Log book and papers of Kurt Ebener.

[455] Papers of Karl-Heinz Langer; estimates of the number of enemy aircraft involved in the attack vary—according to III/JG 3's war diary, 38 Il-2s took part, of which a total of 37 were shot down.

[456] See Prien, JG 53 Part 2, p. 544 and following pages, also p. 1672.

[457] Victories claimed between 4:24 and 4:28 AM; therefore, these machines must have already been airborne when the incursion was detected.

[458] Papers of Kurt Ebener.

[459] With 22 victories I/JG 53 was again the most successful, while *Stab*/JG 3 scored one and III *Gruppe* four more victories. Compare in detail Prien, JG 53 Part 1, p. 545.

[460] OKW War Diary 1942, Part I, Army Group B situation report from 15 August 1942.

[461] OKW War Diary 1942, Part I, p. 596 and following pages; Carell, p. 481 and following pages.

[462] Papers of Kurt Ebener.

[463] See corresponding entries on the weather situation in OKW War Diary 1942, Part I, e.g. p. 614 for 20 August.

[464] Papers of Kurt Ebener.

[465] See OKW War Diary 1942, Part I, p. 635 and following pages.

[466] Papers of Kurt Ebener. These contain the following noteworthy statement, which casts a revealing light on the mood in those days of the last great advance in the east: *"We have been scoring well and were there when, on 22 August 42, the first army units crossed the Don over the two pontoon bridges, and on 23 August 42 the tanks of the XIV Panzer Corps under the command of General Hube reached the*

Volga north of Stalingrad near Rynok in a single day. The objective toward which we have been striving for months is now within reach. We already know that our II Gruppe will soon be transferred to Germany to reequip with new machines. Therefore, we were filled with a sense of satisfaction during our last flight over our armored spearhead on the evening of that 23 August, flying low over the burning steppe, to have finally reached the northern suburb of Stalingrad with the first ground forces. Out of joy and gratitude to our comrades below us, during our return flight to Tuzov we flew rolls and other aerobatics over the advance road being used by the following divisions." No one in the unit could know what tragedy and disaster waited for them there. This ignorance is typified by the following recollection by Helmut Hennig, then Hptm. Brändle's maintenance chief, of an experience with his *Kommandeur:* *"Once, while he sat strapped into his machine, at cockpit readiness in the blazing heat, he appeared to be far away, lost on thought. Then he looked at me and suddenly said, `Hennig, do you know why we're fighting this shitty war? For oil!' He did not expand on this notion, instead he went back to his silent brooding."* Account dated 30/11/1985.

[467] In addition, on 19 September 1942 Fw. Werner Lucas of 4/JG 3, who by 21 August 1942 had achieved a total of 53 victories, was awarded the Knight's Cross.

[468] A further fifteen Bf 109 F-4s had to be released to the aviation industry for repairs; see the inventory lists in the appendices.

[469] Probably the 3 *Jagddivision*; account by Harald Moldenhauer dated 11/8/1986.

[470] Lt. Joachim Kirschner joined 5/JG 3 at the end of 1941. At that time he already had one victory, scored with Erg.Gr./JG 3 (20/8/1941) and scored his second over Malta. He had added 32 more while serving in the east, 12 of them with I/JG 3.

[471] Papers of Hans-Heinrich Brustellin.

[472] The airfield was situated about 20 kilometers northwest of Dugino and roughly the same distance from the Dniepr's source on the east bank of the river.

[473] Papers of Hans-Heinrich Brustellin.

[474] According to Kurt Ebener's log book, the transfer from Königsberg-Neuhausen to Dedyurevo was made via Vilna and Smolensk. He arrived at Dedyurevo on 11 September.

[475] *Luftwaffe-Kommando Ost* had been created on 1 April 1942 from Headquarters, V *Fliegerkorps*; following the withdrawal of VIII *Fliegerkorps*, it took over the former sector of *Luftflotte* 2 in the central sector and supported Army Group Center.

[476] What purpose the *Luftwaffe* command was pursuing with this transfer remains in the dark, for it made no sense to pull a recently reequipped *Jagdgruppe* out of the southern sector of the Eastern Front, in particular the battle zone around Stalingrad, which was clearly the point of main effort, and transfer it to one of the quietest sectors of the front. No offensive operations were planned in that sector, and there was no visible association with the drive by Army Group North to take Leningrad and create a land bridge to Germany's ally Finland, which at that time was still planned for mid-September. A clue to the reasons behind this move may lie in a report by Generaloberst von Richthofen, the commanding general of VIII *Fliegerkorps*, dated 25 August 1942. Displaying a total misappreciation of the facts, he declared that, *"there can be no more talk of strong enemy forces at Stalingrad."* He was quoted by Warlimont, OKW War Diary 1942, Part I, p. 684, who characterized the statement as an *"irresponsible false report".*

[477] See OKW War Diary 1942, Part I.

[478] See Aders, JG 51, p. 112 and following pages, esp. p. 121.

[479] Log book of Gerd Schaedle.

[480] WASt. casualty report; Obermaier, p. 116.

[481] Concerning the career of Paul Stolte with I/JG 1 see Prien/Rodeike, JG 1/11; on 25 September 1942 he was still signing as acting *Gruppenkommandeur* of I/JG 1. The transfer obviously took effect on 30 September 1942, as revealed by an entry in the papers of Hans-Heinrich Brustellin under 29/9/1942.

[482] Obviously after a brief stop at Vitebsk; for example, according to his log book, Kurt Ebener was there from 23 to 26 September 1942.

[483] See Prien/Stemmer, III/JG 3, p. 152 and following pages.

[484] The purpose of the Soviet attack was to relieve the Russian front in the area of Leningrad—Lake Ladoga—Schlisselburg. After a major Soviet offensive and a German counterattack, which began on 20 September, the area was the scene of heavy fighting. While this ended in a German victory by 2 October 1942, it ate up all of the reserves needed for the planned attack on Leningrad and the advance on the Isthmus of Karelia. Consequently, the entire German offensive had to be called off; see OKW War Diary 1942, Part I. The German attack at Demyansk, "Operation Winkelried", was concluded by 10 October.

[485] Gerd Schaedle's log book records a total of 18 missions from _olzy during the period between 27 September and 31 October. Ten of these were free chases and eight were bomber and transport escort missions.

[486] WASt. casualty report.

[487] See OKW War Diary 1942, Part I.

[488] As in the case of Oblt. Waldhelm, Wendt's lack of success may have been partly responsible for him being relieved; according to the contemporary guidelines, the successes of the *Staffelkapitäne* in combat were supposed to provide an inspiration for their pilots and spur them on to similar successes.

[489] According to Gerd Schaedle's log book, he flew his first mission from Smolensk on 27 November 1942.

[490] Cartier, Vol. II, p. 568-569.

[491] In spite of the fact that fighting was still going on in the Stalingrad area, on 14 October 1942 Hitler ordered his armies in the east to hold their present lines at all costs in order to be able to use them as the starting point for a new offensive in 1943—OKW War Diary 1940-41 Part II, p. 800 and following pages, p. 1434 and following pages.

[492] An in-depth examination of the truly indescribable fighting that developed in the Battle of Stalingrad would exceed the scope of this book; for further information on this topic the reader is referred to Cartier, Vol. II, p. 568 and following pages, and Carell, p. 502 and following pages.

[493] See Cartier, Vol. II, p. 573 and following pages.

[494] See Prien/Stemmer, III/JG 3, p. 196.

[495] Papers of Kurt Ebener. He wrote: *"The rumor that German troops had been encircled at Stalingrad was first confirmed at Millerovo on 12 December while our machines were being refueled before our flight to Morozovskaya to join our parent Geschwader."*

[496] The 6th Army had placed its minimum daily requirement at 700 tons of munitions, fuel and rations, while the *Luftwaffe*'s maximum daily transport capacity was 350 tons; Göring assumed that 500 tons per day would be enough and made his fateful promise based on this. However, several obvious facts should have made it clear to everyone that supplying the 6th Army from the air was absolutely impossible, even for a short period. At least 500 transport aircraft would be needed for the task, while only 289 were available in *Luftflotte* 4's entire area and many of these were unserviceable. Furthermore, the operation of such a number of transport aircraft required a sufficient number of suitable airfields at both ends of the air bridge, while in fact only the makeshift airfields of Morozovskaya and Tazinskaya were available outside the pocket and Pitomnik and Gumrak inside. Finally, the inclement Russian winter weather had to be taken into consideration; the predictable interruptions in air transport traffic due to bad weather would mean doubled efforts on the remaining days, which must lead to another rise in the number of required aircraft. Compare in detail Jacobsen and Rohwer, p. 303 and following pages; Cartier, Vol. II, p. 578.

[497] Whose opinion was not revealed to Hitler on express orders from Luftwaffe Chief of Staff Jeschonnek; Compare in detail Jacobsen and Rohwer, p. 304, especially Footnote 41.

[498] The Messerschmitts were usually fueled from the wing tanks of the transport aircraft—papers of Alfred Gerdes; a detachment of 14 men under Uffz. Gerhard Jansen was stationed at the airfield, obviously to service the aircraft of the *Gruppe* that landed there.

[499] The following is from the papers of Kurt Ebener, who was to become the most successful pilot of the *Pitomnik-Staffel*, finishing up with 35 victories scored over the area of the pocket: *"A combination of cold and inadequate rations and the much greater stress of flying in Stalingrad quickly led to physical exhaustion. The Airfield Defense Staffel had to battle tremendous difficulties. Almost all of the heater trucks used to pre-heat the engines were unserviceable and there were no spare parts. Most of the Me 109s had bullet damage, and with the constant enemy air activity it was very difficult to make them operational again. Fuel shortages did not make themselves felt until later, when the front line outside the pocket had to be moved farther and farther back. With the longer approach routes, the supply aircraft used up their fuel themselves and were no longer able to provide us with any. The bitter cold and the dwindling rations scale which we, pilots and ground crew, shared with the ground troops, made it equally difficult for us. In this degree of cold our engines had to be cranked up several times before starting, provided that they had been preheated in time by the heater truck. But the aircraft mechanics usually collapsed from hunger and cold after twice cranking up the starter. The airfield was attacked almost constantly day and night, and our machines were repeatedly damaged by bomb splinters, because in spite of the cold they sat unprotected in the open at the dispersal assigned to us at the northwest end of Pitomnik."*

[500] See Cartier, Vol. II, p. 581 and following pages; Carell, p. 532.

[501] Papers of Kurt Ebener.

[502] Compare in detail Schumann, Vol. 3, p. 54 and following pages; Kehrig, *Stalingrad*, p. 532 and following pages; Cartier, Vol. II, p. 584 and following pages; Jacobsen and Rohwer, p. 305 and following pages. If this choice of objectives is questionable from a strategic point of view, it was "necessary" only because of Hitler's military idiocy and that of the *Wehrmacht* command which remained true to him, which instead of withdrawing the 6th Army from its exposed and militarily totally useless position on the Volga allowed an entire army to be squandered for the sake of a questionable prestige victory in taking the city that bore Stalin's name. The myth that the sacrifice of the 6th Army made military sense because its valiant struggle played a major role in the Russians' ultimate failure to destroy all of Army Group South is one of the most repugnant and untruthful smokescreen legends later promulgated by the German generals in order to obscure their own sad role in the drama of Stalingrad—especially their hesitation in ordering the army to break out

against Hitler's wishes. In January 1943 the 6th Army was still tying down a total of 55 Soviet rifle divisions and brigades, the numerical strength of a Soviet division being about a half to two-thirds of a German one. On the other hand, there were only three tank brigades in the pocket front, which suggests that the 6th Army was unable to tie down any of the tank and motorized units required for the Russian drive into the rear of Army Group A (the oft-quoted figure of 90 major Soviet units still at the pocket front on 19 January is completely absurd). Another reprehensible aspect of this tragedy was the promise made to the command of the 6th Army at the end of December-beginning of January by Adolf Hitler, against his better judgment, of another relief effort, planned for February or the beginning of March at the latest, and an extensive increase in the air supply effort. The 6th Army can justly be seen as the betrayed army. Strictly speaking it was betrayed several times, first when it was left on its own in Stalingrad when this no longer made any sense militarily, then when it was promised that it would be supplied by air and relieved at the proper time, again when the local commander refused to order a breakout against Hitler's will as long as this was still possible, and finally when it was ordered not to surrender and thus save as many of the soldiers of the 6th Army as possible. In no way does Hitler alone bear the guilt for this tragedy; a full measure also belongs to the leading officers in the OKW and those on the scene, especially Marshals Paulus and von Manstein. Finally, the way the battle ended left a bitter taste, in that the vast majority of the leading generals of the 6th Army, whose blind obedience and in some cases draconian measures to prolong the battle were largely responsible for the fighting continuing as long as it did, went into captivity in good shape and returned safe and sound, while only about 6,000 of the common soldiers survived the Russian prison camps.

[503] See Kurt Ebener's papers for a detailed account of his actions in the Stalingrad pocket.

[504] Uffz. Buttstädt flew this mission in Fw. Ebener's machine; he got off with minor burns and was flown out of the pocket in a Ju 52 the same day.

[505] The third man injured was Uffz. Hans Staufferth of 6/JG 3, who crashed at Smolensk-North as a result of engine trouble on 16 December 1942. He was en route to Morozovskaya, flying a machine that had been initially left behind as unserviceable.

[506] Also see Jacobsen/Rohwer, p. 175 and following pages, and Bekker, *Angriffshöhe 4000*, p. 369 and following pages.

[507] According to his log book, Gerd Schaedle flew this mission, his last from Morozovskaya for the time being, on 20 December. He later returned to Morozovskaya and flew his last mission from there—low-level attacks in the Uryupin area—on 27 December.

[508] WASt. casualty report.

[509] Papers of Kurt Ebener.

[510] The New Year's order from the commanding general of VIII *Fliegerkorps*, GenLt. Fiebig, to JG 3 is quoted as follows in the papers of Karl-Heinz Langer: " *'Hold on in the face of the storm!' is our battle solution for the beginning of 1943. Heil to the Führer! Signed: Fiebig."*

[511] Russian tanks reached and overran Tazinskaya on 24/12/1942, destroying numerous transport aircraft there (a total of 30 according to a daily report by the *Luftwaffe* General Staff dated 27/12/1942). In the days that followed, however, this Russian battle group was wiped out, and on 28/12/1942 Tazinskaya airfield was again reported "*firmly in our hands*". OKW War Diary 1940-41 Part II, p. 1024.

[512] See the papers of Kurt Ebener in the appendices.

[513] See Cartier, Vol. II, p. 590 and following pages.

[514] The Quartermaster-General's loss returns describe these machines as "blown up", however this was not possible given the conditions that existed during the rushed evacuation of the airfield. Also see the papers of Kurt Ebener as well as Bracke, p. 62, with the report by Hans Grünsberg, then a *Feldwebel* pilot and member of the Pitomnik *Staffel*. Five more aircraft belonging to *Stab*/JG 3 were blown up or abandoned at Pitomnik on this day.

[515] Papers of Kurt Ebener; in addition to Fw. Steinicke, the *Schwarm* included *Unteroffiziere* May, Schick and Fischer. GFM Milch, the organizer and director of the air bridge to Stalingrad, wrote: "*29/1/1943: Arrival of 5 Bf 110s of 1/ZG 1 under Oblt. Tratt and 6 Bf 109 G-2s of Stab/JG 3 under Maj. Wilcke at Rovenkie. 30/1/1943: Mission to Stalingrad by all eleven machines from 10:45 to 11:15 AM. Two victories. Oblt. Tratt injured in landing crash caused by engine failure. 31/1/1943: Mission by two Bf 109 at 10:45 AM. Aborted on account of low cloud in the Don bend."*

[516] Account by Karl-Heinz Steinicke, appendix to the papers of Kurt Ebener.

[517] Grid Square 34 East N 99/7/6.

[518] See the inventory lists in the appendices; 19 aircraft were new production machines, the rest were repaired airframes or hand-me-downs from other units.

[519] Including the victories by the *Schwarm* from 6 *Staffel* at Svyerevo.

[520] Of the approximately 230,000 men who according to the 6th Army's strength return of 22nd December were surrounded in the pocket, 42,000 were flown out by 24 January 1943—wounded, sick and specialists. Approximately 20,000 men were captured by the Russians prior to the surrender on 3rd February. 91,000 men were

taken prisoner after the fighting ended, the rest were killed or missing. Compare in detail Jacobsen and Rohwer, p. 310; Carell, p. 458-459.

[521] The effort to supply the Stalingrad pocket from the air was also an extremely costly operation for the *Luftwaffe*; a total of 488 transport aircraft were lost during supply missions to Stalingrad between 24/11/1942 and 31/1/1943: 266 Ju 52s, 165 He 111s, 42 Ju 86s, 9 Fw 200s, 5 He 177s and 1 Ju 290. As well, about 1,000 aircrew were forced to pay with their lives for their commander in chief's arrogant and irresponsible promise.

[522] Operations order issued by Army Group South on 19 February 1943, cited in extract in Schumann, Vol. 3, p. 86-87.

[523] Note the widely-dispersed locations of the losses—evidence of how in those days the weak *Luftwaffe* forces were rushed here and there in the role of "fire brigade" in an effort to provide some measure of fighter cover for the hard-pressed ground forces.

[524] See Schumann, Vol. 3, p. 87 and following pages.

[525] See Schumann, Vol. 3, p. 89; Cartier, Vol. II, p. 597 and following pages.

[526] For example, Gerd Schaedle's log book records six missions from Makeyevka for the period 6 to 17 March 1943, three escort and three free chase missions. Two of the latter were carried out over the front along the Mius north of Taganrog, the rest in the Slavyansk—Izyum area.

[527] See Prien/Stemmer, III/JG 3, p. 204.

[528] Which resulted in the creation of the southern sector of the Kursk salient, which was to be the scene of the great summer battle of 1943; see Schumann, Vol. 3, p. 91.

[529] Also see Prien/Stemmer, III/JG 3, p. 204.

[530] The seventh machine was Oblt. Stolte's "Yellow 1", which was obviously sent for repairs after being damaged on 25 March.

[531] Reporting date 30/3/1943, German Order of Battle, Statistics as of Quarter Years.

[532] The exact date of the transfer to Anapa is not known, however the first missions were apparently flown from there on 10/4/1943. See the combat report by Uffz. Cech. As well, the forward airfield at Gostagayevskaya was sometimes used as an alternate airfield.

[533] Also see OKW War Diary 1942, Part I, p. 283 and following pages.

[534] To these must be added non-combat-related losses, two Messerschmitts destroyed in accidents or through mechanical failure and seven more with varying degrees of damage. See loss lists in the appendices.

[535] Such disparities between victories and losses undoubtedly contributed to the oft-described sense of superiority which the German pilots felt toward their Soviet opponents. As impressive as they undoubtedly were, they could not conceal the fact that, in spite of continuous heavy losses, the Russian air forces were growing stronger and that the days of German air superiority over the main fronts in the east were already long gone. And unlike the *Luftwaffe*, which was incapable of making good its losses, the Soviet air force was able to replace its losses while continuing to catch up in the areas of technology and flight training. As a result, it ultimately surpassed the *Luftwaffe* in every respect, a fact which was underlined by the German air force's final defeat in the east in early 1945. This chain of events was only possible because of faulty personnel planning and training by the *Luftwaffe*, whose leading officers obviously did not understand the signs of the times. It is typical that those who were responsible maintain an embarrassed silence in their postwar memoirs as to how it could have happened that the *Luftwaffe* failed so completely in this vital area. In particular, the autobiography of the former *General der Jagdflieger* (*The First and the Last*), who was at least partly responsible for the state of the fighter arm, offers no rational explanation, apart from the usual assignment of blame to Hitler and Göring. Instead, in these memoirs the loss of technical and personnel superiority to the Soviet air force never takes place. The fact is, however, that the Russian air force had almost doubled in size by July 1943. 35,000 combat aircraft were built in 1943, almost one-third of them Il-2s. In this year the Russians introduced the La 5 FN with a more powerful engine, the Yak 9 D, a variant of the Yak 9 with a heavier cannon armament, the Yak 3, and a version of the Il-2 with a dorsal gunner, more powerful engine and a 37-mm cannon. Thus, by this time the Russians fighters had overtaken their German counterparts in speed, rate of climb and firepower and had also caught up in the area of tactics, employing flights of two or four fighters as the Germans did.

[536] For information concerning the planning for the summer offensive of 1943 see OKW War Diary 1942, Part I, p. 1619 and following pages; Schumann, Vol. 3, p. 518 and following pages.

[537] After the near catastrophe of the winter of 1942-43, which was only averted by GFM von Manstein's brilliantly planned and executed counteroffensive which ended in a German tactical success, given the erosion of German strength, it had to be realized that if the war could not be brought to a quick conclusion, the only possibility of continuing the war in the east was mobile warfare. This would have entailed a drastic shortening of the front, however, and a withdrawal of German forces to the Dvina and the Dniepr, from where the numerical and material superiority of the Red Army could be outmaneuvered by means of fast counterattacks. Such a strategy,

which at least made military sense, would also have given the Reich time to negotiate a cease-fire under acceptable conditions. This could not be reconciled with the ideas and plans of an Adolf Hitler, however, for whom the voluntary surrender of the Ukrainian industrial region, all of Central Russia and the salient at Leningrad were as unacceptable as ending the war without destroying the Jews within the German area of power.

[538] Hitler "sold" this idea to his general staff, arguing that a German success in the east would make it impossible for the Red Army to take the offensive, which would give the *Wehrmacht* time to smash the threat to the Reich from the west. See Cartier, Vol. II, p. 635.

[539] Also see Schumann, Vol. 3, p. 525 and following pages.

[540] See OKW War Diary 1942, Part I.

[541] Log book of Gerd Schaedle; victory claims by Oblt. Kirschner and Oblt. Lucas.

[542] The point and purpose of this transfer are not apparent, for there was heavy fighting along the front of the Kuban bridgehead at this time, while the Kharkov front was relatively quiet, with neither major Soviet attacks nor German counterattacks in preparation. See the Special Directive for the Period from 29 April to 5 May 1943 in the OKW War Diary 1942, Part I, p. 436. It is noteworthy that, at about the same time, I/JG52 was transferred into the same battle zone, namely to Varvarovka airfield. It remained there for 14 days before returning to the Kuban bridgehead.

[543] See, for example, the victory claims by Oblt. Lucas and Oblt. Kirschner.

[544] According to the WASt. casualty report, Uffz. Von Langendorff's machine was last seen spinning down with one wing gone, and no parachute was observed. In fact, Uffz. von Langendorff was taken prisoner by the Soviets.

[545] See Prien/Rodeike/Stemmer, III & IV/JG 27, p. 207. Certain animosities between Ettel and the *Gruppe* command purportedly played a role in this transfer. It is noteworthy that Ettel did not receive the Knight's Cross until he reached 120 victories, while previously it had been standard practice to award the decoration for 50 to 55 victories. Oblt. Gustav Frielinghaus was another Knight's Cross candidate who was "got rid of through promotion"; see immediately below.

[546] Grid Square 34 east N 51/7/9, roughly 27 km southwest of Graivoron.

[547] Log book of Gerd Schaedle.

[548] For example, the service record of Oblt. Lucas of 4/JG 3 records several fighter-bomber missions in May and June 1943, in each case with four 50-kg bombs.

[549] Combat report by Hans Grünberg.

[550] See the description of the formation of the new IV *Gruppe* in Prien, IV/JG 3, p. 1 and following pages.

[551] See the combat reports of Franz Cech of 6/JG 3, who single-handedly scored three victories in this engagement.

[552] The Russian side did not need information from secret traitors in high places in the German command to determine German intention, as some incorrigible historians maintain to this day; instead, all they needed do was look at a map. Furthermore, the Russian network of informants and their partisan army meant that no major German troop movement remained a secret.

[553] Which included the bulk of KG 1, 27, 51, 55 and 100, StG 2 and 77, II and III/JG 3, *Stab*, I and III/JG52 plus various anti-tank *Staffeln* equipped with the Hs 129.

[554] See Groehler, *Luftkrieg*, p. 364. Nearly the same number of aircraft was concentrated in the tiny section of front at Kursk, just 150 kilometers wide, as the *Luftwaffe* had amassed on the entire Eastern Front prior to the start of the invasion of the Soviet Union.

[555] Groehler, *Luftkrieg*, p. 364.

[556] Log book of Gerd Schaedle.

[557] From which he did not return.

[558] Of a total of 37 examples of the new series which were allocated to II/JG 3 in July 1943; see aircraft complement list in the appendices.

[559] See the specification accompanying Line Drawing 8 on p. 201.

[560] *Stab*/JG 3 and I *Gruppe* had already been withdrawn to the Reich for service in the Defense of the Reich.

[561] However, elements of II/JG 3 had already taken off on a free chase at 3:10 AM and after the approaching units were detected they were hastily recalled to their "Garden Fence". See the accompanying combat report by Fw. Hans Grünberg of 5/JG 3, who scored four victories during this mission.

[562] Carell, *Angriffshöhe*, p. 384.

[563] On 5 July 1943 the German side claimed a total of 432 victories, the Russians 173. Top scorer of the day was Obfw. Hubert Strassl of JG 51 with 15 victories, followed by Lt. Wiese and Lt. Krupinski, both of JG 52, with 12 and 11 victories respectively.

[564] Groehler, *Luftkrieg*, p. 369.

[565] See Cartier, Vol. II, p. 635 and following pages, especially 641-642.

[566] Recognized as such, although in fact it was II/JG 3's 2,035th victory; see the victory lists in the appendices.

[567] The cessation of the attack was not noted in the *Wehrmacht* Command Staff's war diary until 19 July 1943; however, this may just have been a confirmation of what had already happened days earlier.

[568] The division of the *Gruppe* into the parts moved to Kutelnikovo and the one left at Rogany was obviously done across *Staffel* lines, as a result of which elements of all three *Staffeln* were present at both airfields. In the days that followed, the *Gruppe* was further split apart when individual *Schwärme* were sent to operate from Ugrim and Varvarovka. See log book of Gerd Schaedle and combat reports by Hans Frese.

[569] See Prien/Stemmer, III/JG 3, p. 212.

[570] See OKW War Diary 1942, Part II, p. 802 and following pages.

[571] It appears that some pilots operated from Rogany for a few days and then from Kutelnikovo again, for example Oblt. Lucas and Fw. Frese of 4/JG 3 and Uffz. Thyben of 6/JG 3.

[572] See information concerning weather-related reductions in *Luftwaffe* activity in the OKW War Diary 1942, Part II, for example on 23 and 26 July 1943.

[573] See the accompanying combat report by Lt. Hermann Schuster and the letter of condolence written by Oblt. Werner Lucas.

[574] See OKW War Diary 1942, Part II, p. 867 and following pages.

[575] See Prien/Stemmer, III/JG 3, p. 213.

[576] His last words over the radio were: *"Damn it, I haven't scored yet!"*

[577] Account by Helmut Hennig, 30/11/1985.

[578] It is very likely that a significant number of pilots reported missing were actually taken prisoner; they remain officially missing, however, because there was no official confirmation of their prisoner of war status and they died while captive.

[579] See Prien/Stemmer, III/JG 3, p. 214 or the corresponding loss information in Prien, JG 53 Part 2 concerning I/JG 53's activities in the east in the summer of 1942, and in JG 77 Part 2 for JG 77's losses in the east in 1942.

[580] It is noteworthy that all three losses occurred during II/JG 3's last month of operations in the east.

[581] It is striking that the total number of non-combat-related losses clearly exceeds the figure for losses due to enemy action. Among the 54 machines with degrees of damage between 31% and 60%, 37 are "o.F", meaning not due to enemy action, while the 10% to 30% group includes another 33 such losses. The total works out to 105 non-combat-related losses against 81 due to enemy action.

Engine maintenance on the aircraft of the Gruppenkommandeur *of II/JG 3, Hptm. Kurt Brändle, on Chuguyev airfield at the end of May 1942. The machine is Bf 109 F-4 WerkNr. 8665; it had previously been flown by Hptm. Krahl from Sicily before he took charge of a new aircraft a short time before his death. Below: A II Gruppe technician on a Bf 109 F-4, photographed on a forward airfield in the east in spring 1942. Note the circular wheel wells, the covered firing port in the propeller spinner for the engine-mounted cannon, and the antenna mast for the FuG 25 under the fuselage. (Hennig/Fischer)*

Hptm. Kurt Brändle at Gorschechnoye airfield after returning from a successful mission at the beginning of July 1942. The aircraft is a Bf 109 F-4 trop which Brändle began flying after his previously illustrated machine was damaged. Unlike the previous and subsequent machines flown by him, this one wears a black staff marking. Also note the black finish in the wing root area intended to conceal exhaust staining, the Gruppe *emblem in front of the cockpit, and the attachment points left behind by the supporting struts for sand filter, which has since been removed. In the photo at the top of the page Helmut Hennig, Hptm. Brändle's maintenance chief, is seen standing on the wing. (Hennig)*

Lt. Hans Fuß, Staffelführer *of 6/JG 3 since 1 August 1942, photographed at Frolov airfield on 7 August 1942. On the rudder of his machine are 67 rather unevenly applied victory bars. Note the marking on the fuselage sides aft of the* Balkenkreuz; *unfortunately the entire emblem cannot be seen, however it obviously includes a pair of wings. (BA)*

Above: "Black 6", the aircraft of Obfw. Alfred Heckmann of 5 Staffel, photographed after 10 July 1942, probably on the forward airfield at Marijewka. Thirty-eight victory bars may be seen on the rudder; Heckmann scored his 35th to 38th victories on the early morning of 10 July 1942, just prior to the Gruppe*'s move to Marijewka. The machine wears a gray-green camouflage scheme with rather dense mottling on the fuselage sides supplemented by a narrow yellow band on the aft fuselage. The* Gruppe *emblem appears in front of the cockpit, the* Geschwader *emblem on the engine cowling. Below: Uffz. Hans Frese of 4/JG 3 in the cockpit of his Bf 109 F-4; the aircraft's considerably modified finish and the partly overpainted aircraft number, which was changed from a "10" to a "13", suggest that this machine may have been one of the "Friedrichs" taken over from other* Gruppen *in July 1942. Once again note the* Geschwader *emblem on the engine cowling. (Fischer)*

A pair of II Gruppe *aircraft which sustained heavy damaged when struck by a Ju 87 of I/StG 2 which ground-looped while taking off from Kantemirovka airfield on 13 July 1942. Five of 4/JG 3's mechanics were killed in this accident, another mechanic and a pilot were seriously injured, and a total of four Messerschmitts sustained significant damage. Above a Bf 109 F-4 of 4 Staffel with a broken fuselage, and below another seriously-damaged machine, in front of which lies the wreckage of the Ju 87 D responsible for this catastrophe. (Hennig)*

Hptm. Kurt Brändle with another machine, a Bf 109 F-4 with the WerkNr. 13 387, which he flew in August 1942. These photographs were taken at Tuzov airfield in mid-August. This aircraft once again wears white staff markings; also note the Gruppe *and* Geschwader *emblems, the narrow yellow band on the aft fuselage and the total of 95 white victory bars on the rudder. (Hennig)*

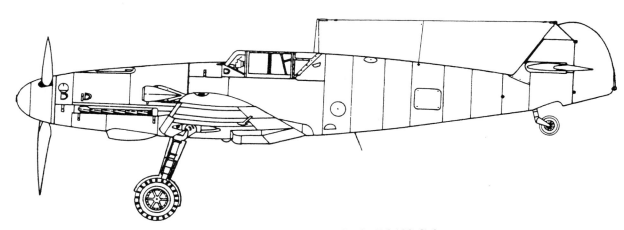

Line Drawing 6: Messerschmitt Bf 109 G-2

In September 1942 II/JG 3 received its first examples of the Bf 109 G-2, which was to be the *Gruppe*'s main equipment until March 1943, when it was replaced by the G-4 series. The main differences between the G-2 and the preceding F-4 were the installation of the more powerful DB 605 A-1 engine and various detail changes such as sturdier cockpit framing, which was necessary to replace the previous externally-mounted armor-glass panel with an integral 50-mm armored windscreen, and the transfer of the fuel filler point to the fuselage spine.

Length: 8.94 m   Engine: Daimler Benz DB 605 A-1, 1,475 H.P.   Empty weight: 2 330 kg

Wingspan: 9.92 m   Takeoff weight: 3 400 kg

Height: 2.60 m   Armament: 1 MG 151/20, 2 MG 17

Winter-camouflaged Messerschmitts of 5/JG 3, photographed on a forward airfield somewhere in the southern sector of the Eastern Front during the winter of 1942-43. (Ebener)

The aircraft of the Kommandeur *of II/JG 3 in a white winter camouflage finish; even the propeller spinner and the forward faces of the propeller blades have been oversprayed white. Hptm. Kurt Brändle flew this Bf 109 G-2 on missions into the Stalingrad area from Morozovskaya and Tazinskaya in December 1942. Note the red dot beneath the* Geschwader *emblem, an addition that was often seen on II* Gruppe *aircraft from this time. In the background is "Black 1" of 5/JG 3, likewise in a winter white camouflage scheme. (Stiflung Prussian culture collection)*

Above: With the help of rubber and wooden mallets, two ground crew free one of II/JG 3's Bf 109 G-2 from its coat of ice in preparation for the next mission. For the "black men," working almost constantly in winter conditions of ice, snow and often biting wind was a tremendous hardship. Below: Congratulations for Hptm. Brändle at Rowenkie following his return from a sortie on the morning of 2 February 1943, during which he scored his 126th to 129th victories. Note the unusual staff marking, obviously applied over an earlier marking, on this Bf 109 G-2, which still wears an unmodified gray-green camouflage scheme in spite of the winter conditions. (MBB/Hennig)

The following photographs depict several Bf 109 G-2s of II/JG 3, some with underwing cannon, which were captured by Russian troops in flyable condition on Pitomnik airfield on 17 January 1943. Although the original finish has been overpainted in the area of the German national insignia, the Geschwader *emblem (in red outline form) remains with the red dot beneath it as seen on II* Gruppe *aircraft. (Petrick)*

The machine with the WerkNr. 14 513 was subsequently restored to flying condition and was tested extensively at the Moscow flight test center. Prior to this, the Messerschmitt became part of a propaganda fairy tale published on 21 January 1943. As the story went, the Messerschmitt's pilot shot down an Il-2 flown by Lt. Kuznetsov and forced it to make a crash-landing, then set down next to the burning Il-2 and inspected the crash, seeking a trophy. Meanwhile, Lt. Kuznetsov climbed into the Messerschmitt unnoticed and flew it back to his home base. Although this story was pure invention, it was eagerly picked up by the Allied press agencies, which held it up as a shining example of the courage and inventiveness of their Russian allies.

Above: Hptm. Kurt Brändle with one of his Gruppe's Messerschmitts in the middle of an engine change, photographed on a forward airfield in the east in spring 1943. Below: Kurt Brändle, since promoted to Major, in the cockpit of his Bf 109 G-4 "Black Double Chevron" during preparations for takeoff, photographed at Anapa on 17 April 1943; note the two clip holders for a sun umbrella beneath the cockpit, which suggests that this machine was originally delivered as a tropical variant. (BA/Wahl/Hennig)

"White 2" of 4/JG 3, a Bf 109 G-2, after a belly landing in spring 1943. The aircraft wears an obviously modified gray-green finish with a yellow fuselage band which was applied right next to the Balkenkreuz. *Noteworthy marking details include the red dot beneath the* Geschwader *emblem and the combination of black* Gruppe *bar and white aircraft number; the latter was standard practise in II/JG 3, for from this time on the* Gruppe *bar was always black, regardless of the* Staffel *color. Finally, note the finish of the propeller spinner, which was red with a white tip. (Wahl)*

Above left: Lt. Ernst-Heinz "Bubi" Löhr of 6/JG 53 describes one of the two victories he scored on 20 April 1943 for a propaganda service photographer; Anapa, 6 May 1943. Note the dot (in this case possibly yellow) beneath the Geschwader *emblem. Above right and below: Pre-flight preparations by Lt. Hermann Schuster of 4/JG 3, photographed on a forward airfield in the east on 28 May 1943. (Ewald/Wahl)*

Above: A Bf 109 G-4 of 5 Staffel, probably "Black 10". Note the considerable contrast in the shades of gray that make up the splinter scheme; photographed at Anapa in May 1943. The wing crosses, black with a narrow white surround, are unusual for a Bf 109 G. Understandably, the pilots always wore life vests on missions flown from Anapa; note the old kapok life vests worn by the pilots depicted here. Below: The pilots of 5/JG 3 toast the Staffel's 500th victory; the photo must have been taken in May 1943. Gathered in front of "Black 12", a Bf 109 G-2, are, from right, Fw. Grünberg, Obfw. Brocks, unidentified, Lt. Bohatsch (with accordion), Staffelkapitän Oblt. Kirschner, unidentified, and Uffz. Fischer. (Wahl)

Above: The camouflage finish of this Bf 109 G-4 of 4/JG 3 ("White 10") has been oversprayed with a dark color in order to increase the camouflage effect; the white aircraft number and the white surround of the Balkenkreuz *were not spared in the process. Also note the lighter area behind the fuselage cross, probably part of a band on the underside of the fuselage only. Kharkov-Roganj, May-June 1943. Below: Leopold Münster, promoted to* Leutnant *at the beginning of May 1943, on his Bf 109 G-4 "White 3", photographed on a forward airfield in the east in May-June 1943. This machine's finish has also been considerably augmented on the upper surfaces, and once again the aircraft number has been oversprayed. The reason for these efforts to increase the effectiveness of the camouflage may have been the numerous attacks by Russian close-support aircraft on airfields occupied by the* Luftwaffe. *(Wahl)*

Above: A Bf 109 G-4 of the Gruppenstab, *photographed at Kjarkov-Roganj in the early summer of 1943. Part of the aircraft's black chevron marking is just visible above the wing. The engine cowling underside must be yellow, the propeller spinner possibly red. Note the* Geschwader *emblem with the red dot beneath it. Below: Pilot and tecnicians of II* Gruppe *seek shade beneath a "Gustav", Kharkov, July 1943. Once again note the red dot beneath the* Geschwader *emblem. (Wahl)*

Above: While at cockpit readiness, Uffz. Thomas Ametsbichler, a pilot in 4/JG 3, uses a sun umbrella to protect himself from the heat in the cramped cockpit of his Bf 109 G-4; the photo was probably taken at Kharkov. Note the sealed air inlet beneath the windscreen assembly and the absence of the rectangular cockpit ventilation flap in the fuselage side. Below: The stained fuselage sides of this 4 Staffel Messerschmitt ("White 2" or "3") suggest that the forced landing was caused by engine failure or engine damage; the folding hood, in particular, appears to be especially heavily "pasted over" with oil. Scarcely still visible is the fuselage band aft of the Balkenkreuz, while the white aircraft number once again appears to have been oversprayed. Where and when this photo was taken is not known, probably in the Kharkov area in spring 1943. (Ametsbichler/Wahl)

Above: Maj. Kurt Brändle and Oblt. Joachim Kirschner, two of the outstanding "experts" of II/JG 3, photographed in the east in summer 1943. Below: Oblt. Kirschner interrogated a Russian pilot who was captured after being shot down. (Petrick)

Above left: Oblt. Förster, officer in the Geschwaderstab of JG 3, in front of a Bf 109 G of II Gruppe; note the aircraft's very dark camouflage scheme. Above right: Another shot of Uffz. Ametsbichler of 4/JG 3 in the cockpit of his "Gustav", a Bf 109 G-4. This view reveals details of the cockpit, including the cockpit air inlet beneath the windscreen structure on the right side only. Also note the thin tube of the windscreen washer in front of the windscreen. Below: Congratulations for Oblt. Kirschner's 150th victory on 5th July 1943. (Wahl/Ring)

Above and below left: Two photographs of a 6 Staffel *pilot in the cockpit of his Bf 109 G-4, photographed at Kharkov in July 1943. This aircraft also lacks the ventilation inlet beneath the windscreen; here it has been replaced with a circular cover, as was sometimes seen. Below right and following page: These photographs were purportedly taken on the forward airfield at Besonovka on 5 July*

1943 after Maj. Kurt Brändle returned from a mission in which he shot down two Il-2s for his 150th and 151st victories. Brändle gives his maintenance chief the first account of the air battle while still sitting in the cockpit; meanwhile, several mechanics are busy themselves with the engine so as to ready the machine, a Bf 109 G-6 with the code "Black Chevron Triangle", for its next sortie. (Wahl)

A drink to the Gruppenkommandeur*'s "milestone victory"; the pilot in the middle is holding* II Gruppe*'s congratulatory card and the bouquet of flowers. The common German soldier, who at this time was literally lying in the mud in fierce fighting on the first day of "Operation Citadel," would probably have shaken his head in amazement at such ceremonies, for which he and many others had no time. (Wahl)*

Messerschmitts of II Gruppe *parked on Kharkov airfield at the beginning of July 1943; in the left foreground is "Yellow 1", a Bf 109 G-6 of 6/JG 3. Note the combination, typical for II/JG 3, of aircraft number in the* Staffel *color and black* Gruppe *bar. The engine cowling underside is yellow, however the panel in front of it is unusually dark. Note that neither a yellow fuselage band or the* Gruppe *or* Geschwader *emblem is to be seen. (Wahl)*

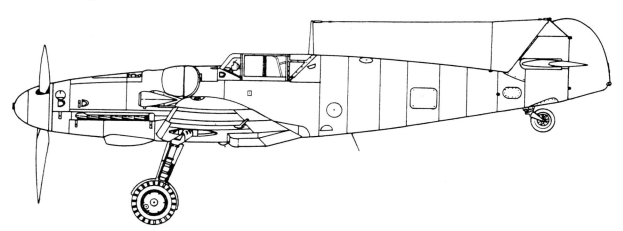

Line Drawing 7: Messerschmitt Bf 109 G-6

II/JG 3 began receiving its first examples of the Bf 109 G-6 at the beginning of July 1943 and it soon replaced the G-4 which had been the unit's principal equipment until then. The most significant difference between the G-6 and its predecessor was the new variant's more powerful armament, the result of replacing the MG 17s above the engine with two MG 131s.

Length: 8.94 m   Engine: DB 605 A, 1,475 H.P.   Empty weight: 2 330 kg
Wingspan: 9.92 m   Takeoff weight: 3 400 kg
Height: 2.60 m   Armament: 1 MG 151/20, 2 MG131

The machine illustrated here is an early production example as delivered to II/JG 3 in the east, still with a tall antenna mast and all-metal head armor in the folding hood.

Oblt. Werner Lucas, Staffelkapitän of 4/JG 3, photographed at Kharkov at the beginning of July 1943. On the left he is seen sitting on an auxiliary fuel tank, above in front of the ordnance sergeant's tent, in front of which crates of ammunition have been lined up. Right of the tent are several more external fuel tanks. In the background is "White 6", a Bf 109 G-4 of 4/ JG 3; this aircraft quite obviously lacks a yellow fuselage band. (Wahl)

This and the following page: Three photos taken on 12 July 1943; Uffz. Walter Stienhans had previously scored his 5th, and—allegedly—II/JG 3's 2,000th victory, here seen being celebrated in appropriate fashion in the presence of a propaganda service cameraman. Above Uffz. Stienhans may be seen on the far left, in the middle Maj. Brändle and on his right Lt. Löhr, who scored

his 27th to 29th victories during the same mission. Below Lt. Löhr once again and in the foreground the certificate produced by the Gruppe *to mark its 2,000th victory, which was presented to Uffz. Stienhans on this day. Below: Running up the engine of a 4* Staffel *Bf 109 G-6 armed with underwing cannon. Note the absence of the* Geschwader *emblem and the finish on the propeller spinner with the tip in the* Staffel *color white, which was standard until the* Gruppe *returned to the Reich in August 1943. (Hennig/de Visser)*

8

Operations in the Defense of the Reich
September 1943 to June 1944

The commencement of daylight raids by heavy bombers of the American 8th Air Force against targets in the occupied western territories in the summer of 1942 marked the beginning of a new chapter in the air war, one which soon posed another serious threat to the German war effort[581]. The first daylight raid against a target inside the Reich, albeit with relatively modest forces, took place on 27 January 1943, when a force of 55 Boeing B-17s bombed the port of Wilhelmshaven[582]. In the weeks and months that followed, the weight of the American attacks against targets inside the Reich grew considerably; not only was there a steady increase in the number of heavy bombers attacking Germany, but the depth of penetration by the bomber formations was gradually increased as well. And so, in March 1943, the American 8th Air Force launched its first strikes against targets in the western part of the Reich[583]. One of the few remaining weaknesses of the American heavy bombers was their lack of fighter escort all the way to the target; the range of the available escort fighter, the P-47, and the Spitfires of the RAF was only sufficient to escort the "heavies" as far as the areas of Netherlands and Belgium adjacent to the borders of the Reich. As a result, once over Germany the formations of B-17s and B-24s had to fend for themselves against the German fighters and destroyers.

The first American daylight raids encountered a very weak German fighter defense. Since the start of the war, the *Luftwaffe* had irresponsibly failed to expand its fighter force to keep pace with the demands of the air war[584]. Consequently the available fighter resources were already insufficient to protect the fronts in the east, south and west, and there was a total lack of immediately available forces or even reserves which could be used over the home war zone. At the beginning of 1943 the *Luftwaffe* had just one *Jagdgeschwader*, JG 1, with which to guard all of the Reich; its four *Gruppen* had to defend the entire coastline from Holland to the south of Norway. In addition, there were two units stationed in the occupied western territories, JG 2 and JG 26, which were under the command of *Luftflotte* 3 and responsible for the defense of France and Belgium. Following the start of the American daylight raids, the *Luftwaffe* command did make some effort to bolster the Defense of the Reich, transferring a number of *Jagdgruppen* from the east[585], however in the face of the concentrated power of the American bomber fleets on the other side of the Channel this was little more than patchwork.

The level of devastation inflicted by the catastrophe at Hamburg in July and August 1943 and the obvious ineffectiveness of the defensive effort had to unsettle and frighten the German command, and in fact the shock of Hamburg caused a fundamental debate within the ranks of the *Luftwaffe* command about the future conduct of the air war. In the end, however, there was no decision for a clear concentration of effort to create an effective air defense over the Reich; instead, a basic misunderstanding of the prevailing conditions led to a vague and consequently ineffective compromise in which the Defense of the Reich was to be significantly strengthened and expanded, while at the same time the *Luftwaffe*'s offensive forces would be bolstered for a resumption of attacks against Great Britain[586]. Since there were no effective short-term alternatives anyway, the *Luftwaffe* command did the only thing it could to counter the bombing terror. It reached out for the forces that were available to it and ruthlessly stripped the eastern and southern fronts of further fighter forces, transferring units to the Reich. This resulted in five more *Jagdgruppen* joining the Defense of the Reich in the following weeks—three *Gruppen* of JG 3 from the east and from Italy[587] together with II/JG 27 and II/JG 51, both of which also came from the Italian theater[588]. In addition, the remaining *Zerstörer* units were transferred back to the Reich from the fronts in the east and south, as the *Luftwaffe* command believed that the heavily-armed Bf 110 would prove very effective in combating the combat boxes of heavy bombers[589].

****

On 3 August 1943[590] the bulk of II/JG 3's air element[591] and all of the Ju 52s carrying the key technical personnel[592] arrived at Uetersen, where, in the weeks that followed, the *Gruppe* was to receive a hasty overhaul. Meanwhile, the main column of ground personnel, which was supposed to follow by rail, was stuck in Dnepropetrovsk until 11 August, consequently it was not expected to arrive at Uetersen until about the 20th[593]. One of the *Gruppe*'s first tasks was to exchange its complement of Bf 109 G-4s and recently acquired G-6s for the latest model Bf 109 G-6s. In keeping with its planned employment as a so-called "light *Gruppe*", the unit's aircraft were not equipped with the underwing 20-mm cannon usually associated with the anti-bomber role. On the other hand, several of the *Gruppe*'s Messerschmitts were outfitted with the extra radio equipment needed for the "Y-Method" of ground control[594]. Externally, installation of the FuG 16 ZY was indicated by the presence of an antenna mast beneath the fuselage[595]. On 9 August the 23 machines which were to be turned in departed for Cracow, from where they were later passed on to units in the east. Meanwhile, the allocation of new machines was initially very slow[596], and by the end of August 1943 II/JG 3 had received just ten Bf 109 G-6s to join the eight Messerschmitts that had not been turned in[597].

When it arrived at Uetersen, II/JG 3 was down to 25 pilots fit for duty[598], as a result of which it was assigned a number of young replacement pilots. As soon as they arrived, the newcomers began working themselves into the *Gruppe* unit. In the beginning, training aircraft also had to be used for this purpose because of the shortage of Messerschmitts[599]. There were no changes in the command structure of II/JG 3 at first, and consequently it looked like this[600]:

II/JG 3 List of Officers on 1 September 1943

Gruppenkommandeur	Maj. Kurt Brändle
Gruppenadjutant	Lt. Max-Bruno Fischer
Staffelkapitän 4/JG 3	Oblt. Werner Lucas[601]
Staffelkapitän 5/JG 3	Hptm. Joachim Kirschner
Staffelkapitän 6/JG 3	Hptm. Paul Stolte

At this point in time, the *Gruppe* was at the peak of its fighting strength in terms of personnel, for its ranks included a large number of experienced and very successful pilots. When the *Gruppe*'s deployment in the west began, *Gruppenkommandeur* Hptm. Brändle, a wearer of the Oak Leaves since August 1942, had 170 victories. The *Kapitän* of 5/JG 3, Joachim Kirschner, had the same number of victories, and his success had resulted in his promotion to the rank of *Hauptmann* and the awarding of the Oak Leaves on 2 August 1943. Oblt. Werner Lucas, *Kapitän* of 4/JG 3, had 105 victories and wore the Knight's Cross, while Hptm. Paul Stolte of 6/JG 3 had 40 victories to his credit. The *Gruppe* also possessed a

number of other "*Experten*" with considerable victory totals. There was Lt. Leopold "Poldi" Münster of 5/JG 3 who had 76 victories and wore the Knight's Cross, Fw. Hans Grünberg of 5 *Staffel* with 61 victories, Fw. Helmut Rüffler of 4 *Staffel*[601] with 51, Fw. Hans Frese of 4/JG 3 with 41, FhjObfw. Josef Schütte of 5 *Staffel* with 40, Oblt. Ernst-Heinz Löhr[603], also of 5 *Staffel*, with 33, while Fw. Franz Cech and Uffz. Gerhard Thyben, both of 6 *Staffel*, each had 32 victories.

At the beginning of September 1943 the *Gruppe* was still in the overhaul phase at Uetersen. Happily, there were no serious incidents and no personnel or material losses. Slowly, new machines arrived, including the first fourteen Bf 109 G-5s. Unlike the G-6, the Bf 109 G-5 had a pressurized cockpit for high-altitude operation[604]. By 12 September 1943 the *Gruppe*'s aircraft complement had swelled to 41 machines, 14 Bf 109 G-5s and 27 G-6s. On that day the *Gruppe* began moving to its new base of operations at Schiphol, a large air base 10 kilometers south of Amsterdam. For operations in the Defense of the Reich, II/JG 3 was initially attached to the *JaFü Holland/Ruhrgebiet* (Fighter Commander Holland/Ruhr Region) based at Deelen, while for day to day operations it was to be under the command of JG 1, which was in turn part of 3 *Jagddivision*[605]. From this point on, the primary mission of II/JG 3 would be to engage the fighters escorting American heavy bombers attacking targets in Reich territory. These were mainly American P-47s, but large numbers of RAF Spitfires[606] also operated in this area. A secondary task was defending against the by now almost ceaseless attacks by British fighter-bombers and light bombers against German coastal shipping and targets in the coastal region of Holland. Since Schiphol airport was close to the sea and right in the main approach route used by the heavy bombers, it was obvious that the *Gruppe* was facing a difficult task.

Things began quietly, however, for after the heavy losses incurred in the last major daylight raids on 17 August and 6 September[607], there was a temporary halt to incursions by the heavy bombers of the 8th Air Force while considerable efforts were made to increase the range of the fighter escort[608]. The first mission from Schiphol by II/JG 3 to result in contact with the enemy took place in the early evening on 16 September 1943[609]. Eight Messerschmitts of 4 *Staffel* under the command of Lt. Ruhl were providing fighter cover for a minesweeper group in the waters off Den Helder and the island of Texel, when a group of Beaufighters escorted by several RAF Mustangs appeared at low-level and headed toward the minesweepers. Both *Schwärme* immediately turned to attack, whereupon the Beaufighters turned away to the west and tried to flee at low level. The Messerschmitts closed, however, and Lt. Ruhl (21) and FhjFw. Frese (42) each shot down one of the twin-engined machines. Hits were also scored on a Mustang, however it was not seen to crash. 4/JG 3 sustained no losses.

The days that followed were largely uneventful. On 21 September 1943 there was a scramble to intercept reported enemy in-

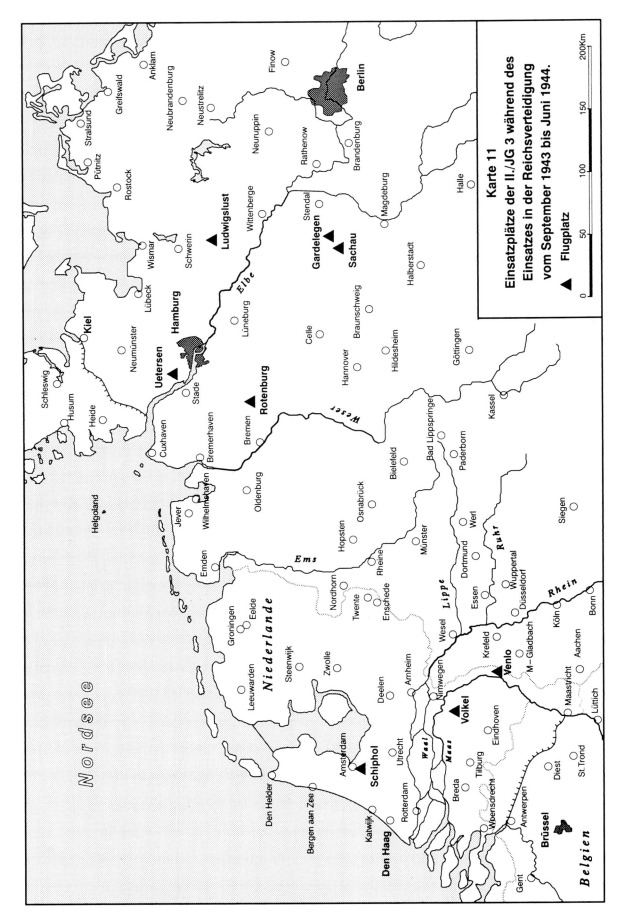

Karte 11

Einsatzplätze der II./JG 3 während des
Einsatzes in der Reichsverteidigung
vom September 1943 bis Juni 1944.

▲ Flugplatz

cursions; the machine of Uffz. Rudolf Scheibe of 5 *Staffel* developed engine trouble and he was forced to put it down on its belly near Halfweg, sustaining minor injuries. No enemy aircraft were encountered[610]. The next day, 22 September 1943, there was again a whole series of incursions by British and American formations[611], and II/JG 3 was one of the units sent up to intercept them. The end result for the *Gruppe* was one victory and one loss: while Uffz. Koch of 4 *Staffel* was able to shoot down a P-47 for his first victory, Uffz. Eduard Bartsch, also of 4/JG 3, was forced to bail out after his machine was hit in combat with Spitfires near Giessendamm. Bartsch was not injured. After a scramble and subsequent mission on the 23rd failed to produce contact with the enemy[612], on 24 September the *Gruppe* had its first encounter with American heavy bombers. At 4:44 PM 24 Bf 109s of II/JG 3[613] scrambled from Schiphol. They were subsequently guided by Y-control to intercept a formation of 80 to 100 B-17s heading home over the sea. The American formation had not made an attack, instead it was on the return leg of a practice mission[614] when, at about 5:15 PM, II/JG 3 made its attack east of Yarmouth[615]. A total of three victories was subsequently claimed, these going to Hptm. Stolte (41), who was leading the *Gruppe* on this day, Hptm. Kirschner (171) and Lt. Ruhl (22). The *Gruppe* suffered no losses.

After two largely uneventful days—apart from a fruitless scramble[616]—on 27 September 1943 units of the 8th Air Force carried out their first major daylight raid with fighter escort all the way to the target and back[617]. At 10:20 AM three large formations of heavy bombers, consisting of 308 B-17s, and their fighter escort were detected west of Terschelling. The bombers were flying east toward Emden, where they were to bomb shipyards and industrial targets. The German side mobilized a total of seven *Jagdgruppen* against this incursion, including II/JG 3[618]. After a brief period of cockpit readiness, at 10:33 AM every serviceable machine scrambled from Schiphol. The following account of the mission is from Lt. Franz Ruhl's combat report:

> Guided by Y-control, at 10:55 AM we sighted three or four groups of heavy bombers, 250 altogether, which were coming in from the west at an altitude of 8 500 meters. Above them were about ten enemy fighters, whose condensation trails made them clearly visible. Following the Kommandeur, I attacked the two formations, however I turned in too soon and had to fire while I was still in the turn. As a result, I was only able to hit one Boeing in its right outboard engine and another in the fuselage. From this point west of the Friesian Islands to the area of Aurich, I made eight frontal attacks on individual groups. Near Emden we flew through the barrage fire put up by the flak; they had the altitude right, however their shells were exploding to the side. So far I had hit eight different machines[619]. One of them immediately began to smoke heavily

> and dropped out of formation; from 6 000 meters I could see it clearly, over the coast at a height of 2 000 meters, descending toward the sea. The various formations assembled over Aurich and turned around, appearing to drop bombs. In order to frustrate their aim, I attacked one formation along the 'stairway of aircraft.' In the process I closed from 500 to 50 meters on the second or third Boeing of the flight on the right, firing the whole while. I scored approximately 15 to 20 hits with explosive ammunition[620] on the left wing, both engines, cockpit and fuselage center-section. The inner left wing was already burning when I pulled up and over the aircraft. While climbing away along the 'stairway of aircraft,' I was hit in the engine from the left front and then in the right wing. Since escaping coolant prevented me from seeing anything in front, I jettisoned the canopy and was able to see the bomber peeling out of formation. I then landed at Bad Zwischenahn.

When the mission was over, the *Gruppe*'s machines, low on fuel or with battle damage, landed at airfields scattered over the German-Dutch border area. Some aircraft which could be made ready in time apparently took part in a second mission against the withdrawing formations of heavy bombers; in the afternoon the *Gruppe* reassembled at its base of operations. When the fighting was over, II/JG 3 claimed five four-engined bombers shot down and one forced to leave formation[621,622]. The *Gruppe*'s losses were one pilot missing, one seriously wounded and one slightly injured plus three machines written off with greater than 80% damage. All three pilot casualties were from 6 *Staffel*. Uffz. Fritz Schwalbach failed to return following combat with B-17s over the sea north of Groningen and was reported missing. Fw. Franz Cech was badly wounded when his aircraft "Yellow 10" was hit in the cockpit; he subsequently put his machine down on its belly north of Groningen. Although he was immediately taken to hospital in Groningen, Cech's injuries proved to be so serious that he was no longer fit to fly. More fortunate was *Staffelkapitän* Hptm. Paul Stolte: his aircraft was shot up and he was forced to make a belly landing northwest of Marx. Stolte sustained minor injuries but was able to remain with the *Gruppe*[623].

The rest of the month was relatively quiet; on the evening of 29 September, two *Schwärme* were scrambled to intercept low-flying British aircraft over the Scheldt Estuary but failed to make contact[624]. On the afternoon of 2 October 1943 Emden was again the target of a major daylight raid by heavy bomber units of the 8th Air Force; escorted by 227 Thunderbolts, a total of 349 B-17s dropped over 950 tons of bombs on the harbor area and industrial facilities between 3:57 and 4:03 PM. The target area was obscured by a thick layer of cloud, but H2S target-finding radar allowed the bombers to achieve a high degree of accuracy and damage on the ground was correspondingly heavy[625]. The German defensive effort was seriously hampered by the bad weather; I *Jagdkorps* was able to muster 263 fighters, destroyers and night fighters against the incoming bombers, but in the end only a fraction of them made contact with the enemy[626]. II/JG 3 was one of the few *Jagdgruppen* to actually make contact with the bombers, shooting down four heavies in a bitter battle of the East Friesian coast in the area of Nordeney—Emden[627]. This success came at the cost of two pilots killed: Fw. Rudolf Blomann and Obgefr. Günter Wollenweber, both of 4 *Staffel*, were shot down in combat with the American fighter escort between Aurich and Leer and went down with their machines.

The number of missions increased noticeably in the first days of October 1943. On 3 October 1943 the *Gruppe* was scrambled three times against reported incursions by Allied bombers. The first saw fourteen Messerschmitts take off from Schiphol at 11:59 AM after several formations of bombers were detected approaching Dutch airspace. These turned out to be about 140 Marauders with a strong escort of P-47s and Spitfires; the Allied formations were en route to attack German air bases at Schiphol, Woensdrecht and Haamstede[628]. Less than twenty minutes after takeoff, the small II/JG 3 formation encountered an approaching group of Marauders. It was unable to close with the bombers, however, as it was engaged in a fierce dogfight by the escorting Spitfires and P-47s. Three victories were scored, while one Messerschmitt was shot down and another damaged and forced to make a belly landing. The pilots of both aircraft escaped without serious injury. Nothing is known about the effects of the attack on Schiphol airfield, however II/JG 3 does not appear to have suffered any damage. In the afternoon there were two more missions against reported incursions by large formations of enemy fighters[629], each involving nine aircraft, but neither resulted in contact with the enemy.

4 October 1943: Two separate attacks by the 8th Air Force on this day were directed at targets near Frankfurt/Main and in the Saar region. The two attack forces, which consisted of 323 B-17s escorted by 223 P-47s[630], set out in the morning and passed over Holland on their way to Germany. II/JG 3 was among the defending units[631]. The *Gruppe*'s mission on this day fits almost seamlessly into the overall picture of the German defensive effort, which was an almost total failure[632]. The German units once again failed to deflect the attackers from their targets and as a result considerable damage was inflicted, especially in Frankfurt, while their own score, 14 enemy aircraft claimed shot down, was unimpressive[633]. II/JG 3 pursued the combat boxes of bombers as they made their way southeast. It was unable to close effectively with the bombers, as the fighter escort broke up its attacks before they could begin and forced the Messerschmitts away from the bombers. As a result, in the end II/JG 3 claimed just three enemy aircraft shot down in return for one casualty. Fw. Alfred Kalitta of 6/JG 3 was shot down north of Aachen and bailed out with minor wounds[634]. When the mission was over, most of the *Gruppe*'s aircraft landed at airfields in the

Frankfurt—Wiesbaden area. Later in the day they flew back to Schiphol, where at 4:30 PM GenMaj. Josef Schmid, the commanding general of I *Jagdkorps*, arrived for a brief visit accompanied by Obstlt. Walter Oesau, then on the staff of I *Jagdkorps*[635].

Operationally, the next three days were uneventful for II/JG 3. The unit's next defensive mission came on 8 October and was directed against a daylight raid by units of the 8th Air Force. In the afternoon the Americans first dispatched 344 B-17s with a strong fighter escort against Bremen and soon afterward a second force of 55 B-24s was sent to attack the Vegesack U-boat yard near Bremen[636]. The incursion by the heavy bombers ran into a determined German defense by elements of four fighter and one destroyer *Geschwader*, a total of 441 aircraft[637]. The German defensive effort was directed mainly against the first force of bombers attacking Bremen. II/JG 3, which scrambled from Schiphol at 2:08 PM[638], was one of the first *Gruppen* to make contact with the enemy. Shortly after 3 PM, over the Ijsselmeer the Messerschmitts encountered a formation of B-17s guarded by P-47s. Two bombers were subsequently claimed shot down by Lt. Ruhl (24-25) and one P-47 by Fw. Thyben. The *Gruppe* lost one pilot killed: Lt. Horst Feder of 4/JG 3 was shot down and killed near Anderen, south of Groningen. When its fuel ran low (II/JG 3's Messerschmitts did not carry drop tanks and thus had an endurance of barely an hour), the *Gruppe* was forced to break off the battle and return to its "Garden Fence." There the machines were hastily rearmed and refueled so that they could take off to intercept the bombers on their way home. There were further fierce battles with the withdrawing bombers, which were now flying southbound in looser formations and isolated groups. For II/JG 3 the result was one enemy aircraft shot down by Uffz. Stienhans of 6/JG 3 over the sea north of Ameland (8) and one bomber forced out of formation southwest of Groningen by Uffz. Lucks (4) for no losses[639].

The next incursion by units of the 8th Air Force took place the very next day, 9 October 1943, when a large force of bombers was dispatched to strike targets on the Baltic coast, especially Anklam, Danzig, Marienburg and Gdingen[640]. The bombers made their approach far out to sea along the Dutch—East Friesian coast. A strong escort of Thunderbolts accompanied the bombers to the limit of their range, while other fighters were supposed to rendezvous with them on the return flight. It appears that II/JG 3 did not intercept the bombers until they were heading home, for in the early afternoon the *Gruppe* claimed two B-17s shot down without loss. The bombers were shot down over the sea 70 kilometers northwest of Terschelling and were credited to Fw. Draeger (6) and Lt. Münster (78). The next day, on 10 October 1943, Münster was the target of a heavy daylight attack by 274 B-17s escorted by 216 P-47s of the American 8th Air Force[641]. A total of eleven day fighter *Gruppen* and elements of two destroyer and several night fighter *Gruppen* were mustered by the defenders, and these flew a total of 346 sorties. II/JG 3's defensive mission was directed against the incoming formations of heavy bombers, whose leading elements reached the Dutch coast near Goeree at 2:18 PM. The bombers subsequently flew east over s'Hertogenbosch toward their target area. The *Gruppe* became involved in a running battle with the fighter escort as far as German territory; II/JG 3 failed to score, while two Messerschmitts were shot down. Lt. Karl-Ludwig Seewald of 6/JG 3 was shot down at 2:40 PM; he was still in the cockpit of his "Yellow 3" when it crashed at Zaltbommel north of s'Hertogenbosch. Fw. Paul Draeger of 5 *Staffel* was more fortunate; he was badly wounded and came down by parachute near Keppeln. After the P-47s had reached their range limit east of the line Wesel—Bocholt, elements of II/JG 3 closed with the bombers. Two were shot down by Lt. Münster (79-80) the *Gruppe*'s only claims on this day[642].

For the next three days weather prevented further combat missions from being flown. On 14 October 1943 the Americans launched another major daylight raid against the Schweinfurt ball-bearing factories, dispatching a total of 291 B-17s of the 1st and 3rd Bombardment Divisions. As in the first attack on 17 August, bad weather over southeast England and parts of the occupied western territories once again hampered the operation and in the end only 229 four-engined bombers escorted by two fighter groups reached German-occupied territory[643]. This incursion by the heavy bombers met the fiercest resistance yet from the German day fighter arm, which mustered no less than 20 *Gruppen* from ten day fighter *Geschwader* as well as elements of three destroyer and six night fighter *Geschwader* and various training and industrial defense units. The defending aircraft flew a total of about 800 sorties, with some pilots flying more than one sortie on this day.

Little is known about II/JG 3's part in the defensive effort. The *Gruppe* was obviously supposed to intercept the approaching bombers over Holland, where its primary task was to engage the fighter escort, draw it away from the bombers and force it to return early, clearing the way for the following *Jagdgruppen* to attack the bombers over the western part of the Reich, however the mission was seriously hampered by the misty, hazy weather that covered much of Holland. In fact, II/JG 3 did not claim a single victory on this day. One of the *Gruppe*'s machines was damaged when poor visibility forced its pilot to make a belly landing near Zwolle[644].

After the attack German victory claims placed the American losses at 121 aircraft, mainly four-engined bombers, while their own casualties amounted to 20 pilots killed and 15 wounded plus 40 aircraft written off due to enemy action[645]. In spite of the devastation that their attack had caused on the ground[646], to the Americans 14 October 1943 represented the bitterest defeat so far in their bombing campaign against Germany; by their own admission they lost 67 B-17s and five P-47s on this mission, which meant the loss of 605 aircrew. On the other hand they claimed to have shot down 227 German fighters and damaged another 94[726]. As a result of this disaster an immediate halt was called to further deep penetration raids; no further missions would be flown beyond the range of the

escort fighters until suitable long-range fighters were available (the first P-38s, which had a range of about 830 kilometers, arrived in England in October and the first examples of the new P-51 were soon to follow).

This decision, which in the following weeks brought a period of relative quiet for the German fighter units stationed farther inland, did II/JG 3 no good on account of its forward position. Its next mission against reported Allied incursions took place the very next day, 15 October 1943. Early in the afternoon, radar detected approximately 60 to 100 enemy aircraft approaching in several waves. The German side scrambled every available aircraft of at least eleven *Gruppen*[648]. II/JG 3 was first into the air; eleven Messerschmitts—every serviceable machine—took off from Schiphol at 2:53 PM. No contact was made with the enemy and the fighters returned to base. The mission was also uneventful for the other units that took off.

The next two days were largely quiet ones for the *Gruppe*; in spite of mainly cloudy weather, a number of shipping escort missions were flown off the coast[649] and all were uneventful. There were, however, two important changes at the command level. Hptm. Joachim Kirschner, *Kapitän* of 5/JG 3 and the *Gruppe*'s most successful pilot, was transferred to IV/JG 27 as *Gruppenkommandeur*[650]. His place as leader of 5 *Staffel* was taken by Hptm. Heinrich Sannemann. The latter had returned to II/JG 3 at the beginning of October after 17 months with the LKS Werder and had at first flown with the *Gruppenstab* for "refamiliarization." At the same time, Hptm. Werner Lucas returned to the *Gruppe* and again took command of 4 *Staffel*, while Lt. Münster returned to 5/JG 3.

On 18 October the weather appeared to have improved significantly over large areas of the Reich and the occupied western territories, and the 8th Air Force prepared to launch further strikes. A large group of B-17s took off to attack Düren[651], while a short time earlier a smaller formation of B-24s had taken off on a diversionary mission over the North Sea to draw away the German fighters[652]. The latter was at least partly successful, for the unescorted Liberators were detected while forming up and tracked as they flew north, about 150 kilometers off the West Friesian coast. At Schiphol, II/JG 3 received the order to scramble at 12:45 PM. Once airborne, it was supposed to be guided on to the heavy bombers, which had meanwhile turned south off Borkum[654]. No contact was made with the enemy, however another disaster awaited the *Gruppe*. Dense fog had formed over the Dutch coast; the *Gruppe* formation became dispersed and the fog made it impossible for the fighters to find their way back to their base. They were also unable to fly around the fog bank, as most were already running low on fuel. In the end, ten machines ran out of fuel and made forced landings wherever their pilots could locate a suitable field in the dense fog. Four more Messerschmitts failed to reach land and crashed into the sea[655]. The result was a catastrophe for the *Gruppe*, for this shambles of an operation cost it four pilots killed or missing and one injured, plus eight machines with 70% or greater damage. Six less seriously damaged aircraft were recovered and put back into service by the *Gruppe*. Hardest hit was 6/JG 3, which had three total losses: *Staffelkapitän* Paul Stolte and Lt. Rudolf Schröder were listed missing and in all likelihood crashed into the sea with their machines, while Uffz. Uwe Michaels crashed near Sneek, southwest of Leeuwarden, and was killed. Uffz. Herbert Dehrmann was luckier, surviving a belly landing near Sneek with only minor injuries. 5 *Staffel* lost Obfw. Werner Kloss, who crashed into the North Sea, probably after running out of fuel. His body was recovered soon afterwards. Hptm. Sannemann succeeded in getting his *Schwarm* as far as Schockland, where all four pilots made successful belly landings.

The death of Hptm. Paul Stolte was a painful blow to the *Gruppe*; he was an experienced and responsible unit commander who had led the *Gruppe* into action often in recent weeks. His death resulted in another shuffle in the *Staffelkapitän* positions: Hptm. Sannemann assumed command of his old *Staffel*, 6/JG 3, while Lt. Münster was named *Staffelführer* of 5/JG 3.

II/JG 3 was assigned a number of new machines to make good the losses of 18 October and thus did not need to be pulled out of action[656]. The next defensive mission by the *Gruppe* occurred on 20 October, when a force of four-engined bombers was sent to attack Düren, a repeat of the aborted mission of two days earlier[657]. Once again the German defensive effort was hampered by bad weather; a total of 221 fighters and destroyers was sent into action, however only elements of the 3 *Jagddivision* based in Holland, including II/JG 3, made contact with the enemy. The *Gruppe* scrambled from Schiphol at 1:50 PM[658] and subsequently encountered an escorted formation of B-17s over the German-Dutch border near Venlo. It was immediately engaged by a superior number of P-47s, which scattered the *Gruppe*. Three Messerschmitts were shot down, while II/JG 3 failed to score. Two pilots of 4 *Staffel* were subsequently placed on the casualty list: Uffz. Heinz Kiy and Uffz. Eduard Bartsch went down with their machines near Roermund and west of Mönchen-Gladbach, respectively[659]. The Messerschmitt of Lt. Koch, who was flying with the *Gruppenstab*, was shot up, however he was lucky and pulled off a successful belly landing at Venlo airfield. Elements of the *Gruppe* later engaged the heavy bombers as they withdrew. Two B-17s were shot down, one of them by Oblt. Lucas (106). Out of ammunition and running low on fuel, the machines of II/JG 3 landed at airfields all over Holland and the northwestern part of the Reich. There was no second mission, as the American formations were already too far to the west. Nevertheless, 4/JG 3 suffered another casualty. The engine of Uffz. Hugo Lucks' machine quit suddenly as he was taking off from Venlo to return to Schiphol, and the Messerschmitt crashed into a house at the edge of the airfield. The seriously injured pilot was pulled from the wreckage and taken to hospital in Mühlhausen.

While 21 October 1943 was mainly quiet[660], on the afternoon of the 22nd sixteen Bf 109s were scrambled[661] after radar detected formations of Bostons, Marauders and fighters approaching the coastal area between the Scheldt Estuary and the northern French coast near St. Valéry. In the evening the pilots of II/JG 3 were ordered to Deelen in anticipation of a visit by the *Reichsmarschall* the next day. Göring was on a tour of the fighter units stationed in the west, inspecting them and urging them to redouble efforts. Early in the afternoon of 23 October a group of pilots, including those of II/JG 3, were assembled in one of the big hangars of Deelen air base. Göring arrived accompanied by *Generalfeldmarschall* Milch, *Generaloberst* Loerzer, *Generalmajor* Schmid and *Generalmajor* Galland. Decorations were presented to deserving pilots[662], after which Göring delivered a lengthy speech in which he expressed extreme dissatisfaction with the results the pilots had so far achieved in combat over the homeland[663]. The entire production was part of a campaign by Göring calculated to improve his standing with Hitler, which had suffered because of the *Luftwaffe*'s repeated failures[664]. Totally incapable of recognizing the true reasons behind the *Luftwaffe*'s lack of effectiveness, much less of rectifying them, he tried to solve the problem by scolding the air crews. Göring berated their lack of success and blamed them for the recent setbacks. Thus inspired by their commander-in-chief, in the early afternoon the pilots of II/JG 3 returned to Schiphol prior to resuming operations the next day.

24 October 1943 saw II/JG 3 engaged mainly in convoy escort for shipping traffic off the Dutch coast. There was no contact with the enemy, however the *Gruppe* did suffer one loss: while flying low in very hazy conditions, Gefr. Erich Zeitlinger of 4/JG 3 inadvertently struck the water just off the coast near Den Helder. He survived the crash, and in spite of serious injuries managed to free himself from his sinking machine. Zeitlinger pulled himself into his inflatable dinghy and was rescued by a navy ship a short time later. Later in the afternoon several formations of single- and twin-engined aircraft were detected approaching the area of the Schelde Estuary. One incursion was aimed at the Schiphol area, and at 4:30 PM elements of II/JG 3 were scrambled to intercept[666]. The enemy aircraft turned out to be a formation of about twenty Spitfires, and a fierce dogfight developed south of Haarlem. 4 *Staffel* lost two pilots killed, while failing to score itself. One of the dead was *Staffelkapitän* Hptm. Werner Lucas. He was shot down near Lejden and went down with his "White 7" into the city. Uffz. Günther Weck was shot down between Katwijk and Scheveningen and also went down with his machine. With the death of Werner Lucas, who had been promoted to *Hauptmann* shortly before his death, II/JG 3 lost its second unit leader in six days. While serving in 4/JG 3 he had worked his way up from *Unteroffizier* to *Staffelkapitän* and amassed a total of 106 victories. After the death of Hptm. Stolte and Hptm. Lucas and the transfer of Hptm. Kirschner, the *Gruppe* had lost all three of its *Staffelkapitäne* within a very short time. These men were impossible to replace, and their loss represented a serious weakening of the unit as experienced unit commanders were al-

ready becoming a rare commodity within the day fighter arm. Lt. Franz Ruhl assumed command of 4/JG 3 in place of Hptm. Lucas.

In the days that followed, bad weather provided a brief respite, with the Allied airmen also confined to the ground for most of the time. The only incursions were by lone, high-flying reconnaissance aircraft[667]. II/JG 3 used this period to improve its technical readiness, which had suffered in recent days, carrying out the extensive maintenance and repair work which had become necessary. At the end of the month the *Gruppe* had available 32 Messerschmitts, fifteen of them Bf 109 G-5s and the rest G-6s.

Continued bad weather on the first two days of November limited activities to occasional escort missions for coastal convoys, all of which were uneventful[668]. Then, on 3 November, a slight improvement in the weather enabled the Americans to send their heavy bombers on another daylight raid over Germany. The target of this attack, which involved 556 heavy bombers, the strongest force assembled so far, was the port facilities at Wilhelmshaven. Guarded by a total of 387 P-47s and P-38s, the bombers came in on a broad front between Bergen and Vlieland, with the leading groups of four-engined bombers crossing the coast at 11:37 AM. The continued poor weather, with multiple cloud layers and ceilings between 600 and 1 000 meters[669], meant that the German response was a weak one. Only four day fighter and one night fighter *Gruppen* saw action and, severely outnumbered, they were unable to achieve much against the attackers[670]. II/JG 3 was scrambled at 12:05 PM. After forming up over Schiphol it climbed to its assigned altitude of 7 000 meters and headed southwest toward the area of the Zuider Zee. At 12:23 PM the aircraft of II/JG 3 encountered a group of P-47s, aircraft of the 4th Fighter Group, near De Kooy. The result was a fierce dogfight which lasted more than half an hour. The *Gruppe* shot down four of the enemy, including two by Maj. Brändle (171-172), without loss to itself. With fuel running low, II/JG 3 was forced to break off the action and return to its "Garden Fence".

The day was not yet over, however, and there was no opportunity to celebrate the success of the first mission[673]. Barely two hours after the unit's Messerschmitts had returned from the first defensive mission against the heavy bombers, radar detected two formations of twin-engined bombers with a strong fighter escort approaching Den Helder from the west[674]. II/JG 3 scrambled at 3:40 PM[675]—the scramble order had apparently become hung up somewhere on the line of communication, for a large formation of Marauders suddenly appeared over Schiphol just as the last fighters were taking off[676]. As far as can be determined, II/JG 3 was spared any serious damage on the ground, however it suffered painful losses in the course of its defensive mission. The fighters had no time to form up after taking off, and the situation quickly deteriorated into numerous individual combats. The Spitfires of the fighter escort had all the advantages on their side: superior numbers, orderly formation and altitude. The result for II/JG 3 was five pilots killed and eight aircraft shot down, of which six had to be written off. Undoubtedly

the most serious blow was the death of *Gruppenkommandeur* Maj. Kurt Brändle. He was last seen racing after the withdrawing medium bombers at full throttle, and he probably fell victim to a Spitfire over the sea. He was at first reported missing, but several days later his body washed ashore and his fate became a sad certainty. Hptm. Sannemann's 6/JG 3 lost three pilots: Lt. Horst Brock, Fw. Walter Stienhans and Gefr. Hans-Wilhelm Hahn were all shot down and killed in combat with the escort fighters. Before he was shot down, Fw. Stienhans had brought down a Spitfire for his tenth victory. Uffz. Horst Kirschner of 4 *Staffel* suffered the same fate; he died when Spitfires shot him down into the sea 20 kilometers west of Harlem[677].

Not only was Maj. Brändle II/JG 3's most successful pilot, he was also one of the most experienced and capable unit commanders in the entire *Luftwaffe*, a man who enjoyed the admiration and respect of every member of his *Gruppe*, from the pilots to the most junior member of the regular personnel[678]. After Brändle failed to return, as the senior *Staffelkapitän*, Hptm. Sannemann assumed temporary command of the *Gruppe*. Hptm. Wilhelm Lemke, then *Kapitän* of 9/JG 3, was named to succeed Brändle as *Kommandeur* of II *Gruppe*. Several days later Lemke, then the most successful pilot of III/JG 3 with 130 victories, arrived at Schiphol to take command of II/JG 3[679].

II/JG 3 flew its next defensive mission on 5 November 1943, before its new *Kommandeur* arrived. On this day a large force of almost 500 heavy bombers of the 8th Air Force escorted by 383 P-47s and P-38s attacked targets in Gelsenkirchen and Münster. The sky was almost cloudless and visibility excellent. To meet this incursion, I *Jagdkorps* mustered elements of five *Jagdgeschwader* as well as a number of destroyers and close-support aircraft (!), which flew a total of 429 sorties[680]. II/JG 3 was scrambled at 12:20 PM[681] and was supposed to be vectored on to the incoming formations of B-17s. The mission was fruitless, however, for in spite of an extended search the *Gruppe* was unable to establish contact with the enemy. Instead, after eighty minutes in the air and with tanks almost dry, the unit's fighters landed at Venlo and Deelen. One machine ran out of fuel and crashed while attempting a dead-stick landing at Venlo.

In the days that followed, persistent cloudy weather hindered further operations. During this time the *Luftwaffe* staffs responsible for the air defense of the Reich held a series of conferences to discuss the alarming rise in losses and the noticeable drop in the number of enemy aircraft being shot down by the day fighter arm[682]. The discussions were marked by a sense of bewilderment and helplessness. The increased range of the escort fighters and their constantly growing numbers, the potential impact of which had been clearly demonstrated in the attack on Emden on 27 September, clearly shocked most of the leading officers of the fighter arm. They had absolutely no idea how to effectively cope with this now obvious threat. If one examines the outcome of the debates held in these days it becomes clear that the inventiveness of the general staff officers was quite limited, for just two measures were adopted in response to the latest developments. One called for the *Jagdgruppen* stationed in the western approaches of the Reich to be pulled back to areas that could not (yet) be reached by the Allied escort fighters. The other ordered several heavy *Gruppen* reclassified as light *Gruppen*, their new role being to engage the enemy escort fighters (this move had provoked heated arguments during the discussions). The latter measure was a clear indication of the hopeless situation facing the *Luftwaffe*, for it was a tacit admission that it would be unable to throw additional forces into the battle in the short or the medium term, and instead would have to make do with its existing units. This measure would of course result in a reduction in the number of day fighters available to engage the heavy bombers and further exacerbate the existing numerical inferiority of the fighter defense. Whereas the Germans had previously believed that they could commit the bulk of their day fighter *Gruppen* against the American bombers[683], a considerable part of the limited day fighter forces was now to be diverted to engage the escort fighters. At the same time, the number of heavy bombers continued to grow and the inferiority of the German fighter defense became more obvious.

The consideration given to the subsequent employment of II/JG 3 at the staff conferences illustrates the prevailing lack of planning: at a conference held by the *Luftwaffe* Commander Center on 7 November it was decided that the *Gruppe* would be pulled back from Schiphol to Hilversum. The next day at the headquarters of *I Jagdkorps* this decision was overturned and II/JG 3 was instructed to remain at Schiphol in the role of light *Gruppe*. The following is from the minutes of that conference:

> It was proposed by Oberst Lützow that, because of its heavy losses of late, II/JG 3 should be taken out of action and brought back up to strength, while Oberst Oesau was of the opinion that the available aircraft and crews should be assigned to other Gruppen in order to bolster the fighting strength of such units. As an immediate solution, it was proposed that the Schiphol Gruppe would remain up front for the time being[...][684]

So much for the command situation in the day fighter arm. The pilots of II/JG 3 knew nothing of this proposed move, although in view of the desperate state of their unit many must have thought about it. The *Gruppe*'s experiences so far were reason enough for a transfer to a more rearward location; it had very quickly become apparent that, in the majority of cases, II/JG 3 did not receive sufficient warning for the *Gruppe* to form up and reach sufficient altitude to engage the Allied escort fighters with some prospect of success. Instead, most of the time the *Gruppe* contacted the enemy while it was still climbing, and consequently was forced to engage

the Spitfires and Thunderbolts from an inferior position. As well, the unit's fighters were usually outnumbered by those of the enemy[685]. As a result, as described above, most of II/JG 3's missions were unsuccessful; it sustained unbearable losses in men and materiel while achieving only limited success. Moreover, the *Gruppe*'s efforts had no impact on the effectiveness of the Anglo-American fighter escort.

On 11 November 1943, 347 B-17s took off from bases in England with an escort of 401 P-47s and P-38s. The plan of attack called for the bombers to form up into two groups and strike targets in Münster and Wesel almost simultaneously. However, bad weather forced the formation assigned to attack Wesel to abort the mission, and, following the loss of the pathfinder aircraft, only a few of the aircraft from the Münster force were able to reach the target area and drop their bombs[686]. The German air defense was also seriously hindered by the weather. Nine *Jagdgruppen* were mobilized against the enemy incursions[687], however only five of these made contact. II/JG 3 scrambled at 1:15 PM and was guided toward the formations of heavy bombers bound for western Germany[688], however only elements of the *Gruppe* made contact. While achieving no result, II/JG 3 lost one Messerschmitt of 5 *Staffel* which was shot down in air combat near Düsseldorf. The aircraft's pilot, Uffz. Wolfgang Polster, who was on temporary assignment to II/JG 3 from JG 26, was not hurt and was able to parachute to safety.

In spite of continued dreary autumn weather, the 8th Air Force launched its next strike two days later, on 13 November. Two large formations, totaling 272 B-17s and B-24s escorted by 390 P-47s and P-38s, were supposed to bomb targets in Bremen and in the area of Schleswig-Holstein. In the end, however, only about half of the strike force reached the northwestern coastal region, where they scattered their bomb loads over a wide area[689]. On the German side, ten day fighter and two heavy fighter *Gruppen* were mobilized to intercept, and these flew a total of 314 sorties[690]. For II/JG 3, operations began at 9 AM with a transfer of the air element to Volkel, a spacious airfield approximately 20 km southwest of Nijmegen and base of operations of III/JG 1. This step was taken after American heavy bombers were detected forming up at 8:20 AM. The transfer placed the *Gruppe* approximately 90 kilometers further inland so as to increase the advance warning of the anticipated incursions, and was obviously a result of the decisions taken at the most recent staff conferences. The *Gruppe*, which on this day was being led by Hptm. Lemke for the first time, scrambled from Volkel at 11:15 AM[691] and was subsequently vectored over the sea toward the force of B-17s flying east-southeast toward Bremen. The *Gruppe* was supposed to accompany III/JG 1[693]. The inclement weather prevented the fighters from locating the bombers, however, and the *Gruppe* was forced to return to Schiphol empty-handed. Shortly after 1 PM elements of the *Gruppe* took off on a second mission against withdrawing heavy bombers. Lt. Münster shot down a B-17 (81), the *Gruppe*'s only success on this day. On the other hand, II/JG 3 sustained no losses.

Kommandeurbesprechung

am 20.11.43   19.30 Uhr in Driebergen

Teilnehmer:
General	Schmid
Oberst	Grabmann
Oberst	Ibel
Oberst	Lützow
Oberst i.G.	Christian
Oberst	Hettler
Oberstleutnant	Hermann
Oberstltn. i.G.	Wittmer
Oberstleutnant	Hülshoff
Major i.G.	Seeliger
Major i.G.	Dyrchs
Major i.G.	Müller-Trinbusch
Major	Böhm-Tettelbach
Major	Streib
Major	Radusch
Stabsing.	Hinzpeter
Hauptmann	Prinz Wittgenstein
Major Dr.	Heynen.

Von General Schmid wurden folgende Punkte besprochen:

Truppendienstlich.

1.) Eine negative Einstellung zum Krieg und seinen Ausgang kann innerhalb des Korps nicht geduldet werden. Gegen Offiziere und Soldaten, die sich defaitistisch äußern und damit praktisch dem Gegner helfen, ist sofort mit allen Mitteln einzuschreiten.

2.) Es wird nochmals befohlen, daß von den Divisionen und Geschwadern alle Dienststellen daraufhin überprüft werde ob junge felddienstfähige Leute, die kein Spezialpersonal sind, vorhanden sind. Derartige Leute sind zwar bis zum Jahrgang 1901 einschließlich abzugeben und nach Mög-lichkeit durch weibliches Personal zu ersetzen.

Einsatz.

1.) Tagjagd.
Es ist damit zu rechnen, daß auch in nächster Zeit die Zuführung an Flugzeugen zahlenmäßig gering sein wird, so daß weiterhin eine Unterlegenheit gegenüber den Eng-ländern und Amerikanern bestehen bleiben wird. Es ist deshalb von den vorhandenen Flugzeugen darauf zu achten, daß mit den Verbandsführern vorsichtig umgegangen und jeder Verlust vermieden wird. Bei Feindeinflügen ist es wichtig, daß die 3. Division rechtzeitig Fühlungs-halter in die Luft setzt, die melden, wo der Feindver-band fliegt und ob er durch Jäger gesichert ist. Da-durch soll vermieden werden, daß die Nachtjäger in feind-liche Jäger geführt werden. Beabsichtigt ist, zu jeder Division eine Aufklärungsstaffel zu geben, die aus Füh-lungshaltern für den Tageinsatz und Aufklärern für den Nachteinsatz besteht. Außerdem soll angeordnet werden, daß bei jeder Taggruppe ein Flugzeug als Lotsenflugzeug fungiert, das bei Schlechtwetter durch die Wolken durch-zieht und die übrigen Flugzeuge zu sich heranführt, so daß wieder geschlossene Verbände über den Wolken vor-handen sind. Den Nachtjägern wird befohlen, daß sie für den Tageinsatz Versammlungen über Funkfeuer üben, ins-besondere auch bei Schlechtwetter.

Auf den vorn gelegenen Flugplätzen sollen nur noch kleine Jagdkommandos liegen, während die Masse der Jäger auf die ebenfalls weiter rückwärts gelegenen Plätze verlegt wird.

2.) Nachtjagd.
Da bei der derzeitigen Wetterlage im allgemeinen eine Bekämpfung der Feindflugzeuge nur im "Himmelbett" mög-lich ist, ist darauf zu achten, daß die Besetzung der "Himmelbetten" nicht zu spät erfolgt. Im Gegensatz zu früher müssen die Besatzungen darauf eingestellt sein, daß die Möglichkeit besteht, daß sie aus dem "Himmelbett" auf einen fremden Platz zu landen haben.

Bei der "Zahmen Sau" ist darauf zu achten, daß die ein-gesetzten Flugzeuge mit SN-2 so früh wie möglich in den eng gebündelten Strom der Feindflugzeuge eingeführt werden. Aus diesem Grunde müssen N.J.G.1 und N.J.G. 2

After this, the cloudy autumn weather at first prevented further daylight raids by units of the 8th Air Force[694]. There was also a clear drop in the number of incursions by British fighters and light bombers, and for II/JG 3 the following days were relatively quiet. Whenever the weather permitted, maintenance test and practice flights were carried out and occasionally *Schwarm-* or *Rotte-*strength escort missions were flown in support of coastal convoys[695]. During one such mission on the early afternoon of 23 November 1943, west of Texel a *Rotte* made up of Lt. Ruhl and Fw. Florian of 4/JG 3 engaged a group of Beaufighters attacking a German convoy[696]. Three enemy aircraft were shot down, two of them by Lt. Ruhl (26-27). Toward the end of the battle several Spitfires appeared and immediately attacked the two Messerschmitts. The Spitfires pursued the German fighters until they were over the coast near Den Helder, scoring hits on Lt. Ruhl's "White 2". The Messerschmitt caught fire and Ruhl was forced to bail out. Luckily he survived the incident without injury.

Three days later, on 26 November, Bremen was again the target of a large daylight raid by units of the 8th Air Force. A total of 505 four-engined bombers was dispatched to strike the ancient Hanseatic city, however in the end only 440 reached the target area[697]. Against these the German side mobilized 294 fighters, destroyers and night fighters, including the bulk of 13 day fighter *Gruppen*[698]. Following early detection of the heavy bombers as they were forming up, at 9 AM II/JG 3 was again ordered to Volkel, from where it scrambled at 10:45 AM[699]. Contact was subsequently made with the enemy, however no results were achieved and after about an hour the *Gruppe*'s aircraft landed at several airfields in northwestern Germany and Holland. Elements of the *Gruppe* took off on a second mission against the bombers as they withdrew, however it was also unsuccessful[700].

After two relatively quiet days[701], on 29 November 1943 the Americans launched another heavy daylight raid on Bremen. The strike force, which was to bomb industrial targets, consisted of 360 B-17s with an escort of 352 fighters, however bad weather prevented all but 154 bombers from finding the target area. About 450 tons of bombs were scattered over the target area, inflicting little damage. The German defensive effort consisted of ten day fighter *Gruppen* plus a few destroyers and elements of Ekdo. 25[702]. II/JG 3's operational day began at 8:30 AM, when the air element was again moved to Volkel[703], this time well before the first enemy bombers were detected forming up. The *Gruppe* scrambled at 1:30 PM and was subsequently vectored on to the first of three waves of bombers, which crossed the Dutch coast north of Bergen at 1:45[704]. Again there were fierce dogfights with the escorting fighters, the bulk of them P-38s of the 55th Fighter Group. Lt. Münster shot down two Lightnings (82-83), however the Messerschmitts were unable to close with the heavy bombers. The *Gruppe*'s losses totaled one pilot missing and one slightly injured plus two machines destroyed and two moderately damaged. Uffz. Fritz Kostenbader

of 5/JG 3 failed to return; he was last seen in combat with the fighter escort in the Hengelo area. More fortunate was Uffz. Karl-Heinz Lintermann of 6 *Staffel*: his "Yellow 9" was damaged in combat, however he was able to make a successful belly landing southeast of Groningen with his engine on fire. Lintermann sustained minor injuries in the landing, however his machine was a complete writeoff[705].

The last day of the month brought another major daylight raid by units of the US 8th Air Force. A force of 381 heavy bombers with an equally strong escort was supposed to attack Solingen, however the continued bad weather resulted in the raid becoming a total failure. Just 80 heavy bombers reached the western area of the Reich, where they dropped their bombs, mainly on targets of opportunity, inflicting no significant damage. The German defensive effort was also severely restricted by the weather. Several *Gruppen* from all three *Jagddivisionen* in the northwest of the Reich were scrambled to intercept, however this did not result in any large-scale air battles[706]. II/JG 3's actions on this day were as follows: in the morning the air element was again ordered to Volkel. The *Gruppe* arrived there at about 9:40 AM with about 20 Messerschmitts[707,708]. Radar then detected the approach of large numbers of heavy bombers, which overflew the coast between Hoek-van-Holland and Blankenberghe at 10:35 AM. II/JG 3 was scrambled from Volkel at 10:40 AM and was subsequently guided into the Breda area by Y-control. There, at about 11:20 AM, contact was made with a gaggle of 40 to 50 P-47s approaching at an altitude of 9 000 meters. After taking off, the Messerschmitts had had sufficient time to climb to 10 500 meters and were thus able to attack the Thunderbolts from above and behind. Two of the American fighters were shot down on the first pass by Hptm. Lemke (131) and Obfw. Grünberg (62). In the ensuing fighting the *Gruppe* forced two B-17s to leave formation and destroyed another P-47. Its losses amounted to two Messerschmitts damaged in belly landings after running out of fuel[709].

On 1 December 1943 the bombardment divisions of the 8th Air Force launched another daylight raid against Solingen (a similar attempt the previous day had been frustrated by bad weather). Late in the morning almost 300 four-engined bombers escorted by 416 P-47s and P-38s overflew the Scheldt Estuary bound for the western Reich. In contrast to the day before, in the area of I *Jagdkorps* alone the defenders mobilized thirteen day fighter and two destroyer *Gruppen* with a total of 184 aircraft[710], including II/JG 3. That morning the *Gruppe* again moved its air element to Venlo[711], where it was to await further developments and stand by to take off. The *Gruppe* was ordered to scramble at 10:50 AM[712]. After takeoff, the fighters were guided over the German-Belgian border region toward the incoming heavy bombers. The ensuing engagement with two formations of twenty P-47s and thirty P-38s of the fighter escort was unsuccessful. Lt. Ruhl claimed to have shot down one of the enemy, however there was no witness and the claim was not submitted for confirmation[713]. On the other hand, the *Gruppe* lost one aircraft: FhjFw. Hans Frese of 4/JG 3 was shot down by enemy fighters north of Liège and forced to bail out, sustaining minor injuries in the process[714]. "White 2", the aircraft of Lt. Franz Ruhl, *Staffelführer* of 4/JG 3, was shot up by enemy fighters and he was forced to make a belly landing 100 meters to the side of the runway at Melsbroek near Brussels. The landing was a smooth one; the machine sustained 15% damage and Ruhl escaped injury.

The next two days were uneventful, the only daylight incursions being made by lone reconnaissance aircraft. The heavy bombers of the US 8th Air Force also stayed on the ground on 4 December, however in the early afternoon there was an incursion by two strong forces of Allied fighter aircraft totaling approximately 200 Typhoons and P-47s. The enemy fighters attacked the *Luftwaffe* airfield at Gilze-Rijen and surprised two *Staffeln* of KG 2 during a training mission, shooting down five Do 217s and compelling another to make a forced landing[715]. The German side was able to mobilize a total of 55 fighters to intercept these incursions, including II/JG 3. The *Gruppe* scrambled from Volkel at 2:10 PM[716] and over the Arnhem area ran into a strong force of Thunderbolts. In the ensuing fierce dogfight, the *Gruppe* suffered grievous losses while failing to shoot down any of the enemy. Especially hard was the loss of *Gruppenkommandeur* Hptm. Wilhelm Lemke, who was shot down and killed near Dodewaard west of Nijmegen. Also killed was FhjObfw. Josef Schütte of 5/JG 3, another of the *Gruppe*'s "*Experten*" with 41 victories to his credit. He went down with his aircraft "Black 8" near Apeldoorn[717]. More fortunate was Uffz. Kurt Soßdorf, also of 5/JG 3: he was shot down over the Zuider Zee but escaped injury and bailed out. The loss of its second *Kommandeur* in just under a month was an especially bitter blow for the *Gruppe*, as it represented the loss of another, now virtually irreplaceable, unit leader. Hptm. Heinrich Sannemann was placed in temporary command of II/JG 3 pending the appointment of a new *Gruppenkommandeur*[718].

The onset of bad weather meant that there were no further daylight incursions into the airspace over the northwest of the Reich until 11 December 1943. On that day a degree of improvement in the weather allowed the US 8th Air Force to launch another major daylight raid on Emden. The attack force consisted of 538 four-engined with an escort of 388 fighters; for the first time the escort included P-51 Mustangs, 44 of which took part. The German response consisted of eight day fighter and three destroyer *Gruppen* with a total of 307 machines, of which 147 ultimately made contact with the enemy[719]. Relatively little is known about II/JG 3's mission on this day. Late in the morning a small force of aircraft was scrambled to intercept one of the three waves of incoming bombers coming in over Texel. In the Groningen area the *Gruppe*'s fighters engaged a group of B-17s, two of which were forced to leave formation. In return the *Gruppe* was forced to report one of its pilots missing, after Gefr. Friedrich König of 6/JG 3 failed to return fol-

lowing combat over Groningen. His element leader last saw him turning away over a solid layer of cloud[721]. As well, one machine was obliged to force-land after running out of fuel, however the pilot was not hurt[722].

The next major daylight raid by the US 8th Air Force on 13 December met little resistance on account of the prevailing very poor weather conditions[723]. II/JG 3 apparently played no part in the defensive effort. Then, in the early afternoon, radar detected the approach of another large group of bombers. The enemy force consisted of 208 Marauders of the US 9th Air Force which, escorted by about 350 fighters, were en route to attack II/JG 3's base at Schiphol. The enemy's approach was detected too late to allow the *Gruppe* to take off to intercept, and consequently the air element was ordered to Deelen[724]. As a result, the attack by the American twin-engined bombers met no defending fighters, the only opposition coming from anti-aircraft guns, which shot down two B-26s and damaged many more. The carpet of 787 1,000-lb bombs inflicted severe devastation on the ground. Hangars, the workshop area and headquarters buildings were heavily damaged by direct hits, while dispersals, taxiways and the runway were so badly cratered that the airfield was temporarily rendered unusable[725]. In spite of the scale of the devastation, II/JG 3 appears to have gotten off lightly, for the records reveal no personnel losses in the raid on Schiphol, while material losses were limited to two Messerschmitts. After the loss of its base of operations, the next day, 14 December, the *Gruppe* was ordered to send its air element and a small technical detachment to Volkel. Fifteen of the unit's Messerschmitts arrived there and these were temporarily subordinated to III/JG 1 for subsequent operations[726].

16 December 1943: Bremen was once again the target of an attack by 631 heavy bombers. Escorted by 201 fighters, 535 four-engined bombers reached the target. Shortly after 1 PM they dropped more than 1,500 tons of bombs on the target area, inflicting further damage on the already battered city and port facilities. Continued bad weather meant that the German response was weak. Just 91 fighters got airborne[727], including those of II/JG 3. The latter scrambled from Volkel at 1:40 PM and apparently failed to make contact with the enemy. About one hour after takeoff, II/JG 3 returned to Volkel empty-handed[728]. The next major daylight raid by the Americans against Bremen came four days later, on 20 December. Once again II/JG 3 was one of the day fighter *Gruppen* committed against the attackers, however its defensive effort on this day produced no tangible result[729,730]. Two days later, on 22 December, further daylight raids were launched against targets inside the Reich. Under mostly cloudy skies, Münster and Osnabrück were struck by virtually simultaneous attacks delivered by 574 four-engined bombers of the US 8th Air Force. The German side once again mustered eight day fighter and three destroyer *Gruppen* which together put up a total of 194 aircraft. In the end, however, only 140 of the defending fight-

ers made contact with the enemy[731]. On this day II/JG 3's handful of serviceable machines saw action together with those of III/JG 1 and once again they achieved no success. After scrambling at 1:10 PM, the small formation swung far to the south in order to climb above the dense cloud overlying the coastal region. It was then guided by Y-control toward an incoming, strongly-escorted formation of Boeings, with which it made contact north of Hengelo at 1:50 PM. In the ensuing engagement with the P-38s and P-47s of the fighter escort, two P-38s were shot down by III/JG 1. At 2:03 PM Lt. Ruhl of II/JG 3 shot down a P-47 near Nordhorn, however there was no witness[732, 733].

The defensive mission on 22 December was to be II/JG 3's last from bases in Holland. Three days later, on 25 December 1943, the *Gruppe* began moving to Rotenburg/Wümme, a well-laid-out air base 40 kilometers east of Bremen[734]. There it was to undergo a brief rest and refit. Early on the afternoon of the 25th, the last 16 Messerschmitts of II/JG 3 took off under the command of Hptm. Sannemann to fly to the *Gruppe*'s new base of operations[735]. The transfer was marred by a fatal crash, however. For reasons unknown, Uffz. Kurt Hörlücke of 5/JG 3 went down out of a turn northeast of Osnabrück and died when his "Black 12" struck the ground. Meanwhile, on 27 December 1943 IV/JG 3 was transferred from southern Germany to Grimbergen where it was to replace II *Gruppe* until further notice[736].

If one draws up an interim balance after the first four months of operations in the Defense of the Reich, it becomes clear that II/JG 3 had suffered losses in a relatively short period of time which were sufficient to considerably erode the substance of its flying personnel. In the course of those four months the *Gruppe* had lost 23 pilots killed or missing plus ten put out of action by wounds. The loss of five of the *Gruppe*'s most important officers was an especially heavy blow (Maj. Brändle and Hptm. Lemke, both *Gruppenkommandeure*, Hptm. Lucas and Hptm. Stolte, two experienced *Staffelkapitäne*, and Hptm. Kirschner, who was transferred out of the unit[737]). Such losses in experienced and successful unit leaders could not be made up from within the *Gruppe* or even from the ranks of the *Luftwaffe*. II/JG 3's serious losses should also have been a clear warning signal for the *Luftwaffe*'s command, for it had been one of the most successful and experienced fighter units whose unit leaders were among the best the *Luftwaffe* had and whose ranks included a significant number of outstanding *Schwarm* and *Rotte* leaders. Yet it had been decimated in a relatively short time in combat against the Anglo-American air forces[738] while achieving relatively little. Since the start of its tour of duty in the Defense of the Reich, II/JG 3 had registered a total of 53 enemy aircraft shot down or forced out of formation[739]. Furthermore, there was no way of replacing the losses suffered to date with comparable personnel[740] or of avoiding similar losses in the future. In that autumn of 1943 the battle of attrition in the skies over the Reich had already assumed such proportions that it made a collapse of the day fighter

arm a definite possibility and caused the beginning of this collapse to move into the foreseeable future[741].

1944 was to bring the peak of the Allied bombing attacks against the Reich; compared to the previous year the quantity of bombs dropped was to increase fourfold[742]. At the same time the spring and summer of 1944 would become the phase of the air war in which the Allied air attacks had the most profound influence on the course of military events in the European theater[743].

As the new year began the *Luftwaffe* faced three main tasks, specifically:

1. to establish an effective air defense over the Reich,

2. to defend against all Allied landing attempts on the European mainland, and

3. firm up the air situation over the German-Soviet front.[744]

By this time even the officers of the *Luftwaffe* general staff could no longer refuse to acknowledge that "*an intact air defense is a necessary condition for the successful continuation of the war.*"[745] Since the day fighter arm formed the core of the Defense of the Reich, on 6 January 1944 *Generaloberst* Hans-Jürgen Stumpff, a leading air officer, replaced *Generaloberst* Wiese of the flak artillery as *Luftwaffe* Commander Center. Moreover, only a short time later this post was renamed "*Luftflotte Reich*"[746]. At the beginning of 1944 *Luftflotte Reich* had at its disposal six day fighter *Geschwaderstäbe*[747] which commanded 19 *Gruppen* and a number of independent *Staffeln*; altogether these units had available 549 fighter aircraft, although only 407 of these were serviceable. As well there were the units of *Luftflotte* 3 based in the western territories, which included another seven day fighter *Gruppen*[748], several of which were always available for defensive missions against incursions into Reich territory.

While there was no sign of any significant technical innovations at the beginning of 1943 (the day fighter *Gruppen* were still equipped exclusively with the Bf 109 G and Fw 190 A[749]), there was a change in the area of tactics. Based on recent experiences in engaging the bomber streams and the realization that individual *Jagdgruppen*, which could rarely muster more than 20 aircraft, now had little chance of breaking through the numerically superior escorts to get at the bombers, effective immediately an attempt was to be made to concentrate the existing forces. So-called *Gefechtsverbände*, or "battle units," each consisting of several *Gruppen*, were to be formed as soon as incursions were detected, promising a significant increase in penetrative power. Such battle units could consist of three or more *Gruppen* and were to include the remaining destroyer *Gruppen*. At the same time there was to be a sort of "division of work," in which the heavy *Gruppen* attacked the bombers while the light *Gruppen* would be responsible for engaging the American escort fighters and preventing them from attacking the heavy *Gruppen*. The objective of the defensive mission was clearly to destroy as many heavy bombers as possible. At the same time a series of increasingly sharply worded orders forbade the day fighter units from engaging the fighter escort; this was undoubtedly a serious error, for it robbed unit leaders of much of their freedom of action in carrying out their missions and forced the day fighter *Gruppen* into an inappropriate defensive role against the American escort fighters.

*****

II/JG 3 enjoyed several quiet weeks at Rotenburg during which the *Gruppe* was brought up to strength in personnel and equipment. At the end of December 1943 it turned in its surviving Bf 109 G-6s and retained only ten Bf 109 G-5s. Then, in January 1944, the *Gruppe* received a full complement of the latest production version of the Bf 109 G-6. A total of 53 aircraft were received during the month, after which all of the Bf 109 G-5s had to be handed in[750]. Unlike II/JG 3's previous equipment, from now on all aircraft were fitted with external mounts for drop tanks in order to increase the *Gruppe*'s range and endurance. Underwing 20-mm cannon also became standard equipment on the *Gruppe*'s aircraft.

At the beginning of January 1944 II/JG 3's new *Gruppenkommandeur* arrived at Rotenburg. He was Hptm. Detlev Rohwer, most recently *Staffelkapitän* of 2/JG 3, a wearer of the Knight's Cross since July 1941 with 35 victories to his credit. He relieved Hptm. Heinrich Sannemann, who returned to 6 *Staffel*. As a result of these changes, at the beginning of 1944 the *Gruppe*'s command list looked like this:

II/JG 3 List of Officers January 1944	
Gruppenkommandeur	Hptm. Detlev Rohwer
Gruppenadjutant	Lt. Max-Bruno Fischer
Staffelkapitän 4/JG 3	Lt. Franz Ruhl
Staffelkapitän 5/JG 3	Lt. Leopold Münster
Staffelkapitän 6/JG 3	Hptm. Heinrich Sannemann

Refurbishment of the *Gruppe* lasted into the first days of February 1944. During this period, whenever the winter weather permitted, numerous practice missions were flown for the usual variety of purposes: *Schwarm* or *Staffel* exercises, air-to-air and air-to-ground gunnery, orientation and radio check flights, and many others. Most of these were completed without serious incident, although two Messerschmitts were written off in accidents or as a result of mechanical trouble[751]. Fortunately, neither pilot was harmed. With its transfer to Rotenburg, the *Gruppe* left the command of 3

Jagddivision and was attached to 2 *Jagddivision* whose headquarters and command post were in Stade.

II/JG 3 flew its first post-workup mission on 10 February 1944. On that day Brunswick was again the target of an attack by B-17s. The attack force consisted of 169 bombers escorted by 466 fighters, however only 143 of the bombers arrived over the target area on account of the continued poor weather conditions. The German side detected the bombers while they were still forming up over the south coast of England; as the B-17s crossed the English Channel in two large formations and flew over Holland in the direction of Lingen on the German border, the fighter units in the northwest and west of the Reich were first placed at 15-minute readiness before being ordered to cockpit readiness at about 10:00 AM. All in all, on this day the *Luftwaffe* was able to muster eleven fighter and two destroyer *Gruppen* to meet the enemy incursions. These units put a total of 303 aircraft into the air, however only 231 made contact with the enemy[752]. II/JG 3 scrambled from Rotenburg at 11:54 AM and within fifteen minutes of taking off it sighted a large force of B-17s. The enemy bombers were at an altitude of 7 000 meters, flying west without fighter escort. There was an air battle north of Osnabrück in which the *Gruppe*'s fighters shot down four B-17s and finished off another. A short time later, after the bombers had linked up with their fighter escort, a P-47 was also brought down, probably by Hptm. Rohwer (36). Two Messerschmitts were shot down in combat and three were damaged for reasons other than enemy action. All of the pilots involved escaped injury[753].

The next daylight raid by the 8th Air Force came on the following day. On 11 February 1944 Frankfurt was once again the destination of the Americans, where the selected targets were railway facilities in the area surrounding the city. The attack force consisted of 223 four-engined bombers, and of these 212 made it to West-German airspace where they dropped their bomb loads on Frankfurt am Main, Ludwigshafen, Saarbrücken and several other towns which suffered as targets of opportunity. A total of 606 long-range fighters provided escort all the way to the bombers' targets and back. The American incursions were met by a German defense consisting of elements of eight day fighter, one destroyer and one night fighter *Geschwader*. Bad weather appears to have seriously hampered the defenders once again, for of the 187 aircraft committed just 70 made contact with the enemy[754]. Very little is known about II/JG 3's defensive mission on this day. The *Gruppe* scrambled at 10:55 AM[755] and was subsequently guided towards the bombers, which by then were already withdrawing in a southerly direction. Over the area north of Frankfurt a fierce dogfight developed with a group of Lightnings. Four of the enemy fighters were shot down without loss, three by Fw. Thyben (35-37) and the fourth by Fw. Hoyer (2), both of 6 *Staffel*[756,757].

For the next eight days continuous bad weather prevented further incursions by the American heavy bombers; as a result, things were quiet for II/JG 3 and activity was limited to practice and maintenance test flights whenever the weather permitted. Apparently, these were all completed without incident.

Meantime, the Allied air command had put the finishing touches to plans for a bombing campaign against the German aviation industry. The idea was based on the realization that gaining air superiority over the Reich and the occupied western territories was a necessary precondition for the subsequent Allied military efforts in their struggle against the German Reich; not only would bombing the German factories cut off the production of new aircraft, it would also force the German day fighters to come up and fight[758]. At the beginning of 1944 German fighter production was clearly a primary target of the Allied bombing campaign, and for the first time the efforts of the American 8th and 15th Air Forces were to be coordinated. The centerpiece of the bombing offensive against German fighter production was a planned one-week series of day and night raids against selected key factories involved in the production of fighter aircraft. The operation was code named "Argument. The American 8th Air Force was assigned a total of 21 aircraft factories, repair facilities and airfields, while RAF Bomber Command was allocated nine metropolitan areas which were more or less directly associated with air armaments[759]. It was planned to launch "Argument," which is better known by its unofficial title of "Big Week," as soon as weather conditions permitted. One of the most important requirements of the Allied plan was good ground visibility over the target areas, without which the desired precision bombing of the German aircraft factories would not be possible.

After the bad weather of the first half of February, the desired conditions finally developed at the end of the second ten-day period. On the night of 19-20 February the Royal Air Force carried out a heavy raid against Leipzig which marked the beginning of "Big Week." The heavy bombers of the American 8th Air Force followed the next day. For the first time a force of over 1,000 Fortresses and Liberators was dispatched, and the bombers' targets were aircraft factories in Tutow, Leipzig, Oschersleben, Brunswick and Bernburg. A total of 835 escort fighters was sent to guard the bombers[761], while numerous RAF fighter squadrons provided fighter cover near the British Isles. The operation was thus the biggest strategic undertaking by the 8th Air Force to date. The *Luftwaffe* defensive effort involved a total of seventeen day fighter and five destroyer *Gruppen* as well as elements of four night fighter *Gruppen* and several industry defense *Schwärme*. These units flew a total of 367 sorties, of which only 155 resulted in contact with the enemy, however[762]. In spite of the considerable number of units involved, the German defensive effort was seriously hampered by the tactics employed by the Allies; the heavy bombers came in several independent formations simultaneously, as a result of which the German units were split up, making a concentration of effort impossible[763].

II/JG 3 scrambled from Rotenburg at 10:35 AM and was then vectored east toward the incoming formations of heavy bombers[764].

Apparently only part of the *Gruppe* subsequently made contact with the B-24s of the 2nd Bombardment Division[765] en route to Brunswick, Gotha and Oschersleben. 5 *Staffel* intercepted the four-engined bombers near Helmstedt and subsequently claimed three Liberators, all by *Staffelkapitän* Lt. "Poldi" Münster (85-87). In return, 5/JG 3 suffered painful losses in this engagement, with one pilot killed, three wounded and three Messerschmitts written off. Uffz. Helmut Dillmann was shot down near Helmstedt and went down with his machine. Fw. Rudolf Scheibe was also shot down near Helmstedt, however he was able to abandon his stricken machine. Scheibe struck the tailplane while bailing out and suffered minor injuries. Lt. Walter Bohatsch was shot down and wounded near Königslutter, while Uffz. Maximilian Reichenberger was forced to belly-land his aircraft "Black 14" near Eitzum after it was shot up, sustaining minor injuries in the process. Some aircraft took off a second time to intercept the withdrawing heavy bombers but failed to make contact.

At the end of the day the *Luftwaffe* counted a total of 59 victory claims, 51 of them heavy bombers which were claimed shot down, forced to leave formation or finished off after having been damaged. Losses amounted to 74 machines written off in action and 29 damaged[766]. For its part, on 20 February 1944 the US 8th Air Force admitted the loss of 26 heavy bombers and six escort fighters while claiming 166 enemy aircraft shot down.

The attacks on 21 February were supposed to strike several of the most important air bases in the northwest of the Reich used by German air defense units, including the airfields at Gütersloh, Lippstadt, Werl, Münster-Handorf and Achmer, however an almost solid layer of cloud over the target area prevented the mission from being carried out as planned. As a result, only 186 of the total of 861 bombers committed were able to drop their bombs over their assigned targets, while insufficient ground visibility forced another 576 to bomb targets of opportunity. The fighter escort for the bombers, which once again operated in several distinct groups, consisted of 679 P-47s, P-38s and P-51s. The German defensive effort essentially consisted of thirteen day fighter and two destroyer *Gruppen*, which together mustered 282 aircraft. The rather bad weather south of a line from the mouth of the Weser through Hamburg to Stettin prevented the *Gruppen* from forming into battle units, and the German units once again had to be thrown into the battle piecemeal[768], a fact that was also appreciated by the Allies. II/JG 3 scrambled from Rotenburg at 1:18 PM and after forming up with IV/JG 3 it was guided by Y-control into the Holzminden area on to a group of B-17s with an escort of P-47s and P-51s. Contact was made at 2:01 PM. The two *Gruppen* of JG 3 subsequently carried out several attacks against the heavy bombers, which were flying in seven waves. IV/JG 3 claimed one B-17 shot down and another forced to leave formation, while II/JG 3 claimed one bomber shot down and another finished off after it had been forced out of formation by Oblt. Kutscha of 12/JG 3. Both of these were credited to Obfw. Roller (12) of 6/JG 3. In addition, a P-51 of the fighter escort was destroyed by Lt. Münster (88). On the other side of the coin 4 *Staffel* suffered two losses: Lt. Siegfried Stahl, who had only recently arrived from III *Gruppe*, was shot down and killed by American fighters near Bad Münder. Gefr. Hans Kupka was forced to abandon his "White 13" after a shell exploded in the barrel of the engine-mounted cannon and caused the motor to catch fire. Kupka sustained minor injuries when he came down not far from Dasseln near Eimbeck.

The *Luftwaffe* claimed 33 enemy aircraft shot down on this day[771]; its own losses were 30 machines lost in action and another 16 with significant damage. On the other side, the American 8th Air Force admitted the loss of 23 heavy bombers and 8 escort fighters, while its units claimed the destruction of 73 German fighters[772]. In spite of the fact that almost 2,000 tons of bombs were dropped, very little damage was done. The 8th Air Force in particular failed to destroy any significant number of German fighter aircraft on the ground; indeed German records reveal that nowhere was a German fighter or destroyer *Gruppe* hit by the bombing. The only units with fighters to be affected were Ekdo. 25 and FlÜG 1 at Achmer and Diepholz, which lost five Bf 109s, four Fw 190s and twelve aircraft of other types.

On the third day of "Big Week" the factories of German aircraft manufacturers were once again the targets of the heavy bombers. For the first time in "Operation Argument," units of the American 15th Air Force based in Italy also intervened in events, their assigned targets being the Messerschmitt production facilities in Regensburg-Obertraubling and Prüfening[773]. The targets of the 8th Air Force, on the other hand, were once again aircraft factories in central Germany, located in Aschersleben, Bernburg, Halberstadt and Oschersleben, while the bomb groups of the 3rd Bombardment Division were supposed to attack factories around Schweinfurt producing ball-bearings. A total of 799 B-17s and B-24s from all three bombardment divisions were mobilized for these attacks (mission number 8 AF 230) along with 659 escort fighters. In the end, however, only 99 bombers reached their assigned target areas, because once again the weather over northwestern Europe was anything but favorable. While the 333 Boeings of the 3rd Bombardment Division were recalled prior to reaching the European mainland, the 177 B-24s of the 2nd Bombardment Division did not receive the recall order until they were over the German-Dutch border. The units then turned back, but not before they unloaded 208 tons of bombs on targets of opportunity in the Enschede—Arnhem—Nijmegen area. Only the 289 Fortresses of the 1st Bombardment Division continued their mission, but solid cloud over the target prevented them from carrying out their attacks as planned and once again most of the bombs fell on targets of opportunity. The very poor weather had one other negative effect on the Americans, for it seriously hindered the fighter escort. As a result the heavy bombers were on their own for much of the way. The *Luftwaffe* was able to muster a total of sixteen day fighter and four destroyer *Gruppen* as well as elements of several night fighter, training and replacement training units to meet the incursions by the 8th Air Force; these

units flew a total of 332 sorties[774].

II/JG 3, which was led by Hptm. Sannemann on this day, scrambled 18 Messerschmitts from Rotenburg at 12:45 PM[775]. After forming up and climbing, these joined other fighter and heavy fighter *Gruppen* to form a battle group, which was then guided by Y-control over the Deister and Solling area where, at 1:20 PM, an approaching group of B-17s was sighted at a height of 7 000 meters. The *Gruppen* closed in and began their attacks. The heavy fighters opened up on the combat boxes in the middle of the formation, while the Messerschmitts attacked those at the front. II/JG 3 made several fruitless attacks against the first box[777]. The German fighters clung stubbornly to the bombers and continued to attack after they had dropped their bombs in the Eisenach area and turned west. II/JG 3 scored two victories, credited to Obfw. Roller (13) and Hptm. Sannemann (21), both of 6/JG 3. One Messerschmitt was shot down and another was obliged to make a forced landing, but in each case the pilot escaped injury.

When the fighting on 22 February 1944 was over, the *Luftwaffe* claimed no fewer than 119 enemy aircraft shot down, 95 of them four-engined bombers bombers[778]. This figure also included victories scored while defending against the 15th Air Force's incursions over the south of the Reich and the "Protectorate." The defending fighter and destroyer *Gruppen* lost 52 aircraft written off and another 22 damaged. The 8th Air Force admitted the loss of 45 heavy bombers and 12 escort fighters on this day; in view of the fact that only 255 heavy bombers actually dropped their bombs, the outcome of this day's fighting may be seen as a German defensive success, for the American loss rate was almost 18%. For their part, the Americans claimed to have shot down 118 German aircraft[779].

There were no daylight incursions by 8th Air Force heavy bombers on 23 February. The main reason for this was bad weather over much of Germany, which hindered large-scale offensive operations, however another factor was the 8th Air Force's low level of serviceability after the past three days of attacks. Many of the heavy bombers had sustained damage during the "Big Week" operations or simply required an overhaul[780]. The Germans were grateful for this respite. The day was an uneventful one for II/JG 3 apart from an accident involving Hptm. Sannemann. In the evening, while returning from a practice mission to Jever, he crash-landed his "Yellow 1" on the airfield.

On 24 February 1944 the skies cleared over large areas of central and southern Germany. This was immediately followed by further daylight raids by the American 8th Air Force from the northwest and the 15th Air Force from the south[781]. A total of 809 four-engined bombers took off from bases in England; escorted by 767 long-range fighters, they set course for their targets inside Germany. The 3rd Bombardment Division, whose 307 B-17s had to fly without fighter escort, was supposed to attack aircraft factories in Tutow, Posen and Kreising, while the target of 266 B-17s of the 1st Bombardment Division was once again the Schweinfurt ball-bearing factories[782]. And finally the 2nd Bombardment Division, which put

239 Liberators into the air, was supposed to attack the Gothaer Waggonfabrik, where the Bf 110 was produced[783]. On this day the Americans once again came in several distinct formations. To meet these incursions by the 8th Air Force, the *Luftwaffe* mobilized seventeen day fighter and three destroyer *Gruppen* as well as elements of several night fighter *Gruppen*. These units put a total of 336 aircraft into the air, however only 220 made contact with the enemy[784].

II/JG 3 scrambled from Rotenburg at 12:15 PM and afterwards assembled over Brunswick with other *Jagdgruppen*[785]. The combined force was then guided south toward an incoming force of heavy bombers[786]. Barely an hour after takeoff, the formation sighted two large groups of B-24s flying south. Soon afterwards, the bombers turned onto a west heading. The German units positioned themselves for a frontal attack and west of Gotha they made several passes through the boxes of B-24s. II/JG 3 subsequently claimed seven bombers shot down and two knocked out of formation[787]. Its own losses—one pilot slightly injured and two machines written off—were minimal. Uffz. Franz Glassauer of 6/JG 3 forced a B-24 to leave formation for his second victory, however his own machine was shot up and he was obliged to make a forced landing near Schotten on the Vogelsberg. While Glassauer was only slightly injured in the landing, his "Yellow 14" was a complete write-off.

The *Luftwaffe* claimed to have shot down 59 enemy aircraft in defending against the incursions by the US 8th Air Force, 52 of them in air combat[788]. A further 26 victories were scored in the south of the Reich by units committed against the 15th Air Force. German losses were 45 machines written off and 29 damaged on operations from various causes. On the other hand, while admitting the loss of 51 four-engined bombers and 10 escort fighters, the Americans claimed to have shot down 144 German aircraft[789]. The 15th Air Force's losses were placed at 19 heavy bombers and two fighters.

On 25 February 1944 the weather over large areas of the Reich was again good, with mainly clear skies, and this allowed the Americans to conduct further large-scale raids against the German aircraft industry. Once again attacks were to be made both by units of the 8th Air Force based in England and the 15th Air Force from Italy, with the focal point being the factories in the south of Germany. The 8th Air Force was able to muster 745 heavy bombers, which were escorted by 899 long-range fighters. The 1st Bombardment Division dispatched 268 Fortresses to strike the Messerschmitt works in Augsburg and factories near Stuttgart, while the Messerschmitt AG's two large factory complexes at Regensburg-Prüfening and Obertraubling were to be bombed in rapid succession by units of the 15th and the 8th Air Force. The former committed 158 B-17s and B-24s escorted by 125 P-38s and P-47s, and the latter 209 B-17s of the 3rd Bombardment Division. Finally, the 196 Liberators of the 2nd Bombardment Division were to attack aircraft factories near Fürth[790]. Since the focal point of the American

attacks lay over the south of the Reich, the German defensive effort involved units based in the northwest and the south, the latter including the *Gruppen* of *Luftflotte* 2 based in northern Italy. The Italian-based units engaged the heavy bombers of the 15th Air Force on the way to and from their targets[791]. Consequently, on 25 February 1944 the *Luftwaffe* was able to commit 22 day fighter and eight destroyer *Gruppen* to meet the enemy incursions plus the operational *Staffeln* of several training units. As a result, the American units met fierce resistance as they approached their targets in the early afternoon. As was standard practice in attacks on targets in the south and southwest of the Reich, the 8th Air Force heavy bombers made their approach over French territory. Consequently, II/JG 3 was far from the scene of events. Surviving records show that only a few of its aircraft saw action on this day. No contact was made with the enemy and one machine was lost in a non-combat-related incident[792,793].

The improvement in the weather over western Europe was short-lived, for the arrival of a new weather front on 26 February prevented the Allies from continuing their series of attacks. The bad weather lasted until month's end and thus brought "Big Week" to a premature end. Even so, the efforts of the USAAF during the previous six days had been impressive enough: between 20 and 25 February 1944 the bomber fleets of the 8th and 15th Air Forces had attacked 21 aircraft factories, repair facilities and airfields, in the process flying more than 3,300 heavy bomber and 3,673 fighter escort sorties[794] and dropping approximately 8,300 tons of bombs[795]. The Americans admitted the loss of 266 heavy bombers and 28 fighters during "Big Week" together with a total of 2,600 aircrew[796].

The most important result of "Big Week" was one which had not been anticipated by the Allied command[797], for the main impact of these attacks was not so much the damage inflicted on the aircraft industry, but the fact that they forced the *Luftwaffe* to engage in a battle which threatened the very substance of its day fighter arm[798]. The fighter arm increasingly found itself helpless against the ever greater number of American bombers; no longer able to maintain even local air superiority, it was increasingly forced on to the defensive—the German hunters had become the hunted. Two main developments were responsible for the decisive turn in affairs to the disadvantage of the *Luftwaffe*: one was the change in American tactics to simultaneous incursions by heavily-escorted formations. This meant that the German fighter pilots were no longer able to engage the bombers on a broad front as they had done before; instead the *Luftwaffe* fighter command now found itself forced to concentrate on attacking individual heavy bomber formations without fighter escort, while ignoring incursions against less important targets or heavily-escorted formations[799]. This attempt by the *Luftwaffe* to husband its dwindling resources[800] was quickly recognized as such by the Americans, and this immediately resulted in another change in tactics by the USAAF, and with it a further reason for the coming defeat of the day fighter arm. Exploiting their growing numerical superiority, the Americans immediately began relieving a considerable portion of their long-range fighters of their direct escort role, instead sending them on fighter sweeps ahead of the bombers in search of German fighters. From this point on German fighters were subject to attack by the P-38s, P-47s and P-51s anytime, anywhere and were never safe. Another element of this new mode of operations called for the American fighters to strafe German airfields whenever the opportunity arose[801].

For the *Luftwaffe*, "Big Week" had brought a period of unprecedented strain. Compared to the previous month, the number of sorties flown had risen from 3,315 to 4,242, while the loss rate had climbed equally sharply—from 5.4% in January to 8.2% in February 1944[802]. Expressed in absolute numbers, in February 1944 the Defense of the Reich had lost a total of 200 aircrew killed and 155 wounded from the day fighter and destroyer units, while material losses amounted to 349 machines written off with 60% or greater damage[803]. Under this continuous pressure and with losses constantly rising, the German day fighter arm threatened to disintegrate; just as the night fighter arm was gradually gaining the upper hand against the RAF night raids, daylight air superiority was clearly being lost to the USAAF[804]. Based at Rotenburg, II/JG 3 was one of the units in the heart of the action and, consequently, it was considered a "front-line *Gruppe*" by *I Jagdkorps*. For II/JG 3 the previous days' missions had been much less costly than for other front-line *Gruppen* based in the northwest of the Reich[806]; in the course of five defensive missions it had lost two pilots killed, four slightly wounded and nine Messerschmitts. On the positive side, during "Big Week" II *Gruppe* shot down or forced out of formation 16 enemy aircraft and finished off one cripple.

For the *Luftwaffe* command, the latest developments in the defensive battles over the Reich had led to clear consternation. Among the German day fighter units there was considerable uncertainty as a result of the appearance of the first long-range escort fighters and the losses they had caused. This was accompanied by a tangible decrease in offensive spirit, something that *General der Jagdflieger* Galland characterized as "fighter fright." An entire series of staff conferences was held in spring 1944 to search for answers to it. Already, on 23 February, *I Jagdkorps* had held a lengthy conference whose main topic was measures to increase the effectiveness of the German air defense by day[807]. The first important measure, adopted because of the constantly increasing depth of penetration by the Allied escort fighters, was a fundamental redistribution of forces. This would include moving the *Gruppen* of the various *Geschwader* closer together than before. In addition to this, each *Geschwader* was to convert or form one "light" *Gruppe* for the high-altitude fighter role, its primary mission to engage the American escort fighters at high altitude. These units would be equipped with high-altitude versions of the Bf 109 G[808,809]. One result of this conference was the concentration of the *Stab* and all four *Gruppen* of JG 3 within the area of 1 *Jagddivision*, whose command also included JG 301, JG 302 and ZG 26. The units would be stationed on airfields in the Brandenburg—Burg—Magdeburg—Gardelegen area[810].

As a result of this redistribution of forces, on 26 February 1944 II/JG 3's air element and its leading technical personnel moved from Rotenburg to Ludwigslust. They did not remain there long, however, for on 1 March the *Gruppe* moved again, this time to Gardelegen in the Altmark district, a spacious, well-equipped air base with permanent hangars and buildings and paved taxiways[811]. An advance detachment had been busy there since 18 February preparing the airfield to accept the *Gruppe*, and Gardelegen was to be its base of operations for subsequent air defense missions. However, the presence on the airfield of IV/KG 54, a bomber training unit, seriously restricted the *Gruppe*'s activities, and a search was soon begun for an alternate airfield in the vicinity which could accommodate elements, at least, of the *Gruppe*. The Sachau landing field, a small grass airfield about 10 km southwest of Gardelegen, was later put into operation and was occupied by elements of the *Gruppe*[812].

II/JG 3 did not take part in the defensive effort against the 8th Air Force's daylight raid on Frankfurt/Main on 2 March 1944[813]. Instead the unit's first defensive mission from its new base of operations took place on the following day. Mission 8 AF 246 was the 8th Air Force's first raid against Berlin, where the bombers were supposed to strike industrial facilities within the city itself as well as in Oranienburg and Erkner[814]. In the morning 748 four-engined bombers from all three bombardment divisions took off from their bases in southeast England and set course for Berlin. 730 fighters of VIII Fighter Command provided the escort, supported by numerous RAF fighters near the British coast[815]. Weather proved to be a problem while the bombers were still en route to the target, for unusually high cloud formations seriously hampered formation flying and navigation and ultimately led to the order to abort the mission[816]. By the time this order was issued, the leading formations of heavy bombers were already over the northwestern coastal area of Germany; a total of 79 heavy bombers dropped their bombs on targets of opportunity, 61 of them on Wilhelmshaven, prior to returning to England[817]. As a result of the weather, the German defensive effort on this day was once again relatively weak. It appears that elements of JG 1, JG 3, JG 11, JG 27, NJG 3 and ZG 26, a total of 213 aircraft, went into action against the formations of heavy bombers detected over the northwestern coastal region. Very little is known about II/JG 3's activities on this day. At 11:07 AM the *Gruppe* scrambled from Gardelegen and it subsequently encountered a formation of bombers with fighter escort over Mecklenburg. The *Gruppe* lost two Messerschmitts while failing to score. Uffz. Hans Staufferth of 5 *Staffel* was shot down near Parchim and forced to take to his parachute. He struck the tail of his aircraft while bailing out and suffered serious injuries. When the fighting was over, the Germans claimed a total of 21 enemy aircraft shot down by flak and fighters; their own losses amounted to 20 machines lost in aerial combat and 4 more lost for reasons other than enemy action. The USAAF admitted the loss of 11 four-engined bombers and 8 fighters (including six P-51s) while claiming 13 victories[318].

On 4 March 1944 the 8th Air Force made another attempt to bomb the Reich capital by day, however it, too, was a failure, mainly on account of the weather. A total of 502 Boeings of the 1st and 3rd Bombardment Divisions took off from their bases in southeast England to strike industrial targets in Klein-Machnow, a suburb in the southwest of Berlin situated on the Teltow Canal. Long-range escort was provided by 770 fighters. Once again, however, towering cloud formations prevented the bombers from forming up as planned, and after some time the order was issued to abort the mission. Some of the units did not receive the recall order, however; while all of the B-17s of the 1st Bombardment Division subsequently aborted the attack[319], 30 B-17s of the 13th CBW pressed on to Berlin, escorted by elements of three P-51 groups. Consequently the first daylight raid on Berlin by the 8th Air Force ended up being a very modest one. In fact, at 1:42 PM 68 tons of high-explosive and incendiary bombs fell on to the southwestern outskirts of Berlin, inflicting minor damage. The defensive effort by the German fighter units also suffered considerably as a result of the bad weather; it was only possible to mobilize nine *Gruppen* with just 149 aircraft to meet the incursion by the heavy bombers[320].

II/JG 3 scrambled from Gardelegen at 12:20 PM[321] and approximately one hour later it encountered thirty B-17s of the 13th Composite Bomb Wing and their escort of Mustangs over the Döberitz area. The *Gruppe* scored several victories in the ensuing combat, a B-17 and a P-51 shot down by Lt. Münster, the *Kapitän* of 5 *Staffel* (90-91), and a P-51 by Uffz. Wahl (1). On the negative side was one pilot killed and one seriously wounded, both from 6 *Staffel*. Gefr. Rolf Lenk was shot down and killed by Mustangs, while Obfw. Robert Roller bailed out seriously wounded and came down near Döberitz. In addition to II/JG 3, the *Stab* and IV/JG 3 also engaged the bombers, subsequently claiming four shot down for the loss of one aircraft[322, 323].

The next day bad weather again prevented the attack on Berlin from being conducted as planned, but on 6 March 1944 there was an improvement in the weather which allowed the American 8th Air Force to launch Mission No. 250 in the morning. Involving a total of 730 heavy bombers from all three bombardment divisions plus 801 escort fighters, its targets were industrial facilities in and around Berlin. Because of the great distance to the target the heavy bombers had to take the shortest route and approached the target in one long stream. The American units crossed the coast north of Amsterdam near Egmond and flew east into the Celle area, where they were to make a turn to the east-southeast[324]. The American incursion encountered a determined defense involving all of the available fighter units stationed in the northwest of the Reich as well as elements of 4 *Jagddivision* based in the western territories.

Those stationed in the south of the Reich were only marginally involved[325]. Also involved in the German defensive were a number of destroyer and night fighter *Gruppen* based deeper in the interior. In the end nineteen day fighter, three destroyer and four night fighter *Gruppen* saw action, along with elements of various other units[326] and together they flew a total of 528 sorties[327]. The result was the fiercest air battle ever fought over Reich territory.

II/JG 3 scrambled sixteen machines from Gardelegen at 11:36 AM[328]. It initially flew to Magdeburg, where units of 1 and 7 *Jagddivision* were supposed to form into a battle unit. In the end, this included 41 heavy fighters of II and III/ZG 26 and I and II/ZG 76, plus 72 Messerschmitts and Focke Wulfs of I, II and IV/JG 3, *Sturmstaffel 1*, JG 302 and *Jasta Erla*. The battle unit was led by the *Kommandeur* of III/ZG 26, Maj. Kogler[329]. At 12:42 PM over Tangerhütte, south of Gardelegen, contact was made with the leading elements of the American bomber stream, the B-17s of the 1st and 94th Composite Bomb Wings. After the initial head-on pass, the engagement developed into a long running fight. Hptm. Sannemann described it as follows in his combat report:

After the battle unit's initial attack (south of Gardelegen) my wingman was gone. Alone, I escorted eight heavy fighters, which swung out to the south and then carried out another attack on a formation of Boeings southeast of Berlin. At about 1:20 PM, at an altitude of 7 000 meters roughly in Grid Square FI 1, I made a frontal attack on the right outer Boeing of the top flight. I scored effective hits in the fuselage and wings. It veered out of formation smoking slightly. I subsequently made three attacks from behind, but in part with machine-guns only. By this time the Boeing had descended to 2 000 meters. After my third attack I was attacked by two Mustangs and lost sight of the Boeing, which was flying on a southwest course. After I landed at 1:45 PM, a Boeing flew southeast past the airfield at a height of 100 meters. I assume that it was the Boeing I had shot up and that it belly-landed in GH/GI.

In addition to the bomber claimed by Hptm. Sannemann (22), Uffz. Agricola of 5/JG 3 accounted for a B-17 (1), while *Gruppenkommandeur* Hptm. Rohwer claimed the destruction of a P-38 (37). Given the ferocity of the fighting, the *Gruppe*'s losses, two Messerschmitts shot down in combat, were relatively light. Uffz. Edmund Britzlmair of 4/JG 3 was the only casualty: he was slightly injured when forced to bail out near Möckern east of Magdeburg after his "White 7" was shot up by American fighters.

The 8th Air Force's losses on 6 March 1944 were the heaviest suffered in any attack against Germany; by its own admission it lost 75 four-engined bombers and 14 escort fighters. The *Luftwaffe* claimed to have shot down a total of 140 enemy aircraft, including 118 heavy bombers[330]. Its own losses were 36 pilots killed and 27 wounded plus a total of 65 aircraft written off[331]. The Americans claimed the impressive figure of 214 German aircraft destroyed[332].

On 7 March the skies over the Reich were quiet. II/JG 3 nevertheless suffered one casualty: Gefr. Heinz Schmeling of 4 *Staffel* died when his machine crashed and exploded south of Gardelegen while on a maintenance test flight. The cause of the crash was not determined.

Two days after its first major daylight raid on Berlin the 8th Air Force launched a second strike against the capital. On 8 March 1944 it mobilized 623 heavy bombers from all three bombardment divisions to attack the VKF ball-bearing factories in Erkner, a suburb in the southeast of Berlin. The raiders were accompanied by 891 escort fighters, including 174 P-51s from six of the nine fighter groups that had reequipped with the type. As in the previous attack the bombers followed the shortest route, so that the incoming bomber formations overflew the coast near Amsterdam in a long stream and from there headed east toward their target. The incursion by the heavy bombers once again encountered determined opposition from units of the Reich air defense. Altogether the German side was able to mobilize 20 day fighter and two destroyer *Gruppen* as well as elements of various night fighter, test and other units, but these were only able to put 282 aircraft into the air[833].

II/JG 3 scrambled from Gardelegen at 12:44 PM and subsequently assembled with the remaining elements of JG 3 and ZG 26 to form a battle unit[834]. The first enemy aircraft were sighted west of Magdeburg at 1:20 PM, a group of escorted B-17s flying at an altitude of 7 000 meters. In the ensuing combat the *Gruppe* recorded two bombers shot down and one forced to leave formation by Lt. Ruhl (30-31) and Lt. Münster (92), while Hptm. Rohwer brought down a P-38 (38). The *Gruppe*'s losses were again bearable, two machines lost in combat and one pilot with minor injuries. Uffz. Ulrich Stingl of 4/JG 3 was injured when enemy fire blew off his canopy; despite his injuries, Stingl was able to bail out safely.

When the fighting was over, the German side placed its successes at 112 enemy aircraft shot down[835], including 66 heavy bombers; on the other hand its own losses were 55 aircraft written off, while the day fighter *Gruppen* alone lost 33 pilots killed[837]. The 8th Air Force admitted the loss of 40 heavy bombers and 34 escort fighters, while its own claims (167 German aircraft shot down) were once again extremely optimistic[838].

The American 8th Air Force's third major daylight raid against the Reich capital took place on 9 March 1944. A force of 526 four-engined bombers was mobilized[839], however a solid overcast prevented the planned precision attacks and only the B-17s of the 1st and 3rd Bombardment Divisions dropped their bombs on Berlin at all, while the Liberators of the 2nd Bombardment Division dropped their loads on secondary targets in the Hanover—Brunswick—Nienburg area[840]. The bad weather prevented the German day fighter and destroyer *Gruppen* from mounting any defensive effort on this day as the low-lying cloud, which in some places reached almost to the ground, made it impossible for them to take off[841].

In the days that followed, the weather remained poor for the most part, seriously hampering operations by both sides[842]. As a result, II/JG 3's next defensive mission was not flown until 23 March

1944[843]. On this day 768 B-17s and B-24s, escorted by 841 long-range fighters, were supposed to bomb aircraft factories in Brunswick and other targets (of opportunity) in Münster, Osnabrück and Achmer. The incursions met very heavy resistance from the German day fighter units based in the northwest of the Reich; the *Luftwaffe* was able to muster 13 day fighter *Gruppen* with a total of 259 aircraft on this day, while the decimated destroyer units had to be left on the ground[844].

The heavy bombers came rather early on this day, and at Gardelegen the order for II/JG 3 to scramble was issued at 9:50 AM. After takeoff, the *Gruppe* formed up with IV/JG 3 and *Sturmstaffel 1* in the usual way[845]. The formation was subsequently vectored west into the area southeast of Münster, where at about 11 AM it encountered enemy aircraft, B-17s of the 1st BD with a strong escort of Mustangs. The American bombers were en route to their target, Münster. The German fighters attacked at once[846] and in the ensuing battle II/JG 3 shot down three enemy aircraft and forced three bombers to leave formation. Its own losses were one pilot killed and three Messerschmitts. Uffz. Heinz Rehm of 6 *Staffel* was shot down and killed; he went down with his machine, which crashed near Nateln, about 10 km northeast of Werl. Gefr. Theo Burchardt of 4/JG 3 was luckier. While attacking a B-17, he rammed the enemy bomber and both aircraft went down. Burchardt was able to bail out in time, however he landed hard and sustained several sprains. In the end, low on fuel, the machines of II/JG 3 landed at airfields all over the northern Rhine region and Westphalia. Most returned to Gardelegen the same day.

When the fighting ended on 23 March, the German side claimed a total of 51 enemy action shot down, including 44 four-engined bombers[847]; its own losses were 16 pilots killed—including the *Kommodore* of JG 3, *Oberst* Wolf-Dietrich Wilcke—and six wounded plus 33 aircraft[848]. The American 8th Air Force admitted the loss of 29 heavy bombers and 5 escort fighters while claiming 62 German aircraft shot down and another 2 destroyed on the ground[849].

On 24 March 1944 230 B-17s of the 1st Bombardment Division launched yet another attack on the ball-bearing factories around Schweinfurt. Weather severely limited the German defensive effort and II/JG 3 saw no action at all[850]. For the next four days there were no more incursions over the Reich by the heavy bombers of the 8th Air Force. The onset of another period of winter weather provided the sorely tried day fighter and destroyer units with a badly needed rest. In spite of the bad weather, maintenance test, practice and radio flights were carried out whenever possible. For II/JG 3 these flights were uneventful.

On 29 March 1944 there was a weak daylight attack on Brunswick. A total of 236 B-17s of the 1st Bombardment Division were sent to attack the Luther Works again, as well as airfields and repair facilities in and around Brunswick. The fighter escort consisted of 428 aircraft. The *Luftwaffe* responded to this incursion with eleven day fighter *Gruppen* and a total of 238 aircraft[851]. II/JG 3 scrambled from Gardelegen at 12:55 PM and was subsequently vectored into the Nienburg—Weser area, where it became involved in a costly engagement with American fighters escorting a group of incoming B-17s. The *Gruppe* lost four pilots without scoring a single victory. Worst of all was the loss of its *Gruppenkommandeur*: Hptm. Detlev Rohwer was shot down by Mustangs and was forced to belly-land his aircraft "Chevron Triangle" near Ibbenbühren. The landing was successful, however the Mustangs attacked again, wounding Rohwer so seriously that he died the next day[852]. 4 *Staffel* suffered two total losses: Uffz. Hermann Beck was listed missing after combat with P-51s, while Uffz. Karl-Heinz Cichoracky was shot down and killed southeast of Nienburg. 6/JG 3 placed Gefr. Friedrich Simchen on the casualty list after he was shot down and killed by Mustangs near Rohrsen. After the loss of Hptm. Rohwer, Hptm. Sannemann again assumed temporary command of the *Gruppe*.

At the end of the day the *Luftwaffe* reported a total of 22 enemy aircraft shot down from the force attacking Brunswick, including 12 heavy bombers[853]; its own losses were 21 pilots killed and 6 wounded with 30 machines written off and another 14 with serious damage[854]. The 8th Air Force admitted the loss of 10 heavy bombers and 18 escort fighters while claiming 59 German aircraft destroyed in the air and another 20 on the ground[855].

There were no more incursions by units of the 8th Air Force prior to the end of the month. March of 1944 had been characterized by predominantly bad weather, which had a detrimental effect on both air forces although with very different outcomes. Whereas the 8th Air Force had continued to increase the number of sorties flown compared to the previous month (from 9,884 to 11,590, of which 8,773 were "effective"[856]), the clearly reduced operational strengths of the German day fighter units after "Big Week" and their lack of bad weather training resulted in a reduction in sorties from 4,242 to 3,672. Nevertheless, the loss rate continued to rise inexorably and, with 349 total losses in this month, reached 9.4%. The 8th Air Force lost almost the exact same number of machines, 347, in March 1944, however this equated to a loss rate of just 3.3% compared to 3.8% the month before[857]. For II/JG 3, the bad weather in March resulted in defensive missions being flown on just six days. The *Gruppe* claimed 15 enemy aircraft shot down or knocked out of formation, while suffering serious losses—seven pilots killed or missing and 18 Messerschmitts written off. The *Gruppe*'s battered state is reflected in the strength report of 31 March 1944[858]. While it shows 44 Messerschmitt Bf 109 G-6s on strength, of which 37 (84%) were serviceable, four above authorized strength, the *Gruppe* had just 24 pilots fit for operations, just 60% of its authorized personnel strength.

During the first week of April, continued poor winter weather over the northwest and west of the Reich prevented the 8th Air Force from carrying out major daylight raids over Germany. Instead, on 5 April 1944 strong fighter forces of the 8th Air Force operating in several waves carried out low-level attacks on German airfields inside the Reich. Bad weather limited the German response to the American incursions, which were carried out by a total of 456 P-38s, P-47s and P-51s; in the area of I *Jagdkorps*, for example, only 36 aircraft could be mustered. These included elements of II/JG 3 which were scrambled early in the afternoon and subsequently engaged a unit of Mustangs. One Mustang was claimed shot down by Obfw. Grünberg of 5/JG 3 (66); the *Gruppe* suffered no losses[859]. Not until 8 April did a marked improvement in the weather allow the next daylight incursion to take place. A total of 664 heavy bombers were committed to attack airfields in the northwest of Germany and, once again, aircraft factories near Brunswick. Among the targets were the air bases at Oldenburg, Quakenbrück, Achmer, Rheine and Twente[860]. The bombers were escorted by a total of 780 fighters, including 206 Mustangs. On the German side 20 day fighter *Gruppen* were mobilized to defend against this incursion, while the destroyer and night fighter units were left on the ground. A total of 417 German aircraft saw action[861].

II/JG 3 scrambled from Gardelegen at 1 PM and afterwards formed up with *Stab*, I and IV/JG 3 plus *Sturmstaffel 1* to form the *Gefechtsverband*. The combined force was then vectored northwest toward the incoming formations of heavy bombers[862], the leading elements of which had crossed the Dutch coast between Noordwijk and Texel at about 12 PM. At 2 PM northwest of Brunswick contact was made with several waves of B-24s flying east accompanied by a powerful escort of fighters. The German fighters launched their frontal attack before the bombers reached their targets and a fierce air battle developed in the area between Celle and Brunswick. Twelve heavy bombers and two P-51s were shot down or forced out of formation[863], with two B-24s and the two Mustangs being credited to II/JG 3. Both enemy fighters were claimed by Fw. Florian of 4 *Staffel* (4-5). On the other side of the coin, the *Gruppe* lost four Messerschmitts in combat with the Mustangs. Luckily, three of the pilots escaped injury. The other, Gefr. Johannes Kupka of 4/JG 3, was seriously wounded when shot down between Brunswick and Helmstedt.

When the fighting was over, the German side claimed a total of 87 enemy aircraft shot down, 65 of them heavy bombers[864]; its own losses amounted to 42 pilots killed and 13 wounded plus 78 aircraft destroyed. To these losses must be added 7 machines which were destroyed on the ground[865]. The 8th Air Force admitted the loss of 36 four-engined bombers and 25 escort fighters while claiming at least 158 German aircraft shot down and 55 more destroyed on the ground[866].

In spite of worsened weather conditions, units of the 8th Air Force carried out their next daylight incursions the very next day, 9 April 1944, Easter Sunday. 542 four-engined bombers from all three bombardment divisions with an escort of 719 long-range fighters were dispatched to attack aircraft factories and airfields in Marienburg, Tutow, Posen, Warnemünde and Rostock. The American incursion encountered a defense consisting of 11 day fighter *Gruppen*; as well (probably on account of the poor weather) for the first time in some while night fighters and destroyers also took part in the defensive effort (elements of NJG 3 and ZG 26). All in all, the German side committed 354 aircraft on this day[867]. II/JG 3 scrambled at 10:35 AM, after which it formed up as usual with the *Stab* and the other two *Gruppen*. The battle unit was then vectored over the Baltic coast near Rügen, where it engaged the heavy bombers and their escort of Mustangs[868]. The participating elements of JG 3 subsequently claimed ten enemy aircraft shot down or forced out of formation, however II/JG 3 came up empty handed[869].

After a day with no enemy incursions, II/JG 3's next mission took place on 11 April 1944. On this day a total of 917 heavy bombers were mobilized to strike aircraft factories in Oschersleben, Bernburg, Halberstadt, Sorau, Cottbus and Arnimswalde producing the Focke Wulf 190 and Ju 88. The escort for the bomber force, which came in several separate formations, consisted of 819 aircraft, including six P-51 groups which put a total of 241 Mustangs into the air. The Germans, on the other hand, mustered eighteen day fighter, two destroyer and elements of two night fighter *Gruppen*, which together put 432 aircraft into action[870].

II/JG 3 scrambled from Gardelegen at 10:05 AM with instructions to rendezvous with the units of the *1* and *3 Jagddivision* over the Brocken Mountains. Contact was subsequently made with large formations of B-17s and B-24s and their escorts over the area between Brunswick and Halberstadt. A bitter air battle raged there from 11:00 to 11:30 AM, extending over a large area and resulting in heavy losses to both sides. When it was over, JG 3 alone claimed 34 enemy aircraft shot down or forced out of formation. II/JG 3's share was two B-17s and two P-51s, all credited to 5 *Staffel*[871]. The *Gruppe*'s own losses were quite serious, with four pilots killed in combat with the American escort fighters and another wounded, plus six Messerschmitts written off. 4/JG 3 lost Uffz. Alfred Beutel, who was shot down and killed west of Gardelegen. 5 *Staffel* lost two pilots: Obfw. Rudolf Traphan, an experienced *Schwarmführer* with 13 victories to his credit, was shot down and killed near Bernburg, while Uffz. Rudolf Stephan fell near Warnenau northeast of Brunswick. 6 *Staffel* suffered two casualties: Fw. Waldemar Eyrich, another very successful *Schwarmführer* with 31 victories, was shot down and killed by Mustangs west of Magdeburg. Uffz. Karl-Heinz Lintermann was luckier: wounded by enemy gunfire, he nevertheless made a successful belly landing near Gardelegen in his "Yellow 3". Elements of the *Gruppe* were sent up a second time to intercept the bombers as they withdrew, however the only result was an inconclusive dogfight with the American fighter escort.

After the fighting was over, the German side initially claimed a total of 129 enemy aircraft shot down, including no less than 105 four-engined bombers[872]. In contrast its own losses were 38 pilots killed and 15 wounded plus 57 aircraft destroyed. Another 7 machines were destroyed on the ground. The 8th Air Force's actual

losses on 11 April 1944 were 69 heavy bombers and 16 escort fighters, a loss total which almost equaled that of its first daylight raid on Berlin on 6 March. On the other hand the Americans claimed to have shot down 153 German machines and destroyed another 65 on the ground[873].

The American daylight raids now came without letup, insofar as the weather permitted. The next major daylight attack was supposed to be flown on 12 April, and in fact that morning 455 heavy bombers took off from their bases in southeast England. Three separate bombing forces were supposed to strike industrial targets in Schweinfurt, Oschersleben, Zwickau, Halle and Leipzig. Once again, however, the operation had to be aborted on account of bad weather and the bomber units recalled. In contrast to the previous day, on 13 April 1944 the 8th Air Force was able to carry out its daylight incursion as planned; on this day 626 four-engined bombers were dispatched to attack the Schweinfurt ball-bearing factories, the Messerschmitt AG facilities in Augsburg, the Dornier factories in Oberpfaffenhofen, and Lechfeld airfield. The bombers were escorted by 871 fighters. At the same time a force of 342 B-24s of the 15th Air Force was to attack aircraft factories and airfields near Budapest, while another force of B-17s was sent to attack similar targets near Raab. The Germans were able to muster a total of 18 day fighter *Gruppen* and one destroyer *Gruppe*, a total of 412 aircraft, to meet the incursions from the northwest and south[874].

II/JG 3 scrambled seventeen Bf 109s from Gardelegen at 12:58 PM. After they had formed up with the *Stab*, I and IV/JG 3, the *Geschwader* battle unit was directed by Y-control toward an approaching group of heavy bombers with a strong fighter escort. Shortly before 2 PM contact was made with four waves of B-17s east of Giessen. The bombers were flying east at 6 500 meters leaving condensation trails and were escorted by numerous Mustangs. After positioning themselves ahead of the enemy formations, at 2 PM the *Gruppen* of JG 3 launched a frontal attack on the Boeings of the third wave, with II/JG 3 attacking the lowest combat box. Two bombers were claimed shot down by the formation leader, Hptm. Sannemann (23), and Lt. Reinartz of 4/JG 3 (4); another was forced out of formation by Uffz. Jäger of 5 *Staffel* (1). The *Gruppe*'s only combat-related loss was a Messerschmitt damaged in air combat, however another aircraft was written off and two more damaged in non-combat-related incidents. When the mission was over, most aircraft landed at Eschborn near Frankfurt. From there, at 5:00 PM elements of II/JG 3 were scrambled against reported incursions. The mission that followed led to an inconclusive skirmish with Mustangs, after which II/JG 3 returned to Eschborn. In the early evening the *Gruppe* returned to Gardelegen[875].

The *Luftwaffe* claimed a total of 91 enemy aircraft shot down, 74 of them heavy bombers[876], in its battles against the daylight incursions on 13 April 1944. Its own losses amounted to 11 pilots killed, 15 wounded and 46 aircraft written off[877]. The American 8th Air Force admitted the loss of 41 four-engined bombers and 11 escort fighters[878] while claiming 64 German fighters shot down and another 21 probables. The Americans also claimed to have destroyed 35 aircraft on the ground[879].

After the attacks of 13 April, the onset of further bad weather prevented the Americans from carrying out further daylight raids on targets within the Reich for four days. II/JG 3 was apparently not committed against an Allied fighter sweep on 15 April which was made in several waves[880]. Three days later, on 18 April 1944, units of the 8th Air Force launched another major daylight raid against industrial targets in the Berlin area in spite of the fact that the weather remained poor. The Americans mobilized a total of 776 heavy bombers from all three bombardment divisions under the protection of 634 escort fighters[881]. The bad weather had a decidedly negative affect on the German defensive effort. The heavy cloud layer that covered most of Germany made it impossible for the units to be employed in concentration; only a few fighter *Gruppen* got into the air and of the 144 aircraft committed only about half made contact with the enemy. JG 3, II/JG 302 stationed near Berlin and *Sturmstaffel 1* were the only units vectored onto the approaching heavy bombers of the 3rd Bombardment Division, and after a bitter air battle these units claimed a total of 26 heavy bombers shot down[882,883]. II/JG 3, which scrambled from Gardelegen at 1:17 PM[884], accounted for three B-17s shot down, however its own losses—three pilots killed and four Messerschmitts written off—were much worse. One loss occurred during the scramble: the engine of "Black 15", the machine of Uffz. Karl Krenkel of 5/JG 3, oversped during takeoff. Krenkel was then killed when he crashed while attempting a forced landing a few kilometers north of Gardelegen airfield. Lt. Friedrich-Wilhelm Schmidt of 6 *Staffel* was shot down by P-51s northwest of Berlin, while Uffz. Edmund Britzlmair of 4/JG 3 was shot down and killed by Mustangs while attempting to land at Gardelegen.

19 April 1944: The 8th Air Force dispatched a total of 772 four-engined bombers to attack factories producing aircraft and aero-engines as well as air bases in Westphalia and Hesse[885]. The fighter escort consisted of 697 aircraft. The weather had not improved significantly and, while the *Luftwaffe* was able to muster 13 day fighter *Gruppen* with a total of 220 aircraft, in the end only 96 of these actually engaged the enemy[886]. During the late morning, the *Gruppen* of JG 3 based in the area of 1 *Jagddivision* engaged incoming B-17 formations of the 1st Bombardment Division and their escort, shooting down or forcing out of formation six B-17s and three P-51s. II/JG 3, which scrambled from Gardelegen at 9:35 AM[887], contributed two B-17s shot down and one forced out of formation plus two P-51s[888]. This was a good day for the *Gruppe*, as it suffered no casualties of any kind.

After two days of bad weather, on 22 April 1944 the heavy bombers of the 8th Air Force returned in large numbers to attack targets inside the Reich. A force consisting of 803 bombers from all

three bombardment divisions was mustered to attack transportation targets in the west of the Reich, in particular the marshalling yards at Hamm, but also the city of Hamm itself. Bad weather delayed the order to take off for a long time, and when the heavy bombers finally took off it, was clear that they would not be able to make it back until after dark. The bombers were escorted by 859 fighters. The German reaction to these incursions was relatively weak; just eight day fighter *Gruppen* with a total of 198 aircraft could be mobilized to intercept the American heavy bomber units and their escorting fighters over West Germany[889]. II/JG 3 was scrambled from Sachau at 6:35 PM to intercept the incoming bombers. It engaged a formation of B-17s, however it failed to achieve any results and all of the *Gruppe*'s aircraft returned to Sachau after almost two hours in the air[890]. Incidentally, this mission was the last by Hptm. Heinrich Sannemann as a member of II/JG 3. After a brief rest leave he was to join JGr. West at Stargard[891]. That same day the new *Kommandeur* of II/JG 3, Hptm. Hermann Baron von Kap-herr, arrived at Gardelegen to take command of the *Gruppe*. He had previously served with the *Stab* of III/JG 3. Appointed *Staffelführer* of 6/JG 3 was Lt. Oskar Zimmermann, who came from IV/JG 3 and had 16 victories to his credit.

24 April 1944: Weather conditions remained less than favorable, however 745 four-engined bombers of the 8th Air Force escorted by 867 fighters carried out attacks against aircraft factories and air bases in the south of the Reich. A force of 281 B-17s of the 1st Bombardment Division was to bomb Landsberg airfield and factory installations at Oberpfaffenhofen, while at the same time 243 Fortresses of the 3rd Bombardment Division attacked aircraft production and other industrial targets in Friedrichshafen on Lake Constance. Finally the air bases at Gablingen and Leipheim were the targets of 230 Liberators of the 2nd Bombardment Division. To meet these incursions, the *Luftwaffe* mobilized a total of 18 day fighter *Gruppen* and one destroyer *Gruppe* as well as elements of training and industrial defense units for a total of 381 aircraft, 301 of which made enemy contact[892].

II/JG 3, which was led by its new *Kommandeur* Hptm. von Kap-herr for the first time on this day, scrambled shortly after noon, and after forming up with the *Stab* and the other two *Gruppen* was vectored south toward the formations of heavy bombers. At approximately 1:15 PM contact was made north of Augsburg with a large formation of B-17s escorted by numerous Mustangs. The battle unit made several firing passes against these; subsequent claims totaled 24 heavy bombers shot down or forced to leave formation, two cripples finished off and two P-51s shot down[893]. II/JG 3's contributed two B-17s shot down by Fw. Florian (7) and Uffz. Engler (1) and one forced out of formation by Lt. Mietzner (2). These successes came at the cost of two pilots killed and three Messerschmitts shot down in air combat and one badly damaged. Hptm. Hermann Baron von Kap-herr was shot down and killed near Neuburg/Donau, the fourth *Kommandeur* lost by the *Gruppe* in defensive operations over the Reich. Hptm. von Kap-herr had been with II/JG 3 just three days and failed to return from his first combat mission with the *Gruppe*. Also lost was Fw. Heinrich Ständebach of 6/JG 3, who was shot down and killed by enemy fighters near Aichach, not far from Augsburg. After the loss of Hptm. von Kap-herr, the *Kapitän* of 5/JG 3, Lt. Leopold Münster, was placed in temporary command of II *Gruppe*.

When the fighting was over, the German side claimed a total of 97 enemy aircraft shot down while defending against the 8th Air Force's daylight incursions[894]. Its own losses were 39 pilots killed and twelve wounded and 60 aircraft written off. On the other side, the USAAF admitted the loss of 41 four-engined bombers and 18 fighters, while its units claimed the destruction of 79 German aircraft in the air and another 72 on the ground[895].

29 April 1944: After four days with no further daylight raids, on this day the capital of the Reich was once again the target of a total of 679 heavy bombers, 618 of which actually reached the target area. The bombers came in several groups and were accompanied by a total of 814 escort fighters. The *Luftwaffe* was able to mobilize fourteen day fighter *Gruppen* plus elements of one night fighter *Gruppe* and various industrial defense and training units to meet these incursions. These units put a total of 350 aircraft into the air[896].

As usual, the four-engined bomber formations were detected while forming up off the English coast, and at about 9:00 AM the units were ordered to cockpit readiness. One hour later at Sachau, II/JG 3 received the order to scramble. It subsequently joined up with *Stab*, I and IV/JG 3 and was then vectored into the Magdeburg area, where shortly before 11 AM it made contact with an incoming group of B-17s with a powerful fighter escort. The ensuing engagement in grid squares HD/HE resulted in the participating *Gruppen* of JG 3 shooting down no less than 15 enemy aircraft, while 12 were forced out of formation and one cripple was finished off. II/JG 3 accounted for a significant share with five B-17s shot down and three forced out of formation[897]. This success came at the cost of two pilots killed and four aircraft shot down. Both fatalities came from 5 *Staffel*: Uffz. Maximilian Reichenberger was shot down by P-47s east of Halberstadt; he bailed out successfully, however his parachute had been damaged and he fell to his death. Uffz. Heinz Rieckenberg fell victim to American escort fighters near Magdeburg and he was shot down and killed 12 kilometers east of Meseberg.

The *Luftwaffe*'s losses in defending against the raids of 29 April 1944 totaled twelve pilots killed and five wounded and 21 aircraft written off. The American 8th Air Force admitted the loss of 65 heavy bombers and 14 escort fighters, while its units claimed a total of 121 enemy aircraft shot down[898].

The last day of the month brought no further daylight incursions, and things were quiet in JG 3's area of operations. Even though the weather had been less than favorable, the month of April 1944

had seen a further increase in the 8th Air Force's activities over the Reich; 14,464 sorties were flown by the heavy bombers, 11,428 of which were directed against targets within the Reich, on which were dropped 22,829 tons of high-explosive bombs and 4,797 tons of incendiaries[899]. Losses during the same period amounted to 420 four-engined bombers[900] and 140 escort fighters[901], making April 1944 the costliest month of the entire war in terms of heavy bomber losses, even though the loss rate was only 2.9 percent[902]. During the same period the *Luftwaffe* logged a total of 4,505 sorties and recorded 469 losses, equivalent to a loss rate of 9.2 percent, roughly equal to that of the previous month[903]. Expressed in absolute numbers, in April 1944 the Defense of the Reich lost 175 aircrew killed, missing or wounded from the day fighter units and 29 from the destroyer units; 258 fighter aircraft were lost in the same period, 208 of them as a result of enemy action, while another 155 were damaged. The corresponding figures for the destroyers were 45 and 28.

There now followed a week which, for II/JG 3, was quiet apart from an uneventful intercept mission on 4 May[904]. The continued unsettled weather with heavy cloud and frequent rain showers at first prevented the US 8th Air Force from launching further daylight raids. This short pause came just in time for II/JG 3 after the heavy losses it had taken in April. The loss of eleven pilots killed and two wounded in only seven days of flying had continued the process of wearing down the *Gruppe*. The *Luftwaffe*'s inadequate training organization meant that replacing the lost pilots with men of equal ability was impossible. By now there were almost no pilots left from the *Gruppe*'s successful days in the summer of 1942. A vivid example of this situation is provided by the personnel in the *Staffelkapitän* positions. Just six months earlier, all three *Staffeln* had been led by experienced officers of *Hauptmann* or *Oberleutnant* rank (Werner Lucas, Joachim Kirschner and Paul Stolte), two of whom had more than 100 victories and wore the Knight's Cross. Two of these officers had since been killed and the other transferred. Now, at the end of April 1944, all three *Staffeln* were commanded by *Leutnants*, because of a shortage of suitable, experienced officers, and one of these, Lt. Leopold Münster, was even in temporary command of the *Gruppe* on account of the shortage of experienced unit leaders of higher rank[905].

Meanwhile, on 1 May 1944, II/JG 3's new *Gruppenkommandeur*, Hptm. Gustav Frielinghaus, had arrived at Gardelegen. Frielinghaus, who had still not recovered fully from the serious injuries he had suffered in December 1943[906], was transferred to II *Gruppe* from IV/JG 3. He had previously served with II *Gruppe* from the summer of 1941 until his transfer to IV/JG 3 in May 1943. Frielinghaus wore the German Cross in Gold and had 74 victories to his credit, the last eight scored over Sicily and Italy while flying with IV *Gruppe*. Since the new *Kommandeur* was not yet fit to fly, Oblt. Max Bruno Fischer, the *Gruppenadjutant*, had to fly a Bf 108 to Salzwedel to pick him up. For the time being he would lead II/JG 3 from the ground, while Lt. Münster remained in command of the air element[907].

II/JG 3's next defensive mission did not take place until 8 May 1944[908]. On this day Berlin and Brunswick were again the targets of large-scale daylight raids by units of the 8th Air Force, which dispatched 807 heavy bombers from all three bombardment divisions escorted by 855 fighters. Unlike the previous raid, on 8 May the American incursions encountered fierce resistance from German fighter units. Elements of seven day fighter *Geschwader*, a total of seventeen *Gruppen*, were mobilized to intercept the raiders, putting 400 aircraft into the air[909].

II/JG 3 scrambled from Sachau at 8:42 AM. Since central Germany was covered by several layers of heavy cloud, the *Gruppen* of JG 3 were initially vectored into the Hamburg area, where broken cloud made it possible for the *Geschwader* to climb up and assemble into battle unit formation[910]. The *Gruppe* reached the specified area, however after climbing up through the cloud it found itself all alone, with no sign of the other *Gruppen*. II/JG 3 nevertheless set course southwest toward Bremen. The following is from the combat report filed by Lt. Franz Ruhl of 4/JG 3:

We had good ground contact in the Bremen area, however the formation leader of our Gruppe believed that he wasn't being guided properly. He suddenly made a half-roll and dive. In the confusion I lost my formation leader. At the same time I saw the four-engined about 2 000 meters above me and I led approximately eleven Bf 109s into a climb in pursuit.

In the general confusion the *Gruppe* formation apparently became completely dispersed. 4 *Staffel* subsequently engaged a group of B-17s in the Verden area. One B-17 was shot down by Lt. Ruhl (32) and came down near Achim at 10:05 AM. All subsequent attacks were unsuccessful, and with fuel running low 4/JG 3 was forced to break off the battle and land at Lemwerder. Meanwhile, the rest of the *Gruppe* under Lt. Münster had reformed and attacked the heavy bombers. West of Brunswick there was a bitter battle with an incoming formation of B-17s and later, in the Hildesheim area, with a group of B-24s. II/JG 3 recorded a total of nine enemy

Gen.Kdo I Jagd-Korps   15. 5. 1944

Korpstagesbefehl Nr. 28

Am 8. Mai 1944 hat bei Abwehr eines feindlichen Großeinfluges

Leutnant M ü n s t e r, Staffelkapitän 5./J.G. Udet unter Hingabe seines Lebens ein viermotoriges feindliches Kampfflugzeug durch Rammstoß vernichtet. Mit dieser soldatischen opfervollen Tat hat ein an Kampf und Ehre reiches Fliegerleben seinen heldenhaften Abschluß gefunden.

93 auf den verschiedensten Kriegsschauplätzen errungene Luftsiege künden seinen Ruhm und führten zu der hohen Auszeichnung mit dem

Eichenlaub zum Ritterkreuz des Eisernen Kreuzes,

die der Führer diesem bis zum Heldentode bewährten Offizier am 12.5.1944 noch nachträglich als dem 471. Soldaten der deutschen Wehrmacht verliehen hat.

Der Dank, den die Heimat ihren Helden zollt, wird niemals verlöschen!

Das I. Jagdkorps wird diesen Dank beweisen durch die Tat gleich ernster und opferbereiter Pflichterfüllung für Führer und Reich!

gez. S c h m i d

bombers shot down or forced out of formation. With one bomber shot down and one forced to leave formation, Lt. Zimmermann, the *Staffelführer* of 6/JG 3, was the most successful pilot (18-19). Lt. Leopold Münster also shot down one bomber and forced another out of formation (94-95), however he paid for this success with his life. Southeast of Hildesheim he collided with the B-24 he was attacking, whereupon the four-engined bomber exploded and went down. "Poldi" Münster's "Black 1" crashed near Wöllersheim, taking its pilot down with it.

Two other Messerschmitts were shot down in air combat, however neither pilot was injured. 4/JG 3 also recorded one casualty: while taking off on the return flight from Lemwerder to Sachau, Uffz. Rolf Klein collided with a building on the airfield and died in the ensuing fire, which consumed his Messerschmitt.

The Germans claimed 86 enemy aircraft shot down in the fighting of 8 May 1944, including 68 heavy bombers. Their own losses were 23 pilots killed or missing and 11 wounded. Fifty aircraft were written off, 47 of them as a result of enemy action[911]. On the other side of the Channel, the Americans admitted the loss of 44 four-engined bombers and 16 fighters while claiming 155 German aircraft shot down[912].

With the death of Leopold Münster, who was awarded the Knight's Cross with Oak Leaves posthumously[913], II/JG 3 had lost the last of its "*Experten*". His place as commander of 5 *Staffel* was taken by Hans Grünberg, who had been made an officer in recognition of his success. Grünberg also shared with Lt. Franz Ruhl the responsibility for leading the *Gruppe* formation in the air.

12 May 1944 marked the beginning of a new phase in the Allied bombing campaign against the German Reich. On this day the American 8th Air Force began a series of attacks against targets within the Reich associated with the fuel industry; the Americans had previously begun bombing the Romanian oil fields and refineries in the area around Ploesti on 5 April 1944[914]. Whereas the most recent attacks had been directed against the German aviation industry, the German fuel industry was now to become the number one target for the American bombers (in addition to preparatory attacks for the invasion of France). The rationale behind the attacks was sound: a decisive fuel shortage as a result of attacks on refineries and synthetic fuel plants must inevitably have a serious effect on the *Luftwaffe*'s operational readiness, while a continuation of such attacks might paralyze the entire *Wehrmacht*[915]. Of course the Allies were also aware that the Reich's fuel supplies were vulnerable[916], and so the hydrogenation plants in which synthetic fuel was produced[917], which were scattered all over the Reich, became targets of the first order for the American 8th and 15th Air Forces. In order to make the first strike against the German fuel industry as effective as possible, the series of raids was to begin with an attack by every available heavy bomber in the best possible weather, which would allow for visual bombing. The desired conditions existed on 12 May, for on this day an almost cloudless blue sky stretched over the majority of the Reich. The 8th Air Force command took advantage of this to dispatch 886 four-engined bombers to attack five of the most important hydrogenation plants in Central Germany (Leuna, Merseburg, Böhlen and Zeitz) and the "Protectorate" of Bohemia and Moravia (Brüx). The heavy bombers were accompanied by a total of 980 fighters[918], including 500 Mustangs[919]. The B-17s and B-24s of all three bombardment divisions flew in one long bomber stream from their assembly areas off the southeast coast of England southeast to abeam Cochem, where they turned east. The incursions met a determined German defense; sixteen day fighter and two destroyer *Gruppen*, a total of 470 machines[920], were mobilized by the *Luftwaffe*, and the result was one of the fiercest air battles of the war over Reich territory.

The approaching American bombers were detected in the morning, and the units of the three *Jagddivision* in the northwest and center of the Reich were brought to readiness and the assembly areas for the coming defensive mission were laid down. The *Jagdgruppen* in the area of 1 *Jagddivision* were to assemble into a battle unit over Eberswalde, then fly in the direction of Frankfurt and engage the incoming bombers there[921]. Under the command of Lt. Ruhl, II/JG 3 scrambled from Sachau at 11:20 AM. After joining the other units in the battle unit, which on this day was led by the *Kommodore* of JG 3 Maj. Heinz Bär, the *Geschwader* was vectored southwest toward the approaching heavy bombers. At about 12:15 PM contact was made in the Frankfurt-Giessen area with a group of B-17s flying in several waves, whereupon the battle unit moved to position itself for a frontal attack. The following account is from the combat report of Lt. Franz Ruhl, who was flying with II *Gruppe* somewhat above and to the left of the *Geschwaderstabsschwarm*:

> In the area of the Rhine, we were vectored on to a bomber unit from almost directly in front. Since I was flying above on the left, I was unable to get all the way down for the first attack, and I was unable to close with the second formation because it was flying somewhat further to the right and because the position of IV Gruppe's aircraft made it impossible for me to make a direct attack. During the second attack I saw six Boeings off to my left. My Staffel and I were the first to attack these and we had time for a proper approach. As a result, I was able to position my Staffel directly in front of this formation. I approached from slightly above and opened fire from a distance of approximately 800 meters. I was able to see strikes in the cockpit, in the right inner engine, in the dorsal turret and fuselage. When I had pulled up and looked around, I was able to see two of the Boeings we had attacked go down in flames and explode, including the trailing Boeing which I had fired on. The downing took place at 12:40 PM in Grid Square PI and was filmed.[922]

The *Gruppen* of JG 3 made several firing passes and in spite of the Mustangs accompanying the four-engined scored numerous successes. The battle unit subsequently claimed 22 B-17s shot down, 15 forced out of formation and one crippled finished off, plus two P-51s shot down[923]. II/JG 3 was particularly successful on this day, claiming no fewer than twelve enemy aircraft shot down and two forced out of formation. The majority of the victories were credited to young replacement pilots: Uffz. Burchardt and Uffz. Gehrke of 4/JG 3 and Fw. Busch of 5 *Staffel* each accounted for two enemy aircraft shot down or forced to leave formation[924]. The *Gruppe*'s losses were one pilot killed, one seriously wounded and five machines shot down. Gefr. Alfred Währisch of 4/JG 3 was shot down and killed in combat with the American fighter escort and came down near Rod on the Weil. More fortunate was Lt. Fridolin Reinartz, also of 4 *Staffel*: his Messerschmitt was hit by return fire from a B-17 and set ablaze, and he was forced to make a belly landing near Steindorf in the area of Wetzlar. Reinartz escaped injury, however his machine was completely destroyed. 6 *Staffel* also had two losses: Gefr. Heinz Elschner was shot down near Loleschied. Though seriously wounded, he was able to parachute to safety. Immediately after shooting down a B-17 for his first victory, Uffz. Heinz Geisthövel was hit by return fire from other bombers in the formation. He was forced to bail out near Rod on the Weil, however the experience left him none the worse for wear[925].

With their ammunition gone and fuel running low, the *Gruppen* of JG 3 were forced to break off the engagement, and the aircraft subsequently landed in twos, fours or singly at various airfields in the Frankfurt Basin. It appears that they were not sent up on the second mission against the withdrawing bombers, in which 51 machines took part. When the day's fighting was over, the German side claimed a total of 91 enemy aircraft shot down from the 8th Air Force's daylight incursions, 78 of them four-engined bombers[926]. Casualties among the day fighter units totaled 28 pilots killed and 24 wounded with 80 aircraft written off and 22 seriously damaged[927]. On the other side, on 12 May 1944 the 8th Air Force admitted the loss of 55 heavy bombers and ten escort fighters while its fighter groups claimed to have shot down 70 enemy aircraft[928]. For the German military command the effects of the bombing on the synthetic fuel plants were far more significant than the victory claims made by the two sides; for as a direct result of the bombing on this day the hydrogenation plants at Brüx and Tröglitz were knocked out 100%, Leuna 60% and Böhlen 50% and daily production sank from the previous 5,645 tons to just 4,821 tons, a drop of 14%. At the same time approximately 25,000 tons of fuel went up in flames[929]. While feverish efforts during the following two weeks largely repaired the damage, allowing production to return to the level of before 12 May 1944, there could be no denying that the bombing of the hydrogenation plants had forced the German command into a race against time. This was determined by the need to always stay one step ahead in the repairing of the hydrogenation plants, before

they again became the targets of devastating air attacks[930]. Even though the loss in production from the hydrogenation plants hit on this day and the fuel destroyed could at first be made good from existing reserves, this new Allied tactic undeniably posed another deadly threat to the German armaments industry and war effort—not least because of the American bombing campaign against the Romanian oil production and processing industry in the Ploesti area, which had begun on 5 April 1944[931].

8th Air Force plans called for further attacks on fuel industry targets on the following day, 13 May 1944. A force of 289 B-17s of the 1st Bombardment Division was dispatched to bomb oil targets in Western Poland, however the attack was frustrated by heavy cloud over the target area. The bombers instead attacked secondary targets along the Baltic coast, in particular port facilities at Stettin and Stralsund, on which 762 tons of bombs were dropped. At the same time 261 Liberators of the 2nd Bombardment Division were committed to attack the Focke Wulf factory complex at Tutow, while the 3rd Bombardment Division put another 199 Boeings into the air to bomb rail targets near Osnabrück. The escort for these formations consisted of 1,107 fighters. The *Luftwaffe*'s defensive effort against these incursions totaled seven day fighter *Geschwader* with a total of 17 *Gruppen* plus one destroyer *Gruppe*. These units put a total of 247 machines into the air for the first mission[932].

At 10:15 AM two groups of bombers were detected forming up in the Great Yarmouth area (Grid Square HC/GB), as were four others whose precise location could not be determined. Beginning at 10:30 AM, the units of the Defense of the Reich were brought to 15-minute readiness. The *Gruppen* of JG 3 were instructed to assemble over Müritz Lake, however almost three hours passed before the scramble order was issued. For II/JG 3 at Sachau, this set off a familiar train of events: the *Stabsschwarm* and the *Staffeln* took off straight across the airfield from their dispersals around the perimeter. Afterwards, the *Gruppe* formed up in a wide, sweeping turn and, climbing all the while, set course for the designated assembly area. Over Müritz Lake it rendezvoused with the rest of the *Geschwader*, which then set out to engage the heavy bombers. The battle unit was directed northwest in the direction of the Anklam—Demmin area, where at about 2:20 PM it sighted a large enemy formation, B-17s of the 1st BD and their escort of Mustangs. In the air battle which began over Demmin, the *Gruppen* of JG 3 shot down five B-17s and two P-51s and forced other two bombers to leave formation. II/JG 3's share was one B-17 and one P-51 shot down, by Lt. Zimmermann (20) and Lt. Schmidt (1). On the other side of the coin, this mission cost the *Gruppe* five Messerschmitts. Only two of these losses were the result of combat, while the other three were lost for reasons other than enemy action. Fw. Wolfgang Fleischer of 5 *Staffel* was seriously wounded in air combat near Demmin. Uffz. Gerhard Benne of 4/JG 3 ran out of fuel and crashed while attempting to land at Prenzlau; his aircraft overturned and he suffered serious injuries.

When the fighting was over, the German side claimed a total of 41 enemy aircraft shot down over the Reich and the occupied western territories. Its own losses amounted to 18 pilots killed and eight wounded plus 40 aircraft written off as total losses[933]. The 8th Air Force admitted the loss of just twelve four-engined bombers and ten escort fighters, while its units claimed to have shot down 75 German fighters[934].

Bad weather moved in over large areas of the Reich, preventing the 8th Air Force from mounting any significant daylight raids for the next five days. Not until 19 May 1944 did the weather permit a resumption of daylight attacks against targets in the interior of the Reich. The 8th Air Force command reacted immediately and dispatched 888 four-engined bombers to attack Berlin and Brunswick (referred to in American slang as the "Two Big B"s). The heavy bombers came in two separate formations and were escorted by 964 long-range fighters[935]. The *Luftwaffe*'s defensive effort included elements of eight day fighter *Geschwader* with a total of 18 *Gruppen* and 451 aircraft[936].

Once it was realized that the heavy bombers were coming in two separate groups, the command of I *Jagdkorps* decided to commit the bulk of its forces against the larger of the two formations, which was approaching over the Zuider Zee, and to deploy only the units of 1 *Jagddivision* against the formation coming in farther north, the B-17s of the 1st Bombardment Division[937]. Consequently the *Gruppen* of JG 3 again received orders to form up over Müritz Lake before being vectored toward the heavy bombers approaching from the northwest. II/JG 3, which on this day was again commanded by Lt. Ruhl, scrambled from Sachau at 12:24 PM, after which it formed up with the other *Gruppen* of JG 3 as per orders. On this day Lt. Zimmermann, the *Staffelführer* of 6/JG 3, assumed command of the *Geschwader* battle unit[938]. After the German command recognized that the northern incursion was aimed at Berlin, the battle unit received orders to proceed west and subsequently encountered enemy units in the Parchim area. The rest of the mission is described in the combat report of Lt. Franz Ruhl:

At about 1:30 PM we sighted enemy formations above us at an altitude of about 7 000 m. We climbed higher and, flying east to west, we passed beneath the formation, which was flying northwest to southeast, and overtook it on the right. I saw a very strong fighter escort, consisting mainly of Mustangs, at our altitude. While overtaking on the right we were continually attacked by Mustangs and I saw several Bf 109s go down. Our left-hand attack turn was rather too wide and I never got a chance to fire at the first formation. I therefore attacked the Boeing flying on the extreme right of the second formation as seen from my position; it was at the same altitude and flying somewhat off to the right.

Pressured by the P-51s of the fighter escort, the Messerschmitts of JG 3 made repeated attempts to close with the B-17s, resulting in fierce air battles extending over a wide area. The Mustangs clung to the Messerschmitts like leeches. In many cases, they pursued the German fighters, which flew away in ones and twos after completing their attacks on the "heavies", right to their home base. The German fighter pilots had great difficulty shaking them off prior to landing. When the fighting was over, JG 3 claimed to have shot down nine heavy bombers and seven escort fighters. One heavy bomber had been forced out of formation and one cripple finished off. II *Gruppe*'s share was three four-engined bombers and one P-51 shot down[939]. The clash with the Mustangs had been a costly one, for the *Gruppe* subsequently reported the loss of ten aircraft, almost half of those which had taken off. One pilot was listed missing, while three more, all of 4/JG 3, were wounded. Lt. Otto Siebenrok failed to return after combat with Mustangs and was reported missing, while Uffz. Heinrich Barisich, Uffz. Ekkehard Raschke and Uffz. Theo Burchardt were all seriously wounded in combat. These three came down by parachute near Kyritz, Wachau and Bohnitz, respectively. Lt. Oskar Zimmermann, who had led the Gefechtsverband on this day, also ended the mission in his parachute. After completing the first firing pass, Zimmermann had been rammed by his wingman while in the turn. His aircraft lost a wing and he bailed out at an altitude of 7 000 meters, after which he allowed himself to fall to about 3 000 meters in order to avoid the unwanted attentions of the P-51s. He landed unhurt and soon afterwards came upon his wingman, who had likewise survived the crash of his Messerschmitt unhurt.

When the fighting was over, the *Luftwaffe* claimed to have shot down 71 enemy aircraft on this day, the majority of them four-engined bombers[940]. Its own losses were 28 pilots killed or missing and 14 wounded along with 64 machines written off as total losses. The 8th Air Force admitted the loss of 30 heavy bombers and 21 fighters while claiming 74 German aircraft destroyed in the air and another 20 on the ground[941].

24 May 1944: While the B-24s of the 2nd Bombardment Division once again carpet-bombed airfields in France, 616 B-17s of the 1st and 3rd Bombardment Divisions carried out another major daylight raid on Berlin escorted by 953 fighters. At the same time, strong heavy bomber units of the 15th Air Force attacked several airfields and aircraft factories in Austria, tying down the *Jagdgruppen* based in the south of the Reich and preventing them from intercepting the incursions by the 8th Air Force. The *Luftwaffe* was able to mobilize fourteen day fighter *Gruppen* against the heavy bomber units attacking Berlin[942].

II/JG 3 scrambled from Sachau at 9:40 AM and, as usual, it subsequently formed up with the other *Gruppen* of the *Geschwader* over Müritz Lake. On this day the *Geschwader* battle unit was supposed to be joined by a number of heavy fighters[943]. II/JG 3 had just 20 serviceable aircraft[944]. The formation was vectored south toward a unit of B-17s with fighter escort and battle was joined north of Berlin. While closing with the combat boxes of heavy bombers, the *Gruppen* of JG 3 came under heavy fire from anti-aircraft guns. As far as may be determined, however, there were no losses as a result. Once again there was a fierce battle with the escort fighters, P-51s and a few P-38s, and the Messerschmitts had a difficult time closing with the bombers. While II *Gruppe* held its own against the American fighters and did not lose a single machine in combat, one pilot was lost in a midair collision. In the confusion of the dogfight, Uffz. Johann Fröhlich of 5/JG 3 collided with another German fighter. He and his aircraft "Black 5" fell near Neustrelitz. On the positive side, Lt. Ruhl knocked a B-17 out of formation (34) and Uffz. Glassauer of 6 *Staffel* shot down a P-38 (3).

On 24 May 1944 the German day fighter *Gruppen* claimed a total of 64 heavy bombers and 24 fighters shot down as well as 29 bombers forced to leave formation. Losses in defending against the Berlin raid were twelve pilots killed and five wounded plus 25 aircraft, of which five were lost for reasons other than enemy action. After the attack on Berlin, the 8th Air Force admitted the loss of 34 B-17s and 16 escort fighters while its units claimed to have shot down 40 enemy aircraft. Total losses for the 8th and 15th Air Forces on 24 May 1944 were 53 four-engined bombers and 25 escort fighters[945].

For the next three days there were no further incursions into 1 *Jagddivision*'s area of operations; after the difficult missions of the past few days, II/JG 3 was grateful for this brief respite.

28 May 1944, Pentecost Sunday:, the 8th Air Force launched its second strike against the fuel industry's factories inside the Reich. A total of 1,341 heavy bombers were dispatched to attack targets within Reich territory, although in the end only 864 actually dropped their bombs[946]. The main targets on this day were the hydrogenation plants at Ruhland-Schwarzheide, Böhlen, Magdeburg-Rothensee, Lützkendorf, Leuna and Tröglitz, as well as the oil storage facilities at Königsberg bei Magdeburg and various aircraft factories, including the Junkers Works at Dessau[947]. The heavy bombers, which came in several separate formations, were escorted by 1,224 fighters. The German side was able to muster a total of eighteen day fighter *Gruppen*, elements of one destroyer *Geschwader* and individual *Schwärme* from training and replacement training units. I *Jagdkorps* put a total of about 330 machines into the air, of which 266 made contact with the enemy[948].

Little is known about II/JG 3's activities on this day. The *Gruppe* was committed as part of the *Geschwader* battle unit as usual and took part in the defensive mission over the area northwest of Magdeburg, where it engaged a unit of B-17s with fighter escort. One B-17 and one P-51 were subsequently claimed shot down, plus three B-17s forced to leave formation. The *Gruppe*'s own losses were three Messerschmitts. One pilot, Uffz. Rudolf Schneider of 5/JG 3, was seriously injured when he was forced to abandon his aircraft near Halberstadt and struck the tailplane of his aircraft while bailing out. After the battle the *Luftwaffe* claimed a total of 75 enemy aircraft shot down, including 50 heavy bombers[949]. Its own losses totaled 19 pilots killed and 14 wounded plus 50 aircraft written off and 22 damaged. The balance for the 8th Air Force at the end of the day: 33 heavy bombers and 17 escort fighters lost, while its own units claimed a total of 124 enemy aircraft shot down[950]. Although only about 400 bombers actually dropped their loads on the hydrogenation plants on this day, the effect of the attacks was much greater than the first strike sixteen days earlier. Combined with the attacks on Ploesti the same day, the bombing of the hydrogenation plants inside the Reich on 28 May 1944 resulted in a fifty percent drop in fuel production[951].

The attacks by the American bomber fleets now came fast and furious. The bombardment divisions of the 8th Air Force launched another major daylight raid against targets within the Reich the very next day. A total of 993 heavy bombers escorted by 1,265 fighters were dispatched to attack aircraft factories in Leipzig, Sorau and Posen, Tutow airfield, and the Pölitz synthetic fuel plant[952]. At the same time, in the south the 15th Air Force launched attacks on the Messerschmitt Works in Wiener-Neustadt, its subcontractor in Atzgersdorf, and Wollersdorf airfield, all in Austria, and inflicted considerable devastation there[953]. The defenders mobilized twelve day fighter and two destroyer *Gruppen* to meet the incursions by the 8th Air Force as well as elements of training and replacement training units[954]. A total of 351 fighters and destroyers were committed under the command of I *Jagdkorps*, however only 208 made contact with the enemy.

In the early morning American heavy bombers were detected forming up off the south coast of Britain, and at about 8:15 AM the units of the Defense of the Reich were brought to fifteen-minute readiness. II/JG 3 was scrambled from Sachau shortly after 11 AM. The *Gruppe* subsequently rendezvoused with the *Stab* and I and IV *Gruppe* to form the *Geschwader* battle unit. On this day the JG 3 battle unit also included the remaining resources of ZG 26, whose three *Gruppen* put a total of about 30 Me 410s and Bf 110s into the air. Thus bolstered, the battle unit totaled upwards of 100 fighters and destroyers. After forming up over the Magdeburg area, the battle unit was guided northeast in the direction of the approaching heavy bombers. In the process, 5/JG 3 and most of the destroyers missed a turn by the battle unit and found themselves all alone in the open sky with no sign of the rest of the battle unit[955]. Lt. Grünberg subsequently assumed command of the group and, after learning via the Reich Fighter Frequency that Pölitz was being attacked, he set course for there. Contact was made with enemy aircraft over Wollin, where Grünberg's small force engaged a group of heavy bombers temporarily without fighter escort. A number of enemy bombers were shot down, especially by the heavily-armed destroyers[956]. The rest of the battle unit also became heavily engaged with heavy bombers and their escorts in the area north of Stettin. On this day II/JG 3 claimed a total of five enemy aircraft shot down and one forced to leave formation. Its own losses were one pilot killed and three Messerschmitts shot down in air combat. Uffz. Eberhard Reußner of 4 *Staffel* was initially reported missing; his body was found several days later, confirming his unfortunate fate[957].

At the end of the day the German side claimed a total of 94 enemy aircraft shot down while defending against the Allied incursions from England and Italy[958]. The *Luftwaffe*'s losses were 45 aircrew killed and 18 wounded; 22 were killed and 18 wounded in missions against the US 8th Air Force, while 39 aircraft were lost. The Americans admitted the loss of 76 aircraft on this day, 57 four-engined bombers and twelve fighters[959], while their units claimed 140 German aircraft destroyed[960].

On this day Maj. Hans-Ekkehard-Bob, who had been selected as the new *Gruppenkommandeur* of II/JG 3, arrived at Salzwedel to report to the *Stab* of the "UDET" *Geschwader*. While there he witnessed the fatal crash involving the *Kommodore*, Maj. Müller. Ekkehard-Bob was subsequently placed in temporary command of the *Geschwader*, making it impossible to take over command of II/JG 3 for the time being[961].

30 May 1944: The continued fine early spring weather enabled the units of the 8th Air Force to launch large-scale daylight attacks against targets inside the Reich for the third day in a row. Aircraft factories and airfields were once again on the heavy bombers' list of targets; factories in Dessau, Halberstadt and Oschersleben and the Oldenburg and Rotenburg/Wümme airfields experienced the horrors of carpet bombing. Further attacks were directed against railway installations in the northeast of France and Belgium. The 8th Air Force committed a total of 928 four-engined bombers, of which 919 dropped their bombs. The fighter escort consisted of 1,309 aircraft[962]. The German defensive effort against these incursions amounted to twelve day fighter *Gruppen* and one destroyer *Gruppe*[963].

Again relatively little is known about II/JG 3's defensive mission. The *Gruppe* was once again committed as part of *1 Jagddivision*'s battle unit and took part in the air fighting over the Dessau—Magdeburg—Brunswick area. It claimed to have shot down two B-17s, one B-24 and one P-51, while one of its Messerschmitts was damaged. On this day German fighters claimed to have shot down twelve heavy bombers and eleven P-51s and forced nine bombers to leave formation; losses totaled 18 pilots killed and eight wounded as well as 43 aircraft written off[964]. Eight German fighters were also destroyed on the ground. The 8th Air Force admitted the loss of 15 heavy bombers and 14 fighters, while its units claimed 66 enemy aircraft shot down[965], 55 by the escort fighters and just 13 by the bomber gunners. This ratio of claims was a clear indication of the effectiveness of the fighter escort on this day, when German fighters rarely got through to attack the bombers.

31 May 1944: On this day more than 1,000 four-engined bombers from all three bomb divisions were supposed to once again attack aircraft factories inside the Reich as well as railway installations in Western Germany, Belgium and the northeast of France. Their fighter escort consisted of 1,329 fighters. A significant worsening of the weather, which had been fine of late, prevented a considerable number of the planned attacks from being carried out, however, and in the end only sub-units of the 1st and 3rd Bombardment Divisions were able to reach their targets. Many groups dropped their bombs on targets of opportunity during the return flight[966]. The German defensive effort against these raids was very weak; only the units of the 3rd Bombardment Division, which in the early evening bombed marshalling yards in Schwerte, Hamm, Oesede and Osnabrück, were attacked at all. It is not known whether II/JG 3 took any part in the defensive action against these incursions; the *Gruppe* reported neither victories nor losses on this day. One machine was damaged due to mechanical failure.

Thus ended May 1944, the hardest and most costly month so far for the units of the German air defense. Under the nearly ceaseless onslaught of the numerically far superior American bomber streams and their escort, the German day fighter defense had been threatening to break down for weeks and at the end of May 1944 it was in fact on the verge of collapse[967,968]. In addition to the serious combat losses, the outlook for the future was bleak: while the bombing of the German fuel industry posed a deadly threat to the entire German war effort, but especially to the *Luftwaffe*, an Allied invasion of France had to be expected at any time and it was anticipated that this would force the *Luftwaffe* into its hardest battle ever against an unprecedented numerical superiority.

With nine pilots killed and four wounded (most of them seriously) and 42 Messerschmitts lost in action, May 1944 had been another costly month for II/JG 3. While the boosted output of fighters meant that aircraft losses could be easily replaced, the *Gruppe* receiving 46 Bf 109 G-6s during the course of the month, it proved impossible to keep pace with the continual drain on personnel. The air defense mission of 30 May 1944 was to be II/JG 3's last as part of the Defense of the Reich for some time. In the week that followed, there were no daylight incursions into German airspace by the US 8th Air Force in the north or the 15th Air Force in the south. While the German fighter units based in the Reich gratefully enjoyed this respite, the American bomber units were conducting the last preparatory raids against targets in northeastern France in preparation for the Allied invasion slated to begin on 6 June 1944[969]. II/JG 3 nevertheless suffered one casualty: on 3 June 1944, shortly after taking off on a transfer flight from Halle-Nietleben to Sachau, Gefr. Franz Nolden of 5/JG 3 stalled from out of a turn for reasons unknown and crashed. He was killed in the crash and ensuing fire.

For II/JG 3, its nine-month tour of duty in the Defense of the Reich had been an unprecedented ordeal which had resulted in extremely painful losses which were out of all proportion to the results achieved. In the period from 16 September 1943 to 31 May 1944 the *Gruppe* had claimed a total of 164 enemy aircraft shot down or forced to leave formation, while its own losses were 49 pilots killed and 31 wounded plus 141 Messerschmitts[970]. The considerable personnel losses had fundamentally changed the face of the *Gruppe*. Very few of the pilots with which the *Gruppe* began its tour of duty in the Defense of the Reich in September 1943 were left, and almost all of the *Experten* with the *Gruppe* at that time had since been killed, put out of action by wounds or transferred to other units. Experienced unit leaders such as Kurt Brändle, Wilhelm Lemke, Detlev Rohwer, Joachim Kirschner, Paul Stolte, Werner Lucas, Leopold Münster and Heinrich Sannemann and *Schwarm* leaders like Franz Cech, Walter Stienhans, Josef Schütte, Gerhard Thyben, Rudolf Traphan and Waldemar Eyrich were impossible to replace. The wearing down of the *Gruppe* was visible in another way: during its most successful periods in the east, the *Gruppe* had as many as five Knight's Cross wearers in its ranks at one time. At the end of May 1943, apart from *Kommandeur* Hptm. Frielinghaus, who was still unfit to fly, the only wearer of the Knight's Cross was Obfw. Rüffler, and he had earned the decoration while serving with I *Gruppe* in the east. The German Cross in Gold was also rare: only the *Staffelführer* of 4 and 5/JG 3, *Leutnante* Ruhl and Grünberg, two of the few remaining "old hands," wore this decoration. Most of the pilots who now filled the ranks of the *Staffeln* were very young replacement pilots fresh from the replacement training *Gruppe*, with no combat experience. Most were *Unteroffiziere*, although there were increasing numbers of *Gefreite* pilots as well as some officer cadets. The newcomers gathered round the few remaining "veterans," most of whom had less than a year's combat experience. The *Gruppe*'s personnel complement was thus a mere shadow of what it had been barely nine months earlier.

Notes:

[581] Since an in-depth examination of the development of the German air defense would unquestionably exceed the scope of this work, the reader is referred to the following basic sources on the subject: Groehler, *Bombenkrieg*; Schumann, *Deutschland im Zweiten Weltkrieg*; Freeman, *Mighty Eighth*. An account combining many of the published and unpublished sources on this theme may be found in Prien and Rodeike, *JG 1/11*.

[582] Compare in detail Prien and Rodeike, JG 1/11 Part 1, p. 219 and following pages.

[583] See Bekker, *Angriffshöhe*, p. 406 and following pages; Aders, *Nachtjagd*, p. 150 and following pages; Prien/Rodeike, *JG 1 / 11*, p. 375 and following pages; Groehler, *Luftkrieg*, p. 389 and following pages; Irving, *Milch*, p. 297 and following pages.

[584] JG 1 and JG 5 were the only new units created after 1940.

[585] The *Stab* along with I and III/JG 54 had been transferred from the east to the Reich or the west; the latter was exchanged for I/JG 26, which was transferred to the east. Elements of I/JG 27 also saw service in the west for a time.

[586] See detailed account in Prien/Rodeike, *JG 1 / 11*, p. 414 and following pages. Although criticism of the measures taken by the *Luftwaffe* command is fully justified, the fact cannot be overlooked that even if the *Luftwaffe* had made strenuous efforts to build up a powerful air defense and had concentrated all its forces for this purpose, defeat in the battle over the Reich could not have been averted. The reader is referred to the in-depth examination of this theme in Prien/Rodeike, *JG 1 / 11*, p. 418 and following pages.

[587] The latter unit was IV/JG 3, newly formed in June 1943; see Prien/Stemmer, IV/JG 3, p. 43 and following pages.

[588] These moves exhausted this reservoir of strength, however. Further reinforcements for the fighter defense could only come from new formations, however the necessary human and material resources were lacking. For the foreseeable future, therefore, the *Jagdwaffe* would have to carry on the battle against the growing superiority of the Allies with the forces available to it. A sober examination of the state of affairs should have revealed that the ultimate hopelessness of the efforts by the units in the Defense of the Reich was both predictable and unavoidable.

[589] ZG 26 was reformed from *Gruppen* withdrawn into the Reich (*Stab*/ZG 2, I and III/ZG 1 and III/ZG 26), while ZG 76 was created at the end of August 1943 from various reconnaissance, training and destroyer *Staffeln*. Dierich, p. 44, 88; Galland, *Geschichte der Zerstörerwaffe*, p. 7.

[590] Writings of Günther Lützow, entry made on 9/8/1943 on the occasion of an inspection of the *Gruppe* at Uetersen. Consideration had been given to moving II/JG 3 to Kassel, however this idea was not pursued.

[591] A total of 24 machines, while two Messerschmitts were left behind at Staaken on account of engine trouble.

[592] According to the writings of Günther Lützow a total of 135 men.

[593] As Helmut Hennig remembers it, the main column arrived at Uetersen on 23/8/1943 *"after numerous detours"*. Account dated 30/11/1985

[594] The Y-control method enabled German fighter controllers to locate and guide their units. This was done with the aid of the FuG 16ZY radio, which was usually installed in four to eight aircraft of a day fighter *Gruppe*. Each unit was assigned a frequency a few megahertz lower than its transmitter frequency and the FuG 16ZY transmitted this continuously, enabling ground stations to determine the position of the unit. Aircraft equipped with the FuG 16ZY were designated *"Pilots"* or *"Locomotives,"* the official radio code-name. In action only one FuG 16ZY equipped aircraft had its set switched on at any time; if the equipment or aircraft went unserviceable, one of the other Y-machines would its place. Since it was also possible for the other side to home in on the FuG 16 ZY, the role of *"Engineer"*—indeed the use of the Y-system in general—was very unpopular with the pilots.

[595] Sometimes also referred to as the *"Morane-Antenna"*—see Line Drawing 9.

[596] According to the strength report of 19/8/1943, on this day II/JG 3 had just four serviceable Bf 109 G-6s, while the number of pilots had already grown to 45. Writings of Günther Lützow.

[597] See the information contained in the inventory lists in the appendices.

[598] Plus thirteen who were not with the *Gruppe* on account of wounds or temporary assignment elsewhere. II/JG 3's total actual strength on 9/8/1943 was actually 38 pilots.

[599] Helmut Hennig recalls that this even included a Fw 58; account dated 30/11/1985.

[600] On 9/8/1943 Günther Lützow wrote of Hptm. Stolte as possible future *Gruppenkommandeur*, while the *Staffelkapitän* reserve included Oblt. Löhr, Lt. Bohatsch and Lt. Ruhl.

[601] Oblt. Werner Lucas was not with the *Gruppe* in mid-October, however; during this period his *Staffel* was led by Lt. Ruhl and then Lt. Münster, in both cases in an acting capacity.

[602] Fw. Helmut Rüffler was transferred to 4/JG 3 on 1 September 1943. He had most recently served as a fighter instructor with JGr. West, having previously flown with III/JG 3 from February 1941 to April 1942 and I/JG 3 from July to December 1942. Rüffler was awarded the Knight's Cross on 23 December 1942. See Obermaier, p. 190.

[603] Oblt. Löhr was later transferred to I/JG 3, to which FhjObfw. Schütte was attached at that time.

[604] For technical specifications see Line Drawing 9.

[605] It is noteworthy that II/JG 3 was not assigned to *Stab*/JG 3, which was based at Mönchengladbach and which had I/JG 3 under its command.

[606] At this time, however, the distribution of responsibilities between the light and the heavy *Gruppen* was largely theoretical in nature, for the defensive units were not yet being formed into battle units, instead the *Gruppen* were usually committed individually. As a result, II/JG 3—like the other units of the Defense of the Reich designated as light *Gruppen*—was regularly called upon to engage the heavy bombers, even though its aircraft were too lightly armed (one 20-mm cannon and two 13-mm machine-guns) for this purpose. The only actual difference between the light and heavy *Gruppen* may have been that the former were not bound by the standing order to engage bombers only and avoid combat with the escort fighters. Instead, when enemy fighters did appear, it was the principal task of the light *Gruppen* to engage them. One other difference was that the light *Gruppen* always flew without drop tanks.

[607] See Prien/Rodeike, *JG 1 / 11*, p. 432 and following pages; Prien/Stemmer *III/JG 3*, p. 268 and following pages.

[608] See Freeman, *Mighty Eighth*, p. 69.

[609] Takeoff time 6:45 PM, mission: escort for five M-boats of the 21st Minesweeper Flotilla. Contact with the enemy at 6:59. While 4/JG 3 claimed two victories, the 21st Minesweeper Flotilla claimed to have shot down four enemy aircraft while crediting one to the fighters. The British force was estimated to number twenty aircraft. See Naval Command War Diary Vol. 49, p. 331; War Diary I Jagdkorps, 16/9/1943; combat report by Lt. Ruhl and witness report by Uffz. Bartsch.

[610] Mission times from the logbook of Rudolf Scheibe 7:00 - 7:30 PM; the enemy aircraft were identified as two P-51s.

[611] A total of 19 incursions was reported between 7:41 AM and 7:30 PM; 65 aircraft and "*ten formations*" (?) were recorded. War Diary *I Jagdkorps*.

[612] Takeoff time 6:10 PM, 23 Bf 109s committed. War Diary *I Jagdkorps*.

[613] War Diary *I Jagdkorps*, 24/9/1943. I/JG 1 and two Messerschmitts of the high-altitude *Staffel* also saw action, however these did not contact the enemy.

[614] Freeman, *Mighty Eighth*, p. 116; the purpose of the mission was to practice the use of H2S target-finding radar.

[615] Grid Square 05 East S /FF-4; combat report by Lt. Ruhl, witness report by Hptm. Kirschner.

[616] On 26/9/1943, takeoff time 6:23 PM, 24 Bf 109s committed; War Diary *I Jagdkorps*.

[617] This was made possible by the first use by Thunderbolts of 108-gallon drop tanks. 187 such machines were committed, bolstered by 47 Spitfires which picked up the returning formations. Freeman, *Mighty Eighth*, p. 118-119.

[618] In addition to II/JG 3, JG 1 and JG 11, each with three *Gruppen*; see Prien/Rodeike, *JG 1 / 11*, p. 461.

[619] The high closing speeds involved in frontal attacks allowed for very short bursts only, otherwise Ruhl would surely not have had enough ammunition. The Bf 109 G-5 and G-6 carried 200 rounds for the engine-mounted MG 151/20 cannon and 300 rounds per gun for the two MG 131s installed above the engine (see the handbook Bf 109 G-5 Part 8A, Fixed Weapons Installation). Theoretically this was sufficient for a duration of fire of 20 seconds for the MG 131s at a rate of fire of 900 rounds per minute and 17 seconds for the engine-mounted cannon at a rate of fire of 720 rounds per minute.

[620] "*Minenmunition*" was the designation for thin-cased ammunition which delivered the maximum possible explosive charge to the target at the cost of fragmentation effect.

[621] In order to claim an *Herausschuss* a four-engined bomber had to be damaged to the extent that it was forced to leave its formation. An *Herausschuss* counted the same as a victory and after the point system for rating victories came into general use in the second half of 1943 counted for two points. For a detailed discussion of the German victory confirmation and ratings system see Prien and Rodeike, *JG 1/11* Part 1, p. 621 and following pages.

[622] From a total of 15 enemy aircraft claimed shot down by the German side. OKW report dated 28/9/1943. According to the Naval Command War Diary Vol. 49, p. 541, 13 victories were claimed while 388 (?) German machines were committed.

[623] As far as can be determined, all of II/JG 3's losses occurred in combat with the heavy bombers, while engagements with the fighter escort produced no result. II/JG 3's action thus differed quite significantly from that of JG 1 and 11, for II/JG 11 suffered badly, losing nine pilots killed or missing, two wounded and ten aircraft; see Prien/Rodeike, *JG 1/11*, p. 464 and following pages. II/JG 3's relatively favorable performance earned it special mention in Corps Order of the Day No. 135 dated 14/10/1943—more on account of its low rate of loss than the noteworthy number of enemy aircraft shot down: "*I wish to express my appreciation to the Kommandeur of II/Jagdgeschwader 3 for the circumspection and skill with which he led his Gruppe in battle against the enemy, who on 27/9/1943 appeared over the German Bight with a strong fighter escort for the first time, and to all the pilots of the Gruppe.*"

As a direct result of the grievous losses suffered in the clash with the American fighter escort, it was decided at a I Jagdkorps staff conference on 29/9/1943 that three *Gruppen* were to be "disarmed". Furthermore, the minutes of the conference stated, "*...and these Gruppen are to be assigned the task of engaging enemy fighters to the extent possible.*" Not long afterwards, on 8 October at another conference at the headquarters of the *General der Jagdflieger*, this measure was extended further, so that there were five light *Gruppen* in the area of *2* and *3 Jagddivision* compared to just three heavy *Gruppen*.

[624] War Diary of *I Jagdkorps*, 29/9/1943. Takeoff time 6:55 PM, enemy formation consisted of seven machines, detected between 6:44 and 7:04 PM.

[625] See Naval Command War Diary Vol. 50, p. 29-30, which contains detailed damage information; for further details of the attack see Freeman, *Mighty Eighth War Diary*, p. 120 and Prien/Rodeike, *JG 1 / 11*, p. 473 and following pages.

[626] War Diary of *I Jagdkorps*, 2/10/1943.

[627] The German victory claims on this day were very contradictory; see Prien and Rodeike, *JG 1 / 11* Part 1, p. 479, FN 1. The individual victory claims of the units engaged reveal eight B-17s and one P-47. On the other hand the Americans admitted the loss of just two B-17s; see Freeman, *Mighty Eighth War Diary*, p. 121.

[628] Freeman, *Mighty Eighth War Diary*, p. 121.

[629] Takeoff time for the first mission 4:12 PM, reported incursion by 15 to 20 Typhoons into the Woensdrecht area; second mission began at 5:15 PM, reported

incursion by a large number of aircraft into the Dunkirk—Brussels—Ghent area; War Diary of *I Jagdkorps*, 3/10/1943.

[630] Freeman, *Mighty Eighth War Diary*, p. 121.

[631] Altogether the German side committed 226 fighters, 89 destroyers and five night fighters, including, in addition to II/JG 3, JG 1 and 11 and II/JG 27; see Prien/Rodeike, *JG 1 / 11*, p. 479 and following pages.

[632] This failure, which was further exacerbated by the damage inflicted on Frankfurt by an RAF night raid on 5 October, resulted in another serious crisis in the command of the Defense of the Reich; see Prien and Rodeike, *JG 1 / 11* Part 1, p. 488 and following pages. Of special significance to II/JG 3 were the staff conferences held on 7 and 8 October, where *Oberst* Lützow obviously attempted to have the *Gruppe* withdrawn from its exposed position in the approach lanes used by the four-engined bombers and transferred further inland. This is revealed by the brief comments made in his notes, such as: "*Schiphol to the rear! Get out!*" or "*Have an order issued to the effect that __forward__ defense is no longer required.*" The latter was undoubtedly a reference to the controversy raging in the *Luftwaffe* command between proponents of a peripheral air defense and those who favored a centralized system.

[633] From the attack on Frankfurt; another three B-17s were shot down from the force which raided the Saarland, while JG 11 claimed eleven heavy bombers shot down while intercepting a diversionary attack in the north.

[634] Alfred Kalitta flew a Bf 109 G-5 on this mission; the following entry in the writings of Günther Lützow dated 7/10/1943 is significant: "*109 G-5 is rejected. Cockpit ices up and is difficult to jettison.*"

[635] War Diary of *I Jagdkorps*; nothing more is known about the course and results of the inspection.

[636] See Freeman, *Mighty Eighth War Diary*, p. 123; Naval Command War Diary Vol. 50, p. 168; War Diary of *I Jagdkorps*, 8/10/1943; Prien/Rodeike, *JG 1 / 11*, p. 492 and following pages.

[637] War Diary of *I Jagdkorps*.

[638] Combat report by Lt. Franz Ruhl.

[639] At the end of the day the German side initially claimed 56 enemy aircraft shot down, however this was later reduced to 48; the Americans admitted the loss of 32 heavy bombers and three P-47s. On the other hand German losses totaled 21 pilots killed and 12 wounded as well as 24 aircraft lost in action. The Americans claimed 189 "certain" victories, the lion's share (167) by the bomber gunners as usual. See Prien and Rodeike, *JG 1/11* Part 1, p. 501.

[640] See in detail War Diary of *I Jagdkorps*, 9/10/1943; Naval Command War Diary Vol. 50, p. 194; Prien/Rodeike, *JG 1 / 11*, p. 501 and following pages; Freeman, *Mighty Eighth War Diary*, p. 124.

[641] See in detail Hawkins; War Diary of *I Jagdkorps*, 10/10/1943; Prien/Rodeike, *JG 1 / 11*, p. 505 and following pages; Freeman, *Mighty Eighth War Diary*, p. 124.

[642] The German side claimed a total of 50 enemy aircraft shot down on this day against the loss of 20 pilots killed, 12 wounded and 29 aircraft written off in action; the corresponding figures from the American side are 34 B-17s and 1 P-47 lost against claims of 183 German aircraft shot down by the bomber gunners and 19 by the escort fighters.

[643] See Prien and Rodeike, *JG 1/11* Part 1, p. 511 and following pages; *Mighty Eighth War Diary*, p. 126; *I Jagdkorps* War Diary, 14/10/1943. The following German units saw action: JG 1, JG 2, JG 3, JG 11, JGr. 25, JG 26, I and II/JG 27, JGr. 50, II/JG 51, III/JG 54, elements of ZG 26, ZG 76 and ZG 101, 14/KG 2, elements of NJG 1, NJG 2, NJG 3, NJG 4, NJG 6, NJG 101 and JG 104 and JG 106.

[644] Another aircraft is named in the Quartermaster-General's reports. It was allegedly lost as a result of a collision with an enemy aircraft near Hammelburg, however it appears that it is the result of a copying error, especially since the *Werknummer* of the machine in question does not "fit" the complement of II/JG 3.

[645] OKW communiqué of 15/10/1943, and OKW War Diary 1943 Part II, p. 1201. Also see the list in Prien and Rodeike, *JG 1/11* Part 1, p. 515, of all 148 victory claims made by the participating units (not all of which survived the subsequent confirmation process). The units of *I Jagdkorps* claimed 74 B-17s and five P-47s.

[646] Also see in detail Speer, p. 298 and following pages; Groehler, *Bombenkrieg*, p. 137 and following pages.

[647] See *Mighty Eighth War Diary*, p. 126; elsewhere the same source mentions a total of 79 heavy bomber losses—62 which crashed in German-occupied territory, 7 which crashed in England as a result of battle damage and another 12 which were wrecked on landing and subsequently treated as total losses ("Cat. E"). [648] War Diary of *I Jagdkorps*, 15/10/1943; elements of JG 1, 3, 11, 26 and 54 plus ZG 26 participated.

[649] See, for example, the logbook of Heinrich Sannemann under 17 October.

[650] Compare in detail Prien/Rodeike/Stemmer, *III & IV JG 27*, p. 370 and following pages.

[651] Bad weather later forced the bombers to abort the mission and return to base.

[652] Freeman, *Mighty Eighth War Diary*, p. 130.

[653] Mission times from the logbook of Heinrich Sannemann.

[654] War Diary of *I Jagdkorps*, 18/10/1943; the interception was supposed to take place in Grid Square 05 East N / UK-1 northwest of Terschelling; WASt. casualty report for Hptm. Stolte.

655 Given the recently reported operational strength of II *Gruppe*, this may have been all of the aircraft committed.

656 A total of 29 Messerschmitts was assigned to II/JG 3 in October, 16 Bf 109 G-5s and 13 Bf 109 G-6s—see aircraft complement list in the appendices.

657 See in detail Freeman, *Mighty Eighth War Diary*, p. 131; Prien/Rodeike, *JG 1 / 11*, p. 520 and following pages; War Diary of *I Jagdkorps*, 20/10/1943.

658 Logbooks of Heinrich Sannemann and Rudolf Scheibe.

659 Crash times 2:24 and 2:43 PM respectively—war diary Luftgau Holland, 20/10/1943.

660 Entry in War Diary of *I Jagdkorps*: *"Nothing out of the ordinary."* Entry in the logbook of Hptm. Sannemann: *"Convoy escort flight, no enemy contact."*

661 Mission time from the logbook of Heinrich Sannemann 3:50 – 4:40 PM, no enemy contact; War Diary of *I Jagdkorps*, 22/10/1943.

662 Including the awarding of the German Cross to Fw. Thyben—see Corps Order of the Day No. 3 of 4/11/1943 (award date 23/10/1943).

663 Part of Göring's speech has survived (see Irving, p. 332 Fn. 31) in the form of Erhard Milch's shorthand notes; in his speech Göring reminds the assembled pilots of an assurance supposedly given when the units were withdrawn from the east and the south into the Reich: *"We were supposed to let the four-engined crates come, then have a fine party shooting them down! Well, they have come, but there has been no party. Now, you must bear one thing in mind: the German people have suffered unspeakably under the terror of the enemy bombers, by day and night. At night the German people still have a measure of understanding, because they tell themselves that finding the bombers at night is difficult. What they cannot understand, however, is failing to find them by day, especially in clear weather. The people have written me countless letters telling me that they have seen how you people fight and that they are convinced that I must have brought sick people back to the Reich to serve in the air defense. I have no intention of singling out a single Gruppe or Staffel and depicting it as especially bad. But I can assure you of one thing: I will not have cowards in my arm […] I will root them out."* For a more detailed account of this address see Prien/Rodeike, *JG 1 / 11*, p. 522 and following pages. 664 In the first half of October the *Luftwaffe* held a series of command-level conferences which dealt with the problems of the Defense of the Reich and where Göring's accusations of lack of fighting spirit on the part of the fighter crews were discussed. The following is an extract from Günther Lützow's personal papers concerning a conference held on 8 October 1943. *"16.) Question: Are the fighters getting in close or not? It is obvious that some are attacking bravely but using incorrect tactics, attacking singly or in pairs, and as a result are shot down. From this it is concluded that attacks must not be rushed, formations must be assembled, reasonable tactical position achieved, targets assigned and post-attack procedures laid down. Call for installation of simple automatic and cine cameras to assess firing passes. After missions, Gruppenkommandeure are to report to the fighter commander on the performance of their pilots. To date this point has been badly neglected. For checking of combat heights, barographs are to be installed and diagrams evaluated. […] 17.) Basic training of fighter pilots: selection must be made according to the stricter guidelines demanded by the Reichsmarschall. The material currently available is not up to requirements."* The use of the cynical term *"material"* is indicative of the spirit of the times. Another demand on the part of Galland which appears in Paragraph 3 concerns the employment of so-called *"Commissars."* These were *"reliable"* officers who were to monitor defensive missions by German units from a safe distance, so as to be able to report afterwards on those *Gruppen* which, in their opinion, had not attacked with sufficient "zeal." It cannot be overlooked that that the fighter command adopted at least part of Göring's accusations as their own and did not shy away from resorting to extremely questionable measures aimed at forcing the pilots to give the often cited "all-out effort." Also see Prien/Rodeike, *JG 1 / 11*, p. 488 and following pages.

665 Unfortunately, II/JG 3's reaction to these statements by Göring was not recorded; it is known, however, that the reaction of the pilots of JG 1 ranged from a certain degree of understanding to outright rejection.

666 Mission times from the logbooks of Heinrich Sannemann and Rudolf Scheibe 4:30 – 5:05 PM.

667 See the corresponding entries in the War Diary of *I Jagdkorps* for the period from 25/10 to 2/11/1943.

668 See the logbook of Heinrich Sannemann, two such missions on 2/11, both uneventful.

669 As well as fog which covered the north of Holland and spread east of the Ems.

670 In addition to II/JG 3, the three *Gruppen* of JG 1 saw action as did II/NJG 1. See Prien/Rodeike, *JG 1 / 11*, p. 525 and following pages; Freeman, *Mighty Eighth War Diary*, p. 133; Rohwer/Hümmelchen, p. 400; War Diary of *I Jagdkorps*, 3/11/1943.

671 Mission times from the logbooks of Heinrich Sannemann, Rudolf Scheibe and Gerd Schaedle 12:05 – 1:10 PM.

672 For information on the defensive mission by the *Gruppen* of JG 1, which contacted the enemy some time after II/JG 3, see Prien/Rodeike, *JG 1 / 11*, p. 527 and following pages.

673 To present-day observers—especially those who are not members of the wartime generation—the way in which successes, but often enough simply the fact that one had survived, were celebrated or toasted with appropriate quantities of alcohol, may seem strange or even repugnant. However, a reasonable observer will realize that a multitude of emotions were released at these moments, that tension and fear were washed away, and that the feeling of luck at having one's life spared again caused much to be forgotten or pushed aside. It was not the fault of those young men that they were placed in such a situation, and one should take care not to make sweeping condemnations, especially when they assume a degree of maturity and insight which many of these young men simply did not possess.

674 War Diary of *I Jagdkorps*.

675 Mission times from the logbooks of Heinrich Sannemann and Rudolf Scheibe 3:40 – 4:45 PM.

676 See the article in *Jägerblatt* 4/XI, April 1962, p. 16-17, where Brändle's last mission is described based on information provided by Gerhard Thyben and Karl-Heinz Steinicke.

677 Uffz. Kirschner was a member of III/JG 26 and was only attached to II/JG 3 at this time.

678 Account by Helmut Hennig, 30/11/1985.

679 Based on his logbook, Wilhelm Lemke made his last combat mission as *Staffelkapitän* of 9/JG 3 on 2 November and his first as *Kommandeur* of II/JG 3 on 13 November. For information on Lemke's career with III *Gruppe* see Prien/Stemmer, *III/JG 3*.

680 See Freeman, *Mighty Eighth War Diary*, p. 134; War Diary of *I Jagdkorps*, 5/11/1943; Prien/Rodeike, *JG 1 / 11*, p. 528 and following pages.

681 Mission times from the logbook of Heinrich Sannemann 12:20 – 1:40 PM, landing at Deelen. Return from there to Schiphol 2:10 – 2:20 PM. Uffz. Scheibe had a similar experience, landing at Rotenburg and returning to Schiphol from there.

682 See conference minutes, which are repeated in the War Diary of *I Jagdkorps*.

683 And at no time did the German fighter defense ever come close to achieving the four to one numerical superiority advocated by *Generalfeldmarschall* Milch in his memo of 29/6/1943.

684 War Diary of *I Jagdkorps*, conference transcript of 8/11/1943, De Breul command post.

685 The German fighter command faced another problem, in that II/JG 3's endurance was limited to an hour at best because its machines had to operate without external tanks. The available flying time was further reduced by the need to climb to altitude as quickly as possible, which further increased fuel consumption. Consequently, the order to scramble had to be delayed as long as possible so as to avoid the *Gruppe* having to return to base for lack of fuel before making contact with the enemy.

686 See *Mighty Eighth War Diary*, p. 137; *I Jagdkorps* War Diary, 11/11/1943; Prien and Rodeike, *JG 1/11* Part 1, p. 534.

687 The total effort in *I Jagdkorps*'s area amounted to 190 aircraft. The ratio of opposing forces clearly illustrates the decisive numerical inferiority of the defending fighters that already existed, for the 190 German fighters encountered 347 four-engined bombers and 401 fighters. In other words: the four to one ratio demanded by *Generalfeldmarschall* Milch existed in reverse, with the Allied fighter escort twice as strong numerically as the entire German fighter defense.

688 Mission times from the logbook of Heinrich Sannemann 1:15 – 2:25 PM, uneventful.

689 See *Mighty Eighth War Diary*, p. 138; *I Jagdkorps* War Diary, 13/11/1943; Prien and Rodeike, *JG 1 / 11* Part 1, p. 537 and following pages.

690 *I Jagdkorps* War Diary, 13/11/1943. The following units took part in the defensive mission in addition to the named fighter and destroyer *Gruppen*: elements of Ekdo. 25, of NJG 3 and the Focke Wulf factory's Industry Defense *Schwarm*.

691 Mission times from the logbook of Heinrich Sannemann 11:15 AM – 12:30 PM.

692 Logbook of Wilhelm Lemke.

693 III/JG 1 scrambled from Volkel seven minutes before II/JG 3. Obviously the two *Gruppen* failed to rendezvous, for III/JG 1 engaged the heavy bombers' fighter escort during the course of its defensive mission—see Prien/Rodeike, *JG 1 / 11*, p. 549.

694 On 19 November bad weather prevented a raid by units of the US 8th Air Force from being intercepted.

695 See logbooks of Heinrich Sannemann and Wilhelm Lemke.

696 Combat report by Lt. Franz Ruhl, takeoff from Schiphol at 2:41 PM; War Diary of *I Jagdkorps*, 23/11/1943; witness report by Oblt.z.S. Bormann, Vp 812—according to whom the enemy formation consisted of 26 Beaufighters.

697 See in detail Freeman, *Mighty Eighth War Diary*, p. 142; OKW War Diary 1943, Part II, p. 1313; War Diary of *I Jagdkorps*, 26/11/1943; Prien/Rodeike, *JG 1 / 11*, p. 543 and following pages.

698 War Diary of *I Jagdkorps*, 26/11/1943.

699 Logbooks of Heinrich Sannemann and Wilhelm Lemke; obviously this mission, like the others from Volkel, was flown together with III/JG 1.

[700] On 26 November 1943 the *Luftwaffe* claimed 41 enemy aircraft shot down over the Reich and another 13 over the occupied western territories while admitting the loss of 23 machines in action. On the other hand, the US 8th Air Force admitted the loss of 32 four-engined bombers and 7 escort fighters while claiming 58 German fighters, 36 of them by the escort fighters.

[701] Apart from the awarding of the Oak Leaves to Hptm. Lemke, who had to report to GenMaj. Schmid in the headquarters of *I Jagdkorps* to receive the decoration on the evening of 27 November. The official award date was 25 November 1943.

[702] Also see in detail Freeman, *Mighty Eighth War Diary*, p. 143; OKW War Diary 1943, Part II, p. 1322; Prien/Rodeike, *JG 1 / 11*, p. 547; War Diary of *I Jagdkorps*, 29/11/1943. The latter contains no reference to the number of aircraft committed, however.

[703] Logbook of Heinrich Sannemann.

[704] War Diary of *I Jagdkorps*, 29/11/1943; mission times from the logbook of Heinrich Sannemann 1:30 – 3:00 PM.

[705] Seen from the German viewpoint, the balance of the end of the day was 33 enemy aircraft shot down for the loss of 25 pilots killed and 18 wounded plus 39 machines lost in action; the Americans, on the other hand, put their losses at 16 four-engined bombers and 17 escort fighters while claiming 45 German fighters shot down by fighters and bomber gunners—see in detail Prien/Rodeike, *JG 1 / 11*, p. 550.

[706] See in detail Freeman, *Mighty Eighth War Diary*, p. 145; War Diary of *I Jagdkorps*, 30/11/1943; Prien/Rodeike, *JG 1 / 11*, p. 550 and following pages.

[707] On 30 November II/JG 3 reported its strength as 26 Bf 109s, 10 G-5s and 16 G-6s.

[708] Logbooks of Wilhelm Lemke, Heinrich Sannemann; combat report by Hans Grünberg.

[709] On this day the Germans claimed 8 enemy aircraft shot down of forced to leave formation; in addition to the victories registered by II/JG 3, III/JG 26 claimed two fighters and II/JG 27 one heavy bomber; the US 8th Air Force admitted the loss of 6 heavy bombers (three of which were Cat. E) and 6 fighters—Freeman, *Mighty Eighth War Diary*, p. 145.

[710] See *Mighty Eighth War Diary*, p. 145-146; *I Jagdkorps* War Diary, 1/12/1943; Prien and Rodeike, JG 1/11 Part 1, p. 553. A further 67 machines from units in the area of *Luftflotte 3* were also committed; see Naval Command War Diary Vol. 52, p. 13.

[711] Logbooks of Wilhelm Lemke and Heinrich Sannemann, ferry flight 9:00 – 9:20 PM.

[712] Logbook of Heinrich Sannemann; combat report by Franz Ruhl.

[713] Combat report by Franz Ruhl.

[714] The participating *Luftwaffe* units claimed a total of 42 victories on this day against losses of 13 pilots killed, 14 wounded and 23 aircraft lost in action; on the other hand the American 8th Air Force admitted the loss of 24 heavy bombers and seven escort fighters while its units claimed 33 German fighters shot down. See Prien and Rodeike, *JG 1 / 11* Part 1, p. 556.

[715] See Balke, KG 2 Part II, p. 280; War Diary of *I Jagdkorps*, 4/12/1943; Naval Command War Diary Vol. 52, p. 62; Freeman, *Mighty Eighth War Diary*, p. 146.

[716] Logbooks of Heinrich Sannemann and Wilhelm Lemke.

[717] In recognition of his success to date, on 25 November 1943 FhjObfw. Schütte was awarded the German Cross in Gold—Corps Order of the Day No. 11 of 28 January 1944; in the meantime, he had seen action with 3/JG 3, shooting down a B-17 on 12 August 1943.

[718] The German side claimed no victories on this date, while the three Messerschmitts lost by II/JG 3 tally exactly with the claims made by the participating American fighter groups.

[719] See in detail Freeman, *Mighty Eighth War Diary*, p. 149; War Diary of *I Jagdkorps*, 11/12/1943; Naval Command War Diary Vol. 52, p. 188; Prien/Rodeike, *JG 1 / 11*, p. 557.

[720] Franz Ruhl wrote of this mission in his combat report: *"At 12:00 PM on 11/12/1943 I led a Rotte from Volkel airfield to intercept reported enemy aircraft. Guided by Y-control, I sighted the enemy at 12:35 PM. Large formations of Boeing Fortress IIs were flying away to the west. Above them a fighter escort of Thunderbolts up to 12 000 meters. I climbed to the same altitude and attacked a group of Thunderbolts flying below me in line astern. I approached a Thunderbolt from the five o'clock high position and saw several strikes in the cockpit and fuselage. It rolled over to the right, went straight down, and made no attempt to recover. Time 12:50 PM, altitude 11 500 m. I last saw the Thunderbolt about 2 000 meters below me in the dive, however I then had to turn my attention to the rest of the Thunderbolts, which now attacked me. My wingman had turned back at 11 500 meters prior to engaging the enemy on account of engine trouble."* Because he had no witness, Ruhl's victory was not submitted for confirmation.

[721] WASt. casualty report.

[722] The *Luftwaffe* subsequently reported 24 enemy aircraft shot down against 18 of its aircraft lost in action; the US 8th Air Force admitted the loss of 19 heavy bombers and 6 escort fighters. Given the weak German response, its claim to have shot down 129 German fighters was quite extraordinary.

[723] See in detail Prien/Rodeike, *JG 1 / 11*, p. 560; all of 47 machines saw action in *I Jagdkorps*'s area of operations.

[724] According to the logbook of Heinrich Sannemann, takeoff was at 2:25 PM, immediately before the start of the bombing raid.

[725] See in detail Rust, 9th Air Force, p. 51; Naval Command War Diary Vol. 52, p. 222; War Diary of *I Jagdkorps*, 13/12/1943.

[726] II/JG 3 arrived at Volkel with 15 Bf 109 Gs, 1 Fi 156 and 1 Go 145 plus 4 officers, 14 non-commissioned officers and one enlisted man—see War Diary of Luftgau Holland, 14/12/1943.

[727] See in detail Freeman, *Mighty Eighth War Diary*, p. 152; War Diary of *I Jagdkorps*, 16/12/1943; Naval Command War Diary Vol. 52, p. 270; Prien/Rodeike, *JG 1 / 11*, p. 561 and following pages.

[728] Mission times from the logbook of Heinrich Sannemann 1:40 – 2:45 PM.

[729] Attack on Bremen by 546 four-engined and 491 escort fighters; German claims totaled 45 enemy aircraft shot down compared to admitted American losses of 27 heavy bombers and 6 fighters—see in detail Prien/Rodeike, *JG 1 / 11*, p. 565 and following pages.

[730] 5/JG 3 did report a Spitfire shot down by Obfw. Grünberg (63) on this day, however no further details are known.

[731] See in detail Freeman, *Mighty Eighth War Diary*, p. 155-156; War Diary of *I Jagdkorps*, 22/12/1943; Naval Command War Diary Vol. 52, p. 365; Prien/Rodeike, *JG 1 / 11*, p. 567 and following pages.

[732] Combat report by Franz Ruhl dated 22/12/1943.

[733] In the end the *Luftwaffe* claimed 28 enemy aircraft shot down, 21 of them heavy bombers, compared to admitted American losses of 22 bombers and 4 fighters.

[734] See Ries/Dierich, p. 55 and 260.

[735] War Diary of Luftgau Holland; logbook of Heinrich Sannemann, 1:35 – 2:35 PM; the War Diary of *I Jagdkorps* contains a note to the effect that the transfer took place on 26/12/1943.

[736] War Diary of *I Jagdkorps*, 29/12/1943; see in detail Prien, *IV/JG 3*, p. 49 and following pages.

[737] As well, other experienced pilots were transferred out of the *Gruppe* to other units: in autumn 1943 Oblt. Löhr went to I/JG 3, Oblt. Schaedle to II/JG 2 and Fw. Bringmann to IV/JG 3.

[738] II/JG 3's exposed position meant that it made contact with the enemy much more frequently than units stationed further inland; not only did it have to deal with the American heavy bombers and their escorts, but the bombers, fighters and fighter-bombers of the 9th Air Force and the RAF as well.

[739] See the victory list in the appendices.

[740] One of the most serious weaknesses of the *Luftwaffe* was its totally inadequate training organization, which proved incapable of meeting the demands of the multi-front war in which Germany found herself after 1941. In particular, the training organization proved incapable of supplying the day fighter arm with sufficient numbers of solidly-trained replacement pilots. The *General der Jagdflieger*, whose responsibilities included the fighter training organization, placed the blame elsewhere. The following is from the minutes of a conference of division commanders held by I *Jagdkorps* on 28 December 1943: *"General Galland: shortage of aircrews due to weather situation to date—supply of aircraft very unfavorable."* The *General*, too, used the weather as a scapegoat, when in fact fundamental omissions on the part of the *Luftwaffe* command were responsible for the existing crisis situation.

[741] See the detailed account in Prien/Rodeike, *JG 1 / 11*, p. 574 and following pages.

[742] OKW War Diary 1944/45, Part I, p. 968. According to it, in 1943 the British and American air forces dropped a total of 226,500 tons of bombs, while in 1944 the figure was 1,188,580 tons. For a survey of the state of the opposing air forces at the beginning of 1944 see Prien/Rodeike, *JG 1 / 11*, p. 646 and following pages.

[743] Groehler, *Bombenkrieg*, p. 210.

[744] Groehler, *Luftkrieg*, p. 417.

[745] ibid.

[746] On 5 February 1944; also see Studie 8.Abt./Genst.d.Lw. of 21/9/1944, p. 10 and following pages.

[747] Including the *Stäbe* of JG 300, 301 and 302; later, following the disbandment of the 30 Jagddivision, the former single-engined night fighter units were transferred to the day fighter arm and assigned to the other divisions—see Studie 8.Abt., p. 11.

[748] Three *Gruppen* of JG 2, I and II/JG 26, II/JG 27 and I/JG 3.

[749] Of the later type the A-7 version was at the point of introduction, while the G-6 and, less commonly, the G-5 versions of the Bf 109 were being flown.

[750] See the aircraft inventory lists in the appendices.

[751] See the loss lists in the appendices.

[752] Also see Freeman, *Mighty Eighth War Diary*, p. 178; War Diary of *I Jagdkorps*, 10/2/1944; Prien/Rodeike, *JG 1 / 11*, p. 713 and following pages.

[753] As usual both sides drew up a balance when the fighting was over, and once again as usual the results were quite different. While the German side claimed a total of 51 enemy aircraft shot down (including 32 heavy bombers), its losses on this day were 30 pilots killed or missing, 19 wounded, 40 aircraft written off and 27 damaged from various causes. On the other hand the 8th Air Force admitted the loss

of 41 aircraft (30 heavy bombers and eleven escort fighters) while claiming the impressive total of 129 victories.

[754] See in detail Freeman, *Mighty Eighth War Diary*, p. 180; War Diary of *I Jagdkorps*, 11/2/1944; Prien/Rodeike, *JG 1 / 11*, p. 720 and following pages.

[755] Logbook of Heinrich Sannemann.

[756] Fw. Gerd Thyben had returned to his *Staffel* from the *Gruppenstabsschwarm* at the beginning of January 1944.

[757] The German side subsequently claimed 26 enemy aircraft shot down against 26 of its own aircraft lost; the 8th Air Force admitted the loss of eight heavy bombers and seventeen fighters while its units claimed 35 victories.

[758] See in detail Prien/Rodeike, *JG 1 / 11*, p. 703 and following pages.

[759] Piekalkiewicz, p. 339; Groehler, *Bombenkrieg*, p. 213 and following pages, *Luftkampf*, p. 404.

[760] The 8th Air Force's target catalogue included a total of 28 airframe and 13 aero-engine factories, mainly in the Brunswick—Leipzig area and around Regensburg, while the RAF raided Leipzig, Stuttgart, Schweinfurt, Steyr and Augsburg by night. See the detailed account in Groehler, *Bombenkrieg*, p. 213 and following pages.

[761] Including the first mission over the Reich by the 357th FG, the first unit of the 8th Air Force to operate the P-51. The 354th FG, a unit of the 9th Air Force, had been operating the Mustang since December 1943.

[762] Draft by Walter Grabmann, p. 39.

[763] See *Mighty Eighth War Diary*, p. 183-184; I *Jagdkorps* War Diary, 20/2/1944; Piekalkiewicz, p. 340; Groehler, *Luftkampf*, p. 404 and *Bombenkrieg*, p. 217; Prien and Rodeike, *JG 1/11*, p. 727 and following pages.

[764] Mission times from the logbook of Heinrich Sannemann 10:35 AM – 12:35 PM (note the significantly greater mission duration made possible by the use of external fuel tanks).

[765] According to the logbook of Heinrich Sannemann 6/JG 3 did not encounter any enemy aircraft during its mission.

[766] The OKL placed the German successes at 39 enemy aircraft shot down in combat, 27 of them four-engined bombers, while the OKW claimed 49; see the detailed list in Prien/Rodeike, *JG 1 / 11*, p. 727.

[767] War Diary of *I Jagdkorps*, p. 183-184; MACR; the losses included five bombers and two fighters Cat. E. The breakdown of American claims was 65-33-29 for the bombers and 61-7-37 for the fighters.

[768] See in detail War Freeman, *Mighty Eighth War Diary*, p. 184-185; Diary of *I Jagdkorps*, 21/2/1944; Prien/Rodeike, *JG 1 / 11*, p. 736 and following pages.

[769] Logbook of Heinrich Sannemann, combat report by Franz Ruhl.

[770] A claim for a B-17 shot down by Lt. Franz Ruhl was rejected by 2 JD even though he had a supporting witness, Lt. Herbert Zschiegner.

[771] OKW communiqué, 22/2/1944; according to the OKL's situation report, 27 enemy aircraft were claimed shot down, including 20 heavy bombers.

[772] Freeman, p. 184-185; among the losses were seven and three "Cat. E." The American bombers claims were 19-16-14, those of the fighters 33-5-18.

[773] Protected by 122 P-38s and 63 P-47s a total of 118 B-24s and 65 B-17s attacked the Messerschmitt factory complex at Regensburg; Rust, p. 14.

[774] See Freeman, *Mighty Eighth War Diary*, p. 185-186 and *Mighty Eighth*, p. 109; *I Jagdkorps* War Diary, 22/2/1944; Prien and Rodeike, *JG 1 / 11*, p. 741 and following pages.

[775] Logbook and combat report by Heinrich Sannemann.

[776] These obviously consisted of II/JG 11, III/JG 54 and I, II and III/ZG 26. The *Luftwaffe* command continued to send the *Zerstörer* units to the slaughter, even though it was well aware (since 1940 at the latest) of the Bf 110's inability to cope with single-engined fighters by day. The catastrophic losses being suffered by the heavy fighters at this time are characterized by the following entry in the war diary of III/ZG 26: *"Eight Bf 110s took off at 12:22 PM, assembly area Steinhuder Lake. Formed up there with I/ZG 26. Contact with enemy aircraft in Bielefeld area. Losses: 6 Bf 110s were shot down. Own successes: 2 B-17s."* It should be noted that two days earlier the *Gruppe* had lost 11 of 13 Bf 110s committed; two days later it put all of four machines into the air. Among those lost on 22 February 1944 was Hptm. Eduard Tratt, *Kommandeur* of II/ZG 26 and with 38 victories the most successful *Zerstörer* pilot in the *Luftwaffe*.

[777] "Combat Box" was the term for an American bomber formation. Initially consisting of nine bombers, by this time a "Combat Box" was made up of 18 heavy bombers. The boxes were staggered vertically and horizontally to provide the maximum mutual defensive fire.

[778] OKW communiqué 23/2/1944. In contrast the OKL's situation report cited just 65 victories in aerial combat, including 55 four-engined bombers. See the list in Prien and Rodeike, *JG 1 / 11*, p. 742; this contains 48 heavy bombers, 9 bombers forced to leave formation, 3 cripples finished off and 12 fighters.

[779] Freeman, p. 185-186. Among the losses were four B-17s and one P-38 "Cat. E." The breakdown of victory claims was 59-7-25 for the fighters and 34-18-17 for the bombers.

[780] Freeman, *Mighty Eighth*, p. 110. On this day the 15th Air Force carried out an attack on the Steyr roller bearing factory in Austria; see Rust, p. 14.

[781] The 15th Air Force's attack was once again directed at Steyr, where the target was the Steyr-Daimler-Puch factories, a major subcontractor in the production of fighter aircraft; see Rust, p. 14.

[782] Schweinfurt was supposed to be the target of a "Double Blow" attack; during the night of 25 February RAF Bomber Command had sent 622 heavy bombers to attack the city however the raid was a total failure. The objective of "double blow" attacks was to prevent valuable installations that survived the first attack from being salvaged prior to subsequent attacks. See Piekalkiewicz, p. 340.

[783] Freeman.

[784] See Freeman, *Mighty Eighth War Diary*, p. 186-187 and *Mighty Eighth*, p. 110; I *Jagdkorps* War Diary, 24/2/1944; Prien and Rodeike, *JG 1 / 11*, p. 746 and following pages.

[785] Obviously the three *Gruppen* of JG 11; see Prien/Rodeike, *JG 1 / 11*, p. 751.

[786] Logbook of Heinrich Sannemann, combat report by Franz Ruhl with eyewitness Uffz. Hermann Beck.

[787] As well as one bomber forced to leave formation by Lt. Ruhl; this claim was not confirmed.

[788] OKL situation report. The figure contained in the OKW communiqué was 166 victories, 143 of them four-engined bombers, which included those achieved against the RAF's night raid on Schweinfurt. See the list in Prien and Rodeike, *JG 1 / 11*, p. 746; it records 68 four-engined bombers shot down, 9 forced to leave formation, 1 a.s.m. and 12 fighters.

[789] Freeman, p. 186-187. Among the bomber losses were two "Cat. E"; the breakdown of claims was 38-1-14 for the fighters and 83-22-42 for the bombers.

[790] See Freeman, *Mighty Eighth War Diary*, p. 188-189 and *Mighty Eighth*, p. 112; Rust, p. 14; I *Jagdkorps* War Diary, 25/2/1944; Prien and Rodeike, *JG 1 / 11*, p. 752 and following pages.

[791] For details of I/JG 53's involvement see Prien, *JG 53* Part 3, p. 1090, for I/JG 77 Prien, JG 77 Part 4, p. 1889, and for III/JG 3 Prien and Stemmer, *III/JG 3*, p. 285.

[792] On Page 753 of *JG 1 / 11* by Prien/Rodeike, a B-17 is credited to II/JG 3; this is based on inaccurate information and should be disregarded.

[793] When the fighting was over the German units involved in the defense against the incursions by the American 8th and 15th Air Forces claimed a total of 112 enemy aircraft shot down or forced to leave formation, 109 of them heavy bombers. It may be assumed that a large number of these claims were either disallowed during the confirmation process or were downgraded to *Herausschüsse* or cases of finishing off a crippled machine. On the negative side the *Luftwaffe* lost 48 aircraft in action together with 33 fighters and destroyers with significant damage. The Americans admitted the loss of 74 four-engined bombers (34 by the 8th and 40 by the 15th Air Force) as well as nine fighters (five by the 8th and four by the 15th Air Force); the 8th Air Force's claims for enemy aircraft shot down were 49-11-26, while the corresponding figures for the 15th Air Force were 93-17-15.

[794] Freeman, *Mighty Eighth*, p. 112; Rust, p. 15-16; Groehler, *Bombenkrieg*, p. 216 with reference to Craven/Cate, Vol. 3, p. 43.

[795] Of a total of 19,177 tons of bombs dropped on the Reich by the USAAF and RAF during this period; of the 6,333 tons of bombs intended for German aircraft factories during these attacks a considerable percentage were dropped on targets of opportunity due to poor weather conditions. See Freeman.

[796] Groehler, *Bombenkrieg*, p. 216.

[797] The leading officers of the American 8th Air Force were convinced that "Big Week" had delivered a decisive blow to the German air armaments industry and created a very important precondition for achieving air superiority over Western Europe. In particular they believed that the bombing of aircraft factories had deprived the German fighter pilots of their material base or at least seriously weakened it. These hopes were to prove unfounded and deceptive, however, for the effects on the German aviation industry were not nearly as serious as first believed. In fact there was only a temporary and not very serious drop in German fighter production as a result of the attacks. Expressed in absolute figures, German aircraft production dropped from 2,445 in January to 2,015 in February, but in March 1944 rose again to an output of 2,607 machines. In April this figure climbed even higher, to more than 3,000. If one looks at the corresponding figures for fighter production, which was the target of the "Big Week" attacks, there was a drop of from 1,555 in January 1944 to 1,104 in February, but then in March production climbed back up to 1,638 machines. The actual effects of "Big Week" on German fighter production lay in the fact that 700 aircraft under construction were destroyed, the planned expansion of fighter production was stopped for one month and slowed for several more. That the effects were not significantly more far-reaching was due in large part to the evacuation and dispersal of the German aircraft industry begun in summer 1943. Since then production in many areas was conducted in bomb-proof installations such as tunnels and mines, while prefabrication and the manufacture of components had been transferred to small and very small concerns and to a quite considerable degree into the territory of the "Protectorate" of Bohemia and Moravia which had so far not been visited by the bombing campaign.

[798] Groehler, *Bombenkrieg*, p. 217.

[799] Piekalkiewicz, p. 341; Groehler, *Bombenkrieg*, p. 217.

[800] Freeman, *Mighty Eighth*, p. 113.

[801] Groehler, *Bombenkrieg*, p. 217; Freeman, *Mighty Eighth*, p. 113; Piekalkiewicz, p. 341. It is noteworthy that at this point the Americans (finally) drew the only correct conclusion regarding the correct conduct of fighter escort—the *Luftwaffe* command had been unable to decide on this step in 1940 over England.

[802] Groehler, *Bombenkrieg*, p. 218, with reference to the USSBS, Statistical Appendix, p. 29, as well as BA RL 2/v. 3157.

[803] See Prien and Rodeike, *JG 1 / 11*, p. 759.

[804] See Piekalkiewicz, p. 341.

[805] The leaders of *I Jagdkorps* considered exchanging these "Front-line *Gruppen*" for less battle-weary units based further inland after a certain period, however in practice this was rarely carried out.

[806] See the overview of losses in Prien/Rodeike, *JG 1 / 11*, p. 760.

[807] *I Jagdkorps* War Diary, 23/2/1944. It is noteworthy that one of the greatest fears was that the British might also turn to daylight raids following the crippling of the German defense.

[808] Scheduled for conversion were III/JG 1 in *3 Jagddivision*, II/JG 11 in *2 Jagddivision* and (somewhat later) I/JG 3 in *1 Jagddivision*. Initial equipment was to be the Bf 109 G-5 and G-6 with GM-1, to be replaced from April 1944 with the Messerschmitt Bf 109 G-6/AS equipped with the DB 605 AS high-altitude motor.

[809] How the *General der Jagdflieger* imagined this happening is revealed in his "*Series of Tactical Thoughts*" contained in the conference record: "*The enemy fighter escort is to be intercepted at the Rhine and attacked from behind. Rotten and Schwärme must always attack from the highest possible altitude in order to maximize the element of surprise.*" The *General* went on to make the following significant statement: "*Clever tactics are needed to overcome the fear of enemy fighters that exists in all fighter units. We must request that forces be formed, equipped and trained for the fighter-versus-fighter role in order to engage the enemy escort. Suitable types are the Bf 109 G-6 and G-5 with GM-1. These Gruppen have to get to altitude early. From this superior position they will have an easy battle.*"
The result of these discussions clearly reveals the inability or unwillingness of the leading representatives of the fighter arm to face up to the facts. Furthermore, the transcripts of these conferences that have survived provide excellent insight into the thought and planning processes of the *Luftwaffe* command, which is characterized here by above quoted statements by GenMaj. Adolf Galland. These statements were made more or less independently of the facts, for there was no possibility of readying additional forces *"for fighter-versus-fighter combat"*—and it is well known that this did not happen—nor was it sufficient to engage the American escort fighters with "*Rotten and Schwärme*". The fighter general's view that the German fighters would then have "an easy time of it" would have caused most fighter pilots to shake their heads. Nevertheless: these statements by the legendary *General der Jagdflieger* hardly fit the picture portrayed by him after the war, of a crystal-clear analyst whose rational and reasonable proposals for increasing the effectiveness of the fighter defense went unheard because they ran up against the narrow-mindedness and inability of the high command.

[810] In fact even after this directive III/JG 3 remained in the south of the Reich; see Prien and Stemmer, *III/JG 3*, p. 284, Footnote 549.

[811] See Ries / Dierich, p. 32 and map on p. 133.

[812] Account by Helmut Hennig, 30/11/1985; he recalls that the move took place in mid-March, while surviving records indicate that II/JG 3 began operations from Sachau roughly in the second half of April.

[813] See in detail Prien/Rodeike, *JG 1 / 11*, p. 762 and following pages.

[814] Targets were the Robert Bosch electrical works in Klein-Machnow, the Heinkel Works in Oranienburg and the VKF ball-bearing factory in Erkner; Ethell and Price, p. 8.

[815] Freeman, *Mighty Eighth War Diary*, p. 192 and *Mighty Eighth*, p. 113.

[816] Ibidem; obviously the recall order did not reach all units and so it was that the 89 P-38s of the 20th, 55th and 364th FGs became the first American aircraft to appear over Berlin by day. Also see Ethell and Price, p. 8.

[817] Freeman, *Mighty Eighth War Diary*, p. 192.

[818] Freeman, *Mighty Eighth War Diary*, p. 192; among the losses was one P-47 "Cat. E"; the breakdown of American claims was 3-1-1 for the bombers and 8-1-3 for the fighters.

[819] Though 219 B-17s dropped their bombs on targets of opportunity in the Cologne—Bonn—Düsseldorf area.

[820] See Freeman, *Mighty Eighth War Diary*, p. 193 and *Mighty Eighth*, p. 113; I *Jagdkorps* War Diary, 4/3/1944; Prien and Rodeike, JG 1/11, p. 768 and following pages.

[821] Logbook of Heinrich Sannemann.

[822] Compare to IV *Gruppe*'s mission—Prien, *IV/JG 3*, p. 81.

[823] While there were no major air battles over the area around Berlin and the northwest of the Reich, the withdrawing units of the 1st Bombardment Division were at times heavily engaged over Western Germany; consequently most of the 41 victories claimed by the German side on this day were scored in the air battles fought there. The *Luftwaffe*'s losses over the Reich on this day amounted to ten pilots killed with thirteen aircraft shot down in aerial combat and another ten lost for reasons other than enemy action. The 8th Air Force admitted the loss of 16 four-

engined bombers and 28 escort fighters on 4 March 1944; on the other hand the Americans claimed 19 enemy aircraft shot down.

[824] Freeman, *Mighty Eighth War Diary*, p. 195; Ethell and Price, p. 37 and following pages.

[825] See for example II/JG 53's defensive mission on this day in Prien, *JG 53* Part 3, p. 1294.

[826] See the list in Prien and Rodeike, JG 1/11, p. 770.

[827] I *Jagdkorps* War Diary, 6/3/1944; Price and Ethell, p. 143; of these 528 sorties only about 370 resulted in enemy contact.

[828] Heinrich Sannemann, logbook and combat report.

[829] Price and Ethell, p. 69 and following pages. JG 3 contributed 55 Bf 109s to the mission, the *Sturmstaffel* seven Fw 190s, JG 302 eight Bf 109s and *Jasta Erla* two Bf 109s.

[830] OKW communiqué 7/3/1944. See the list above (p. 770). Many of the 110 victory claims cited there were unquestionably downgraded or completely rejected, however the precise number of victories scored on 6/3/1944 is not known.

[831] See the list in Prien and Rodeike, *JG 1 / 11*, p. 770.

[832] Freeman, *Mighty Eighth War Diary*, p. 195; Price and Ethell, p. 142. The figures contained in the latter differ slightly from those of Freeman, but see the exact breakdown of American claims is 97-28-60 for the bombers and 81-8-28 for the fighters.

[833] See Freeman, *Mighty Eighth War Diary*, p. 196-197; I *Jagdkorps* War Diary, 8/3/1944; Prien and Rodeike, *JG 1 / 11*, p. 782 and following pages.

[834] Logbook of Heinrich Sannemann; combat report by Franz Ruhl with Obfw. Helmut Rüffler as witness.

[835] OKW communiqué 9/3/1944.

[836] See the list in Prien/Rodeike, *JG 1 / 11*, p. 782.

[837] WASt. casualty report; Summarized Loss Reports RL 2/III/852 and following pages.

[838] Freeman, *Mighty Eighth War Diary*, p. 196-197. Among the losses were three heavy bombers and sixteen escort fighters; the majority of the latter were lost in collisions and crashes over England. Breakdown of victory claims: 63-17-19 for the bombers and 79-8-25 for the fighters.

[839] It should not be overlooked that not even the 8th Air Force could remain unaffected by the loss of 115 four-engined bombers with 1,050 crewmen killed or missing in two days of operations (6 and 8 March) plus another 575 bombers damaged. This was reflected in the reduced number of aircraft available for operations; whereas 730 four-engined bombers had been available on 6 March 1944, on the 8th this figure was down to 623 and on the 9th to 526. Had the *Luftwaffe* been able to go on inflicting this rate of loss, even the Americans would have had to reconsider the wisdom of continuing with their attacks.

[840] Freeman, *Mighty Eighth War Diary*, p. 197 and *Mighty Eighth*, p. 115.

[841] War Diary of *I Jagdkorps*, 9/3/1944: "*No missions flown on account of bad weather.*"

[842] Units of the US 8th Air Force were; however, able to attack Berlin on 9 March and Münster on 11 March; neither raid was intercepted by German day fighters.

[843] It is not clear if II/JG 3 took part in the defensive effort against units of the US 8th Air Force which attacked Brunswick on 15 March 1944.

[844] See in detail Freeman, *Mighty Eighth War Diary*, p. 206; War Diary of *I Jagdkorps*, 23/3/1944; Prien/Rodeike, *JG 1 / 11*, p. 805 and following pages.

[845] Mission times from the logbook of Heinrich Sannemann 9:50 – 11:54 AM; at the same time, *Stab* and I/JG 3 were committed against units of the 3rd Bombardment Division bound for Brunswick.

[846] The following extract from the combat/witness report filed by Uffz. Maximilian Reichenberger of 5/JG 3 is noteworthy: "*At 10:40 AM my Schwarmführer had to return to base after running low on fuel. Our Schwarm broke up and I attached myself to a Schwarm of IV/JG Udet. At about 10:50 we saw the bomber formations heading west. We overtook the formation on the left. While turning towards them I lost the Schwarm. To the right of me were bomber formations heading west, left of me bombers flying east, and above me Mustangs.*"

[847] OKW communiqué, 24/3/1944. The daily reports by the *Jagddivisionen* show 1 *Jagddivision* with 12 four-engined bombers and 4 fighters, 2 *Jagddivision* with 9 four-engined bombers plus two probables, and 3 *Jagddivision* with 8 four-engined bombers and 5 probable victories.

[848] See list in Prien/Rodeike, *JG 1 / 11*, p. 806.

[849] Freeman, *Mighty Eighth War Diary*, p. 206-207. Among the losses were one bomber and one fighter "Cat. E". The breakdown of American claims was 33-8-1 for the bombers and 20-1-6 for the fighters.

[850] See Freeman, *Mighty Eighth War Diary*, p. 207; I *Jagdkorps* War Diary, 24/3/1944.

[851] See Freeman, *Mighty Eighth War Diary*, p. 211; I *Jagdkorps* War Diary, 29/3/1944; Prien and Rodeike, *JG 1 / 11*, p. 811 and following pages.

[852] Attacks against German airmen in their parachutes and on the ground became more frequent in the spring of 1944. Since the war this unpleasant practice has been of great concern to all those involved; while the German fighter pilots almost

unanimously deny that their side employed such practices, most American publications more or less discretely avoid dealing with this thorny subject. The killing—or more accurately the shooting—of defenseless pilots in parachutes was undoubtedly one of the most repugnant aberrations of the war, defying the most basic humanitarian rules, and at the same time was further proof of the type of perversions that went along with a total war of destruction. It is difficult to imagine what might have been going through the heads of the young American fighter pilots while they engaged in these pitiless, inhuman shootings, which as the war went on would be extended to include farmers working in the fields and harmless cyclists and individuals. Of course they were influenced by persistent accounts in official reports and in the press, according to which downed bomber crews had been shot by the Germans. They were also surely aware that the Nazi Party had urged the civilian population to adopt lynch justice against Anglo-American flyers (see Groehler, *Bombenkrieg*, p. 368 and following pages, and in particular Joseph Goebbel's speech in Nuremberg on 4/6/1944 in which he spoke of acts of lynch justice by civilians with understanding and promised that none of the participants would be prosecuted—Goebbel's Speeches, p. 323 and following pages, p. 337). And finally, toward the end of the war, there were even official instructions not to spare bailed-out Me 262 pilots. But none of this is sufficient to justify the "killer mentality" displayed by some Anglo-American fighter pilots.

The anger and disgust of the German fighter pilots is therefore quite understandable. This reaction was strengthened by a feeling of disappointment over an unfair opponent who did not adhere to the unwritten rule of the *"chivalrous duel man against man"* and the rule of the *"noble hunt."* This romantic transfiguration and unjustified elevation of the special place held by the fighter pilot's role is still sometimes encountered today.

Leaving the ethical-moral aspect aside for a moment, one cannot escape the conclusion that shooting at bailed-out airmen is just a part of the war whose objective after all was the destruction of the enemy's air forces. From the point of view of the Americans, an enemy pilot hanging in his parachute had not surrendered and provided that he had not been wounded would soon be back in the air in another fighter aircraft. The shooting of pilots in parachutes was therefore nothing more than the logical consequence of waging a total war. German propaganda had been calling for just that since Goebbel's unholy speech in the Sports Palace on 18 February 1943, in which he said that there was no place for "notions of humanity" in total war. The German reaction to the enemy's ruthlessness seems very inconsistent, especially if, consciously or unconsciously, it happened as a form of retribution for the unspeakable cruelties committed in the name of and in justification of Germany. Furthermore it should not go unmentioned that there were certainly also incidents (though to a much lesser extent) where German fighter pilots shot at bailed-out Anglo-American airmen; the cases involving German fighter pilots which are known to the author were mainly on the level of spontaneous, impulsive acts of revenge.

[853] OKW communiqué, 30/3/1944. *1 Jagddivision*'s daily report read one B-17, one B-17 probable and one fighter. The figures for *2 Jagddivision* were six B-17s, three B-17 probables and six fighters, while *3 Jagddivision* claimed three fighters.

[854] See list in Prien and Rodeike, *JG 1 / 11*, p. 812.

[855] Freeman, *Mighty Eighth War Diary*, p. 211. Among the losses were one four-engined bomber and six fighters "Cat. E", while the breakdown of claims was 8-3-6 by the bombers and 44-4-13 by the fighters.

[856] Freeman, *Mighty Eighth*, Appendix. "Effective" missions were those in which the machine actually dropped its bombs, whether on the intended "primary" target or a target of opportunity.

[857] Groehler, *Bombenkrieg*, p. 218, with reference to the USSBS, Statistical Appendix, p. 29; BA RL/2 v. 3157.

[858] Reporting date 31/3/1944, German Order of Battle, Statistics as of Quarter Years; also see the inventory list in the appendices.

[859] See Freeman, *Mighty Eighth War Diary*, p. 213; *I Jagdkorps* War Diary, 5/4/1944; Naval Command War Diary, Vol. 56, p. 115 with the corresponding degrees of damage.

[860] From the Naval Command War Diary, Vol. 56, p. 186: *"Attacked was the city of Brunswick, where the main railway station was seriously hit and five factories hit. A moderate attack with incendiaries was directed against the Volkswagen factory in Fallersleben. Systematic attacks were made against a large number of north-German airfields, where in some cases considerable damage was inflicted and numerous aircraft destroyed or damaged."* These attacks and those that began on airfields and transportation targets in the occupied western territories were correctly interpreted as the beginning of preparations for an invasion in the west.

[861] See Freeman, *Mighty Eighth War Diary*, p. 214 and *Mighty Eighth*, p. 129 and following pages; *I Jagdkorps* War Diary, 8/4/1944; Prien and Rodeike, *JG 1 / 11*, p. 835 and following pages. According to the Naval Command War Diary, Vol. 65, p. 206 (report dated 9/4/1944) the number of German aircraft committed was 497, which probably included the forces made available from *Luftflotte 3*'s area of command.

[862] Mission times from the logbook of Heinrich Sannemann 1:00 – 2:40 PM.

[863] *Sturmstaffel 1* was credited with four B-24s; these were mistakenly omitted from the summary in Prien and Rodeike, *JG 1 / 11*, p. 835.

[864] OKW communiqué, 9/4/1944. Initial reports indicated 72 certain and 30 probable victories, including 20 certain by the flak. Naval Command War Diary, Vol. 56, p. 206.

[865] The number of ground losses applies to the day fighter units; a total of 72 aircraft were destroyed on the ground on this day and another 45 damaged; *I Jagdkorps* War Diary. Of the aircraft destroyed on the ground 45 belonged to front-line units; Naval Command War Diary, Vol. 56, p. 206.

[866] Freeman, *Mighty Eighth War Diary*, p. 214. Among the losses were two bombers and two fighters "Cat. E"; the breakdown of claims was 58-9-32 by the bombers (2nd Bombardment Division only, figures for 1st and 3rd Bombardment Divisions not available) and 88-3-46 by the fighters, which also claimed 49-6-38 on the ground.

[867] See Freeman, *Mighty Eighth War Diary*, p. 215; I Jagdkorps War Diary, 9/4/1944; Naval Command War Diary, Vol. 56, p. 206 (which claims 361 German sorties); Prien and Rodeike, *JG 1 / 11*, p. 844 and following pages.

[868] Mission times from the logbook of Heinrich Sannemann 10:35 AM – 12:35 PM.

[869] The German side ultimately claimed 71 enemy aircraft shot down (including those brought down at night), with 35 certain and 10 probables during the day. Losses amounted to twelve pilots killed and five wounded with 24 aircraft as total losses. On the other hand the 8th Air Force admitted the loss of 42 four-engined bombers and 14 escort fighters while claiming 74 German aircraft shot down.

[870] See Freeman, *Mighty Eighth War Diary*, p. 217-218 and *Mighty Eighth*, p. 133; *I Jagdkorps* War Diary, 11/4/1944; Prien and Rodeike, *JG 1 / 11*, p. 851 and following pages.

[871] *Stab JG 3*: two B-17s; I/JG 3: one B-17, one B-17 *Herausschuss*, one P-51; II/JG 3: two B-17s, two P-51s; IV/JG 3: twelve B-17s, 4 B-17 *Herausschüsse*, four B-17 a.s.m. III/JG 3, which arrived from the south a short time later, claimed four B-24s shot down; Prien and Stemmer, II, III and IV/JG 3.

[872] OKW communiqué, 12/4/1944. According to initial reports claims were made for 108 certain and 136 probable victories, including 17 and 13 by the flak; Naval Command War Diary, Vol. 56, p. 251. How severely these claims of success were later reduced may be seen in the summary of victories by unit in Prien and Rodeike, *JG 1 / 11*, p. 852.

[873] Freeman, *Mighty Eighth War Diary*, p. 217-218. Among the losses were five four-engined bombers "Cat. E", while nine B-17s sought refuge in Sweden. Victory claims totaled 73-24-23 by the bombers and 51-5-25 by the fighters.

[874] See Freeman, *Mighty Eighth War Diary*, p. 219 and *Mighty Eighth*, p. 134; Rust, p. 21; *I Jagdkorps* War Diary, 13/4/1944; Naval Command War Diary, Vol. 56, p. 291; Prien and Rodeike, *JG 1 / 11*, p. 862; Prien and Stemmer, *III/JG 3*, p. 299-300.

[875] Logbook and combat report by Hptm. Heinrich Sannemann with Obfw. Hans Grünberg and Lt. Mietzner as witnesses. Hptm. Sannemann flew aircraft "Yellow 12" on this mission, a Bf 109 G-6/U4 equipped with an engine-mounted 30-mm MK 108 cannon.

[876] OKW communiqué, 14/4/1944. Contained therein are the victory claims relating to an incursion by the 15th Air Force. After this defensive mission the units of *7 Jagddivision* claimed 13 certain and 2 probable victories, including 11 and 1 heavy bombers. *I Jagdkorps* War Diary.

[877] Including four total losses not due to enemy action; operations against the US 8th Air Force only.

[878] Of which 16 four-engined bombers and two fighters came from the ranks of the 15th Air Force.

[879] Freeman, *Mighty Eighth War Diary*, p. 219. Among the losses were three four-engined bombers and two fighters "Cat. E," while another 13 heavy bombers made emergency landings in Switzerland. The American victory claims were 22-13-24 by the bombers and 42-8-10 by the fighters.

[880] See in detail Prien/Rodeike, *JG 1 / 11*, p. 865 and following pages; Naval Command War Diary, Vol. 56, p. 343.

[881] Freeman, *Mighty Eighth War Diary*, p. 221 and *Mighty Eighth*, p. 136.

[882] *I Jagdkorps* War Diary, 18/4/1944; concerning JG 3's battle with the B-17 formations of the 3rd Bombardment Division see *Mighty Eighth*, p. 135. The next day the OKW communiqué made special mention of JG 3's action under Maj. Friedrich-Karl Müller and credited it with the destruction of an entire unit of heavy bombers; a total of 44 enemy aircraft were claimed shot down including 40 four-engined bombers.

[883] On this day the 8th Air Force admitted the loss of 19 heavy bombers and eight escort fighters, three of the latter "Cat. E". On the other hand its units claimed 38 enemy aircraft shot down, 13-5-6 by the bombers and 20-0-12 by the fighters. See Freeman, *Mighty Eighth War Diary*, p. 221.

[884] Mission times from the logbook of Heinrich Sannemann 1:17 – 3:10 PM.

[885] While 227 B-17s of the 1st Bombardment Division were supposed to strike industrial targets in Kassel, Bettenhausen, Eschwege and Altenbauna, an attack by another 246 B-17s of the 3rd Bombardment Division was directed against the large airfields of Werl and Lippstadt. And finally, the units of the 2nd Bombardment Division, which put up 249 Liberators, were supposed to attack the air bases of Gütersloh and Paderborn.

[886] See Freeman, *Mighty Eighth War Diary*, p. 222 and *Mighty Eighth*, p. 135; *I Jagdkorps* War Diary, 19/4/1944; Prien and Rodeike, *JG 1 / 11*, p. 875 and following pages.

[887] Mission times from the logbook of Heinrich Sannemann 9:35 – 11;15 AM.

[888] To the victory figures for II/JG 3 in Prien/Rodeike, *JG 1 / 11*, p. 876, should be added one B-17 shot down and another forced to leave formation, both credited to Obfw. Rüffler of 4/JG 3 (57-58).

[889] See Freeman, *Mighty Eighth War Diary*, p. 224 and *Mighty Eighth*, p. 135; *I Jagdkorps* War Diary, 22/4/1944; Prien and Rodeike, *JG 1 / 11*, p. 878 and following pages.

[890] When the fighting was over on this day the *Luftwaffe* reported a total of 37 enemy aircraft shot down by fighters and flak, the majority of them heavy bombers. Its own losses totaled 24 killed, seven wounded and 33 machines written off as total losses. The 8th Air Force put its losses at 30 four-engined bombers and 14 fighters while its units claimed 62 victories.

[891] Documents of Heinrich Sannemann.

[892] See Freeman, *Mighty Eighth War Diary*, p. 226 and *Mighty Eighth*, p. 135; *I Jagdkorps* War Diary, 24/4/1944; Prien and Rodeike, *JG 1 / 11*, p. 889 and following pages.

[893] In addition to II *Gruppe*'s victories, *Stab*/JG 3 claimed five B-17s; I/JG 3 one B-17, one B-17 finished off, two P-51s; IV/JG 3 seven B-17s, seven B-17 *Herausschüsse*, one B-17 finished off. III/JG 3, which was committed within *7 Jagddivision* at the same time, claimed five more B-17s, five B-17 *Herausschüsse*, one B-17 a.s.m. and one P-51.

[894] OKW communiqué 25/4/1944.

[895] Freeman, *Mighty Eighth War Diary*, p. 226. Among the losses were one heavy bombers and one fighter "Cat. E," while the American victory claims were 20-1-36 by the bombers and 58-0-38 by the fighters. The latter also claimed 66-6-20 on the ground.

[896] See in detail Freeman, *Mighty Eighth War Diary*, p. 232-233 and *Mighty Eighth*, p. 136. From the latter: *"If, in selecting Berlin as the target for the mission of April 29th the Eighth Air Force hoped to flush the Focke Wulfs and Messerschmitts, they were certainly successful. Not since the early March missions had the enemy responded in such strength to a threat against his capital."* War Diary of *I Jagdkorps*, 29/4/1944; Prien/Rodeike, *JG 1 / 11*, p. 897 and following pages.

[897] Oblt. Bohatsch also claimed to have finished off a crippled B-17; although he was attached to I/JG 3 at this time, the success was credited to 5/JG 3.

[898] Freeman, *Mighty Eighth War Diary*, p. 232-233. Among the losses were two four-engined bombers and one fighter "Cat. E," while the breakdown of American claims is as follows: the bombers claimed 73-26-34 and the fighters 16-6-9 in the air and 6-1-5 on the ground.

[899] Freeman, *Mighty Eighth*, Appendix; of the total of 14,464 sorties 9,945 counted as "effective." Groehler, *Bombenkrieg*, p. 218 with reference to the USSBS Statistical Appendix, p. 29 and BA/MA RL 2/v. 3157.

[900] According to 8th Air Force estimates at the time 314 of these were credited to the German fighters, 105 to flak and one loss was not credited—Freeman, *Mighty Eighth*, Appendix. Interestingly, adding the losses in *Mighty Eighth War Diary* produces only 362 missing aircraft, while the number of heavy bombers written off as "Cat. E" was 45, which suggests that the daily losses contained in the book must actually be lower than the actual loss figures.

[901] Sixty-seven P-51s, 42 P-47s and 31 P-38s—MACR 8th Air Force for the month of April 1944. In this case adding the figures in Freeman results in 194 missing and 22 "Cat. E." The difference may be partly explained by the losses of the IX Fighter Command within the 8th Air Force.

[902] 2.9% based on the total number of sorties flown but 4.2% based on the number of sorties considered "effective." While the loss of 186 heavy bombers in the notorious month of October 1943 was equal to a loss rate of 9.2%, the subsequent huge increase in the available number of four-engined bombers meant that the loss of almost twice as many aircraft resulted in a rate of loss equivalent to only about a third of the earlier month's. See Freeman, *Mighty Eighth*, p. 139.

[903] Groehler, *Bombenkrieg*, p. 218, with reference to BA/MA RL 2 / v. 3157. The loss figure obviously includes losses from units of *Luftflotte* 3 engaged in Defense of the Reich duties; also see the information from the files of *Oberst* Lützow immediately following.

[904] A planned attack on Berlin by the US 8th Air Force on this day had to be aborted on account of bad weather; a total of 197 machines in *I Jagdkorps*'s area were mobilized against these incursions, and there were isolated clashes with American fighters in the areas of *2* and *3 Jagddivision*—see in detail Prien/Rodeike, *JG 1 / 11*, p. 911.

[905] The filling of *Kapitän* positions with junior *Leutnants* was a result of the fighter arm's inadequate reserves; this problem was the subject of various fighter command staff conferences. Stop-gap measures were sought, however the conclusions that were drawn were highly questionable, as the following extract from the staff conference of 16/11/1943 clearly shows: *"(3.) General Schmid proposed that the General der Jagdflieger select the **usable material** from the soldiers and officers from the corps who have volunteered to serve as aircrew, since at the present time*

*there is **too little good human material** in the day fighters. (4) General Schmid proposed that the General der Jagdflieger undertake an evaluation of the Staffelkapitäne, since in many cases these are too young to lead a Staffel. He suggested that if necessary individual Staffeln be combined, since in many cases Staffel strengths are too low."* (Author's emphasis)

[906] On 19 December 1943, while serving as *Staffelkapitän* of 11/JG 3, Oblt. Frielinghaus was seriously injured in a takeoff collision.

[907] Letter written by Gustav Frielinghaus, 18/5/1959; account by Helmut Hennig 30/11/1985.

[908] The bad weather prevented the *Luftwaffe* from intercepting a large-scale daylight raid on Berlin by the 8th Air Force on 7/5/1944. II/ZG 26 with 28 aircraft was the only German unit to see action, however it could not be guided to the bombers. See *I Jagdkorps* War Diary, 7/5/1944.

[909] See Freeman, *Mighty Eighth War Diary*, p. 239. VIII Fighter Command provided 729 of the escort fighters while another 126 came from IX Fighter Command. *I Jagdkorps* War Diary, 8/5/1944, Prien and Rodeike, *JG 1 / 11*, p. 914 and following pages.

[910] *I Jagdkorps* War Diary, 8/5/1944; combat report by Lt. Franz Ruhl with witness report by Lt. Reinartz.

[911] See list at top of Page 915; success figures from OKW communiqué of 9/5/1944.

[912] Freeman, *Mighty Eighth War Diary*, p. 239; among the losses were eight four-engined bombers and two fighters "Cat. E," while the breakdown of American claims was 76-16-16 by the bombers and 59-4-20 by the fighters.

[913] See Corps Order of the Day No. 28 of 15 May 1944 reprinted above.

[914] See Gundelach, *Treibstoff*, p. 686 and following pages; Groehler, *Luftkampf*, p. 222 and following pages; Piekalkiewicz, p. 350 and following pages; Speer, p. 357 and following pages; Freeman, *Mighty Eighth*, p. 141; OKW War Diary 1944/45, Part I, p. 942 and following pages. For an account of the bombing of the Romanian oil fields see Prien, *JG 53*, Vol. 3, p. 1158 and following pages and *JG 77*, Vol. 4.

[915] See the description in Freeman, *Mighty Eighth,* p. 141.

[916] The German Reich had virtually no sources of crude oil of its own and was therefore completely dependent on the importation of foreign crude oil and the production of synthetic fuels. While the first sources dried up when the war began (apart from the Romanian and, until 1941, Russian deliveries), the hydrogenation plants built to produce synthetic fuel were inadequate to meet the considerable fuel requirements of the armed forces and especially the *Luftwaffe* (see the detailed account in Gundelach, *Treibstoff*, p. 686 and following pages). The German command nevertheless managed with difficulty to build up a strategic reserve of fuel; until May 1944 the reserve of high-grade aviation gas was 540,000 tons, which was good for about three months.

[917] This of course leads to the question of why these attacks were only begun now, three weeks before the start of the invasion of France, and not much earlier. Until the Allied planning and command documents are made publicly accessible it will only be possible to speculate as to the reasons behind this. One of these must surely be that had the effort to cut off the German fuel supply succeeded begun one year earlier it would only have benefited the Soviet Army. This would have presented the Soviets with an opportunity to advance far to the west against an immobilized enemy. By this time Allied planners were certain that their invasion of France and the subsequent advance into Germany would be a success, thus preventing the Russians from reaching to the Atlantic Coast.

[918] 735 from VIII Fighter Command and another 245 from the 9th Air Force.

[919] Freeman, *Mighty Eighth War Diary*, p. 242 and *Mighty Eighth*, p. 141 and following pages; Gundelach, *Treibstoff*, p. 691 and following pages; OKW War Diary 1944/45, p. 954.

[920] 419 in the first mission and 51 in the second; *I Jagdkorps* War Diary.

[921] *I Jagdkorps* War Diary, 12/5/1944.

[922] Combat report by Lt. Franz Ruhl with Lt. Reinartz as witness. The reference to the filming of the downing concerns the installation of a cine camera in the leading edge of the left wing; it was coupled with the weapons and operated when the guns were fired. Unlike the USAAF, which used gun camera film to confirm victory claims, the *Luftwaffe* used gun cameras mainly to provide instructional material for the training of fighter pilots; consequently, they were most often installed in the aircraft of the "*Experten*".

[923] Credited to *Stab*/JG 3: three B-17s; I/JG 3: two B-17 *Herausschüsse* and two P-51s; IV/JG 3: eight B-17s, eleven B-17 *Herausschüsse*, one B-17 a.s.m. For an account of III/JG 3's mission see Prien and Stemmer, *III/JG 3*, p. 305.

[924] For all three pilots these were their second and third victories; as well, Uffz. Barisch, Uffz. Geisthövel and Lt. Siebenrock all recorded their first victory.

[925] See Geisthövel's detailed account in Bracke, p. 139 and following pages.

[926] OKW communiqué, 13/5/1944.

[927] See the list in Prien and Rodeike, *JG 1 / 11*, p. 929.

[928] Freeman, *Mighty Eighth War Diary*, p. 243; among the losses were nine heavy bombers "Cat. E" while no victory claims by the bombers are known on this day.

[929] OKW War Diary 1944/45, Part I, p. 954; Speer, p. 357; Groehler, *Bombenkrieg*, p. 227; Gundelach, *Treibstoff*, p. 692.

[930] Groehler, *Bombenkrieg*, p. 226.

[931] See Gundelach, *Treibstoff*, p. 690 and following pages; OKW War Diary 1944/45, p. 942 and following pages; Prien, *JG 53*, Part 3, p. 1158 and following pages and *JG 77*, Part 4.

[932] See Freeman, *Mighty Eighth War Diary*, p. 243-244 and *Mighty Eighth*, p. 142; *I Jagdkorps* War Diary, 13/5/1944; Prien and Rodeike, *JG 1 / 11*, p. 940 and following pages.

[933] See the list in Prien and Rodeike, *JG 1 / 11*, p. 938; among the total losses were six not due to enemy action.

[934] Freeman, *Mighty Eighth War Diary*, p. 243-244; among the fighters was one "Cat. E" loss ("battle damage"). The breakdown of claims was 11-2-0 by the bombers and 58-4-13 by the fighters. Noticeable on this day is the wide discrepancy between the admitted American losses and German claims for P-47s shot down—three (not counting IX Fighter Command) against no less than twelve.

[935] Freeman, *Mighty Eighth War Diary*, p. 245 and *Mighty Eighth*, p. 142. By now Mustangs had become the most numerous escort fighter; there were approximately 500 in action on this day.

[936] 425 aircraft in the first and 26 in the second mission. *I Jagdkorps* War Diary; also see the detailed account in Prien and Rodeike, *JG 1 / 11*, p. 946 and following pages.

[937] The description of II/JG 3's mission is based on information in the War Diary of *I Jagdkorps* and on Lt. Franz Ruhl's combat report (Lt. Reinartz witness).

[938] Notes from Robert Skawran to Oskar Zimmermann.

[939] *Stab*/JG 3: one B-17, one P-38; I/JG 3: one B-24, five P-51s; IV/JG 3: four B-17s, one B-17 finished off.

[940] OKW communiqué, 20/5/1944.

[941] Freeman, *Mighty Eighth War Diary*, p. 245. Among the losses were one bomber and one fighter "Cat. E" while all of the victories were claimed by the fighters (Freeman lists the victory claims by bombers as "0", however it is not certain whether this simply means that no claim is available).

[942] See Freeman, *Mighty Eighth War Diary*, p. 248-249 and *Mighty Eighth*, p. 143; Rust, p. 23; Prien and Rodeike, *JG 1 / 11*, p. 960 and following pages.

[943] Combat report by Lt. Franz Ruhl, who also led II/JG 3 on this day, with Gefr. Pelletier as witness.

[944] From an actual strength of 31 Bf 109 G-6s—strength report of 24/5/1944 from documents of the *Luftwaffe* Study Group/FüAl Bw.

[945] See Prien and Rodeike, *JG 1 / 11*, p. 967.

[946] Freeman, *Mighty Eighth War Diary*, p. 252; Groehler, *Bombenkrieg*, p. 227 with reference to the Public Records Office London, Air 40/353, 376, 378.

[947] See the target summary in Groehler, p. 227.

[948] War Diary of *I Jagdkorps*.

[949] OKW communiqué of 29/5/1944; according to it another nine victories were scored over the occupied western territories and the waters around England. Interestingly the report makes reference to "extremely tough air battles" on this day.

[950] Freeman, *Mighty Eighth War Diary*, p. 252-253; among the losses were one four-engined bomber and three fighters "Cat. E," while the breakdown of American claims was 37-29-24 by the bombers and 57-1-16 by the fighters.

[951] Speer, p. 359; also see Gundelach, *Treibstoff*, p. 692 and following pages.

[952] Freeman, *Mighty Eighth War Diary*, p. 253-254 and *Mighty Eighth*, p. 144.

[953] Rust, p. 23-24.

[954] Also see the list in Prien and Rodeike, *JG 1 / 11*, p. 980.

[955] Also see in detail Bracke, p. 169, where Hans Grünberg is quoted about this mission. *"Suddenly he didn't see the other Staffeln any more, only the `One-Tens'*

were still there. Lt. Grünberg and his Staffel were the only ones still with them. But that can't be possible! Has your radio failed? Have the other Staffeln received an order of which you know nothing? These thoughts raced through his head. He slowly became afraid. This could quickly turn into something for which he would have to answer before a court-martial." The final comment is very revealing, for at this time the *Luftwaffe's* leading offices were already employing the threat of court-martial as a "means of command". For a more detailed discussion of this theme see Prien/Rodeike, *JG 1 / 11*.

[956] On this day ZG 26 claimed a total of 10 bombers shot down and 4 forced to leave formation; two P-51s were also claimed shot down. See the list in Prien/Rodeike, *JG 1 / 11*, p. 982.

[957] WASt. casualty report.

[958] OKW communiqué, 30/5/1944.

[959] Freeman, *Mighty Eighth War Diary*, p. 253-254; Rust, p. 24; M.A.C.R. of 29/5/1944; the 15th Air Force admitted the loss of 20 four-engined bombers and nine fighters on this day.

[960] Freeman, *Mighty Eighth War Diary*, p. 253-254—of the losses three B-24s were Cat. E and eight heavy bombers made forced landings in Sweden; American victory claims were 62-37-29 by the bombers and 39-1-5 by the fighters.

[961] Letter from Hans-Ekkehard Bob, 31/8/1996.

[962] Freeman, *Mighty Eighth War Diary*, p. 254.

[963] See list in Prien/Rodeike, *JG 1 / 11*, p. 984.

[964] Nine machines were also damaged, half of which crashed for reasons other than enemy action.

[965] Freeman, *Mighty Eighth War Diary*, p. 254—of the losses three heavy bombers and two fighters were Cat. E. Victory claims were 8-5-1 by the bombers and 50-3-2 for the fighters.

[966] Groehler, *Bombenkrieg*, p. 217.

[967,968] May 1944 had seen another increase in activity by the 8th Air Force against targets inside the Reich and in the neighboring areas of Belgium and Northeastern France. The heavy bombers recorded a total of 19,285 sorties during the month, of which 13,975 were considered "effective" and during which 38,029 tons of bombs were dropped. During the same period the 15th Air Force flew 14,432 sorties in the south, of which 11,584 were considered 'effective." The quantity of bombs dropped during these was 30,355 tons (Freeman, *Mighty Eighth*, Appendix). On the negative side the 8th Air Force lost 376 four-engined bombers and 171 fighters, to which must be added a number of losses by the P-51 groups of the 9th Air Force temporarily attached to VIII Fighter Command, which reported a total of 78 fighter losses in May 1944, and 175 aircraft of the 15th Air Force. This represented a loss rate of just 2.7% relative to the "effective" sorties flown by the bombers and just 1.9% of the overall figure. On the other hand in May 1944 the *Luftwaffe* recorded 3,805 sorties in the area of *Luftflotte* Reich compared to 4,505 in April. This clearly reflects the drop in the fighting strength of the *Jagdgruppen*, for the number of major combat days (nine) was the same for both months. German losses totaled 446 machines, which equated to a loss rate of 11.7%.

[969] See details in Freeman, *Mighty Eighth War Diary*, p. 256 and following pages, and *Mighty Eighth*, p. 144 and following pages.

[970] Of the 49 pilots killed or missing, 39 were the result of enemy action, while 10 died from non-combat-related causes; the corresponding number of wounded and injured was 26 and 5. Of the 141 Messerschmitts written off as total losses, 99 were lost due to enemy action and 42 from other causes. 13 and 33 machines sustained damage between 30 and 60%, 7 and 16 were reported with degrees of damage between 10 and 30%.

A photograph taken in the days shortly after II/JG 3's arrival in Uetersen in August 1943; seen here from the left are Gruppenkommandeur *Maj. Brändle, the commander of Uetersen air base, Lt. Max-Bruno Fischer (*Gruppen-Adjutant *of II/JG 3), and the air base commander's adjutant. (Hennig)*

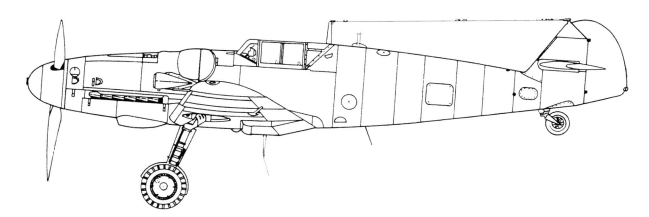

Line Drawing 8: Messerschmitt Bf 109 G-5 Y

In addition to the Bf 109 G-6, dring its rest and refit in August-September 1943 II/JG 3 received a large number of G-5 series aircraft. As successor to the G-1 and G-3 series, it was equipped with a pressurized cockpit but otherwise was similar to the Bf 109 G-6.

Length: 8.94 m	Engine: DB 605 A, 1,475 H.P.	Empty weight: 2 375 kg
Wingspan: 9.92 m	Takeoff weight: 3 435 kg	
Height: 2.60 m	Armament: 1 MG 151/20, 2 MG 131	

A photograph taken in Schiphol in early autumn 1943; in the center is the Kapitän *of 5/JG 3 Hptm. Joachim Kirschner and left Hptm. Paul Stolte, who commanded 6* Staffel.

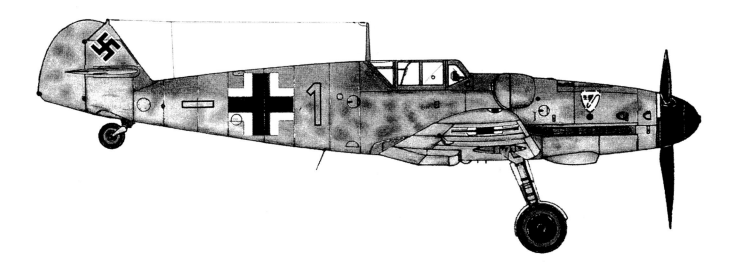

Line Drawing 9: Messerschmitt Bf 109 G-5 of II/JG 3 in gray camouflage scheme, as the aircraft appeared in autumn 1943 during operations in Holland.

There follows a series of photographs of "Black 1", the aircraft of Hptm. Joachim Kirschner, Kapitän of 5 Staffel. The machine, a Bf 109 G-6 with the WerkNr. 18 802, wears the standard dappled gray finish with a heavy overspray on the fuselage sides, which caused the gray blotches to form a very dense camouflage scheme. The aircraft number is unusual, consisting of black outlines only; this style of marking was occasionally seen on II/JG 3 aircraft in the autumn of 1943 and was probably intended to enhance the camouflage effect. The aircraft also has a tall antenna mast with no DF loop behind it and all-metal head armor. Clearly visible is the Geschwader emblem with red dot beneath it. In the photo at the top of the page several technicians of 5/JG 3 are standing in front of the aircraft; below the pilots of 5/JG 3 have gathered in front of it. (all: Wahl)

Above: Hptm. Kirschner sitting in front of the cockpit of his "Black 1". Kirschner was transferred to IV/JG 27 as Kommandeur soon after these photographs were taken. On 17 December 1943 he was shot down in air combat; Kirschner bailed out successfully but was killed by Yugoslavian partisans. Below: Fw. Helmut Notemann of 5/JG 3.

Above: Lt. Horst Brock of 6/JG 3, killed in air combat over the North Sea on 3 November 1943; below Uffz. Hugo Lucks of 4/ JG 3.

Above: Fw. Paul Draeger of 5/JG 3, killed in combat with P-51s over Halle on 2 November 1944, by which time he had been promoted to Leutnant. *Below: Obfw. Werner Kloss, also of 5/JG 3, posted missing on 18 October 1943 after a mission over the North Sea; he probably went down into the sea with his machine after running out of fuel.*

Above left: Hptm. Joachim Kirschner, Staffelkapitän *of 5/JG 3, above right Fw. Helmut Notemann. Below: The* Gruppenkommandeur *with his three* Staffelkapitäne—*from the left Hptm. Werner Lucas, Maj. Kurt Brändle, Hptm. Joachim Kirschner and Hptm. Paul Stolte, photographed on Schiphol airfield in autumn 1943. (Hennig/Wahl)*

The following four photographs depict the last machine flown by Gruppenkommandeur *Maj. Kurt Brändle, who was killed on 3 November 1943, shortly after it was delivered to the* Gruppe *at Schiphol at the end of October. After delivery the machine, a Bf 109 G-6 with the WerkNr. 26 058, was retrofitted with a clear-vision hood (the so-called "Erla hood") and the Y System in the maintenance facility located on the airfield. Interestingly, the original short antenna mast was exchanged for the older, tall mast; this was mounted on the fuselage spine behind the cockpit, which was standard practice when an aircraft was retrofitted with the Erla Hood.*

The aircraft wears a densely-mottled gray camouflage finish; in contrast to the Messerschmitts illustrated previously, the Kommandeur's *aircraft has an eye-catching white rudder, which was supposed to identify it as the aircraft of a formation leader. Also note the staff markings and* Gruppe *bar, which were painted as black outlines only. Curiously, as part of the modification work in the Erla facility the* Geschwader *emblem was "turned around." Whereas the emblem had previously been applied in II/JG 3's standard style with the "U" facing aft, later photographs show the emblem in its "correct" form, facing forward. The antenna mast for the FuG 16 ZY may be seen beneath the fuselage.*

Above: Maj. Brändle's machine once again; sitting in the cockpit is Fw. Helmut Hennig, mechanic in charge of the Kommandeur's *aircraft. Standing is Uffz. Paul Aderhold. (Hennig)*

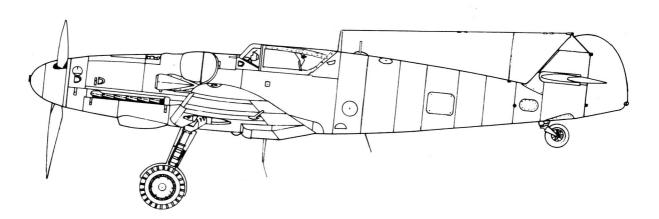

Line Drawing 10: Messerschmitt Bf 109 G-6 Y

In autumn 1943 several of II/JG 3's Messerschmitts were retrofitted with the so-called "clear vision hood," also known as the "Erla Hood," in the Erla facility on Schiphol airfield. This modification replaced the heavily framed folding canopy and the fixed rear portion with a large, glazed folding hood. The latest metal and armor-glass head armor was usually fitted. When the Erla Hood was retrofitted, the antenna mast was mounted on the fuselage spine directly aft of the cockpit; its sat on a metal plate, which in turn was attached to a tubular frame around the sloped rear wall of the cockpit. Illustrated here is a Bf 109 G-6 with retrofitted "Erla Hood," a short antenna mast on the fuselage spine, and the Morane antenna mast for the FuG 16 ZY under the fuselage.

This and top of the following page: The aircraft of the adjutant of II/JG 3, an obviously brand-new Bf 109 G-6; part of the black chevron is just visible above the wing. Beneath the Geschwader *emblem once again is a red dot, which causes the emblem to resemble a question mark. Bottom of following page: Fw. Gerhard Thyben's "Chevron Bar" in its dispersal box on Schiphol*

airfield, photographed in autumn 1943; Thyben was detached from 6 Staffel to the Gruppenstab at that time. The finish worn by this Bf 109 G-6 is relatively pale compared to the machine previously illustrated; once again the staff markings are in outline form. Note the absence of the Geschwader emblem on the engine cowling. (Wahl/Hennig)

Two photographs taken on 2 November 1943 at Osterbegrafplatz, a cemetery near Amsterdam, during the burial of Hptm. Lucas, Hptm. Stolte and Uffz. Weck, who died on 18 and 24 October. On the left in front of the assembled men is Maj. Kurt Brändle. (Wahl)

The graves of pilots of II/JG 3 who were killed in the fierce air battles over Holland in autumn 1943, including Hptm. Wilhelm Lemke, Hptm. Paul Stolte, Hptm. Werner Lucas and Fw. Walter Stienhans. (Wahl)

The following series of photographs depict aircraft of 5/JG 3 and were taken at Schiphol airfield on 11 November 1943. On this page one can see four 5 Staffel Messerschmitts, two Bf 109 G-5s ("Black 8" and "4") and two G-6s ("Black 2" and "10"). All of these aircraft wear a heavily-dappled gray finish with no significant variations. As was standard practice in the Gruppe at this time, the aircraft have no prominent colored markings; the propeller spinner are overall black and the familiar yellow finish on the engine cowling undersides is missing. As well, the white tail markings introduced by the day fighter units in autumn 1943 to identify the machines of formation leaders were not used by the Gruppe or at best only in isolated cases. Instead everything possible was done to increaze the effectiveness of the camouflage finish. Unusual, however, and typical for II/JG 3, was the mirror image version of the Geschwader emblem on the left side of the engine cowling, beneath which was painted the red dot which had originated on the Eastern Front. In the photograph above is Lt. Leopold Münster, one of the "experts" of the Gruppe; the pilot in the bottom photo is Lt. Walter Bohatsch, like Münster a member of 5 Staffel. (Wahl)

The following photos depict Lt. Leopold Münster's "Black 6", a Bf 109 G-5 with the WerkNr. 26 007; this machine also wears a heavily-dappled gray finish. Visible beneath the fuselage is the antenna for the FuG 16 ZY. (Wahl)

Here Walter Bohatsch with "Black 6". Note the head armor in the folding hood, to which an additional plate with a headrest has obviously been affixed.

Six pilots of 5/JG 3 on the way to one of their "Gustavs," a Bf 109 G-6; from the left: Lt. Leopold Münster, Lt. Walter Bohatsch, Obfw. Josef Schütte, Gefr. Rudolf Stephan, Uffz. Bönisch, unidentified, and Uffz. Rudolf Scheibe.

The same six pilots once again in front of a Bf 109 G-6. (all: Wahl)

Above: Lt. Walter Bohatsch (with peaked cap) and Lt. Leopold Münster in front of "Black 2", a Bf 109 G-6 of 5 Staffel. Below left: Obfw. Josef Schütte, one of the most experienced and successful pilots of II/JG 3, seen here soon after returning to his Staffel *after recovering from wounds suffered on 5 July 1943. Below right: Uffz. Rudolf Scheibe. (Wahl)*

Above left: Lt. Bohatsch and Fw. Kalitta, the latter of 6/JG 3, in front of "Black 2". Above right: Gefr. Stephan. Below: Two shots of Fw. Alfred Kalitta of 6/JG 3 with a Bf 109 G-6 of 5 Staffel; on the engine cowling is Obfw. Helmut Rüffler of 4 Staffel. (Wahl)

Uffz. Jäger, another pilot of 5/JG 3, seen in and beside a Bf 109 G-5; in particular note the Geschwader *emblem, painted as a mirror image, and the red dot beneath it. (Wahl)*

Two more photographs of Uffz. Rudolf Scheibe on "Black 2".

The following photographs depict the Bf 109 G-5 of Obfw. Hans Grünberg, another of 5 Staffel's "experts," seen here with a mechanic in front of his machine. Clearly visible are the identifying features of the pressurized cockpit: vertical head armor and silicagel capsules; note the two triangular armor-glass inserts in the head armor and the additional armor plate attached to the front of it. (Wahl)

Above left: Lt. Bohatsch (left) and FhjObfw. Grünberg in front of the same aircraft; the antenna mast for the FuG 16 ZY is clearly visible beneath the fuselage. Above right: Lt. Münster on the engine cowling of a Bf 109 G-6, probably "Black 6" once again; the red dot beneath the Geschwader emblem may just be seen. In the photo above right note the bulge over the air compressor for the pressurized cockpit, located in front of and below the machine-gun bulge; this was seen both on G-5s and G-6s, even though in the latter case it was superfluous. Below: Parked Messerschmitts of 5/JG 3 with a flight of three Ju 88s passing low overhead. (Wahl)

Above: One of II/JG 3's "Gustavs" makes a low-level, high-speed pass over Schiphol airfield; as usual when a Messerschmitt was in a "real hurry," the machine is leaving a clearly visible dark exhaust trail behind it. Below: One of 5/JG 3's pilots on the engine cowling of his "Gustav"; once again note the aircraft number, which consists of a black outline only. The identifying features of the pressurized cockpit—silicagel capsules in the cockpit glazing and the sealed back armor—are just visible behind the pilot. Conversely, the Geschwader *with the red dot beneath it is easily seen; on this machine, however, the emblem is pointing in the "right" direction. (Wahl)*

Above: Lt. Franz Ruhl of 4/JG 3 and a mechanic in front of his "White 10", a Bf 109 G-6 with the rare combination of tall antenna mast and DF loop. Note the unusual, obviously retouched, finish in the area behind the cockpit. Also noteworthy is the "sawtooth" pattern on the upper surface of the wing. Visible on the engine cowling is the Geschwader *emblem with the usual red dot beneath it. Below: A 4* Staffel *pilot in front of his "Gustav," a Bf 109 G-6 with the aircraft number "White 4". This machine has the short antenna mast but lacks the DF loop on the fuselage spine. (Wahl)*

Above: Two 5 Staffel *pilots with several mechanics in front of a Bf 109 G-5; note the short antenna mast and DF loop on the fuselage spine. Below: FhjObfw. Hans Grünberg of 5/JG 3, one of the few* Gruppe *'experts" left after the autumn of 1943, photographed in spring 1944. Soon after this picture was taken he was promoted to* Leutnant *and was placed in command of 5* Staffel *on 8 May 1944 following the death of Lt. Münster. Grünberg held this position until the* Gruppe *was renamed I/JG 7 at the end of 1944. (Wahl)*

Above: A Bf 109 G-5, photographed during the winter of 1943-44; the aircraft must have originally belonged to 6/JG 3 and then was later passed on to another unit in the east, where this picture was taken. It wears the standard gray camouflage scheme, which has clearly been modified in the area of the rudder. Clearly visible is the combination, typical for II/JG 3, of yellow aircraft number "12" and the short black Gruppe *bar. Below: Front view of one of II/JG 3's "Gustavs" revealing the antenna mast for the FuG 16 ZY beneath the fuselage. Also note the "Burbelschnauze" (a broad white spiral on the propeller spinner), a feature introduced after the* Gruppe's *return to the Reich and its brief rest and refit at the beginning of 1944. Rotenburg, spring 1944. (Punka via Petrick/Wahl)*

Right: Hptm. Heinrich Sannemann, who once again assumed command of 6 Staffel *following his return to II/JG 3 in October, photographed after returning from a sortie; the area of his face not covered by the mesh-type helmet is clearly darker than his forehead, possibly the result of smoke caused by engine trouble entering the cockpit. Below: Changing the engine of a Bf 109 G-6 of II/JG 3, photographed at Rotenburg in February 1944. Note the retrofitted Erla hood, the unusual finish in the area of the cockpit and the absence of a white fuselage band. Instead it appears that the machine has a narrow, dark fuselage band directly aft of the* Balkenkreuz. *Part of the black* Gruppe *bar is also just visible. (Hennig/Wahl)*

6 Staffel shortly before taking off on a mission, photographed in Rotenburg in February 1944. All of these aircraft wear a densely-mottled gray camouflage scheme and the broad white Defense of the Reich fuselage band introduced at the beginning of the year. However, in each case the band has been oversprayed gray in the area of the fuselage spine, probably to enhance the effectiveness of the camouflage. Also note the Geschwader *emblem in mirror image form and the black* Gruppe *bars on all of the Messerschmitts. (Wahl)*

Above and above left: Obfw. Helmut Rüffler and Gefr. Hans Kupka of 4/JG 3 with "White 13", a Bf 109 G-6 with the WerkNr. 411 279, photographed at Rotenburg in February 1944. This machine was lost in action on 21 February 1944 while being flown by Gefr. Kupka; during an engagement near Eimbeck a shell exploded in the barrel of the engine cannon, injuring the pilot and forcing him to bail out. Below left: More 4 Staffel pilots, photographed at Rotenburg on the same occasion. Below right: Lt. Walter Bohatsch; this photograph was probably taken in front of the dispensary in Rotenburg, where he received medical treatment after sustaining minor wounds on 20 February 1944. Bohatsch's joy at having survived his ordeal is evident in the photo. (Wahl)

Above and Following: Four photos of Lt. Max-Bruno Fischer, the Gruppen-Adjutant *of II/JG 3, taken following his return from a defensive mission on 24 February 1944 in which he shot down a B-24 for his sixth victory. His aircraft, a Bf 109 G-6 with the staff marking "Black Chevron", wears the familiar, heavily-mottled gray finish. Clearly visible are the broad white spiral on the propeller spinner, the mirror image* Geschwader *emblem with the red dot beneath it, and the retrofitted Erla hood with the antenna mast on the fuselage spine behind it. (Fischer/Wahl)*

Above: "Black 5", a Bf 109 G-6 of 5/JG 3, photographed at Rotenburg in the spring of 1944; this machine also wears a dappled gray finish and has been retrofitted with an Erla hood. Note the octane triangle, partly superimposed on the aircraft number. Below: "Yellow 12" of 6 Staffel. Pilot Fw. Johannes Hoyer was obliged to make a wheels-up landing as a result of battle damage sustained in combat with heavy bombers at the beginning of 1944 and fortunately survived the incident unhurt. Just visible is the white fuselage band with the short black Gruppe bar superimposed on it. (Wahl/Lächler)

Two young pilots of II/JG 3 in a Bf 109 G-6, photographed in spring 1944; both photos reveal details of the cockpit area. (Wahl)

Above: One of II Gruppe's *"gunboats" after a one-wheel landing at Gardelegen in the spring of 1944; not surprisingly the propeller has sustained significant damage. The aircraft's short black* Gruppe *bar is superimposed on a white fuselage band, which has been overpainted gray in the area of the fuselage spine. Below: "Black 12", a Bf 109 G-6 of 5/JG 3 equipped with underwing cannon, photographed at Gardelegen on 18 March 1944. The* Gruppe *bar is superimposed on a white fuselage band, most of which has been overpainted gray. (Wahl)*

Above: aircraft of the Gruppenstab *of II/JG 3 at Gardelegen airfield; on the left is the machine of* Gruppenkommandeur *Hptm. Detlev Rohwer, which obviously does not wear a horizontal* Gruppe *bar. Next to it are two machines with number codes, while the Messerschmitt on the far right apparently has no codes at all. Note that every aircraft with a white fuselage band has had this overpainted gray on the fuselage spine. Below: Lt. Franz Ruhl,* Staffelkapitän *of 4/JG 3, photographed at Gardelegen in spring 1944; he is wearing the German Cross in Gold, which was awarded to him in February 1944. (Lächler/Wahl)*

Right: Lt. Leopold Münster, Kapitän *of 5/JG 3, in the leather flight suit which was first issued in spring 1944. This machine clearly wears the mirror image version of the* Geschwader *emblem. Below: One of II/JG 3's technicians dozes on a "dummy cow"; such mock-ups were placed on landing fields in an attempt to deceive Allied reconnaissance pilots into mistaking second-line airfields for pastures. (Wahl)*

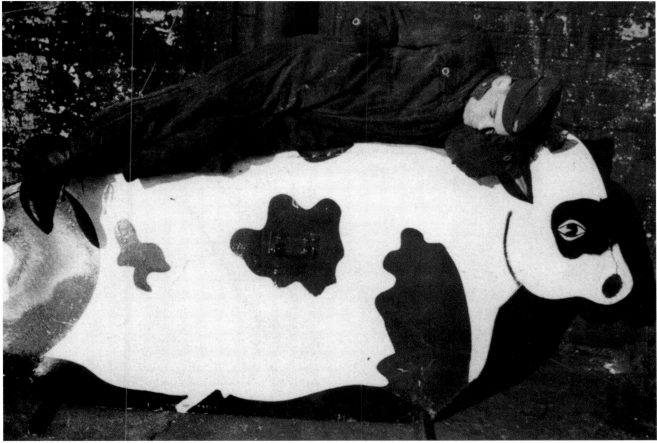

These photographs are purported to show Lt. Leopold Münster's crash site near Hildesheim after the wreckage of his machine had been collected and transported away. (Wahl)

The remains of Lt. Münster's "Black 1" collected on the surface are transported away in the back of a truck; some pieces of the rear fuselage can be made out. (Wahl)

The following photos depict "Yellow 3", a Bf 109 G-6 of 6/JG 3, at Sachau in May 1944. Several of the Staffel's pilots have gathered in front of the aircraft. Above, from left to right, are Uffz. Franz Glassauer, Fw. Albert Zanterl, Fw. Johannes Hoyer, Uffz. Berges, FhjFw. Walter Becker and Uffz. Josef Wester. Note the broad white spiral on the propeller spinner, the underwing cannon and comparatively pale and very lightly mottled finish on the fuselage sides. (Wahl)

Two of 6/JG 3's most experienced pilots during this most difficult period in the Defense of the Reich were Fw. Zanterl (above left) and FhjFw. Becker, seen here on "Yellow 3".

Above and below left: "Yellow 3" of 6 Staffel *once again. Below right: Another of 6* Staffel's *Bf 109 G-6s, this time with neither underwing cannon nor drop tank mount. (Wahl)*

Right: Uffz. Heiner Geisthövel, a pilot in 6/JG 3, on the nose of his aircraft, a Bf 109 G-6. On 12 May 1944, a few days after this photo was taken, Geisthövel was shot down in air combat over the Taunus Region but was able to parachute to safety. Note that this machine does not have the white spiral standard at this time, instead the otherwise dark propeller spinner has a relatively "soft-edged" pale segment. Below: View of II/JG 3's airfield at Sachau. One machine is visible in front of the forest edge, obviously undergoing an engine change; another Messerschmitt, pushed into the forest edge, is visible in the center of the photo. (Geisthövel via Bracke/Wahl)

9

Operations Against the Invasion of France
6 June to 22 August 1944

"Operation Overlord," the Allied invasion on the coast of Normandy, began on 6 June 1944. Supported by overwhelming air and sea forces, on the very first day the Allies were able to put ashore 156,000 troops with heavy weapons and large amounts of materiel[971].

On the German side, plans had existed for some time to meet an anticipated Allied landing on the continent. These called for the *Luftwaffe* to transfer a total of nineteen day fighter *Gruppen* from *Luftflotte Reich* to *Luftflotte 3* based in France; this would result in 800 to 1,000 fighters being available to counter the invasion. To accommodate these units, one hundred forward airfields had been prepared within a 500-kilometer radius of Normandy, the majority of them on either side of Paris. The transfer of the units from *Luftflotte Reich* was supposed to take place immediately after the start of the landings[972].

Among the units earmarked for counter-invasion operations was II/JG 3[973]. While the remaining elements of the *"UDET"* *Geschwader* were assigned airfields west of the Seine in the Evreux area, placing them closer to the actual landing area (only about 100 km from the coast) than any other unit. With the transfer to France, the *Geschwader* was subordinated to *II Fliegerkorps*, which was responsible for the close-support units assigned to defend against the Allied invasion. In the first days of June, with the Allied invasion of the European mainland expected to begin any day, an attempt was made to quickly raise the *Gruppe*'s strength by increasing allocations of men and machines[974, 975]. As a result, on 6 June 1944 II/JG 3 had approximately fifty serviceable Messerschmitts. All preparations for defensive operations against the expected Allied invasion took place under conditions of maximum secrecy and were code-named *"Dr. Gustav West"*[976].

The *Luftwaffe*'s contingency plans called for the affected fighter and fighter-bomber units to fly to their designated airfields in France as soon as the invasion began, and in fact the necessary orders were issued on 6 June[977]. In spite of this, II/JG 3 did not begin its transfer until the following day, 7 June 1944, probably on account of the bad weather which covered large areas of northwestern and western Germany. Several Ju 52s transported the leading technical personnel from Sachau to Evreux, where they were to prepare the airfield to accept the *Geschwaderstab* and II/JG 3. The flight apparently proceeded without serious problem; meanwhile, the bulk of the ground personnel were supposed to follow in trucks. The transfer flight by the air element did not proceed quite so smoothly, however. *Gruppenkommandeur* Hptm. Frielinghaus was still not fit to fly, and Oblt. Max-Bruno Fischer, the *Gruppe-Adjutant*, was placed in charge of the flight, which turned into a complete disaster. After an en route stop at Frankfurt-Eschborn, bad weather caused the *Gruppe* formation to become completely dispersed. A number of aircraft crashed or made forced landings on account of bad weather and lack of fuel. As well, the inadequate training which the young replacement pilots had received resulted in many of them getting lost, which caused further forced landings. In the end, Oblt. Fischer was the only pilot of the *Gruppe* to reach Evreux by the direct route[978]. Fortunately for the *Gruppe*, the cost of this debacle was just one pilot killed and another who was temporarily reported missing but who later turned up with minor injuries. Losses in machines totaled two Messerschmitts written off and eight with varying degrees of damage. Both personnel losses affected 6/JG 3: Uffz. Kurt Steinacker flew into the ground in conditions of poor visibility near Letzlingen, while Uffz. Egon Spinner was slightly injured when he belly-landed his machine near Romilly for reasons unknown[979]. The disastrous transfer flight had consequences for Oblt. Fischer, for as the formation leader he had to submit himself to an investigation by a court-martial. The matter was dropped after the energetic intervention of Maj. Kurt Bühligen, the *Kommodore* of JG 2. Bühligen argued that they absolutely should not punish Oblt. Fischer, the only pilot who reached his specified destination. Instead, those who should answer for their actions were the pilots who had become separated from their unit and subsequently had to put down their machines "somewhere in the countryside"[980].

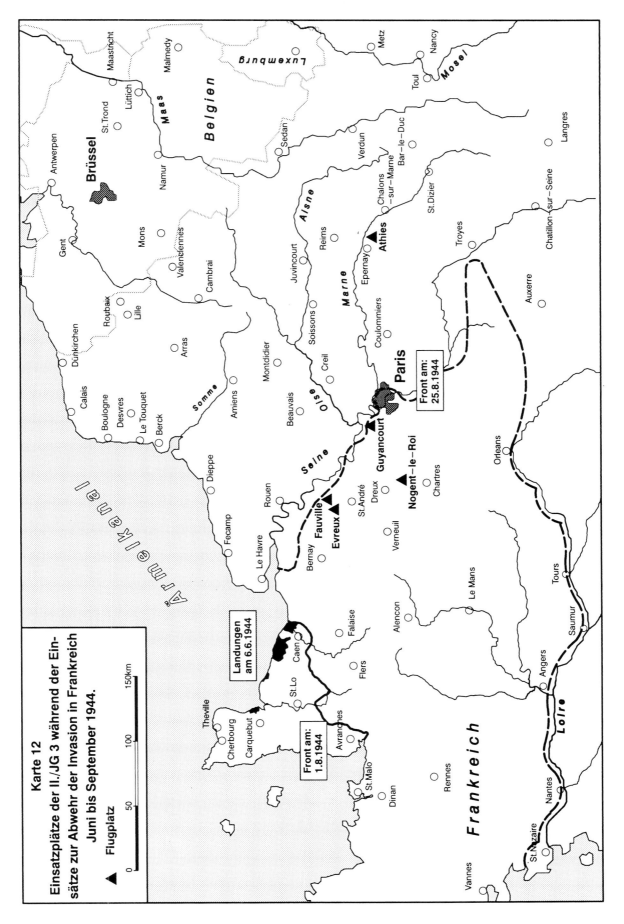

Karte 12

Einsatzplätze der II./JG 3 während der Einsätze zur Abwehr der Invasion in Frankreich Juni bis September 1944.

▲ Flugplatz

Armelkanal

Front am: 25.8.1944

Landungen am 6.6.1944

Front am: 1.8.1944

The operational conditions which II/JG 3 found at Evreux left the men no time to reflect on the events of their transfer; the airfield was only about 80 kilometers from the eastern landing zones in the Seine Bay and consequently it was watched almost constantly by British and American fighters and fighter-bombers. This proximity to the front was the unavoidable consequence of using II/JG 3 as a *Jabogruppe* (III *Gruppe* faced a similar situation). While carrying bombs, the Messerschmitts were left with just their internal fuel, which meant that they could not be based further inland if they were to reach their targets—landing craft and transports in the Seine Bay. After the machines which had landed elsewhere straggled into Evreux on 7 June, the technical personnel immediately had their hands full fitting the Messerschmitts with the external bomb racks flown in by the Ju 52s. In most cases this was completed by early the next morning.

Command List II/JG 3 on 7 June 1944	
Gruppenkommandeur	Hptm. Gustav Frielinghaus
Gruppenadjutant	Oblt. Max-Bruno Fischer
Staffelkapitän 4/JG 3	Lt. Franz Ruhl
Staffelkapitän 5/JG 3	Lt. Hans Grünberg
Staffelkapitän 6/JG 3	Lt. Oskar Zimmermann

The *Gruppe* flew its first missions over the landing area on 8 June 1944. The events of this day provided both the pilots in the air and the ground crews with a clear and immediate demonstration of the ratio of forces which would mark the defensive mission in France during the following weeks. Once the Allies realized that Evreux was occupied by an operational German unit, their virtually omnipresent fighters and fighter-bombers (mainly P-51s and P-47s but also Spitfires and Typhoons in large numbers) made it impossible for the *Gruppe* to conduct regular operations. Under these conditions, takeoff times were dictated by the brief gaps in Allied air coverage over the airfield, not by the orders issued by the commanders of *II Fliegerkorps*. II/JG 3's mission orders on this day read: attack shipping and enemy forces north of Caen in the area of the Orne estuary[981]. These orders resulted in fierce battles with numerically-superior formations of Allied fighters. The end result was two pilots killed and five machines lost, while the *Gruppe* failed to shoot down any enemy aircraft and achieved little with the bombs it dropped. Both pilot casualties came from 5 *Staffel*. Lt. Walter Marizy and Uffz. Heinz Schmidt were initially reported missing after air combat, however both were later found dead. The picture was the same on 9 June: in spite of mainly cloudy weather with frequent periods of rain, the *Gruppe* once again had to mount fighter-bomber attacks against shipping targets and ground troops in the area north of Caen and in the Orne estuary. The *Gruppe* suffered no pilot casualties on this day and the only aircraft loss was a Messerschmitt which crashed for reasons other than enemy action.

On the other hand, the *Gruppe* was again unable to claim any successes for itself.

On the following day, 10 June 1944, the Allied troops succeeded in expanding their landing zones into a continuous bridgehead. After a strong counterattack by Panzer Group West had to be broken off without success on 9 June, the success of the Allied landing in France was assured and the hope of a rapid counterattack to drive the invasion forces back into the sea with was already gone for good[982]. On this day the *Luftwaffe* had available 475 Messerschmitts and Focke Wulfs, of which 290 were serviceable. Four days after the start of the invasion, therefore, the *Luftwaffe*'s strength in France was still far from what the plans for the defense of the west had stipulated for the first day; in spite of ruthlessly stripping the Defense of the Reich, it never succeeded in altering the ratio of forces over the invasion area to less than 1 : 25 to the disadvantage of the *Luftwaffe*[983].

A war diary entry[984] concerning the enemy's activities made on this day reveals a certain hopelessness:

Enemy Activity: Over the entire beachhead and the hinterland four-engined bombers and fighter units active continuously from dawn until dark.

The enemy activity referred to in the war diary entry included a mission by a total of 883 heavy bombers of the US 8th Air Force. Guarded by a powerful fighter escort, the bombers carried out destructive attacks on a series of *Luftwaffe* airfields inland from the landing zones[985]. II/JG 3 felt the effects of the American heavy bombers first hand, for in the morning a group of 65 Liberators placed 65 tons of bombs[986] on Evreux, devastating the airfield. Miraculously, the *Gruppe* escaped serious damage. Another carpet bombing raid struck III/JG 3's base at St. André, wrecking the airfield and "bombing out" the *Gruppe*, as the unit war diary recorded laconically[987]. This was the only cause for relief, however, for the outcome of the day's missions can only be characterized as catastrophic. Once again the mission orders called for fighter-bomber attacks against targets in the area north of Caen[988], and once again the result was bitter dogfights with far-superior groups of American fighters. The *Gruppe*'s losses on this day totaled seven pilots killed plus ten Messerschmitts written off and two damaged. The only victory recorded by the *Gruppe* was a Mustang shot down by Uffz. Agricola of 5 *Staffel* (3). 4 *Staffel* lost three pilots killed: Obfw. Kurt Kundrus, Uffz. Ulrich Gehrke and Uffz. Robert Kanthak were all shot down and killed in the area of Caen. 5/JG 3 reported two pilots killed: Uffz. Bernhard Haupt and Uffz. Kurt Wahl[989] were shot down by enemy fighters during a fighter-bomber mission into the Douvres area, crashing at Huest and Normanville, respectively. They had probably been intercepted by Mustangs en route to the target, and in their bomb-laden Messerschmitts they had no chance against their American attackers. 6 *Staffel* also lost two pilots: Lt. Albert Zanzerl and Uffz. Berthold Zürtz failed to return after air combat and were later found dead.

During the day, the main column of ground personnel arrived at Evreux, where the technicians immediately set to work repairing those Messerschmitts which the advance detachment had lacked the resources to tackle. After just three days of operations in France, the number of serviceable Messerschmitts had already dropped by one half; as a result, *Gruppe* missions (usually three per day) were limited to about 15 to 20 machines[990].

On 11 June 1944 the number of sorties flown by German aircraft over the invasion zone sank to just 317. In spite of the reinforcements received in the previous days, this was exactly two less than the weak forces already in France had been able to fly on 6 June, the day the invasion began[991]. The fighter units fared even worse: compared to the 172 sorties flown on 6 June, the fifteen *Gruppen* now in France flew just 126 sorties—less than ten per *Gruppe* on average! The first cries of *"Where is the Luftwaffe?"* were heard from the hard-pressed army units, which by day they were exposed to almost ceaseless attacks by American and British fighter-bombers, making their life a living hell[992]. These conditions were made even worse by the fact that the Allies immediately set about establishing landing fields in their bridgeheads; the first makeshift airfield at St. Croix-sur-Mer went into operation on 10 June. The more the Allied fighter-bombers could operate from these airfields, the more obvious became their numerical superiority over the battlefields of Normandy, for while an Allied fighter-bomber's average sortie lasted only ten minutes, most of the German fighters had to fly more than 150 kilometers from their bases around Paris in order to reach the battle zone—provided they were not intercepted first[993,994].

Very little is known about II/JG 3's activities on this day. It appears that further *Jabo* missions were flown against the Allied landing zones; the *Gruppe* reported neither successes nor casualties in the air, one machine was damaged in a belly landing after it developed mechanical trouble.

12 June 1944: Some elements of the German command were finally coming to the realization that the landing operations under way since 6 June were in fact the main Allied attack and the necessary reserves and reinforcements were being sent to the west[995]. Meanwhile, in the western sector of the landing zone, American units were on the point of breaking through to the west coast of the Cotentin Peninsula, which would isolate the port of Cherbourg from the German front. This would have fatal consequences for the German defensive effort, for with the large, deep-water port of Cherbourg in their hands, the Allies would no longer have to land men and materiel on the coast.

On this day masses of Allied aircraft were again active over the landing zone and the rear areas. The four-engined bombers of the US 8th Air Force alone flew 1,442 sorties against 16 airfields and six railway bridges in the area around the landing zone, while just under 1,000 fighters of VIII FC flew fighter sweeps and fighter-bomber sorties. Units of the 9th Air Force and the RAF were also active in large numbers[996]. By the end of the day the number of sorties flown by the Allied units since the start of the invasion had reached 49,000, in the course of which they had dropped approximately 42,000 tons of bombs[997]. On 12 June 1944 the units of *Luftflotte 3* flew a total of 460 sorties, with the lion's share, 400, by the day fighter *Gruppen*[998].

II/JG 3 was apparently untouched by the American bombing on this day, for it reported no losses on the ground. Things were much different in the air, however. The *Gruppe* was again ordered to attack targets in the battle zone north of Caen, carry out free chases and engage enemy fighter-bombers over the area behind the front[999]. Losses were heavy, with two pilots killed, one wounded and five aircraft shot down in air combat[1000]. 4/JG 3 lost Fw. Paul Kipulski[1001], who was shot down by enemy fighters during a free chase mission in the Caen area, crashing near La Bataille. 5 *Staffel* reported two casualties: Obgefr. Heinz Wagner and Gefr. Johann Elwischger were both shot down by enemy fighters during a fighter-bomber mission into the area north of Caen. Wagner went down with his "Black 10" near Val-David, while Elwischger was more fortunate, bailing out severely wounded near Orgeville east of Evreux. 6/JG 3 suffered no casualties and was able to shoot down three P-47s, which fell to Lt. Zimmermann (23), Uffz. Löhlein (1) and Lt. Hecker (4) in an engagement north of Dreux.

The picture was much the same on 13 June 1944: by day the sky over the invasion area belonged to the bombers, fighter-bombers and fighters of the Allied air forces, which again carried out attacks against road and rail targets, bridges and airfields[1002]. Once again the number of sorties flown by the *Luftwaffe* was only a fraction of those logged by the Allied units—a total of 761 sorties were recorded on 13 June 1944, the majority of them (476) by the day fighters. So far the missions by the fighter units assigned to *II Fliegerkorps* in the fighter-bomber role had been largely unsuccessful and costly. Beginning on this day, therefore, the fruitless fighter-bomber missions by the day fighter *Gruppen* were abandoned and the focus of operations instead shifted to keeping enemy fighters and fighter-bombers away from the army's main supply roads[1003]. The concentration of forces in support of the army went so far that Allied bomber units were virtually given a free hand to carry out their attacks on transportation targets, troop concentrations, airfields and any other worthy tactical targets[1004]. Even after this change in tactics, the German fighters remained hopelessly outnumbered, and their efforts were unable to significantly alter the situation. At the same time, the various German command authorities had very different ideas about what the mission of the German fighters should be. While the *Luftwaffe* command was mainly interested in shooting down enemy aircraft, *II Jagdkorps* reached the conclusion that a limited fighter screen over the battlefield would be more effective in assisting the army. Behind this was the realization that the most favorable loss ratio achieved to date had been 1 : 1. Whereas the loss of 50 aircraft was not particularly serious to the overpowering Allied air forces, for the German side it represented approximately 10 percent of its actual strength[1005].

Following the order halting fighter-bomber missions, II/JG 3 received instructions to immediately retrofit all machines for the fighter role. At the same time it left the command of *II Fliegerkorps* and was attached to *5 Jagddivision* under *Oberst* Hentschel. The experiences of the fighter units in the first week of the battle in France also led to some fundamental changes in tactics. From now on, several *Gruppen* would be combined into battle units as had been done in the Defense of the Reich. The purpose of this was to enable the German fighters to penetrate the powerful Allied fighter screen to reach the forward combat zone and the army forces in need of air support[1006].

By this date II/JG 3 had accounted for all of four victories—of the 195 claimed by the *Jagdgruppen* in France[1007]. But as brave and self-sacrificial as the efforts of the German fighters were, against the overwhelming Allied air presence such meager successes had little effect. Furthermore, these successes were out of all proportion to their own losses. The losses in men and materiel[1008] were such that they could scarcely be made good, and consequently the *Gruppe*'s fighting power and combat strength had very quickly fallen to worrying levels.

The next day, 14 June 1944, the US 8th Air Force repeated its attacks on the *Luftwaffe*'s ground organization in the hinterland of Normandy, dispatching 1,525 heavy bombers and 908 fighters and fighter-bombers. At the same time, large numbers of twin-engined bombers and fighter-bombers of the 9th Air Force and the RAF were in action in the skies over Normandy. On the German side, beginning on this day efforts were made to send the *Jagdgruppen* into action in the maximum concentration possible. In the days to come II/JG 3 would often see action with III/JG 3, which was now based at the Francheville landing strip, but also with elements of JG 11, 26, 27, 53 and 54. Little is known about this day's activities; apart from two Messerschmitts damaged as a result of mechanical problems, there were no significant results. The next day, 15 June, the *Gruppe* fought a pitched battle with a mixed group of P-47s and P-51s during an early morning mission west of Evreux. Four enemy machines were shot down, two of them by Fw. Otto Florian (11-12), while the *Gruppe*'s losses amounted to two machines. Fortunately, the pilots of both machines escaped injury.

After the next two days' missions proved fruitless, on 17 June 1944 II/JG 3 received orders to move to a landing field near Fauville, northeast of Evreux[1009]. The purpose of this move was obviously to escape the almost constant surveillance which had made operational conditions at its previous base completely unbearable. The fact that the *Gruppe* had so far escaped any losses on the ground was sheer luck[1010]. At Fauville the *Gruppe* was widely dispersed, with quar-

ters spread among the surrounding villages, some of them several kilometers from the airfield. Furthermore, on account of the constant danger of carpet bombing, the order was issued that, in addition to the pilots, only the most necessary technical personnel and equipment were to be kept at the airfield. Much energy was devoted to digging slit trenches and one-man holes.

Very little is known about II/JG 3's operational activities between 18 and 20 June. Bad weather restricted the activities of both sides on these days, while since 18 June the units of the US 8th Air Force had resumed their attacks on targets within the Reich. Only rarely would they intervene in the fighting in France[1011]. During an evening free chase mission in the Caen area on 20 June, west of the city the *Gruppe* engaged a number of P-51s. One enemy fighter was shot down by Uffz. Engler of 4 *Staffel* (4) in return for the loss of three machines. Fw. Otto Florian of 4/JG 3, one of the *Gruppe*'s experienced pilots with twelve victories, was reported missing after he was last seen west of Bernay[1012]. On 20 June the air element of II/JG 5 was supposed to arrive at Evreux, where it was to be placed under the operational control of II/JG 3. During the transfer flight from Wiesbaden, however, the *Gruppe* became completely dispersed, and only three Messerschmitts arrived at Evreux. The rest followed the next day[1013].

After a return to better weather, in the days that followed II/JG 3 saw action over the eastern and central sectors of the invasion front around Caen and Bayeux together with II/JG 5. The majority of the missions flown were free chases and sweeps in search of enemy fighter-bombers. Enemy aircraft were encountered on almost every mission, and in spite of the fact that the *Gruppe* had been moved back, the Messerschmitts were repeatedly intercepted by superior numbers of Allied fighters long before they reached the front and engaged in tough, costly dogfights. While successes were few (a total of six victories between 21 and 25 June 1944), the *Gruppe* continued to lose men and machines. Three aircraft were lost in air combat on 22 June, another on the 23rd and five more on the 24th; II/JG 3 scored no victories on any of these days. Luckily for the *Gruppe*, there were no pilot casualties. 25 June 1944 was a black day for the *Gruppe*[1014]. Late in the morning II/JG 3's base at Evreux-Fauville was bombed and strafed by 43 P-47s of the VIII FC; ten Messerschmitts were damaged on the ground, but fortunately there were no casualties. The surviving machines scrambled after the attackers, which resulted in a fierce dogfight south and east of Evreux with the P-47s and some Mustangs which had apparently been summoned by radio. II/JG 3 scored six victories, however these came at the cost of four pilots killed or missing and one seriously wounded plus eleven Messerschmitts, of which eight were written off as total losses. 4/JG 3 lost two pilots killed: Uffz. Gerhard Siegmund and Uffz. Emil Scheidt failed to return following combat in the Dreux area and were reported missing[1015]. 5 *Staffel* also lost two pilots: Uffz. Johann Vahle[1016] and Gefr. Helmut Eckart were shot down east of Dreux and went down with their machines. 6

Staffel got off relatively lightly with one pilot seriously wounded: Uffz. Günter Tippel was shot down in air combat and came down near Marcilly.

After the morning's heavy losses the *Gruppe* was no longer capable of operations, and it was apparently for this reason that the order was issued the same day for it to be withdrawn from action. II/JG 3 was to go to Guyancourt, a well-equipped air base west of Paris[1017], where the air element was to be completely reequipped. In the days that followed, the *Gruppe* received a complete complement of new Messerschmitts, which were hastily accepted, checked over and test flown. Four days later II/JG 3 was sent back into action[1018]. At the same time it received a new *Gruppenkommandeur*: in place of Hptm. Gustav Frielinghaus, who was still not fit for duty, Maj. Hans-Ekkehard Bob, who had been flying with the *Geschwaderstab* since the end of May 1944, was placed in command of the *Gruppe*[1019,1020]. At this time Bob had 60 victories to his credit, most of them scored on the Channel in 1940-41 and in the east, and he had worn the Knight's Cross since March 1941[1021].

The *Gruppe*'s stay at Guyancourt was a brief one, for on 29 June 1944 an order was issued for II/JG 3 to return to operations. That same day the *Gruppe* was supposed to transfer to Nogent-le-Roi, a forward airfield about 15 kilometers south-southeast of Dreux, where, in the meantime, the ground personnel that had been left behind when the air element moved from Dreux to Guyancourt had prepared the field for the air element's arrival[1022]. The very next day, 30 June, II *Gruppe* resumed operations from Nogent-le-Roi. That evening, during a *Gruppe*-strength armed reconnaissance and free chase mission over the area of the Seine Estuary between Caen and Lisieux (Grid Square UU / UA), there was a fierce dogfight with a unit of Thunderbolts which was soon joined by some Mustangs. Four victories, including Obfw. Rüffler's 60th, were scored for the loss of two pilots killed, two wounded and seven Messerschmitts. 4 *Staffel* reported two casualties: Obgefr. Helmut Hötzel was shot down and killed by enemy fighters, while Obgefr. Helmut Dieter was severely wounded and came down 10 kilometers southeast of Breuil-en-Auge. 5/JG 3 reported Uffz. Gerhard Koslowski missing after he failed to return following combat with P-47s and P-51s. 6 *Staffel* recorded one pilot casualty: Gefr. Walter Bonder was shot down near Port Audemer and seriously wounded[1023,1024]. At the end of the day the *Gruppe*, which had just been brought up to strength, still numbered 44 Messerschmitts, of which 22 were serviceable. Personnel strength was reported as 42 pilots, of which just 22 were with the *Gruppe*[1025].

At the end of June the front line of the Allied bridgehead in Normandy ran from east of the mouth of the Orne approximately 20 kilometers inland, then in a gentle arc north of Caen to Villiers, and from there in a generally northwest direction in front of St. Lô to a few kilometers south of Barneville on the west coast of the Cotentin. The focal point of the fighting continued to be the Caen area in the British sector and, after the fighting had ended on the northern tip of the Cotentin west of Cherbourg, in the area around St. Lô. Immediately after the end of the battle for Cherbourg, the Allies set about clearing the port, and in spite of the extensive devastation they soon succeeded in putting the port into operation, using it to deliver troops and supplies.

In the first two weeks of July 1944 the focal point of II/JG 3's operations was the eastern invasion zone between the mouth of the Orne and the area around Bayeux. The most common missions were free chases and fighter-bomber hunts, low-level attacks in support of the army or fighter cover over army units and supply lines in the rear, favorite targets of the Allied fighter-bombers. In many cases missions were flown together with the remnants of III/JG 3[1026]. For II/JG 3, conditions at Nogent-le-Roi were not significantly better than they had been at Evreux. Its new base of operations was even closer to the front, and the *Gruppe* remained the most forward-based unit, most of the others having meanwhile been withdrawn to airfields in the Paris area and on the Loire. At Nogent-le-Roi, too, the Mustangs and Thunderbolts lurked near the airfield almost continuously, ready to pounce on any Messerschmitt taking off or returning with empty tanks[1027]. The results of the missions in the first week of July were depressing and demonstrated clearly the almost powerless inferiority of the German fighters: without scoring a single victory, II/JG 3 lost one pilot killed, two wounded and twelve Messerschmitts in action. Three more aircraft were seriously damaged as a result of accidents or mechanical malfunctions. On 5 July, while escorting a reconnaissance aircraft, two Messerschmitts of 5 *Staffel* were shot down in a fierce battle with Allied fighters in the Caen area. Uffz. Franz Hametner came down near Evreux with severe wounds; he was recovered but died later in hospital. Uffz. Kurt Poppitz was more fortunate. He was reported missing after his "White 11" was shot down, however he was later able to rejoin his *Gruppe* unhurt[1028]. There were two more casualties at the conclusion of the mission. Uffz. Heinz Pelletier, also of 4/JG 3, overturned on landing at Sucy and sustained serious injuries, while Obfhr. Werner Schulze was killed when his aircraft overturned on landing at Villacoublay. The second week of July represented something of a counterpoint, for during this period II/JG 3 reported no casualties in the air or on the ground; it also failed to achieve any successes.

At this time the *Gruppe* was reinforced through the assignment of an additional *Staffel* which was to be subordinated to II/JG 3 for subsequent defensive operations. It was 4/JG 52, commanded by Lt. Hans Waldmann. The *Staffel* had been withdrawn from the Eastern Front as part of measures taken at the end of May 1944 to bolster the Defense of the Reich[1029]. Now it joined II/JG 3 at Nogent-le-Roi. The new unit's most successful pilot was *Staffelführer* Lt. Hans Waldmann, who had 125 victories to his credit and had worn the Knight's Cross since February 1944[1030]. Within II/JG 3 the unit was known as the "Waldmann *Staffel*". There was also a change in the command of 4 *Staffel* after Lt. Franz Ruhl was temporarily taken out of action because of mental and physical exhaustion and sent to hospital[1031]. His place was taken by Hptm. Herbert Kutscha. Herbert Kutscha had been *Staffelkapitän* of 12/JG 3 until 24 February 1944, when he was seriously wounded. On that date he had 32 victories to his credit. Kutscha had been awarded the Knight's Cross in September 1942 while serving as a *Zerstörer* pilot with II/ZG 1. He received the decoration in recognition of his 22 victories and many successful low-level attack missions in the east[1032].

II/JG 3's range of missions remained unchanged in the second half of the month, which meant that the unit's remaining weak forces mainly flew free chases and fighter-bomber hunts over the area of front on either side of Caen, low-level attacks against tank and vehicle concentrations, escort for reconnaissance aircraft, and road protection missions. The *Gruppe* frequently flew missions with the remnants of JG 1, 2 and 26 as well as with III/JG 3. The latter unit had been transferred to the rear and was operating from a second-line airfield near Chartres[1033]. Almost every mission during this period resulted in contact with the enemy. In the face of overwhelming Allied superiority in the air, even the concentration of the *Luftwaffe*'s remaining fighter forces had little effect. On those rare occasions when German fighters did break through the Allied fighter screen, their low-level attacks had no effect whatsoever on the fighting on the ground and went almost unnoticed by the hard-pressed German ground forces. The number of air victories also remained low, while losses continued to mount and reached shocking levels. In the skies over Normandy the fighter arm for the first time experienced losses which were comparable to what the infantry had been enduring for a long time. Consequently, a description of the *Gruppe*'s activities during this time is essentially nothing more than a survey of its losses.

During the period from 15 to 21 July 1944, II/JG 3 reported just nine victories, however in the same time its losses were seven pilots killed and two wounded plus twenty aircraft, eleven of which were written off. After the experiences of recent days, 16 July brought a brief ray of hope, for on this day the *Gruppe* claimed six Spitfires shot down in return for two Messerschmitts damaged in combat. Two days later, however, on 18 July, the superiority of the P-51 again turned the tables. During a free chase mission into the Caen area the *Gruppe* fought a fierce battle with a gaggle of Mustangs and subsequently reported the loss of five pilots killed, two wounded, and eleven aircraft. All that it could manage in return was three victories. 4/JG 3 reported one pilot seriously wounded: after shooting down two P-51s (62-63), Obfw. Helmut Rüffler was shot down 45 km southeast of Caen. His wounds put him out of action for several months[1034]. Thus, within a short period of time, 4 *Staffel* had thus lost its two remaining *"Experten"* (Rüffler, who had often led the unit in the air in recent weeks, and Lt. Ruhl)[1035]. While 5 *Staffel* was spared any losses on this day, 6 *Staffel* was hit very hard, with three pilots killed. Lt. Robert Roller, Uffz. Lorenz Stephan and Uffz. Alfred Lenz were shot down and killed in air combat near Caen. Three casualties were also sustained by 4/JG

52, its first in the west. Lt. Manfred Fedgenhäuer and Flg. Alfred Feistel were killed in combat with Mustangs, while Fw. Walter Ehrhardt was forced to belly-land his shot-up "Blue 1" near Chérisy. The latter sustained such serious injuries that he later died in hospital in Chartres. The next day, on 19 July, Gefr. Emmerich Berger of 4/JG 3 was killed in air combat northeast of Laval, and on the 20th Uffz. Rudolf Wick of 5 *Staffel* was shot down and killed by Spitfires near Amfreville during an escort mission for a *Gruppe* of Focke Wulfs. All in all, the shattering balance for the last three days was three victories scored in return for seven pilots killed, two wounded and eleven machines written off. Given the *Gruppe*'s weak state, the loss of nine pilots represented almost half of its available strength. Inevitably, this had an effect on the morale of the survivors: after seeing so many of their comrades go down in blazing machines or die when their machines exploded under fire from Mustangs or Spitfires, it is inevitable that many of the pilots began placing more importance on their own survival than on plunging into aerial combat without regard for their own safety[1036]. Another factor was the catastrophically poor level of training of the new pilots sent to the front. Many were just capable of taking off and landing, and in combat against a technically-superior and more experienced foe they had no chance. We will never know how many of these inexperienced pilots become separated from their units and then simply froze when they found an enemy fighter on their tail[1037].

At this time, shortly after 20 July 1944, there was another change in the command of II/JG 3. Maj. Bob, who had led the *Gruppe* for barely a month[1038,1039], was replaced by Hptm. Herbert Kutscha, who had most recently been *Staffelführer* of 4/JG 3. Some time later Lt. Franz Ruhl rejoined his *Gruppe* after completing his rest leave and once again assumed of his old *Staffel*[1040].

On the ground, in the days that followed, operations were focused in two areas. One was the area around St. Lô, the shattered remains of which had fallen into American hands during the night of 19 July[1041] and where the Americans were trying to break out of the western landing zone into Brittany. The other was the Caen area, where British forces had launched a new offensive ("Operation Goodwood") on 18 July. Its immediate objective was the capture of Caen, while the operation's long-range goal was to breach the German front or at least tie down strong German forces so as to prevent their transfer to the St. Lô area. A number of German units were overrun or wiped out in the bitter fighting near Caen, however the grim resistance put up by the German regiments once again prevented the British from achieving a decisive success[1042]. On the other hand, the critical situation in the western part of the front near St. Lô continued to become more acute.

Accordingly, at the end of the month the focal point of II/JG 3's activities shifted to the battle zone around St. Lô, with the *Gruppe* flying free chase missions and fighter-bomber sweeps, but also a growing number of low-level attack sorties in support of the army troops. On 24 July, however, the *Gruppe* fought another bitter battle with Mustangs over the Caen area (the now notorious Grid Square UU). One Mustang was shot down by Lt. Zimmermann (24), however the *Gruppe* lost three of its own aircraft. Fortunately no pilots were lost.

On the next day, 25 July 1944, the American 1st and 3rd Armies began an offensive west of St. Lô. As planned, the operation began with destructive air attacks on German defensive positions west of St. Lô between Amigny-la-Chapelle and Le-Mesnil-Eury. Large numbers of fighter-bombers appeared first[1043], followed by 1,581 four-engined bombers of the US 8th Air Force, which dropped 3,400 tons of bombs over the attack area at 9:30 AM. Then the twin-engined bombers of the 9th Air Force appeared, dropping roughly another 800 tons of bombs before, at about 10 AM, another 400 fighter-bombers attacked what was left of the German positions. The first phase of the air assault ended at about 11:30 armament, when 380 twin-engined bombers appeared and dropped 650 tons of high-explosive, phosphorus and napalm bombs. The German defense front crumbled under this torrent of steel, which literally pulverized trenches, gun positions, tanks and munitions dumps. When the air attacks ended, approximately 1,000 guns opened up a barrage on the German positions, firing 140,000 shells. In spite of all this, when the attack began the American assault troops encountered unexpectedly heavy return fire, and by the end of the day they had gained only three kilometers. This could not alter the fact that the German defense front had been decisively shattered and faced collapse should American armored forces drive through the gap in the front[1044].

The *Luftwaffe*'s defensive effort against the incursions by the Allied air forces over the St. Lô area was pitifully weak. Among the few *Gruppen* mustered was II/JG 3. It appears that it failed to penetrate to the St. Lô battle zone, in each case being intercepted by American fighters well before reaching its target and engaged in fierce dogfights. In the late morning 6 *Staffel* was ordered to fly a free chase mission over the St. Lô area with a single *Schwarm* (all its serviceable Messerschmitts). The *Schwarm* took off, but immediately afterwards, while at a height of 300 meters, it was literally run over by seven Mustangs which had been lurking nearby. In the ensuing dogfight, which drifted southeast over the Rambouillet area, *Staffelführer* Lt. Oskar Zimmermann was able to shoot down a P-51 for his 25th victory. Immediately afterwards, however, another Mustang registered strikes on his machine's engine and cockpit, forcing him to bail out. Just before he jettisoned the canopy, further strikes tore the back armor from its supports and drove it into Zimmermann's back, injuring him slightly. In spite of this he was able to abandon the aircraft[1045]. Lt. Helmut Glaaß was less fortunate: he was shot down and killed near Dourdan, 20 km southeast of Rambouillet. 4/JG 52, which engaged Mustangs near Argentan during a free chase mission into the St. Lô area, reported two casualties. Uffz. Josef Wüst was shot down and at first reported missing. Several days later he rejoined his *Staffel* unhurt. Gefr. Werner

Henselien was slightly injured when his "Blue 7" was shot up by enemy fighters and he was forced to put the aircraft down on its belly northwest of Argentan. A third machine was lost in air combat and two were damaged in non-combat-related incidents. II/JG 3 continued its operations over the St. Lô battle zone on the following day, 26 July 1944. Few details are known, however the *Gruppe* lost three Messerschmitts while failing to shoot down any of the enemy. Although there were no combat-related casualties on this day, 4/JG 52 did loose another pilot. Uffz. Hans Fischer was on approach to land at Chaudon after a maintenance test flight when his engine failed. The aircraft rolled over to the right and crashed, and Fischer died in the resulting explosion and fire.

Heavy fighting continued in the area west of St. Lô in the days that followed. While leading American units continued to drive south, reaching Nôtre-Dame-de-Cenilly and le Mesnil-Herman on 27 July, the units of the German 7th Army in the west fought their way through to the east to retain contact with their own forces[1046]. During these days II/JG 3 continued in action over the St. Lô battle zone, its missions including free chases, fighter-bomber sweeps and low-level attacks against the assembly areas used by American troops. The *Gruppe* lost one machine in combat on 27 July, but the missions of the next two days were completed without loss. No victories were claimed on any of these days.

On 30 July 1944 the spearheads of the American 4th Armored Division reached Avranches, completing the breakout of Allied forces from the bridgehead area. After weeks of fierce positional warfare in the hedgerows of Normandy, all of Brittany and western and central France now spread out before the American armored units, scarcely defended by German troops. Notwithstanding this, the bitter fighting on the Americans' eastern flank continued, while the German command made desperate efforts to establish a new defense position south of Avranches with whatever forces it could scrape together. Allied aircraft were over the west coast of the Cotentin all day, supporting Allied ground forces. The already badly battered German regiments, which again had to fight almost without air support, were quickly wiped out[1047].

For II/JG 3, the missions on the last two days of the month began without incident, apart from a skirmish with Mustangs on 31 July. The *Kapitän* of 4/JG 52, Lt. Waldmann, scored hits on a Mustang but he was unable to watch it crash. The missions of July 1944 had witnessed the continuation of the unhappy train of events which had begun at the outset of the *Gruppe*'s deployment to France. Losses (ten pilots killed or missing and nine wounded) were once again unbearable and out of all proportion to the successes achieved (eleven enemy aircraft shot down). For the second month in a row, the *Gruppe*'s losses in pilots killed and wounded were almost equal to its complement at the beginning of the month. The number of veteran pilots had fallen even further; the loss of a *Staffelführer* and several *Schwarmführer* could not be made good from within the *Gruppe*'s own ranks. In spite of substantial deliveries of new machines, combat losses (50 machines destroyed or seriously damaged) further reduced the *Gruppe*'s aircraft complement. On the last day of the month the *Gruppe* had available 32 Messerschmitts, of which about half were serviceable[1048].

As a result of the American breakthrough at Avranches, the fighting of August 1944 was to be fundamentally different than that of the past almost eight weeks. The war diary of the OKW summed it up as follows:

> Thus the way was paved for an entirely new situation: the war of two more or less fixed fronts with great expenditures of materiel, reminiscent of 1918, is now giving way to a war of movement whose speed might possibly surpass that of 1940.[1049]

The very first day of the new month underlined the correctness of this assessment: American armored spearheads drove through the gap in the front near Avranches/Pontaubault, driving south and west into Brittany, meeting little resistance from German troops. There was also movement in the British sector: southwest of Caen, le-Bény-Bocage fell into the hands of the British 2nd Army, which drove on towards Falaise[1050].

In the first days of August the remnants of II/JG 3 continued to operate over the west coast of the Cotentin Peninsula from the unit's base at Nogent-le-Rois. Its operational tasks remained unchanged: free chases, sweeps in search of enemy fighter-bombers and low-level attacks in support of the army, principally in the Avranches area and near Mortain, but also over the Caen area. While failing to score itself, between 1 and 5 August 1944 the *Gruppe* lost two pilots killed, two wounded and four Messerschmitts. On the 1st Uffz. Josef Selbertinger of 4/JG 52 was shot down by enemy fighters during a free chase mission in the Caen area. He was obliged to make a forced landing near Valletot, sustaining serious injuries in the process. On the following day, 2 August, the *Gruppe* flew several low-level attack missions against advancing American armor south of Avranches. Numerous vehicles and infantry columns were strafed effectively[1051]. While no aircraft were lost to enemy ground fire, the *Gruppe* nevertheless suffered two pilot casualties. While maneuvering in preparation for landing, Uffz. Kurt Poppitz of 4/JG 3 and Fw. Wolfgang Blum of 5/JG 3 collided north of Nogent-le-Roi. Both pilots were killed when their Messerschmitts crashed. 6 *Staffel* reported one loss on 3 August: Uffz. Josef Wester was seriously wounded when he was shot down by enemy fighters while on a free chase in the Alençon area.

The next two days saw the *Gruppe* engaged mainly in low-level attacks in the area south of Avranches. These were all completed without loss. On 6 August II/JG 3 was at first instructed to continue flying missions in support of the army west of Avranches. The order for the early mission read: escort rocket-armed machines[1052] and conduct low-level attacks in the Mortain area. Two

casualties were subsequently reported: Lt. Fridolin Reinartz of 4/JG 3 and Obfw. Herbert Dehrmann of 5 *Staffel* were both shot down and killed in combat with superior numbers of enemy fighters, falling at Villemeux and north of Chaudon respectively. At 11:43 AM the order came to scramble against incoming heavy bomber formations[1053]. Every available machine was put into the air, and north of Paris[1054] battle was joined with a group of Liberators with fighter escort. The engagement lasted 45 minutes, and II/JG 3's handful of Messerschmitts shot down one B-24 and forced another to leave formation. Lt. Waldmann recorded his 126th victory in this action, in which the *Gruppe* suffered no losses. In the afternoon, during a free chase mission over the western breakthrough area by 6/JG 3, Uffz. Berkes claimed to have shot down a P-47 for his first victory.

During the night of 7 August 1944 the German 5th Panzer Army launched a counterattack (the "Mortain Offensive") which was supposed to cut off the American 3rd American near Avranches. In the dark of night the German units achieved a ten-kilometer-deep penetration into the American lines and took the town of Mortain. The German advance continued into the early morning hours. At that time 300 German fighters were supposed to provide air cover for the German armored groups; however, because of the effective fighter screen thrown up around the battle zone and the known German fighter bases, not a single German fighter reached the Mortain area[1055]. Instead, it was the Allied fighters and fighter-bombers which commanded the skies over the battle zone. Low-level attacks by Allied tactical aircraft, especially rocket-firing Typhoons, halted the German armor and were a significant factor in the German decision to call off the attack on the evening of 7 August 1944. The attack units lost about 90 tanks and 200 vehicles and were forced to return to their start positions[1056].

It appears that the remnants of II/JG 3 were also drawn into the attempt by the *Luftwaffe* to provide the army with air support. From Nogent-le-Roi the *Gruppe* was ordered to fly low-level attack missions in the area of Avranches/Mortain. While suffering no losses itself, at the end of the day the *Gruppe* claimed two victories, an Auster shot down by Lt. Waldmann during a low-level attack mission south of St. Lô (127) and a P-47 shot down by Lt. Grünberg during an afternoon engagement near Dreux (71). Nothing is known about the results of the *Gruppe*'s low-level attack missions. In the days that followed, the *Gruppe* continued to operate over the battle zone around Mortain. Apart from vehicles destroyed in low-level attacks, it achieved no further successes. On the other hand, by 10 August it had lost two pilots killed, two missing and two seriously wounded. 4 *Staffel* reported one casualty on 8 August: while taking off on a free chase mission into the Mortain area from the landing strip at Mauzaise near Dreux[1057], Uffz. Karl Clauß ground-looped his "White 2" and suffered severe injuries. The next day, 9 August, 4/JG 3 suffered another casualty: Uffz. Günter Schmedes failed to return after air combat in the Mortain area and was reported missing. 5 *Staffel* also reported one casualty: shortly after taking off on a ferry flight from Chartres to Nogent-le-Roi, the Messerschmitt flown by Obfw. Franz Busch stalled and crashed. The pilot was seriously injured and died the next day in hospital. Finally, on 10 August Uffz. Georg Handrich of 6/JG 3 failed to return from a free chase mission in the Mortain area after combat with enemy fighters and was reported missing.

On the evening of the same day, with American armored spearheads already nearing Chartres, II/JG 3 was forced to abandon the Nogent-le-Roi airfield. Because the airfield was watched by Allied fighters and fighter-bombers all day, the remaining Messerschmitts were not able to take off for Athis, a forward airfield near Epernay, until dusk was falling. A detachment of ground personnel had gone ahead and was waiting for the fighters when they arrived[1058]. As far as can be determined, the transfer of the air element was completed without incident and there were no losses in men or machines.

Effective 10 August 1944, II/JG 3 underwent a reorganization which was intended to bring it into line with recently-introduced regulations[1059]. The *Gruppe* was enlarged to four *Staffeln* through the addition of 4/JG 52. The changes are summarized in the following table:

Stab II/JG 3	remained	*Stab* II/JG 3	Hptm. Herbert Kutscha
4/JG 3	became	7/JG 3	Lt. Franz Ruhl
5/JG 3	remained	5/JG 3	Lt. Hans Grünberg
6/JG 3	remained	6/JG 3	(not known)
4/JG 52	became	8/JG 3	Lt. Hans Waldmann

Coincident with the addition of a fourth *Staffel*, the authorized strength of the *Gruppenstabbschwarm* was doubled and each of the four *Staffeln* was enlarged to four *Schwärme* instead of the previous three. The result was an increase in the *Gruppe*'s authorized strength from 40 to 72 machines; however, in view of the conditions prevailing in France, this remained purely a theoretical exercise.

Meanwhile, the American had rapidly expanded their breakthrough near Avranches and were advancing vigorously to the west and south. On 10 August units of XX Corps of the US 3rd Army liberated Nantes and Anger, while the XV Corps drove north from Alençon toward Argentan. In conjunction with the British drive towards Falaise, this was the beginning of the encirclement of the bulk of the 5th Panzer Army and the German 7th Army. On the following day, which was actually supposed to see the start of another German drive toward Avranches, the German command recognized the deadly danger facing the elements of the 5th Panzer Army and the 7th Army still in the Mortain area and ordered their retreat to the east. The way there led through the now dangerously narrow gap between the advancing British forces in the north and the forces of the American 1st Army driving from the south through Alençon[1060].

II/JG 3's mission orders in the following days read: in conjunction with III/JG 3, support the army in its withdrawal movements south of Falaise and conduct free chase, anti-fighter-bomber and anti-spotter missions in the Falaise-Argentan area[1061]. A number of vehicles were destroyed in low-level attacks near Alençon and Argentan on 11 and 12 August, otherwise the *Gruppe* recorded neither successes nor losses. On the 13th, however, two pilots were reported missing: Uffz. Kurt Soßdorf and Uffz. Richard Quinten, both of 5/JG 3, failed to return from an early evening escort mission into the Chartres area in support of rocket-armed machines (probably of JG 26). Both survived, though wounded. Richard Quinten was shot down by a Spitfire while strafing a column of fuel trucks. Wounded in the arm, he belly landed his machine in no-man's-land. Under cover of darkness Quinten reached a French farmhouse, where he was given first-aid. Before daybreak one of the farmer's took him back to the German lines, where he received medical treatment[1062]. Kurt Soßdorf also returned to his *Staffel*, however the circumstances are not known. The next day, 14 August 1944, II/JG 3 claimed four victory without loss. In the morning Lt. Grünberg shot down a P-38 for his 72nd victory. Then, in a late afternoon free chase and anti-fighter-bomber mission south of Dreux, 8/JG 3 shot down three Thunderbolts, two by Lt. Waldmann (128-129) and the third by his wingman Fw. Schicketanz.

American forces had meanwhile occupied Chartres and Orléans; Dreux, in the approaches to Paris, had also been lost. Meanwhile, the heavy fighting in went on undiminished in the Falaise area, where, in the days that followed, the Allies were still unable to close the pocket around the German troops. Conditions in the battle zone were frightful: every village abandoned by German units, every road leading east, every crossing—even makeshift ones—over the Orne and the Dives was a picture of horror and devastation. Shot-up and burnt-out trucks, cars, tanks and horse-drawn vehicles littered the streets and roads. Bloated, decaying bodies lay everywhere[1063].

Apart from four machines damaged in non-combat-related incidents, 15 August 1944 was an uneventful day for II/JG 3. Then, late on the afternoon of 16 August, there was an encounter with a group of P-47s. Lt. Grünberg, *Kapitän* of 5 *Staffel*, shot down one of the American fighters (73), while the *Gruppe*'s lost one machine damaged in air combat. In the days that followed, the *Gruppe*'s missions were unchanged: free chases and fighter-bomber hunts in the approaches to Paris and over the battle zone around Falaise. On 18 August there were two fierce dogfights with American fighters, in the course of which II/JG 3 shot down seven of the enemy for the loss of four machines and two pilots temporarily reported missing. In the early afternoon the *Gruppe* was sent into the Falaise area on a combined free chase mission and anti-fighter-bomber sweep. While en route to the assigned area, it was intercepted by a larger formation of P-47s and P-51s and engaged in a bitter battle near

Versailles. Four victories were subsequently claimed, including a pair of P-47s by Lt. Waldmann (130-131). On the other side of the coin, Uffz. Alwin Boch of 5/JG 3 was shot down by enemy fighters southwest of Versailles; he was later able to return to the *Gruppe* (probably wounded)[1064]. In the evening the *Gruppe* was supposed to fly a low-level attack mission in the Falaise area, but once again it failed to reach the target area. Instead, while forming up with III/JG 3 southeast of Beauvais[1065], the Messerschmitts were attacked by P-51s and engaged in a fierce dogfight. Three P-51s were shot down by Lt. Grünberg (74), Uffz. Geisthövel (4) and Uffz. Berkes (2), while Fw. Hans Löhlein of 6/JG 3 was shot down. Though initially reported missing, Löhlein was later able to return wounded to his *Staffel*. In spite of periods of inclement, rainy weather, on 19 August the *Gruppe* flew further missions into the area around Falaise, where in the morning there was a fierce dogfight with a large number of American fighters west of Rouen. II/JG 3 lost five Messerschmitts in return for two P-47s shot down by Lt. Waldmann (132) and Obfw. Reiser (5). This time 7 *Staffel* was especially hard hit, with three casualties. Uffz. Norbert Preusler, Uffz. Kurt Möllerke and Gefr. Ernst Fleischhacker were all reported missing after being shot down west of Elbeuf and near Brionne. While Preusler's fate was never explained, Möllerke and Fleischhacker both returned wounded to the *Gruppe* a few days later. The fourth casualty came from 8/JG 3: Fw. Otto Schicketanz was placed on the casualty list after he was shot down and killed by Thunderbolts near Epernon.

20 August 1944: The heavy fighting in the eastern portion of the Falaise pocket raged on in pouring rain. While elements of the II SS Panzer Corps undertook a relief advance from the east, near St. Lambert the remnants of two other SS panzer divisions and the II Parachute Corps attempted to break through the encircling ring from the inside. During the night of 21 August further substantial forces (20,000 men, approximately half of those still trapped inside the pocket) broke out of the pocket and reached the German lines. It was the end of the Battle of Falaise and at the same time the end of the Battle of Normandy. The badly battered remnants of the German units fell back towards the Seine, barely managing to retain their cohesion; it now seemed as if everything was collapsing, as if everything was in disintegration[1066]. In Paris, where the approaching end of the occupation made an uprising all the more likely, on this day the military commander of the city, *General* von Choltitz, signed a cease-fire agreement with the insurgents so as to avoid an open uprising at the last moment and save the city from destruction[1067].

Bad weather severely restricted the activities of the air forces of both sides[1068]. Nevertheless, in the early afternoon II/JG 3 was ordered to fly an anti-fighter-bomber sweep in support of army units in the Falaise-Argentan area. Once again the *Gruppe* was intercepted by a numerically superior formation of P-47s, which attacked and scattered the Messerschmitts. The planned mission had to be abandoned and the fighters engaged the Thunderbolts. Four of the enemy fighters were shot down, including one by Lt. Hans Grünberg for his 75th victory, for the loss of three Messerschmitts. Fhr. Paul Budde of the *Gruppenstab* was shot down in air combat; seriously wounded, he died three days later. Fw. Harald Wojnar was extremely lucky: after shooting down a P-47, he was pursued at treetop height by four other Thunderbolts. His shot-up machine finally crashed into a wood; seriously injured, he was soon pulled from the wreck of his Messerschmitt by German paratroopers and taken to hospital[1069].

The missions of 20 August were to be II/JG 3's last during its deployment in the west, for that same day its relief, III/JG 76, arrived at Athis. The *Geschwaderstab* and II/JG 3 were then ordered home to rest and refit. On 21 August II/JG 3 accompanied the newly-arrived *Gruppe* on several familiarization flights over the area of front west of Paris; one machine was damaged in air combat. After turning in its last remaining Messerschmitts[1070], the *Gruppe* set out for the Reich. Some ground personnel did have to stay behind at Athis, however, to service III/JG 76's aircraft pending the arrival of that unit's ground elements, whose arrival had been delayed by the chaotic transport conditions in the rear areas[1071]. It appears that II/JG 3 also left behind a small detachment of pilots; these were assigned to III/JG 3 to fill gaps in that unit's roster, however the names of the pilots affected are not known[1072].

The withdrawal of the *Gruppe* spared it participation in the final battles associated with the total collapse of the German defense front in the west. In the days that followed, the Allies crossed the Seine and on 25 August American and French troops occupied an intact Paris. On 26 August British troops crossed the lower Seine and advanced into the area of Pas-de-Calais, while one day later American units reached the Marne near Château-Thierry and crossed the river without delay. All the dams of the German defense now began to break, and the roads were filled with columns heading east, train units and rear-echelon troops, plus ground elements of II/JG 3, which became completely dispersed. It was weeks before they reached their destination, Ziegenhain, where the *Gruppe* was to be thoroughly rested and reequipped in the coming weeks[1073].

Thus ended two and a half months of defensive operations in France. In this ten-week period II/JG 3 had suffered grievous losses, which for the first time in the unit's history exceeded its own victories. Between 6 June and 21 August 1944 II/JG 3 had lost 38 pilots killed or missing[1074] and 22 wounded or injured, while none of its pilots was captured. In the same period at least 106 Messerschmitts were written off or sustained damage in excess of 60%, 86 of them as a result of enemy action, while another 74 suffered significant damage[1075,1076]. On the plus side, the *Gruppe* registered 54 victories in the same period. As a result of the severe personnel losses, at the end of its deployment in France II/JG 3 was a mere shadow of the unit which went into battle against the Allied invasion on 6 June 1944. Scarcely any of the pilots who had accompanied the unit to France survived the fierce fighting in Normandy unscathed, for example the *Kapitän* of 5 *Staffel* Lt. Hans Grünberg or the *Gruppen-Adjutant* Oblt. Max-Bruno Fischer. In its few weeks in action, 4/JG 52, which did not join the *Gruppe* until July, also suffered extremely painful losses. In the end, it was left with just a handful of inexperienced pilots. These rallied round their *Staffelkapitän*, Lt. Hans Waldmann, who with six victories over France was also the *Gruppe*'s most successful pilot.

Notes:

[971] For more information on the Allied invasion of France and the *Luftwaffe* reaction see Jacobsen and Rohwer, p. 424 and following pages; Cartier, Vol. 2, p. 747 and following pages; Rohwer and Hummelchen, p. 453; Gundelach, Dr. G.W., p317 and following pages.

[972] After 6 June 1944 the focus of *Luftwaffe* operations was to be shifted to the west by ruthlessly stripping the Defense of the Reich. All that was left in the Reich was four active day fighter *Gruppen*, weak destroyer forces and the operational *Staffeln* of four training *Geschwader* and the "Wild Boar" units, which were now employed almost exclusively in the day fighter role. At the same time, on 6 June the American 15th Air Force stepped up its attacks on targets in southern Germany in order to prevent further fighter forces from being moved to France and to take advantage of the already weakened fighter defenses to strike oil targets in the south and southeast of the Reich. See Gundelach, Dr. G.W., p. 326.

[973] All in all the plan of 27/2/1944 (including the addenda worked out by April) called for the transfer of two tactical reconnaissance *Staffeln*, five bomber *Gruppen*, nineteen day fighter *Gruppen*, two more fighter *Staffeln*, five fighter *Geschwaderstäbe*, one close-support *Gruppenstab* and two *Gruppen*, and two night fighter *Geschwaderstäbe* and eight *Gruppen*. Where JG 3 was concerned, however, only II and III *Gruppe* saw action in France for any length of time. I *Gruppe* temporarily sent a detachment to France, however the bulk of the unit stayed behind in the Reich. IV/JG 3 was recalled from France after only a few days for continued operations in the Defense of the Reich.

[974] See the aircraft inventory lists in the appendices. According to these, in June 1944 II/JG 3 was allocated no fewer than 118 Messerschmitts, some of which were received before the *Gruppe* was transferred to France. As well, a number of pilots were assigned to II/JG 3 from other *Gruppen*, including IV/JG 3, II/JG 5 and 2/JG 51. As a result, when the invasion began, the *Gruppe* was far above its authorized strength.

[975] Other units received similar allocations, at least those which were not bolstered through the subordination and later incorporation of entire *Staffeln* of units based on the Eastern Front and from the south; see Prien/Rodeike, *JG 1 / 11* Part 2, p. 989, for JG 27, the same, p. 260.

[976] This designation stood for **Drohende Gefahr West** (Impending Danger West).

[977] Concerning the transfer of III/JG 3, see Prien and Stemmer, *III/JG 3*, p. 358 and following pages.

[978] Account by Helmut Hennig dated 30/11/1985. Richard Quinten, who joined 5/JG 3 as an *Unteroffizier* pilot in March 1944, remembers that the bulk of the *Gruppe* got through to Evreux. However, because of bomb damage to the airfield surface, it was redirected and only then did it split up, resulting in numerous belly landings in open country. Several Messerschmitts did land at Evreux, but these sustained damage after landing when they ran into fresh bomb craters. Account dated 18/8/1986.

[979] II/JG 3's disastrous transfer was not an isolated incident. Indeed, the transfer of *Gruppen* from the Defense of the Reich to France was characterized by numerous delays, failures and crashes. For example, of the 22 aircraft of III/JG 54 which set out for France, just two landed at Villacoublay as planned, while in spite of assistance from two pilot aircraft, just 3 of 53 Messerschmitts of II/JG 5 arrived at their destination airfield of Evreux. The rest became scattered and nine machines made belly landings. The latter led to the following entry in the papers of General Koller: "*It is to be assumed that the weather situation, thick fog, was the cause. Obstlt. Trautloft has initiated court-martial proceedings. In future General Galland will personally take charge of transfers.*" K.113.407-3/0660, 0705. How Galland was to do this has not been recorded, however.

In view of this, the order of the day issued by Göring on 14 June 1944, in which he gives high praise to the *Luftwaffe* staffs for their leading role in the preparations for the defensive struggle in the west, has a comical ring to it: "*Following the exemplary and problem-free execution of the planned measures for the expected attack on Europe by our Anglo-Saxon foe, I express my special appreciation to the members of my Luftwaffe operations staff for the conscientious and forward-looking way in which they handled all the decisions necessary for the case 'Imminent Danger West'. All of the orders which made possible the short-notice redeployment of the flying units and the flak artillery to the western theater to defend against the landing were prepared in months of painstaking detail work. All gears engaged as planned, making it possible for transfers and transport movements to proceed as anticipated. This success was the Luftwaffe operations staff's reward for its selfless work. I know for certain, that in the future I will be able to continue relying on the loyalty and dedication of each individual, until the final victory crowns our struggle for a free Greater Germany in a free Europe. Heil to the Führer! Göring, Reichsmarschall of the Greater German Reich.*" Koller Documents, K.113.407-3/0507. When one considers that Göring had not had a single good word to say about his once so pampered fighter pilots since 1940, this florid speech of praise to his desk-bound warriors strikes one as especially disgusting.

[980] Account by Helmut Hennig, 30/11/1985.

[981] Information contained in the WASt. casualty reports for the two pilots of 5/JG 3 killed on this day.

[982] OKW War Diary 1944/45, Part I, p. 313. This realization was also spreading among some officers at the highest level of the German command. For example, on this date *Grossadmiral* Dönitz confided to his staff: "The invasion has succeeded. The second front is a reality." Quoted in Irving, *Rommel*, p. 513.

[983] Gundelach, p. 319. This applies to the number of available aircraft, while the ratio of missions flown was "only" 1 : 12 at best.

[984] War Diary of III/JG 3, which was stationed at St. André de l'Eure airfield a few kilometers to the southeast. See Prien/Stemmer, *III/JG 3*, p. 361.

[985] Freeman, *Mighty Eighth War Diary*, p. 262-263.

[986] As above.

[987] See in detail Prien/Stemmer, *III/JG 3*, p. 361.

[988] This day's targets probably included several bridges over the Orne, on which three hits were scored—writings of Robert Skawran, 7/1/1945.

[989] Bernhard Haupt was a member of IV/JG 3, Kurt Wahl of 2/JG 51. Both were assigned to II/JG 3 and were thus among the pilots sent to the *Gruppe* as reinforcements in the first days of June in preparation for its expected defensive mission in the west.

[990] Between 8 and 12 June 1944 Lt. Oskar Zimmermann flew a total of 15 fighter-bomber missions, an average of three per day— writings of Robert Skawran, 7/1/1945.

[991] See the list in Prien/Rodeike, *JG 1 / 11* Part 2, p. 1051.

[992] Characteristic in this context is the situation assessment made by the OB West at the end of this day, in which he declared that the enemy's air superiority was the most serious obstacle for the conducting of operations and estimated the enemy's air activity at 27,000 sorties per day. OKW War Diary 1944/45, Part I, p. 314.

[993] Gundelach, Dr. G.W., p. 323.

[994] The writings of Robert Skawran made after a conversation with Oskar Zimmermann on 7 January 1945 reveal that while flying fighter-bomber missions in those days (June 1944), II/JG 3 was repeatedly intercepted en route to the target and had to jettison its bombs in preparation for the unavoidable engagement with enemy fighters.

995 See in detail OKW War Diary 1944/45, Part I, p. 314-315; Irving, *Rommel*, p. 515 and following pages. In his situation assessment of 13 June GFM von Rundstedt (Commander-in-Chief West) once again referred to the danger of another large-scale Allied landing in the area of the Somme or on the Belgian coast. See OKW War Diary 1944/45, Part I, p. 315.

996 Freeman, *Mighty Eighth War Diary*, p. 264.

997 Piekalkiewicz, p. 355.

998 The Americans were certainly aware of this. For example, Freeman writes (p. 264): *"Luftwaffe operated in strength for the first time since D-Day."*

999 Information contained in the WASt. casualty reports for the pilots killed or wounded on this day.

1000 As well, there were two Messerschmitts which were damaged in air combat and subsequently made forced landings; see the lost list in the appendices.

1001 Fw. Kipulski was a member of 10/JG 3 and was attached to 4 *Staffel* (see above).

1002 See Freeman, *Mighty Eighth War Diary*, p. 264-265.

1003 Gundelach, Dr. G.W., p. 321. By 28 June all day fighter *Gruppen* formerly under the command of *II Fliegerkorps* were reassigned to *II Jagdkorps*, while *II Fliegerkorps* was disbanded on this day.

1004 See the information in Freeman, *Mighty Eighth War Diary*, p. 264 and following pages. From this, it is apparent that the heavy bomber units of the US 8th Air Force met almost no resistance from German fighters during their missions over the landing zone and the rear areas; consequently, losses were light. Also see Gundelach, Dr. G.W., p. 322-323.

1005 As above, p. 321-322.

1006 On this topic, the following interesting entry appears in the war diary of III/JG 3 under this date: *"The enemy's numerical superiority, to say nothing of his technical superiority, is such that takeoffs in Schwarm or Staffel strength lead to unbearable losses. The enemy has an efficient air reporting service and operations organization, as a result of which our units are detected immediately and in no time at all find themselves engaged in air combat with superior enemy forces, which are constantly reinforced. Because the operational area is under almost constant surveillance from the air, our machines can only take off in those few moments when the air is clear, so as to avoid being attacked during takeoff or betraying the location of the base of operations, which would result in bombing and strafing within a few hours. The installation of a radio-telephone in a foxhole next to the takeoff and landing strip to monitor takeoffs and landings has proved an outstanding success and has saved the lives of many pilots. Based on recent fighter experience, on order of the Inspector of Day Fighters Oberst Trautloft, battle units are to be formed from the Jagdgeschwader in the area. These are to consist of fighter-bomber Gruppen, close-escort Gruppen and high cover Gruppen and are intended to make it possible to carry out missions and meet the enemy with a concentrated fighting force."*

1007 Prien/Rodeike, *JG 1 / 11* Part 2, p. 1051.

1008 The allocation of 118 new Messerschmitts in this one month alone did nothing to change this, for operational losses in the same period totaled 103 machines! 1009 Account by Helmut Hennig, 30/11/1985, where he mistakenly refers to the airfield as *Cambrai*. According to an official summary of airfields assigned to the flying units, between 18 and 24 June 1944 II/JG 3 was at Salzwedel. This can only be explained (if at all), if the elements based there consisted of a clean-up detachment or a party sent to collect new machines.

1010 The *Geschwaderstab* of JG 3 apparently moved at the same time as II/JG 3.

1011 According to Uffz. Heiner Geisthövel, on 19 June he shot down a B-17 near Rambouillet, however no further information is available. The date is probably in error, for a victory fitting this description was scored on 22 June 1944.

1012 According to the WASt. casualty report, Otto Florian is still officially listed as missing.

1013 See Footnote 974.

1014 Because of the extraordinary contradictions contained in the surviving records, compiling a precise, binding description of the day's events affecting II/JG 3 is impossible, as the following examples will illustrate: the records are completely contradictory even where the unit's base of operations is concerned, for the available, usually reliable, official and private sources name four different airfields, namely Evreux-Fauville, Dreux-Mauzaise, Guyancourt and Gardelegen! Assuming that the *Gruppe* was in fact at Evreux-Fauville on this day, there followed the attack by the stated 43 P-47s of VIII Fighter Command—the latter dropped 12.5 tons of bombs and reported neither successes nor losses, while II/JG 3 reported 21 losses and 6 victories. Furthermore, American loss records (M.A.C.R.) show that the US 8th Air Force did not lose a single P-47 on this day, while the 9th Air Force lost two; on the other hand, the 9th Air Force did not carry out any attacks on airfields near Evreux on 25 June 1944. This may serve as a graphic illustration of the difficulties that can be encountered in trying to accurately reconstruct events which happened more than fifty years ago.

1015 Both pilots, who were on detachment from 4/JG 5 to 4/JG 3, were declared legally dead after the war—WASt. casualty report.

1016 Uffz. Vahle was a member of 5/JG 5 and was detached to 5/JG 3.

1017 Consequently, in the evening report on this day the *Gruppe* was entered as "in rest and refit"—documents of the *Luftwaffe* Study Group of the FüAk Bw. One part of the air element—probably elements of II/JG 5, which had been subordinated to the *Gruppe*—continued to operate from Evreux for several days, for according to RL 2 / III / 852 (Reports on Aircraft Losses), operational losses were reported on 27 and 28 June 1944. The documents of Gen. Koller reveal that consideration had already been given on 16 June to withdrawing the *Gruppe* and after this losses the idea was raised again. The suggestion was that II/JG 3 be exchanged with II/JG 5, which had been left behind in the Reich as a so-called "collection *Gruppe*". K.113.403-7, Bl. 0618, 0624.

1018 Meanwhile, II/JG 5's air element had already returned to the Reich, where on 30 June 1944 the *Gruppe* appears as part of *Luftflotte* Reich again, based at Salzwedel. It had apparently handed its remaining machines over to II/JG 3 prior to leaving France, for aircraft movement reports reveal that the 50 Messerschmitts assigned to II/JG 3 during the month of June 1944 came from other *Gruppen* (according to this, II/JG 5 only transferred six Bf 109s to other *Gruppen*).

1019 After temporarily taking over the *Geschwaderstab*, Maj. Bob had on several occasions been called upon to function as battle unit commander, whereas the logbook of Maj. Heinz Bär, the new *Kommodore* of JG 3, reveals that he flew no missions at this time. These missions were very difficult for Hans-Ekkehard Bob, who came from the Eastern Front and had experience neither in leading a large battle unit nor in combat against the western powers. In a letter to the author dated 31 August 1996, he wrote: *"I came from the Eastern Front and I was immediately made responsible for every shortcoming, no matter where or when it happened. Not only did I have to fly missions against the Americans, who enjoyed a ten to one superiority in the air, I also had to engaged in `close combat' with my superiors. All very unpleasant."*

1020 The first time Maj. Bob signed the *Gruppe*'s loss report as "*Major and Gruppenkommandeur*" was on 26 June 1944—WASt. casualty reports.

1021 See in detail Obermaier, p. 90.

1022 Account by Helmut Hennig, 30/11/1985.

1023 The losses suffered in this air battle cast a revealing light on the catastrophic personnel situation faced by the fighter arm, whose leading officers did not hesitate to send large numbers of half-trained replacement pilots, who now formed the bulk of the arm's personnel, into the defensive struggle. Against a foe who enjoyed the advantages of far superior equipment, numbers and training these men had no chance and they were sacrificed as cannon fodder in predictably useless and pointless missions.

1024 While the *Gruppe* was literally being chewed up in pointless and ineffective missions such as this one, the *Luftwaffe* was coming under increasing pressure from the army command, which expected more support against the Allied fighter-bombers that were paralyzing all movement on the ground. This was expressed in the following radio message from the headquarters of 5 *Jagddivision* which was received by the *Gruppen* of JG 3 at this time: 1) Hard-fighting army demanding the full support of the fighter arm. I demand that Geschwaderkommodore and Gruppenkommandeure commit everything available in order to get powerful battle units through to the target area. Principal mission: engage fighter-bombers and artillery spotters. Low-level attacks are to be flown against worthwhile targets whenever possible. The army needs our support, we will spare no effort to give it.

2) No unauthorized changes to this mission order without a compelling reason! 1025 German Order of Battle, Statistics as of Quarter Years, reporting date 30 June 1944.

1026 Writings of Karl-Heinz Langer, former *Gruppenkommandeur* of III/JG 3, who produced an abridged copy of the *Gruppe* war diary.

1027 Writings of Robert Skawran about Oskar Zimmermann, 7/1/1945.

1028 His survival was no more than a short reprieve, however, for exactly one month later, on 2 August 1944, Kurt Poppitz was killed in action—see below.

1029 As a further attempt to bolster the forces of the Defense of the Reich, on 25 May 1944 an order was issued for every *Jagdgeschwader* deployed in the east and south to transfer one full-strength *Staffel* (less aircraft) to *Luftflotte Reich* for air-defense operations. The *Staffeln* thus made available were to be used to raise the authorized strength of those day fighter *Gruppen* already in the Defense of the Reich from three to four *Staffeln*, as had been done with JG 2 and 26 in France in the autumn of 1943. While this measure was meant to increase the operational strengths of the units, it was also intended to address the lack of suitable unit leaders, a result of the loss of so many successful and experienced *Kommodore* and *Kommandeure*. This made it necessary to increase the size of the units commanded by the surviving unit leaders. See in detail Prien/Rodeike, *JG 1 / 11*, p. 994 and following pages. Most of the *Staffeln* released from the east and south as a result of this measure (officially referred to as *"Personnel Jagdstaffeln"*) arrived in the area of *Luftflotte Reich* by mid-June 1944. After receiving new aircraft, most were assigned to *Jagdgruppen* deployed in France.

1030 See Obermaier, p. 220; concerning the career of Hans Waldmann see Bracke, where cited.

1031 The precise date of Ruhl's departure is not known; it appears that it was the end of June-beginning of July 1944. The following, an extract from an account by

Oskar Zimmermann, appears in the records of Robert Skawran: *"Z assumes that R was not only [...], but also had some kind of illness (stomach or lung). After eight days on the invasion front he was completely exhausted after roughly six missions."*

[1032] See Obermaier, p. 152.

[1033] See Prien/Stemmer, *III/JG 3*, p. 368.

[1034] After his recuperation Obfw. Rüffler did not return to II/JG 3, instead, at the beginning of 1945, he retrained on the Me 262. He did not see action in the jet fighter, however, instead he was with JG 51 in the east when the war ended.

[1035] The effects which the loss of its *Staffelführer* and two experienced *Schwarmführer* (Rüffler and Florian) had on the *Staffel* is obvious: during the rest of its deployment in the west 4/JG 3 scored just one victory while losing five pilots killed or missing.

[1036] On this topic, the number of aircraft losses with no corresponding pilot casualty rose significantly in July. Based on information from other *Staffeln* at this time, it seems likely that in some cases pilots escaped the certain destruction of their machines by bailing out. In the brash parlance of the pilot: *"Better a coward for five minutes than dead for a lifetime."*

[1037] It is one of the darkest chapters in the story of the *Luftwaffe* command that it sent unprepared pilots into action, even though it was obvious to any reasonable person that they could achieve nothing while suffering frightful losses. These young men had to pay for an inept and unscrupulous command with their lives and their health; however, while hundreds of them died or were crippled, none of the seniors officers who sent them into action were ever called to account. On the contrary, most of them survived the war in safe staff positions and subsequently had time to recount their war experiences in bars or publish them in book form and memorialize the fallen in numerous wreath-laying ceremonies, in most cases omitting any sort of self-criticism. An in-depth examination of this theme would exceed the scope of this book, however.

[1038] Hans-Ekkehard Bob recalled the circumstances of his recall as follows: *"The commanding general of our Fliegerkorps summoned me and told me that the people in Berlin had become very nervous on account of our powerlessness against the invading masses and they therefore wanted to make an example of a responsible air officer. They had me in mind—what an honor! But I had nothing to fear, he was going to make sure of that. My staff and I were summoned to the corps and interrogated. It was degrading, and we didn't get much support from our Kommodore. After a few days we were allowed to return to our unit as if nothing had happened."* Bob did not remain long with the *Gruppe*, however, instead he was assigned to the staff of *General* Kammhuber, who commanded a unit for the testing of jet aircraft.

[1039] According to information provided by Helmut Hennig, Bob was relieved immediately after the 20th of July 1944 (account dated 30/11/1985). On 26 July 1944 Herbert Kutscha signed the *Gruppe's* loss reports as *"Hauptmann and m.d.W.d.G.b. (entrusted with the duties of the commander)"* for the first time.

[1040] Franz Ruhl was awarded the Knight's Cross on 27 July 1944. A congratulatory telegram from Maj. Bär, the *Kommodore* of JG 3, to Franz Ruhl dated 2 August has survived, indicating that he was already back with the *Gruppe* on that date. This is confirmed by statements made by the then Obfw. Reiser in a letter to Hans Ring (undated).

[1041] The plans for "Operation Overlord" called for the city to be taken on the sixth day, whereas 43 days had passed since the landing when the city finally fell. 19 July 1944 also saw the first vessels discharge their cargoes in the port of Cherbourg, resulting in a bolstering of the Allied supply effort.

[1042] OKW War Diary 1944/45, Part I, p. 326; Piekalkiewicz, *Invasion*, p. 181; Cartier, Vol. 2, p. 782.

[1043] Altogether the Americans mustered 1,581 four-engined bombers, 396 medium bombers and 350 fighter-bombers for these attacks. British Lancaster bombers were not used as these were equipped mainly to carry large-caliber bombs. Experience in the Caen area had shown that the effects of these did more to hinder the advance of Allied troops than promote it.

[1044] See in detail the OKW War Diary 1944/45, Part I, p. 327; Jacobsen/Rohwer, p. 428 and following pages; Cartier Vol. 2, p. 795 and following pages; Piekalkiewicz, *Invasion*, p. 188-189.

[1045] Papers of Robert Skawran, 7 January 1945; after a brief hospital stay, Lt. Zimmermann was transferred to III/JG 3, where he took over 9 *Staffel*—see Prien/Stemmer, *III/JG 3*, p. 370.

[1046] OKW War Diary 1944/45, Part I, p. 329.

[1047] OKW War Diary 1944/45, Part I, p. 328-329.

[1048] For the day fighter *Gruppen* concentrated in France under *Luftflotte 3*, July had brought tough and costly fights with the numerically far superior Allied air forces on an almost daily basis. The units of *Luftflotte* 3 flew a total of 15,345 sorties in that month, 10,728 of them by the day fighter *Gruppen*. This was equal to just under 70 percent of all sorties flown and an average of 346 per day, which was 20 fewer on average per day than in June. In spite of generous deliveries of new aircraft, at no point did the *Luftwaffe* come close to the target figure of 1,000 fighter aircraft in France. On the contrary, by the end of July 1944 the number of available fighter aircraft had sunk to just 313 Messerschmitts and Focke Wulfs, of which 228, or

about 70%, were serviceable. The main reasons for this were the drop in operational strengths and transfers back to Germany to reequip, which affected six *Gruppen*. Another factor was the unfavorable weather in July, which that year was unusually cold and wet, seriously hampering the air activities of both sides. In July 1944 the German day fighters lost 206 pilots killed, 128 wounded and 16 captured. Material losses totaled 495 aircraft written off and 271 with varying degrees of damage. Not a single aircraft was destroyed on the ground. Against these losses, German fighters claimed to have shot down approximately 440 enemy aircraft.

While the *Luftwaffe's* efforts in France were proving to be generally ineffective, in July 1944 the resumption by the American 8th and 15th Air Forces of their strategic bombing campaign against targets within the Reich caused additional difficulties which were to prevent any further strengthening of fighter forces in the west. In that month the Americans flew destructive bombing raids against industrial targets inside the Reich on eighteen days. The fuel industry was especially hard hit, with the result that in July 1944 the production of aviation gas dropped to just 35,000 tons, while consumption remained unchanged at about 190,000 tons. In a detailed memo dated 28 July 1944 Reichsminister Albert Speer, the man responsible for the armaments industry, declared unequivocally that the existing reserves would be used up by September, or October at the latest. Assuming that the Allies were able to go on crippling the production of synthetic fuel as they had done in recent weeks, from that point on the *Luftwaffe* would no longer be capable of normal operations. From this Speer drew the conclusion that every effort must immediately be made to provide fighter cover for the hydrogenation plants inside the Reich, if need be by ruthlessly stripping the western front, so that partial production at least might be assured. The alternative was the imminent and irrevocable destruction of the entire fuel production industry, which in turn must cripple the entire German war effort. Nr. 2460/1944 Secret Reich Matter dated 28/7/1944, 4 copies; see Speer, p. 360-361 and Gundelach, *Treibstoff*, p. 697 and following pages.

[1049] OKW War Diary 1944/45, Part I, p. 329.

[1050] Piekalkiewicz, *Invasion*, p. 194-195.

[1051] Bracke, p. 152, with reference to the logbook of Lt. Hans Waldmann.

[1052] At this time elements of JG 2 and JG 26 were carrying out low-level attacks with BR 21 rockets; it is likely that II/JG 3 flew escort for JG 26 on this day.

[1053] Logbook of Hans Waldmann. The heavy bombers were most likely a force of 91 Liberators of the 3rd BD, which attacked V 1 launch sites in the Calais area on this day. See Freeman, *Mighty Eighth War Diary*, p. 316.

[1054] Grid Square UE, Méru area.

[1055] A widely-accepted version of this day's events asserts that most of the 300 fighters promised by *Luftflotte 3* were engaged by Allied fighters immediately after takeoff and many were shot down (see Piekalkiewicz p. 374 or Cartier Vol. 2, p. 853). This version of events can hardly be reconciled with the German loss reports for this day, according to which the total losses of **all** day fighter *Gruppen* stationed in France amounted to just 14 machines; see RL 2/III/852 and following pages.

[1056] See the account in Piekalkiewicz, *Invasion*, p. 202. This was the first time in the western theater that an operation by a strong armored force had been defeated solely by air power. Soon afterwards the Commander-in-Chief West, GFM von Kluge, reported: *"Faced with the complete mastery of the air by the enemy air forces, I see no way of finding a strategy which will allow us to neutralize their destructive effect if we do not withdraw from the battlefield."* Also see the detailed description in Jacobsen/Rohwer, p. 429.

[1057] Which, obviously, elements of the *Gruppe* sometimes used as an alternate airfield in August 1944; account by Helmut Hennig, 30/11/1985.

[1058] According to Hans Waldmann's logbook, he arrived at Athis at 9:30 PM. To facilitate landing in the approaching darkness, the technicians had set up a flare path next to the runway consisting of five to seven flare pots. This enabled the air element to land without incident. See in detail Bracke, p. 160.

[1059] The order to expand the *Jagdgruppen* from three to four *Staffeln* was carried out in stages. In October 1943 the *Gruppen* of the two *Jagdgeschwader* based in the west, JG 2 and 26, were enlarged to four *Staffeln* each, then at the end of May—beginning of June 1944 a number of *Jagdgruppen* in the Defense of the Reich were assigned a fourth *Staffel*. In July 1944 *Gruppen* taken off operations and sent home to rest and refit received an additional *Staffel*, which was associated with the necessary renumbering. The official deadline for reorganization was 15 August 1944 and on this day *Staffeln* which so far had only been subordinated to the affected *Gruppen* were renamed. Based on available victory and loss reports, II/JG 3 had completed the renumbering process by 10 August. The final stage of the process took place in September 1944, when the remaining *Gruppen* were enlarged, for the most part with personnel from disbanded bomber units. In each case the office which issued the orders was the OKL Genst./GenQu., 2. Abt.; see corresponding orders in RL 2/III/62.

[1060] OKW War Diary 1944/45, Part I, p. 341-342; Piekalkiewicz, *Invasion*, p. 204.

[1061] Bracke, p. 162 and following pages; logbook of Hans Waldmann.

[1062] Account by Richard Quinten, 18/8/1996; according to him, he was first transferred by rail to Lebach and later to Karlsbad. In October 1944 he returned to 5/JG 3 by way of the combat pilot assembly point in Quedlinburg.

[1063] Piekalkiewicz, p. 221.

[1064] The exact circumstances of Boch's return are not known; in particular, the WASt. casualty report omits the date of his return.

[1065] Grid Square TE; see II/JG 3's victory reports.

[1066] OKW War Diary 1944/45, Part I, p. 356-357; Cartier, Vol. 2, p. 864-865; Piekalkiewicz, *Invasion*, p. 222.

[1067] He did so in direct contravention of an order he had just received from Hitler. Considering that the assassination attempt of 20 July was only one month in the past and that the consequences of resistance and disobedience were obvious to everyone, this act required considerable personal courage.

[1068] It is noteworthy that on 20 August 1944 *Luftflotte 3* reported the highest number of fighter aircraft at any time during the fighting in France; 581 day fighter aircraft were available on this day, 344 were serviceable. See Gundelach, Dr. G.W., p. 327.

[1069] See in detail Bracke, p. 162-163.

[1070] The number of Messerschmitts still available at this time is not known. Some information is provided by the movement reports for the month of August 1944, however these are incomplete; see aircraft complement lists in the appendices.

[1071] See in detail Bracke, p. 162-163.

[1072] See in detail Prien/Stemmer, *III/JG 3*, p. 380; writings of Karl-Heinz Langer.

[1073] Account by Helmut Hennig, 30/11/1985. Hennig, together with part of the technical personnel which left Athis several days after the main column, did not arrive at Ziegenhain until 12 September 1944.

[1074] Including the pilots of IV/JG 3, II/JG 5 and I/JG 51 who were attached to the *Gruppe*; the number of fallen also includes those pilots who were first reported as wounded but subsequently died as a direct result of their wounds.

[1075] According to the aircraft movement reports, during operations in France II/JG 3 lost a total of 188 Messerschmitts written off or returned to the aviation industry for major repairs.

[1076] It is noteworthy that II/JG 3 fared rather less poorly than III *Gruppe*, whose losses in pilots killed or missing were almost twice as high, as were its losses in aircraft. See in detail Prien/Stemmer, *III/JG 3*, p. 382-383.

A Messerschmitt of the Gruppenstab *of II/JG 3 prepares to take off on a fighter-bomber mission, photographed during the first days of the* Gruppe's *defensive operations from Evreux. The pilot of this Bf 109 G-6 with the code "Black Chevron 1" was probably Oblt. Max-Bruno Fischer, II/JG 3's* Gruppen-Adjutant. *The machine wears a standard gray camouflage finish with a broad white fuselage band. Contrary to standard II* Gruppe *practise the* Geschwader *emblem on the engine cowling has been applied facing in the "right" direction. This and the unusual marking for an aircraft of the* Gruppenstab *suggest that this machine was taken over from the* Geschwaderstab *when, under the command of Maj. Heinz Bär, it converted to the Fw 190. (BA No. 493-3362-20 ff)*

29 August 1944: American soldiers of the Air Technical Intelligence Field Unit inspect Nogent-le-Roi airfield, designated A-67 by the Allied side, where among the aircraft it found left behind was this "White 10" of II/JG 3 see the following report dated 29/9/1944. The aircraft, a Bf 109 G-6 with the WerkNr. 166 224, wears a standard gray camouflage scheme with no significant variations. The propeller spinner is black with a broad white spiral. The very crudely painted last two digits of the aircraft's Werknummer *may just be discerned aft of the black* Gruppe *bar, while the entire number from the 166 000 production lot appears on the rudder. The green (according to the Allied crash recovery report) number 97 on the rudder is unusual. (I.W.M.)*

K-77667

Copy No ___33

CONFIDENTIAL

ADVANCE HEADQUARTERS
AIR SERVICE COMMAND
UNITED STATES STRATEGIC AIR FORCES IN EUROPE
APO 633
Director of Technical Services

AAF Sta 379
28 September 1944

TECHNICAL INTELLIGENCE
REPORT NOS...A-67 thru A-70.

SUBJECT: Inspection of Airfields.

1. The following enemy aircraft were inspected by the Air Technical Intelligence Field Unit on 29 August 1944:

RPT NO.	LOCATION	TYPE OF A/C MARKINGS	ENGINES	ARMAMENT	REMARKS
A-67	Nogent-le-Roi Map Ref R/420220	Me 109 G. 10(White)+ —(black). No. 24 behind the cross painted over. Werks Nr: 166224 painted on bottom rudder in 6" black Nos. Abv Werks No. on rudder painted in lge green Nos. Camouflage: Top: Mottled grey. Bottom: Light blue. 4" white spiral on black spinner.	DB 605 A-1 No. 27797	2 x MG 131/13mm, 2 x AP, 1 x HE (night trace) repeating. 1 x MG 151/20mm 1 x I, 1 x HE, 2 x AP/I, Repeating. Standard armor plate plus BP glass plate behind pilot's head.	All internal equipment removed. Aircraft fitted with wooden tail assembly.
		Me 109 G. 10 + (white numbers). Werks No: 163987 painted on the fin. Camouflage: Top: mottled grey. Bottom: Light blue. White spiral on black spinner. Red wheels.	DB 605 A-3 No. 007 07724	2 x MG 131/13mm, 2 x AP/I, 1 x HE, 1 x I repeating. 1 x MG 151/20mm, 1 x AP, 1 x HE, repeating. Standard armor plate plus BP glass behind the pilot's head.	Aircraft was fitted with a wooden tail. A tank was fitted into the rear fuselage for purpose of holding water and menthol for greater performance at high speeds. Tire Markings: Port (outside): 660 x 150 Lt. No 044 G-0013-1 (Inside): (PTL) 660 x 150 G-0013-1 Stbd (outside): 660 x 150 G-0013-1 26100-044 MPO 1006

10

Rest and Refit and Subsequent Employment in the Defense of the Reich October and November 1944

At the beginning of September 1944[1077] II/JG 3 assembled at Ziegenhain air base in Hesse, approximately 30 kilometers west-northwest of Bad Hersfeld. There, in the weeks that followed, the *Gruppe* was brought up to strength and reequipped[1078]. The pilots and ground personnel were quartered in the surrounding villages, in particular Kirtorf and Treysa. The *Gruppenstab* installed itself in the hotel *"Zur Burg"* in Treysa. After the heavy losses sustained in the defensive mission in France very few of the old pilots were left. The *Gruppe* was now assigned large numbers of replacement pilots, most of them inadequately trained youngsters. Many were officer cadets (*Fähnriche*) or *Unteroffiziere*, though some held the rank of *Gefreite* or *Obergefreite*. Some of the pilots wounded in France also began making their way back to their units after leaving hospital. These usually received a warm welcome from the few "survivors", who were happy to see a familiar face amid the sea of nameless replacements. Several veteran pilots were also transferred to II/JG 3 at this time. They came from disbanded bomber units or from transport or strategic reconnaissance units after receiving a hasty conversion course to fighters. Most of these new additions to the *Gruppe* had two things in common: a desire to fight and a lack of experience as fighter pilots. And so, while they were able to help the unit reach a strength it had never enjoyed before, they had little chance of success or even survival against Allied fighter pilots who enjoyed the advantages of superior numbers, training and equipment. Consequently, under the given circumstances, the task facing Hptm. Kutscha and the four *Staffelkapitän* or *Staffelführer*, to rebuild the air element around the few remaining veteran *Schwarmführer*, was an impossible one.

In the month of September II/JG 3 received a total of 64 brand-new Messerschmitts. All were of the G-14 variant[1079], which had begun replacing the Bf 109 G-6 on the production lines in August 1944 but which differed from the earlier version only in detail[1080]. Training began as soon as the first new aircraft arrived, with the objective of working the many new pilots into the unit. The program followed the familiar pattern, with training exercises in *Schwarm*, *Staffel* and, finally, *Gruppe* strength. While at Ziegenhain the *Gruppe* was able to conduct its refit and unit training in near peacetime conditions in, for the most part, pleasant late-summer weather. Some of the training activities were carried out from Kirtorf, where the *Gruppe* had put into operation a landing strip to serve as an alternate airfield. The flying program did, however, suffer from the now universal fuel shortage which had resulted from the Allied bombing offensive against the German fuel industry. There were two serious accidents during the unit's refit at Ziegenhain, one of them fatal. Oblt. Herbert Zschiegner of the *Gruppenstab* was killed on 14 September 1944, when his aircraft overturned while landing after a training sortie. The pilot's injuries were so severe that he died at the scene of the accident.

The refurbishment period at Ziegenhain ended after just under two months. The *Gruppe* was to return to action even though it was far from operational and the unavoidable fact that most of the *Gruppe*'s new pilots were inadequately trained. On 10 October 1944 II/JG 3 received the order to transfer to Alperstedt near Erfurt[1081]. The air element and an advance detachment of technical personnel moved there the next day, while the bulk of the ground personnel followed by road. This transfer was the first step in a plan to bring the *Gruppen* of JG 3 together in central Germany, where the *Geschwader* would be subordinated to the *3 Jagddivision* for air defense missions in the *Reichsverteidigung*. The following is II/JG 3's command list at that time:

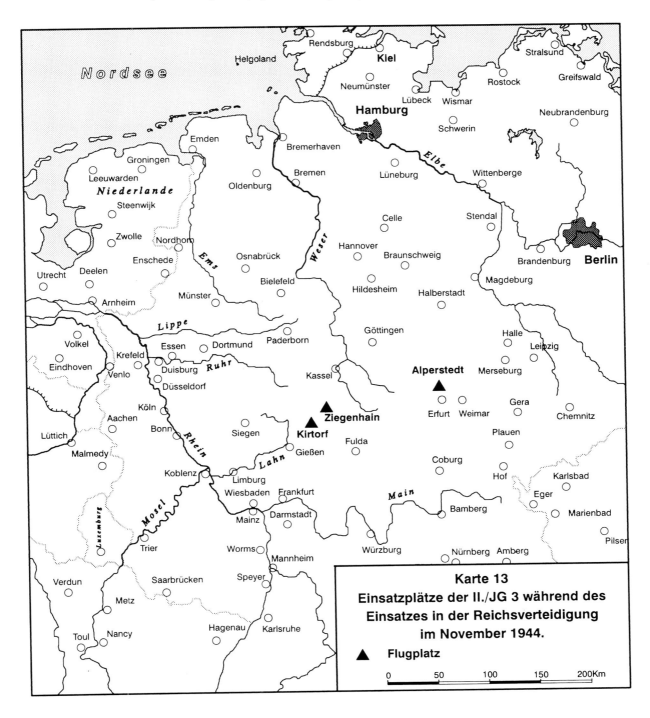

Karte 13
**Einsatzplätze der II./JG 3 während des
Einsatzes in der Reichsverteidigung
im November 1944.**

▲ **Flugplatz**

II/JG 3 List of Officers on 10 October 1944

Gruppenkommandeur	Hptm. Herbert Kutscha
Gruppenadjutant	Oblt. Max-Bruno Fischer
Staffelkapitän 5/JG 3	Lt. Hans Grünberg
Staffelführer 6/JG 3	Lt. Walter Becker
Staffelführer 7/JG 3	not known
Staffelkapitän 8/JG 3	Lt. Hans Waldmann

Only five days after arriving at Alperstedt, on 16 October 1944, the *Gruppe* flew its first air defense mission in the *Reichsverteidigung*. On that day the American 15th Air Force dispatched several attack groups from bases in Italy to attack various fuel and industrial targets in Austria and Bohemia. One of these was the hydrogenation plant at Brüx, which was the target of a large force of B-17s and its powerful escort of Mustangs[1082]. The German side mustered elements of four day fighter *Geschwader*, at least nine *Gruppen*, to meet the enemy incursions. Among the defending units was JG 3, which put up the *Stab* plus I, II and IV *Gruppe*[1083]. The *Geschwader* was ordered to assemble into battle unit formation over the Kyffhäuser prior to being vectored east toward the combat boxes of B-17s, which had positioned themselves to approach Brüx from the east[1084]. Before it made contact with the heavy bombers, however, the JG 3 formation was bounced by Mustangs east of Görlitz and engaged in costly dogfights. Seven machines were lost, however there is no information on claims by JG 3[1086]. II *Gruppe* was hardest hit, with three pilots killed, one seriously wounded and three Messerschmitts written off. Lt. Grünberg's 5 *Staffel* reported three losses: FhjFw. Leonhard Wenzel and Uffz. Johann Elwischger were shot down and killed near Lauban, while Uffz. Fleischer was very fortunate to escape unharmed after his *Gustav* was shot down. 7/JG 3 reported one pilot killed: Uffz. Günter Lehnik fell victim to Mustangs near Gross-Walditz and went down with his "Yellow 11". 8 *Staffel* had one pilot seriously wounded: after his Messerschmitt was damaged in combat with P-51s, Uffz. Hans Schunk was forced to belly-land the machine, sustaining considerable injuries[1087].

There were no more defensive missions prior to the end of the month. The weather was mainly cloudy, which seriously limited operational activities. It also prevented the American heavy bombers from launching major raids against targets in central Germany. The *Luftwaffe* command took advantage of this period of relative calm to carry on with the rebuilding process after the debacle in France.

For II/JG 3 these two weeks passed uneventfully. On 1 November 1944, however, the *Gruppe* was forced to place a pilot on the casualty list. During a ferry flight from Alteno to Alperstedt, Uffz. Heinrich Barisich of 7 *Staffel* encountered fog and flew into the ground near Münchberg, 15 km south of Hof. He died in the crash and subsequent fire.

II/JG 3 flew its next defensive mission the following day, 2 November 1944, when the 8th Air Force dispatched 1,174 heavy bombers and 968 escort fighters to attack fuel and transportation targets in western and central Germany[1088]. The German side responded with a total of 490 machines from *I Jagdkorps*, most of them from JG 3, 4 and 27, of which 305 ultimately made contact with the enemy[1089]. JG 3's defensive mission on this day, the first ever to involve the *Stab* and all four *Gruppen*, was directed against the B-17 units of the 1st and 3rd Bombardment Division, whose targets were the hydrogenation plants at Merseburg/Leuna. Shortly after midday contact was made with the strongly-escorted bomber formations over the Halle—Dessau area northwest of Leipzig, whereupon the German units were engaged in extremely costly dogfights by the American escorts. The Messerschmitt units, in particular, were heavily engaged and prevented from getting through to the bombers. 2 November 1944 was a black day for JG 3, especially for II and IV *Gruppen*, for this mission cost the *Geschwader* 26 pilots killed and eleven wounded plus 49 machines written off. Its own claims amounted to about twenty, the majority of them by the *Sturmgruppe*[1090]. This mission cost II/JG 3 twelve pilots killed and one seriously wounded plus 23 Messerschmitts, 17 of which had to be written off. The *Gruppenstab* alone lost three pilots: Lt. Adolf Briedl, Fhr. Eugen Bohler and Uffz. Heinrich Hess were all shot down and killed by Mustangs. In these circumstances 5/JG 3, which lost one pilot killed, got off the most lightly: Lt. Paul Dräger, one of the few remaining "old hands", was shot down and killed by Mustangs in the Halle area[1091]. Dräger had been a member of the *Staffel* since 1943 and had been promoted to the officer ranks on account of his operational experience and his success in combat. 6 *Staffel* reported three pilots killed, including its *Staffelführer*, Lt. Walter Becker, who was shot down and killed by Mustangs in the Halle/Leipzig area. Also killed were Fhr. Helmut Moll and Uffz. Kurt Müller. 7 *Staffel* emerged with two killed and one slightly wounded: Lt. Gerhard Schweiger and Uffz. Franz Planek were shot down and killed near Aschersleben, while Uffz. Günther Machalosowitz was also shot down but managed to parachute from his crippled "Black 12" near Halle, injuring himself in the process. 8/JG 3 reported three casualties: Lt. Erwin Gottert, Uffz. Ernst Sereinig and Obgefr. Hermann Röge were shot down by P-51s and crashed south of Dessau, near Hornburg and west of Halle.

The defensive mission of 2 November 1944 ended in a devastating defeat for the participating German forces, which lost a total of 72 pilots killed or missing, 32 wounded plus 133 machines. Based on the number of aircraft which actually made contact with the enemy (305), material losses were a catastrophic 44%! German successes (about 60 of the total of 82 enemy aircraft claimed shot down over the Reich by day fighters must have fallen in the air battle over Central Germany[1092]) were not nearly enough to offset such losses. According to the Americans, the force that attacked Leuna lost forty heavy bombers and fourteen Mustangs; as well, two B-17s crashed during the return flight[1093]. The 8th Air Force fighters claimed 102 German aircraft shot down for certain and two probables as well as 25 damaged; they also claimed to have destroyed 25 aircraft on the ground[1094].

After this, attacks were made on an almost daily basis against fuel targets all over the Reich as well as in the so-called "Protectorate", and the units of the 8th Air Force were joined by the heavy bombers of the Royal Air Force Bomber Command and those of the American 15th Air Force[1095]. In contrast to the attacks of 2 November, the daylight raids during the remainder of the month encountered little resistance from German fighters. The principal reason for this, apart from the serious losses the fighter arm had suffered on 2 November, was the incisive fuel shortage which now also forced the Defense of the Reich to ground its units for lengthy periods[1096]. And finally defensive operations were also hindered by the inclement autumn weather, for as previously stated, unlike the American air force the *Luftwaffe* was still not capable of all-weather operations.

For II/JG 3 this meant that the following two weeks were occupied mainly with training sorties, insofar as the weather and fuel situation permitted. As well, new Messerschmitts were received to make good the most recent losses. During the month the *Gruppe* received eight Bf 109 G-14s and 36 examples of the new G-10 series[1097]. On 5 November 1944, just three days after the disastrous mission of the 2nd, II/JG 3 was scrambled against a reported incursion by heavy bombers, however on this day there was no contact with the enemy. In spite of this, the *Gruppe* suffered another casualty: during the scramble from Alperstedt, Obgefr. Wolfgang Klostermayr of 7/JG 3 crashed and was killed for reasons unknown. There was another air defense mission on 19 November, when the *Gruppe* was scrambled against reported incursions. Although the *Gruppe* once again failed to make contact with the enemy, it nevertheless lost one pilot and four aircraft. During takeoff the machine of Obgefr. Herbert Roeske of 5/JG 3 swung to the left. The pilot managed to get his aircraft into the air, however he then flew into the propwash of a preceding machine and collided with another, causing him to crash from low altitude. Roeske did manage to bail out of his "White 7", however his parachute failed to open completely and he was fatally injured when he struck the ground[1098]. The pilot of the other machine was more fortunate and was able to land safely.

The mission on 19 November was to be the last by II/JG 3. On 25 November 1944 the unit was taken completely by surprise when an order arrived for the *Gruppe* to leave JG 3[1099]. II/JG 3 was to be renamed I/JG 7 and convert to the Me 262[1100]. Conversion of the pilots began at Landsberg a short time later. There they flew the Si 204 and Bf 110 in order to become familiar with the characteristics of twin-engined aircraft. Actual conversion training on the jet fighter and the equipping of the *Gruppe* with the Me 262 was to follow at Lechfeld. It was planned that the *Gruppe*, now renamed I/JG 7, would return to operations from Brandenburg-Briest on 8 January 1945[1101].

Thus ended the four-and-one-half-year history of II/JG 3 "UDET". On reflection, the story of the *Gruppe*, indeed of the entire *Geschwader*, mirrors the rise and fall of the German *Luftwaffe*. The initial successes in the west in 1940 were followed by the first serious setback in the aerial offensive against Great Britain in the late summer and autumn of 1940. Then, in early summer 1941, the beginning of the unholy war against the Soviet Union marked the start of the lengthy wearing-down process, which at first was overshadowed by the tremendous victory figures. Two years of operations in the east, which ended at Kursk, where the Red Army took the initiative in the east for good, had brought the *Gruppe* considerable success (over 1,500 victories), however it also suffered significant losses. Committed to the Defense of the Reich, the *Gruppe* experienced the hopeless struggle against the growing might of the American bomber streams. It was there that its very substance was whittled away, for while replacement pilots and machines were received in sufficient quantities to maintain the unit at its authorized strength (at least on paper), the *Gruppe* continued losing irreplaceable veteran fighter pilots. The result of this was a steady deterioration in its value as a fighting unit, until in summer 1944 the *Gruppe* was virtually eliminated as an air unit in the battles over the invasion zone and during the retreat in France. The unit that was reformed in autumn 1944 using untrained replacements was a mere shadow of past days and it was shattered in the first murderous battles over the Reich. Finally, the *Gruppe* was withdrawn from operations and left the *Geschwader*. As part of JG 7, the *Luftwaffe*'s first jet fighter *Geschwader*, it experienced the start of a new chapter in the history of air warfare, even though it no longer had any influence on the course of events. But that is another story[1102].

Expressed in plain figures, during its existence II/JG 3 claimed a total of about 2,370 enemy aircraft shot down or forced to leave formation. In the following table this victory total is broken down into individual segments:

Victories by II/JG 3

French Campaign	10/05/40 – 30/06/40	48
Operations on the Channel	01/07/40 – 15/02/41	48
Operations on the Channel	01/05/41 – 07/06/41	1
Summer Campaign in the East	22/06/41 – 31/10/41	504
Operations against Malta	20/01/42 – 30/04/42	6
Operations in the East	19/05/42 – 01/08/43	1,538
Defense of the Reich	12/09/43 – 06/06/44	164
Invasion Operations	07/06/44 – 21/08/44	54
Defense of the Reich	16/10/44 – 27/11/44	5 – 10

Losses by II/JG 3 During Same Period

	Pilots		Aircraft	
	KIA	POW	WIA	60 – 100%
French Campaign	4	2	1	10
Operations on the Channel	10	6	4	29
Operations on the Channel	1	0	2	3
Summer Campaign in the East	10	3	9	27
Operations against Malta	3	3	6	16
Operations in the East 1942/43	26	2	18	72
Defense of the Reich 1943/44	49	0	31	141
Invasion Operations	38	0	22	106
Defense of the Reich	19	0	2	26
	160	16	95	430

Because of incomplete records, caution must be used in citing losses among ground personnel; as far as can be determined, it appears that the ground personnel of II/JG 3 lost nine men killed or missing and 17 wounded[1103].

Three photographs of Lt. Walter Wagner in the cockpit of a Bf 109 G-14 taken during II/JG 3's rest and refit at Treysa in September 1944 following its return from France. Apparently this was a newly-delivered machine, for no codes of any kind have yet been applied. Note the tall fin and rudder and the rudder's counterweight which projected from the opposite side of the fin when the rudder was deflected. (Bracke)

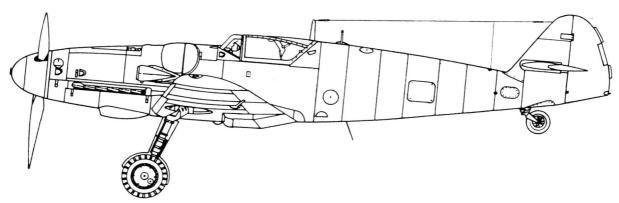

Line Drawing 11: Messerschmitt Bf 109 G-14

During its rest and refit at Treysa in September 1944 II/JG 3 received its first examples of the G-14 series, which for the time being was to form the exclusive equipment of the *Gruppe*. A total of 88 Bf 109 G-14s were assigned to the *Gruppe* before it left the *Geschwader* at the end of November 1944. The new variant did not differ from the final version of the G-6, instead it represented an attempt to standard-ize all of the improvements introduced during the course of G-6 production. Methanol-water injection, which provided a short-term increase in engine output, was supposed to be installed on the production line. Many aircraft were also fitted with an engine-mounted 30-mm MK 108 cannon, which resulted in the designation G-14/U4.

Length: 8.94 m
Wingspan: 9.92 m
Height: 2 60 m

Engine: Daimler Benz DB 605 AM 1,475 H.P.
Takeoff weight: 3 200 kg
Armament: 1 MG 151/20, 2 MG 131

Empty weight: 2 330 kg

The aircraft depicted here has an "Erla Hood", first introduced at the end of 1943 and also known as the "clear-view hood," as well as the enlarged "raised" wooden tail unit.

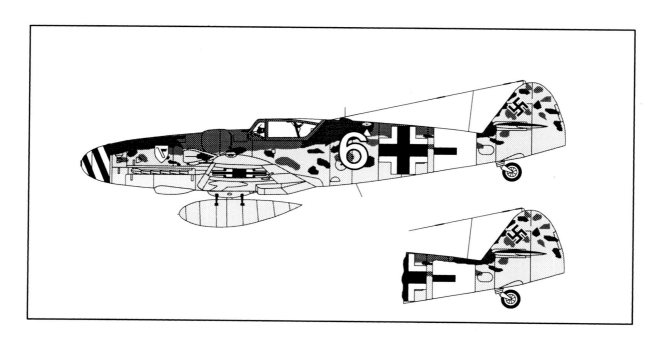

Line Drawing 12: Side view of a Bf 109 G-14 of II/JG 3 in gray finish and the markings standard in autumn 1944.

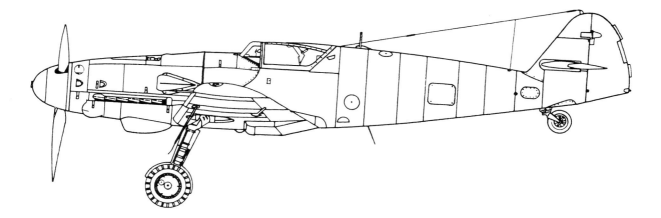

Line Drawing 13: Messerschmitt Bf 109 G-10

II/JG 3 received its first 36 Bf 109 G-10s in November 1944; these were not new-production aircraft, instead they were airframes returned to the manufacturers for repair which were brought up to a technical standard approaching that of the Bf 109 K-4 then being introduced into service. In the weeks that followed, the G-10 was to replace the Bf 109 G-14, which had only recently been placed in service with the *Gruppe*, as its main equipment. Like the K-4 series, most G-10s were powered by the DB 605 D engine; however, a large number of early G-10s were equipped with the DB 605 AS power plant and consequently were designated Bf 109 G-10/AS.

Length: 8.94 m   Engine: Daimler Benz DB 605 D, 1,850 H.P. Empty weight:
Wingspan: 9.92 m   Takeoff weight: 3 300 kg
Height: 2.60 m   Armament: 1 MG 151/20, 2 MG 131

Precise information concerning the G-10's empty weight was not available to the author. The machine illustrated is equipped with the DB 605 D engine.

This photo was probably taken a few days before II/JG 3 left the Geschwader *formation of JG 3; it shows the pilots of 8* Staffel *on a Bf 109 G-10, identifiable by the "chin bulges" on the lower engine cowling. Barely visible is the* Geschwader *emblem, still in use at this time, but without the usual red dot beneath it. On the wing, from left to right, are Lt. Wagner, Obfhr. Toenessen, unidentified, on the engine cowling Fw. Wojnar and standing, from left, unidentified, unidentified, Fhr. Schrey, unidentified, and Uffz. Rach. Alperstedt, second half of November 1944. (Bracke)*

II./*Jagdgeschwader* 3 – New Formation 1944

In order to fill the gap left by the departure of II/JG 3 and bring JG 3 back up to its authorized strength of four *Gruppen*, at the beginning of December 1944 a new II *Gruppe* was incorporated into the *Geschwader*. The new unit originated as I/JG 7 *"Hindenburg"*, which until July 1944 had served as a bomber unit in the east, equipped with the He 177 A and commanded by Hptm. Rohrdantz. When, in August 1944, most bomber units were grounded because of the fuel shortage and subsequently disbanded, II/KG 1 received orders to mothball its He 177 A-5s at Brandis airbase near Leipzig[1104]. Then, on 5 September, it was to transfer to Königsberg/Neumark with its cadre personnel. At the same time, it would be redesignated I/JG 7. The *Gruppe* was supposed be reequipped, first with the Fw 190, then with the Bf 109, however in the end it still had no aircraft of its own well into November 1944[1105]. In any event the *Gruppe* remained at Königsberg until 23 November 1944 before moving to Alperstedt airfield. For the time being it was to retrain for the fighter role, since it was still far from being at a state of operational readiness[1106]. Two days later, on 25 November, the order was issued to rename the *Gruppe* II/JG 3, and this was put into effect at the beginning of December[1107]. The unit's commander was Hptm. Gerhard Baeker, who had been a bomber pilot with KG 1 since the start of the war and who had volunteered to serve in the Defense of the Reich in June 1944. After completing a brief fighter pilot course and taking part in the *General der Jagdflieger*'s unit leader course at Königsberg/Neumark, he assumed command of the *Gruppe*. At this time most of the *Gruppe*'s pilots were also former bomber pilots with minimal fighter training[1108].

The new *Gruppe* apparently took over the entire aircraft complement of the departed II/JG 3[1109] and with these trained for the fighter role for a good two months. There was a serious accident on 1 December: during a training sortie Uffz. Kurt Dürrhammer of 7/JG 3 and Fw. Georg Oberauer of 8/JG 3 collided near Erfurt. Both crashed to their deaths near Grossrudestedt. The period of training apparently ended at the beginning of February 1945 and the *Gruppe* was reported operational. It initially remained at Alperstedt, where it was subordinated to *Luftflotte Reich* for air defense missions against the western allies. And in fact, II/JG 3 did take part in at least one defensive mission against incursions by units of the US 8th Air Force over central Germany. On 9 February 1945 it put up 16 Messerschmitts which joined elements of JG 300 and 301[1110] in intercepting a daylight raid on Magdeburg by 313

Liberators with a strong escort of Mustangs[1111]. Details of II/JG 3's mission are sketchy, in particular it is not known whether the *Gruppe* had any hand in the four Mustangs claimed shot down on this day. On the other hand, the unit's losses amounted to one Messerschmitt slightly damaged in a belly landing at Alperstedt[1113].

This was probably II/JG 3's only mission in the Defense of the Reich, for in mid-February 1945 it received orders to transfer to the east of the Reich to take part in defensive operations against the Russian offensive against Germany which had been under way since mid-January[1114]. It was ordered to the Garz auf Usedom airfield, where the *Stab* and II/JG 1 had been stationed since at the beginning of February[1115]. In those days Garz airfield was completely overcrowded with the remnants of units withdrawing from the east and test units which had evacuated Peenemünde. Conditions on the airfield can only be described as chaotic, and under such circumstances normal operations were virtually impossible. At Garz the *Gruppe* was attached to *1 Fliegerdivision* under GenLt. Fuchs[1116], which in turn was part of *II Fliegerkorps* commanded by *General* Fiebig. The air element made the transfer flight on 20 February and this was overshadowed by several accidents, one of them fatal. Fw. Willi Schreiber of 6/JG 3 went down while taking off from Alperstedt and died in the crash of his Messerschmitt. Four other machines were damaged as a result of mechanical trouble or accidents, however all of the pilots escaped injury.

Operational activity at Garz was extremely limited until the end of the month. On 28 February 1945 at Garz the *Gruppe* reported its strength as 60 Bf 109 G-14s and G-10s, of which 45 were serviceable, and 52 pilots[1117].

There was a noticeable increase in operational activity at Garz in the first days of March 1945 associated with the heavy fighting in Pomerania[1118], especially in the area between Stargard and Rummelsburg. There the Russian armies were attempting to force a breakthrough to the Baltic coast with the objective of encircling all German forces still east of it. In spite of poor weather conditions with low cloud and frequent rain and snow showers, the units of *1 Fliegerdivision* were committed to close-support, escort and low-level attack missions. In the first ten days of March II/JG 3 lost five pilots killed or missing and one captured[1120] while claiming just two victories, including an Airacobra shot down by Lt. Berendes of 7/JG 3 (1) on 3 March 1945. Two pilots were reported missing on 11 March after Lt. Klaus Pajonk and Fw. Heinz Beran, both of 6/JG 3, failed to return from a mission over the Stettin area for reasons unknown.

Operational Activities by II/JG 3 from 1 to 10 March 1945[1119]

1/3/1945	No missions.

2/3/1945   One *Schwarm* fighter escort for tank-destroyers in the Stargard area; attacks on horse-drawn columns, effects not observed due to heavy ground fire. Two machines damaged by anti-aircraft fire.

3/3/1945   Offensive sweep of the airspace around Pyritz. Escort for close-support aircraft and tank-destroyers and low-level attacks on vehicle columns in the Freienwalde—Labes area. Total of 32 Bf 109s committed.

Successes: two victories –

Lt. Berendes	7/JG 3	P-39	(1)	3:07 PM	G.S. 5457
Name unknown	II/JG 3	Yak-9	( )	3:55 PM	G.S. 4964

and two R-5s fired on during low-level attacks on an airfield, results not observed.

Losses: two killed or missing –

Gefr. Claus Günther	5/JG 3	KIA	Freienwalde area
Lt. Gerhard Büker	8/JG 3	MIA	Location not known

Two Bf 109s written off, two others forced landed with bullet damaged.

4/3/1945   No missions.

5/3/1945   Low-level attacks in the Naugard/Rummelsburg area; total of 70 Bf 109s committed.

Successes: numerous vehicles and flak as well as gun positions destroyed, including 34 trucks.

Losses: four pilots.

Lt. Peter Fürbringer	6/JG 3	KIA	near Drewitz.
Obfw. Leo Danetzkii	7/JG 3·	POW	Gölzow area
Gefr. Heinz Abitz	7/JG 3	MIA	Naugard area
Uffz. Rudolf Klotz	8/JG 3	MIA	Gölzow area

Two other Bf 109s belly-landed with battle damage.

6/3/1945   Total of 18 Bf 109s in action, 14 as escorts for tank destroyers, four to reconnoiter the front ahead of the 3rd Panzer Army.

Successes: 4 vehicles destroyed

Losses: 1 Bf 109 force-landed with battle damage.

7/3/1945   No missions

In the second half of the month there was a drastic drop in operational activity, partly because of poor weather but mainly because of the catastrophic fuel situation. As well as isolated sorties over Pomerania, missions were flown in support of aircraft delivering supplies to the German army units cut off in the Courland[1121], after responsibility for defending the waters off Swinemünde was transferred to II *Gruppe* in cooperation with the *Kriegsmarine*.

At the end of March 8 *Staffel* was disbanded and its pilots were divided among the remaining three *Staffeln* of II/JG 3. *Staffelkapitän* Oblt. Grossjohann subsequently assumed command of 6 *Staffel*. At the same time, the *Gruppe* was reinforced through the addition of several pilots of I/JG 3, which had been disbanded a short time earlier. These included Lt. Walter Brandt, a Knight's Cross wearer with 42 victories who flew with a prosthesis after losing a leg[1122]. The pilots of I/JG 3 transferred to II *Gruppe* were trucked from Neubrandenburg to Garz[1123], where they were distributed among the *Staffeln*.

On 3 April, during a mission from Garz, Oblt. Herbert Mielke went down west of the airfield from low altitude and was killed[1124]; Lt. Walter Brandt was subsequently chosen to succeed him as leader of 7 *Staffel*[1125]. The number of missions flown at this time was severely limited. They included several attacks against Russian bridges over the lower Oder by fighter-bombers armed with 250-kg bombs[1126]. The *Gruppe* suffered a tragic loss at this time: on 13 April Uffz. Hermann Picht of 6 *Staffel* was hit by German navy flak shortly after takeoff and forced to return immediately to Garz. As soon as the Messerschmitt touched down, it overturned and burst into flames. Hermann Picht suffered fatal injuries[1127].

A short time later the *Gruppe* received orders to transfer part of the air element to Pillau-Neutief and Brüsterort to support JG 51. In the days that followed, several missions were flown with III/JG 51 under chaotic conditions before the defense front collapsed on 15 April 1945. This was followed by a hurried transfer to Junkertroylhof, a front-line airfield in the Vistula lowlands. After just eight days II/JG 3's detachment returned to Garz, having first handed its machines over to JG 51. The pilots walked across the Frische Nehrung, from where they were taken by ship back to Swinemünde. On 24 April[1129] II/JG 3 sent another detachment to III/JG 51. On that day three *Schwärme* commanded by *Leutnante* Berendes, Ritter and Witt took off for Junkertroylhof, where they were supposed to be subordinated to III/JG 51. Before any missions could be flown, however, most of the Messerschmitts were riddled in the ongoing Russian air raids on the airfield and were left unserviceable. The surviving machines were handed over to III/JG 51. A Ju 52 was supposed to fly the pilots back to Garz, however none was available. An air traffic control vessel subsequently took them as far as Hela, from where a picket boat delivered them to Sassnitz. Finally, a minesweeper took them to Gedser, where they arrived on 1 May 1945[1130].

It appears that the second half of April at Garz was uneventful. Few missions could be flown on account of the catastrophic fuel shortage, the reduced number of available aircraft after the releases to JG 51, and the almost total absence of supplies[1131]. With its remaining machines and fuel reserves, II/JG 3 then intervened in the heavy fighting on the lower Oder. There the Russians had launched another major offensive on 19 April directed against the front of the 3rd Panzer Army. They soon succeeded in establishing a bridgehead on the west bank of the Oder near Stettin, and after heavy fighting this was expanded as far as the area north of Schwedt. This made the situation at Usedom untenable, and on or about 30 April II/JG 3 had ordered to move immediately to Püttnitz. Before the air element departed with the last of the Messerschmitts, the order was issued to elements of the ground personnel still on the airfield, including the signals platoon under Lt. Voigt[1132], to defend the airfield against the approaching Russians. Understandably, the affected ground elements disregarded this insane order and, after the air element had departed Garz, set out along the coast of Mecklenburg/ Schleswig-Holstein. On 5 May they arrived at Klixbüll and experienced the end of the war there. In the first days of May the rest of II/JG 3 with the air element had withdrawn farther to the northwest from Püttnitz. When the cease-fire came into effect on 5 May 1945 the bulk of the *Gruppe* was at Leck airfield[1133], where the remnants of other *Luftwaffe* units had gathered[1134].

Above: Pilots of 6./JG 3 with "Black 7", a Bf 109 G-14, photographed at Gross-Rudelstedt nearErfurt in November 1944. Note the Geschwader *emblem on the engine cowling and the antenna mast for the FuG 16 ZY under the wing. Below: Messerschmitts of 8* Staffel, *including "Blue 8" in the foreground, probably a Bf 109 G-14/AS. None of the aircraft depicted here wear the* Geschwader *emblem or the white Defense of the Reich fuselage band. (Lächler)*

The following series of photographs of 7/JG 3 personnel was taken at Garz auf Usedom in March 1945. In both photos on this page pilots of 7/JG 3 have gathered in front of a Bf 109 G-14 wearing a much modified gray camouflage scheme. Note the obviously overpainted Geschwader *emblem on the engine cowling. Above, standing from left to right, unidentified, unidentified, Obfw. Schwarz, Obfw. Runge,* Staffelführer *Oblt. Mielke, Lt. Berendes, Lt. Niehus and Uffz. Bolte; unfortunately, the names of the three pilots on the wing of the aircraft are not known. (Matthiesen/Meyer-Heintze via Petrick)*

Two more photographs, obviously taken on the same occasion as those on the previous page. Above, from the left, are: unidentified, Uffz. Bolte, Lt. Berendes and Obfw. Schwarz. Second from the right in the photo below is Oblt. Mielke and next to him Uffz. Bolte. Note that aircraft "Yellow 18" wears a white fuselage band with the black Gruppe *bar superimposed, which suggests that not only did the the newly-formed II/JG 3 take over the aircraft of its predecessor* Gruppe *but its marking practises as well. (Matthiesen/Meyer-Heintze via Petrick)*

In these two photographs the much-modified finish worn by "Yellow 18", which was flown by Lt. Helmut Berendes, is plainly evident. Note the octane triangle, which prescribes the use of 100-octane c-3 fuel, as well as the white fuselage band aft of the Balkenkreuz, oversprayed in gray on the fuselage spine. Above Lt. Berendes and Uffz. Bolte stand in front of the machine, below, from left, Lt. Niehus, Oblt. Mielke, Obfw. Runge and Lt. Berendes. (Matthiesen)

Two photographs allegedly taken at Garz on 3 March 1945 depicting Lt. Berendes of 7./JG 3 after returning from an early-afternoon mission during which he shot down a P-39 for his first victory. Several noteworthy details of this Bf 109 G-14 include the row of rivets in front of the cockpit, which suggests that the rectangular fairing associated with the installation of the AS engine was subsequently removed, and the ventilation slot in the rear part of the Erla hood. The latter was designed as a forced-air vent to counter the constant threat of icing, however it did not prove particularly effective. (Matthiesen)

Above left: Lt. Berendes once again, on the cocpit sill of his Messerschmitt, purportedly photographed on the same occasion. Above right: Another pilot of 7/JG 3, possibly Obfw. Schwarz, photographed on the same occasion. Below: Four 7 Staffel pilots with "Yellow 18". (Matthiesen/ Meyer-Heintze via Petrick)

Servicing a Bf 109 G-14 of 7 Staffel, photographed on Garz airfield at the beginning of March 1945; note the external fuel tank and the antenna mast for the FuG 16 ZY under the left wing. (Matthiesen/Meyer-Heintze via Petrick)

This page and top of next: "Yellow 7", a Bf 109 G-10/AS with the WerkNr. 490 629, the aircraft of Lt. Werner Petereit of 7/JG 3. Above Lt. Petereit is seen preparing for a mission at Garz on 11 March 1945, while the two following photos depict the end of this mission, a crash-landing caused by engine failure resulting in the complete destruction of the machine. Werner Petereit was extremely fortunate to escape this crash with only minor injuries. Clearly visible aft of the engine cowling is the style of

fairing typical of the G-10/AS series; once again the external tank may be seen beneath the fuselage as well as the antenna mast for the FuG 16 ZY under the wing. Below: Lt. Petereit with a mechanic under the nose of his Bf 109; note the chin bulge on the lower engine cowling, a feature seen on later variants, specifically the G-10 and K-4, but in many cases on the G-14/AS as well. (Lächler)

Lt. Petereit once again, here riding a bicycle past a row of parked Messerschmitts belonging to II/JG 3. Below: Uffz. Hermann Picht, a pilot in 6/JG 3, in the cockpit of "Yellow 13", a Bf 109 G-14/AS equipped with a bomb rack beneath the fuselage. Both photos were taken at Garz auf Usedom in March 1945. (Lächler)

Above: "Blue 3", a Bf 109 G-10 of 8 Staffel, photographed at Garz auf Usedom in March 1945; note the deep oil cooler under the engine, the large wheel bulges on the wing supper surfaces and the combination of short tailwheel and tall fin and rudder. The aircraft carries neither the Geschwader *emblem or the white fuselage band. Below: "Blue 7", likewise of 8/JG 3, photographed in its dispersal box on Garz airfield; standing in front of the machine is Uffz. Lindemann, the mechanic in charge of the aircraft. Note the* Staffel *standard still bearing the* Staffel *emblem taken over from II/KG 1. (Lächler)*

Above: The Staffelkapitän *of 8/JG 3, Oblt. Günther Grossjohann, in the cockpit of his "Blue 4", a Bf 109 G-10 with the WerkNr. 130 327, photographed at Garz in March 1945. This aircraft's finish has obviously undergone much retouching, its colors are impossible to determine. Clearly visible are the long tailwheel and the standard small undercarriage bulges on the upper surfaces of the wing. Below: Another 8* Staffel *machine was "Blue 1", a Bf 109 G-10/AS with the WerkNr. 490 755. (Lächler)*

Two photographs taken after the war, probably at Leck, to where the remnants of numerous Luftwaffe *units withdrew as the war drew to a close. Visible in the center of the photo are a Bf 109 K-4 and a Bf 109 G-10 whose codes indicate that they belonged to II/JG 3. Note the white fuselage band and the* Geschwader *emblem on the engine cowling. (USAF)*

Two photographs taken at Burg in May 1944. Above: two Bf 109 G-6/AS aircraft of I/JG 3. Tarpaulins have been draped over the aircraft to prevent them from being seen from the air. Note the He 177 on the right. Below: two more Bf 109 G-6/AS.

Three photographs of the aircraft flown by the Kommandeur of II/JG 3, Hptm. Kurt Brändle, a Bf 109 F-4 with the WerkNr. 13 387.

Lt. Hans Fuß, acting commander of 6/JG 3, with his aircraft, a Bf 109 F-4, WerkNr. 13 248. The photograph above suggests that the marking behind the fuselage Balkenkreuz—probably an eagle with talons spread—was also applied on the port side of the fuselage. (See pp. 160-162).

Two photographs taken on 5 July at Kharkov on the occasion of Oblt. Joachim Kirschner's 150th victory. Next to him on the right is Oblt. Förster, who is seen below congratulating Kirschner.

Above: Lt. Münster of 5/JG 3 in front of an earth bunker on the Kharkov airfield, photographed in July 1943. In the background is "Yellow 9", whose markings indicate that it must have belonged to II/JG 52, not II/JG 3. Below: pilots of 5 Staffel, photographed soon after II/JG 3's return to Germany in the late summer of 1943.

Two more pilots of 5/JG 3 on "Black 1", Hptm. Kirschner's aircraft, Schipol, October 1943. Above is Uffz. Rudolf Stephan and below Uffz. Johann Frohlich. (see pp. 230-233).

Two photographs of a group of 5/JG 3 pilots playing cards at Schipol in October 1943. Above, on the left, is Fw. Helmut Notemann, in the center Staffelkapitän Hptm. Joachim Kirschner, and to his right Lt. Horst Brock. Second from the right in the photograph below is Obfw. Hans Grünberg.

Above: Fw. Heinrich Ständebach, a pilot in 6/JG 3, photographed in the cockpit of his aircraft "Yellow 7" in the spring of 1944. Ständebach was shot down and killed near Augsburg on 24 April 1944. Below left: Uffz. Günther Machalosowitz, a pilot in 5/JG 3, photographed in the spring of 1944. Below right: Oblt. Raimund Koch, Kapitän of 8 / 11 Staffel from 16 March 1944 until his death on 2 November of the same year. This photograph was taken at Bad Wörishofen in the late summer of 1943.

Above: Fhr. Herwig Befeldt, a pilot in 8/JG 3, seated on the cowling of his Bf 109 G-6 in the spring of 1944 (also see III/JG 3, Photographs 379 and 380). Below: A Bf 109 G-14 of 9/JG 3 taxis out of its revetment prior to takeoff; Schachten, early December 1944.

Above left: An officer of II/JG 3 in front of a vehicle of the Gruppenstab in the autumn of 1940. Note the Gruppe emblem on the vehicle's fender. Above right and below: Two photographs which appear in black and white as Photographs 115 and 116 in the volume on III/JG 3; the green Gruppe bar is clearly visible.

The following six photographs depict an aircraft of 6/JG 3 which ran out of fuel and made a successful forced landing in the summer of 1942. The aircraft was subsequently refueled and flown back to its base.

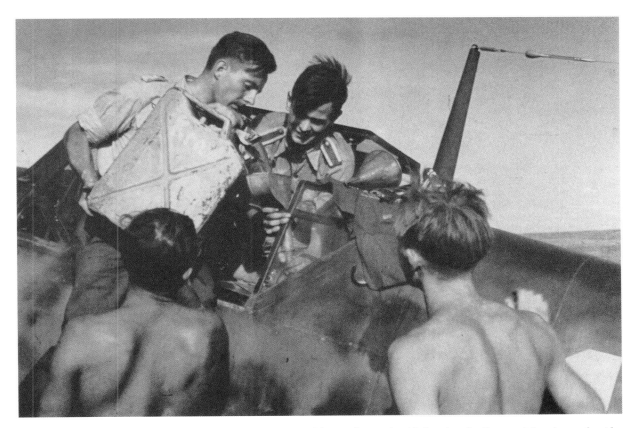

The aircraft is finished in a mottled green-gray scheme. Part of the cowling underside is painted yellow, and the wing undersides are also yellow from the wingtips to the Balkenkreuze. Also visible are the Geschwader and Gruppe emblems and the yellow tip of the propeller spinner.

The aircraft was refueled from canisters, after which the engine was started. Below it is seen turning into the wind in preparation for takeoff.

Appendices

Appendix A:
II./Jagdgeschwader 3 Command Positions

Gruppenkommandeure

Name	Previous Post	Service Dates	Subsequent Post
Hptm. Erich von Selle	GrKdr. II./JG 27	01.02.40 - 30.09.40	Stab NJ-Division
Hptm. Erich Woitke -i. V. -	StKap. 6./JG 3	01.10.40 - 23.11.40	GrKdr. 11./JG 52
Hptm. Lothar Keller	StKap. I./JG 3	241140 - 26.06.41	†
Hptm. Gordon Gollob	StKap. 4./JG 3	27.0641 - 20.11.41	E.-Stelle Rechlin
Hptm. Karl-Heinz Krahl	GrKdr. I./JG 2	21.11.41 - 14.04.42	†
Maj. Kurt Brändle	StKap. 5./JG 53	15.04.42 - 03.11.43	†
Hptm. Heinrich Sannemann - i.V.-	StKap. 6./JG 3	03.11.43 - .11.43	StKap. 6./JG 3
Hptm. Wilhelm Lemke	StKap. 9./JG 3	.11.43 - 04.12.43	†
Hptm. Heinrich Sannemann - i.V.-	StKap. 6./JG 3	04.12.43 - 01.44	StKap. 6./JG 3
Hptm. Detlev Rohwer	StKap. 2./JG 3	02.44 - 30.03.44	†
Hptm. Heinrich Sannemann - i. V. -	StKap. 6./JG 3	30.03.44 - 22.04.44	JGr. West
Hptm. Hermann Frhr, von Kap-herr	Stab III./JG 3	22.04.44 - 24.04.44	
Lt. Leopid Münster - i. V. -	StKap. 5.IJG 3	24.04.44 - 01.05.44	StKap. 5./JG 3
Hptm. Gustav Frielinghaus	Stab IV./JG 3	01.05.44 - 25.0644	
Hptm. Hans-Ekkehard Bob	Stab/JG 3	25.06.44 - 07.44	
Hptm. Herbert Kutscha		07.44 - 30.11.44	Stab IV/JG 27

(*Gruppe* left JG 3 and was renamed I/JG 7)

Staffelkapitäne

4. Staffel

4/JG 3 – from 15/8/1944: 7/JG 3 – from 1/12/1944: 2/JG 7

Name	Previous Post	Service Dates	Subsequent Post
Hptm. Alfred Müller		01.02.40 - 16,08.40	verw.
Oblt. Jost Kipper	4./JG 3	17.08.40 - 29.08.40	†
Lt. Richard von Larisch	4./JG 3	29.08.40 - 31.08.40	†
Oblt. Werner Voigt	5./JG 3	31.08.40 - 08.10.40	KG
Hptm. Gordon Gollob	Stab II./JG 3	12.10.40 - 27.06.41	GrKdr. 11./JG 3
Oblt. Karl Faust	4JJG 3	28.06.41 - 12.07.41	
Hptm. Gerhard Michalek	Stab II./JG 3	15.07.41 - 12.12.41	GrKdr. IJJG 3
Oblt. Walther Dahl	Stab II./JG 3	13.12.41 - 09.0442	Stab/JG 3
Oblt. Albrecht Walz		10.04.42 - 31.07.42	Stab 11./JG 3
Hptm. Gerhard Wendt	Stab/JG 3	01.08.42 - .11.42	Stab Lfl. 4
Hptm. Werner Lucas	4./JG 3	.11.42 - 24.10.43	†
Lt. Franz Ruhl - i.V.-	Stab II./JG 3	09.43 - 09.43	4./JG 3
Lt. Leopold Münster - i. V. -	5./JG 3	09.43 - .10.43	5./JG 3
Lt. Franz Ruhl	4./JG 3	24.10.43 - 07.44	erkrankt
Obfw. Hans Grünberg - i. V. -	5JJG 3	.0444 - 04.44	
Hptm. Herbert Kutscha	StKap. 12./JG 3	07.44 -07.44	GrKdr. 11./JG 3
Lt. Franz Rühl	StKap. 4./JG 3	07.44 -.11.44	StKap. 4./1./JG 3
Lt. Erich Prettner - i.V. -	4./JG 3	10.08.44 -.08.44	VJG 3

5. Staffel

5/JG 3 – from 1/12/1944: 1/JG 7

Hptm. Herbert Kijewski		01.02.40 - 07.41	III./JG 3
Oblt. Harald Moldenhauer	2./JG 3	07.41 - 30.09.42	Stab Lfl. 3[1]
Oblt. Joachim Kirschner	5./JG 3	.09.42 - 18.10.43	GrKdr. IV./JG 27
Hptm. Heinrich Sannemann	Stab II./JG 3	18.10.43 - 20.10.43	Stab II./JG 3
Oblt. Leopold Münster	5./JG 3	20.10.43 - 08.05.44	†
Lt. Hans Grünberg	5./JG 3	09.05.44 - 30.11.44	

6. Staffel

Oblt. Erich Woitke		01.02.40 - 23.11,40	GrKdr. II./JG 52[2]
Oblt. Heinrich Sannemann	6./JG 3	23.11.40 - 3L03.42	LKS 3 Werder
Oblt. Hans-Jürgen Waldhelm		01.04.42 - 07,42	1./SG 2
Lt. Hans Fuß	Stab II./JG 3	01.08.42 - 14.09.42	verw.
N.N. - i.V. -		14.09.42 - .10.42	
Oblt. Paul Stolte	stellv, GrFhr. I./JG 1	.10.42 - 18.10.43	†
Oblt. Gustav Frielinghaus - i. V. -	6./JG 3	25.03.43 - 31.05.43	StKap. II/JG 3
Hptm. Heinrich Sannemann	Stab II./JG 3	24.10.43 - 22.04.44	JGr. West[3]
Lt. Oskar Zimmermann	1 IAG 3	22.04.44 - 25.07.44	StKap. 9./JG 3
Lt. Walter Becker		' 07.44 - 02.11.44	†
N.N.		03.11.44 - 30.11.44	

(*Staffel* disbanded on 1/12/1944, pilots probably assigned to I/JG 7)

8. *Staffel*

4/JG 52 – from 15/8/1944: 8/JG 3 – from 1/12/1944: 3/JG 7

Oblt. Hans Waldmann	StKap. 4./JG 52	01.07.44 - 30.11.44	StKap. 3./JG 7

Notes:

[1] According to personnel files, Harold Moldenhauer did not assume command of 5/JG 3 until 26/11/1941, however this appears to have been merely the date he was confirmed as *Staffelkapitän*, for according to statements by several members of the unit he un fact took over the *Staffel* in July 1941.

[2] According to personnel files, Hptm. Erich Woitke was transferred to II/JG 52 on 2/11/1940. However, he apparently remained with II/JG 3 past that date, and on 23-24 November 1940 handed command of the *Gruppe* over to Hptm. Keller. The log book of Oblt. Sannemann, Keller's successor as *Kapitän* of 6 *Staffel*, reveals that he assumed command of 6/JG 3 on the same day.

[3] According to personnel files, Lt. Oskar Zimmermann was named as Hptm. Sannemann's successor on 7/4/1944, however Heinrich Sannemann's personal documents reveal that he retained command of his *Staffel* until 22/4/1944.

II/Jagdgeschwader 3 (new)

List of Command Positions

Gruppenkommandeure

Name	Previous Post	Service Dates	Subsequent Post
Hptm. Gerhard Baeker	Kdr. 11./JG 7	25.11.44 - 08.05.45	

Staffelkapitäne

5. Staffel

Oblt. Werner Seidler	StKap. 4./JG 7	25.11.44 - 08.05.45	

6. Staffel

Oblt. Heyer?		25.11.44 -	

7. Staffel

NN		25.11.44 - 23.12.44	
Hptm. Karl-Heinz Dietsche	StKap. 12./JG 301	24.12.44 - .03.45	StKap. 6/G 300
Oblt. Herbert Mielke	7./JG 3	.03.45 - 03.04.45	†
Lt. Walter Brandt	StKap. 2./JG 3	04.04.45 - .04.45	

8. Staffel

Oblt. Günther Großjohann	StKap. 6./JG 7	25.11.44 - 08.05.45	

Appendix B:
Losses of II./Jagdgeschwader 3
1940-1945

The following loss list for II/JG 3 is based largely on three sources: the casualty reports submitted by the unit, which are presently in possession of the WASt., the Quartermaster-General's loss reports concerning aircraft losses of operational units for the period spring 1940 to December 1943 and January to March 1945, and the summarized aircraft losses of the flying units, which contain the daily losses grouped roughly according to cause. The latter source is of special importance, because the Quartermaster-General's reports for the year 1944 have so far not been found, and because it at least contains the number and cause of purely material losses which did not also involve personnel loss. Further information came from a multitude of individual sources such as log books, crash recovery reports and various other types of reports. The chaotic conditions that existed, especially in the final months of the war, are the reason why so many gaps exist in the loss reports from March 1945 at the latest, although there are many days in February 1945 for which the Quartermaster-General's reports contain no information. The WASt. personnel loss reports go as far as March 1945, differing from *Gruppe* to *Gruppe*, while the summarized loss reports end in January 1945.

Where purely material losses are concerned, the following list is based on the information contained in the summarized loss reports (RL / III/ 852) and follows its groupings in regard to causes of loss without, however, going into all the differences, for example whether or not the loss in question involved the enemy being sighted. Where reference is made to an „*operational loss*," this refers in the broadest sense to losses through accidents of any type, whether on the ground or in the air. Losses due to „*mechanical problem*" during a combat mission are operational losses which were not due to enemy action.

The severity of damage to an aircraft was expressed as a percentage based on the following formula:

under 10%	minor battle damage, which in some cases could be repaired by the chief mechanic
10 – 24%	moderate damage, requiring minor repairs at the unit level
25 – 39%	damage which required an aircraft inspection by the unit
40 – 44%	damage which required the replacement of the engine or systems (hydraulics, for example); in many cases the work could be completed at the unit level.
45 – 59%	heavily damaged aircraft requiring replacement of major components; in some cases the work could be done at the unit level, for example the replacement of a wing.
60 – 80%	unusable aircraft in which usable parts could be removed for further use, aircraft which were temporarily unusable (wrinkled fuselage, for example), or permanently unusable.
81 – 99%	write-off, crashed in friendly territory
100%	write-off (crashed into sea or in enemy territory)

Explanation of Loss Tables:

Column 1:	Date of loss
Column 2:	Component unit within the *Geschwader*: I = I/JG 3, 2 = 2/JG 3 etc.)
Column 3:	Name of pilot, if this is absent, the pilot was as a rule not injured or the injury occurred on the ground; NN = name not known.
Column 4:	Fate of the pilot: + = killed, MIA = missing, (MIA) = reported missing, eventually returned, POW = prisoner of war, W = wounded, Inj. = injured, - = pilot unhurt.
Column 5:	Cause of loss: P = pilot escaped by parachute; D = aircraft damaged, degree not known.
Column 6:	Aircraft type, partial designation indicates subtype of Bf 109 (T for tropical).
Column 7:	Aircraft *Werknummer*.
Column 8:	Tactical code worn by aircraft.

Losses during the Formation Period
1 February to 19 May 1940

30/03/40	II	NN	Inj.	Crashed on landing, Zerbst, 85%	Bf 109 E-1

Losses during Operations in the French Campaign
19 May to 30 June 1940

20/05/40	5	Lt. Peter Wisser	+	Air combat, struck ground 3 km south of Arras, 100%	Bf 109 E-3
21/05/40	4	Lt. Ernst Ewers	POW	Air combat Bloch 152, crashed near Arras, 100%	Bf 109 E
	4	Uffz. Robert Brüchert	POW	Air combat, Bloch 152, crashed near Arras, 100%	Bf 109 E
	6	Lt. Gottfried Pollack	+	Forced landing while returning from combat mission, near Aachen, 100%	Bf 109 E
	II	NN	—	Overturned on landing, Liège, 100%	Bf 109 E-3
25/05/40	5	Uffz. Max Bücher	+	Landing collision, ferry flight, Montécouvez-North, 100%	Bf 109 E
	5	NN	—	Landing collision, ferry flight, Montécouvez-North, 100%	Bf 109 E-1
	II	NN	—	Air combat, location not known, 30%	Bf 109 E
	II	NN	—	Air combat, location not known, 20%	Bf 109 E
06/06/40	4	Lt. Rudolf Heymann	+	Air combat Hurricane, crashed south of Cavillon, P, 100%	Bf 109 E-3
	4	Fw. August-Wilhelm Müller	W	Air combat Potez, crashed near St. Sauflieu, 100%	Bf 109 E-3
	4	Fw. Erwin Dickow	+	Air combat Curtiss P-36, crashed south of Amiens, 100%	Bf 109 E-3
09/06/40	II	NN	—	Landing collision, Valheureux, 70%	Bf 109 E-3
	II	NN	—	Landing collision, Valheureux, 70%	Bf 109 E
10/06/40	II	NN	—	Air combat, Vernon, 70%	Bf 109 E-3
19/06/40	5	Uffz. Fritz Mias	(M)	Air combat Hurricane, south of Cherbourg, forced landing near Brézolles, 100%	Bf 109 E

Losses during Operations on the Channel and over England
July 1940 to February 1941

11/07/40	5	NN	—	Taxiing accident, Baromesnil, 70%	Bf 109 E-3
03/08/40	5	NN	—	Engine failure, crash landing, Aumale, 60%	Bf 109 E-1
05/08/40	5	NN	—	Engine trouble, forced landing Brombois, 5%	Bf 109 E-1
07/08/40	4	NN	—	Forced landing near Samer, 15%	Bf 109 E-1

08/08/40	5	NN	—	Forced landing, Samer, 15%	Bf 109 E-4	
14/08/40	6	Obfw. Erich Labusga	M	Air combat, Dover—Calais area, 100%	Bf 109 E-1	
16/08/40	4	Hptm. Alfred Müller, Stk.	W	Air combat over the sea, 100%	Bf 109 E-4	
	5	Uffz. Walter Ohlrogge	—	Air combat over the sea, crashed south of Dungeness, 100%	Bf 109 E-4	
18/08/40	4	Fw. August-Wilhelm Müller	—	Air combat, forced landing Brombois[1121], 60%	Bf 109 E-1	
	6	Uffz. Friedrich Becker	+	Air combat, forced landing Marquise, 80%	Bf 109 E-4	
	6	Fw. Erich Dobrick	W	Air combat, crash landing Boulogne, 70%	Bf 109 E-4	
19/08/40	4	NN	—	Crashed Brombois, 70%	Bf 109 E-1	
26/08/40	4	Uffz. Willy Finke	+	Air combat, crashed near Reculver, 100%	Bf 109 E-4	5289
	4	Uffz. Emil Müller	M	Combat mission, air combat Canterbury area, 100%	Bf 109 E-1	6221
	5	NN		Engine trouble, forced landing Ossendrecht, 10%	Bf 109 E-4	3317
	6	Uffz. Fritz Buchner	+	Air combat, crashed Thames Estuary, 100%	Bf 109 E-1	3874
27/08/40	6	NN	—	Landing accident, Samer, 75%	Bf 109 E-4	1471
28/08/40	5	Obfw. Horst Götz	W	Air combat between Samer and Boulogne, 100%	Bf 109 E-4	5142
	5	NN	—	Air combat, crashed off Boulogne, 100%	Bf 109 E-4	1449
	5	NN	—	Air combat, crashed into the sea off Boulogne, 100%	Bf 109 E-1	6011
29/08/40	4	Oblt. Jost Kipper, Stf.	+	Air combat, crashed at Hooe near Hastings, 100%	Bf 109 E-1	1134
	4	Uffz. Walter Gericke	+	Air combat Hastings area, crashed into the sea, 100%	Bf 109 E-4	5364
30/08/40	II	NN	—	Tailwheel failure, Wierre-au-Bois, 15%	Bf 109 E-1	3350
31/08/40	4	Lt. Richard von Larisch	+	Air combat south of London, 100%	Bf 109 E-1	3175
	6	Oblt. Karl Westerhoff	POW	Air combat east of Hastings, crashed near Lydd, 100%	Bf 109 E-4	1475
02/09/40	4	NN	—	landing accident Wierre-au-Bois, 10%	Bf 109 E-4	5130
	5	NN	—	Air combat over the sea, forced landing Marquise, 75%	Bf 109 E-4	1443
	6	NN	—	Air combat, forced landing Sangatte, 30%	Bf 109 E-4	1469
05/09/40	Stab II	Oblt. Franz von Werra	POW	Air combat, forced landing near Marden south of London, 100%	Bf 109 E-4	1480	Black < ±
	5	NN	—	Air combat, ditched in sea, 100% Bf 109 E-4 1464		
09/09/40	4	Obfw. August-Wilhelm Müller	POW	Air combat, Dover area, crashed into sea, 100%	Bf 109 E-	6138

	6	NN	—	Crash landing, Wierre-au-Bois, 10%	Bf 109 E-1 6236
11/09/40	6	NN	—	Forced landing, Wierre-au-Bois, 45%	Bf 109 E-4 5056
27/09/40	6	NN	—	Air combat, crashed into sea, 100%	Bf 109 E-4 4141
28/09/40	4	Gefr. Leo Suschko	—	Air combat, Dover area, forced landing on beach near Le Portel, 30%	Bf 109 E-4 6339
	5	NN	—	Crash landing, Het Zoute, 25%	Bf 109 E-1 3588
08/10/40	4	Oblt. Werner Voigt, Stk.	POW	Air combat London area, crashed into sea, 100%	Bf 109 E-4 1656
	6	NN	—	Failed takeoff, St. Omer Arques, 20%	Bf 109 E-4 1154
09/10/44	4	NN	—	Engine trouble, forced landing Arques, 40%	Bf 109 E-4 1463
14/10/40	4	NN	—	landing accident, Arques, 25% Bf 109 E-4 5359	
15/10/40	4	Gefr. Kurt Jahnke	W	Combat mission, engine failure, crashed at Le Portel, 100%	Bf 109 E-4 6100
	5	NN	—	Air combat, forced landing Arques, 20%	Bf 109 E-1 3297
	5	NN	—	Takeoff accident, Arques, 60% Bf 109 E-1 3251	
17/10/40	4	Obgefr. Wert	—	Crash landing, St. Omer Arques, 30%	Bf 109 E-1 4830
29/10/40	5	Obfw. Horst Götz	+	Crashed during ferry flight, near Arques airfield, 95%	Bf 109 E-1 4873
30/10/40	4	Gefr. Leo Suschko	—	Air combat, forced landing Wissant, 30%	Bf 109 E-4 1126
	6	Uffz. Alfred Fahrian	POW	Air combat, crashed near Leylands, 100%	Bf 109 E-4 6360 Yellow 9 ±
	6	Gefr. Eugen Schuller	POW	Air combat, crashed near East Farleigh, 100%	Bf 109 E-4 1474 Yellow 1 ±
11/11/40	6	NN	—	Crash landing, St. Omer Arques, 25%	Bf 109 E-1 3643
02/12/40	6	NN	—	Undercarriage failure, Arques, 30%	Bf 109 E-7 6328
11/01/41	4	NN	—	Pilot error, Arques, 25%	Bf 109 E-4 5359
04/02/41	6	Uffz. Eduard Rybiak	+	Crashed while on maintenance test flight, Vendeville, 100%	Bf 109 E-4 1485
05/02/41	5	NN	—	Engine trouble, Lille, 15%	Bf 109 E-7 4113
08/02/41	4	NN	—	Fighter-bomber attack during takeoff, Arques, 25%	Bf 109 E-4 2036
	4	NN	—	Taxiing accident, Arques, 5%	Bf 109 E7 4093
	6	NN	—	Crash landing, Arques, 10%	Bf 109 E-4 1243
11/02/41	5	NN	—	Crash landing, Arques, 10%	Bf 109 E-4 773

Reequipment and Return to Operations on the Channel
May to June 1941

07/05/41	5	Uffz. Ernst Pöske	W	Air combat, Spitfires, forced landing Etaples, 20%	Bf 109 F-2	12 652	
08/05/41	4	Lt. Joachim Pfeiffer	MIA	Air combat, Spitfires, over the Channel, 100%	Bf 109 F-2		White 9 ±
	4	Lt. Karlheinz Ponec	W	Air combat, ditched north of Gravelines, 100%	Bf 109 F-2	5765	
	6	NN	—	Air combat, forced landing Etaples, 20%	Bf 109 F-2		
10/05/41	5	NN	—	Engine trouble, belly landing Calais-Marck, 10%	Bf 109 F-1	5709	
26/05/41	II	NN	—	Crash landing, Monchy-Breton, 60%	Bf 109 F-2	5748	
	II	NN	—	Crash landing, Monchy-Breton, 10%	Bf 109 F-2	8922	
27/05/41	II	NN	—	Failed takeoff, Wevelghem, 70%	Bf 109 F-2	12 750	

Losses during Operations in the East
June to September 1941

22/06/41	4	Uffz. Leo Suschko	—	Undercarriage failure, belly landing, Hostynne, 20%	Bf 109 F-2	12 601	
	8	Fw. Hermann Freitag	(MIA)	Combat mission, air combat Lvov-Brody area, P, 100% (returned 2/7)	Bf 109 F-2	12 658	Black 9 ±
	II	NN	—	Blown tire, Hostynne, 15%	Bf 109 F-2	6742	
	II	NN	—	Ran out of fuel, forced landing Zamosc, 20%	Bf 109 F-1	5709	
	II	NN	—	Pilot error, Hostynne, 10%	Bf 109 F-2	12 656	
23/06/41	II	NN	—	Crash landing, Hostynne, 25%	Bf 109 F-2	12 648	
	II	NN	—	Crash landing, Hostynne, 50% Bf 109 F-2 5699			
	II	NN	—	Forced landing, Tomasczew, 15% Bf 109 F-2 6739			
	II	NN	—	Taxiing accident, bad surface conditions, Hostynne, 10%	Bf 109 F-2	12 651	
24/06/41	4	Obfw. Erwin Kortlepel	(MIA)	Enemy fire, Kol Knidhinnek, 100% (returned 27/6/41)	Bf 109 F-2	6745	White 6 ±
	5	Uffz. Eduard Kunz	POW	Air combat, crashed 12 km east of Busk, 100%	Bf 109 F-2	12 762	Black 12 ±
25/06/41	4	Obfhr. Albert Helm	W	Enemy fire, Beresteczko, 25%	Bf 109 F-2	8122	
	4	NN	—	Taxiing accident, Hostynne, 40%	Bf 109 F-2	6746	
	5	Lt. Horst Buddenhagen	+	Struck ground during low-level attack, south of Beresteczko, 100%	Bf 109 F-2	8941	
	II	NN	—	Crash landing, Hostynne, 10%	Bf 109 F-2	5482	
26/06/41	Stab II	Hptm. Lothar Keller, Grk.	+	Air combat, collision, crashed west of Stoyanov, 100%	Bf 109 F		

	6	Lt. Ludwig Häfner	Inj.	Crash landing, Beresteczko, 50%	Bf 109 F-1 5728	
	II	NN	—	Crash landing, Hostynne, 30%	Bf 109 F-2 5750	
27/06/41	4	Obfw. Anton Gremm	+	Air combat SB-2, location not known, 100%	Bf 109 F-2 5519	White 9 ±
29/06/41	4	Uffz. Leo Suschko	(MIA)	Air combat SB-2, SE of Dubno, 100% (returned 1/7/1941)	Bf 109 F-2 9608	
30/06/41	II	NN	—	Ran out of fuel, forced landing Wycer, 10%	Bf 109 F-2 5713	
02/07/41	5	Lt. Friedrich Kanzler	+	Crashed after takeoff, Lutsk, 100%	Bf 109 F-2 9602	
03/07/41	II	NN	—	Flak, Lutsk-Rovno area, 20%	Bf 109 F-2 8907	
06/07/41	4	Uffz. Kuno Bälz	—	Enemy fire, belly landing near Wlodzimierz, 40%	Bf 109 F-2 12 646	
08/07/41	5	Fw. Fritz Mias	—	Combat mission, air combat, location not known, 100%	Bf 109 F-2 9599	Black 8 ±
	II	NN	—	Enemy fire, Polonnoye, 70%	Bf 109 F-2 12 703	
	II	NN	—	Pilot error, crash landing, Gleiwitz, 30%	Bf 109 F-2 661?	
10/07/41	II	NN	—	Crash landing, Miropol, 20%	Bf 109 F-2 8112	
11/07/41	4	Obfhr. Albert Helm	—	Ground fire, forced landing just this side of the lines, near Januspol, 65%	Fi 156 C-1 0698[1122]	
	6	Uffz. Horst Beyer	+	Combat mission, cause not known, south of Kiev, 100%	Bf 109 F-2 9156	Yellow 7 ±
	6	NN	—	Air combat, Miropol area, 10%	Bf 109 F-2 12 702	
	II	NN	—	Air combat, belly landing Tyranovka, 25%	Bf 109 F-2 12 708	
12/07/41	4	Oblt. Karl Faust, Stk.	+	Forced landing in enemy territory, Chernyakhov, 100% (shot by Russian soldiers)	Bf 109 F-2 9164	White 5 ±
14/07/41	II	NN	—	Belly landing, Tyranovka, 20%	Bf 109 F-2	
23/07/41	II	NN	—	Air combat with fighters, Stawiscze, 80%	Bf 109 F-2 5540	
	II	NN	—	Enemy fire, belly landing Belaya-Tserkov, 30%	Bf 109 F-2 8993	
25/07/41	4	Uffz. Kuno Bälz	(MIA)	Combat mission, location and cause not known, 100%	Bf 109 F-2 8918	White 7 ±
	6	Lt. Gustav Frielinghaus	W	Air combat bombers, north of Stawuszce, forced landing, 15%	Bf 109 F-2 8996	
26/07/41	II	NN	—	Air combat fighters, Moroszkoad, 25%	Bf 109 F-2 12 667	
	II	NN	—	Flak, Stawiscze, 30%	Bf 109 F-1 5741	
	II	NN	—	Engine trouble, Belaya-Tserkov, 25%	Bf 109 F-2 6811	
01/08/41	4	NN	—	Flak, belly landing Belaya-Tserkov, 60%	Bf 109 F-4 8389	White 7 ±

11/08/41	Stab II	Oblt. Heinrich Schoenefeldt	+	Ground fire during low-level attack, crashed 6 km SE of Ossokorki, 100%	Bf 109 F-4	7145	
	5	Lt. Herbert Glück	POW	Ground fire during low-level attack, forced landing SW of Kiev, 100%	Bf 109 F-4	8393	Black 4 ±
17/08/41	II	NN	—	Air combat, Kirovograd, 20%	Bf 109 F-4	8391	
19/08/41	II	NN	—	Engine failure, Alferovo, 25%	Bf 109 F-4	7153	
24/08/41	II	NN	—	Flak, Yekaterinoslav, 20%	Bf 109 F-4	8371	
25/08/41	II	NN	—	Air combat fighters, Dnepropetrovsk, 15%	Bf 109 F-4	7150	
	II	NN	—	Flak, Alexandrovka, 25%	Bf 109 F-4	7103	
	II	NN	—	Air combat fighters, Dneprodsershinsk, 15%	Bf 109 F-4	7142	
26/08/41	Stab II	Uffz. Kuno Bälz	Inj.	Crashed on takeoff, Stschastliwaja, 95%	Bf 109 F-4	7095	
27/08/41	5	Gefr. Georg Reichhart	+	Crashed on takeoff due to pilot error, Stschastliwaja, 75%	Bf 109 F-4	8377	
29/08/41	II	NN	—	Flak, belly landing Stschastliwaja, 20%	Bf 109 F-4	7143	
01/09/41	4	NN	—	Air combat fighters, Krasnopol, 20%	Bf 109 F-4	8383	White 1 ±
	4	Obfw. Heinrich Brenner	—	Air combat fighters, Derijewka, belly landing, 25%	Bf 109 F-4	8375	
07/09/41	4	Obfw. Heinrich Brenner	+	Air combat I-16, crashed near Miranovka, 100%	Bf 109 F-4	7155	White 8 ±
	6	Lt. Ludwig Häfner	Inj.	Forced landing, overturned, Przsemysl, 80%	Bf 109 F-4		
11/09/41	II	NN	—	Enemy fire, Rublevka, 25%	Bf 109 F-4	7154	
13/09/41	6	Uffz. Edmund Mächler	W	Air combat, west of Derijewka, 100%	Bf 109 F-4	7210	
14/09/41	II	NN	—	Blown tire, crash landing, Miranovka, 35%	Bf 109 F-4	7216	
18/09/41	5	Gefr. Paul Brune	+	Combat mission, cause not known, crashed near Poltava, 100%	Bf 109 F-4	7141	Black 10 ±
19/09/41	II	NN	—	Air combat, Kremenchug, 30%	Bf 109 F-4	8370	
	II	NN	—	Made contact with ground, Kremenchug, 35%	Bf 109 F-4	8386	
	II	NN	—	Pilot error, Miranovka, 25%	Bf 109 F-4	7248	
	4	Fhr. Eckart König	—	Ran out of fuel, forced landing, Kremenchug, 15%	Bf 109 F-4	7151	
20/09/41	4	Lt. Albert Helm	(MIA)	Shot down by Ju 88, Kharkov area, 100% (returned 28/9)	Bf 109 F-4	7238	White 2 ±
	II	NN	—	Enemy fire, Derijewka, 25%	Bf 109 F-4	8390	
23/09/41	6	Uffz. Karl-Heinz Steinicke	(MIA)	Combat mission, cause not known (probably ran out of fuel), Poltava area, 30%	Bf 109 F-4	7152	Yellow 10 ±

24/09/41	II	NN	—	Enemy fire, Krasnograd, 35%	Bf 109 F-4	8387
06/10/41	5	NN	—	Failed takeoff, Sechtschinskaja, 25%	Bf 109 F-4	8452
18/10/41	4	NN	—	Air combat fighters, Chaplinka, 40%	Bf 109 F-4	8449
	5	NN	—	Air combat fighters, Perekop, 25%	Bf 109 F-4	8445
19/10/41	6	Obfw. Helmuth Keller	W	Air combat, Chaplinka, 30%	Bf 109 F-4	7157
24/10/41	4	Fw. Hans-Georg Riedrich	POW	Engine trouble, crashed 30 km SE Juschim, Crimea, P, 100%	Bf 109 F-4	7146
29/10/41	5	Fw. Fritz Mias	Inj.	Failed takeoff, Chaplinka, 100%	Bf 109 F-4	7114
03/11/41	II	NN	—	Ground looped on takeoff, Orel, 50%	Bf 109 F-4	7140

Losses during Operations in the Mediterranean Theater
January to May 1942

22/01/42	II	NN	—	Blown tire on takeoff, Catania, 50%	Bf 109 F-4	8583	
27/01/42	6	Uffz. Edmund Mächler	Inj.	Undercarriage failure, crashed on takeoff, Sciacca, 100%	Bf 109 F-4T	8576	
	6	Uffz. Heinrich Raben	Inj.	Undercarriage failure, crashed on takeoff, Sciacca, 80%	Bf 109 F-4T	8657	
31/01/42	6	NN	—	Collision on takeoff, Bari, 65%	Bf 109 F-4	8664	
	6	Uffz. Alfred Fischer	—	Engine trouble, forced landing near Cap Porto Empedolce, 100%	Bf 109 F-4	8662	Yellow 7 ±
	II	NN	—	Collision on takeoff, Bari, 50% Bf 109 F-4 8690			
13/02/42	Stab II	Lt. Karlheinz Ponec	+	Engine failure, ditched 5 km south of Agrigento, 100% Bf 109 F-4 8571			Black 3 ±
15/02/42	II	NN	—	Ground looped on landing, Sciacca, 15%	Bf 109 F-4T	8658	
22/02/42	II	NN	—	Taxiing accident, Pantelleria, 60%	Bf 109 F-4	8683	
	II	NN	—	Undercarriage failure, Trapani, 20%	Bf 109 F-4	8678	
02/03/42	4	Obgefr. Heinz Golke	Inj.	Crashed near Sciacca, pilot error, 100%	Kl 35	4092	PF + LB
04/03/42	5	Uffz. Benedikt Wegmann	POW	Engine trouble, bailed out 10 km north of La Valetta, 100%	Bf 109 F-4T	8649	Black 3 ±
07/03/42	4	Obfhr. Eckart König	Inj.	Struck obstacle during takeoff, Catania, 100%	Bf 109 F-4T	7367	
08/03/42	4	NN	—	Crash landing, San Pietro, 60%	Bf 109 F-4	8666	
	13	Uffz. Robert Weinländer	—	Ran out of fuel, overturned on landing, Comiso, 60%	Bf 109 F-4	8513	
20/03/42	6	Uffz. Michael Beikiefer	+	Propeller taken off by cement practice bomb during bomb-dropping practice, crashed into sea south of Gela, 100%	Bf 109 F-4T	8667	Yellow 3 ±
	6	NN	—	Crash landing, San Pietro, 15%	Bf 109 F-4T	8647	

Date	Unit	Name	Status	Description	Aircraft	Code
21/03/42	4	Uffz. Wolfgang Buttstädt	Inj.	Engine trouble, ditched 30 km south of San Pietro, 100%	Bf 109 F-4T 8671	
25/03/42	4	Lt. Rudolf Wicklaus	W	Air combat Spitfires, crashed into sea 50 km south of Pozzallo, P, 100%	Bf 109 F-4T 8576	
26/03/42	6	Uffz. Alfred Fischer	—	Flak, crashed near Gozo, P, 100%	Bf 109 F-4T 10 002	
	II	NN	—	Ground looped on takeoff, San Pietro, 50%	Bf 109 F-4T 8586	
01/04/42	5	Uffz. Hans Pilz	POW	Shot down by flak, over La Valetta, 100%	Bf 109 F-4T 8668	Black 11 ±
07/04/42	6	Uffz. Alfred Fischer	—	Crash landing, Martuba, 10%	Bf 109 F-4T	
	6	Uffz. Waldemar Eyrich	—	Crash landing, Martuba, 10%	Bf 109 F-4 T	
08/04/42	6	Uffz. Wolfgang Vogel	—	Crash landing, Arco Philaenorum, 100%	Bf 109 F-4 T	
	6	Uffz. Franz Schwaiger	—	Ground looped on landing, Martuba, 10%	Bf 109 F-4T	Yellow 3 ±
13/04/42	6	Uffz. Josef Fritz	POW	Air combat P-40, El Adem area, forced landing, 100%	Bf 109 F-4T 10 019	Yellow 12 ±
14/04/42	Stab II	Hptm. Karl-Heinz . Krahl, Grk	+	Flak, near Lucqa airfield, 100%	Bf 109 F-4T 8784	Black << ±
25/04/42	6	Uffz. Waldemar Eyrich	—	Flak, also shell exploded in barrel of engine-mounted cannon, crash landing Martuba, 10%	Bf 109 F-4 T	
29/04/42	II	NN	—	Ground looped on takeoff, San Pietro, 70%	Bf 109 F-4 8645	

Losses during Operations in the East
May 1942 to July 1943

Date	Unit	Name	Status	Description	Aircraft	Code
20/05/42	II	NN	—	Engine failure, Kharkov, 20%	Bf 109 F-4 10 008	
21/05/42	6	Uffz. Robert Weinländer	MIA	Flak, crashed 50 km NE of Volchansk, P, 100%	Bf 109 F-4 10 127	
25/05/42	4	Lt. Albert Helm	+	Ground fire, crashed 50 km NE of Mikhailovskaya, 100%	Bf 109 F-4 10 117	White1 ±
01/06/42	4	NN	—	Ground looped on takeoff, Kharkov-Rogany, 50%	Bf 109 F-4 10 097	
13/06/42	4	Uffz. Arthur Fischer	Inj.	Cooling system failure, forced landing Pechenegi, 75%	Bf 109 F-4 8643	
	6	Lt. Hans Fuß	—	Forced landing, cause not known, near Artemovskaya, less than 5%	Bf 109 F-4	
14/06/42	5	NN	—	Flak, Anovka, 15%	Bf 109 F-4Z 7261	
21/06/42	Stab II	Obgefr. Emil Jazbec	MIA	Missing on courier flight from Roganj to Shchigry, cause not known, 100%	Kl 35 3245	PM + XT
	5	Uffz. Berthold Neumann	MIA	as above (passenger)		
	5	NN	—	Engine failure, forced landing Barikova, 20%	Bf 109 F-4 8769	
	5	NN	—	Pilot error, crash landing, Barikova, 80%	Bf 109 F-4 8689	

24/06/42	4	NN	—	Enemy fire, Dolgenkaya, 30%		Bf 109 F-4	8793	
28/06/42	5	NN	—	Crashed, cause not known, Shchigry, 100%		Bf 109 F-4	13 336	
	6	NN	—	Ground looped on takeoff, Shchigry, 40%		Bf 109 F-4	7304	
29/06/42	II	NN	—	Flak, Mamischy, 20% Bf 109 F-4 10 003			
30/06/42		Uffz. Karl Hamm	+	Air combat Il-2, east of Kshen, near Nizhne-Graiworenka, 100%		Bf 109 F-4	10 006	Black 14 ±
04/07/42	6	NN	—	Enemy fire, Nizhne-Graiworenka, 30%		Bf 109 F-4Z	7402	
05/07/42	4	NN	—	Collision while taxiing, Gorshechnoye, 50%		Bf 109 F-4	8766	
	4	NN	—	Collision while taxiing, Gorshechnoye, 10%		Bf 109 F-4	10 120	
08/07/42	4	NN	—	Flak, Perlovka, 15%		Bf 109 F-4	10 018	
09/07/42	Stab II	Uffz. Brinkmann	—	Crash landing, Gorshechnoye, 20%		Bf 109 F-4	8665	White << ±
	6	Uffz. Georg Schiller	MIA	Air combat bombers, 5 km east of Voronezh, 100%		Bf 109 F-4	13 352	Yellow 6 ±
10/07/42	4	Lt. Wolf Ettel	(MIA)	Air combat Bostons, 15 km north of Voronezh, P, 100% (returned 14/7/42)	Bf 109 F-4	8383	White 1 ±
11/07/42	4	Uffz. Arthur Fischer	+	Bombing, Olkhovatka[1123]			
	6	—	—	Bombing, Maryevka, 10%		Bf 109 F-4	10 231	
	II	—	—	Bombing, Maryevka, 40%		Bf 109 F-4	10 080	
	II	—	—	Bombing, Maryevka, 40%		Bf 109 F-4	8750	
13/07/42	4	—	—	Rammed by ground-looping Ju 87, Kantemirovka, 100% Bf 109 F-4	10 018		
	4	—	—	Rammed by ground-looping Ju 87, Kantemirovka, 90% Bf 109 F-4	8770		
	5	Fw. Werner Kloß	Inj.	Rammed by ground-looping Ju 87, Kantemirovka, 40% Bf 109 F-4	10 229		
	6	—	—	Rammed by ground-looping Ju 87, Kantemirovka,40% Bf 109 F-4	10 249		
14/07/42	6	NN	—	Air combat, Millerovo area, 20%		Bf 109 F-4	7642	
16/07/42	4	NN	—	Ran out of fuel, belly landing Baklantovka, 45%		Bf 109 F-4		
	II	NN	—	Undercarriage failure while taking off from Millerovo, 25%		Bf 109 F-4	10 244	
17/07/42	6	NN	—	Inadvertent ground contact, near Millerovo, 30%		Bf 109 F-4	10 065	
20/07/42	5	Uffz. Horst Opalke	+	Collided with parked Ju 52 during takeoff, Millerovo, 100%		Bf 109 F-4Z	7275	
22/07/42	5	Uffz. Ernst Pöske	MIA	Air combat, SE of Melikhovskaya, 100%		Bf 109 F-4	10 209	Yellow 7 ±

23/07/42	4	Fw. Werner Lucas	—	Air combat, belly landing Frolov, grid square 44 East N/29/3/6, 20%	Bf 109 F-4	7649	
25/07/42	6	NN	—	Struck obstacle during takeoff, Morozovskaya, 100%	Bf 109 F-4	10 120	
26/07/42	4	NN	—	Air combat, forced landing south of Oblivskaya, grid square 44 East N/29/6/1, 25%	Bf 109 F-4	7144	
	II	NN	—	Flak, Kalach, 100%	Bf 109 F-4	10 250	
27/07/42	II	NN	—	Ran out of fuel, belly landing grid square 39/1/5/1, 100%	Bf 109 F-4	10 219	
28/07/42	II	NN	—	Bad weather, crash landing Novy-Cholan, 40%	Bf 109 F-4	13 105	
29/07/42	4	NN	—	Ground looped on takeoff, Frolov, 80%	Bf 109 F-4	13 353	
	6	NN	—	Ground looped on landing, Frolov, 70%	Bf 109 F-4Z	7292	
30/07/42	6	NN	—	Air combat, Frolov, 25%	Bf 109 F-4	10 107	
01/08/42	6	Uffz. Wolfgang Vogel	MIA	Cooling system failure, forced landing 5 km north of Surovikino, 100%	Bf 109 F-4	13 335	White 3 ±
05/08/42	6	Obfw. Maximilian Seidler	Inj.	Engine failure, forced landing on enemy side of the lines west of Kalach, recovered by German armored troops and taken to hospital, 100%	Bf 109 F-4	10 233	Yellow 9 ±
	6	NN	—	Pilot error, Frolov, 20%	Bf 109 F-4	7624	
06/08/42	5	NN	—	Ground looped on landing, Frolov, 65%	Bf 109 F-4	13 215	
07/08/42	5	NN	—	Engine failure, crash landing Frolov, 60%	Bf 109 F-4	8653	
08/08/42	6	NN	—	Crash landing, Frolov, 30%	Bf 109 F-4	13 321	
09/08/42	4	NN	—	Flak, belly landing grid square 44 East N/ south of Kalach, 30%	Bf 109 F-4	13 339	
11/08/42	6	NN	—	Engine failure, crash landing grid square 44 East N/39/2/4, near Golubinskaya, 30%	Bf 109 F-4	7624	
14/08/42	II	NN	—	Ground looped on landing, Frolov, 40%	Bf 109 F-4	13 106	
18/08/42	6	Uffz. Egon Spinner	Inj.	Engine fire, crashed, pilot bailed out, grid square 44 East/39/1/3/1, Ossino-Logowskij area, 100%	Bf 109 F-4	13 321	
	II	NN	—	Flak, forced landing grid square 44 East N/39/1/3/6, near Ossinovka, 50%	Bf 109 F-4	7615	
19/08/42	4	NN	—	Air combat, belly landing Tuzov, 40%	Bf 109 F-4	8783	
	6	Uffz. Waldemar Eyrich	(MIA)	Air combat, forced landing grid square 45 East 30/8/8/2, NW of Vertyachiy, 100%	Bf 109 F-4	13 289	Yellow 3 ±
22/08/42	4	NN	—	Ground looped on takeoff, Tuzov, 20%	Bf 109 F-4	10 217	

14/09/42	6	Lt. Hans Fuß, Stf.	Inj.	Air combat, overturned during forced landing, Dedyurevo, 100% (+ 10/11/1942)	Bf 109 G-2 13 758	
23/09/42	5	Uffz. Hans Leskow	(MIA)	Air combat, location and cause not known, 100%	Bf 109 G-2 13 737	Black 3 ±
28/09/42	II	NN	—	Ground fire, Kozlovo, 15%	Bf 109 G-2 13 745	
02/10/42	II	NN	—	Ground looped on landing, Demyansk, 40%	Bf 109 G-2 14 233	
15/10/42	II	NN	—	Flak, forced landing Lokhnaya/Kholm, 10%	Bf 109 G-2 13 759	
17/10/42	II	NN	—	Ran out of fuel, forced landing Grotkino, 35%	Bf 109 G-2 13 738	
31/10/42	6	Oblt. Paul Stolte	Inj.	Poor surface conditions, overturned, Šolzy, 90%	Bf 109 G-2 13 765	
30/11/42	4	NN	—	Crash landing, grid square 25/1/4/3, 20%	Bf 109 G-2 13 724	
03/12/42	II	NN	—	Engine failure, crashed grid square 36/7/2/4, 100%	Bf 109 G-2 13 752	
04/12/42	II	NN	—	Forced landing due to icing, grid square 25/3/1/2, 20%	Bf 109 G-2 13 745	
08/12/42	II	NN	—	Poor surface conditions, belly landing Kharkov, 25%	Bf 109 G-2 13 725	
16/12/42	6	Uffz. Hans Staufferth	Inj.	Crashed on takeoff, engine trouble, Smolensk-North airfield, 80%	Bf 109 G-2 13 818	
	II	NN	—	Engine trouble, Orel, 35%	Bf 109 G-2 13 722	
17/12/42	4	Uffz. Wolfgang Buttstädt	Inj.	Flak, forced landing north of Pitomnik, 10%	Bf 109 G-2 13 698	
18/12/42	4	NN	—	Belly landing, grid square 39/2/6/1, 20%	Bf 109 G-2 13 746	
21/12/42	4	Oblt. Werner Lucas, Stk.	W	Air combat Bostons, crashed north of Morozovskaya, P, 100%	Bf 109 G-2 13 797	White 13 ±
23/12/42	II	NN	—	Bad weather, forced landing grid square 44 East N/19/6/6/2, east of Morozovski, 25%	Bf 109 G-2 13 723	
31/12/42	4	Uffz. Fritz Köhler	MIA	Combat mission, engine trouble, crashed 3 km SW of Urjupin, P, 100%	Bf 109 G-2 13 762	White 8 ±
17/01/43	5	—	—	Blown up, Pitomnik, 100%	Bf 109 G-2 13 696	
	5	—	—	Blown up, Pitomnik, 100%	Bf 109 G-2 13 792	
	5	—	—	Blown up, Pitomnik, 100%	Bf 109 G-2 14 513	
	5	—	—	Blown up, Pitomnik, 100%	Bf 109 G-2 13 891	
	5	—	—	Blown up, Pitomnik, 100%	Bf 109 G-2 14 546	
	5	—	—	Blown up, Pitomnik, 100%	Bf 109 G-2 14 559	
26/01/43	4	NN	—	Collision, Rovenkie, 45%	Bf 109 G-2 13 922	
	II	NN	—	Flak, Kamensk, 70%	Bf 109 G-2 14 618	

28/01/43	6	NN	—	Engine trouble, Konstantinovka, 50%	Bf 109 G-2 13 894
01/02/43	5	NN	—	Ground looped on takeoff, Rovenkie, 80%	Bf 109 G-2 13 967
	6	NN	—	Belly landing, Rovenkie, 30%	Bf 109 G-2 14 581
03/02/43	4	NN	—	Overturned on landing, Rovenkie, 70%	Bf 109 G-2 14 739
04/02/43	5	NN	—	Enemy fire, forced landing, grid square 44 East N/78/4/3, 40%	Bf 109 G-2 13 84?
05/02/43	5	—	—	Bombing, Rovenkie, 10%	Bf 109 G-2 13 741
	6	—	—	Bombing, Rovenkie, 30%	Bf 109 G-2 10 320
	II	—	—	Bombing, Rovenkie, 100%	Bf 109 G-2 14 577
	II	NN	—	Flak, Voroshilovgrad, 30%	Bf 109 G-2 14 549
07/02/43	6	Uffz. Franz Cech	—	Combat mission, cause not known, Rovenkie area, 100%	Bf 109 G-2 13 933
10/02/43	5	Uffz. Günther Mohn	W	Air combat fighters, over Slavyansk, 10%	Bf 109 G-2 13 961
	5	Uffz. Rudolf Scheibe	—	Air combat fighters, Makeyevka area, 50%	Bf 109 G-2 13 969
	5	NN	—	Air combat fighters, Makeyevka area, 10%	Bf 109 G-2 14 820 Black 1 ±
	6	Uffz. Willi Schick	+	Air combat fighters, 10 km SE of Novocherkassk, 100%	Bf 109 G-2 13 751 Yellow 11 ±
16/02/43	4	NN	—	Ground looped on takeoff, Makeyevka, 25%	Bf 109 G-2 14 661
19/02/43	4	NN	—	Mechanical problem, Gorlovka, 30%	Bf 109 G-2 13 884
20/02/43	5	NN	—	Enemy fire, Dimitrov, 40%	Bf 109 G-2 13 844
22/02/43	5	NN	—	Engine trouble, forced landing grid square 44 East N/79/7/8/3, west of Kurakovka, 50%	Bf 109 G-2 13 549
	6	Uffz. Heinrich May	MIA	Air combat, Matwejew-Kurgan, 100%	Bf 109 G-2 13 760 Yellow 3 ±
24/02/43	4	NN	—	Collision while taxiing, Makeyevka, 10%	Bf 109 G-2 13 728
27/02/43	4	NN	—	Taxiing accident, Makeyevka, 30%	Bf 109 G-2 13 894
09/03/43	4	NN	—	Engine failure, grid square 44 East N/89/6/1/3, west of Voroshilovsk, 20%	Bf 109 G-2 13 921
18/03/43	5	NN	—	Undercarriage failure, Kharkov, 25%	Bf 109 G-2 14 601
20/03/43	5	NN	—	Engine trouble, Makeyevka, 20%	Bf 109 G-2 14 672
25/03/43	5	Uffz. Günther Mohn	Inj.	Takeoff collision with Bf 110, Makeyevka, 85%	Bf 109 G-2 13 813 Black 11 ±
	5	Uffz. Heinz Dahms	Inj.	Engine trouble, Makeyevka, 90%	Bf 109 G-2 13 427
	6	Oblt. Paul Stolte, Stk.	W	Air combat fighters, Makeyevka, 15%	Bf 109 G-4 14 936 Yellow 1 ±

11/04/43	5	NN	—	Forced landing, Verkhno, 30%	Bf 109 G-2 13 599
12/04/43	6	NN	—	Ground looped on landing, Anapa, 35%	Bf 109 G-2 14 617
13/04/43	6	NN	—	Air combat, Anapa, 40%	Bf 109 G-2 13 576
17/04/43	4	NN	—	Crash landing, Melitopol, 45%	Bf 109 G-2 13 917
	II	NN	—	Air combat, crash landing Anapa, 40%	Bf 109 G-2 13 763
18/04/43	4	Uffz. Hans Pabst	+	Air combat P-39s, grid square 75/4/3 near Novorossisk, 100%	Bf 109 G-2 14 744 White 2 ±
	6	NN	—	Mechanical problem, forced landing Anapa, 45%	Bf 109 G-2 13 748
19/04/43	5	Uffz. Oskar Fischer	W	Flak, forced landing near Krymskaya, 50%	Bf 109 G-2 14 820 Black 1 ±
	6	Fw. Rasso Förg	W	Flak, south of Novorossisk, grid square 75/4/5/1, 5%	Bf 109 G-4 19 498 Yellow 10 ±
20/04/43	II	—	—	Bombing, Anapa, 50%	Bf 109 G-2 13 884
21/04/43	5	Lt. Lothar Myrrhe	MIA	Air combat, near Novorossisk, 100%	Bf 109 G-2 10 334 Black 4 ±
23/04/43	II	NN	—	Crash landing, Anapa, 45%	Bf 109 G-4 14 890
	II	NN	—	Undercarriage failure, Anapa, 50%	Bf 109 G-2 14 599
24/04/43	II	NN	—	Taxiing accident, Gostagajeskaja, 35%	Bf 109 G-2 14 719
26/04/43	II	NN	—	Undercarriage failure, Anapa, 90%	Bf 109 G-2 10 460
29/04/43	5	NN	—	Engine trouble, Krasny, 100%	Bf 109 G-2 14 705
09/05/43	4	Uffz. Vitmar von Langendorff	POW	Air combat Bostons and fighters, crashed 6 km south of Krymskaya, 100%	Bf 109 G-4 19448 White 5 ±
10/05/43	4	—	—	Bombing, Anapa, 45%	Bf 109 G-4 19 540
11/05/43	4	Lt. Wolf Ettel	—	Flak, west of Anastassiewskaja, grid square 34 East 76/8/8/2, 25%	Bf 109 G-4 19 453 White 10 ±
13/05/43	6	NN	—	Undercarriage failure, Anapa, 60%	Bf 109 G-4 19 264
20/05/43	5	NN	—	Cause not known, Varvarowka, 10%	Bf 109 G-4 19 515 (?)
29/05/43	4	Lt. Richard Scholze	+	Flak, crashed 2-3 km east of Gresnoye airfield, 100%	Bf 109 G-4 19 719 White 6 ±
01/06/43	4	NN	—	Undercarriage failure, Kharkov-Rogany, 30%	Bf 109 G-4 14 943
02/06/43	6	Uffz. Werner Maisch	MIA	Air combat, area south of Kursk, 100%	Bf 109 G-4 19 356 Yellow 7 ±
03/06/43	4	Uffz. Helmut Liebmann	Inj.	Engine fire, crashed 15 km NE of Rogany, P, 100%	Bf 109 G-4 19 447 White 11 ±
	4	NN	—	Engine trouble, belly landing west of Rogany, 25%	Bf 109 G-4 19 606 White 2 ±
	6	Lt. Karl-Ludwig Seewald	W	Air combat Yak-1, crashed 20 km SW of Belgorod, 100%	Bf 109 G-4 19 338 Yellow 8 ±

05/06/43	5	Fw. Horst Lüdtke	+	Air combat, crashed Oboyan area, 100%	Bf 109 G-4 19 724 Black 11 ±
08/06/43	5	Obgefr. Heinz Welsch	MIA	Air combat LaGG-3, 20 km west of Belgorod, 100%	Bf 109 G-4 14 858 Black 2 ±
	II	NN	—	Engine trouble, belly landing south of Belgorod, 35%	Bf 109 G-4 15 199
09/06/43	4	NN	—	Flak, grid square 60/2/6/5, Pechenegi area, 35%	Bf 109 G-2 13 953
16/06/43	5	Lt. Herbert Fürst	+	Engine failure, belly landing 5 km NE of Kharkov-Rogany, 90%	Bf 109 G-4 19 722 Black 5 ±
17/06/43	6	NN	—	Taxiing accident, Varvarowka, 15%	Bf 109 G-4 19 302
18/06/43	6	NN	—	Undercarriage failure, landing, Varvarowka, 60%	Bf 109 G-4 19 498 Yellow 10 ±
27/06/43	4	NN	—	Ground fire, west of Belgorod, grid square 61/3/1, 25%	Bf 109 G-2 13 769
04/07/43	6	Fw. Alfred Fischer	POW	Flak, belly landing 20 km ESE Chuguyev, 100%	Bf 109 G-4 14 940 Yellow 6 ±
05/07/43	4	Uffz. Helmut Liebmann	W	Air combat Yak-1, forced landing 5 km SE Kharkov-Rogany, 40%	Bf 109 G-4 19 965 White 11 ±
	5	Obfw. Josef Schütte	W	Air combat, Kharkov, crashed 10 km SW of Volchansk, 100%	Bf 109 G-4 19 976 Black 7 ±
	6	Lt. Friedrich-Wilhelm Schmidt	W	Air combat, Belgorod area, belly landing Kharkov-Rogany, 10%	Bf 109 G-4 19 323 Yellow 5 ±
	6	Gefr. Hans Schilling	W	Air combat, Belgorod area, belly landing Kharkov-Rogany, 15%	Bf 109 G-4 19 302 Yellow 4 ±
	II	NN	—	Friendly flak, Kharkov area, forced landing, 40%	Bf 109 G-4 15 177
07/07/43	4	Lt. Wolfgang Cichorius	MIA	Air combat, area SW of Prokhorovka, 100%	Bf 109 G-4 19 302 Yellow 4 ±
	II	NN	—	Mechanical problem, belly landing grid square 61/3/9, 30%	Bf 109 G-4 19 537
08/07/43	6	NN	—	Taxiing accident, Kharkov-Rogany, 35%	Bf 109 G-6 15 685
09/07/43	4	NN	—	Air combat, grid square 61/1/6/7, area NW of Belgorod, 60%	Bf 109 G-6 20 060
	6	NN	—	Belly landing, Belgorod, 30%	Bf 109 G-4 19 323 Y5 ±
10/07/43	4	Lt. Hans Reiser	+	Air combat with La-5, 6 km SW of Prokhorovka, 100%	Bf 109 G-6 20 131 White 8 ±
11/07/43	6	Gefr. Hans Schilling	+	Air combat 20 km south of Oboyan, 100%	Bf 109 G-4 19 746 Yellow 1 ±
12/07/43	6	NN	—	Engine failure, forced landing grid square 61/3/9/5, SW of Belgorod, 35%	Bf 109 G-4 19 508
13/07/43	4	—	—	Rammed by Bf 109, Kharkov-Rogany, 15%	Bf 109 G-6 20 204
	4	—	—	Rammed by Bf 109, Kharkov-Rogany, 80%	Bf 109 G-6 15 699
	6	NN	—	Pilot error, Kharkov-Rogany, 15%	Bf 109 G-4 19 780

	6	NN	—	Air combat, grid square 61/1/6/4, NW of Belgorod, 20%	Bf 109 G-4 19 312
	6	NN	—	Air combat, grid square 61/2/7/4, N of Belgorod, 20%	Bf 109 G-6 20 160
14/07/43	4	NN	—	Enemy fire, belly landing Kharkov-Rogany, 70%	Bf 109 G-6 15 680
	5	Uffz. Hugo Lucks	—	Crash landing, grid square 51/6/4/5, south of Graivoron, 60%	Bf 109 G-6 16 652 Black 5 ±
16/07/43	4	—	—	Bombing, Kharkov-Rogany, 40%	Bf 109 G-6 15 684
	4	NN	—	Air combat, grid square 51/3/7, west of Graivoron, 60%	Bf 109 G-6 20 041
	5	NN	—	Air combat, grid square 61/2/3/3, south of Prokhorovka, 20%	Bf 109 G-4 15 209
	4	Fw. Hans Grünberg	—	Air combat Yak-1, engine failure, crashed grid square 61/2/2/0, P, 100%	Bf 109 G-6
18/07/43	4	Uffz. Thomas Ametsbichler	+	Flak, grid square 61/2/1/2, 12 km SE of Prokhorovka, 6:46 AM, 100%	Bf 109 G-6 20 199 White 12 ±
	4	NN	—	Ground looped on landing, Kutelnikovo, 20%	Bf 109 G-4 19 956
	II	NN	—	Ran out of fuel, forced landing, location not known, 60%	Bf 109 G-4 19 957
19/07/43	4	Uffz. Helmuth Schirra	MIA	Air combat Il-2s, grid square 88/2/3/9, 2 km east of Dmitriyevka, 100%	Bf 109 G-4 14 999 White 7 ±
	5	NN	—	Air combat, grid square 88/1/9, 40%	Bf 109 G-6 20 005
20/07/43	5	NN	—	Engine failure, belly landing, Kutelnikovo, 35%	Bf 109 G-4 15 209
21/07/43	4	Lt. Hermann Schuster	+	Air combat Il-2s, grid square 88/2/2, near Pervomaysk, 100%	Bf 109 G-6 15 704 White 8 ±
22/07/43	5	NN	—	Air combat, grid square 88/2/5, 30%	Bf 109 G-4 19 223
24/07/43	5	Uffz. Günther Mohn	Inj.	Flak, bailed out near Kutelnikovo airfield, 100%	Bf 109 G-6 20 136 Black 8 ±
27/07/43	Stab II	Obfhr. Botho Kaatz	MIA	Air combat LaGG-3, Belgorod, 100%	Bf 109 G-6 20 000 Black << ±
31/07/43	5	Lt. Hartwig Dohse	MIA	Air combat, grid square 88/2/6, Marinovka area, 100%	Bf 109 G-6 20 091 Black 7 ±
	6	NN	—	Air combat, grid square 89/8/6/7, 30%	Bf 109 G-6 20 014

Losses during Operations in the Defense of the Reich
August 1943 to June 1944

19/09/43	II	NN	—	Ran out of fuel, overturned during forced landing, Zoetermeer, 40%	Bf 109 G-6 26 016
21/09/43	5	Uffz. Rudolf Scheibe	Inj.	Air combat P-51, engine failure, forced landing Halfweg, 65%	Bf 109 G-6 15 961 Black 12 ±
22/09/43	4	Uffz. Eduard Bartsch	Inj.	Air combat Spitfires, crashed 2 km north of Giessendam, P, 100%	Bf 109 G-6 26 061 White 9 ±

Date		Name		Cause	Aircraft	W.Nr.	Marking
	4	NN	—	Air combat, s'Hertogenbosch, 45%	Bf 109 G-6	15 628	White 5 ±
	II	NN	—	Air combat, forced landing s'Hertogenbosch, 45%	Bf 109 G-6	15 628	
23/09/43	II	NN	—	Engine fire, crashed near Leijden, P, 100%	Bf 109 G-6	18 809	
27/09/43	4	NN	—	Air combat, forced landing Leeuwarden, 10%	Bf 109 G-6	26 023	White 4 ±
	4	NN	—	Air combat, belly landing Schiphol, 15%	Bf 109 G-6	18 840	White 15 ±
	6	Fw. Franz Cech	W	Air combat, forced landing north of Groningen, 80%	Bf 109 G-6	20 610	Yellow 10 ±
	19	Hptm. Paul Stolte, Stk.	Inj.	Air combat, belly landing 5 km NW of Marx, 85%	Bf 109 G-6	26 019	Yellow 5 ±
	6	Uffz. Fritz Schwalbach	MIA	Air combat, north of Groningen, 100%	Bf 109 G-6	20 305	Yellow 6 ±
02/10/43	4	Fw. Rudolf Blomann	+	Air combat, Nordeney-Emden area, 100%	Bf 109 G-6	15 743	White 6 ±
	4	Obgefr. Günter Wollenweber	+	Air combat, Nordeney-Emden area, 100%	Bf 109 G-6	15 760	White 8 ±
	II	NN	—	Air combat, forced landing Königsmoor, 50%	Bf 109 G-6	18 841	
03/10/43	II	NN	—	Air combat, forced landing Bovenkerk, 65%	Bf 109 G-6	20 617	
	II	NN	—	Air combat, crashed near Amstelveen, P, 100%	Bf 109 G-6	19 912	
04/10/43	6	Fw. Alfred Kalitta	W	Air combat, crashed near Geilenburg, 10 km north of Aachen, P, 100%	Bf 109 G-5	26 096	Yellow 6 ±
08/10/43	4	Lt. Horst Feder	+	Air combat, crashed 1.5 km north of Anderen near Assen, 100%	Bf 109 G-6	20 604	White 8 ±
	4	Lt. Franz Ruhl	—	Air combat B-17s, belly landing near Groningen, 80%	Bf 109 G-6		White 7 ±
10/10/43	5	Fw. Paul Draeger	W	Air combat, crashed at Keppeln near Holzminden, P, 100%	Bf 109 G-5	26 074	Black 11 ±
	6	Lt. Karl-Ludwig Seewald	+	Air combat, crashed near Zaltbommel north of s'Hertogenbosch, 100%	Bf 109 G-6	15 651	Yellow 3 ±
	II	NN	—	Ran out of fuel, belly landing Zwolle, 30%	Bf 109 G-6	20 326	
14/10/43	5	NN	—	Poor visibility, crash landing Zutphen, 25%	Bf 109 G-5	15 723	
18/10/43	4	NN	—	Ran out of fuel, forced landing Terschelling, 30%	Bf 109 G-6	27 035	
	4	NN	—	Ran out of fuel, forced landing Terschelling, 30%	Bf 109 G-6	20 203	
	5	Obfw. Werner Kloss	+	Cause not known, probably crashed after running out of fuel, 100%	Bf 109 G-5	15 959	Black 7 ±
	5	Hptm. Heinrich Sannemann, Stk.	—	Ran out of fuel, forced landing Schockland, 70%	Bf 109 G-6	18 802	Black 1 ±
	5	NN	—	Ran out of fuel, forced landing Schockland, 30%	Bf 109 G-5	15 955	Black 8 ±
	5	NN	—	Ran out of fuel, forced landing Schockland, 30%	Bf 109 G-5	15 946	

Date	Unit	Name	Status	Remarks	Aircraft	W.Nr.	Marking
	5	NN	—	Ran out of fuel, forced landing Schockland, 30%	Bf 109 G-5	15 724	
	6	Hptm. Paul Stolte, Stk.	MIA	Cause not known, probably crashed after running	Bf 109 G-5	27 081	Yellow 1 ±
	6	Lt. Rudolf Schröder	MIA	Cause not known, probably crashed after running out of fuel, 100%	Bf 109 G-5	26 098	Yellow 5 ±
	6	Uffz. Uwe Michaels	+	Ran out of fuel, forced landing 7 km north of Sneeck, 100%	Bf 109 G-5	26 087	Yellow 12 ±
	6	Uffz. Herbert Dehrmann	Inj.	Forced landing caused by fuel shortage and bad weather, near Sneeck, 100%	Bf 109 G-5	26 104	Yellow 7 ±
	6	NN	—	Ran out of fuel, forced landing, Uth, 70%	Bf 109 G-5	26 101	
	6	NN	—	Ran out of fuel, forced landing S W of Leeuwarden, 25%	Bf 109 G-5	26 084	
	II	NN	—	Ran out of fuel, forced landing Terschelling, 100%	Bf 109 G-6	20 292	
20/10/43	Stab II	Lt. Karl-Heinz Koch	—	Air combat, belly landing Venlo, 10%	Bf 109 G-6	26 067	White 8 ±
	4	Uffz. Heinz Kiy	+	Air combat fighters, crashed 4 km west of Neer near Roermund, 90%	Bf 109 G-6	15 633	White 3 ±
	4	Uffz. Eduard Bartsch	+	Air combat fighters, crashed near Arsbeck 6 km west of Mönchengladbach, 99%	Bf 109 G-6	26 059	White 1 ±
	4	Uffz. Hugo Lucks	Inj.	Struck obstacle while taking off from Venlo, 95%	Bf 109 G-6	18 840	White 15 ±
24/10/43	4	Hptm. Werner Lucas, Stk.	+	Air combat Spitfires, crashed near Leijden, 4:43 PM, 100%	Bf 109 G-6	27 080	White 7 ±
	4	Uffz. Günther Weck	+	Air combat Spitfires, crashed on to the Scheveningen—Katwijk road, 100%	Bf 109 G-6	26 015	White 6 ±
	4	Gefr. Erich Zeitlinger	Inj.	Contacted water, crashed off Den Helder, 100%	Bf 109 G-6	410 233	White 3 ±
03/11/43	Stab II	Maj. Kurt Brändle, Grk.	+	Air combat over the sea, 100% (body washed ashore 17/1/1944)	Bf 109 G-6	26 058	Black << ±
	4	Uffz. Horst Kirschner	+	Air combat Spitfires, crashed 20 km (III/JG 26) west of Haarlem, 100%	Bf 109 G-6	27 079	White 9 ±
	6	Lt. Horst Brock	+	Air combat over the sea, 100% (body washed ashore 1944)	Bf 109 G-5	26 113	Yellow 5 ±
	6	Fw. Walter Stienhaus	+	Air combat, crashed Zandvoort, 100%	Bf 109 G-5	27 085	Yellow 4 ±
	6	Gefr. Hans-Wilhelm Hahn	+	Air combat Spitfires, crashed on the outskirts of Zandvoort in the direction of Haarlem, 100%	Bf 109 G-6	410 101	White 11 ±
	II	NN	—	Air combat, Schiphol, 25%	Bf 109 G-5	15 947	
	II	NN	—	Pilot error, crash landing Schiphol, 40%	Bf 109 G-6	410 113	
	II	NN	—	Air combat, Schermerhorn, 30%	Bf 109 G-5	15 963	

	II	NN	—	Air combat, Hoofdorp, 100%	Bf 109 G-6 27 102
05/11/43	5	NN	—	Ran out of fuel, forced landing Venlo, 60%	Bf 109 G-5 15 912 Black 4 ±
	II	NN	—	Ground looped on landing, Venlo, 60%	Bf 109 G-5 15 962
11/11/43	5	NN	—	Air combat, crashed near Dusseldorf, P, 100%	Bf 109 G-6 410 105
15/11/43	II	NN	—	Pilot error, crashed near Brussels, 100%	Fw 44 0082
20/11/43	II	NN	—	Mechanical problem, Deelen, 20%	Bf 109 G-6 410 140
23/11/43	4	Lt. Franz Ruhl, Sff.	—	Air combat Spitfires, grid square EK 6/7, Den Helder area, P, 100%	Bf 109 G-6 20 573
	5	NN	—	Ran out of fuel, belly landing grid square GK-3, west of Amsterdam, 10%	Bf 109 G-5 15 724
29/11/43	4	NN	—	Ran out of fuel, belly landing Kleve, 20%	Bf 109 G-6 410 113 White 11 ±
	5	Uffz. Fritz Kostenbader	+	CBB, grid square GO 4/5, Hengelo area, 100%	Bf 109 G-5 27 100 Black 9 ±
	6	Uffz. Karl-Heinz Lintermann	Inj.	Air combat, belly landing 24 km SE of Groningen, 100%	Bf 109 G-5 26 111 Yellow 9 ±
	II	NN	—	Ran out of fuel, belly landing Dalum, 20%	Bf 109 G-6 27 035
30/11/43	II	NN	—	Ran out of fuel, forced landing Nistelrode, 40%	Bf 109 G-5 27 116
01/12/43	4	FhjFw. Hans Frese	Inj.	Air combat, crashed near Hologne, 10 km north of Liège, 100%	Bf 109 G-6 26 023 White 4 ±
	4	Lt. Franz Ruhl, Sff.	—	Air combat, belly landing Melsbroek, 15%	Bf 109 G-6 410 497 White 2 ±
04/12/43	Stab II	Hptm. Wilhelm Lemke, Grk.	+	Air combat P-47s, crashed near Dodewaard, 18 km west of Nijmegen, 100%	Bf 109 G-6 410 558 Black << ±
	5	FhjObfw. Josef Schütte	+	Air combat P-47s, crashed 7 km west of Barneveld near Appeldoorn, 100%	Bf 109 G-5 15 955 Black 8 ±
	5	Uffz. Kurt Soßdorf	—	Air combat P-47s, crashed SE of Amersfoort, 100%	Bf 109 G-5 15 943 Black 11 ±
11/12/43	6	Gefr. Friedrich König	MIA	Air combat, Groningen area, 100%	Bf 109G-5Y 26 116 Yellow 2 ±
	II	NN	—	Ran out of fuel, forced landing Rhigenzandsten-Polder, 30%	Bf 109 G-6 26 067
13/12/43	5	—	—	Bombing, Schiphol, 20%	Bf 109 G-6 410 100
	6	—	—	Bombing, Schiphol, 15%	Bf 109 G-5 19 825
16/12/43	II	NN	—	Ran out of fuel, forced landing Amstelveen, 10%	Bf 109 G-5 15 946
20/12/43	II	NN	—	Air combat, Laken, 40%	Bf 109 G-6 20 389

25/12/43	5	Uffz. Kurt Hörlücke	+	Crashed while on ferry flight, 5 km NE of Osnabrück, 100%	Bf 109 G-6	15 849	Black 12 ±
07/01/44	II	NN	—	Mechanical trouble/accident, location not known, 100%	Bf 109 G		
24/01/44	II	NN	—	Mechanical trouble/accident, location not known, D	Bf 108		
28/01/44	II	NN	—	Mechanical trouble/accident, location not known, 100%	Fw 44		
04/02/44	II	NN	—	Mechanical trouble/accident, location not known, D	Bf 109 G-6		
10/02/44	II	NN	—	Air combat, location not known, D	Bf 109 G-6		
	II	NN	—	Air combat, location not known, D	Bf 109 G-6		
	II	NN	—	Combat mission, not due to enemy action, location not known, D	Bf 109 G-6		
	II	NN	—	Combat mission, not due to enemy action, location not known, D	Bf 109 G-6		
	II	NN	—	Combat mission, not due to enemy action, location not known,	D Bf 109 G-6		
11/02/44	6	Hptm. Heinrich . Sannemann, Stk	—	One-wheel landing, mechanical trouble, Mannheim-Sandhoven, 5%	Bf 109 G-6		Yellow 1 ±
20/02/44	5	Lt. Walter Bohatsch	W	Air combat, near Königslütter/Elbe, 100%	Bf 109 G-6	411 261	Black 6 ±
	5	Fw. Rudolf Scheibe	W	Air combat, crashed near Helmstedt, P, 100%	Bf 109 G-6	410 864	Black 2 ±
	5	Uffz. Maximilian Reichenberger	W	Air combat, belly landing near Eitzum near Helmstedt, 100%	Bf 109 G-6	411 277	Black 14 ±
	5	Uffz. Helmut Dillmann	+	Air combat, Helmstedt area, 100%	Bf 109 G-6	411 426	Black 4 ±
21/02/44	4	Lt. Siegfried Stahl	+	Air combat fighters, crashed near Beber near Bad Münder, 100%	Bf 109 G-6	411 283	White 11 ±
	4	Gefr. Hans Kupka	Inj.	Air combat, explosion of engine cannon, Dassel near Einbeck, P, 100%	Bf 109 G-6	411 279	White 13 ±
	II	NN	—	Air combat, location not known, D	Bf 109 G-6		
	II	NN	—	Air combat, location not known, D	Bf 109 G-6		
22/02/44	II	NN	—	Air combat, location not known, 100%	Bf 109 G-6		
	II	NN	—	Air combat, location not known, D	Bf 109 G-6		
	II	NN	—	Air combat, location not known, D	Bf 109 G-6		
23/04/44	6	Hptm. Heinrich Sannemann, Stk.	—	Crashed while landing at dusk, Rotenburg, D	Bf 109 G-6		Yellow 1 ±
24/02/44	6	Uffz. Franz Glassauer	W	Air combat, forced landing near Nickelbach near Schotten, 100%	Bf 109 G-6	410 860	Yellow 14 ±

	II	NN	—	Air combat, location not known, 100%	Bf 109 G-6	
25/02/44	II	NN	—	Combat mission, not due to enemy action, location not known, 100%	Bf 109 G-6	
26/02/44	II	NN	—	Mechanical trouble/accident, location not known, D	Bf 109 G-6	
	II	NN	—	Mechanical trouble/accident, location not known, D	Bf 109 G-6	
01/03/44	II	NN	—	Mechanical trouble/accident, location not known, 100%	Bf 109 G-6	
03/03/44	5	Uffz. Hans Staufferth	Inj.	Air combat, crashed near Parchim, P, 100%	Bf 109 G-6	411 340 Black 7 ±
	II	NN	—	Air combat, location not known, 100%	Bf 109 G-6	
04/03/44	6	Obfw. Robert Roller	W	Air combat fighters, crashed near Döberitz near Berlin, 100%	Bf 109 G-6	411 229 Yellow 10 ±
	6	Gefr. Rolf Lenk	+	Air combat, crashed near Döberitz, 100%	Bf 109 G-6	411 441 Yellow 8 ±
06/03/44	4	Uffz. Edmund Britzlmair	Inj.	Air combat, crashed near Möckem near Magdeburg, 100%	Bf 109 G-6	411 348 White 7 ±
	II	NN	—	Air combat, location not known, 100%	Bf 109 G-6	
07/03/44	4	Gefr. Heinz Schmeling	+	Went down during maintenance test flight, cause not known, crashed and burned near Dolle, 20 km south of Gardelegen, 100%	Bf 109 G-6	410 113 White 11 ±
08/03/44	4	Uffz. Ulrich Stingl	Inj.	Air combat, crashed at Weidenrode near Celle, P, 100%	Bf 109 G-6	411 386 White 6 ±
	II	NN	—	Air combat, location not known, 100%	Bf 109 G-6	
	II	NN	—	Air combat, location not known, D	Bf 109 G-6	
12/03/44	II	NN	—	Mechanical trouble/accident, location not known, 100%	Bf 109 G-6	
16/03/44	II	NN	—	Mechanical trouble/accident, location not known, D	Bf 109 G-6	
23/03/44	4	Gefr. Theo Burchardt	Inj.	Rammed by four-engined bomber during combat, crashed near Werl, P, 100%	Bf 109 G-6/U4	440 209 White 13 ±
	6	Uffz. Heinz-Ernst Rehm	+	Air combat, crashed near Nateln, 10 km NE of Werl, 100%	Bf 109 G-6	20 293 Yellow 5 ±
	II	NN	—	Air combat, location not known, 100%	Bf 109 G-6	
	II	NN	—	Air combat, location not known, D	Bf 109 G-6	
	II	NN	—	Combat mission, not due to enemy action, location not known, D	Bf 109 G-6	
24/03/44	II	NN	—	Mechanical trouble/accident, location not known, D	Bf 109 G-6	
29/03/44	Stab II	Hptm. Detlev Rohwer, Grk.	W	Air combat, belly landing near Mettingen, D—shot at on the ground and severely wounded (+ 30/3/1944)	Bf 109 G-6/U4	440 295 Black << ±

	4	Uffz. Hermann Beck	MIA	Air combat fighters, location not known, 100%	Bf 109 G-6	411 469	White 9 +—
	4	Uffz. Karl-Heinz Cichoracky	+	Air combat fighters, crashed near Langendamm, 3 km SE of Nienburg, 100%	Bf 109 G-6	410 823	White 1 ±
	6	Gefr. Friedrich Simchen	+	Air combat fighters, crashed near Rohrsen, 7 km north of Nienburg/Weser, 100%	Bf 109 G-6	411 376	Yellow 13 ±
31/03/44	II	NN	—	Mechanical trouble/accident, location not known, 100%	Bf 109 G-6		
05/04/44	II	NN	—	Mechanical trouble/accident, location not known, D	Bf 109 G-6		
08/04/44	4	Gefr. Johannes Kupka	W	Air combat, crashed between Brunswick and Helmstedt, 100%	Bf 109 G-6	410 923	White 3 ±
	II	NN	—	Air combat, location not known, 100%	Bf 109 G-6		
	II	NN	—	Air combat, location not known, 100%	Bf 109 G-6		
	II	NN	—	Air combat, location not known, 100%	Bf 109 G-6		
11/04/44	4	Uffz. Alfred Beutel	+	Air combat fighters, crashed 5 km west of Kakte, west of Gardelegen, 100%	Bf 109 G-6/U4	440 263	White 5 ±
	5	Uffz. Rudolf Stephan	+	Air combat fighters, crashed near Warnenau, NE of Brunswick, 100%	Bf 109 G-6	20 718	Black 9 ±
	5	Obfw. Rudolf Traphan	+	Air combat fighters, crashed 3 km east of Bemburg, 100%	Bf 109 G-6/U4	440 533	Black 12 ±
	6	Fw. Waldemar Eyrich	+	Air combat fighters, crashed near Eilsleben, west of Magdeburg, 100%	Bf 109 G-6	162 541	Yellow 4 ±
	6	Uffz. Karl-Heinz Lintermann	W	Air combat, forced landing near Gardelegen, D	Bf 109 G-6	15 777	Yellow 3 ±
	II	NN	—	Air combat, location not known, 100%	Bf 109 G-6		
	II	NN	—	Air combat, location not known, 100%	Bf 109 G-6		
13/04/44	II	NN	—	Air combat, location not known, D	Bf 109 G-6		
	II	NN	—	Combat mission, not due to enemy action, location not known, 100%	Bf 109 G-6		
	II	NN	—	Combat mission, not due to enemy action, location not known, D	Bf 109 G-6		
	II	NN	—	Combat mission, not due to enemy action, location not known, D	Bf 109 G-6		
14/04/44	II	NN	—	Mechanical trouble/accident, location not known, 100%	Bf 109 G-6		
	II	NN	—	Mechanical trouble/accident, location not known, 100%	Bf 109 G-6		
	II	NN	—	Mechanical trouble/accident, location not known, D	Bf 109 G-6		

16/04/44	II	NN	—	Mechanical trouble/accident, location not known, 100%	Bf 109 G-6	
	II	NN	—	Mechanical trouble/accident, location not known, D	Bf 109 G-6	
18/04/44	4	Uffz. Edmund Britzlmair	+	Shot down by fighters while landing at Gardelegen, D	Bf 109 G-6	411 382 White 2 ±
	5	Uffz. Karl Krenkel	+	Crashed on takeoff as a result of overspeeding the engine, 5 km north of Gardelegen airfield, 100%	Bf 109 G-6	411 354 Black 15 ±
	6	Lt. Friedrich-Wilhelm Schmidt	+	Air combat fighters, location not known, 100%	Bf 109 G-6/U4	440 592 Yellow 5 ±
	II	NN	—	Combat mission, not due to enemy action, location not known, 100%	Bf 109 G-6	
24/04/44	Stab II	Hptm. Hermann Baron von Kap-herr, Grk.	+	Air combat, crashed near Neuburg/Danube, 100%	Bf 109 G-6	411 817 Black << ±
	6	Fw. Friedrich Ständebach	+	Air combat, crashed near Augsburg, 100%	Bf 109 G-6/U4	440 260 Yellow 12 ±
	II	NN	—	Air combat, location not known, 100%	Bf 109 G-6	
	II	NN	—	Combat mission, not due to enemy action, location not known, D	Bf 109 G-6	
	II	—	—	Strafing attack, location not known, 100%	Bf 109 G-6	
25/04/44	II	NN	—	Mechanical trouble/accident, location not known, 100%	Bf 109 G-6	
29/04/44	5	Uffz. Maximilian Reichenberger	+	Air combat P-47s, crashed 15 km east of Halberstadt, bailed out, parachute tore, 100%	Bf 109 G-6	411 926 Black 14 ±
	5	Uffz. Heinz Rieckenberg	+	Air combat, crashed 12 km east of Meseberg, 100%	Bf 109 G-6	18 569 Black 3 ±
	II	NN	—	Air combat, location not known, P, 100%	Bf 109 G-6	
	II	NN	—	Air combat, location not known, 100%	Bf 109 G-6	
04/05/44	II	NN	—	Combat mission, not due to enemy action, location not known, 100%	Bf 109 G-6	
06/05/44	II	NN	—	Mechanical trouble/accident, location not known, D	Bf 109 G-6	
08/05/44	4	Uffz. Rolf Klein	+	Struck building during takeoff, Lemwerder/Bremen, 100%	Bf 109 G-6	15 238 White 7 ±
	5	Lt. Leopold Münster, Stk.	+	Collided with B-24, crashed near Wöllersheim, 28 km SE of Hildesheim, 100%	Bf 109 G-6/U4	441 142 Black 1 ±
	II	NN	—	Air combat, location not known, 100%	Bf 109 G-6	
	II	NN	—	Air combat, location not known, 100%	Bf 109 G-6	
	II	NN	—	Air combat, location not known, D	Bf 109 G-6	

12/05/44	4	Gefr. Alfred Währisch	+	Air combat, crashed near Rod an der Weil, 100%	Bf 109 G-6	411 336 White 4 ±
	4	Lt. Fridolin Reinartz	—	Air combat Frankfurt-Giessen area, belly landing Steindorf, 100%	Bf 109 G-6	
	6	Uffz. Heiner Geisthövel	—	Air combat, crashed near Rod an der Weil, P, 100%	Bf 109 G-6	
	6	Gefr. Heinz Elschner	W	Air combat, crashed near Loleschied, Unterlahn District, 100%	Bf 109 G-6/U4	441 399 no markings
	II	NN	—	Air combat, location not known, 100%	Bf 109 G-6	
	II	—	—	Strafing attack, location not known, D	Bf 109 G-6	
13/05/44	5	Fw. Wolfgang Fleischer	W	Air combat, crashed near Demmin, 100%	Bf 109 G-6/U4	441 310 Black 7 ±
	6	Uffz. Gerhard Benne	Inj.	Ran out of fuel, overturned on landing, Prenzlau, 100%	Bf 109 G-6/U4	441 309 Yellow 10 ±
	II	NN	—	Air combat, location not known, 100%	Bf 109 G-6	
	II	NN	—	Combat mission, not due to enemy action, location not known, 100%	Bf 109 G-6	
	II	NN	—	Combat mission, not due to enemy action, location not known, 100%	Bf 109 G-6	
	II	NN	—	Combat mission, not due to enemy action, location not known, D Bf 109 G-6		
17/05/44	II	NN	—	Combat mission, not due to enemy action, location not known, 100%	Bf 109 G-6	
19/05/44	4	Uffz. Heinz Barisch	W	Air combat, crashed 20 km SW of Kyritz, 100%	Bf 109 G-6/U4	440 587 White 3 ±
	4	Uffz. Ekkehard Rasche	W	Air combat, crashed Wachau, Nauen District, 100%	Bf 109 G-6/U4	441 131 White 2 ±
	4	Uffz. Theo Burchardt	W	Air combat, crashed near Behnitz near Rathenow, 100%	Bf 109 G-6/U4	441 094 White 1 ±
	4	Lt. Otto Siebenrok	MIA	Air combat, location not known, 100%	Bf 109 G-6/U4	441 160 White 6 ±
	6	Lt. Oskar Zimmermann	—	Collided with wingman during combat, crashed south of Wittenberge, P, 100%	Bf 109 G-6	
	II	NN	—	As above, crashed SE of Wittenberge, P, 100%	Bf 109 G-6	
	II	NN	—	Air combat, location not known, 100%	Bf 109 G-6	
	II	NN	—	Air combat, location not known, 100%	Bf 109 G-6	
	II	NN	—	Combat mission, not due to enemy action, location not known, 100%	Bf 109 G-6	

24/05/44	5	Uffz. Johann Fröhlich	+	Midair collision, crashed near Neustrelitz, 100%	Bf 109 G-6/U4	441 380 Black 5 ±
	II	NN	—	Midair collision, crashed near Neustrelitz, 100%	Bf 109 G-6	
	II	NN	—	Combat mission, not due to enemy action, location not known, D	Bf 109 G-6	
	II	NN	—	Combat mission, not due to enemy action, location not known, D	Bf 109 G-6	
24/05/44	II	NN	—	Mechanical trouble/accident, location not known, 100%	Bf 109 G-6	
28/05/44	5	Uffz. Rudolf Schneider	Inj.	Air combat, crashed near Halberstadt, P, 100%	Bf 109 G-6	412 422 Black 7 ±
	II	NN	—	Air combat, location not known, 100%	Bf 109 G-6	
	II	NN	—	Air combat, location not known, 100%	Bf 109 G-6	
	II	NN	—	Combat mission, not due to enemy action, location not known, D	Bf 109 G-6	
29/05/44	4	Uffz. Eberhard Reußner	+	Air combat, location not known, 100%	Bf 109 G-6	411 691 White 4 ±
	5	Obfw. Wilhelm Bergmann	W	Air combat, location not known, 100%	Bf 109 G-6	411 117 Black 13 ±
	6	Obfw. Ernst Siebert	+	Air combat, Laland, 100%	Bf 109 G-6	412 641 Yellow 1 ±
30/05/44	II	NN	—	Air combat, location not known, D	Bf 109 G-6	
	II	NN	—	Mechanical trouble/accident, location not known, 100%	Bf 109 G-6	
	II	NN	—	Mechanical trouble/accident, location not known, D	Bf 109 G-6	
31/05/44	II	NN	—	Mechanical trouble/accident, location not known, D	Bf 109 G-6	
03/06/44	5	Gefr. Franz Nolden	+	Crashed on takeoff, ferry flight, Halle-Nietleben airfield, 100%	Bf 109 G-6/U4	440 308 Black 14 ±
04/06/44	II	NN	—	Mechanical trouble/accident, location not known, D	Bf 109 G-6	
	II	NN	—	Mechanical trouble/accident, location not known, D	Bf 109 G-6	
	II	NN	—	Mechanical trouble/accident, location not known, D	Bf 109 G-6	
06/06/44	II	NN	—	Mechanical trouble/accident, location not known, D	Bf 109 G-6	
	II	NN	—	Mechanical trouble/accident, location not known, D	Bf 109 G-6	

Losses during Operations against the Invasion in France
June to August 1944

07/06/44	6	Uffz. Kurt Steinacker	+	Flew into the ground near Letzlingen during ferry flight, 100%	Bf 109 G-6	163 914 Yellow 16 ±
	6	Uffz. Egon Spinner	(MIA)	Crashed near Romilly during ferry flight, cause not known, 100% (returned injured)	Bf 109 G-6	163 680 Yellow 9 ±

	II	NN	—	Combat mission, not due to enemy action, location not known, D	Bf 109 G-6	
	II	NN	—	Combat mission, not due to enemy action, location not known, D	Bf 109 G-6	
	II	NN	—	Combat mission, not due to enemy action, location not known, D	Bf 109 G-6	
	II	NN	—	Mechanical trouble/accident, location not known, D	Bf 109 G-6	
	II	NN	—	Mechanical trouble/accident, location not known, D	Bf 109 G-6	
	II	NN	—	Mechanical trouble/accident, location not known, D	Bf 109 G-6	
	II	NN	—	Mechanical trouble/accident, location not known, D	Bf 109 G-6	
	II	NN	—	Mechanical trouble/accident, location not known, D	Bf 109 G-6	
08/06/44	5	Lt. Walter Marizy	+	Air combat fighters, north of Caen, 100%	Bf 109 G-6	163 844 Black 1 ±
	5	Uffz. Heinz Schmidt	+	Air combat fighters, north of Caen, 100%	Bf 109 G-6	163 664 Black 12 ±
	II	NN	—	Air combat, location not known, D	Bf 109 G-6	
	II	NN	—	Combat mission, not due to enemy action, location not known, D	Bf 109 G-6	
	II	NN	—	Mechanical trouble/accident, location not known, D	Bf 109 G-6	
09/06/44	II	NN	—	Combat mission, not due to enemy action, location not known, 100%	Bf 109 G-6	
10/06/44	Stab II	Gefr. Heinrich Berger	(MIA)	Air combat, location not known, 100%	Bf 109 G-6	White 15 ±
	4	Uffz. Ulrich Gerke	+	Air combat fighters, north of Caen, 100%	Bf 109 G-6	412 467 White 1 ±
	4	Uffz. Robert Kanthak	+	Air combat fighters, north of Caen, 100%	Bf 109 G-6	163 850 White 13 ±
	4	Obfw. Kurt Kundrus	+	Air combat fighters, St. Gauburge, 20 km WSW of L'Aigle, 100%	Bf 109 G-6	163 688 White 9 ±
	5	Uffz. Bernhard Haupt	+	Air combat fighters, Douvres area, (2/JG 51) crashed Houest near Evreux, 100%	Bf 109 G-6	163 677 Black 17 ±
	5	Uffz. Kurt Wahl (2/JG 51)	+	Air combat fighters, Douvres area, crashed near Normanville, 100%	Bf 109 G-6	412 474 Black 14 ±
	5	Uffz. Werner Talkenberg (2/JG 51)	—	Air combat P-51s, belly landing near Saquenville, 10 km from Evreux airfield, 100%	Bf 109 G-6	Black 7 ±
	6	Lt. Albert Zanzerl	+	Air combat fighters, north of Caen, 100%	Bf 109 G-6	163 875 Yellow 15 ±
	6	Uffz. Berthold Zürtz	+	Air combat fighters, north of Caen, 100%	Bf 109 G-6	163 933 no markings
	II	NN	—	Air combat, location not known, D	Bf 109 G-6	

	II	NN	—	Combat mission, not due to enemy action, location not known, 100%	Bf 109 G-6
	II	NN	—	Combat mission, not due to enemy action, location not known, 100%	Bf 109 G-6
11/06/44	II	NN	—	Mechanical trouble/accident, location not known, D	Bf 109 G-6
12/06/44	4	Fw. Paul Kipulski (10/JG 3)	+	Air combat fighters, crashed near La Bataille, 100% Bf 109 G-6 411 334 White 10 ±	
	5	Gefr. Johann Elwischger	W	Air combat fighters, crashed near Orgeville east of Evreux, P, 100%	Bf 109 G-6 163 694 Black 5 ±
	5	Obgefr. Heinz Wagner	+	Air combat fighters, crashed Val David, 100%	Bf 109 G-6 412 685 Black 10 ±
	II	NN	—	Air combat, location not known, 100%	Bf 109 G-6
	II	NN	—	Air combat, location not known, 100%	Bf 109 G-6
	II	NN	—	Air combat, location not known, D	Bf 109 G-6
	II	NN	—	Air combat, location not known, D	Bf 109 G-6
14/06/44	II	NN	—	Mechanical trouble/accident, location not known, 100%	Bf 109 G-6
	II	NN	—	Mechanical trouble/accident, location not known, D	Bf 109 G-6
15/06/44	II	NN	—	Air combat, location not known, 100%	Bf 109 G-6
	II	NN	—	Air combat, location not known, 100% Bf 109 G-6	
	II	NN	—	Air combat, location not known, D Bf 109 G-6	
	II	NN	—	Combat mission, not due to enemy action, location not known, D	Bf 109 G-6
	II	NN	—	Combat mission, not due to enemy action, location not known, D	Bf 109 G-6
20/06/44	4	Fw. Otto Florian	MIA	Air combat fighters, west of Bernay, 100%	Bf 109 G-6 412 510 White 3 ±
	II	NN	—	Air combat, location not known, 100%	Bf 109 G-6
	II	NN	—	Air combat, location not known, 100%	Bf 109 G-6
21/06/44	II	NN	—	Mechanical trouble/accident, location not known, D	Bf 109 G-6
22/06/44	4	Uffz. Walter Demmig (4/JG 5)	+	Air combat, 60 km S W of Paris, 100%	Bf 109 G-6 161 127 White 9 ±
	II	NN	—	Air combat, location not known, 100%	Bf 109 G-6
	II	NN	—	Air combat, location not known, D	Bf 109 G-6
23/06/44	6	Uffz. Walter Giese (5/JG 5)	W	Air combat P-47s, near Bernay, 35%	Bf 109 G-6 412 519 Yellow 14 ±

24/06/44	5	Lt. Ortwin Meyer (6/JG 5)	MIA	Air combat P-47s, Caen area, 100%	Bf 109 G-6 412 677 Black 4 ±
	5	Lt. Franz von Thienen (5/JG 5)	POW	Air combat P-47s, Caen area, 100%	Bf 109 G-6 163 874 Black 13 ±
	II	NN	—	Air combat, location not known, D	Bf 109 G-6
	II	NN	—	Combat mission, not due to enemy action, location not known, 100%	Bf 109 G-6
	II	NN	—	Combat mission, not due to enemy action, location not known, 100%	Bf 109 G-6
24/06/44	II	NN	—	Air combat, location not known, D	Bf 109 G-6
25/06/44	4	Uffz. Gerhard Siegmund (4/JG 5)	MIA	Air combat, Dreux area, 100%	Bf 109 G-6 412 565 White 15 ±
	4	Uffz. Emil Scheidt (9/JG 5)	MIA	Air combat, Dreux area, 100%	Bf 109 G-6 411 961 White 16 ±
	5	Uffz. Johannes Vahle (4/JG 5)	+	Air combat, Dreux area, 100%	Bf 109 G-6 411 252 Black 3 ±
	5	Gefr. Helmut Eckart	+	Air combat fighters, crashed near Pacy, 10 km east of Evreux, 100%	Bf 109 G-6 412 718 Black 13 ±
	6	Uffz. Günter Tippel	W	Air combat fighters, near Marcilly, 100%	Bf 109 G-6 163 666 Yellow 5 ±
	II	NN	—	Air combat, location not known, 100%	Bf 109 G-6
	II	NN	—	Air combat, location not known, 100%	Bf 109 G-6
	II	NN	—	Air combat, location not known, 100%	Bf 109 G-6
	II	NN	—	Air combat, location not known, 100%	Bf 109 G-6
	II	NN	—	Air combat, location not known, 100%	Bf 109 G-6
	II	NN	—	Air combat, location not known, 100%	Bf 109 G-6
	II	NN	—	Air combat, location not known, D	Bf 109 G-6
	II	NN	—	Air combat, location not known, D	Bf 109 G-6
	II	NN	—	Air combat, location not known, D	Bf 109 G-6
	II	—	—	Bombing, Evreux-Fauville, D	Bf 109 G-6
	II	—	—	Bombing, Evreux-Fauville, D	Bf 109 G-6
	II	—	—	Bombing, Evreux-Fauville, D	Bf 109 G-6
	II	—	—	Bombing, Evreux-Fauville, D	Bf 109 G-6
	II	—	—	Bombing, Evreux-Fauville, D	Bf 109 G-6

	II	—	—	Bombing, Evreux-Fauville, D	Bf 109 G-6	
	II	—	—	Bombing, Evreux-Fauville, D	Bf 109 G-6	
	II	—	—	Bombing, Evreux-Fauville, D	Bf 109 G-6	
	II	—	—	Bombing, Evreux-Fauville, D	Bf 109 G-6	
	II	—	—	Strafing attack, Evreux-Fauville, D	Bf 109 G-6	
27/06/44	II	NN	—	Air combat, location not known, 100%	Bf 109 G-6	
28/06/44	II	NN	—	Combat mission, not due to enemy action, location not known, D	Bf 109 G-6	
	II	NN	—	Combat mission, not due to enemy action, location not known, D	Bf 109 G-6	
	II	NN	—	Combat mission, not due to enemy action, location not known, D	Bf 109 G-6	
29/06/44	II	NN	—	Combat mission, not due to enemy action, location not known, D	Bf 109 G-6	
30/06/44	4	Obgefr. Helmut Hötzel	+	Air combat fighters, area of Seine Estuary, 100%	Bf 109 G-6/U4	441 495 White 10 ±
	4	Obgefr. Helmut Dieter	W	Air combat fighters, crashed 10 km SE of Breuil-en-Auge, 100%	Bf 109 G-6	163 843 White 14 ±
	5	Uffz. Gerhard Koslowski	MIA	Air combat fighters, area of the Seine Estuary, 100%	Bf 109 G-6/U4	441 464 Black 11 ±
	6	Gefr. Walter Bronder	W	Air combat fighters, near Pont Audemer/Eure, 100%	Bf 109 G-6	163 878 Yellow 11 ±
	II	NN	—	Air combat, location not known, 100%	Bf 109 G-6	
	II	NN	—	Air combat, location not known, 100%	Bf 109 G-6	
	II	NN	—	Combat mission, not due to enemy action, location not known, 100%	Bf 109 G-6	
	II	NN	—	Combat mission, not due to enemy action, location not known, 100%	Bf 109 G-6	
	II	NN	—	Combat mission, not due to enemy action, location not known, 100%	Bf 109 G-6	
	II	—	—	Strafing attack, Nogent-le-Roi, D	Bf 109 G-6	
01/07/44	II	NN	—	Mechanical trouble/accident, location not known, D	Bf 109 G-6	
02/07/44	II	NN	—	Combat mission, not due to enemy action, location not known, 100%	Bf 109 G-6	
	II	NN	—	Combat mission, not due to enemy action, location not known, D	Bf 109 G-6	

	II	NN	—	Combat mission, not due to enemy action, location not known, D	Bf 109 G-6	
	II	NN	—	Mechanical trouble/accident, location not known, 100%	Bf 109 G-6	
05/07/44	4	Uffz. Heinz Pelletier	Inj.	Overturned on landing, Sucy, 100%	Bf 109 G-6	163 750 White 8 ±
	4	Uffz. Franz Hametner	W	Air combat fighters, crashed near Evreux, 100% († 29/7/1944)	Bf 109 G-6/U4	441 800 White 12 ±
	4	Uffz. Kurt Poppitz	(MIA)	Air combat fighters, Caen area, 100%	Bf 109 G-6/U4	441 155 White 11 ±
	6	Obfhr. Werner Schulze	+	Overturned on landing, Villacoublay, 100%	Bf 109 G-6	411 679 Yellow 2 ±
	II	NN	—	Air combat, location not known, 100%	Bf 109 G-6	
	II	NN	—	Air combat, location not known, 100%	Bf 109 G-6	
	II	NN	—	Combat mission, not due to enemy action, location not known, D	Bf 109 G-6	
	II	NN	—	Mechanical trouble/accident, location not known, D	Bf 109 G-6	
06/07/44	II	NN	—	Combat mission, not due to enemy action, location not known, D	Bf 109 G-6	
	II	NN	—	Combat mission, not due to enemy action, location not known, D	Bf 109 G-6	
15/07/44	II	NN	—	Combat mission, not due to enemy action, location not known, D	Bf 109 G-6	
16/07/44	II	NN	—	Air combat, location not known, D	Bf 109 G-6	
	II	NN	—	Air combat, location not known, D	Bf 109 G-6	
17/07/44	II	NN	—	Combat mission, not due to enemy action, location not known, D	Bf 109 G-6	
	II	NN	—	Combat mission, not due to enemy action, location not known, D	Bf 109 G-6	
	II	NN	—	Combat mission, not due to enemy action, location not known, D	Bf 109 G-6	
18/07/44	4	Obfw. Helmut Rüffler	W	Air combat fighters, crashed 45 km SE of Caen, 100%	Bf 109 G-6	165 451 White 13 ±
	6	Lt. Robert Roller	+	Air combat fighters, west of Caen, 100%	Bf 109 G-6	165 628 Yellow 6 ±
	6	Uffz. Lorenz Stephan	+	Air combat fighters, west of Caen, 100%	Bf 109 G-6	165 504 Yellow 4 ±
	6	Uffz. Alfred Lenz	+	Air combat fighters, west of Caen, 100%	Bf 109 G-6	163 669 Yellow 10 ±
	4/JG 52	Flg. Alfred Feistel	+	Air combat fighters, west of Caen, 100%	Bf 109 G-6	165 652 Blue 5 ±
	4/JG 52	Lt. Manfred Fedgenhäuer	+	Air combat fighters, west of Caen, 100%	Bf 109 G-6	165 847 Blue 3 ±

	4/JG 52	Fw. Walter Ehrhardt	W	Air combat fighters, belly landing near Cherisy, 80%	Bf 109 G-6 412 904 Blue 1 ±
	II	NN	—	Air combat, location not known, 100%	Bf 109 G-6
	II	NN	—	Air combat, location not known, 100%	Bf 109 G-6
	II	NN	—	Air combat, location not known, D	Bf 109 G-6
	II	NN	—	Air combat, location not known, D	Bf 109 G-6
19/07/44	4	Gefr. Emmerich Berger	+	Air combat fighters, St. Lô area, crashed 25 km NE of Laval, 100%	Bf 109 G-6 165 645 White 9 ±
20/07/44	5	Uffz. Rudolf Wick	+	Air combat Spitfires, crashed near Amfreville, 100%	Bf 109 G-6 165 409 Black 3 ±
	II	NN	—	Flak, location not known, D	Bf 109 G-6
24/07/44	II	NN	—	Air combat, location not known, 100%	Bf 109 G-6
	II	NN	—	Air combat, location not known, 100%	Bf 109 G-6
	II	NN	—	Air combat, location not known, 100%	Bf 109 G-6
	II	NN	—	Air combat, location not known, D	Bf 109 G-6
	II	NN	—	Combat mission, not due to enemy action, location not known, D	Bf 109 G-6
25/07/44	6	Lt. Helmut Glaaß	+	Air combat fighters, crashed near Dourdan, 20 km SE of Rambouillet, 100%	Bf 109 G-6/U4 440 154 Yellow 1 ±
	4/JG 52	Uffz. Josef Wüst	(MIA)	Air combat fighters, St Lô area, 100% (returned injured 3/8/1944)	Bf 109 G-6/U4 Blue 9 ±
	4/JG 52	Gefr. Werner Henselien	W	Air combat fighters, belly landing NW of Argentan, 20%	Bf 109 G-6 165 643 Blue 7 ±
	6	Lt. Oskar Zimmermann, Stk. Inj.		Air combat P-51s, near Nogent-le-Roi, P, 100%	Bf 109 G-6
	II	NN	—	Air combat, location not known, 100%	Bf 109 G-6
	II	NN	—	Combat mission, not due to enemy action, location not known, D	Bf 109 G-6
	II	NN	—	Combat mission, not due to enemy action, location not known D	Bf 109 G-6
26/07/44	4/JG 52	Uffz. Hans Fischer	+	Engine failure during maintenance test flight, crashed on airfield boundary while attempting to land, Chaudon, 100%	Bf 109 G-6 441 503 Blue 6 ±
	II	NN	—	Air combat, location not known, 100%	Bf 109 G-6
	II	NN	—	Combat mission, not due to enemy action, location not known, 100%	Bf 109 G-6
	II	NN	—	Combat mission, not due to enemy action, location not known, 100%	Bf 109 G-6

Date	Unit	Name	Status	Description	Aircraft	W.Nr./Markings
	II	NN	—	Combat mission, not due to enemy action, location not known, 100%	Bf 109 G-6	
27/07/44	II	NN	—	Air combat, location not known, 100%	Bf 109 G-6	
	II	NN	—	Combat mission, not due to enemy action, location not known, D	Bf 109 G-6	
	II	NN	—	Mechanical trouble/accident, location not known, D	Bf 109 G-6	
01/08/44	4/JG 52	Uffz. Josef Selbertinger	Inj.	Air combat fighters, forced landing near Valletot, D	Bf 109 G-6	165 650 Blue 4 ±
02/08/44	4	Uffz. Kurt Poppitz	+	Midair collision while on approach to land at Nogent-le-Roi, 100%	Bf 109 G-6/U4	441 508 White 9 ±
	5	Fw. Wolfgang Blum	+	Midair collision while on approach to land at Nogent-le-Roi, 100%	Bf 109 G-6	165 801 Black 23 ±
03/08/44	6	Uffz. Josef Wester	W	Air combat fighters, crash landing near St. Paul, 25 km SW of Alencon, 100%	Bf 109 G-6	412 258 Yellow 4 ±
06/08/44	4	Lt. Fridolin Reinartz	+	Air combat fighters, crashed 2 km west of Villemeuxm 100%	Bf 109 G-6	412 618 White 8 ±
	6	Obfw. Herbert Dehrmann	+	Air combat fighters, crashed north of Chaudon, 100%	Bf 109 G-6	411 252 Yellow 5 ±
08/08/44	4	Uffz. Karl Clauß	Inj.	Ground looped on takeoff, Mauziaze, 100%	Bf 109 G-6/U4	441 823
09/08/44	4	Gefr. Günter Schmedes	MIA	Air combat fighters, Mortain area, 100%	Bf 109 G-6	412 565 White 15 ±
	5	Obfw. Franz Busch	Inj.	Ferry flight, crashed on takeoff after striking obstacle, Chartres, 100% (+ 10/8/1944)	Bf 109 G-6	163 818 no markings
10/08/44		Uffz. Georg Handrich	+	Air combat fighters, location not known, 100%	Bf 109 G-6	164 936 Black 6 ±
	II	NN	—	Mechanical trouble/accident, location not known, D	Bf 109 G-6	
13/08/44	5	Uffz. Kurt Soßdorf	(MIA)	Air combat, location and cause not known, 100%	Bf 109 G-6	165 513 no markings
	5	Uffz. Richard Quinten	(MIA)	Strafing attack, shot down by Spitfire, belly landing in the Chartres area, 100% (returned 14/8/1944)	Bf 109 G-6/U4	441 017 Black 16 ±
15/08/44	II	NN	—	Combat mission, not due to enemy action, location not known, D	Bf 109 G-6	
16/08/44	II	NN	—	Air combat, location not known, D	Bf 109 G-6	
18/08/44	5	Uffz. Alwin Boch	(MIA)	Air combat P-47s and P-51s, SW of Versailles, 100%	Bf 109 G-6	165 229 Black 10 ±
	6	Fw. Hans Löhlein	(MIA)	Air combat P-51s, Beauvais area, 100% (returned injured 19/1/1944)	Bf 109 G-6	163 653 Yellow 2 ±
	II	NN	—	Air combat, location not known, 100%	Bf 109 G-6	
	II	NN	—	Air combat, location not known, 100%	Bf 109 G-6	

Date	Unit	Name		Cause	Aircraft	Werk Nr. / Markings
	II	NN	—	Mechanical trouble/accident, location not known, D	Bf 109 G-6	
19/08/44	7	Uffz. Kurt Möllerke	(MIA)	Air combat P-47s, east of Brionne, grid square UB-26, 100% (returned injured)	Bf 109 G-6/U4	440 026 White 11 ±
	7	Uffz. Norbert Preusler	MIA	Air combat P-47s, west of Elbeuf, grid square TB-96, 100%	Bf 109 G-6	163 950 White 2 ±
	7	Gefr. Ernst Fleischhacker	(MIA)	Air combat P-47s, east of Brionne, grid square UB-26, 100% (returned injured)	Bf 109 G-6/AS	165 827 White 4 ±
	8	Fw. Otto Schicketanz	+	Air combat P-47s, north of Epernon, grid square BD-5, 100%	Bf 109 G-6/U4	441 833 Blue 4 ±
	II	NN	—	Air combat, location not known, 100%	Bf 109 G-6	
20/08/44	Stab II	Fhr. Paul Budde	W	Air combat, Argentan area, 100% († 23/8/1944)	Bf 109 G-6/U4	440 683 Black 12 ±
	8	Fw. Harald Wojnar	W	Air combat P-47s, location not known, 100%	Bf 109 G-6	
	II	NN	—	Air combat, location not known, 100%	Bf 109 G-6	
21/08/44	II	NN	—	Combat mission, not due to enemy action, location not known, D	Bf 109 G-6	

Losses during Operations in the Defense of the Reich
September to November 1944

Date	Unit	Name		Cause	Aircraft	Werk Nr. / Markings
14/09/44	Stab II	Oblt. Herbert Zschiegner	+	Overturned on landing, Ziegenhain, 100%	Bf 109 G-14	462 960 Red 2 ±
29/09/44	II	NN	—	Mechanical trouble/accident, location not known, 100%	Bf 109 G-14	
13/10/44	II	NN	—	Mechanical trouble/accident, location not known, D	Bf 109 G-14	
16/10/44	5	Uffz. Johann Elwischger	+	Air combat P-51s, crashed near Lauban, 100%	Bf 109 G-14	462 963 White 10 ±
	5	FhjFw. Leonhard Wenzel	+	Air combat P-51s, crashed near Lauban, 100%	Bf 109 G-14	781 126 White 3 ±
	7	Uffz. Günter Lehnik	+	Air combat P-51s, crashed near Gross-Walditz, 100%	Bf 109 G-14	461 421 Yellow 11 ±
	8	Uffz. Hans Schunk	Inj.	Air combat P-51s, forced landing Glück near Halben/Schleswig, 100%	Bf 109 G-14	462 962 Blue 4 ±
	II	NN	—	Combat mission, not due to enemy action, location not known, D	Bf 109 G-14	
17/10/44	II	NN	—	Mechanical trouble/accident, location not known, D	Bf 109 G-14	
	II	NN	—	Mechanical trouble/accident, location not known, D	Bf 109 G-14	
21/10/44	II	NN	—	Mechanical trouble/accident, location not known, D	Bf 109 G-14	
01/11/44	7	Uffz. Heinrich Barisich	+	Crashed during ferry flight, flew into ground 15 km south of Hof, Ahornsberg near Munich, 100%	Bf 109 G-14	464 140 Black 8 ±

02/11/44	Stab II	Lt. Adolf Briedl	+	Air combat fighters, crashed north of Helfta near Eisleben, 100%	Bf 109 G-14 461 322 Black <1 ±
	Stab II	Uffz. Heinrich Hess	+	Air combat fighters, location not known, 100%	Bf 109 G-14 462 748 Black <2 ±
	Stab II	Fhr. Eugen Bohler	+	Air combat fighters, crashed 1.5 km west of Mansfeld, 100%	Bf 109 G-14 462 680 Black <3 ±
	5	Lt. Paul Draeger	+	Air combat P-51s, Halle-Naumburg area, 100%	Bf 109 G-14 460 595 White 8 ±
	6	Fhr. Helmut Moll	+	Air combat fighters, Pretzsch/Elbe, 100%	Bf 109 G-14 460 418 Black 3 ±
	6	Lt. Walter Becker	+	Air combat fighters, Halle-Dessau-Leipzig area, 100%	Bf 109 G-14 461 487 Black 10 ±
	6	Uffz. Kurt Müller	+	Air combat fighters, crashed Gorna, Sangerhausen District, 100%	Bf 109 G-14 461 473 Black 4 ±
	7	Uffz. Günther Machalosowitz	W	Air combat fighters, north of Halle-Saale, P, 100%	Bf 109 G-14 462 720 Black 12 ±
	7	Lt. Gerhard Schweiger	+	Air combat fighters, Aschersleben area, 100%	Bf 109 G-14 462 733 Yellow 7 ±
	7	Uffz. Franz Planek	+	Air combat fighters, Aschersleben area, 100%	Bf 109 G-14 461 982 Yellow 15 ±
	8	Lt. Erwin Gottert	+	Air combat fighters, area south of Dessau, 100%	Bf 109 G-14 461 460 Blue 7 ±
	8	Obgefr. Hermann Röge	+	Air combat P-51s, crashed near Hornburg near Eisleben, 100%	Bf 109 G-14 461 407 Blue 6 ±
	8	Uffz. Ernst Sereinig	+	Air combat P-51s, crashed 3 km west of Halle-Saale, 100%	Bf 109 G-14 460 618 Blue 12 ±
	8	Lt. Walter Wagner	—	Air combat, crashed Halle area, P, 100%	Bf 109 G-14
	II	NN	—	Air combat, location not known, 100%	Bf 109 G-14
	II	NN	—	Air combat, location not known, 100%	Bf 109 G-14
	II	NN	—	Air combat, location not known, 100%	Bf 109 G-14
	II	NN	—	Air combat, location not known, D	Bf 109 G-14
	II	NN	—	Air combat, location not known, D	Bf 109 G-14
	II	NN	—	Air combat, location not known, D	Bf 109 G-14
	II	NN	—	Air combat, location not known, D	Bf 109 G-14
	II	NN	—	Air combat, location not known, D	Bf 109 G-14
	II	NN	—	Air combat, location not known, D	Bf 109 G-14
	II	NN	—	Combat mission, not due to enemy action, location not known, D	Bf 109 G-14
	II	NN	—	Combat mission, not due to enemy action, location not known, D	Bf 109 G-14

	II	—	—	Strafing attack, location not known, D	Bf 109 G-14
03/11/44	II	NN	—	Mechanical trouble/accident, location not known, D	Bf 109 G-14
05/11/44	7	Obgefr. Wolfgang Klostemayr	+	Crashed on takeoff, Alperstedt, 100%	Bf 109 G-14 781 134 Yellow 5 ±
19/11/44	5	Obgefr. Herbert Roeske	+	Midair collision, crashed 15 km east of Weimar, 100%	Bf 109 G-14 464 301 White 7 ±
	II	NN	—	Combat mission, not due to enemy action, location not known, D	Bf 109 G-14
	II	NN	—	Combat mission, not due to enemy action, location not known, D	Bf 109 G-14
	II	NN	—	Combat mission, not due to enemy action, location not known, D	Bf 109 G-14

Casualties Among the Ground Personnel of II/JG 3

25/05/40	HQ Comp II/JG 3	Flg. Paul Fallick	W	Strafing attack on forward airfield Mont Ecouvez South
	6	Uffz. Bernhard Franke	W	Strafing attack on forward airfield Mont Ecouvez South
22/08/40	HQ Comp. II/JG 3	Flg. Otto Köller	+	Accident, Wierre-au-Bois
27/03/42	6	Obgefr. Johann Dauer (armorer)	+	Killed by cannon shell while calibrating the weapons of a Bf 109
11/07/42	HQ Comp. II/JG 3	Flg. Günther Römelt (Schwarmmeister)	+	Bombing, Marijewka
	HQ Comp. II/JG 3	Obgefr. Wilhelm Dorn (armorer)	W	Bombing, Marijewka
	6	Obgefr. Hermann Ellmers (a/c mechanic)	W	Bombing, Marijewka
13/07/42	HQ Comp II/JG 3	Flg. Friedrich Grosser (gen. personnel)	W	Partisan ambush during requisitioning sortie, near Kantemirovka
	HQ Comp. II/JG 3	Obgefr. Theodor Körner (gen. personnel)	W	as above
	4	Gefr. Albert Schröder (a/c mechanic)		Injured by ground-looping Ju 87, Kantemirovka airfield (+ 14/7/1942)
	4	Uffz. Karl Montzka (a/c mechanic)	+	As above, crushed by 500-kg bomb
	4	Obgefr. Gerhard Richter (a/c electrician)	+	As above
	4	Obgefr. Friedrich Helmers (a/c mechanic)	+	As above
	4	Gefr. Gerhard Lichtenberger (a/c mechanic)	+	As above
	4	Obgefr. Heinrich Steinlage (a/c mechanic)	Inj.	As above
14/07/42	4	Obgefr. Walter Aulich (driver)	W	Bombs dropped on German troops by Hs 129 near Millerovo
23/07/42	HQ Comp. II/JG 3	Obgefr. Leo Deiminger (armorer)	W	Drove over mine while on requisitioning sortie, 25 km east of Frolov

29/07/42	6	Uffz. Oskar Nioch (a/c mechanic)	W	Ambushed by partisans while on requisitioning sortie	
02/10/42	HQ Comp. II/JG 3	Obgefr. Paul Aderhold (a/c mechanic)	W	Bombing, Sôlzy	
	27	Obgefr. Kurt Stallmach (a/c mechanic)	W	Bombing, Sôlzy	
27/12/42	HQ Comp. II/JG 3	Fw. Otto Röhring (radio team leader)	+	While fighting off infantry attack 1.5 km NE of Pavlovskaya	
	5	Obgefr. Walter Stallmann (a/c mechanic)	W	While fighting off infantry attack 1.5 km NE of Pavlovskaya	
10/04/43	5	Fw. Hans Evers (tech. personnel)	W	Low-level attack by Il-2s, Anapa	
	5	Obgefr. Wilfried Fritzsch (tech. personnel)	W	Low-level attack by Il-2s, Anapa	
02/05/43	4	Uffz. Kurt Bork (gen. personnel)	+	Killed by accidental fire from submachine-gun, Osnova	
07/06/43	4	Obgefr. Erich Tiedemann	W	Cause not known, Kharkov-Roganj	

II/JG 3 (new)
Losses during the Formation and Training Period
November 1944 to February 1945

01/12/44	7	Uffz. Kurt Dürrhammer	+	Midair collision, near Grossrudestedt, 100%[1124]	Bf 109 G-14 462 800 Yellow 11 ±
	8	Fw. Georg Oberauer	+	Midair collision, near Grossrudestedt, 100%	Bf 109 G-14 464 097 Yellow 14 ±
06/12/44	II	—	—	Bombing, Alperstedt, 100%	Bf 109 G
12/12/44	II	NN	—	Mechanical trouble/accident, location not known, D	Bf 109 G
29/12/44	II	NN	—	Mechanical trouble/accident, location not known 100%	Bf 109 G
	II	NN	—	Mechanical trouble/accident, location not known, D	Bf 109 G
30/12/44	II	NN	—	Combat mission, not due to enemy action, location not known, D	Bf 109 G
	II	NN	—	Combat mission, not due to enemy action, location not known, D	Bf 109 G
31/12/44	II	NN	—	Combat mission, not due to enemy action, location not known, 100%	Bf 109 G
02/01/45	II	NN	—	Mechanical trouble/accident, location not known, 100%	Bf 109 G
05/01/45	II	NN	—	Mechanical trouble/accident, location not known, D	Bf 109 G
	II	NN	—	Mechanical trouble/accident, location not known, D	Bf 109 G
06/01/45	II	NN	—	Mechanical trouble/accident, location not known, 100%	Bf 109 G
08/01/45	II	NN	—	Mechanical trouble/accident, location not known, D	Bf 109 G
16/01/45	II	NN	—	Mechanical trouble/accident, location not known, D	Bf 109 G

	II	NN	—	Mechanical trouble/accident, location not known, D	Bf 109 G
	II	NN	—	Mechanical trouble/accident, location not known, D	Bf 109 G
20/01/45	8	Obgefr. Friedrich Knost	+	Ran out of fuel, crashed while landing at Alperstedt, ferry flight, 80%	Bf 109 G-10 130 386 Blue 9 ±
06/02/45	II	Fw. Hein Berom	—	Mechanical problem, forced landing, Esperstedt, 50%	Bf 109 G-10 130 337
09/02/45	II	NN	—	Crash landing, Alperstedt, 15%	Bf 109 G-10 490 635
	II	NN	—	Air combat, forced landing Eschwege, 20%	Bf 109 G-10 130 286
16/02/45	II	NN	—	Mechanical problem, location not known, 60%	Bf 109 G-14 781 138

Losses during Operations in the East
February to April 1945

20/02/45	6	Fw. Willi Schreiber	+	Crashed while taking off from Alperstedt on ferry flight, 2:55 PM, 100%	Bf 109 G-10 490 430 White 11 ±
	II	NN	—	Mechanical problem, location not known, 10%	Bf 109 G-14 562 905
	II	NN	—	Ground looped on landing, location not known, 70%	Bf 109 G-14 460 655
	II	NN	—	Taxiing accident, location not known, 50%	Bf 109 G-10 490 762
	II	NN	—	Ran out of fuel, belly landing, location not known, 20%	Bf 109 G-10 490 765
03/03/45	5	Gefr. Claus Günther	+	Combat mission, cause not known, Freienwalde area, 100%	Bf 109 G-10 490 628 White 4 ±
	8	Lt. Gerhard Büker	MIA	Combat mission, cause not known, Freienwalde area, missing, 100%	Bf 109 G-10 490 151 Blue 12 ±
	II	NN	—	Enemy fire, belly landing Stavenhagen, 40%	Bf 109 G-10 130 320
	II	NN	—	Enemy fire, belly landing Stettin-Altdamm, 10%	Bf 109 G-10 490 384
05/03/45	6	Lt. Peter Fürbringer	+	Low-level attack, crashed Drewitz, Pomerania, 100%	Bf 109 G-14 461 370 Black 3 ±
	7	Obfw. Leo Danetzki	POW	Low-level attack, crashed area of Gülzow/Tessin, P, 100%	Bf 109 G-14 463 177 Yellow 3 ±
	7	Gefr. Heinz Abitz	MIA	Low-level attack, Naugard area, 100%	Bf 109 G-14/AS 787 486 Yellow 1 ±
	8	Uffz. Rudolf Klotz	+	Low-level attack, crashed 3 km NW of Gölzow, 100%	Bf 109 G-10 130 315 Blue 6 ±
	II	NN	—	Enemy fire, belly landing north of Wollin, 35%	Bf 109 G-14 781 132
	II	NN	—	Flak, belly landing Nemitz, 40%	Bf 109 G-10 611 071
06/03/45	8	NN	—	Enemy fire, belly landing Wahrlang, 50%	Bf 109 G-10 613 053 Blue 22 ±
09/03/45	II	NN	—	Mechanical problem, belly landing Garz, 30%	Bf 109 G-10 611 033

11/03/45	6	Lt. Klaus Pajonk	MIA	Combat mission, Air combat La-5s, Stettin area, 100%	Bf 109 G-10 490 752 Blue 1 ±
	6	Fw. Heinz Beran	MIA	Combat mission, Air combat, Stettin area, 100%	Bf 109 G-10 490 622 Blue 11 ±
	II	Lt. Werner Petereit	Inj.	Overturned during forced landing following engine trouble, S W of Kaseburg, 90%	Bf 109 G-10 490 629 Yellow 7 ±
	II	NN	—	Ground looped on landing, Garz, 40%	Bf 109 G-10 613 072
03/04/45	7	Oblt. Herbert Mielke, Sff.	+	Combat mission, cause not known, Kleines Haff, 4 km west of Garz, 100%	Bf 109 G-14 464 510 Yellow 15 ±
13/04/45	6	Uffz. Hermann Picht	+	Overturned on landing, Kaminke, D	Bf 109 G

Notes:

[1120] As the following lost list illustrates, units did not always strictly adhere to the official guidelines reproduced above. Many crashes which should have been classified as 81 – 99%, were in fact reported as 100%.

[1121] In fact the location was probably Wierre-au-Bois. The same applies to the loss report of 19 August 1940.

[1122] Aircraft of 5 (H)/11.

[1123] The location given in the WASt. casualty report and the GQM Report; in fact the location must have been the Mareyevka airfield.

[1124] Reported under 3 Dec. 1944 as I/JG 7 loss number two, reporting period 26 Oct. – 1 Dec. 1944. Under the Gruppe designation was the note: "I/JG 7 = ex II/KG 2". It also stated, "I/JG 7, expected to be renamed II/JG 3". The Feldpost number was 33549, LgPA Dresden.

Appendix C: II./Jagdgeschwader 3 Victory List

Victories by II/JG 3 during the Western Campaign
19 May to 25 June 1940

20.05.40	Stab II./JG 3	Hptm. Erich von Selle	Hurricane	(1.)	16.27	
	Stab II./JG 3	Lt. Franz von Werra	Hurricane	(1.)	16.29	
	Stab II./JG 3	Hptm. Erich von Selle	Hurricane	(2.)	16.30	
	4./JG 3	Lt. Rudolf Heymann	Hurricane	(1.)	16.30	
21.05.40	4./JG 3	Hptm. Alfred Müller	Morane	(1.)	16.05	
	4./JG 3	Fw. August Müller	Morane	(1.)	16.10	zusammen mit Fw. Nagel
22.05.40	Stab II./JG 3	Lt. Franz von Werra	Bréguet 690	(2.)	12.36	
	Stab II./JG 3	Lt. Franz von Werra	Bréguet 690	(3.)	12.52	
24.05.40	Stab II./JG 3	Lt. Heinrich Sannemann	Morane	(1.)	17.55	
25.05.40	4./JG 3	Uffz. Anton Gremm	Potez-63	(1.)	20.40	
26.05.40	5./JG 3	Uffz. Josef Heinzeller	Hurricane	(1.)	06.50	
27.05.40	6./JG 3	Obfw. Erich Labusga	Blenheim	(1.)	07.35	
29.05.44	4./JG 3	Hptm. Dr. Albrecht Ochs	Hurricane	(1.)		
	4./JG 3	Lt. Rudolf Heymann	Hurricane	(2.)		
	4./JG 3	Fw. Erwin Dickow	Hurricane	(1.)		
31.05.40	5./JG 3	Uffz. Josef Heinzeller	Bréguet 690	(2.)	18.25	
	6./JG 3	Lt. Karl Westerhoff	Blenheim	(1.)	21.15	
	6./JG 3	Oblt. Erich Woitke	Wellington	(1.)	21.15	
	6./JG 3	Uffz. Erich Dobrick	LeO 451	(1.) *		
03.06.40	5./JG 3	Lt. Horst Buddenhagen	Hurricane	(1.)	08.40	
	5./JG 3	Uffz. Hermann Freitag	Hurricane	(1.)	08.45	
	5./JG 3	Lt Horst Buddenhagen	Hurricane	(2.)		
	5./JG 3	Obfw. Horst Götz	Hurricane	(1.) *		
	6./JG 3	Oblt. Erich Woitke	Morane	(2.)	14.40	
	Stab II./JG 3	Lt. Franz von Werra	Morane	(4.)		
	6./JG 3	Oblt. Karl Westerhoff	Morane	(2.)		
05.06.40	Stab II./JG 3	Hptm. Erich von Selle	LeO 451	(3.)	12.40	
	4./JG 3	Hptm. Alfred Müller	Curtiss P-36	(2.)	13.10	
	4./JG 3	Uffz. Eckart König	Curtiss P-36	(1.)		
	4./JG 3	Uffz. Erwin Kortlepel	Curtiss P-36	(1.)		
	4./JG 3	Hptm. Albrecht Müller	Lysander	(3.)		
	6./JG 3	Lt. Karl Westerhoff	Potez-63	(3.)	16.05	
	5./JG 3	Obfw. Horst Götz	Bréguet 690	(2.)	16.45	
06.06.40	4./JG 3	Hptm. Dr. Albrecht Ochs	Blenheim	(2.)		
	4./JG 3	Fw. August Müller	Potez-63	(2.)		
	4./JG 3	Lt. Rudolf Heymann	Curtiss P-36	(3.)		
	5./JG 3	Uffz. Alfred Heckmann	Morane	(1.)	11.10	
	5./JG 3	Oblt. Herbert Kijewski	Spitfire	(1.)	11.10	
07.06.40	5./JG 3	Lt. Werner Voigt	Curtiss P-36	(1.)	06.25	
	5./JG 3	Oblt. Herbert Kijewski	Spitfire	(2.)	19.07	
	5./JG 3	Uffz. Josef Heinzeller	Battle	(3.)	19.08	
	5./JG 3	Uffz. Konrad Nelleskamp	Battle	(1.)	19.10	
	5./JG 3	Uffz. Hermann Freitag	Battle	(2.)	19.15	
11.06.40	4./JG 3	Uffz. Emil Müller	Battle	(1.)		zusammen mit Uffz. König
13.06.40	5./JG 3	Uffz. Konrad Nelleskamp	Blenheim	(2.)	16.45	
14.06.40	5./JG 3	Uffz. Fritz Mias	Potez-63	(1.)	18.45	
15.06.40	6./JG 3	Uffz. Friedrich Becker	Blenheim	(1.)	12.25	
17.06.40	5./JG 3	Uffz. Fritz Mias	Potez-63	(2.)	17.35	

Victories by II/JG 3 during Operations over the Channel and Great Britain
July 1940 to February 1941

15.08.40	5./JG 3	Uffz. Alfred Heckmann	Spitfire	(2.)		
16.08.40	4./JG 3	Uffz. Willy Finke	Spitfire	(1.)		
	5./JG 3	Uffz. Josef Heinzeller	Spitfire	(4.)	13.20	
	5./JG 3	Uffz. Walter Ohlrogge	Spitfire	(1.)	13.20	
18.08.40	6./JG 3	Oblt. Karl Westerhoff	Hurricane	(4.)		
21.08.40	6./JG 3	Uffz. Kurt Gräf	Spitfire	(2.)		

Date	Unit	Pilot	Aircraft		Time
26.08.40	6./JG 3	Oblt. Karl Westerhoff	Spitfire	(5.)	13.15
	6./JG 3	Oblt. Erich Woitke	Spitfire	(3.)	13.20
	5./JG 3	Lt. Horst Buddenhagen	Spitfire	(3.)	13.20
	4./JG 3	Oblt. Jost Kipper	Hurricane	(1.)	13.25
	Stab II./JG 3	Oblt. Heinrich Sannemann	Spitfire	(2.)	13.30
	Stab II./JG 3	Hptm. Erich von Selle	Spitfire	(4.)	
	6./JG 3	Uffz. Kurt Gräf	Hurricane	(3.)	
28.08.40	Stab II./JG 3	Oblt. Franz von Werra	Spitfire	(5.)	
	Stab II./JG 3	Oblt. Franz von Werra	Hurricane	(6.)	
	Stab II./JG 3	Oblt. Franz von Werra	Hurricane	(7.)	
	Stab II./JG 3	Oblt. Franz von Werra	Hurricane	(8.)	
	4./JG 3	Fw. Erwin Kortlepel	Hurricane	(2.)	
	4./JG 3	Fw. Anton Gremm	Hurricane	(2.)	
	5./JG 3	Uffz. Konrad Nelleskamp	Hurricane	(3.)	17.20
	5./JG 3	Uffz. Josef Heinzeller	Defiant	(5.)	17.25
	6./JG 3	Uffz. Kurt Gräf	Spitfire	(4.)	
	5./JG 3	Obfw. Horst Götz	Spitfire	(3.) *	
	6./JG 3	Fw. Erich Dobrick	Spitfire	(2.)	
29.08.40	5./JG 3	Oblt. Werner Voigt	Spitfire	(2.)	16.40
	5./JG 3	Oblt. Herbert Kijewski	Hurricane	(3.) *	
30.08.40	Stab II./JG 3	Hptm. Erich von Selle	Hurricane	(5.)	
05.09.40	6./JG 3	Oblt. Erich Woitke	Spitfire	(4.)	16.30
07.09.40	Stab II./JG 3	Hptm. Erich von Selle	Spitfire	(6.)	
08.09.40	4./JG 3	Fw. Erwin Kortlepel	Hurricane	(3.)	13.30
	5./JG 3	Obfw. Horst Götz	Hurricane	(4.) *	
09.09.40	4./JG 3	Oblt. Werner Voigt	Hurricane	(3.)	
	4./JG 3	Obfw. August Müller	Hurricane	(3.)	
13.09.40	6./JG 3	Uffz. August Dilling	Blenheim	(1.)	20.50
15.09.40	Stab II./JG 3	Oblt. Heinrich Sannemann	Spitfire	(3.)	15.40
	5./JG 3	Obfw. Horst Götz	Hurricane	(5.) *	
18.09.40	6./JG 3	Oblt. Erich Woitke	Spitfire	(5.)	14.35
20.09.40	5./JG 3	Uffz. Alfred Heckmann	Spitfire	(3.)	12.20
27.09.40	6./JG 3	Oblt. Erich Woitke	Curtiss P-36	(6.)	13.30
	5./JG 3	Lt. Horst Buddenhagen	Hurricane	(4.)	13.30
29.09.40	6./JG 3	Uffz. Eduard Rybiak	Hurricane	(1.)	17.25
	Stab II./JG 3	Hptm. Erich von Selle	Hurricane	(7.)	17.30
	4./JG 3	Fw. Erwin Kortlepel	Hurricane	(4.)	17.30
	4./JG 3	Fw. Eckart König	Hurricane	(2.)	17.30
	6./JG 3	Uffz. August Dilling	Hurricane	(2.)	17.30
	4./JG 3	Oblt. Werner Voigt	Hurricane	(4.)	17.35
10.01.41	Stab II./JG 3	Fw. August Dilling	Hurricane	(3.)	14.05
10.02.41	Stab II./JG 3	Hptm. Lothar Keller	Hurricane	(16.)	17.42

Victories by II/JG 3 during Operations on the Channel
May to June 1941

Date	Unit	Pilot	Aircraft		Time
04.05.41	Stab II./JG 3	Oblt. Heinz Schönefeldt	Lysander	(2.) *	
07.05.41	4./JG 3	Oblt. Gordon Gollob	Spitfire	(6.)	11.25
21.05.41	Stab II./JG 3	Oblt. Heinz Schönefeldt	Blenheim	(3.) *	

Victories by II/JG 3 during Operations in the East
June to October 1941

Date	Unit	Pilot	Aircraft		Time
22.06.41	Stab II./JG 3	Oblt. Walther Dahl	I-18	(1.)	04.30
	4./JG 3	Lt. Hans Fuß	I-153	(1.)	06.50
	4./JG 3	Lt. Hans Fuß	I-16	(2.)	07.00
	4./JG 3	Hptm. Gordon Gollob	I-16	(7.)	07.00
	Stab II./JG 3	Hptm. Lothar Keller	I-16	(17.)	07.28
	Stab II./JG 3	Oblt. Franz Beyer	I-16	(4.)	07.29
	Stab II./JG 3	Oblt. Karl Faust	I-16	(1.)	07.30
	Stab II./JG 3	Hptm. Lothar Keller	I-153	(18.)	07.44
	5./JG 3	Fw. Alfred Heckmann	I-153	(4.)	07.45
	6./JG 3	Uffz. Horst Beyer	DB-3	(1.)	09.30
	6./JG 3	Fw. August Dilling	I-16	(4.)	09.31
	Stab II./JG 3	Hptm. Lothar Keller	I-153	(19.)	18.42
	Stab II./JG 3	Oblt. Karl Faust	I-16	(2.)	18.48
	Stab II./JG 3	Hptm. Lothar Keller	I-16	(20.)	18.50
	Stab II./JG 3	Oblt. Franz Beyer	I-153	(5.)	18.55

23.06.41	5./JG 3	Fw. Alfred Heckmann	I-16	(5.)	04.50
	5./JG 3	Lt. Horst Buddenhagen	I-16	(5.)	04.55
	6./JG 3	Oblt. Heinrich Sannemann	DB-3	(4.)	06.00
	6./JG 3	Fw. August Dilling	DB-3	(5.)	06.01
	6./JG 3	Oblt. Heinrich Sannemann	DB-3	(5.)	06.03
	6./JG 3	Uffz. Horst Beyer	DB-3	(2.)	06.03
	6./JG 3	Fw. August Dilling	DB-3	(6.)	06.04
	6./JG 3	Lt. Ernst-Heinz Löhr	DB-3	(1.)	06.07
	5./JG 3	Lt. Horst Buddenhagen	I-16	(6.)	09.40
	5./JG 3	Obfw. Josef Heinzeller	SB-2	(6.)	09.45
	4./JG 3	Lt. Hans Fuß	SB-2	(3.)	09.50
	4./JG 3	Lt. Hans Fuß	SB-2	(4.)	09.55
	5./JG 3	Uffz. Ernst Pöske	SB-2	(1.)	09.55
	Stab II./JG 3	Oblt. Franz Beyer	SB-2	(6.)	09.58
	5./JG 3	Uffz. Ernst Pöske	SB-2	(2.)	10.00
	5./JG 3	Uffz. Ernst Pöske	SB-2	(3.)	10.05
24.06.41	6./JG 3	Lt. Ludwig Häfner	Potez-63	(1.)	13.22
	5./JG 3	Obfw. Josef Heinzeller	I-16	(7.)	19.50
	5./JG 3	Lt. Horst Buddenhagen	1	(7.)	
25.06.41	6./JG 3	Lt. Ludwig Häfner	DB-3	(2.)	07.01
	6./JG 3	Oblt. Heinrich Sannemann	DB-3	(6.)	07.02
	6./JG 3	Fw. August Dilling	DB-3	(7.)	07.04
	6./JG 3	Oblt. Heinrich Sannemann	DB-3	(7.)	07.08
	6./JG 3	Uffz. Horst Beyer	Potez-63	(3.)	07.10
	6./JG 3	Fw. August Dilling	Potez-63	(8.)	07.12
	Stab II./JG 3	Oblt. Franz Beyer	SB-2	(7.)	08.55
	4./JG 3	Hptm. Gordon Gollob	DB-3	(8.)	09.00
	4./JG 3	Lt. Hans Fuß	DB-3	(5.)	09.00
	4./JG 3	Obfhr. Albert Helm	DB-3	(1.)	09.05
	Stab II./JG 3	Oblt. Karl Faust	DB-3	(3.)	09.07
	4./JG 3	Hptm. Gordon Gollob	DB-3	(9.)	09.10
	Stab II./JG 3	Oblt. Franz Beyer	DB-3	(8.)	09.12
	4./JG 3	Lt. Hans Fuß	I-16	(6.)	09.20
	6./JG 3	Uffz. Horst Beyer	I-15	(4.)	15.25
	5./JG 3	Fw. Walter Ohlrogge	I-16	(2.)	19.50
	5./JG 3	Lt. Horst Buddenhagen	1	(8.)	
26.06.41	5./JG 3	Obfw. Josef Heinzeller	DB-3	(8.)	08.05
	5./JG 3	Oblt. Herbert Kijewski	DB-3	(4.)	08.10
	5./JG 3	Fw. Alfred Heckmann	DB-3	(6.)	08.10
	5./JG 3	Oblt. Herbert Kijewski	DB-3	(5.)	08.13
	5./JG 3	Lt. Herbert Glück	DB-3	(1.)	08.15
	5./JG 3	Lt. Herbert Glück	DB-3	(2.)	08.15
	5./JG 3	Obfw. Josef Heinzeller	DB-3	(9.)	08.15
	5./JG 3	Obfw. Josef Heinzeller	DB-3	(10.)	08.25
	5./JG 3	Fw. Alfred Heckmann	DB-3	(7.)	08.30
	6./JG 3	Fw. August Dilling	DB-3	(9.)	12.37
	6./JG 3	Oblt. Heinrich Sannemann	DB-3	(8.)	12.40
	4./JG 3	Obfw. Anton Gremm	DB-3	(3.)	14.20
27.06.41	5./JG 3	Fw. Alfred Heckmann	I-15	(8.)	08.05
	5./JG 3	Obfw. Josef Heinzeller	I-15	(11.)	08.10
28.06.41	6./JG 3	Oblt. Heinrich Sannemann	Pe-2	(9.)	15.58
	6./JG 3	Uffz. Horst Beyer	Pe-2	(5.)	16.01
	6./JG 3	Fw. August Dilling	Pe-2	(10.)	16.05
	Stab II./JG 3	Oblt. Franz Beyer	SB-2	(9.)	18.15
	5./JG 3	Oblt. Herbert Kijewski	SB-2	(6.)	19.00
	5./JG 3	Obfw. Josef Heinzeller	SB-2	(12.)	19.20
29.06.41	5./JG 3	Lt. Herbert Glück	I-16	(3.)	09.35
	5./JG 3	Obfw. Josef Heinzeller	I-16	(13.)	09.45
	4./JG 3	Uffz. Kuno Bälz	Pe-2	(1.)	18.17
	4./JG 3	Oblt. Karl Faust	Pe-2	(4.)	18.19
30.06.41	5./JG 3	Fw. Walter Ohlrogge	1	(3.)	04.20
	5./JG 3	Fw. Alfred Heckmann	I-16	(9.)	14.30
	4./JG 3	Obfw. Erwin Kortlepel	I-16	(5.)	14.35
	4./JG 3	Lt. Hans Fuß	I-16	(7.)	14.45
01.07.41	4./JG 3	Staffelabschuss	I-153	-	05.01
	4./JG 3	Obfw. Erwin Kortlepel	DB-3	(6.)	18.40
	4./JG 3	Obfw. Erwin Kortlepel	DB-3	(7.)	18.45
	Stab II./JG 3	Hptm. Gordon Gollob	Pe-2	(10.)	19.42
02.07.41	Stab II./JG 3	Hptm. Gordon Gollob	ZKB-19	(11.)	05.42
	Stab II./JG 3	Oblt. Franz Beyer	I-16	(10.)	06.05
	4./JG 3	Uffz. Werner Lucas	I-16	(1.)	06.20
	5./JG 3	Fw. Walter Ohlrogge	I-17	(4.)	08.30
	5./JG 3	Lt. Friedrich Kanzler	DB-3	(1.)	08.30
	5./JG 3	Obfw. Josef Heinzeller	Pe-2	(14.)	08.40
	Stab II./JG 3	Oblt. Franz Beyer	I-153	(11.)	09.30
	5./JG 3	Fw. Walter Ohlrogge	I-153	(5.)	09.30
	5./JG 3	Fw. Walter Ohlrogge	I-153	(6.)	09.33
	Stab II./JG 3	Hptm. Gordon Gollob	V-11	(12.)	11.30
	Stab II./JG 3	Oblt. Franz Beyer	V-11	(12.)	11.30
	Stab II./JG 3	Oblt. Franz Beyer	V-11	(13.)	11.35
	Stab II./JG 3	Hptm. Gordon Gollob	V-11	(13.)	11.43

	5./JG 3	Obfw. Josef Heinzeller	I-15	(15.)	11.45
	5./JG 3	Lt. Friedrich Kanzler	SB-2	(2.)	11.50
	5./JG 3	Obfw. Josef Heinzeller	SB-2	(16.)	11.50
	5./JG 3	Lt. Friedrich Kanzler	SB-2	(3.)	11.52
	5./JG 3	Obfw. Josef Heinzeller	SB-2	(17.)	11.55
	4./JG 3	Oblt. Karl Faust	R-10	(5.)	12.14
	5./JG 3	Fw. Fritz Mias	R-5	(3.)	16.25
	5./JG 3	Fw. Alfred Heckmann	R-5	(10.)	16.25
	5./JG 3	Fw. Alfred Heckmann	R-5	(11.)	16.30
	4./JG 3	Uffz. Kuno Bälz	I-153	(2.)	18.10
05.07.41	5./JG 3	Obfw. Josef Heinzeller	SB-2	(18.)	13.10
	5./JG 3	Fw. Walter Ohlrogge	SB-2	(7.)	13.10
	5./JG 3	Fw. Alfred Heckmann	SB-2	(12.)	13.10
	4./JG 3	Oblt. Karl Faust	Pe-2	(6.)	14.42
	4./JG 3	Oblt. Karl Faust	SB-2	(7.)	14.58
	5./JG 3	Fw. Alfred Heckmann	DB-3	(13.)	16.20
	5./JG 3	Fw. Walter Ohlrogge	DB-3	(8.)	16.20
	5./JG 3	Fw. Walter Ohlrogge	DB-3	(9.)	16.20
	5./JG 3	Fw. Walter Ohlrogge	DB-3	(10.)	16.20
	6./JG 3	Fw. August Dilling	DB-3	(11.)	20.05
	6./JG 3	Uffz. Horst Beyer	SB-3	(6.)	20.05
06.07.41	6./JG 3	Oblt. Heinrich Sannemann	SB-2	(10.)	05.30
	6./JG 3	Lt. Gustav Frielinghaus	SB-2	(1.)	05.35
	4./JG 3	Oblt. Karl Faust	Pe-2	(8.)	08.48
	4./JG 3	Oblt. Karl Faust	SB-2	(9.)	12.37
	4./JG 3	Oblt. Karl Faust	SB-2	(10.)	12.38
	6./JG 3	Fw. August Dilling	DB-3	(12.)	13.25
	4./JG 3	Uffz. Leopold Münster	ZKB-19	(1.)	14.52
	4./JG 3	Oblt. Karl Faust	Pe-2	(11.)	17.43
	4./JG 3	Oblt. Karl Faust	Pe-2	(12.)	17.44
07.07.41	Stab II./JG 3	Oblt. Franz Beyer	I-16	(14.)	18.54
	Stab II./JG 3	Oblt. Franz Beyer	I-16	(15.)	18.55
08.07.41	5./JG 3	Oblt. Herbert Kijewski	DB-3	(7.)	17.25
	5./JG 3	Oblt. Herbert Kijewski	DB-3	(8.)	17.30
	5./JG 3	Lt. Friedrich Glück	DB-3	(4.)	17.35
	6./JG 3	Oblt. Heinrich Sannemann	DB-3	(11.)	17.40
09.07.41	5./JG 3	Oblt. Herbert Kijewski	DB-3	(9.)	11.50
	5./JG 3	Oblt. Herbert Kijewski	DB-3	(10.)	11.50
	5./JG 3	Uffz. Ernst Pöske	DB-3	(4.)	11.50
	4./JG 3	Lt. Hans Fuß	DB-3	(8.)	16.10
	4./JG 3	Uffz. Leopold Münster	DB-3	(2.)	16.12
	4./JG 3	Lt. Hans Fuß	DB-3	(9.)	16.13
	4./JG 3	Uffz. Leopold Münster	DB-3	(3.)	16.16
	5./JG 3	Obfw. Josef Heinzeller	I-153	(19.)	16.35
	5./JG 3	Obfw. Josef Heinzeller	I-153	(20.)	16.40
	5./JG 3	Obfw. Josef Heinzeller	I-153	(21.)	16.45
10.07.41	4./JG 3	Obfhr. Kohl	TB-3	(1.)	16.55
	4./JG 3	Lt. Karl-Heinz Ponec	TB-3	(1.)	16.58
	5./JG 3	Oblt. Herbert Kijewski	TB-3	(11.)	17.20
	5./JG 3	Fw. Alfred Heckmann	V-11	(14.)	17.20
	5./JG 3	Oblt. Herbert Kijewski	DB-3	(12.)	17.25
	5./JG 3	Fw. Alfred Heckmann	V-11	(15.)	17.25
	5./JG 3	Obfw. Josef Heinzeller	TB-3	(22.)	17.25
	5./JG 3	Oblt. Herbert Kijewski	V-11	(13.)	17.30
	4./JG 3	Oblt. Karl Faust	I-16	(13.)	18.47
	4./JG 3	Uffz. Werner Lucas	TB-3	(2.)	19.22
	4./JG 3	Uffz. Werner Lucas	TB-3	(3.)	19.30
	Stab II./JG 3	Oblt. Franz Beyer	TB-3	(16.)	19.31
	4./JG 3	Uffz. Werner Lucas	TB-3	(4.)	19.33
	Stab II./JG 3	Oblt. Franz Beyer	TB-3	(17.)	19.35
	6./JG 3	Uffz. Horst Beyer	I-16	(7.)	20.05
	5./JG 3	Obfw. Josef Heinzeller	I-16	(23.)	20.15
	5./JG 3	Obfw. Josef Heinzeller	SB-2	(24.)	20.20
11.07.41	4./JG 3	Obfw. Erwin Kortlepel	V-11	(8.)	05.58
	4./JG 3	Oblt. Karl Faust	V-11	(14.)	06.01
	6./JG 3	Uffz. Horst Beyer	I-16	(8.)	10.08
	6./JG 3	Gefr. Otto Wirth	I-16	(1.)	10.34
	4./JG 3	Obfw. Heinrich Brenner	V-11	(1.)	13.48
	4./JG 3	Obfw. Erwin Kortlepel	V-11	(9.)	16.10
	4./JG 3	Obfhr. Kohl	V-11	(2.)	16.12
	4./JG 3	Obfw. Erwin Kortlepel	V-11	(10.)	16.13
12.07.41	4./JG 3	Lt. Karl-Heinz Ponec	DB-3	(2.)	17.45
	5./JG 3	Fw. Walter Ohlrogge	DB-3	(11.)	17.45
	5./JG 3	Fw. Walter Ohlrogge	DB-3	(12.)	17.45
	4./JG 3	Lt. Hans Fuß	DB-3	(10.)	17.50
13.07.41	Stab II./JG 3	Hptm. Gordon Gollob	I-153	(14.)	06.30
15.07.41	5./JG 3	Obfw. Josef Heinzeller	1	(25.)	19.05
16.07.41	Stab II./JG 3	Hptm. Gordon Gollob	DB-3	(15.)	11.42
	Stab II./JG 3	Oblt. Heinz Schönefeldt	SB-2	(4.)	11.43

	Stab II./JG 3	Hptm. Gordon Gollob	SB-2	(16.)	11.44
	Stab II./JG 3	Oblt. Walther Dahl	I-16	(2.)	15.45
	5./JG 3	Oblt. Herbert Kijewski	Il-2	(14.)	16.25
	5./JG 3	Fw. Walter Ohlrogge	1-mot	(13.)	16.25
	4./JG 3	Oblt. Georg Michalek	RZ	(12.)	18.45
17.07.41	4./JG 3	Obfw. Erwin Kortlepel	DB-3	(11.)	14.40
	4./JG 3	Obfw. Heinrich Brenner	DB-3	(2.)	14.40
18.07.41	4./JG 3	Obfw. Erwin Kortlepel	I-16	(12.)	14.00
	4./JG 3	Uffz. Kuno Bälz	I-16	(3.)	14.01
20.07.41	4./JG 3	Oblt. Georg Michalek	I-153	(13.)	15.40
21.07.41	4./JG 3	Oblt. Georg Michalek	I-153	(14.)	18.45
23.07.41	4./JG 3	Oblt. Georg Michalek	DB-3	(15.)	11.25
	Stab II./JG 3	Hptm. Gordon Gollob	R-5	(17.)	16.35
24.07.41	5./JG 3	Fw. Hermann Freitag	SB-3	(3.)	18.55
25.07.41	Stab II./JG 3	Hptm. Gordon Gollob	DB-3	(18.)	
	6./JG 3	Lt. Gustav Frielinghaus	DB-3	(2.)	14.25
	6./JG 3	Lt. Gustav Frielinghaus	DB-3	(3.)	14.42
	6./JG 3	Oblt. Heinrich Sannemann	DB-3	(12.)	16.43
	5./JG 3	Fw. Walter Ohlrogge	R-5	(14.)	17.45
	5./JG 3	Fw. Hermann Freitag	R-5	(4.)	17.45
26.07.41	4./JG 3	Lt. Karl-Heinz Ponec	I-153	(3.)	06.34
	4./JG 3	Oblt. Georg Michalek	I-153	(16.)	06.35
	4./JG 3	Uffz. Werner Lucas	I-153	(5.)	06.39
	4./JG 3	Uffz. Werner Lucas	V-11	(6.)	10.59
	4./JG 3	Uffz. Kuno Bälz	V-11	(4.)	11.02
	4./JG 3	Oblt. Georg Michalek	V-11	(17.)	11.15
	5./JG 3	Fw. Alfred Heckmann	SB-3	(16.)	17.23
	5./JG 3	Uffz. Ernst Pöske	SB-3	(5.)	17.25
	5./JG 3	Fw. Alfred Heckmann	SB-3	(17.)	17.28
	5./JG 3	Fw. Hermann Freitag	SB-3	(5.)	17.30
30.07.41	5./JG 3	Oblt. Harald Moldenhauer	1	(2.)	17.25
31.07.41	4./JG 3	Oblt. Georg Michalek	I-16	(18.)	12.15
01.08.41	Stab II./JG 3	Oblt. Walther Dahl	I-16	(3.)	13.00
03.08.41	4./JG 3	Oblt. Georg Michalek	I-153	(19.)	13.15
05.08.41	6./JG 3	Oblt. Heinrich Sannemann	R-10	(13.)	15.08
	Stab II./JG 3	Hptm. Gordon Gollob	I-153	(19.)	17.46
	Stab II./JG 3	Hptm. Gordon Gollob	I-17	(20.)	18.22
08.08.41	4./JG 3	Uffz. Leopold Münster	Il-2	(4.)	06.35
	4./JG 3	Lt. Karl-Heinz Ponec	DB-3	(4.)	11.00
	4./JG 3	Uffz. Leo Suschko	I-153	(1.)	11.10
	4./JG 3	Uffz. Leo Suschko	DB-3	(2.)	11.25
	Stab II./JG 3	Hptm. Gordon Gollob	DB-3	(21.)	13.17
	Stab II./JG 3	Oblt. Heinz Schönefeldt	DB-3	(5.)	13.20
	Stab II./JG 3	Oblt. Walther Dahl	DB-3	(4.)	13.30
	Stab II./JG 3	Hptm. Gordon Gollob	DB-3	(22.)	13.32
	4./JG 3	Uffz. Werner Lucas	DB-3	(7.)	13.40
	4./JG 3	Obfw. Heinrich Brenner	DB-3	(3.)	13.42
	4./JG 3	Oblt. Georg Michalek	DB-3	(20.)	14.40
09.08.41	4./JG 3	Uffz. Werner Lucas	DB-3	(8.)	04.50
	4./JG 3	Oblt. Georg Michalek	DB-3	(21.)	09.50
	4./JG 3	Uffz. Leo Suschko	DB-3	(3.)	09.51
	4./JG 3	Oblt. Georg Michalek	DB-3	(22.)	09.53
	4./JG 3	Obfhr. Kohl	DB-3	(3.)	09.54
	Stab II./JG 3	Hptm. Gordon Gollob	DB-3	(23.)	10.55
	6./JG 3	Lt. Ernst-Heinz Löhr	DB-3	(2.)	18.10
11.08.41	4./JG 3	Oblt. Georg Michalek	Pe-2	(23.)	16.18
	4./JG 3	Oblt. Georg Michalek	Pe-2	(24.)	16.20
	4./JG 3	Obfhr. Kohl	Pe-2	(4.)	16.23
	5./JG 3	Oblt. Harald Moldenhauer	I-16	(3.)	17.10
	Stab II./JG 3	Hptm. Gordon Gollob	Bomber	(24.)	18.45
12.08.41	Stab II./JG 3	Hptm. Gordon Gollob	I-17	(25.)	07.20
	Stab II./JG 3	Hptm. Gordon Gollob	SB-3	(26.)	07.25
	4./JG 3	Obfw. Erwin Kortlepel	SB-2	(13.)	07.40
	4./JG 3	Uffz. Werner Lucas	DB-3	(9.)	07.45
	6./JG 3	Lt. Ernst-Heinz Löhr	SB-2	(3.)	07.50
	4./JG 3	Obfw. Erwin Kortlepel	SB-2	(14.)	07.50
	4./JG 3	Obfhr. Albert Helm	SB-2	(2.)	07.55
	4./JG 3	Oblt. Georg Michalek	I-153	(25.)	18.15
13.08.41	4./JG 3	Obfhr. Kohl	Pe-2	(5.)	
14.08.41	5./JG 3	Gefr. Georg Reichardt	Pe-2	(1.)	08.35

16.08.41	6./JG 3	Uffz. Franz Schwaiger	DB-3	(1.)	06.55
	4./JG 3	Obfhr. Albert Helm	R-2	(3.)	08.40
	6./JG 3	Lt. Ernst-Heinz Löhr	R-5	(4.)	10.35
	6./JG 3	Uffz. Egon Graf	R-5	(1.)	10.55
17.08.41	4./JG 3	Oblt. Georg Michalek	DB-3	(26.)	09.05
	4./JG 3	Uffz. Werner Lucas	DB-3	(10.)	09.07
	4./JG 3	Obfhr. Kohl	DB-3	(6.)	09.07 [1131]
	4./JG 3	Uffz. Werner Lucas	DB-3	(11.)	09.08
	4./JG 3	Uffz. Leo Suschko	DB-3	(4.)	09.10
	4./JG 3	Uffz. Leo Suschko	DB-3	(5.)	09.11
	4./JG 3	Obfhr. Kohl	DB-3	(7.)	09.13
	4./JG 3	Uffz. Werner Lucas	DB-3	(12.)	09.15
	5./JG 3	Fw. Walter Ohlrogge	R-5	(15.)	13.25
	4./JG 3	Uffz. Leo Suschko	SB-3	(6.)	17.43
	4./JG 3	Obfw. Heinrich Brenner	SB-3	(4.)	17.45
	4./JG 3	Obfw. Heinrich Brenner	SB-3	(5.)	17.46
	4./JG 3	Obfw. Erwin Kortlepel	SB-3	(15.)	17.46
	4./JG 3	Uffz. Leo Suschko	SB-3	(7.)	17.47
	4./JG 3	Obfw. Erwin Kortlepel	SB-3	(16.)	17.50
	4./JG 3	Uffz. Werner Lucas	SB-3	(13.)	17.50
	4./JG 3	Obfw. Heinrich Brenner	SB-3	(6.)	17.53
	4./JG 3	Uffz. Werner Lucas	SB-3	(14.)	17.55
	4./JG 3	Staffelabschuss	SB-3	(-)	~ 18.00
	5./JG 3	Oblt. Harald Moldenhauer	R-5	(4.)	18.30
	5./JG 3	Fw. Walter Ohlrogge	R-5	(16.)	18.30
	5./JG 3	Gefr. Georg Reichardt	R-5	(2.)	18.32
	5./JG 3	Fw. Walter Ohlrogge	R-5	(17.)	18.33
	5./JG 3	Oblt. Harald Moldenhauer	R-5	(5.)	18.35
	5./JG 3	Fw. Walter Ohlrogge	R-5	(18.)	18.38
	5./JG 3	Fw. Walter Ohlrogge	I-16	(19.)	18.45
18.08.41	5./JG 3	Uffz. Ernst Pöske	R-5	(6.)	17.05
	5./JG 3	Uffz. Ernst Pöske	R-5	(7.)	17.15
19.08.41	6./JG 3	Uffz. Franz Schwaiger	I-153	(2.)	13.55
	4./JG 3	Lt. Kohl	SB-2	(8.)	16.20
20.08.41	5./JG 3	Fw. Walter Ohlrogge	I-16	(20.)	12.38
	6./JG 3	Lt. Ernst-Heinz Löhr	DB-3	(5.)	15.55
	Stab II./JG 3	Hptm. Gordon Gollob	I-16	(27.)	17.45
	Stab II./JG 3	Hptm. Gordon Gollob	DB-3	(28.)	17.47
21.08.41	6./JG 3	Uffz. Franz Schwaiger	DB-3	(3.)	07.55
	6./JG 3	Uffz. Franz Schwaiger	DB-3	(4.)	07.58
	6./JG 3	Oblt. Heinrich Sannemann	DB-3	(14.)	08.00
	5./JG 3	Oblt. Harald Moldenhauer	P-100	(6.)	08.50
	Stab II./JG 3	Hptm. Gordon Gollob	I-26	(29.)	09.10
	Stab II./JG 3	Hptm. Gordon Gollob	R-5	(30.)	11.06
	Stab II./JG 3	Lt. Karl-Heinz Ponec	R-5	(5.)	11.09
	Stab II./JG 3	Hptm. Gordon Gollob	R-5	(31.)	11.09
	Stab II./JG 3	Hptm. Gordon Gollob	DB-3	(32.)	12.00
	5./JG 3	Fw. Walter Ohlrogge	Convoy	(21.)	15.30
	5./JG 3	Fw. Walter Ohlrogge	Convoy	(22.)	15.35
	4./JG 3	Uffz. Werner Lucas	DB-3	(15.)	16.35
	4./JG 3	Obfw. Heinrich Brenner	DB-3	(7.)	16.38
	4./JG 3	Obfw. Heinrich Brenner	DB-3	(8.)	16.40
	4./JG 3	Uffz. Werner Lucas	DB-3	(16.)	16.43
	Stab II./JG 3	Hptm. Gordon Gollob	I-26	(33.)	17.05
	4./JG 3	Oblt. Georg Michalek	DB-3	(27.)	17.50
22.08.41	Stab II./JG 3	Hptm. Gordon Gollob	I-17	(34.)	06.10
	4./JG 3	Oblt. Georg Michalek	R-5	(28.)	09.51
	4./JG 3	Oblt. Georg Michalek	R-5	(29.)	09.52
	4./JG 3	Uffz. Leo Suschko	R-5	(8.)	09.54
	4./JG 3	Oblt. Georg Michalek	RZ	(30.)	09.55
	4./JG 3	Obfhr. Albert Helm	R-5	(6.)	09.58
24.08.41	5./JG 3	Fw. Walter Ohlrogge	V-11	(23.)	06.25
	Stab II./JG 3	Oblt. Walther Dahl	I-180	(5.)	08.55
	Stab II./JG 3	Hptm. Gordon Gollob	I-180	(35.)	09.00
	Stab II./JG 3	Oblt. Walther Dahl	I-16	(6.)	15.55
	5./JG 3	Fw. Walter Ohlrogge	V-11	(24.)	17.55
	5./JG 3	Gefr. Georg Reichardt	V-11	(3.)	18.05
	5./JG 3	Fw. Walter Ohlrogge	R-5	(25.)	18.10
	5./JG 3	Uffz. Ernst Pöske	R-5	(8.)	18.12
	5./JG 3	Oblt. Harald Moldenhauer	R-5	(7.)	
25.08.41	4./JG 3	Uffz. Werner Lucas	Pe-2	(17.)	05.45
	5./JG 3	Uffz. Ernst Pöske	DB-3	(9.)	06.45
	5./JG 3	Fw. Hermann Freitag	DB-3	(6.)	06.47
	4./JG 3	Oblt. Georg Michalek	SB-3	(31.)	11.10

[1131] Auf einer Abschusstafel der 4./JG 3 anstelle Obfhr. Kohl aufgeführt:

4./JG 3	Obfhr. Albert Helm	DB-3	(4.)	
4./JG 3	Obfhr. Albert Helm	DB-3	(5.)	

	4./JG 3	Obfhr. Albert Helm	SB-3	(7.)	11.12
26.08.41	4./JG 3	Obfw. Heinrich Brenner	I-153	(9.)	12.35
	4./JG 3	Uffz. Leopold Münster	I-153	(5.)	12.40
	6./JG 3	Fw. August Dilling	1	(13.)	16.15
	6./JG 3	Lt. Gustav Frielinghaus	I-16	(4.)	16.25
	5./JG 3	Fw. Walter Ohlrogge	R-5	(26.)	17.20
	5./JG 3	Fw. Walter Ohlrogge	R-5	(27.)	17.20
	5./JG 3	Fw. Walter Ohlrogge	R-5	(28.)	17.20
27.08.41	5./JG 3	Uffz. Ernst Pöske	I-16	(10.)	08.45
30.08.41	4./JG 3	Uffz. Werner Lucas	DB-3	(18.)	12.19
	4./JG 3	Obfw. Heinrich Brenner	DB-3	(10.)	12.22
	4./JG 3	Uffz. Werner Lucas	DB-3	(19.)	12.25
	4./JG 3	Lt. Hans Fuß	V-11	(11.)	14.25
31.08.41	Stab II./JG 3	Lt. Karl-Heinz Ponec	R-5	(6.)	09.03
	Stab II./JG 3	Hptm. Gordon Gollob	TB-3	(36.)	09.08
	Stab II./JG 3	Lt. Karl-Heinz Ponec	R-5	(7.)	12.05
	4./JG 3	Obfw. Heinrich Brenner	V-11	(11.)	13.00
	4./JG 3	Oblt. Georg Michalek	V-11	(32.)	13.02
	4./JG 3	Uffz. Leopold Münster	V-11	(6.)	13.03
01.09.41	6./JG 3	Oblt. Heinrich Sannemann	I-16	(15.)	06.03
	4./JG 3	Obfw. Heinrich Brenner	SB-3	(12.)	16.39
	4./JG 3	Oblt. Georg Michalek	SB-3	(33.)	16.40
	4./JG 3	Uffz. Leopold Münster	I-153	(7.)	17.02
02.09.41	4./JG 3	Uffz. Werner Lucas	DB-3	(20.)	06.45
03.09.41	5./JG 3	Obfw. Alfred Heckmann	I-26	(18.)	07.00
	6./JG 3	Uffz. Franz Schwaiger	Pe-2	(5.)	07.55
	4./JG 3	Fw. Werner Lucas	V-11	(21.)	13.38
06.09.41	4./JG 3	Oblt. Georg Michalek	SB-3	(34.)	16.48
	4./JG 3	Uffz. Leopold Münster	SB-3	(8.)	16.55
	4./JG 3	Lt. Kohl	SB-3	(9.)	16.56
	4./JG 3	Fw. Werner Lucas	SB-3	(22.)	18.25
07.09.41	4./JG 3	Fw. Werner Lucas	I-180	(23.)	05.30
	4./JG 3	Lt. Hans Fuß	V-11	(12.)	13.20
	4./JG 3	Obfw. Erwin Kortlepel	I-153	(17.)	15.13
08.09.41	6./JG 3	Uffz. Franz Schwaiger	SB-2	(6.)	13.47
	Stab II./JG 3	Hptm. Gordon Gollob	I-26	(37.)	15.43
09.09.41	Stab II./JG 3	Hptm. Gordon Gollob	Il-2	(38.)	16.50
12.09.41	5./JG 3	Obfw. Alfred Heckmann	I-26	(19.)	10.00
	5./JG 3	Fw. Walter Ohlrogge	I-26	(29.)	10.00
	5./JG 3	Fw. Walter Ohlrogge	I-26	(30.)	10.10
	5./JG 3	Fw. Walter Ohlrogge	I-153	(31.)	11.35
	5./JG 3	Obfw. Alfred Heckmann	I-26	(20.)	14.50
	Stab II./JG 3	Hptm. Gordon Gollob	Il-2	(39.)	14.52
	Stab II./JG 3	Hptm. Gordon Gollob	I-26	(40.)	17.15
13.09.41	5./JG 3	Fw. Walter Ohlrogge	V-11	(32.)	06.54
	5./JG 3	Obfw. Alfred Heckmann	V-11	(21.)	06.55
	5./JG 3	Fw. Walter Ohlrogge	V-11	(33.)	06.55
	5./JG 3	Gefr. Hans Pilz	V-11	(1.)	06.56
	5./JG 3	Obfw. Alfred Heckmann	V-11	(22.)	06.57
	5./JG 3	Fw. Walter Ohlrogge	V-11	(34.)	06.58
	5./JG 3	Obfw. Alfred Heckmann	R-5	(23.)	07.03
	6./JG 3	Obfw. Eberhard von Boremski	1	(25.)	07.50
	6./JG 3	Oblt. Heinrich Sannemann	DB-3	(16.)	07.52
	6./JG 3	Oblt. Heinrich Sannemann	DB-3	(17.)	07.53
	6./JG 3	Oblt. Heinrich Sannemann	DB-3	(18.)	07.55
	6./JG 3	Uffz. Michael Beikiefer	DB-3	(1.)	07.55
	Stab II./JG 3	Oblt. Walther Dahl	I-16	(7.)	09.30
	Stab II./JG 3	Hptm. Gordon Gollob	V-11	(41.)	17.19
	Stab II./JG 3	Oblt. Walther Dahl	V-11	(8.)	17.20
	4./JG 3	Lt. Hans Fuß	V-11	(13.)	17.22
	4./JG 3	Uffz. Leopold Münster	V-11	(9.)	17.24
	4./JG 3	Fw. Werner Lucas	V-11	(24.)	17.25
	Stab II./JG 3	Oblt. Walther Dahl	V-11	(9.)	17.27
	4./JG 3	Lt. Hans Fuß	V-11	(14.)	17.29
14.09.41	Stab II./JG 3	Hptm. Gordon Gollob	I-153	(42.)	05.47
	Stab II./JG 3	Oblt. Walther Dahl	I-153	(10.)	06.05
17.09.41	4./JG 3	Lt. Hans Fuß	I-17	(15.)	15.40
18.09.41	6./JG 3	Obfw. Eberhard von Boremski	R-5	(26.)	14.40
	6./JG 3	Uffz. Franz Schwaiger	Pe-2	(7.)	
19.09.41	Stab II./JG 3	Hptm. Gordon Gollob	R-5	(43.)	13.55
	Stab II./JG 3	Oblt. Walther Dahl	SB-3	(11.)	13.57
	4./JG 3	Lt. Hans Fuß	I-16	(16.)	14.05
	4./JG 3	Lt. Hans Fuß	V-11	(17.)	17.30

20.09.41	5./JG 3	Fw. Walter Ohlrogge	I-26	(35.)	10.52	
	5./JG 3	Fw. Walter Ohlrogge	DB-3	(36.)	10.55	
	5./JG 3	Lt. Max Buchholz	DB-3	(1.)	11.15	
22.09.41	4./JG 3	Obfw. Erwin Kortlepel	DB-3	(18.)	11.40	
23.09.41	5./JG 3	Fw. Walter Ohlrogge	1	(37.)	11.30	
	Stab II./JG 3	Fw. Hermann Freitag	Il-2	(7.)	11.55	
	4./JG 3	Fw. Werner Lucas	I-153	(25.)	16.35	
24.09.41	5./JG 3	Obfw. Alfred Heckmann	I-153	(24.)	08.30	
	4./JG 3	Lt. Hans Fuß	I-17	(18.)	13.37	
25.09.41	4./JG 3	Fw. Werner Lucas	I-26	(26.)	07.23	zusammen mit Fw. Ohlrogge
	4./JG 3	Obfw. Erwin Kortlepel	DB-3	(19.)	07.23	
	4./JG 3	Fw. Werner Lucas	DB-3	(27.)	14.45	
	4./JG 3	Obfw. Erwin Kortlepel	DB-3	(20.)	14.48	
26.09.41	4./JG 3	Obfw. Erwin Kortlepel	R-10	(21.)	07.55	
	5./JG 3	Fw. Walter Ohlrogge	1	(38.)	13.21	
	4./JG 3	Obfw. Erwin Kortlepel	DB-3	(22.)	15.53	
28.09.41	Stab II./JG 3	Hptm. Gordon Gollob	Pe-2	(44.)	12.20	
	Stab II./JG 3	Hptm. Gordon Gollob	Pe-2	(45.)	12.21	
	Stab II./JG 3	Hptm. Gordon Gollob	Pe-2	(46.)	14.46	
	4./JG 3	Fw. Werner Lucas	Pe-2	(28.)	14.47	
	Stab II./JG 3	Fw. Hermann Freitag	Pe-2	(8.)	14.48	
	4./JG 3	Uffz. Josef Schütte	I-61	(1.)	14.48	
	Stab II./JG 3	Hptm. Gordon Gollob	I-61	(47.)		
	Stab II./JG 3	Hptm. Gordon Gollob	I-61	(48.)		
29.09.41	4./JG 3	Obfw. Erwin Kortlepel	I-26	(23.)	06.00	
	4./JG 3	Fw. Werner Lucas	I-180	(29.)	10.25	
04.10.41	Stab II./JG 3	Hptm. Gordon Gollob	russ. Zerst.	(49.)	10.20	
05.10.41	5./JG 3	Obfw. Alfred Heckmann	Pe-2	(25.)	09.55	
	Stab II./JG 3	Hptm. Gordon Gollob	I-61	(50.)	12.25	
	Stab II./JG 3	Hptm. Gordon Gollob	I-61	(51.)	12.26	
	4./JG 3	Fhr. Eckart König	V-11	(3.)		
06.10.41	6./JG 3	Uffz. Franz Schwaiger	Pe-2	(8.)	09.20	
	Stab II./JG 3	Hptm. Gordon Gollob	Pe-2	(52.)	10.15	
	6./JG 3	Lt. Gustav Frielinghaus	Pe-2	(5.)	10.19	
	Stab II./JG 3	Hptm. Gordon Gollob	Pe-2	(53.)	12.15	
07.10.41	Stab II./JG 3	Hptm. Gordon Gollob	Pe-2	(54.)	09.40	
	Stab II./JG 3	Hptm. Gordon Gollob	Pe-2	(55.)	12.40	
	Stab II./JG 3	Hptm. Gordon Gollob	Il-2	(56.)		
08.10.41	4./JG 3	Fw. Werner Lucas	Pe-2	(30.)	13.15	
10.10.41	Stab II./JG 3	Hptm. Gordon Gollob	I-61	(57.)	12.40	
	Stab II./JG 3	Hptm. Gordon Gollob	I-61	(58.)	12.43	
11.10.41	Stab II./JG 3	Oblt. Walther Dahl	SB-3	(12.)	11.55	
	6./JG 3	Lt. Gustav Frielinghaus	SB-3	(6.)	11.57	
17.10.41	Stab II./JG 3	Hptm. Gordon Gollob	I-61	(59.)	09.04	
	4./JG 3	Obfw. Erwin Kortlepel	I-61	(24.)	09.05	
	5./JG 3	Obfw. Alfred Heckmann	I-17	(26.)	09.12	
	Stab II./JG 3	Hptm. Gordon Gollob	I-16	(60.)	09.15	
	4./JG 3	Fw. Werner Lucas	I-26	(31.)	09.15	
	4./JG 3	Lt. Hans Fuß	I-16	(19.)	09.15	
	4./JG 3	Lt. Hans Fuß	I-16	(20.)	09.15	
	Stab II./JG 3	Uffz. Leopold Münster	I-16	(10.)		
	4./JG 3	Lt. Hans Fuß	I-153	(21.)	10.10	
	4./JG 3	Lt. Hans Fuß	Il-2	(22.)	10.30	
	Stab II./JG 3	Hptm. Gordon Gollob	I-61	(61.)	16.05	
18.10.41	Stab II./JG 3	Hptm. Gordon Gollob	I-61	(62.)	07.18	
	Stab II./JG 3	Hptm. Gordon Gollob	I-61	(63.)	07.20	
	Stab II./JG 3	Lt. Karl-Heinz Ponec	I-61	(8.)	10.05	
	Stab II./JG 3	Hptm. Gordon Gollob	I-61	(64.)	10.05	
	Stab II./JG 3	Hptm. Gordon Gollob	I-61	(65.)	10.07	
	Stab II./JG 3	Oblt. Walther Dahl	I-16	(13.)	10.10	
	Stab II./JG 3	Hptm. Gordon Gollob	I-61	(66.)	10.19	
	Stab II./JG 3	Hptm. Gordon Gollob	I-61	(67.)	10.20	
	Stab II./JG 3	Hptm. Gordon Gollob	I-61	(68.)	10.29	
	4./JG 3	Fw. Werner Lucas	I-61	(32.)	13.11	
	4./JG 3	Oblt. Georg Michalek	I-61	(35.)	13.12	
	4./JG 3	Obfw. Erwin Kortlepel	I-61	(25.)	13.12	
	Stab II./JG 3	Hptm. Gordon Gollob	I-61	(69.)	14.46	
	Stab II./JG 3	Hptm. Gordon Gollob	I-61	(70.)	14.48	
	5./JG 3	Obfw. Alfred Heckmann	I-61	(27.)	14.50	
	4./JG 3	Obfw. Erwin Kortlepel	Il-2	(26.)	16.35	
19.10.41	Stab II./JG 3	Hptm. Gordon Gollob	I-61	(71.)	08.55	
	6./JG 3	Oblt. Heinrich Sannemann	I-16	(19.)	09.10	

	Stab II./JG 3	Hptm. Gordon Gollob	Pe-2	(72.)		12.36
	Stab II./JG 3	Lt. Karl-Heinz Ponec	Pe-2	(9.)		12.36
	Stab II./JG 3	Hptm. Gordon Gollob	Pe-2	(73.)		12.37
	4./JG 3	Oblt. Georg Michalek	Pe-2	(36.)		12.38
	4./JG 3	Lt. Hans Fuß	Pe-2	(23.)		12.40
	Stab II./JG 3	Hptm. Gordon Gollob	Pe-2	(74.)		12.42
	Stab II./JG 3	Oblt. Walther Dahl	I-16	(14.)		15.25
	Stab II./JG 3	Hptm. Gordon Gollob	I-61	(75.)		15.35
20.10.41	Stab II./JG 3	Hptm. Gordon Gollob	I-61	(76.)		11.07
22.10.41	Stab II./JG 3	Hptm. Gordon Gollob	I-16	(77.)		06.55
	5./JG 3	Fw. Ernst Pöske	Pe-2	(11.)		07.19
	Stab II./JG 3	Hptm. Gordon Gollob	Pe-2	(78.)		07.20
	4./JG 3	Lt. Hans Fuß	Pe-2	(24.)		07.20
	Stab II./JG 3	Hptm. Gordon Gollob	I-16	(79.)		10.21
	Stab II./JG 3	Hptm. Gordon Gollob	I-16	(80.)		10.22
	4./JG 3	Oblt. Georg Michalek	I-16	(37.)		10.22
	Stab II./JG 3	Hptm. Gordon Gollob	I-61	(81.)		
	5./JG 3	Fw. Walter Ohlrogge	I-61	(39.)		16.22
	5./JG 3	Fw. Walter Ohlrogge	I-61	(40.)		16.35
23.10.41	Stab II./JG 3	Hptm. Gordon Gollob	I-61	(82.)		10.55
	Stab II./JG 3	Oblt. Walther Dahl	I-61	(15.)		10.56
	Stab II./JG 3	Hptm. Gordon Gollob	I-61	(83.)		10.58
	Stab II./JG 3	Oblt. Walther Dahl	I-61	(16.)		11.00
	Stab II./JG 3	Oblt. Walther Dahl	I-16	(17.)		11.20
	Stab II./JG 3	Hptm. Gordon Gollob	I-61	(84.)		11.40
	Stab II./JG 3	Uffz. Leopold Münster	I-16	(11.)		14.55
	Stab II./JG 3	Uffz. Leopold Münster	I-16	(12.)		
	5./JG 3	Fw. Walter Ohlrogge	I-61	(41.)		16.15
	5./JG 3	Fw. Fritz Mias	I-61	(4.)		16.15
	4./JG 3	Lt. Hans Fuß	I-61	(25.)		16.25
	4./JG 3	Obfw. Erwin Kortlepel	I-16	(27.)		16.26
	5./JG 3	Fw. Ernst Pöske	I-15	(12.)		16.28
	5./JG 3	Fw. Walter Ohlrogge	I-15	(42.)		16.32
	5./JG 3	Fw. Ernst Pöske	I-15	(13.)		16.32
24.10.41	6./JG 3	Lt. Gustav Frielinghaus	I-61	(7.)		13.12
	Stab II./JG 3	Hptm. Gordon Gollob	I-153	(85.)		13.50
31.10.41	6./JG 3	Oblt. Heinrich Sannemann	I-61	(20.)		13.33
	5./JG 3	Fw. Ernst Pöske	ARK-3	(14.)		13.35

Victories by II/JG 3 during Operations in the Mediterranean Theater
January to April 1942

15.02.42	6./JG 3	Uffz. Wolfgang Vogel	Beaufighter	(1.)		13.15
22.02.42	4./JG 3	Fw. Leopold Münster	Hurricane	(13.)		
10.03.42	Stab II./JG 3	Hptm. Karl-Heinz Krahl	Spitfire	(19.)		17.10
18.03.42	6./JG 3	Uffz. Michael Beikiefer	Blenheim	(2.)		18.35
26.03.42	5./JG 3	Lt. Joachim Kirschner	Spitfire	(2.)		13.50
	4./JG 3	Lt. Max-Bruno Fischer	Spitfire	(1.)		
01.04.42	4./JG 3	Oblt. Walther Dahl	Spitfire	n.b.		15.30

Victories by II/JG 3 during Operations in the East
May 1942 to July 1943

20.05.42	Stab II./JG 3	Hptm. Kurt Brändle	R-5	(36.)		03.49
	4./JG 3	Fw. Leopold Münster	MiG-1	(14.)		07.57
	4./JG 3	Fw. Leopold Münster	Il-2	(15.)		08.05
	6./JG 3	Lt. Ludwig Häfner	Il-2	(3.)		14.25
	6./JG 3	Uffz. Wolfgang Vogel	Il-2	(2.)		14.25
	6./JG 3	Uffz. Waldemar Eyrich	Il-2	(1.)		14.30
21.05.42	5./JG 3	Lt. Joachim Kirschner	DB-3	(3.)		04.50
	5./JG 3	Uffz. Kurt Opalke	DB-3	(1.)		
22.05.42	6./JG 3	Lt. Gerd Schaedle	I-61	(1.)		14.25
	5./JG 3	Uffz. Horst Opalke	I-61	(2.)		16.07
	5./JG 3	Lt. Joachim Kirschner	MiG-1	(4.)		16.07
23.05.42	Stab II./JG 3	Hptm. Kurt Brändle	I-61	(37.)		07.26
	Stab II./JG 3	Lt. Hans Fuß	I-61	(26.)		07.27
	Stab II./JG 3	Lt. Hans Fuß	I-61	(27.)		07.28
	4./JG 3	Uffz. Kurt Ebener	I-61	(1.)		09.05
	4./JG 3	Gefr. Heinrich May	I-16	(1.)		09.06
	4./JG 3	Gefr. Heinrich May	I-61	(2.)		09.13
	Stab II./JG 3	Hptm. Kurt Brändle	I-61	(38.)		12.17
	4./JG 3	Uffz. Kurt Ebener	I-61	(2.)		14.05

26.05.42	5./JG 3	Uffz. Horst Opalke	MiG-3	(3.)	06.02
	4./JG 3	Fw. Josef Schütte	I-153	(2.)	08.55
	Stab II./JG 3	Hptm. Kurt Brändle	MiG-1	(39.)	08.57
	Stab II./JG 3	Lt. Hans Fuß	1	(28.)	09.35
	4./JG 3	Uffz. Hans Frese	I-61	(1.)	14.40
	4./JG 3	Fw. Josef Schütte	I-61	(3.)	14.50
	Stab II./JG 3	Lt. Hans Fuß	1	(29.)	17.10
	Stab II./JG 3	Hptm. Kurt Brändle	1	(40.)	17.20
27.05.42	6./JG 3	Uffz. Franz Schwaiger	Il-2	(9.)	12.50
	4./JG 3	Uffz. Kurt Ebener	MiG-1	(3.)	15.56
	Stab II./JG 3	Lt. Hans Fuß	MiG-1	(30.)	18.22
29.05.42	5./JG 3	Lt. Joachim Kirschner	MiG-1	(5.)	04.59
	6./JG 3	Lt. Ludwig Häfner	MiG-1	(4.)	06.14
	5./JG 3	Obfw. Maximilian Seidler	R-10	(1.)	10.45
	Stab II./JG 3	Hptm. Kurt Brändle	Pe-2	(41.)	15.49
	Stab II./JG 3	Lt. Hans Fuß	MiG-1	(31.)	15.55
	Stab II./JG 3	Lt. Hans Fuß	MiG-1	(32.)	15.56
	Stab II./JG 3	Lt. Hans Fuß	MiG-1	(33.)	15.58
	Stab II./JG 3	Lt. Hans Fuß	Pe-2	(34.)	16.04
	6./JG 3	Uffz. Franz Schwaiger	V-11	(10.)	18.35
	6./JG 3	Uffz. Wolfgang Vogel	V-11	(3.)	18.36
	6./JG 3	Uffz. Waldemar Eyrich	V-11	(2.)	18.37
	6./JG 3	Uffz. Franz Schwaiger	V-11	(11.)	18.40
31.05.42	5./JG 3	Uffz. Horst Opalke	DB-3	(4.)	09.13
	5./JG 3	Uffz. Horst Opalke	MiG-1	(5.)	19.20
	5./JG 3	Lt. Joachim Kirschner	MiG-1	(6.)	19.22
02.06.42	Stab II./JG 3	Hptm. Kurt Brändle	MiG-1	(42.)	13.14
	Stab II./JG 3	Hptm. Kurt Brändle	MiG-1	(43.)	13.23
	Stab II./JG 3	Lt. Gustav Frielinghaus	1	(8.)	17.49
04.06.42	6./JG 3	Uffz. Wolfgang Vogel	Il-2	(4.)	17.22
	6./JG 3	Uffz. Franz Schwaiger	Il-2	(12.)	17.27
10.06.42	5./JG 3	Obfw. Alfred Heckmann	Il-2	(28.)	13.10
	Stab II./JG 3	Hptm. Kurt Brändle	LaGG-3	(44.)	17.32
11.06.42	6./JG 3	Uffz. Georg Schiller	Il-2	(1.)	03.54
	6./JG 3	Uffz. Wolfgang Vogel	Il-2	(5.)	03.55
	Stab II./JG 3	Hptm. Kurt Brändle	Il-2	(45.)	06.35
	Stab II./JG 3	Hptm. Kurt Brändle	Il-2	(46.)	06.42
	6./JG 3	Fw. Karl-Heinz Steinicke	Il-2	(1.)	12.20
	6./JG 3	Fw. Karl-Heinz Steinicke	Il-2	(2.)	12.23
	6./JG 3	Uffz. Franz Schwaiger	Il-2	(13.)	12.27
12.06.42	Stab II./JG 3	Hptm. Kurt Brändle	Su-2	(47.)	10.54
	Stab II./JG 3	Lt. Hans Fuß	Su-2	(35.)	10.56
13.06.42	6./JG 3	Uffz. Rasso Förg	Il-2	(1.)	10.17
	Stab II./JG 3	Hptm. Kurt Brändle	Il-2	(48.)	10.18
	Stab II./JG 3	Lt. Hans Fuß	Il-2	(36.)	10.19
	6./JG 3	Lt. Ludwig Häfner	Il-2	(5.)	10.23
	Stab II./JG 3	Lt. Hans Fuß	MiG-1	(37.)	10.32
	6./JG 3	Lt. Ludwig Häfner	MiG-1	(6.)	10.43
	5./JG 3	Lt. Joachim Kirschner	MiG-1	(7.)	17.47
	5./JG 3	Fw. Werner Kloß	MiG-1	(1.)	17.55
	5./JG 3	Lt. Joachim Kirschner	Il-2	(8.)	17.58
21.06.42	6./JG 3	Uffz. Wolfgang Vogel	LaGG-3	(6.)	10.55
22.06.42	4./JG 3	Fw. Josef Schütte	MiG-1	(4.)	13.05
	5./JG 3	Lt. Lothar Myrrhe	MiG-1	(1.)	13.20
	4./JG 3	Oblt. Albrecht Walz	R-10	(5.)	17.55
	Stab II./JG 3	Lt. Hans Fuß	1	(38.)	17.55
	6./JG 3	Fw. Karl-Heinz Steinicke	1	(3.)	18.20
23.06.42	6./JG 3	Uffz. Georg Schiller	V-11	(2.)	17.02
	Stab II./JG 3	Lt. Hans Fuß	LaGG-3	(39.)	18.09
	Stab II./JG 3	Lt. Hans Fuß	LaGG-3	(40.)	18.10
	Stab II./JG 3	Lt. Hans Fuß	LaGG-3	(41.)	18.17
	6./JG 3	Uffz. Wolfgang Vogel	Su-2	(7.)	18.48
	6./JG 3	Uffz. Wolfgang Vogel	LaGG-3	(8.)	18.54
24.06.42	4./JG 3	Fw. Josef Schütte	R-5	(5.)	03.10
	4./JG 3	Fw. Josef Schütte	R-10	(6.)	09.53
	Stab II./JG 3	Lt. Hans Fuß	LaGG-3	(42.)	11.27
	Stab II./JG 3	Hptm. Kurt Brändle	LaGG-3	(49.)	11.38
	Stab II./JG 3	Lt. Gustav Frielinghaus	1	(9.)	11.52
	4./JG 3	Lt. Wolf Ettel	Il-2	(1.)	14.13
	4./JG 3	Fw. Leopold Münster	Il-2	(16.)	14.15
	4./JG 3	Lt. Wolf Ettel	Il-2	(2.)	14.17
	4./JG 3	Fw. Leopold Münster	MiG-1	(17.)	18.20
	5./JG 3	Obfw. Walter Ohlrogge	I-16	(43.)	19.50
26.06.42	4./JG 3	Fw. Leopold Münster	MiG-1	(18.)	08.45
	6./JG 3	Uffz. Wolfgang Vogel	P-40	(9.)	09.58
	6./JG 3	Uffz. Georg Schiller	P-40	(3.)	10.00

27.06.42	6./JG 3	Uffz. Wolfgang Vogel	Il-2	(10.)	13.08
28.06.42	4./JG 3	Lt. Wolf Ettel	Il-2	(3.)	16.07
29.06.42	Stab II./JG 3	Hptm. Kurt Brändle	Pe-2	(50.)	18.42
	Stab II./JG 3	Hptm. Kurt Brändle	Pe-2	(51.)	18.44
30.06.42	5./JG 3	Lt. Joachim Kirschner	LaGG-3	(9.)	10.12
	Stab II./JG 3	Lt. Hans Fuß	P-39	(43.)	10.35
	Stab II./JG 3	Lt. Hans Fuß	Boston	(44.)	10.40
	Stab II./JG 3	Lt. Hans Fuß	Boston	(45.)	10.48
	Stab II./JG 3	Hptm. Kurt Brändle	LaGG-3	(52.)	11.38
	4./JG 3	Lt. Wolf Ettel	Jak-1	(4.)	12.45
	4./JG 3	Fw. Leopold Münster	Jak-1	(19.)	12.48
	4./JG 3	Oblt. Albrecht Walz	Jak-1	(6.)	12.51
	4./JG 3	Fw. Leopold Münster	Jak-1	(20.)	12.53
01.07.42	4./JG 3	Uffz. Kurt Ebener	Il-2	(4.)	09.08
	4./JG 3	Uffz. Heinrich May	Il-2	(3.)	09.11
	6./JG 3	Lt. Ludwig Häfner	LaGG-3	(7.)	12.05
	5./JG 3	Obfw. Alfred Heckmann	Il-2	(29.)	13.11
	Stab II./JG 3	Hptm. Kurt Brändle	Il-2	(53.)	16.17
	Stab II./JG 3	Lt. Hans Fuß	Boston	(46.)	16.27
	Stab II./JG 3	Lt. Hans Fuß	Il-2	(47.)	18.52
	Stab II./JG 3	Lt. Gustav Frielinghaus	Il-2	(10.)	18.54
02.07.42	6./JG 3	Lt. Ludwig Häfner	R-5	(8.)	08.04
	4./JG 3	Uffz. Hans Frese	MiG-1	(2.)	10.17
	4./JG 3	Oblt. Albrecht Walz	MiG-1	(7.)	10.22
	5./JG 3	Uffz. Horst Opalke	LaGG-3	(6.)	13.08
	5./JG 3	Fw. Werner Kloß	LaGG-3	(2.)	16.32
	4./JG 3	Uffz. Heinrich May	Il-2	(4.)	16.33
	6./JG 3	Uffz. Georg Schiller	LaGG-3	(4.)	16.37
	6./JG 3	Uffz. Wolfgang Vogel	Il-2	(11.)	16.39
	4./JG 3	Uffz. Heinrich May	U-2	(5.)	16.40
	4./JG 3	Hptm. Gerhard Wendt	MiG-1	(2.)	17.57
03.07.42	Stab II./JG 3	Hptm. Kurt Brändle	Il-2	(54.)	15.10
	4./JG 3	Oblt. Albrecht Walz	Il-2	(8.)	15.50
	4./JG 3	Oblt. Albrecht Walz	Il-2	(9.)	15.55
	4./JG 3	Uffz. Heinrich May	Il-2	(6.)	16.01
04.07.42	5./JG 3	Obfw. Alfred Heckmann	MiG-1	(30.)	03.40
	5./JG 3	Obfw. Alfred Heckmann	MiG-1	(31.)	03.41
	5./JG 3	Uffz. Horst Opalke	MiG-1	(7.)	03.42
	5./JG 3	Obfw. Alfred Heckmann	MiG-1	(32.)	03.43
	Stab II./JG 3	Lt. Hans Fuß	MiG-1	(48.)	10.25
	Stab II./JG 3	Lt. Gustav Frielinghaus	MiG-1	(11.)	10.27
	6./JG 3	Uffz. Rasso Förg	Il-2	(2.)	13.08
	6./JG 3	Lt. Ludwig Häfner	Il-2	(9.)	13.37
	Stab II./JG 3	Hptm. Kurt Brändle	LaGG-3	(55.)	16.58
	6./JG 3	Lt. Gerd Schaedle	SB-2	(2.)	17.05
	6./JG 3	Uffz. Michael Vogel	SB-2	(12.)	17.06
	6./JG 3	Uffz. Michael Vogel	SB-2	(13.)	17.07
	6./JG 3	Lt. Gerd Schaedle	DB-3	(3.)	17.12
	5./JG 3	Lt. Joachim Kirschner	Il-2	(10.)	18.45
	Stab II./JG 3	Lt. Hans Fuß	Pe-2	(49.)	19.21
05.07.42	4./JG 3	Uffz. Heinrich May	Il-2	(7.)	07.45
	4./JG 3	Fw. Leopold Münster	Il-2	(21.)	07.55
	4./JG 3	Fw. Leopold Münster	Il-2	(22.)	07.57
	Stab II./JG 3	Lt. Gustav Frielinghaus	Il-2	(12.)	16.27
06.07.42	Stab II./JG 3	Lt. Gustav Frielinghaus	Il-2	(13.)	11.41
	6./JG 3	Lt. Ludwig Häfner	Jak-1	(10.)	16.52
	Stab II./JG 3	Lt. Hans Fuß	Pe-2	(50.)	18.02
	Stab II./JG 3	Lt. Hans Fuß	Pe-2	(51.)	18.05
	Stab II./JG 3	Lt. Hans Fuß	Hurricane	(52.)	18.25
	6./JG 3	Uffz. Georg Schiller	DB-3	(5.)	18.40
07.07.42	6./JG 3	Uffz. Georg Schiller	Il-2	(6.)	07.25
	Stab II./JG 3	Lt. Hans Fuß	Pe-2	(53.)	17.14
	Stab II./JG 3	Lt. Hans Fuß	Pe-2	(54.)	17.18
08.07.42	6./JG 3	Fw. Karl-Heinz Steinicke	MiG-1	(4.)	12.30
	6./JG 3	Fw. Karl-Heinz Steinicke	MiG-1	(5.)	12.40
	6./JG 3	Uffz. Alfred Fischer	MiG-1	(1.)	
	5./JG 3	Lt. Joachim Kirschner	U-2	(11.)	17.05
	Stab II./JG 3	Lt. Hans Fuß	Pe-2	(55.)	19.22
	Stab II./JG 3	Hptm. Kurt Brändle	Pe-2	(56.)	19.24
	Stab II./JG 3	Lt. Hans Fuß	Pe-2	(56.)	19.26
	Stab II./JG 3	Hptm. Kurt Brändle	Pe-2	(57.)	19.27
	Stab II./JG 3	Lt. Hans Fuß	Pe-2	(57.)	19.30
	Stab II./JG 3	Hptm. Kurt Brändle	Pe-2	(58.)	19.32
09.07.42	5./JG 3	Obfw. Alfred Heckmann	Jak-1	(33.)	13.15
	5./JG 3	Obfw. Alfred Heckmann	Jak-1	(34.)	13.16
	4./JG 3	Lt. Wolf Ettel	Jak-1	(5.)	13.18
	4./JG 3	Lt. Wolf Ettel	Il-2	(6.)	13.30

	6./JG 3	Lt. Ludwig Häfner	LaGG-3	(11.)	17.55
	6./JG 3	Lt. Ludwig Häfner	LaGG-3	(12.)	18.10
	6./JG 3	Lt. Ludwig Häfner	LaGG-3	(13.)	18.13
	5./JG 3	Lt. Joachim Kirschner	LaGG-3	(12.)	18.20
	6./JG 3	Lt. Ludwig Häfner	LaGG-3	(14.)	18.33
10.07.42	6./JG 3	Uffz. Michael Vogel	MiG-1	(14.)	04.05
	6./JG 3	Uffz. Michael Vogel	P-39	(15.)	04.10
	4./JG 3	Lt. Wolf Ettel	Boston	(7.)	04.30
	5./JG 3	Obfw. Alfred Heckmann	Boston	(35.)	04.30
	5./JG 3	Obfw. Alfred Heckmann	Boston	(36.)	04.31
	5./JG 3	Obfw. Alfred Heckmann	Boston	(37.)	04.33
	5./JG 3	Obfw. Alfred Heckmann	Boston	(38.)	04.34
	4./JG 3	Hptm. Gerhard Wendt	Boston	(3.)	04.36
	6./JG 3	Lt. Ludwig Häfner	P-39	(15.)	04.37
	6./JG 3	Lt. Ludwig Häfner	MiG-1	(16.)	09.17
	6./JG 3	Uffz. Michael Vogel	MiG-1	(16.)	09.20
	4./JG 3	Uffz. Hans Frese	Pe-2	(3.)	09.25
	6./JG 3	Oblt. Hans-Jürgen Waldhelm	MiG-1	(1.)	09.27
	Stab II./JG 3	Hptm. Kurt Brändle	Pe-2	(59.)	09.30
	Stab II./JG 3	Hptm. Kurt Brändle	MiG-1	(60.)	09.50
	Stab II./JG 3	Hptm. Kurt Brändle	MiG-1	(61.)	09.52
	Stab II./JG 3	Lt. Hans Fuß	Hurricane	(58.)	09.53
11.07.42	Stab II./JG 3	Hptm. Kurt Brändle	R-5	(62.)	08.55
13.07.42	6./JG 3	Lt. Ludwig Häfner	Pe-2	(17.)	04.55
	5./JG 3	Obfw. Alfred Heckmann	Jak-1	(39.)	08.25
	5./JG 3	Obfw. Alfred Heckmann	Jak-1	(40.)	08.28
	5./JG 3	Lt. Joachim Kirschner	Jak-1	(13.)	08.30
	5./JG 3	Lt. Joachim Kirschner	DB-3	(14.)	08.32
	Stab II./JG 3	Hptm. Kurt Brändle	MiG-3	(63.)	09.07
	4./JG 3	Fw. Josef Schütte	Il-2	(7.)	11.46
	6./JG 3	Lt. Ludwig Häfner	R-5	(18.)	11.55
	6./JG 3	Uffz. Michael Vogel	Il-2	(17.)	12.37
	6./JG 3	Uffz. Michael Vogel	DB-3	(18.)	16.16
14.07.42	6./JG 3	Lt. Ludwig Häfner	Il-2	(19.)	11.22
15.07.42	4./JG 3	Fw. Werner Lucas	DB-3	(33.)	15.15
	4./JG 3	Fw. Werner Lucas	Pe-2	(34.)	16.50
16.07.42	Stab II./JG 3	Hptm. Kurt Brändle	LaGG-3	(64.)	11.45
	4./JG 3	Uffz. Heinrich May	LaGG-3	(8.)	11.45
	Stab II./JG 3	Hptm. Kurt Brändle	Pe-2	(65.)	17.17
	Stab II./JG 3	Hptm. Kurt Brändle	Pe-2	(66.)	17.20
	Stab II./JG 3	Hptm. Kurt Brändle	Pe-2	(67.)	17.23
17.07.42	Stab II./JG 3	Lt. Hans Fuß	Il-2	(59.)	10.11
	Stab II./JG 3	Lt. Hans Fuß	Il-2	(60.)	17.51
19.07.42	6./JG 3	Uffz. Michael Vogel	Il-2	(19.)	19.02
20.07.42	4./JG 3	Oblt. Albrecht Walz	Il-2	(10.)	11.48
	5./JG 3	Obfw. Alfred Heckmann	MiG-1	(41.)	11.58
	4./JG 3	Fw. Werner Lucas	Il-2	(35.)	11.59
	Stab II./JG 3	Hptm. Kurt Brändle	Il-2	(68.)	15.44
	Stab II./JG 3	Lt. Hans Fuß	Il-2	(61.)	15.50
21.07.42	6./JG 3	Fw. Karl-Heinz Steinicke	Il-2	(6.)	05.35
	Stab II./JG 3	Hptm. Kurt Brändle	Il-2	(69.)	09.05
	4./JG 3	Fw. Werner Lucas	Il-2	(36.)	09.07
	Stab II./JG 3	Lt. Gustav Frielinghaus	V-11	(14.)	10.14
22.07.42	6./JG 3	Uffz. Franz Schwaiger	I-16	(14.)	05.00
	5./JG 3	Obfw. Alfred Heckmann	LaGG-3	(42.)	16.15
	5./JG 3	Lt. Joachim Kirschner	Jak-1	(15.)	18.07
	5./JG 3	Lt. Joachim Kirschner	Il-2	(16.)	18.22
	5./JG 3	Lt. Joachim Kirschner	LaGG-3	(17.)	18.28
	5./JG 3	Lt. Joachim Kirschner	LaGG-3	(18.)	18.28
	6./JG 3	Uffz. Michael Vogel	Il-2	(20.)	18.58
23.07.42	6./JG 3	Lt. Ludwig Häfner	Jak-1	(20.)	09.30
	4./JG 3	Uffz. Hans Frese	LaGG-3	(4.)	09.42
	6./JG 3	Uffz. Michael Vogel	LaGG-3	(21.)	09.43
	4./JG 3	Fw. Leopold Münster	LaGG-3	(23.)	09.45
	Stab II./JG 3	Hptm. Kurt Brändle	Il-2	(70.)	13.01
	Stab II./JG 3	Hptm. Kurt Brändle	Il-2	(71.)	13.03
	Stab II./JG 3	Lt. Hans Fuß	Jak-1	(62.)	13.05
	4./JG 3	Fw. Leopold Münster	LaGG-3	(24.)	15.05
	4./JG 3	Uffz. Hans Frese	LaGG-3	(5.)	15.07
	4./JG 3	Uffz. Heinrich May	LaGG-3	(9.)	
	4./JG 3	Fw. Werner Lucas	Il-2	(37.)	17.30
24.07.42	4./JG 3	Fw. Leopold Münster	Il-2	(25.)	06.15
	4./JG 3	Lt. Wolf Ettel	Hurricane	(8.)	06.16
	4./JG 3	Fw. Leopold Münster	Hurricane	(26.)	06.17
	Stab II./JG 3	Hptm. Kurt Brändle	Jak-1	(72.)	11.41
	6./JG 3	Uffz. Franz Schwaiger	Jak-1	(15.)	13.20
	4./JG 3	Fw. Leopold Münster	Il-2	(27.)	13.22

	4./JG 3	Fw. Leopold Münster	Il-2	(28.)	13.24
	4./JG 3	Lt. Wolf Ettel	Il-2	(9.)	13.25
	4./JG 3	Lt. Wolf Ettel	Il-2	(10.)	13.31
	4./JG 3	Fw. Leopold Münster	Il-2	(29.)	13.34
	4./JG 3	Oblt. Albrecht Walz	Il-2	(11.)	18.10
	4./JG 3	Uffz. Kurt Ebener	Il-2	(5.)	18.12
	4./JG 3	Fw. Leopold Münster	Il-2	(30.)	18.15
25.07.42	6./JG 3	Lt. Ludwig Häfner	Jak-1	(21.)	09.55
	6./JG 3	Lt. Ludwig Häfner	MiG-1	(22.)	10.12
	4./JG 3	Uffz. Kurt Ebener	R-5	(6.)	12.32
26.07.42	4./JG 3	Lt. Wolf Ettel	LaGG-3	(11.)	03.55
	4./JG 3	Uffz. Kurt Ebener	LaGG-3	(7.)	03.56
	4./JG 3	Lt. Wolf Ettel	Il-2	(12.)	08.15
	6./JG 3	Uffz. Franz Schwaiger	Il-2	(16.)	08.15
	4./JG 3	Lt. Wolf Ettel	Il-2	(13.)	08.17
	6./JG 3	Uffz. Franz Schwaiger	Il-2	(17.)	08.20
	5./JG 3	Lt. Joachim Kirschner	Jak-1	(19.)	11.25
	5./JG 3	Obfw. Alfred Heckmann	Jak-1	(43.)	11.25
	5./JG 3	Obfw. Alfred Heckmann	Jak-1	(44.)	11.26
	5./JG 3	Lt. Joachim Kirschner	Jak-1	(20.)	11.27
	5./JG 3	Lt. Joachim Kirschner	Jak-1	(21.)	11.28
	5./JG 3	Obfw. Alfred Heckmann	Jak-1	(45.)	11.29
	Stab II./JG 3	Hptm. Kurt Brändle	Il-2	(73.)	12.04
	Stab II./JG 3	Hptm. Kurt Brändle	MiG-1	(74.)	12.09
	4./JG 3	Oblt. Albrecht Walz	Pe-2	(12.)	14.50
	4./JG 3	Fw. Werner Lucas	Pe-2	(38.)	15.14
	Stab II./JG 3	Hptm. Kurt Brändle	Pe-2	(75.)	16.05
	Stab II./JG 3	Hptm. Kurt Brändle	Pe-2	(76.)	16.07
	Stab II./JG 3	Hptm. Kurt Brändle	Jak-1	(77.)	16.11
	6./JG 3	Uffz. Waldemar Eyrich	LaGG-3	(3.)	16.35
27.07.42	4./JG 3	Fw. Leopold Münster	Il-2	(31.)	07.10
	4./JG 3	Uffz. Kurt Ebener	LaGG-3	(8.)	07.15
	Stab II./JG 3	Hptm. Kurt Brändle	LaGG-3	(78.)	09.11
	Stab II./JG 3	Hptm. Kurt Brändle	LaGG-3	(79.)	09.12
	6./JG 3	Uffz. Franz Schwaiger	Jak-1	(18.)	11.40
	4./JG 3	Fw. Werner Lucas	Jak-1	(39.)	16.02
	4./JG 3	Fw. Werner Lucas	Jak-1	(40.)	16.05
	6./JG 3	Fw. Rasso Förg	LaGG-3	(3.)	16.31
	5./JG 3	Lt. Joachim Kirschner	LaGG-3	(22.)	17.42
28.07.42	4./JG 3	Oblt. Albrecht Walz	MiG-1	(13.)	07.35
	4./JG 3	Lt. Wolf Ettel	U-2	(14.)	09.40
	4./JG 3	Fw. Leopold Münster	Il-2	(32.)	09.46
	4./JG 3	Fw. Leopold Münster	Il-2	(33.)	09.47
	4./JG 3	Lt. Wolf Ettel	MiG-1	(15.)	09.48
	4./JG 3	Fw. Leopold Münster	Il-2	(34.)	10.05
29.07.42	6./JG 3	Fw. Rasso Förg	Il-2	(4.)	17.52
	6./JG 3	Lt. Ludwig Häfner	Il-2	(23.)	17.52
30.07.42	6./JG 3	Lt. Ludwig Häfner	LaGG-3	(24.)	05.32
	5./JG 3	Lt. Lothar Myrrhe	MiG-1	(2.)	05.40
	6./JG 3	Fw. Rasso Förg	LaGG-3	(5.)	05.45
	6./JG 3	Lt. Ludwig Häfner	LaGG-3	(25.)	05.47
	6./JG 3	Lt. Ludwig Häfner	LaGG-3	(26.)	05.48
	6./JG 3	Lt. Ludwig Häfner	Pe-2	(27.)	
	4./JG 3	Lt. Wolf Ettel	MiG-1	(16.)	07.10
	4./JG 3	Fw. Leopold Münster	MiG-1	(35.)	07.17
	Stab II./JG 3	Lt. Gustav Frielinghaus	MiG-1	(15.)	11.44
	4./JG 3	Uffz. Kurt Ebener	Jak-1	(9.)	13.04
	4./JG 3	Uffz. Kurt Ebener	Jak-1	(10.)	13.05
	4./JG 3	Fw. Leopold Münster	MiG-1	(36.)	13.07
31.07.42	4./JG 3	Uffz. Hans Frese	Il-2	(6.)	10.50
	6./JG 3	Lt. Ludwig Häfner	LaGG-3	(28.)	13.45
	6./JG 3	Lt. Ludwig Häfner	Il-2	(29.)	13.55
	6./JG 3	Uffz. Franz Schwaiger	Il-2	(19.)	13.55
	6./JG 3	Uffz. Waldemar Eyrich	Il-2	(4.)	13.58
	6./JG 3	Uffz. Franz Schwaiger	LaGG-3	(20.)	14.00
	6./JG 3	Fw. Rasso Förg	Il-2	(6.)	14.05
	6./JG 3	Lt. Ludwig Häfner	Il-2	(30.)	14.05
01.08.42	4./JG 3	Oblt. Albrecht Walz	LaGG-3	(14.)	13.35
	4./JG 3	Uffz. Kurt Ebener	LaGG-3	(11.)	15.37
03.08.42	Stab II./JG 3	Hptm. Kurt Brändle	Jak-1	(80.)	14.55
	Stab II./JG 3	Lt. Gustav Frielinghaus	Jak-1	(16.)	14.57
04.08.42	4./JG 3	Uffz. Heinrich May	Jak-4	(10.)	06.10
	4./JG 3	Fw. Leopold Münster	Il-2	(37.)	15.45
	4./JG 3	Fw. Leopold Münster	Il-2	(38.)	15.55
	4./JG 3	Fw. Werner Lucas	Pe-2	(41.)	17.35
05.08.42	4./JG 3	Fw. Werner Lucas	Pe-2	(42.)	04.30
	4./JG 3	Fw. Werner Lucas	MiG-1	(43.)	04.35
	4./JG 3	Lt. Wolf Ettel	LaGG-3	(17.)	04.37
	4./JG 3	Fw. Leopold Münster	LaGG-3	(39.)	04.37

	4./JG 3	Uffz. Kurt Ebener	Pe-2	(12.)	04.40
	4./JG 3	Uffz. Kurt Ebener	Pe-2	(13.)	04.42
	Stab II./JG 3	Hptm. Kurt Brändle	Jak-1	(81.)	07.12
06.08.42	6./JG 3	Lt. Ludwig Häfner	Pe-2	(31.)	05.35
	5./JG 3	Obfw. Alfred Heckmann	LaGG-3	(46.)	06.50
	4./JG 3	Fw. Leopold Münster	LaGG-3	(40.)	06.53
	Stab II./JG 3	Lt. Gustav Frielinghaus	Pe-2	(17.)	11.23
	Stab II./JG 3	Hptm. Kurt Brändle	Pe-2	(82.)	11.25
	Stab II./JG 3	Hptm. Kurt Brändle	Pe-2	(83.)	11.26
	Stab II./JG 3	Hptm. Kurt Brändle	Pe-2	(84.)	11.35
	Stab II./JG 3	Oblt. Albrecht Walz	Il-2	(15.)	11.40
	4./JG 3	Fw. Werner Lucas	R-5	(44.)	14.40
	4./JG 3	Uffz. Hans Frese	Il-2	(7.)	14.53
	Stab II./JG 3	Oblt. Albrecht Walz	Il-2	(16.)	15.21
	Stab II./JG 3	Lt. Gustav Frielinghaus	Il-2	(18.)	15.23
07.08.42	5./JG 3	Lt. Lothar Myrrhe	Il-2	(3.)	05.42
	6./JG 3	Lt. Ludwig Häfner	Il-2	(32.)	05.47
	6./JG 3	Lt. Hans Fuß	Il-2	(63.)	10.20
	6./JG 3	Lt. Hans Fuß	Il-2	(64.)	10.24
	6./JG 3	Lt. Ludwig Häfner	LaGG-3	(33.)	10.25
	6./JG 3	Lt. Hans Fuß	LaGG-3	(65.)	13.50
	5./JG 3	Lt. Lothar Myrrhe	MiG-1	(4.)	13.56
	6./JG 3	Lt. Hans Fuß	LaGG-3	(66.)	13.57
	6./JG 3	Lt. Hans Fuß	MiG-1	(67.)	13.58
	6./JG 3	Lt. Hans Fuß	MiG-1	(68.)	14.00
	Stab II./JG 3	Hptm. Kurt Brändle	Pe-2	(85.)	14.09
	Stab II./JG 3	Hptm. Kurt Brändle	Pe-2	(86.)	14.10
	Stab II./JG 3	Oblt. Albrecht Walz	Pe-2	(17.)	14.10
	Stab II./JG 3	Hptm. Kurt Brändle	Pe-2	(87.)	14.11
	Stab II./JG 3	Lt. Gustav Frielinghaus	Pe-2	(19.)	14.13
	4./JG 3	Fw. Leopold Münster	Pe-2	(41.)	17.45
	Stab II./JG 3	Hptm. Kurt Brändle	Pe-2	(88.)	17.45
	5./JG 3	Obfw. Alfred Heckmann	Pe-2	(47.)	17.46
	Stab II./JG 3	Hptm. Kurt Brändle	Pe-2	(89.)	17.46
	4./JG 3	Fw. Werner Lucas	Pe-2	(45.)	17.47
	4./JG 3	Lt. Wolf Ettel	LaGG-3	(18.)	17.47
	Stab II./JG 3	Oblt. Albrecht Walz	Pe-2	(18.)	17.47
	4./JG 3	Fw. Leopold Münster	Pe-2	(42.)	17.48
08.08.42	Stab II./JG 3	Hptm. Kurt Brändle	Su-2	(90.)	09.46
	Stab II./JG 3	Lt. Gustav Frielinghaus	Su-2	(20.)	09.47
	Stab II./JG 3	Hptm. Kurt Brändle	Su-2	(91.)	09.48
	Stab II./JG 3	Hptm. Kurt Brändle	Su-2	(92.)	09.50
	Stab II./JG 3	Lt. Gustav Frielinghaus	Su-2	(21.)	09.52
09.08.42	4./JG 3	Fw. Leopold Münster	Il-2	(43.)	05.25
	4./JG 3	Lt. Wolf Ettel	Il-2	(19.)	05.26
	4./JG 3	Lt. Wolf Ettel	Il-2	(20.)	05.35
	6./JG 3	Lt. Hans Fuß	1	(69.)	09.55
	5./JG 3	Lt. Lothar Myrrhe	1	(5.)	09.58
	6./JG 3	Lt. Hans Fuß	1	(70.)	10.05
	Stab II./JG 3	Lt. Gustav Frielinghaus	1	(22.)	14.40
10.08.42	Stab II./JG 3	Hptm. Kurt Brändle	1	(93.)	07.07
	Stab II./JG 3	Hptm. Kurt Brändle	1	(94.)	07.08
11.08.42	Stab II./JG 3	Hptm. Kurt Brändle	1	(95.)	12.06
	Stab II./JG 3	Lt. Gustav Frielinghaus	1	(23.)	12.08
16.08.42	5./JG 3	Obfw. Alfred Heckmann	LaGG-3	(48.)	04.30
17.08.42	4./JG 3	Fw. Werner Lucas	Il-2	(46.)	05.20
	Stab II./JG 3	Oblt. Albrecht Walz	1	(19.)	09.11
	6./JG 3	Uffz. Waldemar Eyrich	1	(5.)	10.56
	4./JG 3	Uffz. Heinrich May	1	(11.)	11.01
18.08.42	5./JG 3	Obfw. Alfred Heckmann	I-16	(49.)	06.45
	5./JG 3	Obfw. Alfred Heckmann	I-16	(50.)	06.50
	4./JG 3	Fw. Leopold Münster	I-16	(44.)	06.51
19.08.42	4./JG 3	Lt. Wolf Ettel	MiG-1	(21.)	04.59
	Stab II./JG 3	Hptm. Kurt Brändle	1	(96.)	11.28
	Stab II./JG 3	Lt. Gustav Frielinghaus	1	(24.)	11.30
	Stab II./JG 3	Hptm. Kurt Brändle	1	(97.)	11.31
	5./JG 3	Fw. Hans Grünberg	DB-3	(1.)	12.35
	5./JG 3	Lt. Lothar Myrrhe	DB-3	(6.)	12.45
	4./JG 3	Fw. Werner Lucas	Il-2	(47.)	17.44
	5./JG 3	Uffz. Arnold Bringmann	Il-2	(4.)	17.46
20.08.42	4./JG 3	Fw. Werner Lucas	Il-2	(48.)	04.33
	4./JG 3	Fw. Werner Lucas	Pe-2	(49.)	04.40
	4./JG 3	Uffz. Heinrich May	Pe-2	(12.)	04.40
	4./JG 3	Fw. Werner Lucas	Pe-2	(50.)	04.42
	4./JG 3	Fw. Werner Lucas	Pe-2	(51.)	04.43
	4./JG 3	Fw. Werner Lucas	Pe-2	(52.)	04.46
	6./JG 3	Lt. Ludwig Häfner	MiG-1	(34.)	06.20
21.08.42	4./JG 3	Lt. Wolf Ettel	Jak-7	(22.)	13.35

	4./JG 3	Uffz. Kurt Ebener	Jak-7	(14.)	13.37
	4./JG 3	Fw. Werner Lucas	Il-2	(53.)	17.45
	6./JG 3	Fw. Rasso Förg	Il-2	(7.)	17.47
	6./JG 3	Fw. Karl-Heinz Steinicke	Il-2	(7.)	17.48
22.08.42	Stab II./JG 3	Hptm. Kurt Brändle	1	(98.)	09.45
	Stab II./JG 3	Hptm. Kurt Brändle	1	(99.)	09.47
23.08.42	Stab II./JG 3	Hptm. Kurt Brändle	1	(100.)	05.43
	Stab II./JG 3	Hptm. Kurt Brändle	LaGG-3	(101.)	08.42
	Stab II./JG 3	Hptm. Kurt Brändle	LaGG-3	(102.)	08.44
	4./JG 3	Fw. Leopold Münster	LaGG-3	(45.)	08.45
	4./JG 3	Uffz. Hans Frese	Pe-2	(8.)	09.30
	4./JG 3	Fw. Leopold Münster	MiG-1	(46.)	
	4./JG 3	Fw. Leopold Münster	MiG-1	(47.)	
	6./JG 3	Lt. Ludwig Häfner	MiG-1	(35.)	
	6./JG 3	Lt. Ludwig Häfner	LaGG-3	(36.)	
10.09.42	4./JG 3	Fw. Josef Schütte	1	(8.)	10.30
13.09.42	4./JG 3	Lt. Wolf Ettel	LaGG-3	(23.)	06.55
	4./JG 3	Fw. Werner Lucas	Pe-2	(54.)	06.58
	4./JG 3	Fw. Werner Lucas	Pe-2	(55.)	07.03
	5./JG 3	Lt. Joachim Kirschner	LaGG-3	(35.)	07.04
	4./JG 3	Lt. Wolf Ettel	Jak-1	(24.)	07.10
	5./JG 3	Fw. Helmut Notemann	LaGG-3	(1.)	
14.09.42	Stab II./JG 3	Lt. Gustav Frielinghaus	1	(25.)	14.55
	6./JG 3	Lt. Hans Fuß	1	(71.)	17.21
	6./JG 3	Uffz. Herbert Dehrmann	1	(1.)	17.26
15.09.42	4./JG 3	Fw. Werner Lucas	Il-2	(56.)	09.12
	4./JG 3	Uffz. Manfred Fedgenhäuer	Il-2	(1.)	09.13
	4./JG 3	Lt. Wolf Ettel	Il-2	(25.)	09.13
	4./JG 3	Lt. Wolf Ettel	Il-2	(26.)	09.16
	Stab II./JG 3	Hptm. Kurt Brändle	Il-2	(103.)	09.44
	Stab II./JG 3	Hptm. Kurt Brändle	1	(104.)	10.00
	Stab II./JG 3	Lt. Gustav Frielinghaus	Pe-2	(26.)	14.40
	Stab II./JG 3	Lt. Max-Bruno Fischer	Pe-2	(2.)	14.41
	4./JG 3	Uffz. Kurt Ebener	Pe-2	(15.)	14.42
	4./JG 3	Fw. Werner Lucas	Pe-2	(57.)	14.44
	4./JG 3	Uffz. Heinrich May	Pe-2	(13.)	14.47
	5./JG 3	Fw. Helmut Notemann	Il-2	(2.)	
21.09.42	Stab II./JG 3	Lt. Gustav Frielinghaus	1	(27.)	11.05
	Stab II./JG 3	Hptm. Kurt Brändle	1	(105.)	11.06
	Stab II./JG 3	Lt. Gustav Frielinghaus	1	(28.)	11.07
	Stab II./JG 3	Fw. Wilhelm Laubenthal	1	(1.)	11.08
	6./JG 3	Lt. Ludwig Häfner	LaGG-3	(37.)	
	6./JG 3	Lt. Ludwig Häfner	MiG-1	(38.)	
22.09.42	Stab II./JG 3	Lt. Gustav Frielinghaus	1	(29.)	10.25
23.09.42	4./JG 3	Lt. Wolf Ettel	LaGG-3	(27.)	07.08
	4./JG 3	Uffz. Martin Fedgenhäuer	LaGG-3	(2.)	07.09
	4./JG 3	Fw. Josef Schütte	MiG-3	(9.)	07.12
	4./JG 3	Lt. Wolf Ettel	MiG-3	(28.)	07.15
	4./JG 3	Fw. Werner Lucas	LaGG-3	(58.)	07.17
	5./JG 3	Obfw. Alfred Heckmann	LaGG-3	(51.)	07.25
	5./JG 3	Lt. Joachim Kirschner	Pe-2	(36.)	10.25
	5./JG 3	Lt. Joachim Kirschner	LaGG-3	(37.)	10.27
	5./JG 3	Uffz. Arnold Bringmann	LaGG-3	(5.)	10.28
28.09.42	5./JG 3	Lt. Joachim Kirschner	LaGG-3	(38.)	10.22
	4./JG 3	Uffz. Heinrich May	1	(14.)	11.15
	6./JG 3	Uffz. Waldemar Eyrich	1	(6.)	13.40
29.09.42	Stab II./JG 3	Hptm. Kurt Brändle	LaGG-3	(106.)	08.59
	Stab II./JG 3	Fw. Wilhelm Laubenthal	LaGG-3	(2.)	09.02
	Stab II./JG 3	Fw. Wilhelm Laubenthal	I-16	(3.)	09.03
	Stab II./JG 3	Hptm. Kurt Brändle	I-16	(107.)	09.08
	Stab II./JG 3	Lt. Gustav Frielinghaus	1	(30.)	
	6./JG 3	Lt. Ludwig Häfner	LaGG-3	(39.)	
	6./JG 3	Lt. Ludwig Häfner	LaGG-3	(40.)	
30.09.42	6./JG 3	Fw. Rasso Förg	1	(8.)	08.35
04.10.42	5./JG 3	Obfw. Alfred Heckmann	LaGG-3	(52.)	13.50
	6./JG 3	Lt. Gustav Frielinghaus	LaGG-3	(31.)	13.52
	4./JG 3	Uffz. Hans Kühnel	LaGG-3	(1.)	13.55
	5./JG 3	Obfw. Alfred Heckmann	LaGG-3	(53.)	13.55
	6./JG 3	Oblt. Paul Stolte	LaGG-3	(5.)	14.00
	5./JG 3	Lt. Joachim Kirschner	Il-2	(39.)	17.21
	5./JG 3	Lt. Lothar Myrrhe	Il-2	(7.)	17.22
	5./JG 3	Lt. Joachim Kirschner	LaGG-3	(40.)	17.24
05.10.42	5./JG 3	Lt. Ernst-Heinz Löhr	LaGG-3	(6.)	07.24
	5./JG 3	Lt. Joachim Kirschner	LaGG-3	(41.)	11.31
06.10.42	4./JG 3	Fw. Kurt Ebener	LaGG-3	(16.)	07.20

07.10.42	5./JG 3	Fw. Josef Schütte	LaGG-3	(10.)	15.55
	4./JG 3	Fw. Leopold Münster	LaGG-3	(48.)	15.57
	4./JG 3	Lt. Wolf Ettel	LaGG-3	(29.)	15.58
	4./JG 3	Fw. Leopold Münster	LaGG-3	(49.)	15.59
	4./JG 3	Lt. Wolf Ettel	LaGG-3	(30.)	16.00
11.10.42	5./JG 3	Lt. Joachim Kirschner	Pe-2	(42.)	17.30
	5./JG 3	Lt. Joachim Kirschner	MiG-1	(43.)	17.35
12.10.42	5./JG 3	Lt. Joachim Kirschner	LaGG-3	(44.)	16.29
15.10.42	4./JG 3	Fw. Werner Lucas	LaGG-3	(59.)	08.58
	4./JG 3	Fw. Kurt Ebener	LaGG-3	(17.)	09.01
	6./JG 3	Uffz. Herbert Dehrmann	LaGG-3	(2.)	09.10
	5./JG 3	Lt. Joachim Kirschner	LaGG-3	(45.)	09.23
	5./JG 3	Lt. Joachim Kirschner	LaGG-3	(46.)	09.25
	5./JG 3	Fw. Hans Grünberg	LaGG-3	(2.)	09.26
17.10.42	5./JG 3	Fw. Hans Grünberg	Pe-2	(3.)	15.50
	5./JG 3	Lt. Joachim Kirschner	Il-2	(47.)	15.57
22.10.42	5./JG 3	Fw. Josef Schütte	LaGG-3	(11.)	12.08
	5./JG 3	Lt. Joachim Kirschner	LaGG-3	(48.)	12.09
	5./JG 3	Lt. Joachim Kirschner	LaGG-3	(49.)	12.11
23.10.42	4./JG 3	Fw. Leopold Münster	Pe-2	(50.)	13.19
28.10.42	5./JG 3	Lt. Lothar Myrrhe	1	(8.)	12.32
	5./JG 3	Fw. Josef Schütte	1	(12.)	12.40
	5./JG 3	Fw. Josef Schütte	1	(13.)	12.48
29.10.42	5./JG 3	Lt. Joachim Kirschner	LaGG-3	(50.)	09.36
	5./JG 3	Fw. Hans Grünberg	LaGG-3	(4.)	09.37
	5./JG 3	Lt. Joachim Kirschner	LaGG-3	(51.)	09.48
30.10.42	5./JG 3	Fw. Hans Grünberg	LaGG-3	(5.)	08.55
	5./JG 3	Fw. Josef Schütte	LaGG-3	(14.)	09.00
	5./JG 3	Fw. Josef Schütte	1	(15.)	09.30
31.10.42	4./JG 3	Fw. Leopold Münster	MiG-3	(51.)	15.57
	4./JG 3	Lt. Wolf Ettel	Il-2	(31.)	16.00
	4./JG 3	Lt. Wolf Ettel	LaGG-3	(32.)	16.40
	4./JG 3	Lt. Wolf Ettel	Il-2	(33.)	16.50
	5./JG 3	Uffz. Günther Mohn	Il-2	(1.)	16.55
02.11.42	5./JG 3	Fw. Helmut Notemann	LaGG-3	(3.)	
07.11.42	Stab II./JG 3	Hptm. Kurt Brändle	1	(108.)	12.29
	5./JG 3	Fw. Helmut Notemann	LaGG-3	(4.)	
08.11.42	5./JG 3	Lt. Joachim Kirschner	LaGG-3	(52.)	14.24
10.11.42	Stab II./JG 3	Hptm. Kurt Brändle	LaGG-3	(109.)	12.27
11.11.42	Stab II./JG 3	Hptm. Kurt Brändle	LaGG-3	(110.)	14.17
26.11.42	4./JG 3	Lt. Werner Lucas	Il-2	(60.)	12.17
	4./JG 3	Lt. Werner Lucas	Il-2	(61.)	12.19
30.11.42	4./JG 3	Lt. Werner Lucas	Il-2	(62.)	13.56
	5./JG 3	Fw. Hans Grünberg	Il-2	(6.)	14.00
03.12.42	4./JG 3	Lt. Werner Lucas	Il-2	(63.)	12.37
	4./JG 3	Fw. Kurt Ebener	Il-2	(18.)	12.40
	4./JG 3	Fw. Kurt Ebener	Il-2	(19.)	12.42
	4./JG 3	Uffz. Georg Pissarski	Il-2	(1.)	12.42
	Stab II./JG 3	Fw. Wilhelm Laubenthal	LaGG-3	(4.)	13.14
	5./JG 3	Fw. Josef Schütte	LaGG-3	(16.)	13.16
16.12.42	5./JG 3	Uffz. Günther Mohn	MiG-1	(2.)	
17.12.42	Stab II./JG 3	Hptm. Kurt Brändle	1	(111.)	10.55
	4./JG 3	Oblt. Werner Lucas	Pe-2	(64.)	11.35
	4./JG 3	Oblt. Werner Lucas	Pe-2	(65.)	11.36
	5./JG 3	Fw. Hans Grünberg	Jak-1	(7.)	12.22
	5./JG 3	Fw. Hans Grünberg	Jak-1	(8.)	12.25
	Stab II./JG 3	Hptm. Kurt Brändle	Jak-1	(112.)	13.10
	Stab II./JG 3	Hptm. Kurt Brändle	Il-2	(113.)	13.17
	4./JG 3	Fw. Kurt Ebener	Il-2	(20.)	13.20
	4./JG 3	Uffz. Georg Pissarski	Il-2	(2.)	13.22
	Stab II./JG 3	Hptm. Kurt Brändle	Il-2	(114.)	13.23
	4./JG 3	Fw. Kurt Ebener	Jak-1	(21.)	13.24
	4./JG 3	Uffz. Wolfgang Buttstädt	Il-2	(1.)	13.26
	Stab II./JG 3	Hptm. Kurt Brändle	Il-2	(115.)	13.30
	5./JG 3	Fw. Josef Schütte	1	(17.)	
18.12.42	4./JG 3	Fw. Kurt Ebener	Il-2	(22.)	12.47
19.12.42	4./JG 3	Oblt. Werner Lucas	Il-2	(66.)	09.30

	4./JG 3	Fw. Hans Frese	La-5	(9.)	09.35
	4./JG 3	Oblt. Werner Lucas	Il-2	(67.)	09.50
	4./JG 3	Uffz. Georg Pissarski	1	(3.)	11.45
	4./JG 3	Fw. Kurt Ebener	LaGG-3	(23.)	12.45
	4./JG 3	Fw. Kurt Ebener	LaGG-3	(24.)	13.52
	4./JG 3	Fw. Kurt Ebener	LaGG-3	(25.)	13.55
	4./JG 3	Fw. Kurt Ebener	Pe-2	(26.)	14.08
	4./JG 3	Fw. Kurt Ebener	Pe-2	(27.)	14.09
20.12.42	5./JG 3	Uffz. Arnold Bringmann	Jak-1	(6.)	09.00
	5./JG 3	Fw. Josef Schütte	1	(18.)	12.07
	5./JG 3	Fw. Hans Grünberg	Il-2	(9.)	12.36
	4./JG 3	Fw. Kurt Ebener	LaGG-3	(28.)	12.38
	Stab II./JG 3	Lt. Max-Bruno Fischer	Il-2	(3.)	
21.12.42	4./JG 3	Fw. Kurt Ebener	Jak-1	(29.)	
	6./JG 3	Lt. Gustav Frielinghaus	Boston	(32.)	12.39
	6./JG 3	Uffz. Waldemar Eyrich	1	(7.)	12.55
22.12.42	5./JG 3	Fw. Josef Schütte	1	(19.)	09.55
	5./JG 3	Fw. Hans Grünberg	Jak-1	(10.)	12.05
	4./JG 3	Fw. Kurt Ebener	Jak-1	(30.)	13.35
25.12.42	4./JG 3	Fw. Kurt Ebener	Il-2	(31.)	13.05
	4./JG 3	Uffz. Georg Pissarski	LaGG-3	(4.)	13.05
	4./JG 3	Fw. Kurt Ebener	LaGG-3	(32.)	13.06
27.12.42	Stab II./JG 3	Hptm. Kurt Brändle	MiG-1	(116.)	11.55
	Stab II./JG 3	Hptm. Kurt Brändle	Il-2	(117.)	12.05
	4./JG 3	Fw. Hans Frese	Il-2	(10.)	13.28
	5./JG 3	Fw. Hans Grünberg	Il-2	(11.)	13.32
28.12.42	4./JG 3	Fw. Kurt Ebener	LaGG-3	(33.)	09.05
	6./JG 3	Lt. Ernst-Heinz Löhr	1	(7.)	14.01
	5./JG 3	Fw. Josef Schütte	1	(20.)	14.02
29.12.42	6./JG 3	Lt. Gustav Frielinghaus	MiG-1	(33.)	11.32
30.12.42	5./JG 3	Fw. Josef Schütte	Il-2	(21.)	06.50
	6./JG 3	Lt. Gustav Frielinghaus	1	(34.)	09.09
	6./JG 3	Lt. Gustav Frielinghaus	1	(35.)	09.13
	4./JG 3	Fw. Kurt Ebener	MiG-1	(34.)	09.45
	4./JG 3	Fw. Kurt Ebener	MiG-1	(35.)	09.48
	4./JG 3	Fw. Kurt Ebener	Il-2	(36.)	12.25
	4./JG 3	Fw. Kurt Ebener	LaGG-3	(37.)	12.27
31.12.42	Stab II./JG 3	Hptm. Kurt Brändle	Il-2	(118.)	07.06
	Stab II./JG 3	Hptm. Kurt Brändle	1	(119.)	07.30
	5./JG 3	Fw. Rudolf Traphan	1	(1.)	07.31
	5./JG 3	Fw. Josef Schütte	1	(22.)	07.36
03.01.43	Stab II./JG 3	Hptm. Kurt Brändle	1	(120.)	07.52
04.01.43	4./JG 3	Fw. Kurt Ebener	LaGG-3	(38.)	13.57
05.01.43	4./JG 3	Oblt. Werner Lucas	La-5	(68.)	07.10
	4./JG 3	Oblt. Werner Lucas	La-5	(69.)	07.20
	6./JG 3	Lt. Gustav Frielinghaus	MiG-1	(36.)	09.42
07.01.43	4./JG 3	Fw. Kurt Ebener	LaGG-3	(39.)	07.47
	4./JG 3	Fw. Kurt Ebener	La-5	(40.)	08.26
	5./JG 3	Fw. Rudolf Traphan	1	(2.)	09.46
10.01.43	4./JG 3	Fw. Kurt Ebener	Il-2	(41.)	07.30
	4./JG 3	Fw. Kurt Ebener	Il-2	(42.)	07.35
	4./JG 3	Fw. Kurt Ebener	LaGG-3	(43.)	07.46
	5./JG 3	Uffz. Arnold Bringmann	LaGG-3	(7.)	08.50
	4./JG 3	Fw. Kurt Ebener	Il-2	(44.)	09.03
12.01.43	5./JG 3	Lt. Walter Bohatsch	LaGG-3	(2.)	09.00
	4./JG 3	Fw. Kurt Ebener	Il-2	(45.)	10.40
	4./JG 3	Fw. Kurt Ebener	Il-2	(46.)	10.42
	4./JG 3	Fw. Kurt Ebener	LaGG-3	(47.)	14.25
13.01.43	4./JG 3	Fw. Kurt Ebener	Il-2	(48.)	10.15
15.01.43	4./JG 3	Fw. Kurt Ebener	DB-3	(49.)	08.28
	4./JG 3	Fw. Kurt Ebener	DB-3	(50.)	08.32
	4./JG 3	Uffz. Georg Pissarski	1	(5.)	09.28
	4./JG 3	Fw. Kurt Ebener	LaGG-3	(51.)	10.21
	4./JG 3	Fw. Kurt Ebener	LaGG-3	(52.)	10.39
	4./JG 3	Uffz. Thomas Ametsbichler	1	(1.)	12.17
	6./JG 3	Lt. Gustav Frielinghaus	DB-3	(37.)	12.32
	4./JG 3	Fw. Hans Frese	PS-84	(11.)	12.57
	4./JG 3	Oblt. Werner Lucas	PS-84	(70.)	13.00
	4./JG 3	Oblt. Werner Lucas	PS-84	(71.)	13.04
	4./JG 3	Oblt. Werner Lucas	PS-84	(72.)	13.08
	4./JG 3	Fw. Hans Frese	PS-84	(12.)	13.09
20.01.43	6./JG 3	Uffz. Heinrich May	1	(15.)	11.35

23.01.43	5./JG 3	Uffz. Günther Mohn	LaGG-3	(3.)	
25.01.43	5./JG 3	Fw. Helmut Notemann	MiG-1	(5.)	
26.01.43	6./JG 3	Fw. Karl-Heinz Steinicke	1	(8.)	09.35
	6./JG 3	Lt. Ernst-Heinz Löhr	1	(8.)	09.37
	Stab II./JG 3	Hptm. Kurt Brändle	1	(121.)	11.47
28.01.43	Stab II./JG 3	Hptm. Kurt Brändle	1	(122.)	09.25
	5./JG 3	Fw. Josef Schütte	1	(23.)	11.48
	6./JG 3	Uffz. Heinrich May	1	(16.)	12.25
30.01.43	6./JG 3	Lt. Gustav Frielinghaus	1	(38.)	12.52
	6./JG 3	Oblt. Paul Stolte	1	(6.)	12.53
	6./JG 3	Uffz. Waldemar Eyrich	1	(8.)	13.05
31.01.43	6./JG 3	Uffz. Alfred Fischer	1	(2.)	13.12
01.02.43	Stab II./JG 3	Hptm. Kurt Brändle	Boston	(123.)	11.05
	Stab II./JG 3	Hptm. Kurt Brändle	Jak-1	(124.)	11.15
	Stab II./JG 3	Hptm. Kurt Brändle	Boston	(125.)	11.22
	6./JG 3	Uffz. Willi Schick	LaGG-3	(1.)	11.40
	4./JG 3	Oblt. Werner Lucas	Boston	(73.)	11.55
02.02.43	4./JG 3	Fw. Hans Kühnel	1	(2.)	09.15
	Stab II./JG 3	Hptm. Kurt Brändle	1	(126.)	09.21
	Stab II./JG 3	Hptm. Kurt Brändle	1	(127.)	09.23
	Stab II./JG 3	Hptm. Kurt Brändle	1	(128.)	09.24
	Stab II./JG 3	Hptm. Kurt Brändle	1	(129.)	09.25
	5./JG 3	Uffz. Arnold Bringmann	1	(8.)	11.11
	5./JG 3	Fw. Rudolf Traphan	1	(3.)	15.10
03.02.43	6./JG 3	Fw. Rasso Förg	1	(9.)	09.25
08.02.43	4./JG 3	Fw. Hans Frese	Boston	(13.)	13.27
10.02.43	4./JG 3	Oblt. Werner Lucas	Il-2	(74.)	09.00
	Stab II./JG 3	Hptm. Kurt Brändle	1	(130.)	09.10
	6./JG 3	Lt. Ernst-Heinz Löhr	1	(9.)	13.33
	5./JG 3	Uffz. Günther Mohn	Boston	(4.)	
12.02.43	6./JG 3	Lt. Gustav Frielinghaus	1	(39.)	08.15
	6./JG 3	Uffz. Herbert Dehrmann	1	(3.)	08.16
	6./JG 3	Uffz. Waldemar Eyrich	1	(9.)	08.18
	5./JG 3	Fw. Josef Schütte	1	(24.)	10.45
	4./JG 3	Lt. Wolf Ettel	La-5	(34.)	14.10
	4./JG 3	Uffz. Georg Pissarski	1	(6.)	15.01
	6./JG 3	Uffz. Alfred Fischer	1	(3.)	15.15
	6./JG 3	Uffz. Heinrich May	1	(17.)	15.20
13.02.43	6./JG 3	Oblt. Paul Stolte	LaGG-3	(7.)	14.25
	6./JG 3	Lt. Karl-Ludwig Seewald	1	(1.)	14.35
	6./JG 3	Fw. Karl-Heinz Steinicke	1	(9.)	14.38
	6./JG 3	Uffz. Heinrich May	1	(18.)	15.25
	4./JG 3	Lt. Wolf Ettel	La-5	(35.)	15.30
20.02.43	5./JG 3	Oblt. Joachim Kirschner	Jak-4	(53.)	10.04
	5./JG 3	Uffz. Rudolf Scheibe	1	(1.)	11.45
22.02.43	6./JG 3	Oblt. Gustav Frielinghaus	1	(40.)	09.32
	5./JG 3	Oblt. Joachim Kirschner	LaGG-3	(54.)	10.40
	5./JG 3	Oblt. Joachim Kirschner	Jak-7	(55.)	10.48
	6./JG 3	Fw. Karl-Heinz Steinicke	LaGG-3	(10.)	11.03
	6./JG 3	Fw. Rasso Förg	LaGG-3	(10.)	11.05
	6./JG 3	Fw. Karl-Heinz Steinicke	LaGG-3	(11.)	11.15
	6./JG 3	Fw. Karl-Heinz Steinicke	MiG-3	(12.)	11.29
	6./JG 3	Oblt. Paul Stolte	Boston	(8.)	12.35
	4./JG 3	Uffz. Georg Pissarski	1	(7.)	13.35
	4./JG 3	Lt. Wolf Ettel	LaGG-3	(35.)	13.55
	5./JG 3	Oblt. Joachim Kirschner	LaGG-3	(56.)	15.40
24.02.43	6./JG 3	Uffz. Waldemar Eyrich	Pe-2	(10.)	14.10
	4./JG 3	Fw. Hans Kühnel	LaGG-3	(3.)	15.16
25.02.43	6./JG 3	Lt. Ernst-Heinz Löhr	Boston	(10.)	10.35
	6./JG 3	Uffz. Franz Cech	Boston	(1.)	10.38
26.02.43	6./JG 3	Uffz. Gerhard Thyben	Boston	(1.)	09.15
27.02.43	5./JG 3	Oblt. Joachim Kirschner	LaGG-3	(57.)	07.37
	5./JG 3	Uffz. Arnold Bringmann	LaGG-3	(9.)	07.40
	6./JG 3	Oblt. Gustav Frielinghaus	LaGG-3	(41.)	15.27
02.03.43	5./JG 3	Fw. Josef Schütte	MiG-3	(25.)	14.40
05.03.43	4./JG 3	Lt. Wolf Ettel	U-2	(37.)	09.00
	5./JG 3	Fw. August Dilling	Il-2	(40.)	
06.03.43	5./JG 3	Fw. August Dilling	Il-2	(41.)	

	5./JG 3	Fw. August Dilling	Il-2	(42.)	
	5./JG 3	Fw. August Dilling	Il-2	(43.)	
09.03.43	5./JG 3	Oblt. Joachim Kirschner	Jak-1	(58.)	08.10
	4./JG 3	Lt. Wolf Ettel	La-5	(38.)	08.30
	6./JG 3	Uffz. Franz Cech	LaGG-3	(2.)	08.35
	4./JG 3	Lt. Wolf Ettel	LaGG-3	(39.)	13.50
	5./JG 3	Oblt. Joachim Kirschner	LaGG-3	(59.)	15.25
	5./JG 3	Fw. August Dilling	LaGG-3	(44.)	15.26
	4./JG 3	Lt. Hermann Schuster	LaGG-3	(1.)	15.35
	6./JG 3	Uffz. Herbert Dehrmann	LaGG-3	(4.)	15.35
	6./JG 3	Lt. Ernst-Heinz Löhr	LaGG-3	(11.)	15.36
10.03.43	5./JG 3	Uffz. Horst Lüdtke	Il-2	(1.)	09.33
	5./JG 3	Uffz. Günther Mohn	Il-2	(5.)	09.34
	5./JG 3	Uffz. Günther Mohn	Il-2	(6.)	09.35
	4./JG 3	Fw. Leopold Münster	I-16	(52.)	10.07
	5./JG 3	Fw. August Dilling	LaGG-3	(45.)	11.55
	5./JG 3	Fw. August Dilling	LaGG-3	(46.)	11.57
	5./JG 3	Lt. Lothar Myrrhe	MiG-3	(9.)	14.55
	5./JG 3	Lt. Lothar Myrrhe	MiG-3	(10.)	14.57
	4./JG 3	Lt. Franz Ruhl	Il-2	(1.)	15.25
	5./JG 3	Uffz. Rudolf Scheibe	Il-2	(2.)	15.29
	Stab II./JG 3	Lt. Max-Bruno Fischer	Il-2	(4.)	
12.03.43	4./JG 3	Lt. Wolf Ettel	Il-2	(40.)	06.50
	4./JG 3	Fw. Leopold Münster	Il-2	(53.)	06.52
13.03.43	4./JG 3	Lt. Wolf Ettel	Il-2	(41.)	06.20
	4./JG 3	Lt. Wolf Ettel	Il-2	(42.)	06.25
	6./JG 3	Uffz. Alfred Fischer	Il-2	(4.)	06.30
	5./JG 3	Lt. Lothar Myrrhe	La-5	(11.)	10.20
	5./JG 3	Uffz. Arnold Bringmann	Il-2	(10.)	10.21
	5./JG 3	Fw. Rudolf Traphan	Il-2	(4.)	10.21
	5./JG 3	Oblt. Joachim Kirschner	Il-2	(60.)	10.27
	5./JG 3	Oblt. Joachim Kirschner	La-5	(61.)	10.28
	5./JG 3	Oblt. Joachim Kirschner	La-5	(62.)	10.29
14.03.43	6./JG 3	Oblt. Gustav Frielinghaus	U-2	(42.)	07.52
	6./JG 3	Oblt. Paul Stolte	LaGG-3	(9.)	13.07
	6./JG 3	Lt. Karl-Ludwig Seewald	LaGG-3	(2.)	14.50
16.03.43	4./JG 3	Lt. Wolf Ettel	LaGG-3	(43.)	14.25
	4./JG 3	Fw. Leopold Münster	LaGG-3	(54.)	14.27
	5./JG 3	Fw. August Dilling	LaGG-3	(47.)	11.55
	5./JG 3	Uffz. Günther Mohn	Boston	(7.)	
17.03.43	6./JG 3	Oblt. Gustav Frielinghaus	Boston	(43.)	10.48
	6./JG 3	Fw. Karl-Heinz Steinicke	Boston	(13.)	10.49
	4./JG 3	Lt. Wolf Ettel	Boston	(44.)	10.50
	5./JG 3	Fw. August Dilling	Boston	(48.)	
18.03.43	4./JG 3	Uffz. Martin Fedgenhäuer	1	(3.)	13.25
	4./JG 3	Lt. Wolf Ettel	LaGG-3	(45.)	15.05
	5./JG 3	Oblt. Joachim Kirschner	Il-2	(63.)	15.14
	5./JG 3	Lt. Lothar Myrrhe	Il-2	(12.)	15.15
19.03.43	4./JG 3	Lt. Wolf Ettel	LaGG-3	(46.)	06.15
	4./JG 3	Fw. Hans Kühnel	LaGG-3	(4.)	06.17
	4./JG 3	Lt. Wolf Ettel	LaGG-3	(47.)	06.45
	6./JG 3	Uffz. Waldemar Eyrich	Pe-2	(11.)	08.58
	4./JG 3	Fw. Leopold Münster	Pe-2	(55.)	10.16
	5./JG 3	Uffz. Horst Lüdtke	La-5	(2.)	12.05
	5./JG 3	Fw. August Dilling	La-5	(49.)	13.40
	4./JG 3	Lt. Wolf Ettel	LaGG-3	(48.)	14.15
	4./JG 3	Fw. Leopold Münster	La-5	(56.)	14.16
	4./JG 3	Lt. Wolf Ettel	Jak-7	(49.)	14.27
20.03.43	4./JG 3	Lt. Wolf Ettel	La-5	(50.)	08.43
	5./JG 3	Fw. Josef Schütte	LaGG-3	(26.)	12.05
	4./JG 3	Lt. Hermann Schuster	LaGG-3	(2.)	15.02
	4./JG 3	Lt. Wolf Ettel	LaGG-3	(51.)	15.05
21.04.43	5./JG 3	Oblt. Joachim Kirschner	Jak-1	(64.)	14.34
	6./JG 3	Uffz. Waldemar Eyrich	La-5	(12.)	14.45
	6./JG 3	Lt. Karl-Ludwig Seewald	LaGG-3	(3.)	14.47
	4./JG 3	Lt. Wolf Ettel	LaGG-3	(52.)	14.57
	5./JG 3	Fw. Werner Kloß	Jak-1	(3.)	14.59
	4./JG 3	Lt. Wolf Ettel	LaGG-3	(53.)	15.00
	4./JG 3	Fw. Leopold Münster	La-5	(57.)	15.04
22.03.43	6./JG 3	Lt. Friedrich-Wilhelm Schmidt	Jak-1	(1.)	05.36
	5./JG 3	Uffz. Arnold Bringmann	Il-2	(11.)	07.35
	5./JG 3	Uffz. Arnold Bringmann	Il-2	(12.)	07.36
	6./JG 3	Oblt. Gustav Frielinghaus	LaGG-3	(44.)	12.05
	6./JG 3	Uffz. Franz Cech	LaGG-3	(3.)	12.06
	6./JG 3	Uffz. Franz Cech	LaGG-3	(4.)	12.16
	5./JG 3	Lt. Hartwig Dohse	LaGG-3	(1.)	12.18
	6./JG 3	Fw. Karl-Heinz Steinicke	LaGG-3	(14.)	12.20
	6./JG 3	Uffz. Alfred Fischer	LaGG-3	(5.)	12.25

	5./JG 3	Fw. August Dilling	LaGG-3	(50.)	
	5./JG 3	Fw. August Dilling	LaGG-3	(51.)	
25.03.43	4./JG 3	Fw. Hans Kühnel	LaGG-3	(5.)	07.46
	4./JG 3	Lt. Wolf Ettel	LaGG-3	(54.)	07.49
	4./JG 3	Lt. Wolf Ettel	Il-2	(55.)	07.50
	5./JG 3	Lt. Lothar Myrrhe	MiG-1	(13.)	08.03
	5./JG 3	Uffz. Hans Staufferth	MiG-1	(1.)	08.07
	5./JG 3	Oblt. Joachim Kirschner	MiG-1	(65.)	08.07
	5./JG 3	Oblt. Joachim Kirschner	Il-2	(66.)	08.08
	5./JG 3	Oblt. Joachim Kirschner	LaGG-3	(67.)	08.16
	4./JG 3	Lt. Wolf Ettel	La-5	(56.)	13.30
	6./JG 3	Oblt. Gustav Frielinghaus	LaGG-3	(45.)	13.30
	6./JG 3	Uffz. Herbert Dehrmann	LaGG-3	(5.)	13.32
	4./JG 3	Lt. Wolf Ettel	LaGG-3	(57.)	13.35
	6./JG 3	Oblt. Paul Stolte	La-5	(10.)	13.43
	6./JG 3	Uffz. Herbert Dehrmann	LaGG-3	(6.)	13.45
	6./JG 3	Uffz. Franz Cech	La-5	(5.)	13.50
	6./JG 3	Uffz. Uwe Michaels	LaGG-3	(1.)	13.50
	4./JG 3	Uffz. Georg Pissarski	LaGG-3	(8.)	13.55
	5./JG 3	Oblt. Joachim Kirschner	LaGG-3	(68.)	14.00
26.03.43	4./JG 3	Lt. Wolf Ettel	LaGG-3	(58.)	07.52
27.03.43	4./JG 3	Fw. Leopold Münster	I-16	(58.)	11.08
	6./JG 3	Oblt. Gustav Frielinghaus	I-16	(46.)	11.12
	4./JG 3	Lt. Wolf Ettel	I-16	(59.)	11.15
	4./JG 3	Fw. Leopold Münster	I-16	(59.)	11.17
	4./JG 3	Lt. Wolf Ettel	I-16	(60.)	11.20
	4./JG 3	Lt. Wolf Ettel	LaGG-3	(61.)	11.30
28.03.43	4./JG 3	Lt. Wolf Ettel	Jak-7	(62.)	10.35
	4./JG 3	Lt. Wolf Ettel	LaGG-3	(63.)	13.12
	4./JG 3	Lt. Wolf Ettel	Jak-7	(64.)	13.15
29.03.43	5./JG 3	Oblt. Joachim Kirschner	R-5	(69.)	12.05
30.03.43	5./JG 3	Lt. Lothar Myrrhe	Il-2	(14.)	13.29
	5./JG 3	Uffz. Arnold Bringmann	Il-2	(13.)	13.30
	5./JG 3	Uffz. Hans Staufferth	Il-2	(2.)	13.31
	6./JG 3	Lt. Karl-Ludwig Seewald	DB-3	(4.)	17.07
31.03.43	5./JG 3	Oblt. Joachim Kirschner	La-5	(70.)	05.48
	5./JG 3	Fw. Josef Schütte	La-5	(27.)	05.50
	5./JG 3	Fw. Rudolf Traphan	La-5	(5.)	05.55
	6./JG 3	Oblt. Gustav Frielinghaus	LaGG-3	(47.)	09.32
	5./JG 3	Oblt. Joachim Kirschner	LaGG-3	(71.)	09.52
	5./JG 3	Oblt. Joachim Kirschner	LaGG-3	(72.)	15.50
	6./JG 3	Uffz. Herbert Dehrmann	1	(7.)	16.05
02.04.43	4./JG 3	Lt. Wolf Ettel	La-5	(65.)	06.42
10.04.43	6./JG 3	Uffz. Waldemar Eyrich	LaGG-3	(13.)	07.28
	6./JG 3	Uffz. Franz Cech	LaGG-3	(6.)	07.30
11.04.43	5./JG 3	Oblt. Joachim Kirschner	I-16	(73.)	05.16
	5./JG 3	Fw. Hans Grünberg	I-16	(12.)	05.18
	5./JG 3	Oblt. Joachim Kirschner	I-16	(74.)	05.24
	5./JG 3	Fw. Hans Grünberg	I-16	(13.)	05.28
	4./JG 3	Lt. Wolf Ettel	P-39	(66.)	09.35
	4./JG 3	Lt. Wolf Ettel	P-39	(67.)	09.37
	4./JG 3	Lt. Wolf Ettel	P-39	(68.)	09.40
	5./JG 3	Oblt. Joachim Kirschner	LaGG-3	(75.)	12.05
	6./JG 3	Oblt. Gustav Frielinghaus	1	(48.)	
	6./JG 3	Oblt. Gustav Frielinghaus	1	(49.)	12.11
	4./JG 3	Lt. Franz Ruhl	P-39	(2.)	12.35
	6./JG 3	Oblt. Gustav Frielinghaus	1	(50.)	13.53
	4./JG 3	Lt. Wolf Ettel	Il-2	(69.)	13.55
	4./JG 3	Lt. Wolf Ettel	LaGG-3	(70.)	14.05
12.04.43	5./JG 3	Oblt. Joachim Kirschner	P-39	(76.)	10.21
	4./JG 3	Lt. Wolf Ettel	P-39	(71.)	10.25
	4./JG 3	Lt. Franz Ruhl	P-39	(3.)	10.35
	4./JG 3	Lt. Wolf Ettel	P-40	(72.)	10.35
13.04.43	6./JG 3	Lt. Friedrich-Wilhelm Schmidt	La-5	(2.)	10.05
15.04.43	5./JG 3	Lt. Lothar Myrrhe	P-39	(15.)	08.30
	5./JG 3	Oblt. Joachim Kirschner	LaGG-3	(77.)	08.36
	5./JG 3	Lt. Lothar Myrrhe	Il-2	(16.)	08.42
	5./JG 3	Lt. Hartwig Dohse	Il-2	(2.)	08.45
	5./JG 3	Uffz. Arnold Bringmann	Il-2	(14.)	08.48
	5./JG 3	Oblt. Joachim Kirschner	LaGG-3	(78.)	08.56
	5./JG 3	Uffz. Horst Lüdtke	LaGG-3	(3.)	08.57
	6./JG 3	Lt. Ernst-Heinz Löhr	P-39	(12.)	09.39
	6./JG 3	Lt. Karl-Ludwig Seewald	LaGG-3	(5.)	09.50
	4./JG 3	Fw. Hans Frese	I-153	(14.)	09.57
	6./JG 3	Oblt. Gustav Frielinghaus	I-16	(51.)	12.35
	6./JG 3	Uffz. Waldemar Eyrich	I-16	(14.)	12.37
	6./JG 3	Oblt. Gustav Frielinghaus	Il-2	(52.)	12.39

	6./JG 3	Uffz. Herbert Dehrmann	P-40	(8.)	12.45
	6./JG 3	Uffz. Waldemar Eyrich	P-39	(15.)	13.02
	4./JG 3	Lt. Wolf Ettel	P-39	(73.)	15.30
	5./JG 3	Fw. Rudolf Traphan	LaGG-3	(6.)	16.10
	4./JG 3	Lt. Wolf Ettel	LaGG-3	(74.)	16.12
	4./JG 3	Lt. Wolf Ettel	LaGG-3	(75.)	16.15
	6./JG 3	Fw. Karl-Heinz Steinicke	LaGG-3	(15.)	16.25
	6./JG 3	Fw. Rasso Förg	LaGG-3	(11.)	16.30
16.04.43	4./JG 3	Fw. Hans Frese	I-16	(15.)	14.30
	5./JG 3	Fw. Hans Grünberg	P-40	(14.)	14.44
	5./JG 3	Oblt. Joachim Kirschner	P-39	(79.)	14.46
	4./JG 3	Lt. Wolf Ettel	P-40	(76.)	14.47
	5./JG 3	Oblt. Joachim Kirschner	P-39	(80.)	14.54
	4./JG 3	Lt. Wolf Ettel	P-39	(77.)	14.55
	6./JG 3	Oblt. Gustav Frielinghaus	LaGG-3	(53.)	16.58
17.04.43	6./JG 3	Oblt. Gustav Frielinghaus	LaGG-3	(54.)	09.20
	6./JG 3	Uffz. Alfred Fischer	LaGG-3	(6.)	11.21
	4./JG 3	Lt. Wolf Ettel	LaGG-3	(78.)	11.30
	5./JG 3	Lt. Lothar Myrrhe	LaGG-3	(17.)	11.32
	4./JG 3	Lt. Wolf Ettel	LaGG-3	(79.)	11.35
	6./JG 3	Oblt. Gustav Frielinghaus	LaGG-3	(55.)	11.42
	4./JG 3	Lt. Wolf Ettel	P-39	(80.)	11.43
	6./JG 3	Lt. Horst Brock	LaGG-3	(1.)	14.04
	6./JG 3	Uffz. Franz Cech	Jak-1	(7.)	15.01
	6./JG 3	Uffz. Alfred Fischer	Jak-1	(7.)	15.03
	5./JG 3	Uffz. Arnold Bringmann	LaGG-3	(15.)	15.03
	5./JG 3	Oblt. Joachim Kirschner	LaGG-3	(81.)	17.37
	5./JG 3	Fw. Werner Kloß	I-153	(4.)	17.40
	5./JG 3	Oblt. Joachim Kirschner	I-16	(82.)	17.43
18.04.43	5./JG 3	Oblt. Joachim Kirschner	LaGG-3	(83.)	06.08
	4./JG 3	Lt. Wolf Ettel	I-16	(81.)	10.05
	5./JG 3	Fw. Rudolf Traphan	1	(7.)	16.15
	5./JG 3	Oblt. Joachim Kirschner	I-153	(84.)	16.44
	4./JG 3	Lt. Wolf Ettel	LaGG-3	(82.)	18.00
19.04.43	6./JG 3	Oblt. Gustav Frielinghaus	Il-2	(56.)	11.52
	5./JG 3	Lt. Lothar Myrrhe	Il-2	(18.)	11.54
	6./JG 3	Oblt. Gustav Frielinghaus	Il-2	(57.)	11.56
	6./JG 3	Oblt. Gustav Frielinghaus	Il-2	(58.)	11.58
	6./JG 3	Uffz. Herbert Dehrmann	Il-2	(9.)	11.58
	6./JG 3	Uffz. Franz Cech	LaGG-3	(8.)	16.55
	6./JG 3	Uffz. Waldemar Eyrich	Il-2	(16.)	17.05
	6./JG 3	Uffz. Alfred Fischer	Il-2	(8.)	17.05
	6./JG 3	Uffz. Franz Cech	Il-2	(9.)	17.10
	5./JG 3	Fw. Hans Grünberg	LaGG-3	(15.)	17.10
	5./JG 3	Uffz. Horst Lüdtke	1	(4.)	17.12
	6./JG 3	Fw. Rasso Förg	1	(12.)	17.15
20.04.43	5./JG 3	Lt. Lothar Myrrhe	LaGG-3	(19.)	05.50
	5./JG 3	Lt. Hartwig Dohse	LaGG-3	(3.)	05.55
	6./JG 3	Lt. Ernst-Heinz Löhr	Jak-1	(13.)	06.20
	6./JG 3	Uffz. Franz Cech	Jak-1	(10.)	06.23
	6./JG 3	Lt. Ernst-Heinz Löhr	Jak-1	(14.)	06.24
	6./JG 3	Lt. Karl-Ludwig Seewald	1	(6.)	08.27
	4./JG 3	Oblt. Werner Lucas	Boston	(75.)	10.04
	4./JG 3	Fw. Leopold Münster	1	(60.)	10.05
	4./JG 3	Fw. Leopold Münster	1	(61.)	10.07
	4./JG 3	Fw. Georg Pissarski	1	(8.)	10.08
	4./JG 3	Uffz. Martin Fedgenhäuer	1	(4.)	10.09
	6./JG 3	Uffz. Alfred Fischer	1	(9.)	10.55
	5./JG 3	Oblt. Joachim Kirschner	LaGG-3	(85.)	11.50
	5./JG 3	Oblt. Joachim Kirschner	Il-2	(86.)	11.52
	5./JG 3	Oblt. Joachim Kirschner	Il-2	(87.)	11.54
	Stab II./JG 3	Maj. Kurt Brändle	LaGG-3	(131.)	11.56
	5./JG 3	Fw. Hans Grünberg	Il-2	(16.)	11.56
	5./JG 3	Fw. Hans Grünberg	Il-2	(17.)	11.57
	Stab II./JG 3	Maj. Kurt Brändle	Il-2	(132.)	11.58
	4./JG 3	Oblt. Werner Lucas	Boston	(76.)	16.00
	6./JG 3	Uffz. Franz Cech	La-5	(11.)	16.00
	5./JG 3	Oblt. Joachim Kirschner	LaGG-3	(88.)	16.01
	5./JG 3	Fw. Josef Schütte	LaGG-3	(28.)	16.02
	5./JG 3	Oblt. Joachim Kirschner	LaGG-3	(89.)	16.02
	6./JG 3	Uffz. Franz Cech	La-5	(12.)	16.03
	5./JG 3	Oblt. Joachim Kirschner	Boston	(90.)	16.04
	4./JG 3	Oblt. Werner Lucas	Boston	(77.)	16.05
	5./JG 3	Oblt. Joachim Kirschner	LaGG-3	(91.)	16.06
	5./JG 3	Fw. Josef Schütte	1	(29.)	16.07
	6./JG 3	Oblt. Gustav Frielinghaus	1	(59.)	16.07
	5./JG 3	Oblt. Joachim Kirschner	Il-2	(92.)	16.08
	4./JG 3	Lt. Franz Ruhl	La-5	(4.)	16.10
21.04.43	5./JG 3	Fw. Hans Grünberg	Il-2	(18.)	11.02
	6./JG 3	Fw. Karl-Heinz Steinicke	Il-2	(16.)	11.05
	5./JG 3	Fw. Hans Grünberg	Il-2	(19.)	11.07
	5./JG 3	Oblt. Joachim Kirschner	Boston	(93.)	18.28

22.04.43	4./JG 3	Lt. Wolf Ettel	LaGG-3	(83.)	14.01
	4./JG 3	Lt. Hermann Schuster	LaGG-3	(3.)	14.03
	4./JG 3	Lt. Wolf Ettel	LaGG-3	(84.)	14.08
	4./JG 3	Lt. Wolf Ettel	LaGG-3	(85.)	14.11
	4./JG 3	Lt. Wolf Ettel	LaGG-3	(86.)	14.20
	4./JG 3	Lt. Hermann Schuster	LaGG-3	(4.)	14.25
23.04.43	5./JG 3	Oblt. Joachim Kirschner	LaGG-3	(94.)	05.12
	5./JG 3	Oblt. Joachim Kirschner	LaGG-3	(95.)	05.17
	4./JG 3	Lt. Wolf Ettel	U-2	(87.)	05.30
	6./JG 3	Lt. Friedrich-Wilhelm Schmidt	1	(3.)	09.11
	Stab II./JG 3	Maj. Kurt Brändle	1	(133.)	09.45
	5./JG 3	Oblt. Joachim Kirschner	Il-2	(96.)	14.38
	5./JG 3	Oblt. Joachim Kirschner	I-16	(97.)	14.39
	5./JG 3	Fw. Helmut Notemann	Il-2	(6.)	
	6./JG 3	Uffz. Waldemar Eyrich	1	(17.)	14.39
	6./JG 3	Uffz. Waldemar Eyrich	1	(18.)	14.40
	5./JG 3	Fw. Hans Grünberg	I-16	(20.)	14.42
	4./JG 3	Lt. Wolf Ettel	LaGG-3	(88.)	17.02
	4./JG 3	Oblt. Werner Lucas	LaGG-3	(78.)	17.04
	6./JG 3	Fw. Rasso Förg	LaGG-3	(13.)	17.04
	4./JG 3	Uffz. Martin Fedgenhäuer	LaGG-3	(5.)	17.05
	4./JG 3	Lt. Wolf Ettel	LaGG-3	(89.)	17.07
	4./JG 3	Oblt. Werner Lucas	LaGG-3	(79.)	17.08
	4./JG 3	Lt. Wolf Ettel	LaGG-3	(90.)	17.10
	Stab II./JG 3	Maj. Kurt Brändle	LaGG-3	(134.)	17.12
	6./JG 3	Fw. Uwe Michaels	LaGG-3	(2.)	17.12
24.04.43	4./JG 3	Lt. Wolf Ettel	I-16	(91.)	05.36
	4./JG 3	Lt. Wolf Ettel	I-16	(92.)	05.37
	5./JG 3	Fw. Werner Kloß	I-16	(5.)	05.37
	4./JG 3	Fw. Leopold Münster	I-16	(62.)	05.38
	5./JG 3	Oblt. Joachim Kirschner	I-16	(98.)	05.39
	5./JG 3	Fw. Hans Grünberg	Il-2	(21.)	05.40
	4./JG 3	Lt. Wolf Ettel	I-16	(93.)	05.42
25.04.43	6./JG 3	Fw. Rasso Förg	1	(14.)	13.30
26.04.43	4./JG 3	Lt. Wolf Ettel	La-5	(94.)	12.19
	4./JG 3	Fw. Leopold Münster	La-5	(63.)	12.20
	4./JG 3	Lt. Wolf Ettel	La-5	(95.)	17.05
	4./JG 3	Lt. Wolf Ettel	La-5	(96.)	17.20
27.04.43	5./JG 3	Fw. Hans Grünberg	LaGG-3	(22.)	13.06
	6./JG 3	Uffz. Waldemar Eyrich	Jak-1	(19.)	15.58
	5./JG 3	Fw. Werner Kloß	1	(6.)	16.10
	6./JG 3	Uffz. Franz Cech	Jak-1	(13.)	16.15
	5./JG 3	Fw. Hans Grünberg	LaGG-3	(23.)	17.23
	5./JG 3	Oblt. Joachim Kirschner	P-39	(99.)	17.25
	5./JG 3	Uffz. Hans Staufferth	LaGG-3	(3.)	17.33
	5./JG 3	Oblt. Joachim Kirschner	Boston	(100.)	17.34
	5./JG 3	Oblt. Joachim Kirschner	LaGG-3	(101.)	17.35
	5./JG 3	Oblt. Joachim Kirschner	Boston	(102.)	17.36
28.04.43	6./JG 3	Oblt. Gustav Frielinghaus	LaGG-3	(60.)	08.56
	4./JG 3	Fw. Leopold Münster	1	(64.)	09.22
	6./JG 3	Lt. Karl-Ludwig Seewald	1	(7.)	10.50
	6./JG 3	Lt. Friedrich-Wilhelm Schmidt	1	(4.)	10.51
	4./JG 3	Lt. Wolf Ettel	LaGG-3	(97.)	12.25
	4./JG 3	Uffz. Georg Pissarski	LaGG-3	(9.)	12.27
	4./JG 3	Lt. Wolf Ettel	LaGG-3	(98.)	12.35
	4./JG 3	Lt. Wolf Ettel	LaGG-3	(99.)	12.40
	4./JG 3	Lt. Wolf Ettel	LaGG-3	(100.)	12.42
	4./JG 3	Lt. Franz Ruhl	LaGG-3	(5.)	16.20
	5./JG 3	Oblt. Joachim Kirschner	Jak-1	(103.)	16.21
	5./JG 3	Fw. Hans Grünberg	Jak-1	(24.)	16.22
	5./JG 3	Oblt. Joachim Kirschner	Jak-1	(104.)	16.25
	5./JG 3	Uffz. Horst Lüdtke	Jak-1	(5.)	16.31
	5./JG 3	Oblt. Joachim Kirschner	Jak-1	(105.)	16.32
29.04.43	5./JG 3	Oblt. Joachim Kirschner	LaGG-3	(106.)	05.31
	5./JG 3	Fw. Hans Grünberg	LaGG-3	(25.)	05.32
	5./JG 3	Oblt. Joachim Kirschner	LaGG-3	(107.)	05.40
	4./JG 3	Lt. Franz Ruhl	LaGG-3	(6.)	05.42
	4./JG 3	Lt. Hermann Schuster	LaGG-3	(5.)	05.43
	4./JG 3	Lt. Franz Ruhl	LaGG-3	(7.)	05.45
	Stab II./JG 3	Maj. Kurt Brändle	Jak-4	(135.)	07.47
	5./JG 3	Lt. Hartwig Dohse	Jak-1	(4.)	07.52
	Stab II./JG 3	Maj. Kurt Brändle	1	(136.)	07.56
	Stab II./JG 3	Maj. Kurt Brändle	1	(137.)	07.57
	Stab II./JG 3	Maj. Kurt Brändle	1	(138.)	07.58
	4./JG 3	Lt. Franz Ruhl	LaGG-3	(8.)	07.58
	5./JG 3	Fw. Rudolf Traphan	1	(8.)	08.05
	6./JG 3	Uffz. Waldemar Eyrich	LaGG-3	(20.)	08.09
	5./JG 3	Uffz. Horst Lüdtke	Jak-1	(6.)	08.10
	6./JG 3	Uffz. Franz Cech	Il-2	(14.)	08.12
	4./JG 3	Lt. Franz Ruhl	LaGG-3	(9.)	08.12
	6./JG 3	Uffz. Franz Cech	LaGG-3	(15.)	08.15
	5./JG 3	Uffz. Horst Lüdtke	Jak-4	(7.)	08.27
	5./JG 3	Oblt. Joachim Kirschner	Jak-1	(108.)	10.06

	5./JG 3	Uffz. Arnold Bringmann	Jak-1	(16.)	10.06
	5./JG 3	Fw. Hans Grünberg	Jak-1	(26.)	10.16
	5./JG 3	Oblt. Joachim Kirschner	Jak-1	(109.)	10.18
30.04.43	5./JG 3	Fw. Josef Schütte	1	(30.)	05.54
	5./JG 3	Uffz. Heinz Dahms	1	(1.)	06.52
06.05.43	6./JG 3	Uffz. Gerhard Thyben	Boston	(2.)	04.15
	5./JG 3	Fw. Josef Schütte	LaGG-3	(31.)	13.24
	5./JG 3	Uffz. Horst Lüdtke	LaGG-3	(8.)	13.25
	5./JG 3	Oblt. Joachim Kirschner	LaGG-3	(110.)	13.25
	5./JG 3	Oblt. Joachim Kirschner	LaGG-3	(111.)	13.29
	4./JG 3	Lt. Wolf Ettel	LaGG-3	(101.)	13.30
	4./JG 3	Lt. Wolf Ettel	LaGG-3	(102.)	13.35
	4./JG 3	Lt. Wolf Ettel	Jak-1	(103.)	13.37
	4./JG 3	Lt. Hans Reiser	LaGG-3	(1.)	
	4./JG 3	Oblt. Werner Lucas	LaGG-3	(80.)	13.45
	5./JG 3	Oblt. Joachim Kirschner	MiG-1	(112.)	13.48
	4./JG 3	Lt. Wolf Ettel	Jak-1	(104.)	14.00
	5./JG 3	Oblt. Joachim Kirschner	Boston	(113.)	14.07
	5./JG 3	Fw. Helmut Notemann	Spitfire	(7.)	
07.05.43	5./JG 3	Oblt. Joachim Kirschner	Spitfire	(114.)	16.02
	5./JG 3	Lt. Hartwig Dohse	I-153	(5.)	16.21
	Stab II./JG 3	Maj. Kurt Brändle	La-5	(139.)	16.26
	4./JG 3	Lt. Hermann Schuster	La-5	(6.)	16.27
	4./JG 3	Oblt. Werner Lucas	La-5	(81.)	16.30
	5./JG 3	Oblt. Joachim Kirschner	LaGG-3	(115.)	18.27
	4./JG 3	Lt. Wolf Ettel	Jak-1	(105.)	18.35
08.05.43	5./JG 3	Oblt. Joachim Kirschner	LaGG-3	(116.)	05.32
	5./JG 3	Fw. Josef Schütte	LaGG-3	(32.)	05.35
	6./JG 3	Uffz. Franz Cech	Spitfire	(16.)	07.50
	6./JG 3	Oblt. Gustav Frielinghaus	Spitfire	(61.)	07.55
	6./JG 3	Uffz. Gerhard Thyben	Spitfire	(3.)	08.00
	Stab II./JG 3	Maj. Kurt Brändle	I-153	(140.)	11.31
	Stab II./JG 3	Maj. Kurt Brändle	I-153	(141.)	11.33
	4./JG 3	Lt. Wolf Ettel	Il-2	(106.)	11.51
	4./JG 3	Lt. Leopold Münster	Il-2	(65.)	11.51
	4./JG 3	Lt. Wolf Ettel	Il-2	(107.)	11.52
	4./JG 3	Lt. Leopold Münster	Il-2	(66.)	11.52
	5./JG 3	Oblt. Joachim Kirschner	Spitfire	(117.)	11.56
	4./JG 3	Lt. Leopold Münster	LaGG-3	(67.)	12.04
	4./JG 3	Lt. Wolf Ettel	LaGG-3	(108.)	12.05
	4./JG 3	Lt. Leopold Münster	LaGG-3	(68.)	12.07
	4./JG 3	Lt. Wolf Ettel	LaGG-3	(109.)	12.09
	4./JG 3	Lt. Hans Reiser	Il-2	(2.)	12.10
	5./JG 3	Oblt. Joachim Kirschner	LaGG-3	(118.)	12.12
	5./JG 3	Oblt. Joachim Kirschner	Il-2	(119.)	12.13
	Stab II./JG 3	Lt. Franz Ruhl	Spitfire	(10.)	12.15
	5./JG 3	Oblt. Joachim Kirschner	LaGG-3	(120.)	14.20
	5./JG 3	Fw. Hans Grünberg	LaGG-3	(27.)	14.20
	5./JG 3	Oblt. Joachim Kirschner	LaGG-3	(121.)	14.24
	6./JG 3	Uffz. Franz Cech	P-39	(17.)	15.15
	6./JG 3	Uffz. Franz Cech	P-39	(18.)	15.20
	Stab II./JG 3	Maj. Kurt Brändle	P-39	(142.)	15.23
	6./JG 3	Uffz. Gerhard Thyben	P-39	(4.)	15.46
	Stab II./JG 3	Lt. Franz Ruhl	Spitfire	(11.)	17.55
	5./JG 3	Fw. Hans Grünberg	LaGG-3	(28.)	18.03
	5./JG 3	Oblt. Joachim Kirschner	LaGG-3	(122.)	18.10
09.05.43	4./JG 3	Lt. Wolf Ettel	Boston	(110.)	08.35
	4./JG 3	Uffz. Martin Fedgenhäuer	Boston	(6.)	
	4./JG 3	Oblt. Werner Lucas	La-5	(82.)	08.57
	6./JG 3	Oblt. Gustav Frielinghaus	1	(62.)	10.10
	5./JG 3	Uffz. Arnold Bringmann	1	(17.)	12.08
	5./JG 3	Fw. Werner Kloß	1	(7.)	12.21
	5./JG 3	Oblt. Joachim Kirschner	Jak-1	(123.)	12.34
	Stab II./JG 3	Lt. Franz Ruhl	Jak-1	(12.)	16.45
	5./JG 3	Oblt. Joachim Kirschner	Il-2	(124.)	16.53
	5./JG 3	Oblt. Joachim Kirschner	Jak-1	(125.)	16.59
	5./JG 3	Uffz. Hans Staufferth	1	(4.)	17.10
	6./JG 3	Fw. Rasso Förg	1	(15.)	17.15
	4./JG 3	Lt. Wolf Ettel	LaGG-3	(111.)	18.07
	4./JG 3	Lt. Wolf Ettel	LaGG-3	(112.)	18.15
10.05.43	4./JG 3	Lt. Wolf Ettel	LaGG-3	(113.)	09.40
	5./JG 3	Uffz. Horst Lüdtke	1	(9.)	12.30
	6./JG 3	Oblt. Gustav Frielinghaus	Jak-1	(63.)	15.27
	4./JG 3	Lt. Wolf Ettel	LaGG-3	(114.)	15.35
	4./JG 3	Lt. Wolf Ettel	LaGG-3	(115.)	15.35
	4./JG 3	Lt. Wolf Ettel	LaGG-3	(116.)	15.37
	4./JG 3	Lt. Wolf Ettel	Jak-1	(117.)	15.50
	4./JG 3	Lt. Wolf Ettel	Jak-1	(118.)	15.55
	5./JG 3	Oblt. Joachim Kirschner	Jak-1	(126.)	16.00
	5./JG 3	Lt. Hartwig Dohse	Jak-1	(6.)	16.01
	5./JG 3	Oblt. Joachim Kirschner	Il-2	(127.)	16.08
	5./JG 3	Oblt. Joachim Kirschner	Spitfire	(128.)	16.13
	5./JG 3	Fw. Rudolf Traphan	1	(9.)	16.35
	6./JG 3	Uffz. Franz Cech	R-5	(19.)	17.35

	6./JG 3	Uffz. Franz Cech	R-5	(20.)	17.36
11.05.43	6./JG 3	Fw. Waldemar Eyrich	1	(21.)	06.25
	Stab II./JG 3	Lt. Franz Ruhl	Jak-1	(13.)	06.30
	Stab II./JG 3	Maj. Kurt Brändle	1	(143.)	11.56
	5./JG 3	Fw. Josef Schütte	1	(33.)	14.40
	6./JG 3	Uffz. Gerhard Thyben	LaGG-3	(5.)	16.23
	4./JG 3	Lt. Wolf Ettel	LaGG-3	(119.)	16.35
	4./JG 3	Lt. Wolf Ettel	LaGG-3	(120.)	16.37
	4./JG 3	Uffz. Martin Fedgenhäuer	LaGG-3	(7.)	
	5./JG 3	Uffz. Horst Lüdtke	1	(10.)	17.13
	5./JG 3	Uffz. Heinz Dahms	1	(2.)	17.13
12.05.43	5./JG 3	Uffz. Rudolf Scheibe	1	(3.)	05.30
13.05.43	5./JG 3	Uffz. Arnold Bringmann	1	(18.)	17.21
	5./JG 3	Uffz. Horst Lüdtke	1	(11.)	17.22
	5./JG 3	Uffz. Horst Lüdtke	1	(12.)	17.24
	5./JG 3	Uffz. Heinz Dahms	1	(3.)	17.24
14.05.43	6./JG 3	Uffz. Gerhard Thyben	Jak-1	(6.)	12.15
	6./JG 3	Fw. Rasso Förg	1	(16.)	12.32
	5./JG 3	Lt. Walter Bohatsch	1	(3.)	13.35
	5./JG 3	Fw. Rudolf Traphan	P-39	(10.)	16.44
	5./JG 3	Oblt. Joachim Kirschner	P-39	(129.)	16.45
15.05.43	5./JG 3	Uffz. Horst Lüdtke	La-5	(13.)	11.15
17.05.43	6./JG 3	Oblt. Gustav Frielinghaus	LaGG-3	(64.)	11.16
	6./JG 3	Lt. Friedrich-Wilhelm Schmidt	LaGG-3	(5.)	11.17
	6./JG 3	Oblt. Gustav Frielinghaus	LaGG-3	(65.)	11.18
	6./JG 3	Oblt. Gustav Frielinghaus	LaGG-3	(66.)	11.21
18.05.43	6./JG 3	Fw. Waldemar Eyrich	Il-2	(22.)	15.43
20.05.43	5./JG 3	Oblt. Joachim Kirschner	LaGG-3	(130.)	13.20
21.05.43	5./JG 3	Fw. Werner Kloß	I-16	(8.)	
22.05.43	6./JG 3	Uffz. Franz Cech	LaGG-3	(21.)	06.20
	6./JG 3	Oblt. Paul Stolte	1	(11.)	15.03
23.05.43	5./JG 3	Fw. Josef Schütte	1	(34.)	06.35
	6./JG 3	Lt. Karl-Ludwig Seewald	LaGG-3	(8.)	06.40
	4./JG 3	Lt. Hermann Schuster	La-5	(7.)	06.51
	5./JG 3	Lt. Hartwig Dohse	La-5	(7.)	06.51
	5./JG 3	Oblt. Joachim Kirschner	La-5	(131.)	06.53
	5./JG 3	Oblt. Joachim Kirschner	La-5	(132.)	06.55
	5./JG 3	Fw. Hans Grünberg	La-5	(29.)	06.57
	6./JG 3	Lt. Ernst-Heinz Löhr	La-5	(15.)	06.59
	5./JG 3	Uffz. Horst Lüdtke	Jak-1	(14.)	07.03
24.05.43	4./JG 3	Lt. Leopold Münster	1	(69.)	04.10
29.05.43	6./JG 3	Lt. Karl-Ludwig Seewald	LaGG-3	(9.)	04.30
30.05.43	6./JG 3	Oblt. Gerd Schaedle	La-5	(4.)	04.30
	5./JG 3	Uffz. Horst Lüdtke	1	(15.)	06.22
31.05.43	Stab II./JG 3	Maj. Kurt Brändle	1	(144.)	06.22
	5./JG 3	Fw. Hans Grünberg	Jak-4	(30.)	06.41
01.06.43	4./JG 3	Lt. Leopold Münster	LaGG-3	(70.)	05.04
	5./JG 3	Oblt. Joachim Kirschner	LaGG-3	(133.)	05.04
	6./JG 3	Uffz. Gerhard Thyben	LaGG-3	(7.)	05.04
	6./JG 3	Lt. Horst Brock	LaGG-3	(2.)	05.05
	5./JG 3	Lt. Hartwig Dohse	1	(8.)	05.10
02.06.43	5./JG 3	Oblt. Joachim Kirschner	1	(134.)	05.22
	5./JG 3	Oblt. Joachim Kirschner	1	(135.)	05.34
	6./JG 3	Oblt. Paul Stolte	1	(12.)	05.35
	6./JG 3	Oblt. Paul Stolte	1	(13.)	05.40
	6./JG 3	Fw. Waldemar Eyrich	1	(23.)	05.42
	4./JG 3	Fw. Hans Frese	La-5	(16.)	10.28
	5./JG 3	Oblt. Joachim Kirschner	1	(136.)	10.40
	6./JG 3	Oblt. Gerd Schaedle	La-5	(5.)	10.42
	5./JG 3	Oblt. Joachim Kirschner	1	(137.)	10.46
	5./JG 3	Fw. Horst Lüdtke	1	(16.)	11.00
	6./JG 3	Obfw. Robert Roller	1	(1.)	11.26
	6./JG 3	Uffz. Alfred Fischer	1	(10.)	13.45
	6./JG 3	Fw. Uwe Michaels	1	(3.)	13.49
	5./JG 3	Uffz. Arnold Bringmann	1	(19.)	17.50
	5./JG 3	Fw. Werner Kloß	1	(9.)	17.53
03.06.43	6./JG 3	Uffz. Gerhard Thyben	La-5	(8.)	03.15
	4./JG 3	Fw. Hans Frese	LaGG-3	(17.)	03.20
	6./JG 3	Uffz. Gerhard Thyben	Jak-1	(9.)	03.22
	6./JG 3	Uffz. Franz Cech	La-5	(22.)	03.23
	6./JG 3	Uffz. Herbert Dehrmann	La-5	(10.)	03.25
	6./JG 3	Uffz. Franz Cech	La-5	(23.)	03.28

	4./JG 3	Lt. Leopold Münster	La-5	(71.)	03.31
	6./JG 3	Uffz. Franz Cech	Jak-1	(24.)	03.35
	6./JG 3	Oblt. Gerd Schaedle	La-5	(6.)	03.36
	6./JG 3	Oblt. Paul Stolte	Jak-1	(14.)	03.37
	6./JG 3	Oblt. Gerd Schaedle	Jak-1	(7.)	03.38
	6./JG 3	Fw. Waldemar Eyrich	La-5	(24.)	03.38
	6./JG 3	Oblt. Paul Stolte	La-5	(15.)	03.38
	6./JG 3	Lt. Friedrich-Wilhelm Schmidt	La-5	(6.)	03.39
04.06.43	5./JG 3	Fw. Horst Lüdtke	La-5	(17.)	17.23
	5./JG 3	Lt. Hartwig Dohse	La-5	(9.)	17.35
	5./JG 3	Fw. Horst Lüdtke	La-5	(18.)	17.36
	5./JG 3	Fw. Hans Grünberg	Jak-1	(31.)	17.50
	5./JG 3	Fw. Werner Kloß	Jak-1	(10.)	17.52
05.06.43	6./JG 3	Fw. Waldemar Eyrich	1	(25.)	14.22
	6./JG 3	Uffz. Franz Cech	La-5	(25.)	18.15
06.06.43	4./JG 3	Lt. Leopold Münster	1	(72.)	17.15
	4./JG 3	Uffz. Martin Fedgenhäuer	1	(8.)	17.20
08.06.43	5./JG 3	Fw. Werner Kloß	1	(11.)	05.18
	5./JG 3	Fw. Werner Kloß	1	(12.)	05.20
	5./JG 3	Oblt. Joachim Kirschner	1	(138.)	05.22
	4./JG 3	Oblt. Werner Lucas	LaGG-3	(83.)	11.12
	5./JG 3	Fw. Josef Schütte	La-5	(35.)	11.14
	Stab II./JG 3	Lt. Franz Ruhl	Jak-1	(14.)	11.15
	5./JG 3	Uffz. Arnold Bringmann	La-5	(20.)	11.17
	Stab II./JG 3	Lt. Franz Ruhl	La-5	(15.)	11.20
	4./JG 3	Oblt. Werner Lucas	La-5	(84.)	11.22
	5./JG 3	Fw. Hans Grünberg	Jak-1	(32.)	18.20
	4./JG 3	Lt. Hermann Schuster	Jak-1	(8.)	18.25
09.06.43	5./JG 3	Fw. Rudolf Traphan	1	(11.)	11.00
	4./JG 3	Lt. Leopold Münster	1	(73.)	16.19
	4./JG 3	Lt. Leopold Münster	1	(74.)	16.22
10.06.43	6./JG 3	Oblt. Gerd Schaedle	La-5	(8.)	03.18
	4./JG 3	Lt. Hermann Schuster	Il-2	(9.)	03.20
	5./JG 3	Lt. Hartwig Dohse	Il-2	(10.)	03.20
	6./JG 3	Lt. Friedrich-Wilhelm Schmidt	La-5	(7.)	03.23
	6./JG 3	Fw. Waldemar Eyrich	La-5	(26.)	03.25
	5./JG 3	Fw. Hans Grünberg	Jak-1	(33.)	05.25
12.06.43	6./JG 3	Uffz. Gerhard Thyben	La-5	(10.)	03.39
	6./JG 3	Uffz. Gerhard Thyben	La-5	(11.)	07.15
14.06.43	5./JG 3	Oblt. Joachim Kirschner	1	(139.)	03.36
	5./JG 3	Oblt. Joachim Kirschner	1	(140.)	05.25
	5./JG 3	Oblt. Joachim Kirschner	1	(141.)	05.31
15.06.43	4./JG 3	Fw. Hans Frese	La-5	(18.)	03.28
16.06.43	4./JG 3	Oblt. Werner Lucas	Jak-1	(85.)	03.35
	4./JG 3	Lt. Leopold Münster	Jak-1	(75.)	03.35
	5./JG 3	Fw. Hans Grünberg	Il-2	(34.)	03.54
	5./JG 3	Oblt. Joachim Kirschner	Il-2	(142.)	03.55
	6./JG 3	Lt. Ernst-Heinz Löhr	Il-2	(16.)	15.26
	6./JG 3	Obfw. Robert Roller	Il-2	(2.)	15.27
	4./JG 3	Lt. Hermann Schuster	1	(10.)	17.02
	4./JG 3	Fw. Hans Frese	Jak-1	(19.)	18.24
17.06.43	6./JG 3	Oblt. Paul Stolte	Jak-1	(16.)	05.17
19.06.43	Stab II./JG 3	Maj. Kurt Brändle	1	(145.)	08.55
	6./JG 3	Uffz. Franz Cech	Jak-1	(26.)	11.03
	5./JG 3	Fw. Hans Grünberg	La-5	(35.)	13.41
	4./JG 3	Oblt. Werner Lucas	Pe-2	(86.)	15.57
	4./JG 3	Lt. Hermann Schuster	1	(11.)	19.20
20.06.43	Stab II./JG 3	Maj. Kurt Brändle	1	(146.)	09.57
	5./JG 3	Lt. Hartwig Dohse	1	(11.)	15.19
21.06.43	6./JG 3	Uffz. Franz Cech	La-5	(27.)	09.58
	6./JG 3	Uffz. Franz Cech	La-5	(28.)	10.03
	4./JG 3	Oblt. Werner Lucas	Il-2	(87.)	14.32
	Stab II./JG 3	Lt. Franz Ruhl	Jak-1	(16.)	14.45
	6./JG 3	Oblt. Paul Stolte	La-5	(17.)	18.35
	6./JG 3	Uffz. Franz Cech	Jak-1	(29.)	18.40
	5./JG 3	Oblt. Joachim Kirschner	1	(143.)	18.46
23.06.43	6./JG 3	Uffz. Gerhard Thyben	Jak-4	(12.)	06.16
	4./JG 3	Lt. Leopold Münster	1	(76.)	17.25
	5./JG 3	Fw. Werner Kloß	1	(13.)	17.35
	5./JG 3	Fw. Rudolf Traphan	1	(12.)	17.37
	4./JG 3	Lt. Hans Reiser	1	(3.)	17.45
	Stab II./JG 3	Lt. Franz Ruhl	Jak-1	(17.)	17.50
	4./JG 3	Lt. Hermann Schuster	Jak-1	(12.)	17.51

24.06.43	6./JG 3	Uffz. Gerhard Thyben	Jak-1	(13.)	05.25
	6./JG 3	Uffz. Franz Cech	Jak-1	(30.)	14.30
	5./JG 3	Oblt. Joachim Kirschner	1	(144.)	17.45
	6./JG 3	Lt. Ernst-Heinz Löhr	1	(17.)	17.53
	6./JG 3	Uffz. Gerhard Thyben	La-5	(14.)	18.05
25.06.43	6./JG 3	Uffz. Franz Cech	Jak-1	(31.)	06.25
26.06.43	5./JG 3	Uffz. Hugo Lucks	Jak-1	(1.)	04.55
	6./JG 3	Uffz. Gerhard Thyben	La-5	(15.)	19.28
	6./JG 3	Uffz. Walter Stienhans	La-5	(1.)	19.34
	6./JG 3	Uffz. Gerhard Thyben	La-5	(16.)	19.43
28.06.43	5./JG 3	Oblt. Joachim Kirschner	1	(145.)	09.53
	5./JG 3	Oblt. Joachim Kirschner	1	(146.)	09.57
	5./JG 3	Fw. Werner Kloß	1	(14.)	10.00
29.06.43	6./JG 3	Uffz. Franz Cech	Jak-1	(32.)	11.28
30.06.43	6./JG 3	Oblt. Paul Stolte	1	(18.)	15.29
	6./JG 3	Fw. Waldemar Eyrich	1	(27.)	15.45
	5./JG 3	Fw. Werner Kloß	1	(15.)	17.26
	5./JG 3	Fw. Hans Grünberg	Il-2	(36.)	17.34
02.07.43	6./JG 3	Uffz. Gerhard Thyben	Boston	(17.)	07.46
	5./JG 3	Uffz. Günther Mohn	La-5	(8.)	
	5./JG 3	Uffz. Günther Mohn	Il-2	(9.)	
03.07.43	6./JG 3	Lt. Ernst-Heinz Löhr	1	(18.)	09.18
	4./JG 3	Lt. Hermann Schuster	1	(13.)	16.36
	5./JG 3	Oblt. Joachim Kirschner	La-5	(147.)	16.47
	5./JG 3	Oblt. Joachim Kirschner	La-5	(148.)	16.52
04.07.43	6./JG 3	Lt. Friedrich-Wilhelm Schmidt	1	(8.)	15.30
	4./JG 3	Fw. Hans Frese	Jak-1	(20.)	15.35
	4./JG 3	Lt. Hermann Schuster	Jak-1	(14.)	15.36
05.07.43	4./JG 3	Oblt. Werner Lucas	Jak-1	(88.)	03.25
	4./JG 3	Uffz. Martin Fedgenhäuer	Jak-1	(9.)	03.25
	5./JG 3	Fw. Hans Grünberg	Il-2	(37.)	03.30
	5./JG 3	Oblt. Joachim Kirschner	Il-2	(149.)	03.30
	5./JG 3	Fw. Josef Schütte	Il-2	(36.)	03.31
	4./JG 3	Fw. Hans Frese	Il-2	(21.)	03.33
	4./JG 3	Lt. Hans Reiser	Il-2	(4.)	03.33
	4./JG 3	Lt. Hermann Schuster	Il-2	(15.)	03.34
	4./JG 3	Lt. Hans Reiser	Il-2	(5.)	03.35
	5./JG 3	Oblt. Joachim Kirschner	Il-2	(150.)	03.35
	4./JG 3	Lt. Hermann Schuster	La-5	(16.)	03.36
	5./JG 3	Fw. Hans Grünberg	Il-2	(38.)	03.37
	5./JG 3	Fw. Josef Schütte	Jak-1	(37.)	03.40
	5./JG 3	Oblt. Joachim Kirschner	Jak-1	(151.)	03.41
	5./JG 3	Fw. Josef Schütte	Il-2	(38.)	03.44
	5./JG 3	Lt. Walter Bohatsch	Il-2	(4.)	03.45
	5./JG 3	Uffz. Arnold Bringmann	MiG-1	(21.)	03.46
	5./JG 3	Uffz. Arnold Bringmann	Il-2	(22.)	03.47
	5./JG 3	Fw. Josef Schütte	Il-2	(39.)	03.48
	Stab II./JG 3	Obfhr. Botho Kaatz	Il-2	(1.)	03.50
	5./JG 3	Fw. Hans Grünberg	Il-2	(39.)	03.52
	Stab II./JG 3	Maj. Kurt Brändle	Il-2	(147.)	03.55
	Stab II./JG 3	Maj. Kurt Brändle	Il-2	(148.)	03.57
	5./JG 3	Fw. Josef Schütte	Il-2	(40.)	04.02
	5./JG 3	Fw. Hans Grünberg	Il-2	(40.)	04.05
	4./JG 3	Oblt. Werner Lucas	Il-2	(89.)	04.05
	5./JG 3	Lt. Hartwig Dohse	Jak-1	(12.)	04.06
	Stab II./JG 3	Maj. Kurt Brändle	Jak-1	(149.)	04.07
	5./JG 3	Fw. Werner Kloß	Il-2	(16.)	04.08
	5./JG 3	Fw. Werner Kloß	Il-2	(17.)	04.42
	6./JG 3	Hptm. Paul Stolte	1	(19.)	07.30
	6./JG 3	Lt. Ernst-Heinz Löhr	1	(19.)	07.35
	6./JG 3	Fw. Waldemar Eyrich	1	(28.)	07.45
	4./JG 3	Oblt. Werner Lucas	Pe-2	(90.)	09.15
	4./JG 3	Oblt. Werner Lucas	Il-2	(91.)	09.30
	4./JG 3	Uffz. Helmut Liebmann	Il-2	(1.)	09.33
	5./JG 3	Oblt. Joachim Kirschner	Il-2	(152.)	09.57
	Stab II./JG 3	Obfhr. Botho Kaatz	Il-2	(2.)	10.20
	Stab II./JG 3	Maj. Kurt Brändle	Il-2	(150.)	10.22
	Stab II./JG 3	Maj. Kurt Brändle	Il-2	(151.)	10.24
	5./JG 3	Uffz. Paul Draeger	Il-2	(1.)	10.30
	6./JG 3	Fw. Waldemar Eyrich	Pe-2	(29.)	12.45
	4./JG 3	Lt. Hermann Schuster	Pe-2	(17.)	12.45
	4./JG 3	Fw. Hans Frese	Pe-2	(22.)	12.50
	4./JG 3	Fw. Hans Frese	Pe-2	(23.)	12.52
	4./JG 3	Uffz. Thomas Ametsbichler	Pe-2	(2.)	12.52
	6./JG 3	Lt. Ernst-Heinz Löhr	Pe-2	(20.)	12.52
	6./JG 3	Obfw. Robert Roller	Pe-2	(3.)	12.53
	6./JG 3	Hptm. Paul Stolte	Pe-2	(20.)	12.53
	4./JG 3	Uffz. Eduard Bartsch	Pe-2	(1.)	12.53
	4./JG 3	Fw. Hans Frese	Pe-2	(24.)	12.54
	5./JG 3	Fw. Hans Grünberg	Il-2	(41.)	14.05
	5./JG 3	Oblt. Joachim Kirschner	Il-2	(153.)	14.15

	4./JG 3	Lt. Fridolin Reinartz	1	(1.)	14.29
	6./JG 3	Uffz. Walter Stienhans	Il-2	(2.)	16.18
	6./JG 3	Fw. Werner Dehrmann	Il-2	(11.)	16.19
	6./JG 3	Uffz. Walter Stienhans	Il-2	(3.)	16.20
	6./JG 3	Fw. Werner Dehrmann	Il-2	(12.)	16.22
	6./JG 3	Fw. Waldemar Eyrich	1	(30.)	17.00
	6./JG 3	Hptm. Paul Stolte	1	(21.)	17.25
	6./JG 3	Uffz. Uwe Michaels	1	(4.)	17.40
	4./JG 3	Lt. Hermann Schuster	Il-2	(18.)	18.03
	4./JG 3	Oblt. Werner Lucas	Il-2	(92.)	18.05
	5./JG 3	Lt. Hartwig Dohse	Il-2	(13.)	18.06
	5./JG 3	Oblt. Joachim Kirschner	Il-2	(154.)	18.10
	5./JG 3	Oblt. Joachim Kirschner	Il-2	(155.)	18.17
	5./JG 3	Oblt. Joachim Kirschner	Il-2	(156.)	18.24
	4./JG 3	Lt. Hermann Schuster	Il-2	(19.)	18.28
	4./JG 3	Lt. Fridolin Reinartz	Il-2	(2.)	18.28
	5./JG 3	Oblt. Joachim Kirschner	Il-2	(157.)	18.32
	4./JG 3	Uffz. Helmuth Schirra	Il-2	(1.)	18.33
	4./JG 3	Uffz. Helmuth Schirra	Il-2	(2.)	18.36
	5./JG 3	Fw. Hans Grünberg	Il-2	(42.)	18.50
	5./JG 3	Fw. Hans Grünberg	Il-2	(43.)	18.55
	5./JG 3	Uffz. Arnold Bringmann	1	(23.)	
	Stab II./JG 3	Lt. Max-Bruno Fischer	Il-2	(5.)	
	4./JG 3	Lt. Hans Rachner	1	(1.)	
06.07.43	6./JG 3	Lt. Ernst-Heinz Löhr	Jak-1	(21.)	09.18
	6./JG 3	Lt. Ernst-Heinz Löhr	La-5	(22.)	09.24
	6./JG 3	Hptm. Paul Stolte	1	(22.)	10.07
	5./JG 3	Lt. Hartwig Dohse	Il-2	(14.)	11.00
	4./JG 3	Uffz. Helmuth Schirra	Il-2	(3.)	11.04
	4./JG 3	Lt. Hermann Schuster	Il-2	(20.)	11.05
	5./JG 3	Uffz. Arnold Bringmann	1	(24.)	12.21
	6./JG 3	Uffz. Gerhard Thyben	La-5	(18.)	12.30
	Stab II./JG 3	Maj. Kurt Brändle	Il-2	(152.)	14.04
	Stab II./JG 3	Maj. Kurt Brändle	Il-2	(153.)	14.07
	4./JG 3	Fw. Hans Frese	Il-2	(25.)	14.08
	4./JG 3	Lt. Hans Reiser	1	(6.)	15.10
	5./JG 3	Fw. Hans Grünberg	Il-2	(44.)	15.10
	6./JG 3	Obfw. Robert Roller	Jak-1	(4.)	16.26
	4./JG 3	Lt. Hermann Schuster	Jak-1	(21.)	16.26
	4./JG 3	Oblt. Werner Lucas	Il-2	(93.)	17.13
	5./JG 3	Uffz. Arnold Bringmann	1	(25.)	17.31
	5./JG 3	Oblt. Joachim Kirschner	La-5	(158.)	17.43
	5./JG 3	Oblt. Joachim Kirschner	La-5	(159.)	17.46
	5./JG 3	Oblt. Joachim Kirschner	Boston	(160.)	17.50
	6./JG 3	Obfw. Robert Roller	1	(5.)	19.02
07.07.43	5./JG 3	Fw. Hans Grünberg	Il-2	(45.)	03.42
	5./JG 3	Oblt. Joachim Kirschner	Il-2	(161.)	03.44
	5./JG 3	Fw. Hans Grünberg	Il-2	(46.)	03.45
	5./JG 3	Oblt. Joachim Kirschner	Il-2	(162.)	03.46
	5./JG 3	Lt. Walter Bohatsch	Il-2	(5.)	03.50
	5./JG 3	Lt. Hartwig Dohse	1	(15.)	04.02
	4./JG 3	Oblt. Werner Lucas	Il-2	(94.)	04.30
	4./JG 3	Oblt. Werner Lucas	Il-2	(95.)	04.34
	4./JG 3	Lt. Hermann Schuster	1	(22.)	04.38
	4./JG 3	Uffz. Helmuth Schirra	1	(4.)	04.30
	6./JG 3	Hptm. Paul Stolte	1	(23.)	05.20
	Stab II./JG 3	Maj. Kurt Brändle	1	(154.)	07.33
	Stab II./JG 3	Maj. Kurt Brändle	1	(155.)	07.55
	6./JG 3	Uffz. Gerhard Thyben	Jak-1	(19.)	07.55
	Stab II./JG 3	Maj. Kurt Brändle	1	(156.)	08.03
	6./JG 3	Uffz. Gerhard Thyben	La-5	(20.)	08.10
	6./JG 3	Hptm. Paul Stolte	1	(24.)	10.20
	5./JG 3	Lt. Hartwig Dohse	1	(16.)	12.26
	4./JG 3	Fw. Hans Frese	Boston	(26.)	15.08
	6./JG 3	Uffz. Gerhard Thyben	La-5	(21.)	17.02
	6./JG 3	Uffz. Gerhard Thyben	La-5	(22.)	17.14
	5./JG 3	Uffz. Hugo Lucks	Il-2	(2.)	17.34
	5./JG 3	Uffz. Arnold Bringmann	1	(26.)	17.35
	6./JG 3	Lt. Ernst-Heinz Löhr	1	(23.)	18.30
	6./JG 3	Lt. Ernst-Heinz Löhr	1	(24.)	19.00
	5./JG 3	Fw. Hans Grünberg	La-5	(47.)	19.43
	5./JG 3	Uffz. Arnold Bringmann	1	(27.)	19.46
08.07.43	5./JG 3	Uffz. Paul Draeger	1	(2.)	04.09
	6./JG 3	Hptm. Paul Stolte	1	(25.)	07.48
	4./JG 3	Lt. Hermann Schuster	1	(23.)	09.48
	4./JG 3	Fw. Hans Frese	Il-2	(27.)	10.38
	5./JG 3	Oblt. Joachim Kirschner	Pe-2	(163.)	13.41
	5./JG 3	Uffz. Günther Mohn	Pe-2	(10.)	13.44
	5./JG 3	Lt. Hartwig Dohse	1	(17.)	17.31
	5./JG 3	Uffz. Arnold Bringmann	1	(28.)	17.32
	5./JG 3	Uffz. Rudolf Scheibe	Jak-1	(4.)	17.40
	6./JG 3	Uffz. Walter Stienhans	1	(4.)	18.38
09.07.43	6./JG 3	Hptm. Paul Stolte	1	(26.)	06.10
	5./JG 3	Fw. Hans Grünberg	La-5	(48.)	06.18
	6./JG 3	Uffz. Gerhard Thyben	La-5	(23.)	06.20
	6./JG 3	Uffz. Gerhard Thyben	La-5	(24.)	06.35

	6./JG 3	Hptm. Paul Stolte	1	(27.)	06.35
	4./JG 3	Lt. Hermann Schuster	1	(24.)	09.11
	4./JG 3	Lt. Hermann Schuster	1	(25.)	12.52
	4./JG 3	Lt. Hans Reiser	1	(7.)	12.56
	6./JG 3	Lt. Ernst-Heinz Löhr	1	(25.)	15.52
10.07.43	4./JG 3	Lt. Hermann Schuster	1	(26.)	17.12
	5./JG 3	Oblt. Joachim Kirschner	1	(164.)	17.12
	5./JG 3	Uffz. Arnold Bringmann	1	(29.)	17.16
11.07.43	5./JG 3	Oblt. Joachim Kirschner	1	(165.)	09.40
	6./JG 3	Hptm. Paul Stolte	La-5	(28.)	10.01
	6./JG 3	Hptm. Paul Stolte	Jak-1	(29.)	10.03
	6./JG 3	Lt. Ernst-Heinz Löhr	La-5	(26.)	10.05
	6./JG 3	Hptm. Paul Stolte	Jak-1	(30.)	10.09
	5./JG 3	Lt. Hartwig Dohse	1	(18.)	11.26
	6./JG 3	Obfw. Robert Roller	1	(6.)	13.18
	5./JG 3	Fw. Hans Grünberg	Pe-2	(49.)	16.32
	6./JG 3	Obfw. Robert Roller	1	(7.)	16.55
12.07.43	5./JG 3	Fw. Hans Grünberg	La-5	(50.)	05.30
	6./JG 3	Lt. Ernst-Heinz Löhr	1	(27.)	15.45
	6./JG 3	Lt. Ernst-Heinz Löhr	1	(28.)	15.46
	6./JG 3	Lt. Ernst-Heinz Löhr	1	(29.)	15.47
	6./JG 3	Uffz. Walter Stienhans	1	(5.)	15.48
	5./JG 3	Uffz. Günther Mohn	Il-2	(11.)	16.50
	5./JG 3	Uffz. Günther Mohn	Il-2	(12.)	16.58
	4./JG 3	Lt. Hermann Schuster	Il-2	(27.)	17.00
13.07.43	6./JG 3	Uffz. Gerhard Thyben	La-5	(25.)	05.56
	6./JG 3	Uffz. Gerhard Thyben	P-40	(26.)	06.02
	4./JG 3	Fw. Hans Frese	Il-2	(28.)	14.12
	4./JG 3	Uffz. Helmuth Schirra	Il-2	(5.)	14.13
14.07.43	5./JG 3	Fw. Hans Grünberg	Il-2	(51.)	04.56
	5./JG 3	Fw. Hans Grünberg	Il-2	(52.)	04.57
	5./JG 3	Lt. Walter Bohatsch	Il-2	(6.)	04.57
	6./JG 3	Hptm. Paul Stolte	Jak-1	(31.)	06.45
	4./JG 3	Lt. Hermann Schuster	Jak-1	(28.)	06.46
	6./JG 3	Uffz. Gerhard Thyben	Jak-1	(27.)	06.47
	4./JG 3	Fw. Hans Frese	Jak-1	(29.)	07.14
	Stab II./JG 3	Maj. Kurt Brändle	1	(157.)	08.35
	6./JG 3	Hptm. Paul Stolte	1	(32.)	08.38
	Stab II./JG 3	Maj. Kurt Brändle	1	(158.)	08.41
	5./JG 3	Lt. Hartwig Dohse	1	(19.)	18.45
	4./JG 3	Uffz. Helmuth Schirra	1	(6.)	18.47
	4./JG 3	Uffz. Helmuth Schirra	1	(7.)	18.48
15.07.43	4./JG 3	Oblt. Werner Lucas	Il-2	(96.)	14.45
	4./JG 3	Oblt. Werner Lucas	Il-2	(97.)	14.50
	4./JG 3	Fw. Hans Frese	Jak-1	(30.)	15.22
	5./JG 3	Fw. Hans Grünberg	Il-7	(53.)	18.50
16.07.43	5./JG 3	Oblt. Joachim Kirschner	La-5	(166.)	05.33
	5./JG 3	Uffz. Günther Mohn	La-5	(13.)	05.34
	5./JG 3	Oblt. Joachim Kirschner	La-5	(167.)	05.35
	5./JG 3	Fw. Hans Grünberg	Jak-1	(54.)	06.15
	4./JG 3	Fw. Hans Frese	Jak-1	(31.)	06.49
	5./JG 3	Lt. Hartwig Dohse	1	(20.)	06.50
	5./JG 3	Fw. Hans Grünberg	Jak-1	(55.)	08.50
	Stab II./JG 3	Maj. Kurt Brändle	1	(159.)	11.40
	4./JG 3	Fw. Hans Frese	Pe-2	(32.)	12.37
	5./JG 3	Uffz. Paul Draeger	Il-2	(3.)	16.08
	4./JG 3	Uffz. Helmuth Schirra	1	(8.)	17.59
17.07.43	5./JG 3	Uffz. Arnold Bringmann	1	(30.)	05.50
	Stab II./JG 3	Maj. Kurt Brändle	1	(160.)	08.13
	Stab II./JG 3	Maj. Kurt Brändle	1	(161.)	14.16
18.07.43	5./JG 3	Lt. Hartwig Dohse	1	(21.)	04.35
19.07.43	4./JG 3	Lt. Hermann Schuster	1	(29.)	11.59
	4./JG 3	Lt. Hermann Schuster	1	(30.)	12.01
	4./JG 3	Oblt. Werner Lucas	Il-2	(98.)	12.20
	4./JG 3	Fw. Hans Frese	LaGG-3	(33.)	15.44
	4./JG 3	Oblt. Werner Lucas	Il-2	(99.)	18.20
20.07.43	6./JG 3	Uffz. Gerhard Thyben	Jak-1	(28.)	04.36
	6./JG 3	Hptm. Paul Stolte	1	(33.)	10.03
	4./JG 3	Lt. Hermann Schuster	1	(31.)	10.05
	6./JG 3	Hptm. Paul Stolte	1	(34.)	10.07
	6./JG 3	Uffz. Gerhard Thyben	Jak-1	(29.)	15.50
	4./JG 3	Lt. Hermann Schuster	1	(32.)	18.34
21.07.43	4./JG 3	Fw. Hans Frese	Pe-2	(34.)	04.34
	4./JG 3	Fw. Hans Frese	Pe-2	(35.)	04.36
	4./JG 3	Oblt. Werner Lucas	Il-2	(100.)	08.05
	6./JG 3	Lt. Ernst-Heinz Löhr	1	(30.)	08.54
	Stab II./JG 3	Maj. Kurt Brändle	1	(162.)	10.12
	Stab II./JG 3	Maj. Kurt Brändle	1	(163.)	10.14

	4./JG 3	Oblt. Werner Lucas	Jak-1	(101.)	14.10
22.07.43	4./JG 3	Oblt. Werner Lucas	Il-2	(102.)	04.13
	5./JG 3	Oblt. Joachim Kirschner	Il-2	(168.)	04.15
	5./JG 3	Lt. Hartwig Dohse	Il-2	(22.)	04.22
	Stab II./JG 3	Maj. Kurt Brändle	Il-2	(164.)	04.26
	6./JG 3	Lt. Ernst-Heinz Löhr	1	(31.)	05.48
	6./JG 3	Oblt. Ernst-Heinz Löhr	1	(32.)	05.55
	4./JG 3	Fw. Hans Frese	LaGG-3	(36.)	09.35
	Stab II./JG 3	Maj. Kurt Brändle	Il-2	(165.)	10.44
	Stab II./JG 3	Maj. Kurt Brändle	Il-2	(166.)	10.55
	4./JG 3	Fw. Hans Frese	LaGG-3	(37.)	17.49
23.07.43	5./JG 3	Lt. Hartwig Dohse	Jak-1	(23.)	08.50
	Stab II./JG 3	Maj. Kurt Brändle	Il-2	(167.)	09.33
	Stab II./JG 3	Obfhr. Botho Kaatz	Il-2	(3.)	09.33
	Stab II./JG 3	Maj. Kurt Brändle	Il-2	(168.)	09.35
	Stab II./JG 3	Obfhr. Botho Katz	Il-2	(4.)	09.37
	5./JG 3	Fw. Hans Grünberg	Il-7	(56.)	12.30
24.07.43	6./JG 3	Uffz. Gerhard Thyben	Jak-1	(30.)	04.42
	6./JG 3	Oblt. Ernst-Heinz Löhr	Il-2	(33.)	15.05
	6./JG 3	Uffz. Walter Stienhans	Il-2	(6.)	15.15
	4./JG 3	Uffz. Eduard Bartsch	Il-2	(2.)	18.31
	4./JG 3	Fw. Hans Frese	Il-2	(38.)	18.32
25.07.43	6./JG 3	Hptm. Paul Stolte	1	(35.)	07.07
	6./JG 3	Hptm. Paul Stolte	1	(36.)	07.08
	6./JG 3	Uffz. Walter Stienhans	1	(7.)	07.10
	6./JG 3	Uffz. Gerhard Thyben	Jak-1	(31.)	18.24
26.07.43	5./JG 3	Oblt. Joachim Kirschner	1	(169.)	16.55
27.07.43	5./JG 3	Oblt. Joachim Kirschner	1	(170.)	15.47
	6./JG 3	Obfw. Robert Roller	1	(8.)	16.07
	Stab II./JG 3	Maj. Kurt Brändle	1	(169.)	18.15
28.07.43	6./JG 3	Hptm. Paul Stolte	1	(37.)	16.17
	4./JG 3	Lt. Franz Ruhl	Jak-1	(18.)	16.30
30.07.43	Stab II./JG 3	Maj. Kurt Brändle	Il-2	(170.)	12.22
	6./JG 3	Uffz. Gerhard Thyben	Jak-1	(32.)	12.43
	6./JG 3	Hptm. Paul Stolte	1	(38.)	15.37
	5./JG 3	Uffz. Paul Draeger	1	(4.)	16.12
	4./JG 3	Oblt. Werner Lucas	Il-2	(103.)	17.12
31.07.43	4./JG 3	Fw. Hans Frese	Jak-1	(39.)	04.46
	4./JG 3	Uffz. Eduard Bartsch	Il-2	(3.)	05.35
	4./JG 3	Lt. Franz Ruhl	La-5	(19.)	05.37
	5./JG 3	Fw. Hans Grünberg	Il-2	(57.)	05.39
	4./JG 3	Lt. Franz Ruhl	Jak-1	(20.)	05.43
	5./JG 3	Fw. Hans Grünberg	Il-2	(58.)	05.56
	6./JG 3	Hptm. Paul Stolte	Il-2	(39.)	10.57
	4./JG 3	Lt. Fridolin Reinartz	Il-2	(3.)	10.59
	4./JG 3	Oblt. Werner Lucas	Il-2	(104.)	11.00
	6./JG 3	Hptm. Paul Stolte	Il-2	(40.)	11.01
	4./JG 3	Oblt. Werner Lucas	Il-2	(105.)	11.13
	5./JG 3	Uffz. Hugo Lucks	Il-7	(3.)	11.15
	5./JG 3	Fw. Hans Grünberg	Jak-1	(59.)	11.21
	5./JG 3	Fw. Hans Grünberg	Il-2	(60.)	11.26
	4./JG 3	Lt. Fridolin Reinartz	1	(4.)	15.38
	4./JG 3	Fw. Hans Frese	Il-2	(40.)	15.45
	4./JG 3	Fw. Hans Frese	Jak-1	(41.)	18.20
01.08.43	5./JG 3	Fw. Hans Grünberg	Il-2	(61.)	18.53

Victories by II/JG 3 during Operations in the Defense of the Reich
12 September 1943 to 6 June 1944

16.09.43	4./JG 3	Lt. Franz Ruhl	Beaufighter	(21.)	19.02
	4./JG 3	FhjFw. Hans Frese	Beaufighter	(42.)	19.04
22.09.43	4./JG 3	Uffz. Karl-Heinz Koch	P-47	(1.)	
24.09.43	5./JG 3	Hptm. Joachim Kirschner	B-17	(171.)	17.18
	4./JG 3	Lt. Franz Ruhl	B-17	(22.)	17.20
	6./JG 3	Hptm. Paul Stolte	B-17	(41.)	17.24
27.09.43	6./JG 3	Fw. Franz Cech	B-17	(33.)	10.59
	5./JG 3	Hptm. Joachim Kirschner	B-17	(172.)	11.10
	4./JG 3	Lt. Franz Ruhl	B-17	(23.)	11.15
	6./JG 3	Lt. Horst Brock	B-17	(3.)	11.22
	4./JG 3	Fw. Rudolf Blomann	B-17 HSS	(1.)	12.09
	6./JG 3	Hptm. Paul Stolte	B-17	(42.)	
02.10.43	6./JG 3	Hptm. Paul Stolte	B-17	(43.)	17.08
	5./JG 3	Obfw. Rudolf Traphan	B-17	(13.)	17.22

	5./JG 3	Hptm. Joachim Kirschner	B-17	(173.)	
	6./JG 3	Obfw. Robert Roller	B-17	(9.)	
03.10.43	5./JG 3	Hptm. Joachim Kirschner	Spitfire	(174.)	12.24
	4./JG 3	FhjFw. Hans Frese	Spitfire	(43.)	12.30
	5./JG 3	Obfw. Werner Kloß	P-47	(18.)	12.36
04.10.43	5./JG 3	Fw. Paul Draeger	Typhoon	(5.)	
	5./JG 3	Hptm. Joachim Kirschner	B-17	(175.)	12.20
	4./JG 3	Lt. Leopold Münster	B-17	(77.)	13.07
08.10.43	4./JG 3	Lt. Franz Ruhl	B-17	(24.)	14.42
	4./JG 3	Lt. Franz Ruhl	B-17	(25.)	15.12
	Stab II./JG 3	Fw. Gerhard Thyben	P-47	(33.)	15.34
	4./JG 3	Uffz. Hugo Lucks	B-17 HSS	(4.)	16.22
	6./JG 3	Uffz. Walter Stienhans	B-17	(8.)	16.28
09.10.43	5./JG 3	Fw. Paul Draeger	B-17	(6.)	13.45
	4./JG 3	Lt. Leopold Münster	B-17	(78.)	13.50
10.10.43	4./JG 3	Lt. Leopold Münster	B-17	(79.)	15.06
	4./JG 3	Lt. Leopold Münster	B-17	(80.)	15.08
18.10.43	6./JG 3	Obfw. Robert Roller	Spitfire	(10.)	13.26
20.10.43	4./JG 3	Oblt. Werner Lucas	B-17	(106.)	14.39
	4./JG 3	Obfw. Helmut Rüffler	B-17	(52.)	14.45
03.11.43	Stab II./JG 3	Maj. Kurt Brändle	P-47	(171.)	12.30
	Stab II./JG 3	Maj. Kurt Brändle	P-47	(172.)	12.31
	4./JG 3	FhjFw. Hans Frese	P-47	(44.)	12.40
	6./JG 3	Fw. Walter Stienhans	P-47	(9.)	13.00
	6./JG 3	Fw. Walter Stienhans	Spitfire	(10.)	16.00
13.11.43	5./JG 3	Lt. Leopold Münster	B-17	(81.)	13.38
23.11.43	4./JG 3	Lt. Franz Ruhl	Beaufighter	(26.)	15.06
	4./JG 3	Lt. Franz Ruhl	Beaufighter	(27.)	15.08
	4./JG 3	Fw. Otto Florian	Beaufighter	(1.)	15.09
29.11.43	5./JG 3	Lt. Leopold Münster	P-38	(82.)	14.28
	5./JG 3	Lt. Leopold Münster	P-38	(83.)	14.30
30.11.43	Stab II./JG 3	Hptm. Wilhelm Lemke	P-47	(131.)	11.25
	5./JG 3	FhjObfw. Hans Grünberg	P-47	(62.)	11.25
	6./JG 3	Fw. Gerhard Thyben	P-47	(34.)	11.40
	6./JG 3	Obfw. Robert Roller	B-17 HSS	(11.)	11.45
	4./JG 3	Fw. Otto Florian	B-17 HSS	(2.)	12.05
01.12.43	4./JG 3	Lt. Franz Ruhl	P-47	n.b.	11.27
11.12.43	4./JG 3	Lt. Franz Ruhl	P-47	n.b.	12.50
	5./JG 3	Lt. Leopold Münster	B-17 HSS	(84.)	
	4./JG 3	Obfw. Helmut Rüffler	B-17 HSS	(53.)	
20.12.43	5./JG 3	FhjObfw. Hans Grünberg	Spitfire	(63.)	
22.12.43	4./JG 3	Lt. Franz Ruhl	P-47	n.b.	14.03
10.02.44	6./JG 3	Obfw. Robert Roller	B-17	e.V.	12.20
	4./JG 3	Lt. Franz Ruhl	B-17	(28.)	12.30
	6./JG 3	Fw. Johannes Hoyer	B-17	(1.)	12.30
	5./JG 3	Uffz. Johann Fröhlich	B-17	(1.)	12.30
	6./JG 3	Uffz. Franz Glassauer	B-17	(1.)	12.30
	Stab II./JG 3	Hptm. Detlev Rohwer	P-47	(36.)	
11.02.44	6./JG 3	Fw. Gerhard Thyben	P-38	(35.)	13.06
	6./JG 3	Fw. Gerhard Thyben	P-38	(36.)	13.07
	6./JG 3	Fw. Gerhard Thyben	P-38	(37.)	13.10
	6./JG 3	Fw. Johannes Hoyer	P-38	(2.)	13.10
20.02.44	5./JG 3	Lt. Leopold Münster	B-24	(85.)	
	5./JG 3	Lt. Leopold Münster	B-24	(86.)	
	5./JG 3	Lt. Leopold Münster	B-24	(87.)	
21.02.44	4./JG 3	Lt. Franz Ruhl	B-17	n.b.	14.24
	6./JG 3	Obfw. Robert Roller	B-17	(12.)	14.35
	6./JG 3	Obfw. Robert Roller	B-17	e.V.	15.05
	5./JG 3	Lt. Leopold Münster	P-51	(88.)	
22.02.44	6./JG 3	Obfw. Robert Roller	B-17	(13.)	13.45
	6./JG 3	Hptm. Heinrich Sannemann	B-17	(21.)	13.55
24.02.44	4./JG 3	Lt. Franz Ruhl	B-24 HSS	n.b.	13.25
	5./JG 3	Lt. Leopold Münster	B-24	(89.)	13.34
	4./JG 3	Fw. Otto Florian	B-24	(3.)	13.40
	4./JG 3	Gefr. Heinz Schmeling	B-24	(1.)	13.42
	4./JG 3	Obfw. Helmut Rüffler	B-24	(54.)	13.42
	4./JG 3	Lt. Franz Ruhl	B-24	(29.)	13.45
	4./JG 3	Uffz. Edmund Britzlmair	B-24 HSS	(1.)	13.48

	5./JG 3	FhjObfw. Hans Grünberg	B-24	(64.)	13.50
	6./JG 3	Uffz. Franz Glassauer	B-24 HSS	(2.)	13.55
	Stab II./JG 3	Oblt. Max-Bruno Fischer	B-24	(6.)	
04.03.44	5./JG 3	Lt. Leopold Münster	B-17	(90.)	13.11
	5./JG 3	Lt. Leopold Münster	P-51	(91.)	13.25
	5./JG 3	Uffz. Kurt Wahl	P-51	(1.)	
06.03.44	5./JG 3	Uffz. Walter Agricola	B-17	(1.)	12.45
	6./JG 3	Hptm. Heinrich Sannemann	B-17	(22.)	13.45
	Stab II./JG 3	Hptm. Detlev Rohwer	P-38	(37.)	14.20
08.03.44	4./JG 3	Lt. Franz Ruhl	B-17	(30.)	13.32
	5./JG 3	Lt. Leopold Münster	B-17	(92.)	13.37
	4./JG 3	Lt. Franz Ruhl	B-17	(31.)	13.50
	Stab II./JG 3	Hptm. Detlev Rohwer	P-38	(38.)	15.12
23.03.44	5./JG 3	Uffz. Maximilian Reichenberger	B-17	(1.)	11.16
	5./JG 3	FhjObfw. Hans Grünberg	B-17 HSS	(65.)	11.20
	6./JG 3	Fw. Waldemar Eyrich	B-17 HSS	(31.)	11.20
	Stab II./JG 3	Uffz. Albert Zanterl	B-17	(1.)	11.20
	4./JG 3	Lt. Horst Mietzner	B-17 HSS	(1.)	11.24
	4./JG 3	Gefr. Theo Burchardt	B-17	(1.)	11.25
05.04.44	5./JG 3	FhjObfw. Hans Grünberg	P-51	(66.)	15.38
08.04.44	4./JG 3	Fw. Otto Florian	P-51	(4.)	14.16
	4./JG 3	Fw. Otto Florian	P-51	(5.)	14.17
	4./JG 3	Obfw. Helmut Rüffler	B-24	(55.)	
	5./JG 3	FhjObfw. Hans Grünberg	B-24	(67.)	
11.04.44	5./JG 3	Lt. Leopold Münster	B-17	(93.)	11.07
	5./JG 3	FhjObfw. Hans Grünberg	B-17	(68.)	11.08
	5./JG 3	Uffz. Maximilian Reichenberger	P-51	(2.)	11.12
	5./JG 3	Uffz. Kurt Wahl	P-51	(2.)	
13.04.44	4./JG 3	Lt. Fridolin Reinartz	B-17	(5.)	14.00
	5./JG 3	Uffz. Jäger	B-17 HSS	(1.)	14.01
	Stab II./JG 3	Hptm. Heinrich Sannemann	B-17	(23.)	14.03
18.04.44	4./JG 3	Uffz. Ulrich Gehrke	B-17	(1.)	14.32
	5./JG 3	Lt. Hans Grünberg	B-17	(69.)	14.33
	4./JG 3	Obfw. Hlmut Rüffler	B-17	(56.)	
19.04.44	4./JG 3	Fw. Otto Florian	B-17	(6.)	10.35
	4./JG 3	Fw. Otto Florian	P-51	(7.)	10.38
	5./JG 3	Uffz. Jäger	P-51	(2.)	10.42
	4./JG 3	Obfw. Helmut Rüffler	B-17	(57.)	
	4./JG 3	Obfw. Helmut Rüffler	B-17 HSS	(58.)	
24.04.44	4./JG 3	Fw. Otto Florian	B-17	(8.)	13.35
	6./JG 3	Lt. Horst Mietzner	B-17 HSS	(2.)	13.35
	4./JG 3	Uffz. Günther Engler	B-17	(1.)	13.35
29.04.44	5./JG 3	Fw. Franz Busch	B-17	(1.)	10.52
	6./JG 3	FhjFw. Walter Becker	B-17	(1.)	11.05
	6./JG 3	Lt. Oskar Zimmermann	B-17	(17.)	11.05
	6./JG 3	Fw. Johannes Hoyer	B-17 HSS	(3.)	11.05
	5./JG 3	Uffz. Maximilian Reichenberger	B-17 HSS	(3.)	11.05
	4./JG 3	Fw. Otto Florian	B-17	(9.)	11.05
	5./JG 3	Uffz. Kurt Sossdorf	B-17 HSS	(1.)	11.05
	4./JG 3	Fw. Otto Florian	B-17	(10.)	11.20
08.05.44	4./JG 3	Lt. Franz Ruhl	B-17	(32.)	10.05
	Stab II./JG 3	Fw. Albert Zanterl	B-17	(2.)	10.14
	5./JG 3	Lt. Leopold Münster	B-17	(94.)	10.15
	6./JG 3	Lt. Oskar Zimmermann	B-24	(18.)	10.17
	5./JG 3	Lt. Leopold Münster	B-24 HSS	(95.)	
	6./JG 3	Lt. Oskar Zimmermann	B-24 HSS	(19.)	10.40
	6./JG 3	Uffz. Josef Wester	B-24 HSS	(1.)	10.40
	6./JG 3	Fw. Johannes Hoyer	B-17	(4.)	10.50
	4./JG 3	Obfw. Helmut Rüffler	B-17 HSS	(59.)	
12.05.44	5./JG 3	Fw. Franz Busch	B-17 HSS	(2.)	12.35
	4./JG 3	Uffz. Ulrich Gehrke	B-17	(2.)	12.40
	4./JG 3	Uffz. Theo Burchardt	B-17	(2.)	12.40
	4./JG 3	Uffz. Theo Burchardt	B-17 HSS	(3.)	12.40
	4./JG 3	Lt. Franz Ruhl	B-17	(33.)	12.40
	6./JG 3	FhjFw. Walter Becker	B-17	(2.)	12.40
	4./JG 3	Uffz. Heinz Barisich	B-17	(1.)	12.40
	4./JG 3	Uffz. Günther Engler	B-17	(2.)	12.40
	4./JG 3	Lt. Otto Siebenrock	B-17	(1.)	12.40
	6./JG 3	Uffz. Heiner Geisthövel	B-17	(1.)	12.40
	5./JG 3	Fw. Franz Busch	B-17	(3.)	12.42
	4./JG 3	Uffz. Ulrich Gehrke	B-17	(3.)	12.43
13.05.44	5./JG 3	Lt. Dietrich Schmidt	B-17	(1.)	14.22
	6./JG 3	Lt. Oskar Zimmermann	P-51	(20.)	14.30
19.05.44	5./JG 3	Uffz. Jäger	P-51	(3.)	13.45

	6./JG 3	Lt. Oskar Zimmermann	B-17	(21.)	13.46
	5./JG 3	Lt. Dietrich Schmidt	B-17	(2.)	13.47
	4./JG 3	Lt. Franz Ruhl	B-17 HSS	(34.)	13.50
24.05.44	6./JG 3	Uffz. Franz Glassauer	P-38	(3.)	11.12
	4./JG 3	Lt. Franz Ruhl	B-17	(35.)	11.15
28.05.44	5./JG 3	Uffz. Jäger	B-17	(4.)	14.15
	6./JG 3	Obfw. Ernst Siebert	B-17 HSS	(1.)	14.18
	4./JG 3	Lt. Fridolin Reinartz	B-17 HSS	(6.)	14.20
	4./JG 3	Uffz. Walter Loos	B-17 HSS	(11.)	14.20
	5./JG 3	Uffz. Jäger	P-51	(5.)	14.25
29.05.44	6./JG 3	FhjFw. Walter Becker	B-24	(3.)	12.20
	4./JG 3	Lt. Fridolin Reinartz	B-24 HSS	(7.)	12.20
	4./JG 3	Uffz. Walter Loos	B-24	(12.)	12.25
	5./JG 3	Lt. Hans Grünberg	B-24	(70.)	12.27
	5./JG 3	Uffz. Walter Agricola	B-24	(2.)	12.27
	4./JG 3	Lt. Wilhelm Mamz	B-24	(1.)	
30.05.44	4./JG 3	Uffz. Kurt Möllerke	B-17	(1.)	11.15
	6./JG 3	Uffz. Franz Glassauer	B-17	(4.)	11.15
	4./JG 3	Uffz. Walter Loos	B-24	(13.)	11.15
	6./JG 3	Lt. Oskar Zimmermann	P-51	(22.)	11.45

Victories by II/JG 3 during Operations against the Allied Invasion of France
7 June to 22 August 1944

10.06.44	5./JG 3	Uffz. Walter Agricola	P-51	(3.)	11.05
12.06.44	6./JG 3	Lt. Oskar Zimmermann	P-47	(23.)	15.12
	6./JG 3	Uffz. Hans Löhlein	P-47	(1.)	15.13
	6./JG 3	Lt. Karl-Dieter Hecker	P-47	(4.)	15.14
15.06.44	4./JG 3	Fw. Otto Florian	P-51	(11.)	06.40
	4./JG 3	Uffz. Kurt Möllerke	P-51	(2.)	06.40
	4./JG 3	Fw. Otto Florian	P-51	(12.)	06.45
	4./JG 3	Uffz. Günther Engler	Spitfire	(3.)	06.50
20.06.44	4./JG 3	Uffz. Günther Engler	P-51	(4.)	18.53
22.06.44	6./JG 3	Uffz. Heiner Geisthövel	B-17	(2.) 1132	
25.06.44	6./JG 3	Fw. Herbert Dehrmann	P-47	(13.)	10.55
	6./JG 3	Uffz. Heinrichs	P-47	(1.)	11.20
	5./JG 3	Uffz. Walter Agricola	P-47	(4.)	11.25
	5./JG 3	Uffz. Willi Stoll	P-47	(1.)	
	6./JG 3	Gefr. Helmut Hötzel	P-47	(1.)	
	5./JG 3	Uffz. Willi Stoll	P-51	(2.)	
30.06.44	6./JG 3	Lt. Johannes Hoyer	P-47	(5.)	20.38
	6./JG 3	Gefr. Walter Bronder	P-47	(1.)	20.39
	5./JG 3	Fw. Jäger	P-47	(6.)	20.40
	4./JG 3	Obfw. Helmut Rüffler	P-51	(60.)	20.50
05.07.44	4./JG 3	Uffz. Josef Wüst	P-51	(10.)	
16.07.44	4./JG 3	Obfw. Helmut Rüffler	Spitfire	(61.)	20.17
	5./JG 3	Uffz. Richard Quinten	Spitfire	(1.)	20.18
	4./JG 3	Hptm. Herbert Kutscha	Spitfire	(36.)	20.20
	4./JG 3	Lt. Wilhelm Manz	Spitfire	(2.)	20.21
	6./JG 3	Fw. Herbert Dehrmann	Spitfire	(14.)	20.22
	6./JG 3	Uffz. Heiner Geisthövel	Spitfire	(3.)	
18.07.44	4./JG 3	Lt. Wilhelm Manz	P-51	(3.)	09.20
	4./JG 3	Obfw. Herbert Rüffler	P-51	(62.)	09.21
	4./JG 3	Obfw. Herbert Rüffler	P-51	(63.)	09.21
24.07.44	6./JG 3	Lt. Oskar Zimmermann	P-51	(24.)	15.31
25.07.44	6./JG 3	Lt. Oskar Zimmermann	P-51	(25.)	11.25
06.08.44	4./JG 3	Uffz. Kurt Möllerke	B-24 HSS	(3.)	12.30
	4./JG 52	Lt. Hans Waldmann	B-24	(126.)	12.31
	6./JG 3	Uffz. Berkes	P-47	(1.)	15.07
07.08.44	4./JG 52	Lt. Hans Waldmann	Auster	(127.)	15.06
	5./JG 3	Lt. Hans Grünberg	P-47	(71.)	18.28
14.08.44	5./JG 3	Lt. Hans Grünberg	P-38	(72.)	07.26
	4./JG 52	Lt. Hans Waldmann	P-47	(128.)	16.45
	4./JG 52	Lt. Hans Waldmann	P-47	(129.)	16.47
	4./JG 52	Fw. Otto Schicketanz	P-47	(.)	16.55

16.08.44	5./JG 3	Lt. Hans Grünberg	P-47	(73.)	17.15
18.08.44	8./JG 3	Lt. Hans Waldmann	P-47	(130.)	14.06
	8./JG 3	Uffz. Weichert	P-47	(1.)	14.07
	7./JG 3	Uffz. Kurt Möllerke	P-47	(4.)	14.07
	8./JG 3	Lt. Hans Waldmann	P-47	(131.)	14.12
	5./JG 3	Lt. Hans Grünberg	P-51	(74.)	19.30
	6./JG 3	Uffz. Heiner Geisthövel	P-51	(4.)	19.30
	6./JG 3	Uffz. Berkes	P-51	(2.)	19.31
19.08.44	8./JG 3	Lt. Hans Waldmann	P-47	(132.)	09.10
	7./JG 3	Obfw. Robert Reiser	P-47	(5.)	09.12
20.08.44	8./JG 3	Uffz. Weichert	P-47	(2.)	15.37
	8./JG 3	Lt. Erwin Gottert	P-47	(.)	15.45
	8./JG 3	Fw. Harald Wojnar	P-47	(5.)	15.48
	5./JG 3	Lt. Hans Grünberg	P-47	(75.)	15.49
.08.44	6./JG 3	Lt. Gustav Sturm	P-51	(17.)	
.08.44	5./JG 3	Lt. Hans Grünberg	1	(76.)	
.08.44	5./JG 3	Lt. Hans Grünberg	1	(77.)	

Victories by II/JG 3 during Operations in the Defense of the Reich October to November 1944

There is no reliable documentation of victories by II/JG 3 during its operations in the Defense of the Reich in the autumn of 1944, however the *Gruppe* probably scored between five and ten, with Lt. Draeger, Lt. Johannes Hoyer and Obfw. Reiser amont the successful pilots.

Victories by II/JG 3 – New Formation – During Operations In the East February to May 1945

There is no reliable documentation of additional victories by the reformed II/JG 3 during its operations in the east in 1945; it is possible that the *Gruppe* scored additional victories in April 1945.

03.03.45	7./JG 3	Lt. Helmut Berendes	P-39	(1.)	15.07
	II./JG 3	N.N.	Jak-9	(.)	15.55

Appendix D:
II./Jagdgeschwader 3 Aircraft Inventory List

Month	Number	Type	Total	New Prod	Repaired	From other Causes	Total	Enemy action	Other causes	Over-hauled	To other units	Number
			Actual strength first of month	Taken on strength end of month				Struck off strength			Actual strength	
03-42	33	Bf 109 F-4 trop	19	19			16	2	8		6	36 [1132]
04-42	36	Bf 109 F-4 trop	11	8	-	3	7	2	1	-	4	40
05-42	40	Bf 109 F-4 trop	4	4	-	-	10	4	5	-	1	34
06-42	34	Bf 109 F-4 trop	2	-	2	-	11	4	6	-	1	25
07-42	25	Bf 109 F-4 trop	32	1	2	29	27	12	15	-	-	30
08-42	30	Bf 109 F-4 trop	21	-	13	8	51	7	7	15	22	0
	0	Bf 109 G-2	7	7	-	-	-	-	-	-	-	7
09-42	7	Bf 109 G-2	37	34	3		11	3	1	7	-	33
10-42	33	Bf 109 G-2	5	-	5		5	1	4	-	-	33
11-42	33	Bf 109 G-2	5	5	-	-	3	-	3	-	-	35
12-42	35	Bf 109 G-2	-	-	-	-	18	6	8	4	0	17
01-43	17	Bf 109 G-2	46	19	1	26	20	13	2	4	1	43
02-43	43	Bf 109 G-2	20	10	2	8	22	6	8	4	4	41
03-43	41	Bf 109 G-2	9	-	2	7	16	-	5	11	-	34
	0	Bf 109 G-4	7	7	-	-	I	I	-	-	-	6
04-43	34	Bf 109 G-2	-	-	-	-	25	6	7	7	5	9
	6	Bf 109 G-4	15	12	1	2	3	-	I	1	1	18
05-43	9	Bf 109 G-2	-	-	-	-	6	-	-	1	5	3
	18	Bf 109 G-4	25	21	1	3	12	4	4	4	-	31
06-43	3	Bf 109 G-2	1	-	1	-	2	2	-	-	-	2
	31	Bf 109 G-4	10	9	1	-	10	4	6	-	-	31
07-43	2	Bf 109 G-2	-	-	-	-	2	-	-	-	2	0
	31	Bf 109 G-4	5	2	2	1	23	12	7	-	4	13
	0	Bf 109 G-6	37	37	-	-	14	12	2	-	-	23
08-43	13	Bf 109 G-4	-	-	-	-	13	-	-	-	13	0
	23	Bf 109 G-6	10	10	-	-	15	-	-	1	14	18
09-43	0	Bf 109 G-5	14	14	-	-	1	-	I	-	-	13
	18	Bf 109 G-6	9	9	-	-	1	1	-	-	-	26
10-43	13	Bf 109 G-5	16	14	-	2	15	2	13	-	-	14
	26	Bf 109 G-6	13	12	1	-	21	14	7	-	-	18

Month	Actual strength first of month		Taken on strength end of month				Struck off strength					Actual strength
	Number	Type	Total	New Prod	Repaired	From other Causes	Total	Enemy action	Other causes	Over-hauled	To other units	Number
11-43	14	Bf 109 G-5	5	2	3		9	7	2			10
	Is	Bf 109 G-6	5	5	-		7	5	2			16
12-43	10	Bf 109 G-5	-	-	-		-	-	-	-	-	10
	16	Bf 109 G-6					16	3	3	-	10	0
01-44	10	Bf 109 G-5					10	-	-	-	10	0
	0	Bf 109 G-6	53	49		4	10	-	2	-	a	43
02-44	43	Bf 109 G-6	-	-		-	15	-	-	-	15	28
03-44	28	Bf 109 G-6	46	31	8	7	30	16	5	3	6	44
04-44	44	Bf 109 G-6	22	18	2	2	34	19	12	3	-	32
05-44	32	Bf 109 G-6	46	35	4	7	49	27	15	7		29
06-44	0	Bf 109 G-5	I	-	-	I	-	-	-	-		1
	29	Bf 109 G-6	117	62	5	50	103	65	38			43
07-44	1	Bf 109 G-5	-	-	-	-	I	-	-	-	1	0
	43	Bf 109 G-6	50	38	12	-	72	30	27	15	-	21
	0	Bf 109 G-6/IJ4	5	5	-	-	-	-	-	-	-	5
	0	Bf 109 G-6/U2	2	2	-	-	-	-	-	-	-	2
	0	Bf 109 G-6 Y	4	4	-	-	-	-	-	-	-	4
08-44	21	Bf 109 G-6					28	20	8	-	-	0
	5	Bf 109 G-6/U4										
	2	Bf 109 G-6/U2										
	4	Bf 109 G-6 Y										
09-44	0	Bf 109 G-14	64	64	-	-	5	2	3	-		59
10-44	59	Bf 109 C-T-14	16	5	1	10	11	3	5	3	-	64
11-44	64	Bf 109 G-14	8	8	-	-	32	30	-	1	1	40
	0	Bf 109 G-10	36	36	-	-	-	-	-	-	-	36
12-44	40	Bf 109 G-14	I	I	-	-	25	-	6	8	11	16
	36	Bf 109 G-10	2	2	-	-	2	-	2	-	-	36

Appendix E:
II./Jagdgeschwader 3 Bases of Operation

The following list contains all known bases of operation used by II/JG 3 from the time of its formation in March 1940 until the end of the war. In each case the location given is the airfield used by the air element, while the location of the ground elements, if these were situated elsewhere, is not. Since transfers, especially over long distances, required more than one day, dates are approximate, with a start or end date of the transfer order (if known) or the first known entry under the new base. Where the air element was divided, the airfield occupied by the individual elements appear indented. An „A" in the right column indicates that the base was used for rest and refit, while „A / E" indicates that missions were also flown from the base after the rest and refit was complete.

Formation and Operations in the West

Zerbst	01/02/1940 – 19/05/1940	A

French Campaign

Philippeville	19/05/1940 – 23/05/1940
Cambrai	23/05/1940 – 24/05/1940
Mont Ecouvez South	24/05/1940 – 04/06/1940
Valheureux	04/06/1940 – 13/06/1940
Doudeville	13/06/1940 – 17/06/1940
Escorpain	17/06/1940 – 18/06/1940
Le Mans	18/06/1940 – 23/06/1940
Brombois	23/06/1940 – 29/06/1940

Operations over the Channel and Great Britain

Brombois	04/07/1940 – 07/08/1940
Wierre-au-Bois	07/08/1940 – 23/09/1940
Arques	23/09/1940 – 14/02/1941

Operations on the Channel, Spring 1941

Darmstadt-Griesheim	20/02/1941 – 04/05/1941
Monchy-Breton	04/05/1941 – 08/06/1941

Russian Campaign 1941

Breslau-Gandau	09/06/1941 – 18/06/1941
Hostynne	18/06/1941 – 26/06/1941
Wlodzimierz	26/06/1941 – 05/07/1941
Lutsk-South	01/07/1941 – 05/07/1941
Dubno	05/07/1941 – 10/07/1941
Miropol	10/07/1941 – 20/07/1941
Berdichev	20/07/1941 – 23/07/1941
Belaya-Tserkov	23/07/1941 – 07/08/1941
Signajewka	07/08/1941 – 17/08/1941
Kirovograd-North	17/08/1941 – 20/08/1941
Stschastliwaja	20/08/1941 – 01/09/1941
Mironovka	01/09/1941 – 15/09/1941
Kremenchug	15/09/1941 – 01/10/1941
Sechtschinskaja	01/10/1941 – 13/10/1941
Chaplinka	16/10/1941 — —/11/1941

Operations in the Mediterranean Theater

Wiesbaden-Erbenheim	—/11/1941 – 07/01/1942	A
Bari	10/01/1942 – 24/01/1942	
Sciacca	19/01/1942 – 22/02/1942	
San Pietro	22/02/1942 – 26/04/1942	
Martuba	07/04/1942 – 26/04/1942	(6/JG 3 only)

Operations in the East

Pilsen	27/04/1942 – 18/05/1942	A
Chuguyev	19/05/1942 – 24/06/1942	
Shchigry	24/06/1942 – 04/07/1942	
Gortschetnoje	04/07/1942 – 10/07/1942	
Mariyevka	10/07/1942 – 15/07/1942	
Kantemirovka	13/07/1942 – 16/07/1942	
Millerovo	15/07/1942 – 21/07/1942	
Novy Cholan	21/07/1942 – 27/07/1942	
Frolov	27/07/1942 – 10/08/1942	
Tuzov	11/08/1942 – 23/08/1942	
Königsberg-Neuhausen	—/08/1942 – 12/09/1942	A
Dedjurewo	12/09/1942 – 27/09/1942	
_olzy	27/09/1942 — —/11/1942	
Smolensk	—/11/1942 – 07/12/1942	
Morozovskaya	12/12/1942 – 23/12 1942	
Pitomnik	12/12/1942 – 17/01/1942	
(Airfield Defense *Staffel*)		
Morozovskaya-South	23/12/1942 – 03/01/1943	
Tazinskaya	03/01/1943 – 05/01/1943	
Shakhty	05/01/1943 — —/01/1943	
Rowenkie	—/01/1943 – 06/03/1943	
Makeyevka	06/02/1943 – 05/04/1943	
Kerch	05/04/1943 — —/04/1943	
Anapa	—/04/1943 – 01/05/1943	
Kharkov-Rogany	02/05/1943 – 07/05/1943	

Anapa	07/05/1943 – 16/05/1943	
Warwarowka	16/05/1943 –04/07/1943	
Kharkov-Rogany	04/07/1943 – 02/08/1943	
Kuteinikovo	16/07/1943 – 02/08/1943	
Warwarowka	29/07/1942 – 02/08/1943	

Operations in the Defense of the Reich

Uetersen	12/08/1943 – 12/09/1943	
Schiphol	12/09/1943 – 13/12/1943	
Volkel	14/12/1943 – 25/12/1943	
Rotenburg	25/12/1943 – 26/02/1944	A/E
Ludwigslust	26/02/1944 – 01/03/1944	
Gardelegen	01/03/1944 – 07/06/1944	
Sachau	27/04/1944 – 07/06/1944	

Operations against the Invasion of France

Evreux	07/06/1944 – 17/06/1944	
Evreux-Fauville	17/06/1944 – 25/06/1944	
Guyancourt	25/06/1944 – 29/06/1944	

Nogent-le-Roi	30/06/1944 – 10/08/1944	
Athis	10/08/1944 – 22/08/1944	

Operations in the Defense of the Reich

Ziegenhain	—/09/1944 – 10/10/1944	A
Kirtorf (auxiliary field)	—/09/1944 – 10/10/1944	A
Alperstedt	10/10/1944 – 30/11/1944	

II/JG 3 (new)

Formation and Operations in the Defense of the Reich

Alperstedt	01/12/1944 – 20/02/1945	A/E

Operations in the East

Garz	20/02/1945 – 30/04/1945	
Püttnitz	30/04/1945 – 03/05/1945	
Leck	03/05/1945 – 05/05/1945	

Bibliography

1. Literature

Aders, Gebhard — *Geschichte der deutschen Nachtjagd*
Motorbuch Verlag, 1977

Bartov, Omer — *Hitler's Army – Soldiers, Nazis and War in the Third Reich*
Oxford University Press, 1992

Bekker, Cajus — *Angriffshöhe 4000 - Ein Kriegstagebuch der deutschen Luftwaffe* - Stalling Verlag, 1964

Boog, Horst (Hrsg.) — *Der Angriff auf die Sowjetunion, aus: Das deutsche Reich und der II Weltkrieg,* Stuttgart, 1983

Brütting, Georg — *Das Buch der deutschen Fluggeschichte Bd. 3,* Drei Brunnen Verlag, 1979

Cartier, Raymond — *Der Zweite Weltkrieg*
R. Piper & Co. Verlag, 1967

Dahl, Walther — *Rammjäger – Das letzte Aufgebot*
Orion Verlag, 1961

Franks, Norman — *The Battle of the Airfields*
William Kimble, 1982

Freeman, Roger — *Mighty Eighth War Diary*
Jane's, 1981

Freeman, Roger — *The Mighty Eighth*
Arms And Armour

Galland, Adolf — *Die Ersten und die Letzten*
Schneekluth, 1970

Groehler, Olaf — *Geschichte des Luftkriegs, 1910 - 1980*
Militärverlag der DDR, 1981

Groehler, Olaf — *Bombenkrieg gegen Deutschland*
Akademie-Verlag, 1990

Gundelach, Karl — *Drohende Gefahr West - Die deutsche Luftwaffe vor und während der Invasion 1944* - Wehrwissenschaftliche Rundschau 1959, Heft 6, S. 299 ff

Gundelach, Karl — *Der alliierte Luftkrieg gegen die deutsche Flugtreibstoffversorgung* - Wehrwissenschaftliche Rundschau 1963, S. 686 ff

Gundelach, Karl — *Die deutsche Luftwaffe im Mittelmeer 1940 – 1945*
Verlag Peter D. Lang, 1981

Haberfellner, Wernfried und Schroeder, Walter — *Wiennaer Neustädter Flugzeugwerke - Entstehung, Aufbau und Niedergang eines Flugzeugwerkes*
Weishaupt Verlag, Graz

Hentschel, Georg — *Die Geheimen Konferenzen des Generalluftzeugmeisters*
Bernard & Graefe Verlag, 1989

Hillgruber, Andreas (Hrsg.) — *Von El Alamein bis Stalingrad*
dtv Dokumente, Nr. 209, 1964

Hofbeck, Franz — *Die Südviertler - Lebensgleise*
Creative Verlag, 1995

Horne, Alistair — *Der Frankreichfeldzug 1940*
Heyne Buch 5816, 1969

Irving, David — *Die Tragödie der Deutschen Luftwaffe,*
Ullstein, 1970

Jackson, Robert — *Air War over France, 1939 - 1940,*
Ian Allan Ltd., 1974

Jacobsen, Hans-Adolf und Rohwer, Jürgen — *Entscheidungsschlachten des zweiten Welkrieges,* Bernard & Graefe, 1960

Jacobsen, Hans-Adolf und Dollinger, Hans — *Der Zweite Weltkieg in Bildern und Dokumenten* - Verlag Kurt Desch, 1968

Jung, Hermann — *Die Ardennen-Offensive 1944/45*
Musterschmidt-Verlag, 1971

Koller, Karl — *Der letzte Monat - Tagebuchaufzeichnungen vom 14/ April bis 27/ Mai 1945,* Wohlgemuth-Verlag, 1949

Kühn, Dieter — *Luftkrieg als Abenteuer*
Kampfschrift – Fischer, 1978

Mason, Francis — *Battle over Britain*
McWhirter Twins, 1969

Obermaier, Ernst — *Die Ritterkreuzträger der Luftwaffe 1939 - 1945, Band I - Jagdflieger*
Verlag Dieter Hoffmann, 1989

Piekalkiewicz, Janusz — *Invasion - Frankreich 1944*
Südwest Verlag, 1979

Piekalkiewicz, Janusz — *Luftkrieg 1939 - 1945*
Südwest Verlag, 1978

Piekalkiewicz, Janusz — *Stalingrad*
Südwest Verlag, 1980

Price, Alfred — *Battle over the Reich*
Ian Allan, 1973

Price, Alfred — *The Hardest Day - 18 August 1940*
McDonald and Jane's, 1979

Price, Alfred und Ethell, Jeffrey — *Target Berlin - Mission 250: 6 March 1944*
Jane's, 1981

Prien, Jochen — *Pik-As - Geschichte des Jagdgeschwaders 53, Teile 1 - 3,*
Eigenverlag, 1989 - 1991

Prien, Jochen — *Geschichte des Jagdgeschwaders 77, Teile 1 - 4,*
struve-druck, 1992 - 1995

Prien, Jochen and Rodeike, Peter — *Messerschmitt Bf 109 F- K - An Illustrated Study,* Schiffer Publ., 1993

Prien, Jochen and Rodeike, Peter — *Jagdgeschwader 1 und 11, Teile 1 – 3,* struve-druck, 1993 - 1994

Prien, Jochen, Rodeike, Peter, und Stemmer, Gerhard — *Messerschmitt Bf 109 im Einsatz bei der III und IV/Jagdgeschwader 27*

Prien, Jochen and Stemmer, Gerd — *Messerschmitt Bf 109 im Einsatz bei der III./JG 3* struve-druck, 1996

Priller, Josef — *Geschichte eines Jagdgeschwaders* Kurt Vowinckel Verlag, 1956

Rahn, Werner und Schreiber, Gerhard (Hrsg.) — *Kriegstagebuch der Seekriegsleitung 1939 - 1945,* Teil A

Ramsey, Winston G. — *The Battle of Britain then and now* After the Battle Publ., 1980

Ries, Karl und Dierich, Wolfgang — *Fliegerhorste und Einsatzhäfen der Luftwaffe,* Motorbuch Verlag, 1993

Ring, Hans — *Die Luftschlacht über England 1940* LUFTFAHRT INTERNATIONAL, Heft 8/1990 S. 327 ff

Ring, Hans, Bock, Winfried and Weiss, Heinrich — *"BATTLE OF BRITAIN" - Die grosse Schlacht, die niemals stattfand?* FLUGZEUG, Heft 3/1990, S. 40 ff

Rohden, Herhuth von — Die Luftwaffe ringt um Stalingrad Limes Verlag, 1950

Rohwer, Jürgen and Hümmelchen, Gerhard — *Chronik des Seekrieges, 1939 - 1945* Stalling Verlag, 1968

Rust, Kenn C. — *Fifteenth Air Force Story,* Historical Aviation album

Rust, Kenn C. — *The 9th Air Force in World War II* Aero, 1970

Saft, Ulrich — *Das bittere Ende der Luftwaffe - "Wilde Sau", Sturmjäger, Todesflieger, " Bienenstock "*

Schramm, Percy E. — *Kriegstagebuch des Oberkommandos der Wehrmacht, 1939 - 1945,* Bernard & Graefe, 1982

Schultz-Naumann, Joachim — *Die letzten dreissig Tage - Das Kriegstagebuch* des OKW April bis Mai 1945 Weltbild Verlag, 1951

Schumann, Wolfgang — *Deutschland im Zweiten Weltkrieg* Akademie-Verlag, 1982

Shores, Christopher — *Fledgling Eagles,* Grub Street, 1993

Skawran, Robert — *Ikaros - Persönlichkeit und Wesen des* deutschen Jagdfliegers m Zweiten Weltkrieg Luftfahrt Verlag Walter Zuerl, 1969

Speer, Albert — *Erinnerungen* Propyläen Verlag, 1969

Thorwald, Jürgen — *Das Ende an der Elbe,* Knaur, 1965

Überschär, Gerd R. und Wette, Wolfram (Hrsg.) — *Der deutsche Überfall auf die Sowjetunion - »Unternehmen Barbarossa« 1941* Fischer, 1991

Warlimont, Walter — *Im Hauptquartier der deutschen Wehrmacht 1939 - 1945,* 2 Bände, Weltbild Verlag

Wegmann, Günter — " *Das Oberkommando der Wehrmacht gibt* bekannt ..." - Der deutsche Wehrmachtbericht 1939 - 1945 - Gesellschaft für Lit. und Bildung, 1989

2. Unpublished Sources

a) Archives – Overview of the most important archival sources used; this does not include a large number of individual reports, accounts and notes, which are, however, recorded in detail in the footnotes.

Various personnel files of former members of JG 3 from the holdings of the BA/MA Kornelimünster.

Casualty reports of the flying units of the Luftwaffe for JG 3 from the holdings of the WASt., Berlin.

Reports on aircraft accidents and losses of the flying units, Gen.Qu. 6/Abt., BA/MA various signatures.

Reports on aircraft losses of the flying units, BA/ MA RL 2/III/852 ff.

Reports on aircraft complement and complement changes (day fighters), March 1942 to December 1944.

War diary I Jagdkorps, preserved for the period 15/9/1943 to 20/5/1944.

Various strength reports by *Luftwaffe* day fighter units from the holdings of the US National Archives, the BA/MA and the Luftwaffe Study Group.

Fragmentary sources on victory claims from the holdings of the Luftwaffe personnel office, microfilmed; presently partly in the holdings of the BA / MA.

War diary Stab/JG 77 - Part 1, 1/10/1939 to 25/ 11/1940; BA / MA RL 10/299.

Air Ministry Weekly Intelligence Summary January / February 1945.

Various A.D.I(K) Reports – Evaluations of the interrogations of German POWs, US National Archives.

The Struggle for Air Superiority over Germany – Study by the Historical Division HQ USAREUR - Air Force Project.

Überblick über die deutsche Luftkriegführung 1939 - 1945 – Study by 8/ Abt. GenSt. Lw. dated 21/9/1944.

Various aircraft handbooks concerning the E, F, G and K variants of the Messerschmitt Bf 109.

Various C-Amt plans concerning the production and delivery of the Bf 109, period 1940 - 1944.

b) Personal Writings from the Wartime and Postwar Periods

Alex, Georg Papers on operations by 4/JG 3.

Brustellin, Hans-Heinrich Hand-written notes from period of service with The staff of the G.d.J., January 1942 to April 1943.

Cronenbroeck, Helmut Jagdgeschwader 3 "Udet" – Chronik der 9. *Staffel* von März 1940 bis zum Waffenstillstand 1945.

Grabmann, Walter Experiences from the German home air defense in the Second World War—May 1958.

Galland, Adolf History of the Zerstörer arm (manuscript), 8/10/1945.

Koller, Karl Writings from his time in the *Luftwaffe* General Staff 1941-44, National Archives, K. 113-403.

Langer, Karl-Heinz Copied extracts from the Gruppe war diary of III/JG 3.

Lützow, Günther Hand-written notes from period of service with the staff of the G.d.J., August 1943 to January 1944.

Schwaiger, Franz Diary.

Skawran, Robert Notes on the fighter pilot Oskar Zimmermann, 7/1/1945 (based on conversations in Bad Lippspringe).

c) Private Sources – the following sources were made available to the author in part directly from the persons named, in part via Hans Ring.

aa) Log Books, Record Books, Combat Report

The log books etc. of the following pilots of II/JG 3 were made available to the author in whole or in part, in the original, as dupilcates, extracts or copies:

Heinz Bär (Stab/JG 3), Franz Cech, Kurt Ebener, Hans Grünberg, Wilhelm Lemke, Werner Lucas, Günther Lützow (Stab and I/JG 3), Franz Ruhl, Heinrich Sannemann, Gerd Schaedle, Hermann Schuster, Hans Waldmann

bb) Letters, Accounts, Writings and Conference Notes (cited with the corresponding date)

Günther Behling (JG 77), Helmut Berendes, Hans-Ekkehard Bob, Max-Bruno Fischer, Alfred Gerdes (III/JG 3), Hans von Hahn (I/JG 3), Josef Heinzeller, Helmut Hennig, Rudolf Klose, Harald König, Harald Moldenhauer, Gerhard Niehus, Heinrich Sannemann, Erich von Selle, Botho Teichmann, Werner Voigt.

d) Photographs

aa) Photographs from former members of the Geschwader

Ametsbichler, Helmut Berendes, Wolfgang Ewald (III/JG 3), Max-Bruno Fischer, Josef Heinzeller, Helmut Hennig, Gisela Lützow (widow of Günther Lützow), Meyer-Heintze, Richard Quinten, Heinrich Sannemann, Dr. Felix Sauer (II/JG 53), Schellhorn, Walter Seiz (I/JG 53), Skibitzki, Karl-Heinz Steinicke, Rudolf Wahl.

bb) Photographs from Archives, Collections and Museums

Bundesarchiv / Bildarchiv, Koblenz; Imperial War Museum, London; Etablissement Cinématographique et Photographique des Armées (E.C.P.A.), Fort d'Ivry; Kent Messenger, Gerhard Bracke, Dr. Koos, Hans Lächler, Jean-Yves Lorant, Walter Matthiesen, Michael Payne, Peter Petrick, Roletscheck, Robert de Visser

Expression of Thanks

My heartfelt thanks to the following members of the *Geschwader* and their families, listed alphabetically, who for more than ten years have made a significant contribution to this project through their generosity in providing documents and photos, and who in the face of efforts of individuals who wished to prevent the production of this work ultimately confirmed that they considered the appearance of a history of their Gruppe more important than an equally incomprehensible and unnecessary controversy.

Alfred Bilek	Herbert Liebig
Rudolf Dannat	Waldo Lösch
Joachim Foth	Gisela Lützow (widow of Günther Lützow)
Walther Hagenah	Franz Mörl
Rudolf Hener	Helmut Rose
Hans Knickrehm	Alfred Seidl
Ernst Laube	Horst Petzschler